The Logic of Violence in Civil War

By analytically decoupling war and violence, this book explores the causes and dynamics of violence in civil war. Against prevailing views that such violence is either the product of impenetrable madness or a simple way to achieve strategic objectives, the book demonstrates that the logic of violence in civil war has much less to do with collective emotions, ideologies, cultures, or "greed and grievance" than currently believed. Stathis Kalyvas distinguishes between indiscriminate and selective violence and specifies a novel theory of selective violence: it is jointly produced by political actors seeking information and individual noncombatants trying to avoid the worst but also grabbing what opportunities their predicament affords them. Violence is not a simple reflection of the optimal strategy of its users; its profoundly interactive character defeats simple maximization logics while producing surprising outcomes, such as relative nonviolence in the "frontlines" of civil war. Civil war offers irresistible opportunities to those who are not naturally bloodthirsty and abhor direct involvement in violence. The manipulation of political organizations by local actors wishing to harm their rivals signals a process of privatization of political violence rather than the more commonly thought politicization of private life. Seen from this perspective, violence is a process taking place because of human aversion rather than a predisposition toward homicidal violence, which helps explain the paradox of the explosion of violence in social contexts characterized by high levels of interpersonal contact, exchange, and even trust. Hence, individual behavior in civil war should be interpreted less as an instance of social anomie and more as a perverse manifestation of abundant social capital. Finally, Kalyvas elucidates the oft-noted disjunction between action on the ground and discourse at the top by showing that local fragmentation and local cleavages are a central rather than peripheral aspect of civil wars.

Stathis N. Kalyvas is Arnold Wolfers Professor of Political Science at Yale, where he directs the Program on Order, Conflict, and Violence. He has previously taught at Chicago, NYU, and Ohio State and has been a visiting professor at the Juan March Institute and a Jean Monnet Fellow at the European University Institute. He is the author of *The Rise of Christian Democracy in Europe* (1996), which was awarded the J. David Greenstone Prize for the best book in politics and history. He has also received the Gregory Luebbert Award for the best article in comparative politics and has been a grant recipient of the Harry Frank Guggenheim Foundation and the United States Institute of Peace.

Cambridge Studies in Comparative Politics

General Editor
Margaret Levi *University of Washington, Seattle*

Assistant General Editor
Stephen Hanson *University of Washington, Seattle*

Associate Editors
Peter Lange *Duke University*
Helen Milner *Princeton University*
Frances Rosenbluth *Yale University*
Susan Stokes *Yale University*
Sidney Tarrow *Cornell University*
Kathleen Thelen *Northwestern University*
Erik Wibbels *University of Washington, Seattle*

Continued after the Index

Publication of this book has been aided by the generosity of the Yale Center for International and Area Studies.

The Logic of Violence in Civil War

STATHIS N. KALYVAS

Yale University

CAMBRIDGE
UNIVERSITY PRESS

CAMBRIDGE UNIVERSITY PRESS
Cambridge, New York, Melbourne, Madrid, Cape Town, Singapore, São Paulo, Delhi

Cambridge University Press
32 Avenue of the Americas, New York, NY 10013-2473, USA

www.cambridge.org
Information on this title: www.cambridge.org/9780521670043

First published 2006
Reprinted 2007, 2008 (twice), 2009

Printed in the United States of America

A catalog record for this publication is available from the British Library.

Library of Congress Cataloging in Publication Data

Kalyvas, Stathis N., 1964–
The logic of violence in civil war / Stathis N. Kalyvas.
  p. cm. – (Cambridge studies in comparative politics)
Includes bibliographical references and index.
ISBN 0-521-85409-1 (hardback) – ISBN 0-521-67004-7 (pbk.)
1. Political violence. 2. Civil war. I. Title. II. Series.
JC328.6.K34   2006
303.6'4 – dc22   2005018158

ISBN 978-0-521-85409-2 hardback
ISBN 978-0-521-67004-3 paperback

Τῆς Ἀγγελικῆς

We are so little accustomed to treat social phenomena scientifically that certain of the propositions contained in this book may well surprise the reader. However, if there is to be a social science, we shall expect it not merely to paraphrase the traditional prejudices of the common man but to give us a new and different view of them; for the aim of all sciences is to make discoveries, and every discovery more or less disturbs accepted ideas.

Emile Durkheim, *The Rules of Sociological Method*

No one engaged in thought about history and politics can remain unaware of the enormous role violence has always played in human affairs, and it is at first sight surprising that violence has been singled out so seldom for special consideration.

Hannah Arendt, *On Violence*

Le nouveau ne se produit jamais par simple interpolation de l'ancien.

Michel Houellebecq, *Les particules élémentaires*

Contents

Tables and Figures

Acknowledgments

This book is the outcome of an unexpected disruption. In 1997 the United States Information Agency told me that I had to spend two years in Greece because of a visa regulation. At the time I was teaching at NYU and did not welcome this prospect. Yet my forced stay in Greece led to exploratory fieldwork that eventually impelled me to shift altogether my research agenda toward the study of civil war and violence. I am indebted to Roger Petersen for discussing with me this fascinating topic just before my departure for Greece and to Adam Przeworski for supporting with enthusiasm what seemed at the time like a highly improbable research venture.

Once in Greece, I relied on a network of friends for my first contacts. Yannis Apostolopoulos, Dimitra Hadjiangelaki, Kostas Heliotis, and Vangelis Kombotis proved immensely helpful. Tasoula Vervenioti was instrumental in convincing me that interviews were both possible and valuable – against the opposite advice I had received from several professional historians in Greece. My friend Nikos Argyropoulos was helpful and supportive, as always. George Mavrogordatos wisely mixed encouragement and criticism. I cannot thank Marina Tsouloucha enough; she, over many years, helped me mine the riches of the Historical Archive of the Argolid. I also thank H. F. Meyer and G. Th. Mavrogordatos for sharing some of the archival material they collected, and the Near East Foundation for retrieving and making available to me the *Village Social Organization in Greece* study.

More people than I can possibly list here listened to my arguments in formal or informal settings, invited me to seminars and workshops where I presented my research, read my work, and offered comments. I want to single out just a few: Lars-Erik Cederman, Kanchan Chandra, Jim Fearon, Manolis Galenianos, Diego Gambetta, Michael Hechter, Macartan Humphreys, Matt Kocher, David Laitin, Nikos Marantzidis, Nikolay Marinov, John Roemer, Nicholas Sambanis, Ignacio Sanchez Cuenca, Jonah Schulhofer-Wohl, Steven Shewfelt, Jim Vreeland, and Elisabeth Wood. Ana M. Arjona was particularly helpful during the final stretch, as were Sandy Henderson and Abbey Steele, who helped edit the manuscript.

Four anonymous reviewers provided valuable feedback. Margaret Levi supported this project from its early stages, as did Lew Bateman. I thank them all.

I started this project at NYU, began writing while at the University of Chicago, and completed the book at Yale. All three institutions provided an excellent intellectual and professional environment. The European University Institute and the Juan March Institute hosted me at crucial times, allowing me to make significant headway; for this, I am very grateful to Daniel Verdier and José Maria Maravall. The H. F. Guggenheim Foundation funded my research in northern Greece, part of which is included here. Thanks to Chrysostomos Mantzavinos and Christoph Engel, I was able to prepare the manuscript for publication in the wonderful environment of the Max Planck Institute for Research in Collective Goods in Bonn. I am very grateful to Ian Shapiro and the Yale Center for International and Area Studies for their support in publishing this book.

I was fortunate to include parts of this book in graduate seminars I taught at Chicago, Juan March, and Yale. My students took my work apart ruthlessly, sending me back repeatedly to fix the problems they identified; this bespeaks the quality of their feedback and their contribution to the final project.

For superb research assistance, I would like to thank Ioannis Evrigenis, Ioanna Karariga, Panayota Koliatsi, Harris Mylonas, Nassos Roussias, Sebastian Saiegh, Andromachi Tsomaka, and Jieun Yoo. Steve Citron-Pousty designed the maps. I acknowledge the permission to use the material in Chapters 6 and 11, whose earlier versions appeared as "The Paradox of Terrorism in Civil War," *Journal of Ethics* 8:1 (2004): 97–138, and "The Ontology of 'Political Violence': Action and Identity in Civil Wars," *Perspectives on Politics* 1:3 (2003): 475–94.

I acquired many friends among the people I interviewed, but I am particularly indebted to the Kalymniou, Skinochoritis, and Yannakou families for their warm hospitality and friendship. At the same time, I owe many thanks to all the people who opened their doors to me in Greece. Many were initially distrustful, but they grew friendly as the conversation went on; they spoke with passion, emotion, and great intelligence about their lives, their beliefs, their suffering, their hopes. This was a life-changing experience for me. This book does very little justice to their remarkably rich and cogent recollections. I am already at work on another book that will be based directly on their stories, as well as the stories that I recovered from the archives.

I would not have been able to carry out this research without the emotional and material support of my parents, Nikos and Margarita Kalyvas, to whom I am, once more, deeply grateful. The book is dedicated to Angeliki Louvi, who was there throughout the entire project, from conception to end. I need not say more, for she already knows.

Abbreviations

AMFOGE	Allied Mission for Observing the Greek Elections
ARVN	Army of the Republic of Vietnam
ASKI, KKE	Archive of Contemporary Social History, Archive of the Communist Party of Greece
AUC	United Self-Defense Forces of Colombia
BLO	British Liaison Officer
DAN	Municipal Archives of Nafplio
DIS/AEA	Directorate of Army History, Archive of National Resistance
DSE	Democratic Army of Greece
EAM	National Liberation Front
EDES	National Democratic Greek League
EES	Greek National Army
EGP	Guerrilla Army of the Poor
EKKA	National and Social Liberation
ELAS	National Popular Liberation Army
ELF	Ethnolinguistic Fractionalization Index
ELN	National Liberation Army
ERP	Revolutionary Army of the People
ETA	Basque Fatherland and Liberty
FARC	Revolutionary Armed Forces of Colombia
FECCAS	Christian Federation of Salvadoran Peasants
FLN	Front of National Liberation
FMLN	Farabundo Martí National Liberation Front
FRELIMO	Liberation Front of Mozambique
FRETILIN	Revolutionary Front of Independent East Timor
GIA	Armed Islamic Group
GVN	Government of the Republic of Vietnam

HAA/DAN	Historical Archive of the Argolid, Municipal Archives of Nafplion
HAA/EDD	Historical Archive of the Argolid, Special Court of Collaborators
HES	Hamlet Evaluation System
INLA	Irish National Liberation Army
IRA	Irish Republican Army
JVP	People's Liberation Front
KKE	Communist Party of Greece
KLA	Kosovo Liberation Army
KMT	Kuomintang
LTTE	Liberation Tigers of Tamil Eelam
MI5	British domestic intelligence service
MPAJA	Malayan People's Anti-Japanese Army
MPLA	Popular Movement for the Liberation of Angola
MRLA	Malay Races Liberation Army
MTLD	Movement for the Triumph of Democratic Freedoms
NDF	National Democratic Front
NEF	Near East Foundation
NGOs	nongovernmental organizations
NKVD	People's Commissariat for Internal Affairs
NPA	New People's Army
NPFL	National Patriotic Front of Liberia
OPLA	Organization for the Protection of People's Fighters
ORDEN	Nationalist Democratic Organization
PASOK	Panhellenic Socialist Movement
PEEA	Political Committee of National Liberation
PF	Popular Forces
PKK	Kurdistan Workers' Party
PPF	Popular Party of France
PRI	Institutional Revolutionary Party
PRO, FO	Public Records Office, Foreign Office Records
PRO, HS	Public Records Office, Special Operations Executive Records
RENAMO	Mozambican National Resistance
RUF	Revolutionary United Front
SB	Security Battalion
SWAPO	South West Africa People's Organization
UNITA	National Union for the Total Independence of Angola
UVF	Ulster Volunteer Force
VC	Vietcong
VCI	Vietcong Infrastructure
ZSt.	Zentrale Stelle der Landesjustizverwaltungen

The Logic of Violence in Civil War

Introduction

The guilty perished, but now there were only the guilty to survive.

Lucan, *Bellum Civile*

All is uniform, though extraordinary; all is monotonous, though horrible.

Germaine de Staël, *Considerations on the Principal Events of the French Revolution*

I.I. FOUR PUZZLES

On the hills that rise gently off the Argolid plain, in the Greek peninsula of the Peloponnese, lie the twin villages of Manesi and Gerbesi (now Midea). Located on the eastern edge of the Plain of Argos, just a few miles from the famous archaeological sites of Tiryns, Mycenae, and Argos, these villages share a social, economic, political, and cultural outlook. In the 1940s this featured a conservative, ethnically and religiously homogeneous population of mainly Albanian descent working on small family farms of roughly equal size and practicing primarily subsistence agriculture. The inhabitants of these two villages developed common reciprocity networks and intermarried frequently; indeed, they share many family names. During the German occupation of Greece, they faced similar choices and challenges: many men from the two villages joined resistance organizations and both villages suffered German reprisals. There is, however, one crucial divergence in their histories. In August 1944 a vicious massacre of five village families, including elderly people and young children, took place in Gerbesi; armed guerillas perpetrated the actual killing, but neighbors and even relatives of the victims took part in the planning. In contrast, neighboring Manesi escaped violence of this kind. Although the same guerrillas came to Manesi looking for victims, they were successfully thwarted by the villagers. Why? How were the people of Gerbesi able to inflict such violence on their neighbors? And how were the people of Manesi, similar, it seems, in every observable aspect to those of Gerbesi, able to prevent this violence?

Microhistorical and anthropological accounts of civil wars are replete with such village dyads, in which violence strikes in a pattern that seems to defy logic. The village of "Los Olivos" in southern Spain lost thirty-eight men to the civil war, all in 1936; they were, for the most part, socialist sympathizers who died not on the battlefield but at the hands of the right-wing Falangists, who found them after receiving information from their neighbors. Nearby "Los Marines," however, a village with a similar political and social outlook, experienced no killings (Collier 1987:163). No other area of the Colombian department of Tolima was more devastated by the civil war known as La Violencia than the *municipio* of Rovira, while Dolores, a similar *municipio* in the same department, as mountainous and politically divided as Rovira, escaped the violence (Henderson 1985:144–5). Guatemala suffered enormous levels of violence during the early 1980s; hundreds of villages were wiped out and thousands of people killed in massacres perpetrated by the army. Yet, the anthropologist Kay Warren (1998:92) found, to her surprise, that the town of San Andrés, her field site, somehow escaped the massacres that occurred in other similar towns – the same puzzle that another anthropologist, John Watanabe (1992:182), encountered during his own field research: "Despite the army occupation, almost no one died in Chimbal, in contrast to all the towns around them.... Whether by collective disposition, acts of personal courage, or even divine intervention, Chimbal survived." Indeed, Linda Green (1995:114) observes that "one of the notable features of the military campaign known as 'scorched earth' [in Guatemala] is that neighboring villages fared quite differently: one might be destroyed while another was left untouched." Jonathan Spencer (2000) was similarly surprised to discover that the village he studied in Sri Lanka had "miraculously" escaped the worst violence even though many surrounding villages did not. The ethnic Albanian village of Bukos in Kosovo suffered Serb violence, but not its equally Albanian neighbor Novo Selo (Gall 1999); likewise, the Chechen village of Primykaniye bore the brunt of Russian violence but not the neighboring Tsentora-Yurt (Gordon 1999b). An IRA cadre in Northern Ireland (Collins 1999:98) recalled that "the IRA had already obliterated every hotel in Newry, and though Warrenpoint was a ten-minute drive from Newry, it could have been in another country, so untroubled was it by the war going on around it." The variation in violence has been detected by several students of the conflict in Northern Ireland (Smyth and Fay 2000:133; O'Leary and McGarry 1993:9).[1]

This variation has also mystified scholars: "Why this should have been," writes Watanabe (1992:x) about the relative absence of violence from his Guatemalan

---

[1] Benini and Moulton (2004), Ron (2000a), and Moyar (1997:307) point to similar variation in Afghanistan, Yugoslavia, and Vietnam, respectively. While conducting ethnographies of civil wars in Mozambique and Liberia, Geffray (1990), Nordstrom (1997), Ellis (1999), and Finnegan (1992) were all surprised to discover oases of peace right in the midst of the most extreme violence. Similar observations have been made about other forms of political violence. The mass killings in Indonesia (1965–6) "were scattered in time and space and whatever we know about one massacre only dimly illuminates the others" (Cribb 1990:23); Hindu-Muslim riots in India likewise display considerable variation (Wilkinson 2004; Varshney 2002), as did the Terror during the French Revolution, where "certain regions bore the brunt of the Terror while others escaped almost unscathed" (Greer 1935:40).

field site, "evades any simple answer." The very existence of variation has been cited as evidence, at worst, of the sheer impossibility of making sense of violence (Kann 2000:401) and, at best, of the inability to move beyond educated guesses.[2] Yet, despite the obvious significance of the matter, there have been few attempts to move toward a systematic explanation of variation in violence – an oversight that has puzzled more than one scholar (e.g., Klinkhammer 1997:29; Getty and Manning 1993:17).[3]

This leads to a second, more general puzzle: the oft-noted and seemingly enduring brutality of civil war. In 1589 Alberico Gentili observed that the "chief incentive to cruelty [in war] is rebellion" (in Parker 1994:44). Montaigne (*Essais* 2:23) argued that "a foreign war is a distemper much less harsh than a civil war," while Adam Smith (1982:155) pointed out that "the animosity of hostile factions, whether civil or ecclesiastical, is often still more furious than that of hostile nations; and their conduct towards one another is often still more atrocious." Why are civil wars so violent–or perceived as such?

A third puzzle is this: almost every macrohistorical account of civil war points to the importance of preexisting popular allegiances for the war's outcome, yet almost every microhistorical account points to a host of endogenous mechanisms, whereby allegiances and identities tend to result from the war or are radically transformed by it. Consider Lynn Horton's findings about the dynamics of allegiance during the Nicaraguan Civil War, from her research in the municipality of Quilalí. She provides plenty of evidence about how political allegiance and geography were linked and shows how the latter tended to shape the former: the contras relied on the weakness of the Sandinista state apparatus in an outlying region to generate popular collaboration with them. First, the contras began to harass Sandinista sympathizers, forcing them to abandon their farms and seek refuge in the town of Quilalí. As a result, some peasants decided to distance themselves from the Sandinista organizations and projects. As a peasant put it, "If you behaved well, you wouldn't have problems [with the contras]." Another peasant stated, "Here we lived very close to those people [the contras]. Maybe inside we felt something else, but we could never externalize it. The Frente Sandinista abandoned us." Horton suggests that had the Sandinistas managed to maintain a greater military and political presence in the region, the political allegiance of most peasants would have been different. In contrast, in the town of Quilalí where Sandinista rule remained effective, "civic political dissent on the part of the anti-Sandinistas was muted during the war years." She argues that this silence reflected practical expediency rather than political preference. In fact, when the

---

[2] In speculating about the causes of variation in violence, Warren (1998:100), Viola (1993:97), Watanabe (1992:183), and Henderson (1985:142–3) point to factors such as the relative isolation of the region, the strategy of incumbents and insurgents, local factionalism and conflict, local tactics to resist the violence, and local leadership in general.

[3] Systematic attempts to analyze variation in violence are a rather recent trend; they include, among others, Greer (1935), probably the first effort to study state repression in a systematic way; Valentino et al. (2004) and Downes (2004) on civilian victimization in war; Wilkinson (2004), Varshney (2002), and Petersen (2002) on ethnic riots; Straus (2004), Verwimp (2003), and Fein (1979) on genocide; and J. Weinstein (2003) and Echandía (1999) on civil war.

war ended, "an anti-Sandinista backlash poured over Quilalí as many residents expressed grievances they had been unwilling or afraid to openly articulate in the 1980s."[4]

Spain under French Napoleonic occupation (1808–14) offers an additional illustration of this puzzle. Lawrence Tone (1994:57) found that the guerrilla war against Napoleon in Spain did not take place in the strongholds of the 1808 summer revolution (towns such as Madrid and Valencia), but in the backward and isolated region of Navarre, one of the quietest provinces of Spain during that revolution. Using detailed data on tax collection and insurgent participation in 116 towns and villages of Navarre, he reports a positive correlation between geographical location (proximity to towns and major roads) and efficacy in taxation by the French, and an inverse correlation between the efficacy of taxation (which was likely to produce considerable grievance) and popular participation in the insurgency. Contrary to what one would expect, where the French were able to tax, and therefore aggrieve, the population, they did not face an insurgency. In contrast, the more remote the region, the more successful was guerrilla taxation and the more likely were men to join the insurgency. Indeed, insurgents came predominantly from the *Montaña*: "They lived in small villages and towns, which the French could not steadily occupy." Tone leaves little doubt as to the direction of causation. Hard-hit town dwellers stayed put despite the exactions, he argues, because "the constant French presence in such places made it difficult for young men to join the insurgency." Even the towns that managed to contribute some volunteers to the insurgency never became sites of armed guerrilla struggle. In a similar fashion, the clergy in Galicia collaborated with the French in the cities but favored the resistance in the countryside.[5] These examples suggest that, contrary to widespread perception, allegiances may be endogenous to the war, and that military control of a locale may result in popular collaboration.

Related to the question of the origins of allegiances is a final puzzle, the oft-noted presence of a disjunction between the macrolevel causes of the war and the microlevel patterns of violence. Consider Palestine in the late 1930s, where a rebellion against the British, known as *thawra* (revolt), has been described as a nationalist insurrection of the Palestinians against British colonialism. In his superb study, Ted Swedenburg (1995) found that the rebel military structure often reflected rather than transcended existing divisions among Palestinians. Because guerrilla bands were based on families or clans, their mobilization triggered all sorts of divisions into new disputes, turning the rebellion against the British into a civil war among the Palestinians. Competing village groups tried to exploit rival rebel factions for their own purposes, each group occasionally denouncing a member of the opposing family group as a spy in order to incite the rebel chieftain with whom it was aligned to punish that group. In the course of these disputes, a significant number of Palestinians ended up collaborating with the British and fighting against their ethnic kin. Rather than being based

---

[4] Horton (1998: 71, 129–30, 219, 205, 221–2, 264).
[5] Tone (1994:160–1, 171, 161, 149, 13).

on ideological or programmatic concerns, this collaboration was motivated by "strictly local, family reasons," including revenge. In the narratives Swedenburg collected, the British were often seen as incidental to the whole story, mere "tools" for settling local feuds; those of his informants who had collaborated with the British described themselves as having manipulated and even outsmarted their supposed principals. In short, the prevailing description of this conflict based on a key cleavage (British versus Palestinian) and a central political issue (nationalism) is partially misleading as to the motivations and identities of many participants and the dynamics of the violence.

In a different formulation, the habitually cited causes of group division (e.g., ideological, social, or ethnic polarization) often fail to account for the actual dynamics of violence: the game of record is not the game on the ground. Consider again the Argolid in southern Greece, which was a remarkably homogeneous place, lacking deep cleavages. Yet it went through a savage civil war that caused the death of close to 2 percent of the rural population. Why would a place lacking all conditions that supposedly cause civil strife experience such a tragedy? This simultaneous absence of deep divisions and presence of mass violence force us to rethink approaches that trace mass violence to such divisions and ask whether violence really is the direct result of deep divisions, even when and where such divisions exist.

I.2. GOALS

This book is simultaneously conceptual and positive, theoretical and empirical. It is difficult to understate the importance of a clear conceptualization of what remains a highly confused set of issues. Emile Durkheim (1938:14–22) noted that because thought and reflection are prior to science, physical and social phenomena are represented and understood by crudely formed "lay" concepts – *notiones vulgares* or *praenotiones*, as Francis Bacon called them. These concepts, Durkheim pointed out, are freely employed with great assurance, as if they corresponded to things well known and precisely defined, whereas they awaken in us "nothing but confused ideas, a tangle of vague impressions, prejudices, and emotions. We ridicule today the strange polemics built up by the doctors of the Middle Ages upon the basis of their concepts of cold, warm, humid, dry, etc.; and we do not realize that we continue to apply the same method to that very order of phenomena which, because of its extreme complexity, admits of it less than any other." Indeed, when it comes to "political violence," currently fashionable terms of practice tend to impose themselves as terms of analysis (Brubaker and Laitin 1998). The emancipation from "empirical categories, which from long continued habit have become tyrannical" (Durkheim 1938:32), requires a clear specification of key conceptual categories and the scope conditions of the argument – an eminently theoretical enterprise.

Civil war is defined as *armed combat within the boundaries of a recognized sovereign entity between parties subject to a common authority at the outset of the hostilities*. Within civil war, my focus is on violence committed intentionally against noncombatants. This sort of violence is a phenomenon that has long remained off research limits because of its conceptual complexity and empirical opacity. To use Antoine De Baecque's (2002:851) felicitous words, my goal is to bring reason to circumstances when reason is pushed to its limits. From a methodological point of view, I show the importance of systematic research at the microlevel. Typically, microlevel evidence tends to be marginalized as irrelevant or too messy. It is commonplace among historians that the "local" must be integrated with the "global" (e.g., Pred 1990:15), yet efforts to do so rarely venture beyond the boundaries of the case study. Here, I show a possible way of achieving this integration.

I begin with a simplified and abstract characterization of violence in civil war, yet one that stands on well-specified conceptual foundations. I analytically decouple *civil war violence* from civil war. I show that despite its many different forms and the various goals to which it is harnessed across time and place, violence in civil war often displays some critical recurring elements. Rather than just posit this point, I coherently reconceptualize observations that surface in tens of descriptive accounts and demonstrate that seemingly random anecdotes tend to be facets of the same phenomenon. The positive component of the book consists of two parts: a theory of irregular war and a microfoundational theory of violence (with two strands: indiscriminate and selective). Unlike existing work, the theory stresses the *joint* character of civil war violence, entailing an interaction between actors at the central and local levels, and between combatants and noncombatants. This interaction is informed by the demands of irregular war, the logic of asymmetric information, and the local dynamics of rivalries. Hence the theory differs from existing accounts of violence that stress exclusively macrolevel motivations and dynamics, pinpoint overarching and preexisting cleavage structures, and characterize violence as "wanton," "indiscriminate," or "optimal" from the users' point of view.

From the theory, I specify a model of selective violence that is consistent with the theoretical characterization, in which the interaction between actors operating at different levels results in the production of violence in a systematic and predictable way. This exercise yields counterintuitive empirical predictions about the spatial variation of violence at the microlevel, which I subject to an empirical test using data I collected in Greece. The empirical test confirms the explanatory power of the theory in a limited setting, whereas evidence from a wide array of civil wars suggests broader plausibility. Of course, the general validity of the theory awaits further empirical testing.

Finally, I explore two implications of the theory, looking first at mechanisms of "intimate" violence and then at how the modalities of violence identified can help inform our understanding of cleavage formation – that is, how and to what degree national-level or "master" cleavages map onto local-level divisions.

On the whole, this book diverges from studies that approach violence in a normative way (Sorel 1921) or via interpretation or hermeneutical reflection (e.g., Sofsky 1998; Keane 1996; Héritier 1996; Arendt 1973; 1970; Friedrich 1972). It also diverges from studies that rely on inductive data analysis (e.g., Harff 2003), do not venture beyond the macrolevel (e.g., Valentino, Huth, and Balch-Lindsay 2004), or rely solely on secondary accounts (e.g., Downes 2004; Valentino 2004) and one actor only, be it the state or the rebels (e.g., J. Weinstein 2003).

This book is a first step. More and better data can be collected to allow broader empirical tests. The theory can be further refined and expanded. Civil wars and their violence are highly complex phenomena that can be tackled only by sustained research. In this book, I restrict my focus to coercive homicidal violence in irregular civil wars. The focus on a specific type of violence acts as a baseline: the goal is to see how much can be explained given the restrictions imposed. It turns out that the theory does quite well and generates implications for noncoercive violent practices, for violence that stops short of homicide (e.g., arrest, torture, displacement), and for other types of civil wars. Still, more research is needed to graft onto the theory those aspects not yet incorporated into it.

Reflecting about civil wars began simultaneously with the writing of history, yet only recently have we been able to use the tools of social science in our investigations. This book will have achieved its goal if it succeeds in establishing a baseline that inspires an ongoing research program.

I.3. ROAD MAP

Wars, and their violence, display enormous variation – both across and within countries and time. The form and intensity of violence used at different points in the conflict by the Reds and Whites during the Russian Civil War, by diverse Serb, Muslim, and Croat factions in Bosnia, or by competing groups in Liberia vary significantly. Ernesto "Che" Guevara (1998:75–6) summarized this variation with cogency: "The enemies of the people act in a more or less intensely criminal fashion according to the specific social, historic, and economic circumstances of each place. There are places where the flight of a man into the guerrilla zone, leaving his family and his house, does not provoke any great reaction. There are other places where this is enough to provoke the burning or seizure of his belongings, and still others where the flight will bring death to all members of his family."

Consider Northern Ireland. Although the British authorities have committed human rights abuses including torture, they "have not ruthlessly and brutally suppressed the population which explicitly or tacitly supports insurrection in the manner experienced by Algerian Muslims, Afghan peasants, Iraqi Kurds, Kashmiri Muslims, Palestinian Muslims and Christians, South African blacks, Sri Lankan Tamils, and Vietnamese peasants" (O'Leary & McGarry 1993:19). As an IRA man was told after his arrest by the security forces, "If this was Beirut we would just take you out into that yard and shoot you" (Collins 1999:188). At the same time, the IRA has "sought to avoid any operations which had obviously sectarian overtones: a policeman could be justified as a legitimate target, his non-combatant Protestant family could not" (Collins 1999:295). In short, there has been considerable reciprocal restraint in Northern Ireland (Toolis 1997:21), unlike in many other civil conflicts.

The sources of this variation are highly complex. Carl von Clausewitz (1976:609–10) remarked that the conduct of war is determined by the nature of societies, as well as "by their times and prevailing conditions." The same is true of civil wars, whose violence appears bewilderingly complex and polysemic

(Apter 1997; Nordstrom 1997). The cross-national variation in levels, types, and practices of violence across wars may be affected by factors that include the specific profile of political actors and their political ideology (J. L. Anderson 2004; Heer and Naumann 2000; Degregori 1998; Bartov 1992; Furet 1981:51);[6] their organizational structure, underlying social basis, and military culture (Gumz 2001; T. Anderson 1999; Livanios 1999; Mazower 1992); their resources (J. Weinstein 2003); their national and local leadership and strategies (Shepherd 2002; Schulte 2000); the type of challenges they face and the assistance they receive from third parties; the prevailing international norms (Ron 2000a); the level of available military technology; and factors such as geography and climate. Furthermore, these factors may converge to produce distinct endogenous dynamics, as violence spirals and rival actors often mimic each other. Isabel Hull (2004:1–2) summarizes the sheer complexity of the issue by pointing to several determinants of violence in war: "The length of war, the sheer number of belligerent nations, the technical stalemate caused by the strength of defensive weaponry, scientific and industrial capacity (which created more, and more lethal, weapons), ideologization (making it hard to end the war and easy to vilify the enemy), bad leadership ('donkeys leading heroes'), and the escalatory force of broad public identification with the war (which meant that the soldiers kept coming and civilians pressed for victory despite increasing sacrifice). Many of these factors have a reciprocal effect; they strengthen each other as they interact over time."

The same variation can be observed with respect to the cultural idioms through which violence is expressed. Political actors draw from a limitless variety of cultural repertoires and models of violence (J.-C. Martin 1998; Richards 1996; Zulaika 1988). Imagination runs wild, and the possibilities seem endless. Thucydides notes that during the civil war in Corcyra "there was death in every shape and form" and "every form of wickedness arose" (*History of the Peloponnesian War* 3.81, 3.83). Pedro Altamirano, a Nicaraguan rebel chieftain in the 1920s, derived much of his notoriety from his frequent use of the "vest cut," in which "victims were decapitated, their arms cut off at the shoulders, and their abdomens sliced open, the corpses thus resembling a waistcoat or vest" (Schroeder 2000:40). insurgents in Sierra Leone resorted to mutilation, Algerian insurgents to throat slicing, Guatemalan soldiers to defacing and mutilating corpses, Filipino militiamen to beheading and "vampirelike bloodletting," Confederate rebels in Missouri to scalping, and so on. The emergence of a vast literature devoted to the detailed documentation of this variation is, therefore, not surprising.

Given current theoretical and empirical limitations, specifying and testing cross-national models of violence remains challenging and, perhaps, premature. Yet, these limitations do not warrant abandoning the task of understanding the dynamics of violence in a systematic way, as sometimes suggested (e.g., David 1997:575).

---

[6] But note that similar ideologies may be associated with different types of violence. Communist violence was centralized and bureaucratic in the Russian and Greek civil wars (Werth 1998; Kalyvas 2000), but decentralized and "anarchic" in the Finnish and Spanish civil wars (Alapuro 2002; Juliá 2000).

An alternative route is a deductive strategy aiming at producing testable hypotheses about empirical variation. This strategy can be traced back to Thucydides' effort to specify a general model of civil war instead of cataloging endless variations (Price 2001:12–14). Although civil wars and their violence vary extensively, core observations from observers, practitioners, and scholars often pinpoint recurring elements, suggesting an underlying logic.[7] The American journalist Peter Arnett, who covered civil wars in Vietnam and Afghanistan, told a Soviet colleague that "traveling around Afghanistan, I always remember the Vietnam War. . . . I covered Vietnam for ten years, and the analogies with Afghanistan were obvious" (Borovik 1991:67). Anthropologists have pointed to "incredible" cross-cultural similarities in practices of political violence (Sluka 2000:9; Zur 1994:13; Nordstrom 1992:262). As one of them points out, "the same basic meaning to violent acts and images is likely to be imputed by people who in other respects subscribe to very different cultural ideas" (Riches 1986:25). Nordstrom (1997:89), who researched several civil war sites, found that, despite pronounced local variation, "themes of terror and hope – however different their manifestation from locale to locale – demonstrate similarities that allow understandings across time and space, village and culture." The presence of an underlying logic has not escaped practitioners either. Although Che Guevara (1998:75–6) pointed to a wide variation in practices of violence, he hastened to add that "the general methods of repression are always the same" – a judgment shared by several British counterinsurgents, such as General George Erskine, who brought to Kenya methods used in Palestine (D. Anderson 2005:200), and Julian Paget, who recalls: "In 1965 I found myself in Aden in a staff appointment directly concerned with the planning of measures, both civil and military, to be taken to defeat the insurgents then operating in those parts. The problems that arose were remarkably diverse and complex, but they were seldom completely new; they had almost all cropped up before in some previous Emergency, such as Palestine, Kenya, Cyprus, or Malaya, and it would have been most helpful to be able to study this past experience and learn from it" (Paget 1967:11).

It makes sense, therefore, to take seriously Eugene Walter's (1969:vii) claim that, although violence "emerges in unique contexts and, in each case, is expressed and understood in a local idiom, conforms to specific values, and serves the needs of a particular power system, it is a universal process formed by recurrent elements and organized in systems with regular structural features." In the same vein, and more generally, this book subscribes to the view that there exists "a deep structure to human conflict that is masked by observable cultural variation" (Gould 2003:101). The challenge is to specify this "deep structure" in terms that are general enough to accommodate the appropriate analysis without falling into the trap of maximal extension and conceptual stretching (Sartori 1970).

Toward this end, I rely on two strategies. First, I match abstract theoretical conjectures and highly specific illustrations from a great variety of empirical contexts to demonstrate the plausibility of these conjectures. Throughout the book, there is a constant dialogue between empirics and theory. I draw from the very

---

[7] E.g., Toolis (1997:76); Riches (1986:25); E. Walter (1969:vii); Jones and Molnar (1966:37); Clutterbuck (1966:177).

best of fine-grained analysis of particular cases to suggest that, while contexts may differ, mechanisms recur. It is often forgotten that theory building should be grounded in credible intuitions, and examples from a broad comparative canvas serve to demonstrate the credibility of each and every building block in this theoretical edifice – though, obviously not the theory's validity, which can only be derived from rigorous testing. Second, I adopt a strategy of disaggregation. I specify three levels of analysis, moving from macro to micro. The first level focuses on interactions between unitary (state and nonstate) political actors; the second level deals with the interaction between political actors and the populations they rule; and the third level concentrates on interactions within small groups and among individuals. Most research on political violence, rebellions, revolutions, and civil wars tends either to conflate these three levels or to focus on just one – usually the first.

The first (or macro) level is the realm of elites, ideologies, and grand politics, where research in history, historical sociology, military strategy, area studies, comparative politics, and international relations is primarily located. Violence is usually merely a sideshow in these studies since it is seen as a natural outcome of war. Macrolevel studies share a key element: they all assume unitary actors. Elites and populations are fused and amalgamated. For example, references to either the Kosovo Liberation Army or "ethnic Albanians" in the context of the Kosovo conflict usually apply to an entity that indiscriminately includes the various factions of ethnic Albanian elites, ethnic Albanian fighters, and the entire ethnic Albanian population. The assumption is that elites determine automatically and unilaterally the course of group actions and that groups are monolithic and behave as such. This shortcut is perhaps necessary when narrating the story of a specific civil war or reflecting on the *grande durée* but is problematic when developing a theory of violence.

Positing coherent, identifiable political groups with clear preferences fails to match the vast complexity, fluidity, and ambiguity one encounters on the ground. The insight that political actors at the top and individuals at the bottom cannot always be lumped together has been provided by applied military research (including insurgency and counterinsurgency perspectives), as well as by microsociological and anthropological studies of civil wars. In short, violence is often used to police groups internally and to achieve the desired (but seldom reached) total "overlap" between specific leaders and organizations, on the one hand, and underlying populations, on the other. The assumption of an unlimited and unwavering support of the population for the political actor who claims to represent it is at odds with the stark and widespread reality of forced recruitment in civil wars: these wars are often fought by conscript armies (including, in the most extreme cases, kidnapped children); desertion from these armies can be pervasive. This is true of grand "classic" civil wars (such as the American, Russian, Spanish, or Chinese civil wars), ethnic civil wars (such as the civil war in Sri Lanka), and minor rural insurgencies (such as the Kachin insurgency in Burma) (Argenti-Pillen 2003; Tucker 2001; Werth 1998; Ranzato 1994). Clearly, the relation between political actors and underlying populations must be problematized rather than assumed away – which defines the content of the second (or meso) level. This analysis requires a theoretical and empirical account of civil wars as processes, including their conduct *qua* wars – a difficult enterprise insofar as basic information on the war-fighting aspects of many civil wars remains scarce (Harkavy and Neuman 2001). Indeed, the study of military operations belongs to a policy-oriented literature that has remained outside the scope of mainstream social science and is primarily concerned with "practical" tasks (e.g., how to defeat insurgencies). As a result, the dynamics of civil wars, though generally understood, have seldom been the object of analytical examination by social scientists.[8]

Even at the mesolevel, however, something important is missing: intracommunity dynamics. Individuals are treated as constituting an entity that must be "won" by political actors, but that entity remains undifferentiated and monolithic. Empirical evidence, however, suggests more often than not that populations (including ethnic groups) are internally divided into competing families, clans, localities, or other factions (Tilly 1964:173; Yang 1945:241). Understanding the behavior of individuals vis-à-vis political actors requires knowledge of the dynamics within and among small groups – a fact well understood by political actors, some of whom have even called on anthropologists to provide them with such knowledge (Lacoste-Dujardin 1997; Wakin 1992). Hence, the need for a focus on a third (or micro) level – mostly the province of anthropological and microhistorical studies, literature, and novels – which opens up the black box of intracommunity dynamics and individual behavior. As I show, such a focus carries several theoretical implications.

The central theoretical and methodological challenge underlying the entire book is the integration of these three levels. I begin with a conceptual focus (Chapters 1 and 2), reviewing several pathologies that recur in the study of violence and civil wars and arguing for the analytical autonomy of violence by discussing three important distinctions: between violence and violent conflict, between violence as an outcome and as a process, and between violence in peace and war. I specify the book's scope conditions, identify a series of problems that plague the study of violence, and point to solutions.

Chapter 3 is devoted to theoretical ground clearing. Two key features tend to set civil wars apart from interstate ones with respect to violence: barbarism and intimacy. Many (though not all) civil wars are particularly atrocious or barbaric, a feature typified by a disproportional victimization of civilians; their violence is also more intimate, in the sense that it often takes place where there is a record of closeness and peaceful interaction between victims and victimizers, even on the individual level. I reconstruct, specify, and contrast four general arguments that link civil war to barbarism, inspired by different theoretical traditions: the Hobbesian account of violence as a by-product of *anarchy*, the view of violence as a response to normative *transgression*, the Schmittian thesis of violence as a result of ideological *polarization*, and the institutional account of violence as a reflection of challenges associated with a particular *technology of warfare*, namely irregular war. Although each tradition has merits, I identify this last one as the

---

[8] The most impressive effort so far remains the work of Leites and Wolf (1970).

most promising theoretical foundation on which to build and elaborate a theory of violence in civil war.

Accordingly, Chapters 4 and 5 lay out a theory of irregular war, which is defined by the twin processes of segmentation and fragmentation of sovereignty: territory is divided into zones monopolistically controlled by rival actors (segmentation) and zones where these actors' sovereignty overlaps (fragmentation). The type of sovereignty or *control* that prevails in a given region affects the type of strategies followed by political actors. Political actors try to shape popular support (or collaboration) and deter collaboration with their rival (or defection). As the conflict matures, control is increasingly likely to shape collaboration because political actors who enjoy substantial territorial control can protect civilians who live in that territory – both from their rivals and from themselves, giving survival-oriented civilians a strong incentive to collaborate with them, irrespective of their true or initial preferences. In this sense, collaboration is largely endogenous to control, though of course, high rates of collaboration spawned by control at a given point in time are likely to reinforce it in the future. For example, incumbents tend to control cities, even when these cities happen to be the social, religious, or ethnic strongholds of their opponents, whereas the insurgents' strongholds tend to be in remote rural areas, even when rural populations are inimical to them. In the long run, military resources generally trump prewar political and social support in spawning control. However, the military resources that are necessary for the imposition of control are staggering and, hence, usually lacking. The rival actors are therefore left with little choice but to use violence as a means to shape collaboration. The use of violence is bounded by the nature of sovereignty exercised by each political actor and generally must be selective rather than indiscriminate. Chapter 6 discusses the logic of indiscriminate violence, including the paradox of its use even when it appears to be counterproductive.

In Chapter 7 I use the theory of irregular war as a foundation for a theory of selective violence. Political actors maximize territorial control subject to the local military balance of power; territorial control in the context of irregular war requires the exclusive collaboration of individual civilians who, in turn, maximize various benefits subject to survival constraints. Irrespective of their sympathies (and everything else being equal), most people prefer to collaborate with the political actor that best guarantees their survival rather than defect by helping the rival actor. Collaboration is much more uncertain, however, in areas of fragmented sovereignty where both sides are present. Because of its value for consolidating control, here the premium on selective violence is particularly steep. Selective violence, however, requires private information, which is asymmetrically distributed among political actors and civilians: only the latter may know who the defectors are, and they have a choice to denounce them or not. Put otherwise, selective violence is the result of transactions between political actors and individuals: it is jointly produced by them.

The theory bridges the meso- and microlevels and predicts the likelihood of violence as a function of control. On the one hand, political actors do not need to use violence where they already enjoy high levels of control and cannot use selective violence where they have no control whatsoever; having no access to information, they may use indiscriminate violence, but it will be counterproductive. Instead, they want to use selective violence in contested areas, where they have incomplete control. On the other hand, individuals want to denounce only where it is safe for them to do so; this is the case where their victims have no access to the rival political actor and, therefore, lack the option of *counterdenunciation*. In turn, this option is related to control: the higher the level of control for one actor, the lower the presence of the rival one and, hence, of the option of counterdenunciation. The prediction is that violence is most likely to occur where one actor is near hegemonic, not where this actor is in full control or is being contested. Violence, in other words, is most likely where the organizational demand for information meets its individual supply. Outside this space, violence is less likely: political actors may demand information but individuals will fail to supply it (or veto its transformation into violence); and individuals may supply information but political actors won't act on it because they know that defection is unlikely. In short, the prediction is, rather ironically, that strategic political actors won't use violence where they need it most (in the most contested areas) and, likewise, strategic individuals will fail to get rid of their enemies where they are most willing to denounce them (in the areas fully controlled by one actor).

The empirical test requires the specification of variables that effectively circumscribe the space of violence. There are two key variables: the likelihood of individuals "defecting" to the opposite side must be high enough for political actors to be willing to resort to violence, and the likelihood of counterdenunciation or retribution facing individual denouncers must be low enough for them to be willing to denounce their neighbors. To an important extent, however, defection and most denunciations tend to be "invisible" processes. Fortunately, the operationalization of these variables exploits an essential feature of control, namely its inverse correlation with defection and denunciation: the higher the level of control, the less likely are individuals to defect (because the risks of getting caught are likewise high) and the more likely they are to denounce (because the risks of retribution are low). I compare the theory's predictions with anecdotal comparative data (Chapter 8) and test the hypotheses with data from a micro-comparative study I conducted in Greece (Chapter 9). The evidence is far from optimal, but optimal evidence does not exist for problems such as those explored in this book. It is, however, extremely suggestive and constitutes an important step in the direction of systematic and comprehensive testing. I also use the theory's mispredictions as a tool for capturing the causal mechanisms at work. Because the theory uses a rationalist baseline, its predictive failures may be a way to grasp the work of noninstrumental factors, such as norms and emotions. Finally, I conduct a series of out-of-sample tests across Greece, including a replication in an ethnically divided area of the country and the testing of additional implications using data on 136 villages collected from local histories, ethnographies, agricultural studies, research papers, and interviews.

The last two chapters explore two implications of the theory. Chapter 10 turns to the "intimate" violence that characterizes civil wars. Although the theory of selective violence accounts for the political actors' demand for information and predicts *where* individuals will denounce, it remains agnostic as to *why* individuals are willing to respond to demands for information by denouncing. I argue that denunciation constitutes a key microfoundation of intimate violence and, hence, civil war. Individuals have strong incentives to exploit the informational asymmetries of civil war in order to reap all kinds of benefits, including settling accounts with personal and local enemies. Though denunciation does not have to be opportunistic, I provide an explanation for why it so often is, one that also accounts for the triviality of disputes that often undergirds it. I also point to the moral hazard aspect of denunciation. While political actors "use" civilians to collect information and win the war, it is also the case that civilians "use" political actors to settle their own private conflicts. Put otherwise, civilians may effectively turn political actors into their own private "contract killers," in a pattern akin to what Jan Gross (1988:118–19) has described in his study of western Ukraine as "privatization of authority." This aspect of civil war, directly implied by the logic of joint violence, turns polarization theories on their head: rather than reflecting the politicization of private life, civil war violence often privatizes politics. Insofar as it reflects local conflicts and personal disputes, the intimate nature of violence in civil war can be seen as the dark face of social capital. From a more general perspective, this account suggests that civil wars are bloody not so much because people are inherently violent, but because they are not: most are repelled by the prospect of acting violently, and so they will not, unless someone else handles the gory details while shielding them. Hence civil war is so violent at least partly because it provides opportunities for indirect violence.

The last chapter explores the theory's implications for our understanding of the notion of cleavage and points to a solution to the problem of the macro-micro disjunction. The link between actors at the center and the action on the ground is usually subsumed in the concept of cleavage, which implies common preferences between central and local actors. This book introduces a different mechanism for mapping national-level cleavages onto the local level, one that is consistent with the observed disjunction between center and periphery: the mechanism of alliance entails an exchange between local and supralocal actors, whereby the latter offer the former military muscle so that they can prevail in local conflicts; in return, local actors supply central ones with essential local resources that help them wage the war. Myriads of local conflicts are thus linked to the overarching conflict of the civil war – its "master cleavage." Seen from this perspective, civil war is, at its core, a process of integration and state building.

I.4. A NOTE ON THE HISTORY OF THE PROJECT

I began with a rather vague idea about researching the process of polarization at the microlevel. In fact, my original intention was to trace the process through which political identities became radicalized and led to violence. In early 1997, I conducted the first exploratory interviews in Athens (my first interview took place on January 27, 1997). While working on other projects, I was able to conduct some more interviews across Greece (summer 1997) and came away rather confused but with two key intuitions: first, local dynamics were of fundamental importance and, second, violence appeared to be less the result of powerful political identities and deep divisions and more their cause. Further reading and thinking led me to shift to a new dependent variable: violence.

In September 1997 I went to Florence, where I spent nine months at the European University Institute as a Jean Monnet Fellow. An initial disadvantage of this fellowship was that it forced me to interrupt my fledging fieldwork; however, this interruption turned into an advantage as I was able to read extensively and distance myself from the field while benefiting from the insights of my exploratory field research. Although I was able to conduct some additional research during a couple of brief visits to Greece, I used my time in Florence to formulate the project's core research question: the variation of violence at the local level. I elaborated my research design, selected the Argolid as my field site, and read extensively, both theoretically and empirically. The theoretical work I conducted in 1997–8 found its first empirical application in an article published by *Rationality and Society* in 1999: "Wanton and Senseless? The Logic of Massacres in Algeria." During this period I came up with the main hypotheses about the spatial variation of violence.

Although my intuitions from the work I had already conducted in Greece informed my readings and thinking, I had not thus far collected any data on violence. In the summer of 1998, I returned to Greece and began to conduct systematic research in the Argolid. I still remember my excitement at discovering that the empirical patterns I uncovered fit many of my theoretical expectations. I conducted the bulk of my research in the Argolid between the summer of 1998 and the summer of 1999, following which I was able to explore Greek and British archives. I returned to NYU in 2000 and conducted additional fieldwork in the Almopia area of northern Greece in the summer of 2000.

The work was far from finished, however. Even though the essential parts of the theory and data were in place, I spent a substantial amount of time refining and clarifying the theory, transcribing interviews, cleaning and cross-checking the data, and going through hundreds of pages of archival material, memoirs, and local histories. I began to work on the manuscript after moving to Chicago in early 2001. The manuscript went through several permutations: the main challenge was the unusual combination of materials that defeated the standard political science presentation scheme of "theory" and "empirical" chapters. I felt that I reached the right balance only in 2004, after I moved to Yale. The book was reviewed during the summer of 2004 and the revisions were completed in May 2005. In sum, a long trip – but worth it.

I

Concepts

[I]t is to no purpose, it is even against one's best interest, to turn away from the
consideration of the affair because the horror of its elements excites repugnance.

Carl von Clausewitz, *On War*

To understand the living ... I found it was necessary to begin with the dead.

Salman Rushdie, *The Jaguar Smile*

This chapter reviews existing accounts of violence and civil war and clarifies
definitional and conceptual issues related to both civil war and violence. I make the
case for the analytical autonomy of violence vis-à-vis conflict and introduce three
important distinctions: between violence and violent conflict, between violence
as an outcome and as a process, and between violence in peace and violence in
war.

1.1. CIVIL WAR

Civil war has attracted considerable scholarly attention from various disciplines –
though considerably less than interstate war. Important bodies of literature have
explicitly or implicitly (as studies of revolution, rebellion, or ethnic conflict)
focused on numerous aspects: onset (Fearon and Laitin 2003; Collier et al. 2003;
Sambanis and Elbadawi 2002; Gurr 1980), resolution (B. Walter 1997), social
bases (Wickham-Crowley 1992; Skocpol 1979), outcome (Leites and Wolf 1970),
political and social consequences (Sambanis 2000), and processes of rebuilding,
reconciliation, and postwar justice (Bass 2000; Nino 1996). A recent boom in
civil war studies has been fueled by the global shift from interstate to intrastate
conflict: of the 118 armed conflicts that have taken place between 1989 and 2004,
only 7 have been interstate wars (Harbom and Wallensteen 2005).

Until recently, however, civil war enjoyed little conceptual autonomy (Ranzato
1994); the term is still used by analysts and observers in multiple, often contradictory, ways. While historians have used it to describe discrete historical events,

they have generally refrained from analyzing civil war as a phenomenon that transcends particular instances. In historical sociology and political science, civil war was until very recently subsumed under phenomena implicitly deemed more important, such as revolution, peasant rebellion, or ethnic conflict. In everyday language, "civil war" (unlike "revolution") is a term that conveys a sense of violent division, often used as a metaphor for extreme conflict and widespread brutality.

Civil war often refuses to speak its name. Euphemisms abound: one hears of "troubles," "emergency," "situation," or simply "violence." Indeed, civil war is often the object of serious semantic contestation. The very use of the term is part of the conflict itself, conferring or denying legitimacy (or status equality) to the parties in the conflict. The American Civil War was called "The War of Rebellion" and "The Second American Revolution," depending on the favored side. During the war, the term is usually sought out by insurgents in search of legitimacy, and denied by incumbents who label their opponents "bad guys," bandits, criminals, subversives, or terrorists – and describe the war as banditry, terrorism, delinquent subversion, and other cognate terms.[1] In fact, the repudiation of the term is common to all incumbent regimes, leftist and rightist, authoritarian and democratic alike (e.g., Horton 1998:11; Pavone 1994). Following a civil war's end, the term is often claimed by the vanquished in their quest for political redemption and inclusion, and denied by the winners who seek the permanent exclusion of the losers from the political, or even national, realm (Bobbio 1992). The spillover effect of this semantic contest has affected research on the topic, as definitions of civil war have tended, until recently at least, to hinge on the war's outcome (Price 2001:33–4).

Civil war is defined here as *armed combat within the boundaries of a recognized sovereign entity between parties subject to a common authority at the outset of the hostilities*. This definition is a broader and more minimal version of existing definitions (Sambanis 2004); it is agnostic about causes, goals, and motivations. "Internal war" is more precise, but civil war is by far the most familiar term. "Armed combat" (implying a degree of organization on both sides and violence of a certain magnitude) serves political aims when it challenges existing authority, even when also serving additional goals (Chapter 11).

The key intuition is the violent physical division of the sovereign entity into rival armed camps. This entails a de facto *territorial* division. At the war's outset, the rivals are subjects to a common sovereign or authority (De Lupis 1987:3; C. Schmitt 1976). After 1648 this refers increasingly to state authority, but prior to the spread of modern state sovereignty civil wars took place within entities perceived as sovereign or "quasi-sovereign," from empires down to city-states and kin-based groups.[2] In fact, historians use the concept of civil war as an analytical category for the pre-1648 period (e.g., Porter 1994).

---

[1] The German occupation authorities in the Soviet Union made this point explicitly in 1942: "For psychological reasons," the term "partisan" was to be replaced by "bandit"; accordingly, antipartisan operations were to be called "antibandit warfare" and areas of suspected partisan presence were referred to as areas "contaminated with bandit groups" (in Heer 2000:113).

[2] Carl Schmitt (1976:32) speaks of "organized units" and Bobbio (in Ranzato 1994:xxvi) of "autarkic entities." Even when sovereignty was fragmented, decentralized, and overlapping (e.g., in medieval

Civil wars have been fought for all kinds of reasons, from "differences of doctrine and intellectual wrangling" (Hobbes, *Leviathan*, appendix 2:30), to differences of ascription (mainly ethnicity and religion), and to plain power grabbing (Collier and Hoeffler 1999). The parties to the conflict may be united or divided, internationally recognized or isolated and obscure, supported by external actors or relying on local resources, seeking to capture the state or to divide it. However, the conflicts that are constitutive of civil wars can be best described as those related to the effective breakdown of the monopoly of violence by way of armed internal challenge. The armed contestation of sovereignty entails mutually exclusive claims to authority that produce a situation of *divided* or *dual sovereignty* (Tilly 1978:191; Trotsky 1965:224) – a concept that can be traced back to Plato, who thought of domestic war or "faction" as the war that arises when "ruling [a city] becomes a thing fought over" (*Republic* 521a), and Grotius (II, 18:2), who pointed to situations whereby "a people has been divided into parts so nearly equal that it is doubtful which of the two sides possesses sovereignty." Divided sovereignty came to be seen as something unnatural (Rousseau, *Social Contract* II, 2:3). In the words of a Vietnamese man: "There cannot be two suns and there cannot be two kings for one country" (in Elliott 2003:749).

Shared membership to a sovereign entity by all belligerents when the war begins is essential (Bouthoul 1970:447). "The American Revolution was a civil war," Shy (1976:183) reminds us, because "in proportion to population, almost as many Americans were engaged in fighting other Americans during the Revolution as did so during the Civil War." Membership is understood here as reflecting basic obligation rather than citizenship and does not require a subjective perception of belonging.

Reflection on civil war is associated with two intertwined intellectual traditions. On the one hand, the concepts of *stasis* (faction) and public discord and division preoccupied writers in smaller sovereign entities, such as city-states; on the other hand, the concepts of sedition and rebellion tended to emerge in larger sovereign entities, such as empires.

The ancient Greeks posited a self-evident link between *stasis* and the *polis* and understood the concept of *stasis* to refer to "a *polis* which is internally divided" (Price 2001:31). Thucydides (3.69–85), Plato (*Republic* 470c–b), and Aristotle (*Politics* V:v–xii) drew a clear distinction between *stasis* and external war.[3] Civil war became the dominant form of war in the late Roman Empire (Brent Shaw 2001) and has been a constant occurrence in Europe since then; these civil wars include factional conflicts of the sort that took place in the Italian medieval republics, as recorded in the writings of Marsilius of Padua, Machiavelli, and others, as well as wars pitting the crown against various corporate entities, such as estates,

---

Europe), there existed entities with recognized jurisdiction, princes that were "supreme and public persons" (in Hale 1971:8). The concepts of "dominium" and "lordship" describe such quasi sovereignty during the Middle Ages (Davies 2003).

[3] There was even a more subtle difference as well: *diaphorá* was a term used to describe civil wars in one's own *polis*, whereas civil wars in a neighboring *polis* were described as *stasis* (Price 2001:35).

religious groups, and cities. Grotius (*On the Law of War and Peace* II, 19:4) made a clear distinction between civil and "foreign" wars, while Hobbes (*Leviathan* 13:8) argued that sovereign authority emerges (and is justified) precisely to ward off civil war: men are in a state of war as long as there is no "common power to keep them all in awe" – a point also made by Grotius (I, 4:2). Indeed, restrictions on the right of resistance to a legally constituted authority were justified by Grotius and other authors on the basis of their consequence, namely civil war.

By this definition, most revolutions, sustained peasant insurrections, "revolutionary" or ethnic insurgencies, anticolonial uprisings, and resistance wars against foreign occupiers are civil wars (Malefakis 1996:18; C. Friedrich 1972:37). On the other hand, violent protests, riots, crime, and low-level banditry, all of which leave sovereignty pretty much intact, are excluded from this category.[4]

1.2. VIOLENCE

Though it may be an intuitive concept, violence is a conceptual minefield. As a multifaceted social phenomenon, it can be defined very broadly and stretched way beyond physical violence (Nordstrom and Martin 1992:8). Some distinguish between violence that preserves the social order ("systemically functional" violence) and violence that destroys it ("dysfunctional" violence) (C. Friedrich 1972; Sorel 1921); others take social and economic oppression (or even competition) to be forms of "structural" violence (Braud 1999; Galtung 1975; Ellul 1969:86). Finally, some think that the range of social acts that qualify as violence is so broad as to include any act that results in mental anguish (Bourdieu 1977:191). This books narrows down the definition of violence to its physical dimension.

At a very basic level, violence is the deliberate infliction of harm on people. Here I further narrow my focus to violence against noncombatants or civilians. This is an ambiguous and contentious category in most civil wars, the object of never-ending legal and philosophical dispute (Nabulsi 1999; Walzer 1997). Because I am interested in intracommunity dynamics, for the purpose of this book I regard as civilians all those who are not full-time members of an armed group, thus including all types of part-timers and collaborators.[5] Noncombatant

---

[4] Many studies of occupation and anticolonial insurgencies stress their civil war dimension (e.g., D. Anderson 2005; Bouaziz and Mahé 2004; Pavone 1994; Shy 1976). Civil wars are distinguished from coups when a certain fatality threshold is crossed, entailing significant military operations. Large-scale insurgencies with a predominantly rural basis should not be confused with a class of events described as "peasant rebellions," including spontaneous peasant uprisings, jacqueries, food riots, and the like. These undisciplined, unstable, anarchic, and decentralized processes (Tilly 1978) are not sustained long enough to challenge sovereign authority effectively. Unless harnessed by skilled organizers, jacqueries are usually repressed (Marks 1984:240). Peasant rebellions develop into civil wars (and possibly social revolutions) when spurred and led by organizations (DeNardo 1985; B. Moore 1966:479). Borderline phenomena such as the Chinese Cultural Revolution may be understood as civil wars (L. White 1989:308).

[5] I explain how I code noncombatants in Appendix B.

fatalities in civil wars are not always violent; famine and disease can be highly lethal. Violent fatalities can also be unintentional, the so-called collateral damage. In this book, I account for the violent and intentional victimization of civilians.

Intentional and direct physical violence takes several forms, including pillage, robbery, vandalism, arson, forcible displacement, kidnapping, hostage taking, detention, beating, torture, mutilation, rape, and desecration of dead bodies. Although I refer to various forms of violence, my primary focus is on violent death or homicide. As just stated, homicide does not exhaust the range of violence, but is an unambiguous form that can be measured more reliably than other forms (Spierenburg 1996:63; Buoye 1990:255), which is why it is used as the primary indicator of violence in quantitative studies (e.g., Poole 1995; Greer 1935). In addition, there is a general consensus that homicide crosses a line: it "is an irreversible, direct, immediate, and unambiguous method of annihilation" (Straus 2000:7); in this sense, death is "the absolute violence" (Sofsky 1998:53).

1.2.1. Violence, Conflict, War

Violence is typically treated as synonymous with cognate but distinct concepts such as "conflict," "revolution," or "war." Hence most references to, say, "ethnic violence" refer to ethnic conflict or ethnic war rather than the actual violence that takes place within the conflict. However, conflicts, wars, and revolutions are phenomena that cannot be simply reduced to large-scale violence. Conversely, violence, as Hannah Arendt (1970:19) pointed out, is "a phenomenon in its own right" that should not be equated with cognate phenomena. David Horowitz (2001:475) echoes Arendt when he points out that "there is good reason to treat conflict and violence separately." Obviously, war "causes" violence. However, a considerable amount of violence in civil wars lacks conventional military utility and does not take place on the battlefield. If anything, there appears to be an inverse relationship between the magnitude of the conflict, as measured by the size of forces and the sophistication of the weapons used, and the magnitude of violence (Harkavy and Neuman 2001:230). Moreover, areas consumed by the same conflict can exhibit substantial variation in violence. Hence, violence should be analytically decoupled from war, echoing the well-established distinction between *jus ad bellum* (lawful initiation of war) and *jus in bello* (lawful conduct of war).

This book places violence at the center of the analysis. The analytical distinction between *civil war* and *violence in civil war* is both its premise and major implication. The causes of violence in civil war cannot be subsumed under the causes of civil war; hence a theory of civil wars cannot be a theory of violence in civil wars – and vice versa.[6] At the same time, the theory of violence presented herein is compatible with different views of civil war onset: it does not matter whether civil wars begin because of mass grievances or opportunities. Simply put, a civil war is likely to open a Pandora's box of violence.

---

[6] Hence it is incorrect to test theories of civil war onset using an indicator of violence, such as fatalities, as the dependent variable (e.g., Murshed and Gates 2005).

1.2.2. Violence as an Outcome and as a Process

The observation that political violence tends to be produced by very small groups of people (Mueller 2004; Valentino 2000:21–5) has led to the conjecture that most people remain uninvolved (Valentino 2000:2); they are an unaware public at best and passive spectators at worst. Likewise, the observation that killers often dehumanize their victims (e.g., Toolis 1997:126) sustains the perception that violence in civil wars is impersonal. Regardless of their empirical accuracy, these conjectures fail to distinguish between violence as an *outcome* and violence as a *process*.

Although political scientists and historians tend to subsume violence under violent conflict, many anthropologists, NGO activists, and journalists tend to perceive violence as an outcome rather than as a process, often effectively "black-boxing" it (e.g., Appadurai 1996). The focus is on instances of violence rather than the complex, and often invisible, nonviolent actions and mechanisms that precede and follow them. Often, the description of very recent acts of violence is accompanied by references to ancient historical events, with no reference to the period in between. Like traditional depictions of Balkan feuding, many descriptions of civil war make no effort "to link one episode to another. Each case is treated as isolated in time and space. Nor do these writers attempt to explain the disproportion that so marks what superficially appears to constitute the relationship of cause to effect" (Black-Michaud 1975:34). Furthermore, little or no information is provided about the victims' histories and lives before the advent of violence (Binford 1996:5). Such a view assumes (and further propagates) a dichotomous world populated only by victims and perpetrators, combined with the flawed perception that victimhood and guilt are mutually exclusive categories – hence victims cannot be guilty. Yvon Grenier (1999:2) portrays the literature on Latin American insurgencies as suggesting "a world inhabited by women, children, and the elderly," a point also made about other civil wars (Cenarro 2002:67; Brovkin 1994:5). Typically overlooked is a large "gray zone" populated by those who partake in the process of violence in a variety of ways without, however, being directly involved in its outcome, as either perpetrators or victims. A corollary is that the line between perpetrators and victims is blurred, as yesterday's victims may turn into tomorrow's victimizers and vice versa (Joshi 2003:xiii; Chang 1992:498). Women and children, usually portrayed as victims, are often active and willing participants in all kinds of activities, including combat (Peterson 2000:112). Tzvetan Todorov (1996:xvi–xvii) tells how conducting a close study of a massacre that took place in the French town of Saint-Amand-Montrond in the summer of 1944 forced him to discover the missing sequence of events and revise his understanding of the massacre:

Little by little I realized that the massacre in question had not occurred at that time and place for no reason but was rather the culmination of a series of no less dramatic events that preceded it during that summer. After a short time I was no longer satisfied with having read the few works that told the various episodes in this story. With the help of a friend from the region, I decided to seek out and ask questions of the various contemporaries and witnesses of these incidents. I ran across some unpublished manuscripts. I read both the daily and weekly press of the period, and I spent several days undoing the strings around the dusty files in the departmental and national archives. I could no longer tear myself away from the story.... In reading about [the fate of the main actors] I became convinced that, when talking about this period, it was imperative to go beyond both the hagiography of the "victors" (which is nevertheless so fitting for official celebrations) and its reverse image, systematic denigration; the same could be said for the "defeated." Instead of a world of black and white, I discovered a series of distinct situations, of particular acts, each of which called for its own separate evaluation.

Approaching violence as a dynamic process allows an investigation of the sequence of decisions and events that intersect to produce violence, as well as the study of otherwise invisible actors who partake in this process and shape it in fundamental ways.

1.2.3. Violence in Peace and in War

As studies of civil war have tended to overlook violence, studies of "political violence," a broad and imprecise concept that covers everything from campus demonstrations to genocide, have tended to disassociate it from civil war. This body of research often intersects with research on social movements – particularly studies of "contentious politics," a term that also includes phenomena ranging from nonviolent collective action to sporadic violence (Tarrow 1994). This work tends to treat violence "either as the unproblematic extension of ordinary social movement processes, or conversely, as a pathological effect of competition or decline within social movements" (Seideman 2001:2).

Conflating violence in the context of contentious action with civil war violence suggests a failure to recognize that war and peace are radically different contexts that induce and constrain violence in very different ways. To be sure, these contexts share many mechanisms (Tilly 2003); however, the way in which these mechanisms are activated as well as their effects' diverges. Most obviously, forming and expressing political preferences are fundamentally different in times of peace and during a war. At the very least, the stakes are much higher in wartime.

The difference between violence in peace and violence in war is clearly one of degree. The total number of deaths in all reported episodes and campaigns of protest is negligible compared with the total number of deaths in all reported rebellions (Gurr 1986:52). Even terrorism involves violence on a much lower scale than civil war (Guelke 1995). Sri Lanka, a country with the misfortune of having experienced both peacetime riots and civil war has experienced significantly more fatalities due to the latter.

More important, the difference between violence in peace and violence in war is a difference in kind. As Vladimir Brovkin (1994:419) reminds us about Russia, "the civil war routinized the unthinkable.... It substituted for politics as usual the politics of war." War structures choices and selects actors in radically different ways than peace – even violent peace. As a former Greek insurgent remarks, "an armed confrontation is not like a [workers'] strike. You can be defeated in a strike once and twice and three times, and still survive. When you opt for an armed rebellion you bet everything you have" (Papakonstantinou 1986 1:583).

Contentious action represents a challenge to the government in place in a context characterized by an undeniable monopoly of violence by the state. In contrast, the defining characteristic of civil war is the absence of such monopoly. Contentious action in democratic settings is causally different from rebellion: whereas the former thrives in the presence of political opportunities, the latter is likely in situations where such opportunities are absent (Goodwin 1999); in ethnically heterogeneous societies at least, the dynamics of riots and demonstrations are the exact opposite to those of rebellion (Bates 1999). Unlike civil wars, riots tend to be a predominantly urban phenomenon (Varshney 2002:10; C. Friedrich 1972:70), lacking significant retaliation (Horowitz 2001:224), heavily influenced by institutional (often electoral) incentives (Wilkinson 2004), and facilitated by crowd anonymity; the ratio of perpetrators to victims tends to be inverse in riots and civil war: in the former participation is public and the victims are an unlucky few, whereas in the latter a few participate directly in victimizing an unlucky public. In Sri Lanka, ethnic riots declined and almost ceased after the civil war began, and there were no riots in Indian Punjab during the Sikh insurgency of 1984–94 (Horowitz 2001:482–5). Varshney (2002:11) is thus right to argue that a theory of civil wars must be "analytically distinguished" from a theory of riots. This is true, even when riots and pogroms take place in the context of war (Petersen 2002). The situation can be compared with the occurrence of genocide and war: although the two almost always intersect, the study of each phenomenon is usually distinct.

1.3. SCOPE CONDITIONS

Available conceptualizations of political violence as an object of research vary depending on the criteria employed: the scale of violence (mass killing; mass crimes; massacres) (Verwimp 2003; Valentino 2004; Sémelin 2000; Levene 1999), its mode and technique (riots, pogroms, reprisals) (Wilkinson 2004; Varshney 2002; Geyer 2000), the motivations of perpetrators (Straus 2000; Fein 1993), or the specific historical and social context of a particular instance (Browning 1998). A careful delineation of scope conditions is, thus, necessary. The intersection of two key features of violence defines the domain of analysis in this book: the aims and the production of violence.

1.3.1. The Aims of Violence

Political actors use violence to achieve multiple, overlapping, and sometimes mutually contradictory goals. Various literatures detail more than twenty uses for violence, including intimidation, demoralization, polarization, demonstration, radicalization of the public, publicity, the improvement of group morale, the enforcement or disruption of control, the mobilization of forces and resources, financing, the elimination of opposing forces, the sanction of cooperation with the enemy, and the provocation of countermeasures and repression (Hovil and Werker 2005; Schmid 1983:97–9, Mallin 1966:59, Molnar 1965:169). Further, violence may be used with no goal in mind, and war may generate violence that is completely independent from the intentions of the main actors and materializes as a by-product of their action, such as looting or certain forms of revenge. Such a profusion of diverse aims can paralyze the analysis.

It is necessary, first, to address the issue of violence that serves no instrumental purpose. Such violence is said to be expressive when its use is restricted to the "strictly consummatory rewards of inflicting pain on one's enemies or destroying a hated symbol" (Rule 1988:190). Often described as anomic or nihilistic, expressive violence is often combined with "identity" or "sectarian" violence, that is, violence directed against persons exclusively on the basis of who they are. This understanding of violence dominates popular accounts that emphasize the madness of violence (e.g., Rosenberg 1991) and is present in many scholarly works stressing the discursive, symbolic, ritualistic, and generally noninstrumental character of violence.[7] Interpretations of violence as expressive motivation can also be found in victims' testimonies: "They killed for killing's sake – like mad dogs going after their prey" (in Tarnopolsky 1999:52).

Individual motivations of violence can be, and often are, expressive (Petersen 2002; Horowitz 2001:123). Greek tragedy is a treasure trove of expressive violence, with *orgē* (anger), *eris* (discord), or *pthonos* (envy) driving violent acts (Bernand 1999). Criminological research recognizes the importance of expressive motivations, because a large part of nonpredatory murders are not premeditated or driven by instrumental means-end motivations and are conducted with an indifference to consequences (J. Katz 1988). Many descriptions of violence in civil wars are apparently devoid of any instrumental significance and fit the expressive template very well. Consider the following parallel recollections, from the Spanish and Lebanese civil wars:

> Later they shot Saturnino along with thirty-six others in reprisal for a civil guard's son who was killed at the front.... When the father heard the news of his son's death, he went to the Toro jail and began saying, "This one, this one, this one!" without knowing who they were. Thirty-six were shot. (Sender Barayón 1989:162–3)

> We're heading straight for the slaughterhouse.... it's just a couple of blocks behind your house. You know the empty lot there. That's where Halabi, the Moslem butcher whose son was kidnapped, is collecting Christian Maronites. He wants his revenge, that man! We'd better stay out of that area. (Tabbara 1979:64–5)

An overriding emphasis on expressive motivation, however, runs into problems. In general, it is extremely difficult to uncover with an acceptable level of accuracy the individual motives behind violent acts (Tilly 1975:512). Deducing motive from behavior is a bad idea, as is replacing evidence with politically motivated classifications, as in the case of "hate crime" (Rothstein 2005:E3): the problem of observational equivalence is common since a particular act may be consistent with several motives. Furthermore, motives are typically subject to (strategic or unselfconscious) reinterpretation and ex post rationalization by the subjects. Even when fully revealed, intentions often turn out to be mixed or even contradictory. For example, individual motivations of violence may mix hatred (of many sorts), peer pressure (Browning 1992), obedience (Milgram 1974), honor,

---

[7] E.g., Mahmood (2000:74–81); Geyer (2000:201); Crouzet (1990); Zemon Davis (1973).

rituals, and collective imaginaries (Nahoum-Grappe 1996; Zemon Davis 1973), greed (Paul and Demarest 1988), revenge (Frijda 1994), or sadistic impulses; they may also result from the consumption of alcohol (Tishkov 2004:139; G. Jones 1989:124) or the use of drugs (Aussaresses 2001; Peters and Richards 1998). Complicating things is the prevalence of correspondence bias – the tendency of observers to draw inferences about enduring individual dispositions from behavior that can be explained by the situation in which it occurs (Gilbert and Malone 1995).

Obviously, these problems apply to all types of motives, instrumental and noninstrumental alike. However, many observers tend to be biased toward interpretations that stress expressive motives. For instance, while several observers were quick to attribute the violence between the Dayaks and the Madurese of West Kalimantan in Indonesia to the ritual reenactment of headhunting, others remarked that violence was strategically deployed in the course of the conflict (Peluso and Harwell 2001). Consider the following remark by Mario Vargas Llosa (1994:428): "I was scribbling the speech . . . [when] the news of the assassination of our leader in Ayacucho, Julián Huamaní Yauli, reached me. . . . His murder was a good example of the irrationality and stupid cruelty of the terrorist strategy, since it was not intended to punish any violence, exploitation, or abuse committed by the extremely modest and previously apolitical Julián Huamaní, but simply to terrify through the crime those who believed that elections could change things in Peru." In a misleading, though extremely common way, Vargas Llosa overlooked the clearly instrumental nature of this murder, which he himself acknowledges, to describe it as an irrational act.

Seneca observed that "no one proceeds to shed human blood for its own sake, or at any rate only few do so" (in Grotius II, 22:2). Indeed, expressive motivations may be less widespread than is often assumed. People involved in the production of political violence appear to lack the kind of "extreme" personality features that tend to correlate with expressive violence. A number of studies of perpetrators of violence have failed to uncover pathological traits (Kakar 1996; Della Porta 1995), whereas others have pointed out that the ritualization of violence often serves instrumental purposes (Richards 1996:xx; Schroeder 1996:432).

The stress on expressive violence may result from a double confusion: between individual and collective motivations and between descriptive and causal accounts. Arguments about the expressive and symbolic aspects of violence claim to address the motivations of collective actors (e.g., why the Hutu attacked the Tutsi) when in fact they only describe the way in which individuals perform violence (e.g., how some Hutu attacked some Tutsi). For example, in discussing the incidents of cannibalism perpetrated in the Liberian Civil War, Ellis (1995:193) points out that "the observation that there is a 'cultic' element to violence of this type does not imply that the militias fight primarily as a form of ritual behaviour." Inge Brinkman (2000:2, 14) first notes that her informants, Angolan refugees in Namibia, interpret the violence of the civil war as primarily senseless and absurd, "deemed to be beyond comprehension"; still, she then reports that her informants were also sharply aware that these practices were used to instill a paralyzing and incapacitating fear: "they do it," she was told, "to frighten people." Likewise, violence in Mozambique was often sadistic and reinforced by drug use, but there is also substantial evidence that it "was co-ordinated and systematic rather than spontaneous" (Vincent 1994:87).

In fact, individual motivations alone are unlikely to result in large-scale violence over a long period of time. The Nazi policy of reprisals across occupied Europe was developed centrally even though it was often implemented by semi-rogue and openly sadistic junior officers (Heer 2000; Mazower 1993). It is, indeed, possible to overlay instrumental action on expressive action by imputing strategic behavior to leaders and expressive behavior to followers (May 1991:253; Coleman 1990:483). Unlike riots, civil wars are contexts that place considerable premium on organization, hence reinforcing interpretations of violence as instrumental.

Violence can be used to exterminate a group or to control it (Sémelin 2000; E. Walter 1969:14). This book focuses on the latter type, also known as coercive violence. Although the methods used to achieve compliance and physical destruction may be similar, these objectives differ. A way to distinguish between the two is to ask whether at least one political actor intends to govern the population it targets for violence; an empirical indicator of this intention is whether the targets of violence have the option to surrender. In many civil wars amnesty programs encourage insurgent defection and spare or even reward civilians who defect and collaborate with them, whereas in genocides the surrender of victims does not prevent their murder but expedites it (Fein 1993:21). Analytically akin to physical destruction is mass deportation, sometimes referred to as "ethnic cleansing."

When violence is primarily used to control a population, it becomes a resource rather than the final product (Gambetta 1993:2). This type of violence entails an analytical distinction between the victims and the targets of violence (E. Walter 1969:9). If someone tortures a child in order to get her to reveal where somebody else can be found, the child is simultaneously a victim and a target. But if the same child is tortured in order to get her father to reveal somebody else's whereabouts of which the child knows nothing, then it is the father who is the target although it is the child who suffers the violence; the father can comply or refuse to comply, whereas the child can do neither (O. O'Neill 1991:172–3). In short, violence is intended to shape the behavior of a targeted audience by altering the expected value of particular actions. Put otherwise, violence performs a communicative function with a clear deterrent dimension – consistent with the description of civil wars as times of fear and eras of terror (Senaratne 1997:145). As Trotsky (1961:88) put it, "the revolution . . . kills individuals and intimidates thousands" – an insight also expressed in the Chinese proverb "kill just one and frighten ten thousand others." Mao Zedong called for "blows to the traitors and collaborators who undermine the army and the people" (in Heilbrunn 1967:145) and Che Guevara (1998:91) justified "assaults on persons" as a means of preventing information leaks. In Grossman's (1995:207) emphatic formulation, "One of the most obvious and blatant benefits of atrocity is that it quite simply scares the hell out of people. The raw horror and savagery of those who murder and abuse cause people to flee, hide, and defend themselves feebly, and often their victims respond with mute passivity." Note, however, that coercive violence is not necessarily massive. In fact, successful terror implies low levels of violence, since violence is "off the equilibrium path." Coercion fails if it merely destroys the subject whose compliance is sought.

Coercive violence may be strategic and tactical at the same time. Targeting a person to eliminate a particular risk (e.g., information leaks) is tactical, but using this act of violence so as to deter others from engaging in similar behavior is strategic. The counterrevolutionary rebels in western France directed their violence against people accused of informing the republican soldiers about their movements; they abandoned the mutilated corpses near republican-held towns and hung a tag around the informer's neck with his name and those of the victims who were avenged by his death; in this way they sought "to make examples in order to deter similar vocations" (Dupuy 1997:161). Martyn Latsis, a Communist leader during the Russian Civil War, asserted that "one must not only destroy the forces of the enemy, but also demonstrate that whoever raises the sword against the existing order of class, will perish by the sword" (Werth 1998:85). In Colombia, summary execution of suspected collaborators is the rule: "An assassin, dispatched day or night, ends any potential for collaboration and closes the case irrevocably, while also sending a crystal-clear message to the local population that the armed group will not tolerate such activities" (Fichtl 2004:5). Consider the following description of an IRA assassination: "Flood had become an RUC military asset who had to die to protect the IRA and deter other would-be informers" (Toolis 1997:202). In a different formulation, coercive violence tends to be both retrospective in its intention to punish an action that has already taken place and prospective in its goal to deter a similar future action by someone else.[8]

Even a cursory reading of descriptive accounts suggests the widespread strategic character of violence in civil war contexts. Consider the following examples. A Zimbabwean peasant explained the murder of a government collaborator by guerrillas by saying that "they only wanted to show the [masses] they had the power to do anything and instill fear so that none would repeat the mistake" (Kriger 1992:156). In Peru, "from the beginning, even without an infrastructure of war weaponry, Shining Path sought to terrorize and paralyze opposition, to inspire fear by displaying overwhelming force that demolished the enemy" (Del Pino 1998:168). Jeffrey Race (1973:135) was told that "the Vietcong use terrorism to instill fear. In a hamlet they will pick out a couple of people who they say cooperate with the Americans, and shoot them, to set an example.... After they kill a few people, the whole hamlet is afraid and the Vietcong can force them to cooperate." A British agent in German-occupied Greece in 1944 stressed the same aspect to describe the violence used by the partisans: they "were masters of the psychology of the 'exemplary atrocity.'... They seem to specialise in picking on the one man whose death or disappearance would cause a whole area to continue its more or less docile support for their cause."[9]

---

[8] Obviously, this logic is part of justice systems everywhere.

[9] "Report by Cpl Buhayar," PRO, HS 5/698. See also Toolis (1997:81) on Northern Ireland, Senaratne (1997:121) on Sri Lanka, Kheng (1983:180) on Malaya, Ortiz Sarmiento (1990:190) on Colombia.

Perpetrators and victims often acknowledge the deterrent character of violence. The following entry from the diary of an Algerian man is telling: "November 29, 1956: Each time a traitor or so-called traitor is executed, anguish seizes the survivors. Nobody is sure of anything anymore. People are really terrified. Terrified of the soldiers, terrified of the outlaws" (Feraoun 2000:155). A Nicaraguan Liberal writing in 1928 about Conservative violence pointed out that "All of the above delinquencies have been committed by Conservative bandits, and per the general opinion to put fear into the Liberals." Michael Schroeder (2000:38) who quotes him, concludes that "the fundamental objective of all political groups" was to instill fear *(para infundir terror)*. This dimension is also consistent with ways of killing that sometimes border on the baroque, such as abandoning corpses in public spaces or stuffing the victim's mouth with banknotes to warn against accepting cash payments from rivals (Dalrymple 1997:123; Crozier 1960:163). Mutilation often serves the same purpose: it is a "walking example" (Leites and Wolf 1970:106). In Sierra Leone, the "cutting off of villagers' hands and fingers inscribe, on the landscape and in the bodies of village people, a set of political messages rather more firmly than if they had been spoken over the radio" (Richards 1996:6). In fact, instances of harrowing and seemingly absurd violence often reflect strategic calculations. Paul Richards (1996:181), an anthropologist who studied the civil war in Sierra Leone, argues that such an analysis makes sense of "patterns of otherwise apparently senseless violence by the RUF." William Finnegan (1992:58), an American journalist, likewise argues that many massacres perpetrated by the insurgents in Mozambique (and which were interpreted as gratuitous by ill-informed observers) were intended to send specific messages to the local population.

Although the underlying logic of coercive violence is similar across contexts, its form varies depending on aims and local cultures. Targets can be prominent local personalities or weak and marginal people, and the intensity of their victimization varies widely. A Northern Irish petty thief recalls how his defiance in the face of the IRA demand that he leave the country led to his abuse (in Smyth and Fay 2000:124): "So, the IRA was blaming me and saying it was my fault because if I hadn't stood up to them, no one would have stood up. There was nobody stood up to them before me."

In short, although violence in civil war may fulfill a variety of functions, the instrumental use of coercive violence to generate compliance constitutes a central aspect of the phenomenon. This is not to say that it is the only one. However, given the present level of theoretical development it makes sense to focus on it.

1.3.2. The Production of Violence

Violence can be produced unilaterally (by one actor, usually the state) or bilaterally/multilaterally (by two or more competing actors). The main difference between unilateral and multilateral settings is that strategic interaction is more critical in the latter. When the population has the option to join or assist existing rival actors, its reaction to violence must be factored in because it is consequential

TABLE 1.1. *A Typology of Mass Political Violence*

Production of Violence	Aims of Violence: Political Actor Intends to Govern the Population Targeted	
	Yes	No
Unilateral	State terror	Genocide and mass deportation
Bilateral (or multilateral)	Civil war violence	Reciprocal extermination

for the outcome of the conflict. Because the villagers of Duc Lap in South Vietnam were mistreated by the government soldiers assigned to protect them, they welcomed the Vietcong who got "them off their backs" (Ellsberg 2003:131). As a Mozambican man put it (in Nordstrom 1997:9), "You know, sometimes when there is only one force, they can do anything they please. There are problems with this, they can begin to throw around their power, make people do things they don't want to do, use violence against people to get what they want. When you have two forces, people now have an option. Each force has to be more responsible. People can say, 'Hey you can't treat us this way, there are others to protect us.'"

The intersection of aims and production of violence generates four ideal types of mass political violence: state terror, genocide and mass deportation, civil war violence, and a type that may be referred to, for lack of a better term, as "reciprocal extermination" (Table 1.1). These categories are not intended to capture the entire spectrum of real-world variation. They provide, instead, a useful way to specify the scope conditions of the book.[10]

Coercion is present in standard definitions of *state terror* (Mitchell et al. 1986:5). As a Spanish inquisitor put it in 1578: "We must remember that the main purpose of the trial and execution is not to save the soul of the accused but

---

[10] State terror may be delivered in a quasi-multilateral fashion by competing state agencies; the goals of compliance and extermination may coexist in the purposive elimination of one group so as to terrorize others; counterinsurgency campaigns launched with the intention of reestablishing government control over rebel-held areas may degenerate into genocidal violence; and governments, such as the Argentine junta, may justify repression by claiming that they are fighting a civil war. For example, Margolin (1999) argues that the Indonesian government's purpose in killing thousands of Communists was intimidation rather than extermination; Gurr (1986:47) disagrees. Díaz-Balart and Rojas Friend (1997:15) describe the violence exercised by Nationalists in the Spanish Civil War as intended to fulfill both intimidation and "often" extermination purposes. Likewise, Ranzato (1988) and de la Cueva (1998) show that the persecution of Catholic clergy by the Republicans during the same war reveals both an intention to scare predominantly Catholic Nationalists into compliance and a desire to exterminate as many priests as possible, simply because they were priests. The White Terror of the Russian Civil War included violence to exterminate the Jews (Figes 1996), while the Red Terror demanded the extermination "to the last man" of certain groups, such as the Cossacks (Brovkin 1994:103). The Nazi occupation of Poland aimed both at the extermination of the Polish elites and the exploitation and control of the masses (Jan Gross 1979:76). Still, it is possible to use this typology to sort out different processes taking place in the same location and time: the Nazis used different methods against partisans and Jews in the Ukraine, and, although both the Tutsi and Hutu were killed in Rwanda, the violence against the two groups followed distinctive patterns (Verwimp 2003).

to achieve the public good and put fear into others" (in Kamen 1998:174).[11] The key feature of state terror is that it is exercised against a population that lacks organized alternatives; this may account for the arbitrary character it sometimes takes. Chang (1992:218) describes how the Maoist "Anti-Rightist" Campaign of 1957 produced categories of "rightists" described in everyday language as "lots-drawing rightists" (people who drew lots to decide who should be named as rightists), "toilet rightists" (people who found they had been accused of being rightists in their absence after they could not restrain themselves from going to the toilet during the long meetings), and the rightists "who had poison but had not released it" (those who were named as rightists without having said anything against anyone). Przeworski (1991:47) cites a Soviet joke: "Three men meet in a gulag. One asks another, 'What are you here for?' 'I was against Radek,' he says. 'And you?' 'I was for Radek.' They turn to the third man, thus far silent. 'I am Radek,' he says."[12]

Genocide is premeditated, purposive, and centrally planned; it aims toward extermination rather than coercion. At its core is "intentional group annihilation" (Straus 2000:2). From this perspective, genocide is neither mere continuation of severe repression through other means nor just mass killing, but a phenomenon of an altogether different kind (Straus 2000; Chalk and Jonassohn 1990). The violent, purposeful, and permanent deportation of populations, usually in the pursuit of nationally pure space ("ethnic cleansing"), is also driven by the logic of group elimination, though the elimination is spatial rather than physical (Snyder 2003).[13]

Reciprocal extermination is a type of violence that emerges in multilateral, inter-state or intrastate contexts where neither political actor intends to govern the

---

[11] Kamen (1998:174) adds that "The coming of the Inquisition to a town was, in principle, designed to cause fear.... The public activity of the Holy Office was thus based on a premise, common to all policing systems, that fear was the most useful deterrent."

[12] Arendt (1973:305) argued that whereas "tyrannical terror" ends once it has paralyzed individuals, and "revolutionary terror" ends when the opposition is destroyed, "totalitarian terror" begins only after the opposition has been destroyed. In this situation, "terror is no longer a means to an end; it is the very essence of government." Violence in totalitarian dictatorships can turn not only against the regime's alleged enemies but against completely innocent people (Gillespie 1995:244) or even its friends and supporters (Arendt 1970:55). McAuley (1992:50) describes Stalinist terror as a completely arbitrary system where it was impossible to know how to avoid arrest and where the most committed supporter of the regime could be arrested and the most apathetic left untouched; the Russian writer Ilya Ehrenburg recalled about this period that "the fate of men was not like a game of chess, but like a lottery" (in Schmid 1983:175). In such extreme environments, violence can easily become a goal in itself. For example, toward the end of 1977, one of the most notorious detention centers of the Argentine military, finding that the "natural" supply of "subversives" was drying up, had been calling factory managers to inquire whether they had any "troublemakers" (Gillespie 1995:244).

[13] Mass population movements should be distinguished from mass deportation when they are the unintended by-product of war or the intended but temporary product (as in "forcible evacuation"). The possibility of returning to one's place once the war has ended provides an acid test for distinguishing between mass deportation and population movements. Mass dislocation that is unrelated to armed conflict is, obviously, a different issue; an estimated 40 to 80 million people have been physically displaced worldwide by the construction of dams (Rajagopal 2001).

population it targets for violence; put differently, political actors hold symmetrical intentions to exterminate each other's "civilian basis." Such intent often entails mass deportation. Often, this type of violence is associated with circumstances of state collapse and a type of warfare I label "symmetric nonconventional" (Chapter 4). Examples include the Balkan Wars (1912-13), the partisan war between Poles and Ukrainians during the Second World War, the partition of India, and the Serb-Croat War. In general, however, exterminatory violence tends to be unilateral rather than reciprocal. In fact, the unilateral nature of genocide appears to be such an empirical regularity as to be part of many definitions (e.g., Chalk and Jonassohn 1990:23).[14]

This book focuses on the final category, *civil war violence*. Unlike state repression and genocide, it is not unilateral: it is produced by at least two political actors who enjoy partial and/or overlapping monopolies of violence. Unlike the unilateral production of violence, targeted individuals often have the possibility of shifting their support and resources to competing actors; this is possible because at least one actor intends to govern the population it targets rather than to exterminate or deport it. This feature turns violence into a process with obvious strategic implications. First, political actors need to anticipate their opponents' strategy and the likely effects of their violence on civilians. Second, violence is not merely state terror multiplied by two; whereas the violence under unilateral provision is more or less a direct expression of the intentions of the actor initiating it, in civil wars it reflects the strategic interaction of at least two actors that are simultaneously present on the same territory.

1.4. CONCLUSION

This chapter has clarified the conceptual terrain. I have supplied working definitions of civil war and violence, discussed their parameters, established a set of crucial conceptual distinctions, and specified the scope conditions of the analysis. The phenomenon under investigation is intentional physical violence against noncombatants that takes the form of homicide, in a context where at least one actor seeks to control the population. The particular subset I examine is coercive violence, which is used to obtain popular compliance – a type of violence that tends to be strategic.

[14] The distinction between civil war violence and "reciprocal extermination" does not overlap with that between the violence of ethnic and nonethnic civil wars. In the majority of ethnic civil wars at least one actor (usually the incumbents) intends to rule over the population that constitutes the ethnic basis of its opponent. Reciprocal extermination appears to be a sub-type of either ethnic or "ideological" civil wars (Kalyvas 2002).

2

Pathologies

The dead are innocent, the killer monstrous, the surrounding politics insane or nonexistent.

Peter Gourevitch, *We Wish to Inform You That Tomorrow We Will Be Killed with Our Families: Stories from Rwanda*

Twenty thousand miles and four days later [U.S. officials] Krulak and Mendenhall read diametrically opposed reports [about the situation in Vietnam] to another NSC meeting at the White House. "You two did visit the same country, didn't you?" Kennedy asked. "I can explain it, Mr. President," Krulak said. "Mr. Mendenhall visited the cities and I visited the countryside and the war is in the countryside."

Neil Sheehan, *A Bright Shining Lie*

A guiding premise of this book is that despite a great deal of academic and popular interest in violence and civil war and the lurid and tragic details associated with them, violence in civil wars remains poorly understood. Extant literature on the subject suffers from a number of pathologies rising from the manner in which violence is conceptualized and the biases brought in either by researchers themselves or by the logistics involved in studying civil war. Specifically, the study of violence in civil war must overcome at least a frequent misconceptualization, referred to here as "madness," and five common biases: the partisan bias (taking sides), the political bias (equating war with peace), the urban bias (overlooking bottom-top processes), the selection bias (disregarding nonviolence), and the overaggregation bias (working at too high a level of abstraction). In the following section, I identify these pathologies, describe their effects, and point toward a solution.

2.1. MADNESS AND "BLOODLESS CONVENTION"

Prevailing accounts of political violence tend to cluster around two poles. One, descriptively rich and highly dramatic, is associated with a view of violence as an irrational and atavistic pathology, whereas the other takes violence to be an outcome of narrowly instrumental goals, in a way that is often tautological. Both are unsatisfactory and misleading.

"This is a book about evil." Bill Berkeley (2001:5) begins his riveting book on African civil wars in a way that sends a powerful signal to the reader, one stressing deviance and deep pathology. Indeed, mainstream perceptions of mass political violence typically emphasize recurring cultural proclivities, anomic randomness, and anarchic irrationality; violence is deprived of meaning beyond its own finality and is equated with madness. No wonder that invocations of Joseph Conrad's *Heart of Darkness* are so frequent (e.g., Ignatieff 1998:5). Because violence is a symptom of "social pathology," medical metaphors abound: violence is a "disease" that "is difficult to predict" and comes in convulsions, spasms, and seizures.[1] This understanding is not exclusive to journalistic descriptions or popular culture; it can also be found among well-informed elites: Abraham Lincoln argued that peace could come back to his war-torn country because "good men ought to come to their senses" (Fellman 1989:85), while international mediators appeared to think that all they had to do in order to stop the war in Bosnia was "to persuade the belligerents of the folly of war" (Silber and Little 1997:159). In a way, this understanding of violence is the contemporary and secular version of ancient perceptions of war as part of a divine plan for punishing the sinful (Hale 1971:8).

Repetitive descriptions of violence stressing its most grotesque aspects substitute emotion for coherent political analysis. The foremost rhetorical devices deployed by many observers and scholars are awe and disbelief.[2] A recurrent consequence is a breakdown of reflexivity. Echoing traditional understandings of banditry, many exercises of cultural analysis join the contemporary public discourse on terrorism in substituting anguish, conjecture, and moral platitude for systematic and rigorous theoretical and empirical analysis. Linking "piety with pathology" (Loyd 2001:4), they reproduce "the media's sensational stories, old mythical stereotypes, and a burning sense of moral wrath" (Zulaika and Douglass 1996:ix).

The prevalence of such a posture is unsurprising: violence is naturally dramatic, "an abiding source of fascination" (Cribb 1990:14). Two additional tendencies reinforce it. The first is sympathy for the victims of violence. Human rights organizations, major providers of detailed accounts of civil war violence, tend to produce a descriptive discourse of victimization that is "contaminated" by a normative discourse of condemnation. This is fine from a normative point of view, but can be fatal from a theoretical one, because condemnation surreptitiously substitutes for explanation.[3] The second tendency misconstrues the description of the symptoms of violence as its explanation, thus substituting effects for causes.

---

[1] Greenberg (2001:A8); Spencer (1992:264); Leiden and Schmitt (1968:30–1); Feldman (1964:111). In many ways, the understanding of violence today parallels the interpretation of conflict in the 1960s, which also stressed factors such as irrationality and pathology (Coser 1956).

[2] "How was so much cruelty, so much death possible?" asks Juliá (1999:11) in the opening chapter of a recent collective volume on the Spanish Civil War.

[3] Consider Browning's (1998:207) depiction of Goldhagen (1996): his claims are "grounded on the emotional impact of his narrative rather than actual comparison. He offers numerous graphic and chilling descriptions of German cruelty toward Jews and then simply asserts to the numbed and horrified reader that such behavior is clearly unprecedented."

As Durkheim (1938:110) pointed out, it is fallacious to explain social phenomena by reference to their manifestation among the states of individual consciousness rather than the social facts preceding them. For instance, the observation that civil war causes civilian victimization or dehumanization often gives rise to circular arguments positing the wish to victimize or dehumanize as the cause of civil war (e.g., Onishi 1999; Prins 1999). The result is a willingness to theorize the inherent complexity of violence into an elemental inability to explain it.[4] Not surprisingly, this generates trivial, if not outright misleading, "lessons" about the importance of tolerance and the immorality of hatred under the overall rubric of "man's inhumanity to man" (Novick 1999:258-9).

It is easy to disparage such popular understandings of violence (e.g., Sadowski 1998). The fact remains that research on violence has had little impact on popular perceptions of violence. Fascination and detail abound, but sound theoretical understanding is in short supply. Despite its centrality, violence remains marginal in studies of civil war. Because of its dramatic and graphic nature, violence appears better suited to description than theory (hence the popularity of the "madness" script), and in those cases where the focus is directly on violence, it tends to be directed toward cognate issues, such as the suffering of victims (Daniel 1996), the narratives of violence (Gilsenan 1996), or the collective memory of past violence (Contini 1997; Portelli 1997). Thirty-six years ago, Leites and Wolf (1970:v) remarked that mass political violence was "a subject whose wealth of detail is accompanied by a poverty of theory." Despite recent progress, their judgment remains largely valid.

In part, this is due to the tendency, among social scientists, to shun and conceal the lurid details that so often accompany the descriptions of violence. This is a natural reaction. As Madame de Staël (1818:112) noted in her account of the French Revolution, "we should be in some measure ashamed of ourselves, if we could contemplate these brutal atrocities sufficiently near to characterize them in detail." In that sense, social science can be said to be ruled by "bloodless conventions" (Kaufman 2001:3). Where descriptive accounts provide direct, detailed, and highly emotional descriptions of violence, social scientists tend to adopt narrowly instrumentalist accounts with a tautological bent. Mad subjects are replaced by instrumental leaders able to manipulate myopic citizens and implement policies of violence to achieve their goals. There is a tendency to argue that violence is used because it "works" (Downes 2004; Valentino, Huth, and Balch-Lindsay 2004).

As bloodless conventions in the general study of political violence often lead social scientists to skirt the very violence they purport to explain, studies of civil wars have tended to overlook the actual *content* of those conflicts (Tishkov 1999:588-9). Violence, arguably a key feature of civil wars, is often left out of the analysis. Although criminal violence and, more recently, the violence of ethnic riots, pogroms, and genocide have been subjected to rigorous social scientific scrutiny, the violence of civil war remains a topic predominantly

---

[4] The most extreme position has been made with respect to the Holocaust, which is often described as inexplicable. Bauer (2000) has rightly castigated this tendency as reducing the Holocaust to a phenomenon relevant to lamentations and liturgy rather than historical analysis.

handled by journalists and human rights activists.[5] Among academic researchers, the violence of civil war as a coherent theoretical *and* empirical phenomenon (as opposed to historical investigation or purely abstract reflections) has attracted the attention mainly of anthropologists and historians whose work is primarily descriptive. Political scientists and economists have, with few exceptions, focused on the causes of war (and civil war) rather than on their violence; likewise, studies of ethnic conflict seldom have displayed an explicit and sustained theoretical focus on violence (Brubaker and Laitin 1998:425–6). Yet, civil war is not called "dirty war" (*sale guerre, guerra basurienta*) for no reason.

2.2. PARTISAN BIAS

If war is the continuation of politics by other means, then studies of civil wars are often a continuation of war by other means: "When guns fall silent, pens take over" (Petitfrère 1981:13). Civil wars have a sticky quality: they are notorious for being a past that won't go away, *ce passé qui ne passe pas*. Their stickiness, often reinforced by their political implications for the present,[6] has produced a "scholarship of combat" by authors who explicitly or implicitly take sides and see their work as one of condemnation and justification. Much writing on this subject takes the dichotomous form of hagiography and anathema (Barrett 2001:15; Leys and Saul 1995:2; Ramsey 1973:3). Sometimes, researchers tend to take the claims of combatants for truth and reproduce them mechanically. Many writers, David Anderson (2005:10) points out, have been inclined to swallow too readily the propaganda of the Mau Mau insurgency and have thus depicted it in a simplistic dichotomous way. In its most extreme, yet frequent, version, this tendency inevitably leads to conclusions in which "glory is monopolized by one's own camp, crime by the other's" (Petitfrère 1981:50). Even seemingly descriptive language tends to be contaminated by partisanship (Rubio 1999:20). In fact, the study of violence is often the preserve of polemicists engaged in competitive discussions of comparative cruelty. Showing that one faction was more violent than the other side is thought to absolve the less violent one (Reig Tapia 1990:11). One can sometimes find a division of labor whereby the atrocities of one side are studied by partisan "experts" of the other (e.g., Casas de la Vega 1994; Reig Tapia 1990). Obviously, the partisan bias has an important implication for the social scientific study of violence since it is a major contributor to the contamination of existing data.[7]

---

5 Recent social science work on various types of violence includes Wilkinson (2004); Downes (2004); Straus (2004); Valentino et al. (2004); Verwimp (2003); J. Weinstein (2003); Varshney (2002); and Petersen (2002).

6 As Rohde (2001:46) notes about the excruciatingly exhaustive search for the victims of the massacre at Srebrenica, "just how many there are is a pivotal issue. The power of the bodies is that they control how history will be told."

7 An example of the wide-reaching and damaging effects of partisan bias can be seen in the official fatality figures for conflicts. Fatality figures tend to be prized items used in competing propaganda claims (Rohde 2001; Okey 1999); the numbers become canonical and, hence, hard to revise; any attempt to do so can easily be portrayed as a way to challenge the real suffering of the victims in the memory of their community – or its representatives. The number of "disappeared" in Argentina

This bias often spills over beyond the direct parties to the conflict. International mass media sometimes are prone to partisanship because their format encourages the production of short, unambiguous, neatly scripted stories, replete with villains and heroes (Khan 1998; Jonassohn 1998). Nor is academic research beyond reproach. Revolutionary sympathies and counterinsurgency predilections color much work on the subject. Gérard Prunier (1995:157) reports how "most genuine foreign specialists of [Rwanda and Burundi] have either been contaminated or at least accuse each other of having been contaminated by Hutu-demonising or Tutsi-hating," while Fredrik Barth (1994:24) condemns the propensity of some anthropologists to become self-appointed "advocates and apologists of ethnic groups and their grievances." So much is clear in the courageous self-criticism of an anthropologist who studied the Salvadoran Civil War: "In this Cold War atmosphere, it was difficult for me to perceive and portray the revolutionary Salvadoran peasants as anything less than innocent victims, at worst, or as noble resistors at best. The urgency of documenting and denouncing state violence and military repression blinded me to the internecine everyday violence embroiling the guerrilla(s) and undermining their internal solidarity" (Bourgois 2001:28).

Investigations by human rights organizations often fail to avoid two forms of partisanship. First, they do not always avoid the temptation of taking sides (Peterson 2000:213; Le Pape 1999; Stoll 1999; Prunier 1995); sometimes they fall prey to manipulative political actors (Hedges 2003:36) and sometimes they consciously exaggerate the amount of suffering in order to achieve a desired policy result (R. Cohen 1994). Often, stressing minority rights causes NGOs to overlook the victimization of majority group members (Tishkov 2004:9). A related problem is to see civilians as objects rather than agents. Guatemalan peasants tended to describe the civil war as "something rural communities were caught in but not of their making" (Warren 1998:93). "The villagers were, as always, the victims of struggles of others rather than the active element of the struggle itself," points out an anthropologist referring to the experience of a Greek village during that country's civil war (du Boulay 1974:237). The term "puppet," used to describe the collaborator army during the Japanese occupation of China and similar situations elsewhere, is telling (e.g., Thaxton 1997; Wou 1994; Henriksen 1983:89). However, such a view denies that there are "instigatees" too, whose participation is essential to transform animosity into violence (Kakar 1996:151).

---

during the "Dirty War" was initially estimated to be as high as 100,000, but eventually stabilized in the canonical figure of 30,000 (e.g., Tarnopolsky 1999), which is likely to be an overestimation (Snow and Bihurriet 1992:361). The Algerian government's long-standing claim that the war of independence cost the lives of 1.5 million Algerians remains canonical, despite careful demographic analysis showing that both that claim and the claim of those critical of the government that 150,000 Algerian collaborators of the French were massacred in 1962 are both wild exaggerations (Meynier and Vidal-Naquet 1999 quoting the research of Mohammed Harbi and Charles-Robert Ageron). The canonical figure for the Bosnian war (200,000 fatalities) emerged in 1993 from the Bosnian Information Ministry (T. Allen 1999:21) and appears unlikely to be revised any time soon. Likewise, claims about the magnitude of displacement and refugee flows tend to be distorted by political considerations (Dale 1997:82).

Second, because fieldworkers are vulnerable to human suffering, they sometimes uncritically reproduce victims' testimonies, a trend reinforced in anthropology by the move away from explanation and toward "meaning"; as a result, "the question of truth does not receive much attention in the many books on fieldwork that have appeared in the last three decades" (Robben 1995:96).

A pervasive form of partisan bias is revolutionary romanticism. François Bizot (2003:21) describes how French intellectuals automatically assumed that the Khmer Rouge insurgency in Cambodia was an "independent and spontaneous popular rebellion" and how French journalists completely disregarded his own direct observations of the conflict when these did not fit into their assumptions. S. P. Mackenzie (1997:1–2) refers, more generally, to "a foundation myth – a tendency to accentuate the positive, the selfless, the heroic, in the revolutionary context, in order to legitimize a particular set of social beliefs." He adds that "at root [this] is a morality tale in which the forces of light ipso facto overcome the forces of darkness." The mirror image of revolutionary romanticism can be found in the bulk of counterinsurgency studies with their stereotypes of revolutionary terror. Jeffrey Sluka (1989:303) castigates the counterinsurgency and terrorism literature for being written from the perspective of those combating insurgents and assuming that those who combat guerrillas are inherently moral and that insurgents are inherently immoral.

Partisanship can be extremely resistant to time, both because sources contemporary to the conflict are biased and because passions outlast the conflict. Major events such as the Saint-Barthelemy massacre of Protestants in Paris in 1572, the civil war in the Vendée during the French Revolution, or the Russian Civil War remain controversial to this day (Jouanna 1998:1262; J.-C. Martin 1998:7; Brovkin 1994:3–4; Petitfrère 1981:13). In sum, partisanship is ubiquitous. Prunier (1995:157) explains it as an expression of our "Manichean fascination with good and evil" and "our compulsive need to take sides."

Some authors believe that intellectual distance is either impossible or undesirable (Reig Tapia 1990:13–14). This perspective is suggested by Ranajit Guha's (1999:108) dictum on the interpretation of peasant insurgency in India: it could reflect only the point of view of either rulers or rebels – or historians thinking as rulers or rebels. Some anthropologists have even called for researchers explicitly to act as intermediaries, to lend their voices on behalf of the victims of terror, to turn monographs into sites of resistance and acts of solidarity. Not to do so, they argue, is an act of indifference and, ultimately, hostility (Falla 1994; Scheper-Hughes 1992). However, as Durkheim (1938) noted a long time ago, social scientists cannot be accused of wishing to condone crime or be devoid of all moral sense just because they study it as a sociological phenomenon and submit it to "cold, dry, analysis." Rather than implying moral relativism, this position posits the formulation of moral judgments as outcomes rather than preconditions of research. In Browning's (1993:xx) words, "Explaining is not excusing; understanding is not forgiving."

It is hard to make a better case in favor of distance than quoting William Finnegan's (1992:262–3) experience in Mozambique: "One of the first former captives of Renamo I interviewed ... subtly but firmly refused to demonize his captors, and I was surprised to find myself annoyed, even appalled, by his reticence, and by the 'moral equivalence' between the two sides that I thought his sad, quiet, apolitical descriptions of the war implied. Subsequent interviews with other former Renamo captives and *deslocados* only added to my confusion, as I continued to get a vastly more nuanced, ambiguous description of the war than I expected to find."

2.3. POLITICAL BIAS

Armed combat between political enemies, Carl Schmitt (1976:33) suggests, is poles apart from "normal" political competition. As Mao Zedong (in Bruno Shaw 1975:223) observed, "war has its own particular characteristics and in this sense it cannot be equated with politics in general." I describe as "political bias" the failure to recognize the fundamental distinction between peaceful political competition and armed combat – put otherwise, the conceptual conflation of civil wars with regular politics. By contributing to a fundamental mischaracterization of civil war, such failure biases the analysis.

The politics of civil wars are often treated as if they were just "normal" peaceful politics – rather than situations deeply affected and shaped by war. For many authors, civil wars are just a different kind of electoral process. Whereas soldiers (and many military historians) describe civil war as largely a matter of tactics, techniques, and firepower while failing to account for its political and social nature, most social scientists typically emphasize political aspects but overlook the importance of the military process. As a result, they neglect a key institution that shapes the social and economic context, structures politics, defines the relevant political actors and their strategies, and determines individual incentives and behavior. War is a social and political environment fundamentally different from peace in at least two crucial ways. First, it entails more constraints and less consent. Second, the stakes are incomparably higher for everyone involved. It is one thing to vote for a political party but quite another to fight (and possibly die) for it.

The key contribution of war is the primacy of violence as a resource, "the virtual equation of power and injury" (Berry 1994:xix). For Mao Zedong (in Bruno Shaw 1975:223–4), "politics is war without bloodshed while war is politics with bloodshed." Civil war induces polarization, introduces uncertainty, alters expectations. "Normal expectations collapsed," writes Michael Fellman (1989:xvi) about the American Civil War in Missouri, "to be replaced by frightening and bewildering personal and cultural chaos. The normal routes by which people solved problems and channeled behavior had been destroyed. . . . Ordinary people, civilians as well as soldiers, were trapped by guerrilla war in a social landscape in which almost nothing remained recognizable or secure."

2.4. URBAN BIAS

Studies of civil war violence are produced by urban intellectuals despite the fact that most civil conflicts are fought primarily in rural areas by predominantly peasant armies. Indeed, civil wars are commonly described as wars "in the hamlets," "the hills," "or the mountains."[8] Hence, violence tends to be disproportionably located in the countryside.[9] Yet, these wars tend to be viewed through a heavily urban lens by both scholars and practitioners; and as James Scott (1977b:4) has pointed out, "there is a systematic slippage between political ideas as understood in the city and as practiced in the village." Note the following observation from Vietnam. "Knowing what needed to be done required an understanding of circumstances at the village and hamlet level no one could acquire sitting in a provincial capital or district town or peering down from helicopters. Not only did you miss a lot that way, flying high enough to avoid snipers, but more important, you visited many parts of the area only rarely. There just weren't that many helicopter flights" (Ellsberg 2003:118). Rather than just a literal reference either to the absence of the countryside from many studies or to misleading inferences about it, urban bias is a term that refers to the more general tendency to interpret civil wars acontextually and in an exclusively top-down manner.[10]

The experience and perspective of ordinary people is remarkably absent from much of the civil war literature, especially theoretical works. Despite an expressed interest in peasants, most studies of rural-based revolutions focus on elites (Horton 1998:311; Collier 1987:13; Kriger 1992:27). In this sense, the literature on civil wars follows and amplifies the more general tendency of disregarding what J. Scott (1977b; 1977c) calls the "little tradition" in favor of the "great tradition." Even successful rural-based movements tend, after their victory, to produce official histories that downgrade or purge their rural origins (Thaxton 1997:xiv). Sometimes, this can cause entire wars to fall into obscurity. Until recently, Bruce Calder (1984:xvii) points out, the insurgency against the U.S. occupation in the Dominican Republic (1916–24) was "shrouded in historical obscurity because neither North Americans nor Dominicans had written more than a few lines about the war. Those who did usually dismissed the guerrillas as bandits and the war as a short-lived affair." The reason is that the guerrillas were nearly illiterate peasants and their testimonies remained largely unwritten. Conversely, the politically conscious and literate Dominicans of the time, even those opposed to the occupation, generally accepted the banditry thesis due to lack of information. After the war, Dominican historians, members of the liberal intellectual establishment, paid little attention to the guerrilla war and devoted their energy to documenting the intellectual and political protest of their own class (Calder 1984).

---

[8] Petersen (2002:238); Derriennic (2001:170); Geffray (1990:114–15); Ziemke (1964:194); R. Berman (1974:33).

[9] For example, 95 percent of the violence in the Salvadoran Civil War occurred in rural areas (Truth Commission in Wood 2003). There are exceptions to this pattern, of course. The violence in Northern Ireland is twice as likely to strike in urban as opposed to rural areas, although given the population distribution the risk of being killed in an urban and rural area is approximately the same (Poole 1990). Urban violence was common in countries like Lebanon (M. Johnson 2001), Liberia, Sierra Leone, and Congo (Harkavy and Neuman 2001:210). Most civil wars, however, are fought in the countryside for reasons developed in Chapters 4 and 5.

[10] The urban bias is, of course, not confined to civil wars. There is a long tradition of explaining rural politics using murky categories, such as "tradition" and "backward political consciousness" (Boswell 1998:56; Swedenburg 1995). The study of state repression is likewise biased by an overly urban perspective (Kuromiya 1993:222).

Urban bias is primarily caused by prejudice and costly information. First, there is a long tradition of interpreting rural violence as a manifestation of primitivism (e.g., Finley 1994:x). This tradition easily migrated to civil wars, assisted by a (partisan) interpretation of rural insurgents as bandits. French Republicans described the insurgent Vendée as "a country two hundred years behind the Revolution" (Dupuy 1997:145), and Parisian journalists echoed them in describing the inhabitants of the counterrevolutionary South as "cannibals and savages, covered in blood from head to foot" (Cobb 1972:52); the "Asian mind" and other clichés about Asia "worthy of the flimsiest tourist guides" became a common "explanation" for insurgent violence in Vietnam and Cambodia (Bizot 2003:34; Schell 1967:56–7); interpretations of violence in African civil wars typically refer to "madmen and mindless savages" (Richards 1996:xx).

Combined with the prevailing emphasis on the cultural and ritual aspects of violence, this tendency is conducive to serious misinterpretations. For example, one encounters a surprising number of baroque interpretations of behavior that can be explained in simpler and more universal terms. Fence-sitting, free-riding, or *attentisme*, all common expressions of risk aversion during civil wars caused by a desire for survival, are interpreted as resulting from bizarre local customs. In Vietnam, such noncommittal behavior was seen as springing from traditional Confucian doctrine and was dubbed the "Will of Heaven" (FitzGerald 1989:29–31). Geoffrey Robinson (1995:2) notes how political violence in Bali was explained by some authors "as the consequence of a religiously rooted 'Balinese' desire to rid the island of evil and restore a cosmic balance. The frenzy with which it was carried out has been attributed to schizophrenic tendencies in the 'Balinese character' and to a cultural predilection for going into a trance. Analyses of the violent conflict of 1965–6 as a political problem with historical origins have been conspicuously absent." The burgeoning literature on so-called new civil wars (Kaldor 1999; Enzensberger 1994) is but the latest manifestation of urban bias (Kalyvas 2001).

The inhabitants of Sarajevo experienced the bitter irony of their own urban prejudice when war hit home. As one of them recalled, "Years ago, we would read about the terrible things going on in Lebanon. You know! 'That's the Middle East,' we would say, they are some kind of animals out there! Now we say, 'Of course they're killing each other in the Krajina! That's the old Military Border, they're aggressive and primitive! Maybe next week we'll be saying, 'Oh that! That's *New* Sarajevo, you know what those people are like! So what will we say when our neighbors in the next building are killing each other?' " (in Hall 1994:236).

Urban prejudice is, of course, as wrongheaded as urban romanticism. The literature is full of descriptive swings from "rural savage" to "noble savage" and brutish Hobbesian thug to noble Tolstoian defender (Starn 1998:226). The counterrevolutionary peasants of the Vendée were described by monarchist authors as exceptional people of a primitive candor (Dupuy 1997:141; Petitfrère 1981:87); Cambodian city folk "who loathed the plow, the soil, the palm groves, and domestic animals, who disliked the open rustic life of the villagers, idealized the Khmer peasant as a stereotype of perpetual revolution: a model of simplicity, endurance, and patriotism" (Bizot 2003:61); and much early writing about the Shining Path insurgency in Peru cast the insurgents as primitive rebels from a "non-Western" world or, in the sensationalizing exoticism of one British journalist, as children of the "magical world of Indians" (Starn 1998:233).

The second cause of urban bias is costly information. Access to the country-side tends to be hard if not impossible (e.g., Hamilton-Merritt 1993:xii). More-over, because sites of violence are notoriously difficult to study, ethnographies of civil war are rare (e.g., Wood 2003; Nordstrom 1997). Constraints are multiple. Jeffrey Sluka (1989:3) points out that "the situation in Belfast of conflict between polarized ethnic communities, did not allow for a participant-observation based study in both a Catholic and Protestant community simultaneously." Moreover, the danger inherent in civil war makes people suspicious toward outsiders and, hence, reluctant to convey information or be frank (Race 1973:xii). A Mozam-bican woman replied to a request for an interview: "We are afraid. I will not say anything. Everything that happens here gets known within the neighbor-hood very easily. This (the request to have an interview) is frightening" (Chin-gono 1996:138). Journalists often succeed in obtaining access but tend to lack the necessary deep regional knowledge. An American journalist who was inves-tigating a massacre in Kashmir recalls that, while he was conducting an inter-view with villagers, they started arguing with each other. His translator leaned over him and whispered: "They are debating whether it is for the greater good of the village to lie to you, and if so, what are the right lies to tell" (Bearak 2000:30).

When possible, access may be contingent on demonstrable political allegiance to the incumbent regime or the insurgent organization in control, and these "stints in the bush" often serve as "propaganda for their respective sponsors" (Kriger 1992:7). As a result, most observers cluster in cities. The Bosnian war was mostly covered from Sarajevo, "which distracted journalists from much of what was happening elsewhere" (Loyd 2001:179). The world's image of what was going on in Mozambique, Geffray (1990:19) points out, reflected "the views of the urban elites, national intellectuals, and foreigners who live in Maputo, the capital of Mozambique, and the big cities of the provinces. Journalists cannot investigate [the war] on the ground, and the international media reproduce the information and analyses produced in these circles." Journalists and other observers on the ground often lack the necessary linguistic skills and local understanding and rely, instead, on elites for both information and interpretations. "Despite the presence of several 'old Vietnam hands' during my military service in Vietnam," recalls Race (1973:x), not a single member of the foreign press spoke Vietnamese, and as a consequence all the output of the foreign press had to be filtered through the limited part of Vietnamese society which spoke Western languages." The same is true for many participants in the conflict: "For most Americans in Vietnam," Herrington (1997:39) recalls, "the dynamics of the Vietnamese villager's dilemma were impossible to grasp, and the barriers to understanding posed by the linguistic and cultural differences between our two peoples were insurmountable."

As a result, information about the countryside tends to be scarce and mislead-ing. The Malayan insurgency looked like a "bewildering labyrinth" (Crawford 1958:180); Vietnam was a "Kafka-like nightmare to anyone seeking facts. Even simple data, the population of a province, for example, were unobtainable. Beyond simply the dearth of statistics lay the domain of obfuscated information.... The falsehoods consisted on the one hand of untruths born of events themselves: the partial account, the uncertain rumor, the contradictory report" (Pike 1966:viii). The Algerian Civil War "has been shrouded in mystery since it began in early 1992, a war concealed by layers of darkness" (Peterson 1997b); "viewed from any angle Northern Ireland is a place of mirrors. Political messages are distorted and refracted by competing groups and interests" (M. Smith 1995:227). F. A. Voigt (1949:167–9) speaks of "a realm of twilight merging in darkness that defies enquiry, whether private or official"; he adds that during the Greek Civil War "most of the massacres perpetrated in Greece remain unknown to the outside world. Even in Greece there are many that never come to be known more than locally.... Many massacres are only heard of from the mouth of eyewitnesses by chance and long after the event." Carolyn Nordstrom (1997:44) reports how she happened to stumble upon a fairly large but now destroyed town in Mozambique where a massacre had just taken place and how this massacre never showed up on any record; a peasant told her (1997:48): "Maybe lots of people who were killed were killed by other people and for other reasons than what is said."

The invisibility of the countryside hardly ends with the war: deaths, massive displacements, and repression hinder research. People often want to forget and be left alone to rebuild their shattered lives. Moreover, scholars generally tend to avoid the required labor-intensive rural fieldwork. A scholar of Colombia (Ramsey 1973:3) concludes that "the violencia, a solidly rural phenomenon that generated relatively few written records, calls for sweaty field research of a type not practiced by many writers on the subject." Not coincidentally, one of the most intensely studied conflicts is Northern Ireland: an English-speaking country with good hotels, very pleasant scenery, temperate climate, tasty local cuisine, and most important, not a high level of danger, thus providing the excitement of being in a "war-zone" with a probability of being the victim of a battle that is far lower than that of being killed in a traffic accident in most places (M. Smith 1995:225–6).

Added to this is a tendency of some researchers to minimize the impact of past conflicts. Even anthropologists, who are best placed to observe and study how civil wars are played out on the ground, often refrain from doing so. They "have traditionally approached the study of conflict, war, and human aggression from a distance, ignoring the harsh realities of people's lives" (Clastres 1999:5; Green 1995:107; Nagengast 1994:112). Robinson (1995:8) notes how Clifford Geertz's famous *The Interpretation of Cultures*, which contains at least three articles specifically about Bali and was published in 1973, devotes only one sentence to the massacres that took place only eight years earlier and cost the lives of about 5 percent of the island's population.

The urban bias is a serious problem because it distorts data and conceptualizations of civil war dynamics; it tends to privilege written sources, "top-down" perspectives, ideological or normative motivations of participants, and fixed, unchanging identities and choices over oral sources, "bottom-top" perspectives, nonideological motivations of participants, and fluid identities and choices.

First, there is an inverse relation between the type of societies where civil war takes place and the type of societies that produce, preserve, and make available written records. Hence, an exclusive reliance on written sources introduces bias. Often, the only available sources are government records, which tend to focus on rebel violence and ignore incumbent violence (Fellman 1989:189). Moreover, exclusive reliance on published memoirs can be a distorting factor, because they tend to be produced by city dwellers and elites with the education and resources to devote time to writing, whose view of people from the countryside is colored by prejudice (Hobsbawm 2001:xvii). According to Barrington Moore (1966:480), "The discontented intellectual with his soul searchings has attracted attention wholly out of proportion to his political importance, partly because these searchings leave behind them written records and also because those who write history are themselves intellectuals." For example, most memoirs and chronicles of the Spanish guerrilla war against Napoleon were produced by pro-French urban elites, the Afrancesados, rather than the mostly peasant Guerilleros (C. Schmitt 1992:209). Nor can the dead write memoirs (Wickham-Crowley 1990:204). Because rural-based movements and peasants do not usually leave behind them many written sources, their actions are overlooked (Brovkin 1994:127) or imputed to other actors who are seen as representing or manipulating them – depending on the author's political preferences (Dupuy 1997:266). In fact, investigations that stress "unauthorized narratives" such as songs and oral recollections often uncover a disjunction between the ascribed attitudes of the rank and file and the real ones (McKenna 1998:279).

A second manifestation of urban bias is the emphasis on "top-down" perspectives, stressing high politics and elite interactions (Bax 2000; Tone 1994:6). Because they fragment space, civil wars are processes that entail important local dynamics. However, histories of civil wars tend to lack this dimension; they are typically located in the realm of high international politics and diplomatic history rather than messy local reality (Merrill 1989:189; Mason and Krane 1989:193; Tilly 1964:340). Historians of the Russian Civil War, Brovkin (1994:127) points out, "have been preoccupied with armies, headquarters, front lines, and governments" and have ignored Bolshevik war against peasants on the internal front whose magnitude "eclipsed by far the frontline civil war against the Whites." Studies of Nazi-occupied Greece, Mazower (1993:xvii) observes, are based on the "implausible assumption that wartime developments inside occupied Greece were determined within the realm of high politics. Ambassadors, generals, senior mission officers, Greek politicians and resistance leaders flit across the pages in a variety of colours, according to the author's sympathies. . . . This is fertile territory for conspiracy theories and heroic epics." However there is a systematic difference between leaders and followers. George Orwell (1937:176-7) remarked that "one of the analogies between Communism and Roman Catholicism is that only the educated are completely orthodox," and Philip Converse (1964:213) points to a gulf between elite and mass beliefs and shows that "the true motivations and comprehensions of the supporters may have little or nothing to do with the distinctive beliefs of the endorsed elite."

A related, and widespread, problem is the propensity to take these elites' descriptions of who they are and who they represent at face value. Because they are aware of this propensity, they manipulate it accordingly. Both journalists and scholars are vulnerable to such manipulations.[11] Finally, a pernicious version of "top-down" perspectives is the tendency of poststructuralist accounts toward "metanarratives" and "teleologies" that "can lead into slipshod analysis that does more to mystify than illuminate the politics of protest" (Starn 1998:236). Overcoming this bias calls for the recognition that the local is not the provincial or the parochial but rather the social and, most importantly, the empirical. Indeed, incorporating the local dimension into the study of civil wars almost always uncovers the plurality and lack of uniformity of civil war experiences and outcomes (e.g., Blackwood 1997; Richardson 1997:11), thus introducing variation that makes empirical investigation both possible and fruitful.

Third, the urban bias is present in explanations of motivations that are heavily biased toward ideology. There is a clear epistemic bias, at least in the sociological and historical traditions, in favor of the assumption that all (or most) participants in conflicts are motivated by ideological concerns. Because "urban" scholars tend to be primarily motivated by ideology themselves, they often assign unambiguous ideological motives to participants, even if this is not the case. As a French officer commented on the American Revolution (in Shy 1976:13): "There is a hundred times more enthusiasm for this Revolution in any Paris café than in all the colonies together."[12] A historian of French fascist movements (Jankowski 1989:ix; xii) remarks that "the protagonists in the debate have focused almost obsessively on ideology" to the exclusion of actual empirical research on mass-level dynamics. Such perspectives result in the assumption that "a strong ideology" is a precondition for guerrilla warfare because it "prepares the population for an absolute war effort. The wide majority must identify with the fate of the country against a real enemy; otherwise, they will not tolerate great sacrifices" (Rohkrämer 1997:513–14).[13]

To be sure, ideology does motivate action (e.g., M. F. Brown and Fernández 1991:98); however, several additional motivations also come into play, which tend to be systematically overlooked in macrohistorical accounts. Popular participation in the guerrilla war against Napoleon in Spain "did not flow from superior patriotism or piety, but from the nature of rural society in Navarre" (Tone 1994:7); what determined the "tentative and reluctant" choice of Macedonian peasants at the beginning of the twentieth century to declare themselves as

---

[11] BBC World Service's influential *Focus on Africa* evening news magazine relied on the commentary of Charles Taylor, the leader of Liberian rebels, because however partial, "it is cleverly expressed in clear and dramatic English. His rivals struggle, linguistically and dramatically, in his wake" (Richards 1996:3). Adams (1994:7) tells of how Congolese politicians in the 1960s credibly described themselves in Western terms, such as "radical syndicalist" even though their conflicts were purely local.

[12] Shy (1976:13) notes that this officer was fully committed to the American side and that, although he exaggerated, "too much other evidence supports the line of his argument to reject it out of hand."

[13] Ironically, because the various aspects of urban bias tend to occur together, the willingness to impute ideological motivations to every peasant rebel is often accompanied by the tendency to deny all rationality to people who appear motivated by religious, ethnic, or "tribal" concerns. This is closely related with the tendency to privilege high politics and macrosocial factors over contextual and local factors.

Greek or Bulgarian "ranged from financial considerations, social cleavages, and local politics, to personal animosities, leaving thus precious little room, if any, for 'national' orientations" (Livanios 1999:197); an individual's decision to side with the Germans or the partisans in the German-occupied Soviet Union was not determined by "abstract considerations and evaluations of the merits and demerits of the two regimes, nor even by likes and dislikes or experiences under the Soviet regime before the occupation" (Dallin, Mavrogordato, and Moll 1964:336); the percentage of those who joined the collaborationist Milice in Marseille out of ideological conviction is estimated, on the (imperfect) basis of judicial records, to have been close to 5 percent; another 5 percent joined under pressure from family and friends, another 10 to take advantage of jobs and privileges, and the rest for multiple and often conflicting reasons (Jankowski 1989: 123–4).

In fact, ordinary people caught in the whirlwind of violence and war are, more often than not, less than heroic: they seek to save one's job, house, family, and, above all, life (e.g., Butalia 2000:76). Timothy Snyder (2003) notes that persecuted Poles in the western Ukraine tended to join the Soviet partisans when they lived in the countryside and the German occupiers when they lived in towns: they wanted to survive or take revenge. As Nordstrom (1992:265) points out about Mozambique and Sri Lanka, "While the ideologues and (para)militaries waging the conflict viewed the distinction of sides and the application of right and wrong to each as lying at the core of the conflict, civilians often had difficulty distinguishing sides, especially according to ideological considerations of just and unjust. Indeed, many of the victims of war – torn from comfort and community, family, and home, too often wounded or bereaved – do not know what the conflict is about or who the contenders are."

Additional light is shed by recent sociological research on religious conversion, a "choice" as amenable to ideological considerations as those made regarding politics. This research shows that doctrinal appeal (i.e., people hearing the message, finding it attractive, and embracing the faith) does not lie at the heart of the conversion process: most people do not really become strongly attached to the doctrines of their new faith until after their conversion (Stark 1997). The frequent endogeneity of ideology to the war finds support in many historical accounts that do not restrict their sources among the elites. In occupied France, "far more maquisards became communist through maquis experience than were communist by motivation at the outset" (Kedward 1993:153), whereas in the western Ukraine during the German occupation, "the experience of directed killing combined with political indoctrination could make loyal and even committed fighters out of apolitical peasants" (Snyder 2003:216). Likewise, most Vietcong recruits were not committed revolutionaries when they entered the organization but had to be "socialized" and "molded" and have "their consciousness raised" through elaborate processes of political and ideological training; even then, ideological commitment failed to materialize for most (Berman 1974:75, 8).

The view that good performance in combat is an indicator of ideological commitment is as problematic as observations that tie joining a movement exclusively to ideology. To begin with, many claims are self-serving. Rebel victories are seen as a sign of moral strength and ideological commitment, whereas rebel defeats are often interpreted as the product of betrayal (Mackenzie 1997). An extensive body of research shows that combatants are usually motivated to fight *not* by ideology or hate or fear but by peer pressure and processes involving regard for their comrades, respect for their leaders, concern for their own reputation with both, and an urge to contribute to their success of the group – in short, what is known as "primary group cohesion."[14] Even when present, ideological motivations are usually filtered though peer dynamics. Finally, war provides its own powerful attractions. The adolescents abducted into serving for the RENAMO rebels in Mozambique displayed high morale, which was partly explained by the excitement of life in RENAMO ranks, including access to looted luxury items and women (T. Young 1997:132). Severe sanctions make sure that people stay put, willingly or not. Desertion is typically punished by death by most armies, regular and irregular alike (e.g., Rubio 1999:115–16).

Although decisions to join are often nonideological, their ex post facto reconstruction by interviewees is likely to be so. This is the case, as Ivan Ermakoff (2001:4) argues, because unsettled periods generate simultaneously a need for strategic nonideological action and an ideological explication of those actions. The ideological bias is reinforced by the impossibility of measuring attitudes and behavior ex post facto. Suppose that an individual is coerced at t_1 into joining the rebels.[15] At t_2 her village is destroyed in an indiscriminate raid by the army and her family killed. As a result, at t_3 she wholeheartedly commits to the rebel cause in order to avenge her family (and also because she has nothing to lose). After the end of the war (t_4) she may reconstruct her initial motivation and claim, and may come to believe sincerely, that she joined the rebels at t_1 out of ideological commitment. An unsophisticated researcher who collects this piece of information at t_4 will base his conclusions on biased evidence. In his study of religious conversion, Rodney Stark (1997:19) warns against this tendency: "Having not gone out and watched people as they converted, we might have missed the point entirely, because when people retrospectively describe their conversions, they tend to put the stress on theology."

The fourth manifestation of the urban bias is the assumption of given, fixed, and unchanging identities, such as "peasant," "Catholic," or "Albanian." This promotes a view of the war between clearly demarcated sides with compact, stable, and loyal social bases. In portrayals of recent civil wars "the ideology is clear-cut, the opponents are obvious, and the fight takes place among delineated factions that are politically recognizable" (Nordstrom and Martin 1992:4). However, there are several problems with this assumption. First, identities are not only exogenous to the war. For example, the label "landlord" in Communist China was a political weapon rather than a neutral class label, often imposed on local opponents. As Helen Siu (1989:134) notes, the lack of clear-cut boundaries between class labels

---

[14] Grossman (1995:89–90); Lynn (1984); Stouffer (1949); Shils and Janowitz (1948); Marshall (1947).
[15] Todorov (1996:113) reports the story of a man posing as a French resister who was arrested by the resistance fighters and forced to kill an occupation official. "The pseudo-maquisard was given amnesty and later became a true resister."

"allowed room for maneuver. Neighbors and kinsmen found themselves locked in anxious negotiations and mutual accusations." On the island of Negros in the Philippines, "'Communist' was a loosely defined and widely defined epithet that could be used to legitimize the murder of just about anyone" (Berlow 1998:xiii). Second, these identities may hide and disguise local identities that are not as visible to the untrained eye (Chapter 10).

The assumption that identities are more or less permanently ascribed becomes a problem because of the pronounced tendency to infer motivations directly from identities (Bayly 1988:119–20; Perry 1980:251; Tilly 1964:7). These motivations are usually based on the group's "external" grievances and disregard its many internal conflicts and divisions, such as gender, lineage, clan, age, and socioeconomic position within the community (Tambiah 1996:316; Kriger 1992). However, even small groups such as peasant communities and small villages are deeply divided (e.g., Lison-Tolosana 1983:39). Academic studies often share with "official historiographies" the tendency to erase these troubling internal divisions, "class fissures, acts of treachery, or peasant initiatives that were independent of elite control" and to smooth over "the past's jagged edges" (Swedenburg 1995:21; Kedward 1993:160).

The same holds true for ethnic groups, which are rarely, if ever, homogeneous. Studying a Belfast area reputed to be an "IRA fortress," Sluka (1989:289) found out that it was, in fact, "a heterogeneous and complex community" with a great mix of political attitudes and with only "a minority" really interested and politically active. Likewise, Thomas McKenna (1998) found that most ordinary Filipino Muslims who supported the Muslim separatist rebellion and even fought in its ranks were not motivated by the nationalism of their leaders: they did not classify themselves as "Moro," the term used by their leaders to denote the citizens of the new nation they wanted to form, and they denied that they were fighting primarily for this new nation. Swedenburg (1995), who studied the memories of the Palestinian uprising of 1936–9, uncovered "collaborationist" memories (of Palestinian rebels who defected and ended up fighting alongside the British), which explicitly contradicted the orthodox Palestinian nationalist version of the past. Mohand Hamoumou (1993) argues that the motivations that drove large numbers of Algerian peasants to fight alongside the French during the Algerian War of Independence were primarily nonideological.

The insight about the endogeneity of identity to war is consistent with an understanding of the power of ideology as deriving from routines of compliance (Earle 1997:8) and residing "less in the set of motivations it creates than in the repertoires of reasons it provides actors to justify their actions" (Ermakoff 2001:4). It is also consistent with the recurring complaints of revolutionary leaders about the low level of political "consciousness" of peasant guerrilla recruits (Wickham-Crowley 1991:52).[16]

---

[16] There are many reports that insurgent fighters rarely discuss politics among themselves (Zimmerman 2000:192; Rubio 1999:117; Hart 1999:264; M. F. Brown and Fernández 1991:137; Kerkvliet 1977:229). Sales of Hitler's *Mein Kampf* rose in Germany after membership in the Nazi Party had increased, not before; apparently possession of the book was a badge of loyalty rather than a

It goes without saying that countering the urban bias should not come at the expense of ignoring developments in the urban centers or at the national level. What is needed, instead, is a way to connect the local and the national, the view from below with the perspective from above – or, to use the terminology of historians of the English seventeenth century, the "main street" with the "parish pump."

2.5. SELECTION BIAS

Durkheim (1938:40) pointed out that "morbidity is not absolutely antithetical to health; these are two varieties of the same phenomenon, and each tends to explain the other." Instances of violence cannot be considered independently of instances where violence does not occur. Indeed, recent large-N studies of civil war (Sambanis 2000; Fearon and Laitin 2000) and ethnic riots (Wilkinson 2004; Varshney 2002) correct for this bias. Micro-oriented studies tend to be particularly vulnerable to selection bias, however, as they often focus on the most violent outcomes and neglect related places and times with more limited violence or none at all.

Another form of selection bias concerns the focus on the actor perpetrating the violence. Many studies assume away or minimize the possibility that insurgents, and not just incumbents, target civilians (e.g., Valentino 2004; Downes 2004; Azam and Hoeffler 2002; Gulden 2002). According to this approach, civilian victimization is only a government strategy, not one used by insurgents. The opposite (a focus on insurgent violence only) has been the case with counterinsurgency studies (e.g., Hosmer 1970) but also with more recent work (J. Weinstein 2003). Besides removing the possibility of explaining the violence of the side not being studied, this problem distorts the analysis by overlooking the crucial interaction process between the rival actors.

2.6. OVERAGGREGATION BIAS AND DATA PROBLEMS

Any study of violence must face the thorny problem of data. Beyond the distortions imposed on the collection and interpretation of data by the urban and partisan biases, data on violence are vulnerable to two problems: most available indicators of political violence tend to be unreliable and inconsistent across nations and over time; and, the available data are overly aggregate. Both problems are likely to bias analyses that rely on available quantitative measures.

Data on violence, when available, can be wildly distorted.[17] These distortions do not appear to be systematic: sometimes fatalities are overestimated and

tool of conversion (Wickham-Crowley 1991:129). It also turns out that the link between political violence and (radical) ideologies is very tenuous even in urban environments, as Della Porta (1995:196) shows in the case of Italian and German 'terrorist' organizations.

[17] Lacey (2005); Harkavy and Neuman (2001:323–4); Tishkov (1999:580–1); Werth (1998:95); Manrique (1998:221); Licklider (1998:122); Nordstrom (1997:43); Schlichte (1997:6); Della Porta (1995); Cranna (1994); Lopez and Stohl (1992); Mitchell et al. (1986); Henriksen (1983); Westing (1982:262).

sometimes they are underestimated, depending on the vagaries of the process of adjudicating between competing partisan claims. More than twice as many people are estimated to have died in Peru's civil war between 1980 and 2000 as previously believed, 69,000 rather than 35,000 (Knight 2003), and Operation "Enduring Freedom" in Afghanistan may have been much costlier in civilian lives than previously thought (Benini and Moulton 2004). The opposite is probably true of the Bosnian Civil War, where informed estimates place the total number of fatalities closer to 60,000 than the figure of 250,000 that is widely believed (Kenney 1995). Rounding tends to inflate numbers: for a long time, the fatalities of the Spanish Civil War were believed to have reached 1 million, a wild overestimation (Barnstone 1995:169). Similar distortions appear in many other cases (e.g., Last 2000:315–16), although we will probably never know the true numbers for most civil wars. These distortions affect not only the total number of fatalities but also each side's share. A recent review of the available evidence on the violence of the Spanish Civil War concludes that the violence of the Right was consistently underestimated and that of the Left overestimated (Juliá 1999:410). Distorted data make it into datasets, contributing to severe measurement bias problems (Dulić 2004; Davenport and Ball 2002).[18]

Much distortion results from the political process, but even in its absence measurement problems are enormous. The Vietnam War was arguably "the most operations-researched conflict in human history" (Fall 2000:110); yet the data on casualties, particularly civilian and North Vietnamese, are spotty to say the least (Moyar 1997:230–41; Thayer 1985:101). Data are just difficult to collect in times of war, and not only in the remote rural areas whose relative invisibility was discussed in the section on urban bias. The proverbial fog of war undermines such efforts, compounded by ineffective or inexistent bureaucracies. The sheer difficulty of the enterprise is suggested by the discovery a few years ago that two Muslim brothers, whose supposed slaying was used as evidence in the most publicized war crimes trial run by the Bosnian government, had been found living in a Sarajevo suburb (Hedges 1997). Of course, these problems are not restricted to war. Natural disasters in developing countries produce very approximate fatality counts. It took months of painstaking work by the effective bureaucracy of an advanced industrial nation to produce an accurate fatality count of the September 11, 2001 attacks or the 2005 New Orleans flood; initial estimates had been wildly off mark and would have never been corrected but for long, meticulous, and labor-intensive counting.

Moreover, available data tend to be overly aggregate and acontextual. Information on the exact circumstances surrounding the violence (who, where, when, how, by whom) is usually missing.[19] Data also tend to truncate instances of

---

[18] In a rare public admission, the Rhodesian intelligence chief acknowledged "cooking the books" when it came to enemy casualties and "chalking up" killings committed by the security forces as killings done by the insurgents (Flower 1987:151, 204).

[19] Absurd quantification exercises sometimes become a substitute for contextual understanding. Goldstein (1992:50) provides a small anthology of such absurdities: among others, a researcher

violence from the crucial events that precede and follow.[20] These are not new problems, as John Shy (1976:189) points out about one of the best studied conflicts, the American Revolution: "The war being fought out, day by day and night by night, in dozens of nasty little raids, ambushes and encounters all over Bergen and Westchester counties [in New York State], was complex and confusing; it is almost impossible to state with certainty what actually happened in many controversial episodes – how many atrocities? Committed by whom? And why?"

Overaggregate and acontextual data are amenable to misinterpretation. For example, an analysis of violence in Colombia that relied on reported homicides would be biased because, as Mauricio Rubio (1999:44–5) has shown, individual decisions to report homicides are not independent of the overall patterns of violence: homicides are more likely to be reported (and be reported accurately) where they are least likely to take place; put otherwise, the higher the violence, the scarcer the data on violence. Likewise, analysts of the violence in Iraq following the American invasion may be tempted to use the number of insurgent roadside attacks against American patrols as an indicator of insurgent activity. However, such an interpretation would be wrong because the U.S. military sharply reduced its patrolling in insurgent strongholds, thus decreasing its vulnerability to roadside attacks: "There are fewer attacks here because we're out on the road less," an officer at the Marine headquarters in Anbar province said in September 2004. "But you shouldn't conclude from that," he added, "that things are any safer" (in Chandrasekaran 2004:A1).

A great deal of information, especially as far as human rights NGOs are concerned, comes exclusively from the victims of violence. Such evidence can be problematic insofar as victimization does not imply full or accurate knowledge of the actions that produced it; in fact, victims' testimonies are not sacred just because they come from victims (Rousso 1998:67). Like everyone else, victims forget,[21] ignore,[22] or misrepresent[23] crucial aspects or the exact sequence of the actions and events that produced their victimization (Wagenaar 1988). Often

---

has attempted to figure out "how many reports of torture are equivalent to one murder," while another one has proposed an indicator that equates 70 murders with 100 "disappearances."

[20] Black-Michaud's (1975:35) assessment of the quality of the data on tribal feuds fully applies to civil war violence: "Accounts that purport to describe actual 'feuds' either only narrate a single sanguinary episode in a long chain of such events, or, alternatively, provide a much abridged 'history' of feud, which usually ignores several variables without which all attempts to give a sociological explanation of the pattern of hostilities in a particular case must remain abortive."

[21] There is very compelling evidence that eyewitnesses of criminal (and other) events are systematically wrong about substantial parts of the events they are called to describe (Dwyer 2001; Gawande 2001). David Tereshchuk (2001), a journalist present during the so-called Bloody Sunday in Northern Ireland in 1972 was certain that a soldier firing toward him was wearing a red beret; however, detailed pictures showed that the soldier was, in fact, wearing a helmet. "After checking more pictures and news film," he notes, "I have come to see that – however certain my recollection – I was simply wrong."

[22] "I don't know who burned my village and killed seventeen people, including my brother's son," a Sri-Lankan refugee told Nordstrom (1992:265).

[23] The tendency to misrepresent one's past in order to appear as a hero is widespread. In the United States, for example, more than 7,000 people have falsely claimed to have been members of Navy Seals units, mostly during the Vietnam War. It is not infrequent for public personalities to be

informants, and especially victims, have a stake in making researchers adopt their truths, especially since they perceive them to be curators of history who will retell their stories and provide them with the halo of objectivity brought by academic status: "Precisely because the experiences are unspeakable, and yet must be spoken, the speakers are sustained by the mediating structures of language, narrative, social environment, religion, politics. The resulting narratives – not the pain they describe, but the words and ideologies through which they represent it – not only can, but must be critically understood" (Robben 1995:97).

Finally, journalistic accounts and individual testimonies sometimes turn out to be completely fabricated (Wyatt 2005; Steinberg 2004; Tyler 2002). Recent efforts by various NGOs and Truth Commissions to systematically report human rights violations are a welcome but only partial corrective. These data can be partial and inaccurate (e.g., Wood 2003:32, 55; Binford 1996:106); often, they are collected with a narrow "applied" focus in mind, in order to publicize and apply pressure (Suárez-Orozco 1992:220), while not allowing systematic comparisons.[24] And, as discussed already, these organizations (including the UN) are not always free of partisan bias, which affects the reliability of their data. In this respect, recent work by groups such as the American Association for the Advancement of Science could prove to be especially useful (Knight 2003). The compound result of these problems is the bifurcation of studies on violence in either case-study formats based on anecdotal evidence or large-N correlational analyses relying on quantitative measures of violence that are most likely totally unreliable.

2.7. CONCLUSION

These problems of bias can be (and have been) daunting; they explain the relative lack of progress in the study of violence, both in civil war contexts and elsewhere. Overcoming them calls for research designs "firmly committed to disaggregation in both data collection and theory building" (Brubaker and Laitin 1998:447). In Chapter 9, I lay out a microcomparative research design that tackles most of the problems identified here. Further discussion of the methodological issues associated with data collection on civil war violence is included in Appendixes A and B.

unmasked as having exaggerated or even invented a false heroic military past (Belluck 2001) or a false victimization story (Wyatt 2005).

[24] Amnesty International has consciously reported its findings in such a way that social science reconstructions of yearly reports could not yield a document that could be comparative across countries within a single year or by country across the years. The organization believes not only that it is impossible to create such accurate reporting but that to do so would be politically unwise (Mitchell et al. 1986:22). As Gourevitch (1998:187) puts it, "According to the human rights orthodoxy of our age, such comparisons are taboo."

3

Barbarism

> These were moments you cannot understand unless you lived through them. The Civil War was a despicable thing. They took people away for nothing!
>
> A Spanish man quoted in Sender Barayón, *A Death in Zamora*

Despite a quasi-universal recognition of an association between civil war and atrocity, there is surprising little in the way of specified links between the two. Exactly why is civil war associated with excessive violence? Put otherwise, what are the sources of barbarism in civil war? Answering this question is a prerequisite for the formulation of a theory of violence in civil war.

In this chapter, I reconstruct, specify, and contrast four general arguments inspired by different theoretical traditions. The first thesis, present in many historical and descriptive accounts, flows from Thomas Hobbes's insight linking the *breakdown* of political order to violence. The second, *transgression*, points to domestic armed challenge as being transgressive of established norms, thus triggering violence. The third account, *polarization*, can be found in historical and sociological research and stresses deep ideological or social divisions, highlighting the predictably violent effects of what Carl Schmitt described as total enmity. The last thesis stresses violent responses triggered by security concerns related to the *technology of warfare* practiced in civil wars. I review several theoretical and empirical facets of these arguments and select the last thesis as the most appropriate theoretical foundation for a theory of violence in civil war.

3.1. BARBARISM AND CIVIL WAR

To say that war "causes" violence is a tautology since war is an instance of collective violence. However, civil war is striking in its perceived association with excessive violence and atrocity. "If war is hell," Mayer (2000:323) asserts, "then civil war belongs to hell's deepest and most infernal regions"; and although ethnic conflict has attracted considerable attention recently, it is important to keep in mind that violence is far from being its exclusive property. Religion was for long seen as the main cause of violence and civil war (Hobsbawm 1997:258), and "ideological" or "revolutionary" civil wars were considered likely to attain the highest reaches of violence (Payne 1987:209; Bouthoul 1970:448). Bernand (1999:273) concludes his analysis of warfare in ancient Greece by pointing out that "ideological conflicts led to astonishing waves of violence."

Civil war is "often the bloodiest and bitterest kind of war"; "cruelty is the steady companion of civil wars," and "naked brutality" is "inherent in any full-fledged civil war" (Mayer 2000:207; Roberts 1994:136; Petitfrère 1981:50). These statements reflect the pervasive view of civil wars as exceptionally brutal and barbaric, a perception going back to writers such as Thucydides, Alberico Gentili, Michel de Montaigne, and Adam Smith.[1] Madame de Staël (1979:10) observed that "all civil wars are more or less similar in their atrocity, in the upheaval in which they throw men and in the influence they give to violent and tyrannical passions." Dupuy's formulation (1997:255) is telling: the Vendée War "was a civil war before anything else, hence violence was its essential component."[2] This view is shared by participants. An Italian partisan wrote in his diary that "the ancients were right when they said that civil wars are much more cruel than foreign ones" (in Pavone 1994:466). Indeed, this belief is so ingrained that the absence of large-scale atrocities in a civil war becomes a puzzle (e.g., Clifton 1999:107; Donagan 1994; Worden 1985:141).

Clearly, describing certain forms of violence as cruel entails a subjective and culturally specific judgment.[3] Moreover, perceptions of cruelty may just be an artifact of the prevalence of civil wars in poor countries. Wealthy countries have the ability to fight what Trinquier (1964:113) calls "modern war," which is more

---

[1] For more recent formulations, see Tishkov (2004:127); Malefakis (1996:28); Bobbio (1992); Bouthoul (1970:448); and Gunther (1949:129).

[2] The governor of South Carolina during the American Revolution termed it an "uncommonly Cruel War"; a politician from the same state pointed out in 1782 that "the good people of this state have not only felt the Common Calamities of War, but from the Wanton and Savage manner in which it has been prosecuted they have experienced such severities as are unpractisd and will Scarcely be Credited by Civilized Nations" (in Weir 1985:77, 78); and a nineteenth-century French counterrevolutionary leader remarked that "excesses are inseparable from wars of opinion" (in Dupuy 1997:237). I was able to find only one explicit comparison that favored civil over interstate war, and even in that case (the Israeli invasion of Lebanon) the interstate war in question entailed strong elements of a civil war (Mouro 1999:44). Sometimes the belief that civil wars are more violent is associated with the perception that civil wars are the only wars worth fighting (Venturi in Pavone 1994:225).

[3] Crozier (1960:158); Barnett and Njama (1966:138). Voigt (1949:71) remarks that "in Spain, both sides massacred because that is the Spanish way of waging civil war." Prunier (1995:140) castigates the Western journalists who covered the Rwandan genocide because they "always insisted that the victims were killed with machetes, as if the use of cold steel rather than a bullet made the killing worse. Nobody ever thought of blaming the Roman army or European medieval knights for their use of the sword, any more than journalists were able to realise that using machetes reflected a certain level of economic functioning rather than cultural barbarity." Richards (1996:xx) concurs, writing about Sierra Leone that "cheap" violence based on killing with knives and cutlasses should not be taken as being inherently worse than "expensive" violence in which civilians are maimed or destroyed with sophisticated laser-guided weapons: "It makes no sense to call one kind of war 'barbaric' when all that is meant is that it is cheap."

impersonal in that it allows "the military to kill more and more of the enemy at greater and greater distances," thus reducing the "cruel and brutal physical contact with the enemy." In contrast, civil wars are low-tech wars with "rugged contact of physical suffering and death individually given and received" – hence they are perceived as more cruel. Nevertheless, the belief that civil wars are particularly barbaric is remarkable less as an objective empirical fact and more as an enduring subjective perception.

Civil wars vary considerably in terms of magnitude of violence.[4] Nevertheless, observers have noted the "strikingly high" mortality rates of recent civil wars (Harkavy and Neuman 2001:323). Ten out of the thirteen deadliest conflicts in the nineteenth and twentieth centuries were civil wars, and major violence was a feature of 68 percent of civil wars as opposed to 15 percent of interstate wars (Magalhães 1996:225; Miall 1992:124). Still, many civil wars produce low fatalities and interstate warfare has produced horrific levels of civilian destruction from time immemorial (Mueller 2004; Bernand 1999; Tilly 1985:173).

Rather than the magnitude of fatalities, it is the victimization of noncombatants that best approximates the perception of excessive violence and atrocity in civil wars – along with the incidence of intimate ("fratricidal") violence (see Chapter 10).[5] High rates of civilian victimization in civil war, relative to overall fatalities, result from the dearth of military engagement and the deliberate targeting of civilians: as an Angolan refugee remarked, "The war has even entered people's homes" (in Brinkman 2000:7). Highly violent civil wars often almost completely lack battles. As in Ireland during the war of independence, "murder was more common than battle" (Hart 1999:18). The battlefield is society itself and civil war is "total war at the grassroots level" (Waghelstein 1985:42).

Although the modern concept of "total war" (especially nuclear war, its most extreme form) entails a total removal of the distinction between combatants and noncombatants, modernity is inextricably linked with the attempt, however imperfect, to draw a line between combatants and civilians, thus limiting violence to the battlefield. Modern conventions on restraint in war, both in theory and practice, emerged in Europe between 1550 and 1700 (Parker 1994:41). European nations were generally successful in acknowledging a distinction between combatants and civilians in the wars that pitted them against each other and took place between the mid-seventeenth century and the Second World War. Yet, for practical as well as normative reasons, this civilizing trend bypassed civil wars. The resistance of civil war to "civilizing" trends in warfare has unquestionably reinforced its association with excessive violence.

---

[4] In 146 civil wars that started in the 1945–99 period, the mean number of estimated deaths is 143,883 and the median number just 19,000; 11 conflicts are estimated to have had fewer than 1,500 deaths (Sambanis 2004).

[5] Eckhardt (1989:92) estimates that interstate wars in the 1900–87 period killed close to twice as many civilians as civil, colonial, and imperial wars combined, and that civilians constitute a higher proportion of the deaths in civil wars. Others point to a trend whereby civilians constitute a higher and increasing proportion of fatalities since the 1960s – a period of predominantly civil wars (Sivard 1996:17–19; Sivard 1987:28–31).

In short, the view of civil war as barbaric is a compound of subjective perceptions and real trends. Although civil wars are not necessarily the most barbaric ones, many civil wars are barbaric at least in that they target primarily civilians, bucking prevailing or emerging international norms. Next, I reconstruct and assess four "conventional wisdoms" that explain the barbaric bent of civil war.

3.2. BREAKDOWN

It has been argued that civil war transforms societies into "Hobbesian playgrounds" (Hedges 2003:163). Following Hobbes, civil war violence has been causally associated with the breakdown of political order, an insight traceable to Thucydides. The underlying theory is that humans are naturally violent and are likely to express their violence unless constrained. Put otherwise, violence is the human condition by default. When belligerency and lawlessness extend to the entire society, barbarism is a predictable and unescapable outcome. On its face, this conjecture is plausible and central to many descriptions of civil war (e.g., Berkeley 2001:14; Barrett 2001:11), as well as scholarly studies (e.g., J. Weinstein 2003). It can also be found in recollections by participants: "All is anarchy and confusion here, everything going to destruction," asserted a Mississippi man during the American Civil War, and another one added: "Every thing at a standstill.... No law, no order, *chaos* & *disorder*" (in Ash 1995:204).

Four mechanisms possibly link the breakdown of political order to barbarism: first, breakdown reveals or creates a culture of generalized brutalization; second, in the absence of institutionalized justice, it leads to an endless spiral of retaliation; third, breakdown generates security dilemmas, leading to mass preemptive violence; and, fourth, it gives rise to undisciplined armed groups that prey on civilians in a fashion reminiscent of medieval warfare.

3.2.1. Brutalization

The argument that civil war either reveals true human nature or alters it in fundamental ways has been popular at least since Thucydides, who turned it into a central feature of *stasis* (Price 2001). For Burke, "civil wars strike deepest of all into the manners of the people. They vitiate their politics; they corrupt their morals; they pervert even the natural taste and relish of equity and justice" (in Keane 1996:157). Ash's description (1988:162) of middle Tennessee in 1864, summarizes this point: the "countryside was a moral as well as a geographical no-man's land, a world without accepted verities and shared convictions, without collective obligations and common rewards, without all the customary formal and informal instruments for commending the virtuous, reproving the wayward, and punishing the wicked. Subject no longer to coercion from authorities above or from peers around, or in many cases from conscience within, individual volition was cast adrift on a turbulent sea of social anarchy." More specifically, civil war produces violence via brutalization in at least five ways: unremitting exposure to violence, removal of social controls, decline of the cost of violent activity, rise in prominence of people with a propensity for violence, and the unlearning of peaceful skills and learning of new violent skills, resulting in the creation of vested interests in the use of violence.

It is well known, first, that war brutalizes combatants (e.g., Ellis 1999:128; Henderson 1985:51). "When you see enough of what man can do to man in the context of warfare," recalled an American who was in Vietnam, "you become desensitized. It was a nasty, bloody conflict, and the people that fought it became very tough, very hard" (in Moyar 1997:98). Lotnik's (1999:54–79) account of the war between Poles and Ukrainians in 1943–4 includes a frank depiction of his own experience: "Men become desensitized very quickly and kill as if they knew nothing else. Even those who would otherwise hesitate before killing a fly can quickly forget that they are taking human lives." War destroys "civilized" principles and dispositions. A French conscript in Algeria recalls how his peers, initially deeply opposed to war, came close to lynching Algerian prisoners: "I am astounded," he noted, "by the insidious transformation that has affected our mindset since we left [France]" (in Butaud and Rialland 1998:132). The recollection of an Italian partisan (in Portelli 1997:139) is suggestive: "When you've been eight, nine months, a year up in the mountains, you come down, you're half a beast. There's no two ways about it. You're not a normal man. Today, I say, I was a beast. I realize that in those times I had lost my reason. You've come down the mountain with that constant hatred, constant war, weapons, always expecting to be shot in the back, always expecting a bullet."

Unlike many interstate wars, civil wars brutalize civilians as well, most obviously by unremitting exposure to violence. A Russian observer (A. Babine in Figes 1989:346) described brutalization as a process of habituation: "People have witnessed so much wanton destruction of human life in the past few years that they are no longer startled by the sight of pools of blood.... People have grown to be unresponsive and callous to the suffering of others.... [They] seem to have acquired a taste for agonizing forms of death." Judge Aedanus Burke was certain at the end of the American Revolution that South Carolinians had become so habituated to violence that they had "reconciled their minds to the killing of each other" (in Weir 1985:76). The bitterness of the American Civil War in Missouri, Fellman points out (1989:57–8), "infiltrated everyday social contact.... In many letters, one reads of what appears on the surface to be an almost matter-of-fact acceptance of violence as a new, accepted norm." A Lebanese man notes the contrast in wartime behavior: "If someone died from cancer or an accident, people would stop talking about it when I came into the room. Now I see friends talking about death in front of their children as if they were talking about bread or wine" (in Dalrymple 1997:259–60). A Lebanese woman recalls a similar experience by way of numerous "snapshots" from the civil war: as a fifteen-year-old child she visited the site of an atrocity and enjoyed the sight of the corpses; militiamen blew up a shop after one of their members was slapped in the face by the owner during an argument; a traffic dispute quickly degenerated into a gunfight; an adolescent brought a human ear to school to impress his classmates. It became difficult, she concludes, to "differentiate between the banal and the extraordinary" (Chamoun 1992:38–9, 55, 61,132–3).

Brutalization affects foreign observers, civilians, and even individuals who decide to fight because they want to put a stop to it. A British journalist (Loyd

2001:24, 204) who covered the war in Bosnia tells how he was affected: when a Bosnian Croat villager killed his puppy after it had taken one of his chickens, he almost went so far as to install a booby trap with a grenade, intending to kill him in revenge. Some refugee camps breed anarchic violence (Crisp 2000). "Those who confront violence with resistance," writes Bourgois (2001:30), "whether it be cultural or political – do not escape unscathed from the terror and oppression they rise against."

Second, civil war destroys the psychosocial mechanisms of self-sanction that serve as guides and deterrents for conduct (Bandura 1990:161). Initially, this may take relatively innocuous forms. A Northern Irish Catholic recalls that, as a teenager, he "ran wild, raking about the estate, making noise and annoying the neighbours. The violent political situation gave us greater opportunities for mischief" (Collins 1999:47). Such behavior can escalate quickly: "With the ordinary conventions of civilized life thrown into confusion, human nature, always ready to offend even when laws exist, [shows] itself proudly in its true colours, as something incapable of controlling passion, insubordinate to the idea of justice, the enemy to anything superior to itself" (Thucydides 3:84).

Third, civil war lowers the cost of violent activity (G. Martin 2000:162; Gilmore 1987:44). By destroying sanctioning institutions, civil war turns violence into a costless and profitable endeavor. Mary Elizabeth Berry (1994:7) describes civil-war-torn medieval Japan as a place where, "with the licensing of violence and private justice at the highest level of power, the rule of force became endemic to all quarrels: differences among villagers over water rights or among towns-people over wells resulted time and again in bloody resolutions that were hardly resolutions at all." In Colombia, where "killing is easy, cheap, and popular," some high school girls sought contract killers in order to "solve" problems of romantic rivalry. Neighbors settled small disputes in the same fashion: "López also knew of a man who was angry at his neighbor, whose new construction was causing water to flood the man's house. The neighbor was richer than he, and the man feared that if he sued, the neighbor would simply pay off the judge. His solution was to hire a *sicario* [contract killer] and have the neighbor killed" (Rosenberg 1991:34). Civil war also destroys social hierarchies that effectively act as social controls. By transferring power from elders to youth, it eliminates what in many traditional societies counts as the most effective informal means of conflict resolution and social control (e.g., Jok and Hutchinson 1999:135).

Fourth, civil war allows the rise in prominence of people with a propensity for violence: in Abraham Lincoln's words (in Fellman 1989:85), these are times in which "every foul bird comes abroad, and every dirty reptile rises up." In a more recent formulation: "The scum [rises] to the surface; the meek and the humane were the war's losers" (Loyd 2001:13). The oft-described process of criminalization of civil wars is a case in point (e.g., Mueller 2004). Backcountry North Carolina during the American Revolution was a place where much violence committed by roving bands of Whigs and Tories appeared to be lacking any clear partisan purpose; a Whig officer wrote of one such band that "I do not learn that they are connected with any party, but... [are] an independent company for the Special purpose of stealing and plundering" (in Ekirch 1985:108). Whereas roadblocks and checkpoints were initially used as a means of population control during the civil war in Congo-Brazzaville, they quickly became a low-risk, high-profit means of extortion (Bazenguissa-Ganga 1999a:47); although the Colombian *Violencia* grew out of a partisan cleavage, it "became an umbrella under which every variety of criminality could be found. As the depredations of men under arms grew even more ghastly, it became clear that large numbers of psychopaths and common bandits had joined those who claimed to be fighting to maintain their political principles" (Henderson 1985:149). Indeed, the most extreme forms of violence may be seen as by-products of looting and predation (Azam and Hoeffler 2002).

Fifth, civil war engenders new actors with a vested interest in the perpetuation of both war and violence. On the collective level, new war economies produce actors with skills in the use of violence, whose existence and power derives from the war (Roldán 2002:227; M. Johnson 2001:226; Keen 1998:22). On the individual level, civil war shrinks the "shadow of the future," thus causing peaceful skills to become "unlearned" (Genschel and Schlichte 1998). Many child soldiers in Sierra Leone made a conscious choice to participate in the war, having grown up in a world of "destroyed families and failed educational systems" where only war appears to offer opportunities (Peters and Richards 1998:210). A Kenyan policeman observed that the Somali refugees in a refugee camp were violent because they "have been brought up without justice and under the rule of the gun" (in Crisp 2000:624). An Afghan explained anarchy and violence in Afghanistan in a similar fashion: "These youngsters have had no school – they know only fighting" (in Weiner 2001:B4); a Lebanese Shia militiaman summarized it all in 1984: "War is my only friend. It's like my wife, I love it. In peace I feel afraid" (in M. Johnson 2001:203).

All these mechanisms converge to generate a culture of lawlessness and violence that can be self-sustaining, in line with Durkheim's (1951:299) quip that "at any given moment the moral constitution of society establishes the contingent of voluntary deaths."

3.2.2. Revenge

The desire to avenge a previous violent or nonviolent act (such as humiliation) is widespread even in societies with working judicial systems (Jacoby 1983). "Revenge is a natural thing to desire," Frijda (1994:283) argues, "and sometimes it is a natural thing to take."[6] It is a feature that recurs in all kinds of settings, from the biblical *lex talionis* ("an eye for an eye, a tooth for a tooth") to the Greek tragedies that take it as their central theme, to Hume's (1978:410–11) assertion that the desire to punish one's enemies is a regular human appetite. Frijda (1994:264) underlines the ubiquitous and universal nature as well as the immense power of "the urge of private vindication." The desire for revenge is certainly exacerbated when these systems disappear, and generates cycles of violence in all civil wars

---

[6] In a 1976 decision, the U.S. Supreme Court made precisely this point: "The instinct for retribution is part of the nature of man" (in Solomon 1994:307).

(e.g., Berry 1994:9; Henderson 1985:226). A Lebanese woman (Tabbara 1979:54) speaks for many others when she describes her emotions during the civil war: "I am Lebanese, Moslem and Palestinian and it concerns me when three hundred and sixty-five Lebanese Moslems are murdered. I feel the seeds of hatred and the desire for revenge taking root in my very depths. At this moment I want the [Moslem militia] or anybody else to give the Phalangists back twice as good as we got. I would like them to go into offices and kill the first seven hundred and thirty defenseless Christians they can lay their hands on."

As a result of such impulses, revenge may quickly dominate the motivations of violence: in North Carolina during the Revolutionary War "vengeance overshadow[ed] policy" (Escott and Crow 1986:391). "As both Unionist and Secessionist bands intensified their operations, violence in East Tennessee became increasingly reciprocal . . . attacks by one side led to retaliation by the other, and the result was an escalating cycle of violence that was difficult to halt" (Fisher 1997:84). In Missouri, "violent reprisals and counter-reprisals . . . had been the very stuff" of the Civil War (Fellman 1989:263). A governor of a Colombian province found it difficult to resist local demands to distribute arms to aggrieved Conservatives, "so that locals might form *chusmas* and gangs that would perpetrate the same actions as the Liberals do and, in this way, apply the law of an 'eye for an eye'" (Roldán 2002:258). In Liberia, "there appears to have been a large number of people who took up arms at some stage during the war, but who may have been victims at other times" (Ellis 1999:133). Revenge is associated with escalation: as a Union man from Missouri wrote in 1863, "The bushwhackers burn a house and then we burn two houses" (in Fellman 1989:184). The title of a book on the Colombian Civil War succinctly alludes to this dynamic: *Matar, rematar y contramatar* (Uribe 1990).

Revenge is probably the most recurrent feature in descriptions of violence in civil war, often leading to the metaphor of blood feud or vendetta;[7] it is a central theme of novels and memoirs and, more generally, of the folklore of civil wars.[8] The Lebanese writer Massoud Younes entitled his book *Ces morts qui nous tuent* (These dead who kill us). Revenge gives civil war violence its irrational and anomic glow and lends support to the perception that violence has become "an end in itself rather than a means to political ends" and that it "escape[s] the control of the actors" who initiate it (Crenshaw 1995:476). For Tracy Chamoun (1992:10, 23) the entire Lebanese civil war was a cycle of revenge: the war "reached a paroxysm because revenge became the reason to live for an entire nation. If one Christian died, then two Moslems were killed, and so on. . . . During these fifteen years of war, we never understood that our hatred begot hatred. When we acted, moved by revenge, we generated the spirit of retaliation. When we were terrorized, we were precisely provoking that which we were so scared of." Indeed, people who have lived through civil wars describe with

---

[7] E.g., M. Johnson (2001:125); Battini and Pezzino (1997:xxii); Pavone (1994:240); Kedward (1993:160); Ortiz Sarmiento (1990:134); Loizos (1988:648–9); Henderson (1985:228).

[8] Ung (2000); Collins (1999); Lotnik (1999); Lebrun (1998); Portelli (1997); Meyer (1995); Cela (1992); Sender Barayón (1989); Gage (1984).

amazement those exceptional situations where revenge *is not* exacted (e.g., Mouro 1999:181).

Individual, personalized revenge is omnipresent in the recollections of participants in civil wars.[9] The Confederate Missouri guerrilla Bill Anderson wrote to citizens of Lexington in 1864 that the Yankees had killed his father and sister and added: "I have fully glutted my vengeance.... I have tried to war with Federals honorably, but for retaliation I have done things, and am fearful will have to do that which I would shrink from if possible to avoid." Fellman (1989:139) comments that "Anderson's was a personal war of vengeance against a personal enemy." This kind of behavior is not restricted to poor, backward, or ethnically divided societies; it is reported by allegedly committed ideologues in Western societies, such as French and Italian partisans and Spanish Republican fighters (Portelli 1997:138; Kedward 1993:160; Zulaika 1988:28).

Revenge operates across many different dimensions of civil wars. It is a direct motivator of violent action, but it is also indirectly connected to violence in that it often acts as the chief motivation for joining armed organizations, which then go on to produce violence. Benedict Kerkvliet (1977:68) quotes Filipino peasants who told him that they had joined the anti-Japanese underground after parents or relatives had been killed by the Japanese. A young militiaman in Sierra Leone made the same point: "One of my smaller brothers was killed by the rebels, that was in 1991.... So after that I tried to join the army as a matter of revenging. I wanted to revenge my people" (in Peters and Richards 1998:189). Revenge may also operate at the collective level, either between an individual and a group or between large groups (e.g., Loizos 1988). Lotnik (1999:70) recalls a former comrade in the Polish guerrilla warfare of 1943–4, whose life "had ceased to mean anything to him after he had lost his sister and his brothers, his parents, his wife and his three little daughters in a [Ukrainian] raid [and] continued to exist only for the purpose of killing and torturing Ukrainians." A U.S. adviser in Vietnam told an American journalist, while troops from his unit were torturing a suspect nearby: "You know, it's a whole cycle of this stuff. Last week in another village near Don Nhon the VC marched five government sympathizers into the marketplace and beat their heads with hammers. So we return it on this guy. It goes on and on" (in Moyar: 1997:97). Sometimes group and individual motivations merge. Often what appears to be purely group violence is, in fact, very individual. Pervanic (1999:80) describes how the Muslim inmates of the Omarska camp in Bosnia constituted a general pool for revenge-oriented violence by the Serbs; but whereas the pool of targets was defined in terms of group ethnic identity, the specific targets tended to be selected on the basis of individual characteristics, such as their past actions.

---

[9] The desire to take revenge for the murder of loved ones seems to be omnipresent, even when it is not (or not intended to be) carried out. When asked if he has ever fantasized about revenge, a man, whose entire family was killed during the "Dirty War" in Argentina, replied: "Oh, yes! About Massera [a member of the junta] I dreamed up magnificent scenarios where I'm walking along the street, just like they do on TV, with a gun and a silencer. I approach Massera and say, 'Good day.' He looks at me strangely and asks who I am. I say, 'You killed my parents and my siblings,' and with that, I wipe him out on the spot" (Tarnopolsky 1999:57).

In extreme situations revenge may degenerate into social anomie bordering on an ideal-typical Hobbesian world, as in Tennessee during the American Civil War: "When a Union foraging squad set fire to her house in January 1865, [a woman] rushed outside and, to her astonishment, found one of her neighbors accompanying the Yankees. He 'said he had joined them,' she reported, '[and said] that he had been broken twice, once by the Rebels and once by the Federals, and he was going to have revenge and didn't care who it was off of'" (Ash 1988:163). When this is the case, revenge becomes another instance of generalized brutalization. In most cases, however, revenge appears to be subject to rules, although targets run the gamut from specific individuals to entire groups.

3.2.3. Security Dilemma

The security dilemma applies to conflict and violence at once (De Figueiredo and Weingast 1999; Hardin 1995; Posen 1993). A security dilemma is said to occur when the breakdown of order creates a situation in which individuals coordinating around focal points (primarily ethnic identities) resort to preemptive violence, or align with warmongering leaders who do so, because of security fears. Incentives for violence are compounded by uncertainty and the extremely high costs of not preempting: they must kill so as not to be killed. The security dilemma argument usually implies two distinct motivations: elites act instrumentally in pursuit of power, while the followers act emotionally, out of fear.

Examples of preemptive violence are not infrequent in descriptions of civil wars. For Abraham Lincoln, the American Civil War in the borderlands was a situation whereby "each man feels an impulse to kill his neighbor, lest he be first killed by him" (in Fellman 1989:85). A Union commander in Missouri pointed out in 1864 that "there is scarcely a citizen in the country but wants to kill someone of his neighbors for fear that said neighbor may kill him" (in Fellman 1989:62). In the immediate aftermath of the Second World War in Malaya, a man recalled that "Once the first clashes were known, the communists in the MPAJA alerted the Chinese in the villages and towns all over the country, to be ready for the Malay rampage. The cry was: 'The Malays are out to kill – so, kill before you are killed'" (Kheng 1983:219).

3.2.4. Medievalization

Civil war is seen not only as "essentially wild and savage" (Mayer 2000:323), but in a way that harks back to medieval wars: warfare is said to be "medievalized" (Münkler 2002; van Creveld 1991). Indeed, the chief prosecutor of the International Criminal Tribunal for the Former Yugoslavia accused Slobodan Milosevic of "medieval savagery" (Rotella 2002:4). Anarchy destroys military organization and discipline, thus opening the door to all kinds of violent excesses (e.g., Schofield 1996:251). Undisciplined armed men, marauding soldiers, troops living off the land, and criminal elements prey on the population with complete impunity, if not encouragement (J. Weinstein 2003; Ignatieff 1998:6; Laqueur 1998:399; Schlichte 1997:5). This argument, which Richards (1996:xiv) dubs the "new barbarism thesis," denies the political dimension of civil wars in favor of its criminal character and is usually applied to recent civil wars in Africa. According to a typical description (Luttwak 1995:9), "The chaos that now engulfs [Sierra Leone] cannot be described as civil war, inasmuch as the contending forces – notably including the 'government' represent nobody but themselves; nor can it be described as a guerrilla war, for no side seriously pretends to be fighting for a cause."

3.3. TRANSGRESSION

Insofar as war is normatively understood to be the exclusive preserve of sovereign actors, organized violence by nonsovereign actors is seen as illegitimate and transgressive. Hence, subjects and citizens who disregard the sharply drawn distinction between sovereign and nonsovereign actors are not legitimate belligerents but criminals who cannot expect the treatment accorded to legitimate belligerents.

Violence is often regulated by norms (Carpenter 2003). The norms that separate "lawful" from "unlawful" violence can be powerful. There is a long normative tradition that sees civil wars as being less "lawful" compared with wars between sovereign entities; its origins lie in the medieval belief that war is permissible only if waged by legitimate authority, which led to a distinction between "public wars" waged by Christian princes, and private wars, vendettas, and *chevauchées* conducted in medieval Europe by local warlords or bands of unemployed or indigent knights (Howard 1994:9). A parallel distinction was made between *bellum hostile* and *bellum romanum* or *guerre mortelle*. The former was the norm in Western Christendom and entailed regulations and restrictions, whereas the latter concerned wars against outsiders, infidels, or barbarians where no holds were barred and all those designated as enemy, whether bearing arms or not, could be indiscriminately slaughtered (Howard 1994:3). The two distinctions came together in civil war, with *guerre mortelle* seen as related to civil conflicts, where it merged with a private legal condition known as "mortal enmity" (Stacey 1994:33).

This distinction was elaborated later on, most notably by the Swiss jurist Emmeric Vattel; the key implication was that rebellion could and ought to be distinguished from belligerency (De Lupis 1987:35). Civilians who rose against the authority of their rightful sovereign "had no rights at all, and if they lost, their activities were judged, and judged very severely, by the criminal law" (Howard 1994:10). Thus rebellion was equated with other forms of transgression and deviance, such as leprosy and heresy, which by then had come to be seen as legitimate targets of extreme violence (R. Moore 1987). As Balthasar Ayala argued in 1582, "disobedience in the part of subjects and rebellion against the prince is treated as heinous offense on a par with heresy. . . . The laws of war, and of captivity, and of postliminy, which apply to enemies, do not apply to rebels" (in Parker 1994:44).[10]

---

[10] In the same line of thought, siege warfare, which produced massive victimization of civilian populations, was viewed not as an act of war but as the enforcement of a judicial sentence against traitors who had disobeyed their prince's lawful command to surrender (Stacey 1994:38).

By transgressing the *jus ad bellum* (the right to wage war), rebels could not hope for protection under the *jus in bello* (the laws of war); they were, instead, subject to the laws of peace (Donagan 1994:1139). Paradoxically, then, it is the application of domestic law (either the law of treason or common criminal law) rather than the laws of war that is seen as the source of barbarism. Indeed, Donagan (1994:1159) explains the relative absence of cruelty during the English Civil War as the result of a conscious choice by the belligerents to follow the rules of "foreign wars" as opposed to the laws of peace and grant each other status of "lawful enemies"; in fact, within the English Civil War, atrocities took place where "civilian law overrode the laws of war."

Hence the treatment of rebels was for a long time excluded from the general trend toward the humanization of warfare (Parker 1994); this was decisively reinforced by the rise of both nationalism and the Clausewitzian distinction between states and peoples based on the principle that organized violence deserved to be called "war" only if it were waged "by the state, for the state, and against the state" (van Creveld 1991:36). Therefore a state that experienced a revolt, insurrection, rebellion, revolution, or civil war was essentially beyond the purview of international law (McCoubrey and White 1995:6). This view was explicitly held by many participants in civil wars: J. Franklin Bell, the commander of U.S. troops in the Philippines at the dawn of the twentieth century, ordered his troops to treat captured rebels like "highway robbers or pirates" (May 1991:253). This perception is also evident in an exchange between Queen Frederika of Greece and the American writer Willis Barnstone (1995:72–3), during the Greek Civil War:

"Why do you execute prisoners of war?" I asked Frederika.
"They are not prisoners of war. They're thieves."
"But they are human beings, and Greece has had enough death."
"They're just common thieves."

This practice was codified in the laws of war. The legal consensus until recently was that civilians were protected only as long as they were passive (Nabulsi 2001). In fact, and until 1949, interstate and civil wars diverged with respect to the application of laws that recognized the enemy as a legitimate opponent; the laws of war applied to interstate conflicts, whereas in civil wars states enjoyed the option of applying domestic criminal laws that view the enemy as an outlaw. According to the draft Russian text at the Brussels Conference of 1874, all civilians who participated in hostilities were considered outlaws and were to be "delivered to justice," and, as a French jurist argued in 1874, "That which is called patriotic insurrections or irregular uprisings by the entire population to harass a legitimate army should always be condemned, without bothering to distinguish between methods used" (in Nabulsi 2001:13, 17). Eventually, the 1899 Hague Convention on Land Warfare restricted the class of person that could represent a belligerent party at war to the professional soldier, thus excluding rebels (Nabulsi 2001:16).[11]

---

[11] The 1949 Geneva Conventions (in particular the Fourth Convention, also known as the "Civilians Convention"), along with protocols I and II added in 1977, have attempted to address this issue only with partial success.

A corollary of this thesis is that the more an army distinguishes between soldiers and civilians, the more implacably it will react against rebels, whom it will treat as criminals (C. Schmitt 1992:240–1). In a way, the transgression thesis is the reverse of the breakdown thesis: whereas the latter maximizes the status of belligerent (extending it to the entire society), the former minimizes it (restricting it to the agents of the sovereign). Nevertheless, both predict barbarism.

3.4. POLARIZATION

Polarization is a well-known link between civil war and barbarism. It refers to the intensity of divisions between groups, "when a large number of conflict group members attach overwhelming importance to the issues at stake, or manifest strongly held antagonistic beliefs and emotions toward the opposing segment, or both" (Nordlinger 1972:9). Polarized conflicts are said to be "no longer over specific gains or losses but over conceptions of moral right and over the inter-pretation of history and human destiny" (Lipset and Rokkan 1967:11); they are "the kind of intense and divisive politics one may refer to by the name of *absolute politics*" (Perez Díaz 1993:6).

Polarization can be conceptualized as the sum of antagonisms between indi-viduals belonging to a small number of groups that simultaneously display high internal homogeneity and high external heterogeneity (Esteban and Ray 1994). The intuition is that if a population is clustered around a small number of distant but equally large poles, it is likely to undergo violent conflict. A typical claim is that "civil wars are by their nature often more savage than international wars, and have a stronger ideological content. The two factors are certainly related" (Hearder, quoted in Close 1995:viii). The underlining mechanism is dislike so intense as to cancel even fraternal ties, imagined or real. "Identity," Buruma (2002:12) writes, "is what gets the blood boiling, what makes people do unspeakable things to their neighbors. It is the fuel used by agitators to set whole countries on fire."

Although typically made about "ideological" conflicts, this argument is also echoed in the "ethnic antipathy" argument as formulated by Horowitz (2001), Kaufman (2001), and others, which implies a similar logic for civil wars associated with ethnic polarization. For example, it is argued that "almost all of our current and recent ethnic conflicts appear to involve high levels of hatred and compulsions to vengeance, with the end result of brutality, massacres, and various forms of savagery" (Harkavy and Neuman 2001:208).

This thesis is related to Carl Schmitt's (1976) insight about politics as a reflection of the fundamental distinction between friend and enemy. The *polit-ical*, he argued, is the most extreme antagonism pitting one fighting collec-tivity of people against another. War is just the natural expression of enmity; as Lenin pointed out, civil war in a class-based society is an extension of the class struggle (in J.-C. Martin 1995:61). It follows that the enemy in civil war is not just circumstantial but absolute – a point that emerges in the fol-lowing exchange between Bizot (2003:111) and his Khmer Rouge warden in Cambodia:

"In a word," I persisted, "you prefer to extend your hand to the Chinese and stir up hatred against your brother, rather than unite with him to find peace."

"You don't understand," he told me calmly, sounding like a schoolmaster about to explain his point again patiently. "He who has betrayed, is no longer my brother. He is merely a lackey of imperialism, and it is he who has turned against me."

Norberto Bobbio (1992:303) observed that the relationship between a just war and a just enemy is inverse: a war is just when the enemy is unjust. Naturally, unjust and absolute enemies demand no mercy whatsoever. Hence barbarism is the result of polarization. A paradigmatic formulation of the link between polarization and barbarism comes from Stanley Payne (1987:209):

It has been observed that civil wars tend to be much more conflicts of principle than are most international struggles, while those of this century have been stimulated by intense ideological and moralistic passion. In the past, civil wars might take a heavy toll on life on the regular battlefield – as in the case of the English conflict of the 1640s or the American Civil War of the 1860s – yet be generally free of atrocities against civilians. This was presumably due to the fact that despite the intense differences in political principle that divided the participants in these earlier conflicts, they continued to share a common world outlook, religion, or sociomoral framework.... By contrast, nearly all the twentieth-century conflicts have reflected the intense civilizational and ideological conflicts that demonize the enemy and serve psychologically and emotionally to legitimate the most extreme and atrocious measures.

In fact, the polarization thesis reasons back from violence to the factors that are believed to have produced it. Linking polarization and violence implies an underlying causal claim that both predicts the relevant perpetrator-victim dyad and assigns a motive to the violence. For example, the relevant dyad in a class war includes the owners of capital and the owners of labor. In an ethnic war, it refers to members of different ethnic groups. According to this logic, a group is targeted because of its position on the relevant cleavage dimension and, subsequently, individuals are victimized because of their membership in this group. Hence polarization explains simultaneously the onset of a conflict, its content, and its violence. This causal link is generally simply assumed rather than empirically confirmed. We either observe an action at the microlevel (e.g., a Sinhala victimizing a Tamil) and conclude that (ethnic) polarization at the macrolevel explains this particular action; or we observe polarization around a given cleavage at the macrolevel and then generalize it to all individual acts of violence at the microlevel.

While the breakdown thesis is privileged in descriptive accounts of civil wars, the polarization thesis lies at the core of most macrohistorical accounts of civil wars that generally subsume violence under a theory of deep group rivalry that precedes and causes the war; hence, this is really a theory of *ex ante* or *prewar* conflict.

The causes of polarization may be found at the intersection of structural conditions, political institutions, and the action of political entrepreneurs who succeed in turning real or perceived differences into polarized politics. At the individual level, polarization manifests itself as "fanaticism": an uncompromising and passionate commitment for a particular cause that overcomes other connections between people and leads to a willingness to shed one's own blood as well as the blood of others. Exemplary statements are encountered in most conflicts. The following examples are from Spain and eastern Tennessee:

> Dedication to the cause and party consciousness broke former bonds of friendship and kinship; there was a tendency to greet and be friendly towards members of the same group, whilst systematically avoiding the others. Quarrels, rivalry and hatred developed out of these estrangements. Each group had its café, its meetings and even its feastdays, religious on the one side and secular on the other. (Fisher 1997:85)

> The internecine strife entered almost all areas of Eastern Tennessee life, and its effects were corrosive. The Unionist-secessionist conflict destroyed families, friendships, and institutions. It pitted family members against each other, split communities into factions, and erased former friendships. (Lison-Tolosana 1983:48)

3.5. THE TECHNOLOGY OF WARFARE

The counsel of two counterrevolutionary French guerrillas explained the violent acts of his clients by pointing to the nature of the warfare they practiced: "The Chouannerie is a new kind of war which was unknown up to now in the regulated nations; it is a war of savages where every individual searches for his enemy in isolation, kills him and loots him everywhere he may find him. The Rebels have been called Brigands because, in truth, they behave in their kind of war like brigands" (in Cobb 1972:21). Likewise, a Union general explained the breakdown of social norms and the ensuing violence in Civil War Missouri as resulting from irregular war: he insisted that "there was something in the hearts of these good and typical American Christian farmers which had exploded when basic social and moral ties had disintegrated under the stress of the guerrilla war" (Fellman 1989:265).

The claim that "guerrilla" warfare and barbaric violence are causally connected is commonplace (e.g., Laqueur 1998:399; Wickham-Crowley 1990:225). This thesis posits barbarism as a product of a particular technology of warfare. Assessing it requires a clear understanding of what "guerrilla" war is. The distinction between conventional (or classic) warfare and its "unconventional," "guerrilla," or "irregular" counterpart is common in the military literature, although the terminology fluctuates. The intuition behind this distinction boils down to this: whereas conventional warfare entails face-to-face confrontations between regular armies across well-defined front lines, "unconventional" warfare features a dearth of large-scale direct military confrontations or "set-piece battles" and the absence of front lines.

Conventional warfare entails either a shared perception of power parity by the rivals, or recognition by the weaker side that it must play by the existing rules and confront its enemy on the battlefield. Without some sort of mutual consent, no conventional battle can take place (Beaufre 1972:12). Historically, front lines emerged as a result of a complex combination of factors. According to Beaufre (1972), war evolved from a highly ritualized clash between small bands into a confrontation between armies in set-piece battles that became a sort of "judiciary duel" whose outcome was binding for the groups represented by the armies.

A convention emerged following which armies acted as "armed delegations" for populations that generally remained on the sidelines. The gradual growth of fire-power caused warfare to shift from column- to front-based and then the front to expand gradually until it covered the entire territory. In some instances, however, the battlefield outcome did not determine the outcome of the war, either because only one side had a regular army (e.g., in colonial wars) or because victorious armies were challenged by local armies relying on "irregular" or "partisan" war-fare – an outcome generally attributed to the nationalist feelings of the population; as a result, conquering armies had to "pacify" the conquered territory. In fact, local resistance against conquerors was common before the age of nationalism (Nabulsi 1999), and the peripheries of empires were rarely pacified.

Irregular warfare, thus, takes place when the weaker actor refuses to face the stronger one directly and, instead, fights by deception. In this sense, irregular warfare is an unambiguously proclaimed manifestation of military asymmetry. This is how a Filipino insurgent described the choice of irregular warfare against the Americans in 1900: "The war we make upon our enemies is formal, and because of their greater numbers and the superior means of warfare which they have at their disposal, the result is disastrous to us, even though we sacrifice the lives of our brothers. The most advisable thing to do at the present time in this campaign is to employ ambush warfare; although it is slow in results, it will enable us to attain our independence" (in May 1991:121).

A stylized description of irregular war is as follows: the state (or *incumbents*) fields regular troops and is able to control urban and accessible terrain, while seeking to engage its opponents militarily in peripheral and rugged terrain; chal-lengers (rebels or *insurgents*) "hover just below the military horizon," hiding and relying on harassment and surprise, stealth and raid (Simons 1999:84). Such wars often turn into wars of attrition, with insurgents seeking to win by not losing, while inflicting incessant pain on incumbents (Henriksen 1983:141; Shy 1976:12). As a Vietnamese Communist told an American official in 1975: "One side is not strong enough to win and the other is not weak enough to lose" (in Thayer 1985:97). Contrary to what is sometimes claimed or implied (e.g., Luttwak 1995:9; C. Schmitt 1992), irregular warfare does not require a specific cause, revolutionary, Communist, nationalist, or otherwise; it can serve any cause.

Irregular war, broadly conceived, has been practiced in "backward" areas invaded by regular armies (e.g., wars of empire and colonization); in areas that had been already colonized (wars of decolonization); in modern states whose regular armies have been defeated on the battlefield (wars of occupation); in weak but modernizing states bent on centralization and the subjugation of their periphery; and in "failing" or "failed" states.

Although military asymmetry stands at the opposite end of conventional war, the reverse is not necessarily true: military symmetry is not always synonymous with conventional war.[12] Symmetric wars can be fought by irregular armies on both sides – sometimes labeled "primitive wars" (Earle 1997:108; Beaufre 1972:9)

---

[12] Likewise, military asymmetry does not always imply irregular war; it includes other forms of armed challenge, including what is often described as "terrorism."

or "criminal wars" (Mueller 2004). Examples include wars in Congo-Brazzaville or Liberia (but also in Lebanon), as well as some civil wars that erupted in the wake of the Soviet Union's collapse (e.g., the wars in Georgia). These "symmetric irregular" wars are often described as "guerrilla" wars, but they differ from typical irregular wars in a number of ways. They feature front lines, though they tend to lack major set-piece battles, at least of the classic kind; and they take place under state collapse: the rival armies typically equip themselves by plundering the arsenal of the disbanded state army (e.g., Tishkov 1999:585). Front lines often take the form of roadblocks and checkpoints that appear immediately following the collapse of the state and may last for years; these wars tend to display the type of violence that I label "reciprocal extermination," featuring indiscriminate raids against enemy territory, as neither actor has the capacity or willingness to control the population associated with its rival (e.g., Lotnik 1999; Ellis 1995).[13]

Despite the many appeals to the technology of warfare as a causal variable in barbarism, the actual link between warfare and violence remains unspecified. It is possible to identify three causal pathways. The first one takes us back to the polarization thesis and points to the revolutionary character of irregular war; the second one goes back to the breakdown thesis and stresses the "medieval" nature of irregular war; the third one points to security considerations that trigger either psychological mechanisms (e.g., frustration and fear) or strategic reactions: in a dangerous environment where one cannot possibly tell civilian and enemy combatant apart, it pays to be violent toward civilians.

3.5.1. Irregular War as Revolutionary War

Because "deep" conflicts are seen as intractable, the wars they produce can be both irregular and highly violent. Carl Schmitt (1992) linked his polarization thesis to "partisan war" by stressing the heavily ideological character of the "National Liberation" movements of the decolonization and Cold War era. His "theory of the partisan" argues that the "limited and domesticated" hostility of conventional war turns into the "real hostility" of partisan warfare because of ideological enmity – an insight that is found in many subsequent works (e.g., Holsti 1996:39).

3.5.2. Irregular War as "Medieval" War

Those who espouse a theory by which irregular war is violent because of its "medieval" character hold that because irregular warfare presupposes a relative absence of formal structures, it causes a breakdown in military discipline, thus turning war into a cover for decentralized looting, banditry, and all kinds of violence against civilians. The absence of professional armies indicates the disappearance of the "warriors' honor" and its replacement with barbarism (Ignatieff

---

[13] Some civil wars combine aspects from both asymmetric and symmetric nonconventional wars. For example, the RENAMO insurgency in central Mozambique was a classic guerrilla war, whereas it looked more like a symmetric nonconventional war in the south, with hit-and-run attacks and no attempt to hold territory (Finnegan 1992:62).

1998). According to this argument, contemporary guerrilla wars "from Colombia to the Philippines" are nothing more than "the work of ragtag bands of ruffians out for their own advantage, hardly distinguishable from the *ecorcheurs* ('skinners') who devastated the French countryside during the Hundred Years' War" (van Creveld 1991:60).

3.5.3. Security

The acute feeling of vulnerability that combatants experience in the context of irregular war provides the third causal link between irregular war and barbarism. This link can be formulated in either a psychological version or a rationalist one.

On the psychological front, the absence of clear front lines and the presence of the enemy behind one's back cause frustration, "endemic" uncertainty, fear, anxiety, even panic (Lary 2001:114; May 1991:147; Cooper 1979:92). The problem facing actors is *identification* – in the words of a Union General in Civil War Missouri, "the utter impossibility of deciding who were guilty and who innocent" (in Fellman 1989:96). This facilitates trigger-happy reactions (Filkins 2005; Grossman 1995:81; Finley 1994:74; Calder 1984:xxii), particularly among troops unused to irregular war. For example, violence in the Appalachians during the American Civil War was closely linked to the fact that local military commanders "saw danger from the rear as well as the front"; as a Confederate officer put it: "When an officer finds himself and men bushwhacked from behind every shrub, tree, or projection on all sides of the road, only severe measures will stop it" (Paludan 1981:66, 94). Violence by disciplined troops, such as the massacre of Vietnamese peasants by U.S. servicemen in My Lai, has been attributed to such psychological processes (Bilton and Sim 1992).

The rationalist variant links violence specifically to an army's inability to identify the enemy: in an environment where it is impossible to tell civilian from enemy combatant apart, it pays to be violent. On the one hand, rebels are vulnerable to infiltration and have a hard time recognizing informers; on the other hand, incumbents face an enemy that refuses to fight conventionally but succeeds in inflicting casualties. Given such constraints, violence against civilians, including collective reprisals, may appear rational. Whether the population acts willingly or not, there is typically a very deep social and geographical overlap between a political actor's "support system" (the source of its military intelligence, food, supplies, and recruits) and the civilian population (Wickham-Crowley 1990:225; C. Johnson 1968:447). Hence, focusing on civilian collaborators rather than fighters (the "sea" rather than the "fish," in the terms of Mao's famous dictum) becomes a primary objective for victory-seeking armies that face high costs (Downes 2004; Valentino, Huth, and Balch-Lindsay 2004).[14] In short, it is not that combatants

---

[14] The recent example of Chechnya is telling. The Russian interior minister pointed out during a trip to Chechnya that "the militants did not simply disappear. They are here among us"; as Colonel Yevgeni Sidorov put it: "You can't say exactly how many militants there are. It all depends on whether you count them in the day or at night. It's not written on somebody's forehead that he is a militant." After suffering a surprise raid by Chechen guerrillas in the village of Shali,

kill people out of frustration (though individual combatants may do so) but that violence addresses a basic strategic problem of irregular war.

3.6. ASSESSMENT

Each of these arguments has something to contribute to our understanding of violence in civil war. Similarly, each has its weaknesses, its inconsistencies, and its discrepancies with regard to the empirical record. As they stand, however, they tend to be too vague and indeterminate to be tested empirically; in fact, some are unfalsifiable. Priority must thus be given to conceptual clarification and theoretical development. Therefore, the discussion that follows is not intended to test these arguments against each other and establish one as the only legitimate frame through which to view the question. A research program must emerge from a clear set of first principles, and, given the available evidence, these arguments do not stand as equals in their ability to generate such principles. In the section that follows, I consider the weaknesses and strengths of each argument and select the security version of the technology of warfare thesis as the most promising basis for theoretical development.

3.6.1. Breakdown

Through its various mechanisms and versions, the breakdown thesis constitutes perhaps the most intuitive account of barbarism, which explains its popularity. Ultimately, however, it raises more questions than it answers.

To begin with, many of the mechanisms discussed previously are correlates of violence rather than its causes. This is clearly the case for brutalization and revenge (but not for the security dilemma). They also suffer from the same problem I identified in the discussion on expressive motivations of violence: individual actions of revenge or brutalization may be consistent with organizational decisions to use violence for instrumental reasons. More generally, breakdown may well be a mischaracterization of most civil war situations. Many ground-level accounts describe a situation in which pockets of (usually relative) disorder coexist with pockets of impressive order. For instance, armed actors are often willing and able to eliminate common crime.[15] In fact, both people who have lived in civil wars (e.g., Mouro 1999:44) and ethnographers and journalists who

in January 2000, a Russian officer declared that "it is not clear where [the rebels] came from. They just popped up among the civilians." As a result, the Russians resorted to violence against noncombatants. According to a Chechen refugee woman: "They bomb us, they kill us, they don't make a difference between militants and civilians" (Gordon 2000a:A3; Gordon 2000b:A4).

[15] Simons (1999:92) observes that anarchy "is nothing more than an intellectual construct" because "at ground level, people always self-organize somehow, and they know who is gunning for whom." In Venezuela, the insurgents policed the area under their control, curbed local violence (stabbings and machete fights), and controlled excessive drinking, truancy among children, and "sleeping around" (Wickham-Crowley 1991:44); crime all but vanished in the areas held by the FARC rebels in Colombia (Rubio 1999:129); crime rates in Northern Ireland are lower than in the rest of the United Kingdom, while public opinion surveys indicate that perceptions and fear of crime are higher in (peaceful) Britain than in (violent) Northern Ireland (Gallagher 1995:50). Similar

have conducted fieldwork in stateless environments (e.g., Nordstrom 1997:12; Finnegan 1992:230) report that everyday life is much more structured than imagined; violence tends to come in bursts rather than being a continuous occurrence and it tends to occur in specific times and places rather than randomly. Daniel Ellsberg (2003:114) recalls his experience in the Vietnamese countryside: "I gradually got the picture that everywhere we went in both the hamlets and the countryside there were little signposts visible to all who knew the neighborhood that said 'To find VC, turn left – about ten feet,' 'This bridge closed for mining, tonight and every night.' The widespread perception of chaos appears to be the result of superficial observation."

The problem of mischaracterization is particularly obvious in the case of revenge. Although violence is often motivated by revenge, revenge tends to be implemented by organized political actors, since most individuals do not or cannot act directly. The presence of armed actors that act as avengers on behalf of individuals *only* if and when violence serves their interests places revenge within a framework that is far from random or anomic.

Furthermore, the existing analogy between civil war violence and blood feuds is incorrect and misleading. Leaving aside that revenge appears to be exceptional even in blood-feud cultures (Gould 2003), civil war transforms blood-feud-prone cultures into settings of unlimited communal violence that "at other times would have been considered reprehensible and dishonourable behaviour" (M. Johnson 2001:61). The available sociological and anthropological evidence on blood feuds (Keiser 1991; W. Miller 1990; Boehm 1984; Black-Michaud 1975) fails to support this analogy. The blood feud turns out to be a social institution with clear rules (about who retaliates, when, how, and against whom), governed by norms that limit the class of possible expiators (women and children are usually excluded) and the appropriateness of responses. Most feuding cultures recognize a rough rule of equivalence in riposte, the *lex talionis* being but one example;[16] there are culturally acceptable means for making temporary or permanent settlements of hostility; potential attacks can be bought off, and men marked for revenge could be granted reprieve if encountered with their family; sanctuary and hospitality rules can be very elaborate. In short, blood feuds are closer to a game than a real fight (Loizos 1988:648), "social power regulators" in societies lacking central authority (Frijda 1994:270). They regulate, limit, and contain conflict and violence; they are institutions of social control, often co-opted by states, rather than instances of social anomie (Wormald 1980). So much was clear to Gerald Curtis, a British political officer who visited Afghanistan in the 1930s: "It can be argued that in a country where there is no Government to enforce sanctions on those whose conduct is injurious to others, the blood feud spares as much life as it destroys. The fear of provoking a feud

---

evidence is provided by Smyth and Fay (2000:123); Manrique (1998:204); Degregori (1998:135); Senaratne (1997:75); Berlow (1998:95); Stoll (1993:80); Jones (1989:127); Kheng (1983:148); Rudebeck (1975:445); Taber (1965:40); Lear (1961:92); Kerkvliet (1977:70;164).

[16] Indeed, the *lex talionis* forbids escalation since desire for revenge is immoderate but revenge must be regulated (Frijda 1994:264).

to be the curse of generations of his descendants must give a man pause" (in Schofield 1984:120).[17]

Studies of civil war in regions that are traditionally blood-feud-prone find that war disorganizes the institutions and rules of feuding and destroys its honor code, which tends to be associated with order rather than disorder (Xanthakou 1998:12–13).[18] Furthermore, civil war violence far exceeds the violence of feuds by breaking the blood-feud norm that excludes women and children from violence (M. Johnson 2001:65; Paludan 1981:20) and by violently dividing clans and families (Xanthakou 1998:12–13). Finally, the violence of civil wars can be extreme in regions lacking a tradition of feuding. The Lebanese Civil War was particularly violent in cities even though a tradition of feuding prevailed in the mountainous countryside (M. Johnson 2001:44), and the Greek region of the Argolid that I studied experienced high levels of violence despite lacking a tradition of feuding. In fact, there is some evidence that feuding is sometimes endogenous to civil war, with a culture of feuding following, rather than preceding, the war (Paludan 1981:20–1; Williams 1975:26). Also, the relationship between feuding practices and civil war violence may be spurious: tight-knight groups are both easier to mobilize for fighting and tend to engage in feuding. In short, although it is clear that revenge is associated with excessive violence in civil war, it would be wrong to connect the two causally.

While the security dilemma mechanism is a plausible explanation for the emergence of violence, like the other "breakdown" mechanisms, it is hard to operationalize and test, and even then it tends to be observationally equivalent with several other mechanisms. One solution entails the derivation of specific testable implications: first, violence is the most likely where populations are most intermixed – ideologically, religiously, or ethnically;[19] second, violence should be launched by substantial minorities that are weak enough to feel threatened, yet strong enough to be able to launch an attack; and, third, violence is the only possible outcome, as opposed to peaceful arrangements, such as local peace deals. We lack systematic evidence, but anecdotal observations do not appear to support these conjectures. For instance, violence in the former Yugoslavia was often exercised by armies and militias rather than among individuals, and only small minorities of the various populations participated in the violence (Mueller 2004);

[17] The same appears to apply to sacrificial violence, which, according to Girard (1977), is a mechanism of social control in premodern societies lacking effective justice systems.

[18] The August 2002 killing of twenty-two members of a single family in Upper Egypt may be an instance of how insurgencies exacerbate, yet disorganize, feuding practices. This was no individualized killing but a quasi-military ambush; and, although it is traced to the enmity of two families, the Hashasbas and the Abdul Haleems, it became intertwined with an Islamist insurgency in the area (BBC News, 10 August 2002). A similar process appears to have taken place in the Chiapas region of Mexico, where the Zapatista insurgency has taken place among communities "torn for generations by struggles over land, religion, and power. The fighting pits fathers against sons, brothers against brothers, neighbors against neighbors" and has resulted in several massacres (G. Thompson 2001:16). Ethnic strife in Kenya and neighboring Somalia may also account for the radicalization of feuding between the Gabra and Borana clans in northeast Kenya (Reuters 2005).

[19] Note, however, that a positive test of this implication would be observationally equivalent with the polarization thesis.

survey data show that minority or majority status did not cause a difference in tolerance levels for enclaved populations, a proxy for the propensity to use violence (Massey, Hodson, and Seculić 1999); and there is evidence that local deals between local groups were reached in several circumstances (Bougarel 1996).

Finally, the "medievalization" thesis does not seem to match the available evidence either. Formulated in a falsifiable way, it predicts that violence is a function of how irregular an army is. In Selesky's (1994:85) formulation, "The greater the distance away from centralized monitoring, and probably also the smaller the numbers involved, the greater the opportunity for men to use violence to settle some personal score which may or may not have anything to do with the goals of the society that has authorized them to use purposeful violence in the first place." However, we know that in numerous civil wars (e.g., El Salvador, Guatemala) the greatest proportion of violence was produced by highly disciplined regular troops rather than insurgent irregulars. Indeed, mass killing tends to be associated with order rather than disorder as suggested, among others, by the Nazi and Japanese occupations during World War II. Atrocities were more common during the English Civil War in times and areas where professional armies rather than militias operated (Coster 1999:95); the single worst massacre in Bosnia, Srebrenica, was executed in a highly organized fashion and mainly by regular troops rather than paramilitary thugs on a rampage. Recent econometric analysis of evidence from Africa also seems to support the contention that violence against civilians is used to achieve military advantage as opposed to loot and prey (Azam and Hoeffler 2002). Last, the medievalization thesis also entails a mischaracterization of many conflicts. The violence of some of the worst recent African civil wars is not necessarily random (Richards 1996; Ellis 1995:184; Geffray 1990).

3.6.2. Transgression

The transgression thesis receives indirect prima facie support from the striking similarities that violence displays in narrowly defined civil wars and civil wars that take place during foreign occupation. Collective reprisals, indiscriminate violence, hostage taking, mass population relocation: these are all features of both types of wars, suggesting that rebellion against any authority calls for a highly violent response. Indeed, the legal discussion about the distinction between combatants and noncombatants took place in the context of debates about the regulation of occupation regimes. This thesis is also consistent with the observation that high levels of violence against "lesser" or "inferior" peoples, as in colonial wars, have been justified on similar normative grounds (Donagan 1994:1139).

There are, however, several problems with this thesis. First, is barbarism caused by the transgressive character of the internal challenge to sovereignty, or is the perception of transgression just a manifestation of other processes, such as polarization or warfare? Second, this argument begs the question of why these particular actions are seen as transgressive in the first place. Third, the empirical record raises questions. There is considerable variation in the reaction to internal challenges to authority – no matter how serious and threatening. For instance, the French demonstrations of May '68, the East European protest marches of 1989, and the internal terrorist challenges in Europe (Red Brigades, ETA, IRA, etc.) were handled moderately despite the threat they posed and the norms they may have transgressed. Fourth, this thesis fails a critical empirical test: the violence exercised by rebels or between competing rebel groups is often as barbaric as that meted out by the state against the rebels. The violence between monarchist and Communist partisans in Yugoslavia during the Second World War is a good case in point. Finally, it appears that massive violence by states is often a direct response to threats, trumping considerations such as regime type or normative considerations (Downes 2004). In short, the transgression thesis appears to capture the process whereby barbarism rather than its causes is rationalized.

3.6.3. Polarization

Polarization is analytically superior to both breakdown and transgression because it can easily subsume them; it also captures an important aspect of civil war. However, a theory of deep divisions is only so useful as a theory of violence.

Stated empirically, the polarization thesis predicts that civil wars with deep preexisting cleavages should be, *ceteris paribus*, more barbaric than civil wars motivated by more shallow cleavages. Likewise, variation in levels of violence within the same civil war should covary with the depth of cleavages. This hypothesis is hard to test, given the difficulty of measuring the depth of cleavages independently from the conflict and its violence. As a result, systematic evidence is scant.[20]

Prewar polarization is linked to barbarism in two ways: in its broad version, it is seen as causing civil war and, by implication, its violence; in its narrow version, it provides the epistemological basis for intense violence once a civil war is on. Either way, violence results from deep prewar divisions.

A critique of the broad version asserts that the link between polarization and civil war is tenuous even when prewar polarization runs deep. A significant body of empirical research suggests that high levels of social, religious, or ethnic polarization fail to explain the outbreak of civil war; they appear to be neither necessary nor sufficient conditions (Collier et al. 2003; Laitin 2001; Fearon and Laitin 2000; Sartori 1969:81). Furthermore, the absence of a good indicator for polarization has concealed the fact that even in societies that are seen as deeply polarized, only a minority can really be described as cleaving tightly to one pole or the other, while the majority tends to remain uncommitted or weakly committed, part of a

---

[20] I know of two partial exceptions, both from microlevel studies. In his ongoing analysis of violence across villages of Aragón during the Spanish Civil War, Ledesma (2001) finds some relation between polarization and violence. However, it is unclear how polarization is measured, and alternative hypotheses are not tested. Chacón (2003) finds that prewar polarization as measured by electoral returns at the municipal level is a good predictor of violence during the first phase of the Colombian *Violencia*. However, this was a period during which the conflict was not militarized and resembled more a generalized launching of pogroms. Indeed, he finds that polarization ceases to be a good predictor of violence in the second period of the *Violencia*, when the conflict evolved into a full-fledged armed conflict. During this period, geographical and military variables appear much more significantly related to violence.

"gray zone" between the two poles.[21] When more systematic data are available, as in Yugoslavia, the link between prewar polarization and war appears tenuous. From a cross-sectional point of view, there was an inverse relationship between prewar polarization and civil war, with Bosnia scoring very high on interethnic tolerance (Hodson, Seculić, and Massey 1994); from a time-series point of view, there was little change in mass indicators of nationalism in Croatia from 1984 to 1989, suggesting that polarization increased either just before the war or after the war erupted (Seculić 2005).

Nevertheless, it may be that *where* civil war does erupt, prewar polarization is causally linked to observed intense violence. However, "even when violence is clearly rooted in preexisting conflict," Rogers Brubaker and David Laitin (1998:426) warn, "it should not be treated as a natural, self-explanatory outgrowth of such conflict, something that occurs automatically when the conflict reaches a certain intensity, a certain 'temperature.'" This point is supported by the observation that what causes civil war onset may not be what sustains it (Pfaffenberger 1994). Indeed, the perceived depth of prewar cleavages may often be an artifact of retrospective assessments contaminated by the war (Brubaker and Laitin 1998:426). Moreover, deep polarization need not precede civil wars; intense violence may emerge in places that lack prior cleavages. Whereas in certain cases, like Spain or El Salvador, the political conflict was fully activated before the outbreak of the civil war, in other cases, like Russia or Greece, cleavages were formed during the course of the civil war. The Quindío region in Colombia lacked intense partisan conflicts until the end of the 1940s, yet suffered from violence that led to thousands of deaths (Ortiz Sarmiento 1990:22). Likewise, the region of Aragón in Spain experienced plenty of violence during the process of collectivization initiated by the Anarchists, even though it was not characterized by "a high level of social polarization or conflict" (Casanova 1985:59); this violence, Julián Casanova (1985:315) found, was the result of "the exceptional circumstances of the context of war" related to military factors, most notably the presence of Anarchist troops from Catalonia. In contrast, the region of Levante in Valencia experienced less violence than Aragón despite a higher degree of class polarization (Bosch Sánchez 1983).[22]

In addition, the assertion of a link between prewar polarization and violence is vulnerable to two methodological critiques. First, civil war violence may be erroneously linked to prewar polarization via inference biases, such as the extrapolation from the aggregate to the individual level and the privileging of target information, as opposed to base-rate information. As a result, interaction effects,

[21] A point made forcefully by Edward Malefakis (1996:26) about the Spanish Civil War: "In every civil war, the majority of the population probably belongs, at least at the beginning of the conflict, to something equivalent of what came to be called, in 1936-9, the *third Spain*: they did not believe in any cause with sufficient intensity as to be willing to shed their blood for it." Seidman (2002) provides plenty of evidence to support this point.

[22] Therefore it may be costly to infer individual risks exclusively from prewar polarization. When Amparo Barayón returned to her hometown of Zamora in the first months of the Spanish Civil War, she did so "because she didn't think there would be trouble. Zamora had always been so peaceful"; soon after, however, she was denounced, arrested, and executed (Sender Barayón 1989:165).

spurious effects, and nonobserved variables are overlooked. Second, violence may emerge out of dynamics that inhere in civil wars and are either indirectly connected or totally unconnected to prewar polarization via two processes, *endogenous polarization* and *endogenous violence*. Abraham Lincoln observed about the American Civil War that with "actual war coming, blood grows hot, and blood is spilled. Thought is forced from old channels into confusion" (in Fellman 1989:85). Lincoln's observation suggests that violence may be *endogenous* to the war and independent of the cleavages that produced the war in the first place. Complicating things more, polarization may *also* be endogenous to the civil war, its effect rather than its cause.

3.6.3.1. Inference Biases

Explanations of violence that reason back to the factors that are believed to produce it are vulnerable to an inference bias akin to ecological fallacy: they extrapolate from the aggregate to the individual level in the absence of individual-level data about particular acts of violence. Raymond Boudon (1988) has shown that even in a homogeneous society of equals, it is possible to generate processes of competition (and hence violence), which would appear on the aggregate level to have been generated by deep cleavages; likewise, it has been pointed out that competition effects between groups may be merely by-products of a selection bias: even in a world where ethnicity plays no role whatsoever in defining either the likely interactions among individuals or the proclivity of individuals to engage in violence, we would still see significant violence, wrongly perceived as resulting from ethnic competition (Dion 1997). Hence, interpretations of violence require fine-grained contextual data. When such data are available, as in Northern Ireland, they suggest a disjunction between the violence of the conflict and the religious cleavage that informs it (O'Leary and McGarry 1993).[23] It may also be the case that individual identities observed from "above" may well have been fully fabricated either below or ex post facto. For example, many persecuted kulaks (wealthy peasants) during the Stalinist terror were not kulaks at all: "During this time and after," Lynne Viola (1993:65–6) tells us, "for a glass of vodka or a bottle of *samogon* (moonshine), a kulak could be transformed into a poor peasant or, in absence of a glass of vodka or a bottle of *samogon*, a poor peasant could be transformed into a kulak.... The kulak seemed to be largely in the eye of the beholder."

The contextual data needed to establish the inference have to be fine-grained. For example, the observation that an individual landlord was killed in a rebel-held zone does not suffice to establish this action as a reflection of the class cleavage; that would require detailed information about the actual motivation behind this particular act of violence.[24] It is also necessary to avoid the widespread

[23] They find that violence does not correlate with levels of religious practice across space and time, violent actors do not define themselves in religious terms, and violence is not directed against religious symbols.

[24] This is hard to obtain. An investigative journalist, Berlow (1998), wrote an entire book describing his quest for clues about two murders related to the insurgency in the island of Negros, in the Philippines (one was the murder of a landowner). He eventually failed to find any conclusive evidence.

fallacy of truncation – ignoring the remote and abstract base-rate information in favor of the vivid and concrete target information. What is needed, instead, is the ratio of observed victimization and observable (but usually ignored) rates of nonvictimization within the same population: how many landowners were killed and how many not?[25] If just one landowner was killed (and if, moreover, a landless peasant was also killed by the same group), then we ought to question the extent to which this is an instance of "class violence."[26]

Furthermore, motivations may be mixed: a person may have been victimized both because of her group membership *and* because of a particular action that may or may not be connected to her membership. During his investigation into a number of violent events during a leftist insurgency in the Philippine island of Negros, Alan Berlow (1998:166) was told by an informant that a landlord named "Serafin was targeted [by the rebels] because he was helping the Army.... That was the main reason he was shot." "Landlords" killed in northern China by Communist-led peasants during the civil war were often just better-off peasants who had collaborated with the government supporters, while those who refrained from any action, including "real" landlords, were not harmed; as a Communist cadre put it, a local landlord would not have been persecuted "if he had not returned with the Kuomintang to threaten our cadres. We agreed that the rich peasants were not the object of our struggle" (Thaxton 1997:289–90). There is extensive evidence from Vietcong documents drawing a clear distinction between landlords and landlords "who are wicked agents of the enemy" and recommending different treatment for each (Race 1973:126); Vietcong cadres also divided peasants into two political classes based on security criteria that did not overlap with the class cleavage (Elliott 2003:954–60). The extent of the variation between identity and behavior is likely due to the willingness of an actor to distinguish between the two, which may be unrelated to polarization.

Finally, it is often the case that a person is victimized both because of politics (her identity *and* actions) and because of nonpolitical causes, such as personal animosities and feuds. For instance, a baker in a small Guatemalan town was abducted by a death squad and killed *both* because he had openly criticized the army and because of a personal vengeance exacted by a death squad member (Paul and Demarest 1988:126).

3.6.3.2. Endogenous Polarization

The polarization thesis implies that the distribution of popular support during the war is a faithful reflection of (prewar) cleavages; in times of high polarization, the "carrying capacity" of political actors reaches its maximum value, producing an almost total overlap between the goals of political actors and the goals of the

---

[25] This is the core of Louie's (1964) critique of Greer's analysis of the French Terror.

[26] Local studies of the Spanish Civil War find that many landowners were spared by the Republicans for reasons that remain puzzling (Estrada i Planell 1995:39), while poor peasants were frequently targeted by them (Ledesma 2001:254). Ledesma (2004:291–2; 311–12) concludes that, although class informed the Republican violence, it was never a simple instance of class violence, with class understood less in a narrow economic way and more as a complex web of interlinked political loyalties. Argenti-Pillen (2003:77) makes the same case about ethnic violence in Sri Lanka.

population they claim to represent. Hence, landless peasants naturally support leftist insurgents and landowners right-wing governments; Tamils join the Tamil Tigers and Sinhalas side with Sri Lanka's government; Catholics support the IRA and Protestants the Unionists; and so on. It follows that collaboration and support are fixed and given exogenously with respect to the war; hence, determining their distribution requires only access to relevant census data.

Yet there is substantial evidence that polarization is often endogenous to the conflict. Thucydides (3.83–4) pointed to "the violent fanaticism which came into play *once* the struggle had broken out. . . . *As the result* of these revolutions, there was a general deterioration of character throughout the Greek world. . . . Society *had become* divided into two ideologically hostile camps, and each side viewed the other with suspicion" (emphasis added). This insight is present in many contemporary studies.[27] From a theoretical point of view, René Girard (1977) has suggested a mechanism of endogenous polarization: as rivalry becomes acute, the rivals tend to forget the initial cause of the rivalry and instead become more fascinated with one another; as a result, the rivalry is purified of any external stake and becomes a matter of pure prestige.

During the war, political actors make concerted efforts to mobilize the population around the cleavage dimension they represent, because they know both that the population is divided in a multitude of contradictory ways and that civilians tend to avoid risky commitments. The Kosovo Liberation Army had to find ways to unite ethnic Albanian village clans often divided by bitter blood feuds, and the Chinese Communists had to convince poor villagers that their identity lay with other poor villagers rather than with the wealthy members of their own lineage.[28] Such mobilization is no easy task to accomplish and usually violence shows itself to be more effective than persuasion. This claim is consistent with the observation that insurgent violence in ethnic rebellions "is usually directed primarily against their own people, in order to ensure their support for the revolt, however reluctant or however passive" (Paget 1967:32). New cleavage dimensions become successfully institutionalized, usually after the war has been won.[29] Hence, what is often taken to be the cause of a civil war may well be its outcome.

At the beginning of a civil war, most people have initial predispositions and preferences that flow directly from prewar politics, but these predispositions shift with the dynamics of the conflict. Sometimes, following its well-known reductionist logic, war reinforces these initial predispositions by "hardening" identities (Van Evera 2001:21; O. Roy 1999:233; Kaufmann 1996; Fawaz 1994:5) and

---

[27] See also M. Johnson (2001:60); Rubio (1999:79); Collins (1999:177); Genschel and Schlichte (1998); Licklider (1998:127); Byrne (1996:2); Ellis (1995:185); Ranzato (1994); Simmel (1955:30).

[28] In a southern Chinese village, "the poorer Chens themselves would have to set aside the traditional notion of lineage solidarity. They would have to be convinced to join outsiders in attacks against kinsmen. They would have to learn to express themselves in terms of 'hatred' " (Chan et al. 1992: 19–20).

[29] Identities thus spawned may become naturalized and form the basis of an organic community with inherited attributes. In China, for instance, class labels imposed in the 1950s have become inheritable in the male line: a poor peasant may be called a "landlord" even though he owns no land (Chan et al. 1992:21).

increasing their saliency (T. Allen and Seaton 1999:3).[30] Most Missouri farmers were "conditional Unionists" before the Civil War, yet the war "destroyed the middle ground and threw the unwilling as well as the committed into a maelstrom which surpassed understanding"; this was a place where "new loyalties superseded an earlier, more tolerant attitude" (Fellman 1989:22; 28). Protestant testimonies from Cork County during the Irish Revolution illustrate the incremental heightening of ethnic polarization: "During this time the gap between Us and Them had been steadily widening until in the end it seemed to be quite unbridgeable. They became not only different from us, they were against us" (in Hart 1999:312–13). According to a Tajik shop owner of Herat city in Afghanistan, "There was no problem in the city, but after the fighting there are ethnic problems" (in Waldman 2004:A3). A Lebanese student recalls:

I was at the university when the war broke out. I was studying to be an architect. All I wanted to do was to start my life. Then suddenly this strange mentality developed: everything became polarized into Christian versus Muslim. All my life I had never asked anyone whether he was a Christian or not. Then quite suddenly you had to give up half your life: half your friends, half the places you knew. I still have more Muslim friends than Christian ones. When the war broke out, I suddenly could not see them, could not speak to them. (in Darlymple 1997:259)

Civil war may simultaneously reinforce some prewar cleavages while weakening or altering others. In Voigt's (1949:75) comprehensive formulation, it "widens the fissures and augments the stresses that exist in every human society.... It divides and confounds loyalties, it fortifies some, it weakens others, and it evokes new loyalties." Christian Geffray's (1990) and Michel Cahen's (2000) analyses of the civil war in Mozambique point precisely to such a process. This finding is consistent with the "conflict trap" thesis, whereby the eruption of civil conflict increases the risk of further future wars (Collier et al. 2003), and with the local cleavage thesis, which stresses the role of local cleavages activated by the war, including ties of kinship and place that cut across master cleavages (Kalyvas 2003).[31]

Often, civil war politicizes innocuous or nonviolent prewar cleavages. In Uganda, ethnic group membership was irrelevant "in local level intercourse" until government soldiers started killing people (T. Allen 1989:61); the ethnically plural society of Malaya "remained fairly harmonious" prior to the Japanese occupation, which triggered a civil war along ethnic lines (Kheng 1983:16–18).[32] In fact, civil war may create altogether new cleavages, independent of the prewar cleavages. "The essential feature of the first century of warfare," during

---

[30] This insight has been incorporated into practical theories of insurgency: the view that fighting itself catalyzes the struggle is central to Debray's (1967) thinking.

[31] Several local studies of civil wars suggest that local cleavages tend to trump prewar cleavages (Hart 1999:307; Moyar 1997:70–1; Paul and Demarest 1988:152; Gerolymatos 1984:78).

[32] Interestingly, the Japanese did not deliberately promote ethnic animosity between Malays and Chinese; this animosity, Kheng (1983:41) points out, was an unintended outcome of the occupation. The occupation created social tensions and led to local interpretations of these tensions, which caused a bitter ethnic conflict.

the civil war in medieval Kyoto (Berry 1994:xviii), "was rupture itself – rupture so extensive that it opened cleavages in every unit of the polity and the society." The frequent observation that violence is often unrelated to the master cleavage, however, is not evidence that deep prewar cleavages are at work (e.g., Lubkemann 2005:500). The fact that violence is often a reflection of local cleavages is fully consistent with a process of endogenous polarization (see Chapter 11).

At the individual level, it is possible to find many stories about individuals whose political identity was forged in and by the war. Figes (1996:697) tells how the tsarist general Alexei Brusilov joined the Bolsheviks during the Russian Civil War. He was a prisoner of the Bolsheviks, so his only son joined the Cheka to spare his father's life. However, he was captured by the Whites and executed. Brusilov blamed himself for his son's death and joined the Bolsheviks to avenge it. Figes' comment: "Blood, if not class, had made him Red." The role of incumbent prisons in turning people wrongly incarcerated into real insurgents has been amply documented (e.g., D. Anderson 2005:52).

Civil war may even generate completely new ethnic identities. Such is the case of the Algerian Harkis. Originally designating the Algerian auxiliaries who fought on the side of the French during the war of Algerian independence, the term became ethnicized and hereditary through the years (Hamoumou 1993). Eventually, the Harkis became a quasi-ethnic group, whose members live in France; they do not think of themselves as primarily Algerians and tend not to intermarry with other Algerians. Another example is provided by the inhabitants of the Panjshir valley in Afghanistan (O. Roy 1999:231). The Panjshiri identity existed in prewar Afghanistan, but it had limited uses and a nonpolitical character: it designated rural migrants who came to Kabul from the valley but was not used in the Panjshir valley itself; politically, Panjshiris thought of themselves as *farsiwan*, that is, Iranophone Sunnites. The Panjshiri identity became a salient political identity only when the valley became a military front under a unified political command.

This process is especially clear in the case of class. Charles Tilly (1964:305, 330) shows that whereas the initial configuration of parties in southern Anjou during the French Revolution ran along class lines and had crystallized "long before" the outbreak of the counterrevolutionary rebellion, in 1793 "participation in the counterrevolution cut boldly across class lines. Therefore, no simple scheme of class alignment can account adequately for the division of forces in 1793." Empirically, most efforts to predict support (mainly for rebels) on the basis of preexisting sociostructural characteristics have produced rather meager returns.[33] At the very least, these studies suggest that social structure generally

---

[33] The general absence of an easily identifiable overlap between peasants and rebels has spawned a large literature, which has sought to specify in increasingly narrow terms the precise sociostructural location (middle peasants, sharecroppers, migratory estate laborers, producers of cash crops, etc.) that produces peasant support for rebellions (e.g., Perry 1980; Paige 1975; Wolf 1969). From a theoretical point of view, this literature generally fails to problematize and, instead, assumes away

fails to explain the connection between underlying cleavages and support for belligerents in civil wars.

Well-designed microsociological studies further undermine these conjectures (e.g., Wood 2003). A classic ecological study of Chinese Communism (Hofheinz 1969) demonstrates that sociostructural variables cannot satisfactorily account for Communist mobilization during the civil war.[34] A study of Vietnam in 1964–5 suggests that insurgent control was more likely in areas where landholdings in prior years had been of more equal size and owner cultivation more prevalent than tenant cultivation (Mitchell 1968); likewise, poor villages in the Mekong Delta that had initially welcomed the Vietcong reacted more strongly to the draft and agricultural tax imposed by them, precisely because of their poverty (Elliott 2003:1017). Carlos Cabarrús's (1983) detailed analysis of peasant allegiances in seven Salvadorean villages just prior to the civil war shows class relations to be a poor predictor of allegiances compared with factors such as kin, conjuncture (who gets to organize peasants first), and micropolitics (the ability of organizations to manage intracommunity conflicts).[35] When the war started, additional factors kicked in, such as the ability of political actors to provide protection for their supporters.

Endogenous polarization is consistent with the frequent observation that the outbreak of violence and war takes people by surprise, that polarization is abrupt and unexpected, and that violence appears totally baffling to them, more like a natural phenomenon, "random, inexplicable, indelible, like a lighting bolt or wildfire" (L. White 1989:5), than the result of human action. A woman describes the violence of the Spanish Civil War: "Looking at her face while she recalls [the killings] it would seem she is visualizing utter darkness.... If anything, these killings appear in her conversation as beyond comprehension"; the war is perceived as "a sudden outburst erupting like a volcano" (Joseba Zulaika 1988: 21, 34). A Guatemalan Indian concluded the recollection of his ordeal during 1980–2 by saying that "he and his neighbors fell victim to temporary madness" (Annis 1988:173). "It was as if Beirut had gone totally mad," Gladys Mouro

---

four critical links: from individual interest to group interest, to group conflict, to group (violent) action, and finally to individual (violent) action.

34 Hofheinz found that Chinese Communists achieved success in three kinds of areas: in two of them ("radical hotbeds" and "border area bases"), historical, political, and social variables were important; however, in the third and most crucial one ("great rear areas"), background social factors were the least relevant. As he puts it (1969:76): "Because of the security provided by terrain and distance, the rear area base counties were able to achieve the highest rates of mobilization and participation in Communist politics."

35 Cabarrús (1983) found that poor peasants (*semiproletarios*) were more likely to join any side as compared with wealthier peasants (*campesinos medios*) and agricultural workers (*jornaleros*), who were more likely to be apolitical. When they did take sides, wealthier peasants and agricultural workers were more likely to join the rightist organization ORDEN, whereas poor peasants tended to join the leftist organization FECCAS. About half of FECCAS members were poor peasants, whereas ORDEN's membership was almost equally divided among the three groups. There was also considerable variation in the social composition of these organizations across the villages.

(1999:20) recalls about the start of the civil war in Lebanon. Consider the following observations from the English Civil War, Chechnya, and Bosnia:

It is strange to note how we have insensibly slid into this beginning of a civil war, by one unexpected accident after another. (in McGrath 1997:91)

At first I failed to recognize the war for what it was. I thought for a long time that it was some kind of misunderstanding. It never occurred to me that such a thing was possible. (in Tishkov 2004:132)

I thought about other similar situations. Lebanon, Angola, Romania. Before, I would watch the news on TV about what had been happening there – and then I would switch the TV off and continue my everyday business thinking: "There's nothing I can do about it."... I certainly never expected, not even remotely, that events in Bosnia might take the shape of what was actually happening now. (Pervanic 1999:148)

Indeed, both Bosnian Muslims and Croats complained of "a kind of madness taking people over, and changing them unexpectedly" (Loizos 1999:119). "We always lived together and got along well; what is happening now has been created by something stronger than us" (in Bringa 1995:4). Survey research conducted in Yugoslavia during the mid–1990s found that only 7 percent of the respondents believed that the country would break up (Oberschall 2000:988). Noel Malcolm (1998) summarizes these observations: "What comes across most strongly from [the] personal histories [of the Bosnian War] is the sense of bewilderment most people felt. The outbreak of the war took them by surprise, and the transformation of neighbors into enemies seemed to have no basis in their previous experience. Their favorite metaphor was that a whirlwind had come out of nowhere and blew their lives apart."

3.6.3.3. Endogenous Violence
Beyond polarization, violence may also be endogenous to the war in the sense of being unconnected to its causes. Once the war begins, the spiral of violence described in accounts stressing breakdown kicks in: violence becomes a "monster which leads to continuous escalation of violence" (C. Friedrich 1972:76); it is "cross-fertilized" (Senaratne 1997:145) and acquires a logic of its own that is disproportionate or even independent of the war's initial causes – and even the war's conduct and aims (Scheffler 1999:178). War takes on "a life of its own, like the Thirty Years' War as portrayed in Bertold Brecht's Mother Courage, with people forgetting what it was about, and trying to do no more than survive, even if survival meant collaborating with the impersonal machinery of mobilization" (Shy 1976:14). As a South Carolina politician remarked in 1789: "Once the Dogs of Civil War are let loose it is no easy matter to Call them back" (in Weir 1985:76). There is some systematic evidence about this process. A quantitative analysis of politically motivated homicides in Northern Ireland points to "a process of localised social reproduction of violence," whereby violence causes and sustains more violence (Poole 1995:42). This is also suggested by the finding that incumbent violence is a better predictor of insurgent political violence in Northern Ireland than economic deprivation (R. White 1989).

In short, the universalization of the distinction between friend and enemy is often a consequence of the war, a by-product of its violence. The responses of political actors and individuals to the dynamics of war (and the responses to their responses) shape violence, the war, and the prospects for peace in a way that is often quite independent of the proximate causes of the conflict.

Acknowledging that both violence and polarization can be endogenous to war implies a strong qualification of the view that violence arises exclusively from prewar cleavages. At the same time, just ascribing violence to war and reverting to the breakdown mechanisms would be unsatisfactory for the reasons discussed in section 3.6.1. A better way to understand the dynamics of endogenous violence requires that we take into account the institutional environment within which violence unfolds, which is to say the technology of warfare in civil war.

3.6.4. The Technology of Warfare

A striking empirical observation is that very few civil wars are fought by means of conventional warfare (e.g., United States, Spain) – with some mixing irregular and conventional warfare (e.g., Russia, China, Vietnam) (Derrienic 2001:166). Conversely, almost all interstate wars are fought conventionally.[36] In short, there is a high degree of overlap between civil and unconventional war – of both the irregular and the "symmetric" kind. Hence, the observation that the high levels of violence are linked with civil war through unconventional war appears plausible.

Stated as a hypothesis, the warfare thesis predicts that violence should be a direct function of the irregular character of the war. However, the evidence is mixed: a few conventional interstate wars, such as the German-Soviet clash during the Second World War, have been highly barbaric, as was the Spanish Civil War, a conventional civil war. At the same time, not all irregular wars produce barbaric violence; those, however, that cross a certain threshold of magnitude do (Valentino 2004). Indeed, the claim is made that where guerrilla warfare and mass violence coincide, they are causally linked (Valentino et al. 2004).

The American Civil War provides a partial, but critical, test for the warfare hypothesis. In some parts of the country (mainly in Missouri, east Tennessee, West Virginia, and east North Carolina, but also in Georgia, Alabama, Kentucky, Louisiana, and Arkansas), it was fought irregularly (Beckett 2001:10–11; Fellman 1989; Paludan 1981); this was the case for reasons that had nothing to do with the type of prewar politics and everything to do with geographical location. This irregular civil war was vastly different from the much better-known conventional one, in which war was fought on battlefields and left civilians largely alone, as the following description of the war in east Tennessee suggests: "This struggle pitted region against region, community against community, and members of the same community against each other. It was decentralized, local, and often surprisingly detached from the conventional war, and its character varied from place to place"

[36] A few irregular interstate wars are reported, but they mostly consist of low-intensity border skirmishes, such as the Libya-Chad War and the war between Belize and Guatemala (Harkavy and Neuman 2001:18–19).

(Fisher 1997:3). William Auman (1984:70) concludes his account of the Civil War in the Randolph County area of North Carolina by remarking that "this contest of neighbor against neighbor and brother against brother . . . was characterized by murder, arson, torture, intimidation, robbery, and pillage." The American case suggests that the technology of warfare may possibly be a sufficient cause of barbarism, though not a necessary one.

Yet the exact causal mechanism between barbarism and irregular war must still be identified. Three mechanisms have been suggested: irregular war as revolutionary war, a variant of the polarization argument, in which ideological enmity imbues irregular warfare with a particularly nasty character; irregular war as "medieval" war, in which the lack of military discipline among irregular fighters leads to violent excesses; and the vulnerability inherent to irregular war, in which actors attempt to use violence to minimize exposure to deadly risk.

In terms of the first mechanism, Schmitt fails to draw an explicit link between polarization and partisan warfare: why is it that polarization must be expressed through this form of warfare? Furthermore, he was generalizing from a particular historical period and failed to recognize that violence and irregular war have a broader historical connection going beyond the revolutionary movements of the decolonization period and the Cold War.[37] The obvious empirical limitation of this argument is that it cannot explain the extreme violence of the many civil wars that seem to be unconnected to preexisting polarization, including so-called greed wars.

The second mechanism is similar to the "medievalization" variant of the breakdown thesis, only with warfare as an intervening variable. As noted in section 3.6.1, this argument mischaracterizes many civil wars. More damningly, it fails to account both for the violent behavior of disciplined regular armies practicing counterinsurgency and for the violence of conventional civil wars. In fact, some scholars apply the available evidence to make the opposite argument. Carl Schmitt (1992:240–1) argues for a direct link between army discipline and high levels of violence, while Rothenberg (1994:87) argues that popular participation in wars and the concomitant growth of citizens' armies, a feature of modernity rather than primitivism, have contributed to unrestrained violence.

Formulating the security thesis as a testable hypothesis makes barbarism a function of the degree of insecurity faced by armed actors. As opposed to the other theories, this thesis has the advantage of explaining the behavior of both incumbents and insurgents, and of accounting for the patterns of violence in conventional civil wars and symmetric irregular wars (though not interstate conventional wars). For example, most of the violence against civilians during the Spanish Civil War took place in the initial months of the conflict when high uncertainty and the presence of real or suspected "fifth-columnists" (a term invented during this war) behind one's back subverted the logic of front lines and generated a sense of acute

---

[37] Irregular war far preceded Mao Zedong or Che Guevara. Guerrilla movements (and theorists) of the early nineteenth century were mostly conservatives rather than revolutionaries. Trotsky used examples from the Russian Civil War to argue that guerrilla warfare is not peculiar to a revolutionary army (Laqueur 1998).

vulnerability. Once the front line was stabilized, violence decreased (Ledesma 2001:256; Ucelay da Cal 1995:84; Ranzato 1994:li). This was also the case in Finland (Upton 1980:292), Korea (Yoo 2002:20), and Bosnia (Kalyvas and Sambanis 2005). In occupied Italy, Colombia, and Afghanistan indiscriminate violence against civilians correlated closely to proximity to the front line, another indicator of insecurity (Forero 2002:A9; Waldman 2002b:A9; Klinkhammer 1997).

Additionally, the security variant of the technology of warfare thesis allows predictions about the spatial distribution of violence: where armed actors are most vulnerable, they are most likely to use violence. However, this argument does not allow predictions about the type of violence used. Violence can be either selective or indiscriminate, and there is no definitive logic by which to adjudicate whether an increase in security would lead to an increased proportion of one or the other type. The operationalization of "vulnerability" remains, obviously, a key issue.

3.7. CONCLUSION

Four different theoretical accounts for violence in civil wars – breakdown, transgression, polarization, and warfare – have been identified, reconstructed, and discussed in this chapter, in order to clarify the choice of foundation on which to build the current theory of violence in civil wars. Each account has great merit and continues to stand as a strong basis from which to answer a variety of questions surrounding civil war and violence. Violence is a complex phenomenon, and it clearly encompasses multiple processes and mechanisms. Ultimately, they must be operationalized and tested empirically. Nevertheless, a deductive theory of violence in civil war must arise from a simple and clear foundation.

From a theory-building perspective, the thesis pointing to the technology of warfare is an optimal foundation. Breakdown is not well suited to explaining the initial emergence of violence in an area, nor do its implications – more violence in areas where neither party is in control, more violence where populations are more heterogeneous, more violence the more irregular the army – seem to match the available evidence. Similarly, transgression cannot account for the empirical reality of rebel violence against both civilians and other rebels and requires an as-yet-unarticulated account for why rebellion is so transgressive, as opposed to other offenses. Although polarization is a compelling account, able to subsume both transgression and breakdown, it remains very difficult to identify empirically without resorting to the tautology of where there is war, there is polarization, and where there is polarization, there is war; also, it leaves aside both the violence and the polarization that are produced endogenously through the process of war. Although the security variant of the irregular warfare hypothesis does not generate predictions about whether violence will be discriminate or indiscriminate, it yields plausible and interesting testable implications and accounts for the actions of both insurgents and incumbents, fitting well the anecdotal empirical record across a number of conflicts. In the next chapter, I turn to the task of specifying a theory of irregular warfare from which a theory of violence in civil war can be built.

Although I build the foundations for a theory of violence in civil war from the technology of warfare thesis, the empirical questions raised in this chapter remain open. I return to these issues in Chapters 8 and 9, where I test many of the empirical implications of all four theoretical accounts. I ask whether there is a positive relationship between the degree of anarchy and the intensity of violence, whether the intensity of violence is related to the demand for revenge, whether there is preemptive violence that matches the logic of the security dilemma mechanism (breakdown thesis), whether the intensity of violence matches prewar polarization (polarization thesis), and whether violence emerges where actors are most vulnerable (technology of warfare thesis).

4

A Theory of Irregular War I

Collaboration

Informers, they ought to be hanged. It is no sin to kill them.

Quoted in Ranajit Guha, *Elementary Aspects of Peasant Insurgency in Colonial India*

You can't tell who's who.

First Lieutenant Quinn Eddy, U.S. Army, Afghanistan, 2001

This chapter lays out the first part of a theory of irregular war as the foundation on which to build a theory of civil war violence. I begin by discussing the relation between irregular war and geographical space and I derive key implications for the nature of sovereignty in civil war. I then turn to the thorny issue of popular support, where I distinguish between attitudinal support (preferences) and behavioral support (actions). I argue in favor of a framework that makes no assumptions about the underlying preferences of the vast majority of the population and only minimal assumptions about behavioral support, in which complex, ambiguous, and shifting behavior by the majority is assumed, along with strong commitment by a small minority. I conclude with a discussion of the institutional context within which interactions between political actors and civilians take place.

4.1. SOVEREIGNTY IN CIVIL WAR

Analytically, the distinct character of irregular war is marked by the lack of front lines. A veteran of the campaigns against the American Indians remarked that "the front is all around, and the rear is nowhere" (in Paludan 1981:40); this feature was captured by a rhyme sung by German soldiers stationed in the occupied Soviet Union:

Russians ahead
Russians behind
And in between
Shooting

(Cooper 1979:92)

However, rather than being nonexistent, the boundaries separating two (or more) sides in an irregular war are blurred and fluid. Put otherwise, irregular war fragments space. This fragmentation can easily be seen on maps depicting countries that are undergoing civil wars: whereas conventional wars neatly divide space into two well defined and clearly demarcated spaces, irregular wars show up as messy patchworks; the more detailed the map, the messier it looks (e.g., Giustozzi 2000:291; Cooper 1979:62; Li 1975:154). Mark Danner (1994:17) describes the region of northern Morazán in El Salvador as a "crazy-quilted map," "where villages 'belonged' to the government or the guerrillas or to neither or to both, where the officers saw the towns and hamlets in varying shades of pink and red."

The fragmentation of space reflects the fact that irregular war alters the nature of sovereignty in a fundamental way. At its core lies the breakdown of the monopoly of violence by way of *territorially based* armed challenge. The simplest way to conceptualize the division of sovereignty in civil war is to distinguish between zones of incumbent control, zones of insurgent control, and zones in which control is contested. Where the government is able to exercise effective control and where its troops and administrators are able to move with safety day and night, we are in a zone of *incumbent control*. Where insurgents are able to effectively prevent the operation of government forces day and night, and the government is absent and unable to perform basic state functions, such as collect taxes and draft young men into its army, we are in a zone of *insurgent control*. In both zones sovereignty is undivided, though the sovereign in each is different.

In between these two zones lies an "intermediate" area, often referred to as a "contested" or "twilight" zone (Armstrong 1964:30). Deemed as the "most important arena of struggle" (McColl 1969:624), this is the zone of *contested control*. Unlike in the two other zones, the nature of sovereignty has been radically altered as conveyed by the following descriptions from the German-occupied Soviet Union and British-controlled Malaya:

A far greater number of people lived in what may be called the twilight zones where neither Germans nor partisans held permanent sway. In some instances, German garrisons would have nominal control, but partisans would be able effectively to raid and take reprisals by night; in others, neither side had sufficient forces to command constant popular obedience. Generally, the Germans would only occasionally send in troops and civilian officials to recruit forced labor, round up food, or simply conduct reconnaissance. (Dallin et al. 1964:330)

The terrorists were secure in their jungle. The Army and Police and Government Administration were secure in their towns. Between was the no-man's-land of village, road, railway, plantation, rubber, paddy. The terrorists at their strongest could paralyze the communications of all Malaya, but they could never hope to take the towns by storm. At their strongest, the security forces could confine the terrorists to deep jungle, but they could never hope to find them all in one massive offensive – the jungle was too thick. (Crawford 1958:82)

Political actors face three distinct population sets: populations under their full control; populations they must "share" with their rival; and populations completely outside their control. These three situations constitute two general types of sovereignty: *segmented* and *fragmented*. Sovereignty is segmented when two political actors (or more) exercise full sovereignty over distinct parts of the territory of the state. It is fragmented when two political actors (or more) exercise limited sovereignty over the same part of the territory of the state.

4.2. THE IDENTIFICATION PROBLEM

Irregular combatants and the spies and agents of either side hide among the civilian population. This feature of irregular war, which can be termed the "identification problem," was concisely described by an American officer patrolling an Afghan village (in Zucchino 2004:A8): "Two out of 10 people here hate you and want to kill you. You just have to figure out which two." An American soldier made the same point during a brutal house-to-house search in Iraq: "I feel bad for these people, I really do. It's so hard to separate the good from the bad" (in Filkins 2005:57). A few years earlier, Soviet soldiers had referred to their Afghan adversaries as *dukhi*, the Russian word for ghosts (Baker 2002:A1), and summarized the problem they faced as follows: "You see me, but I don't see you" (in Wines 2001:B7).

The inability to tell friend from enemy is a recurring element of irregular war, as evidenced by the following observations of U.S. military personnel in Vietnam in 1968, in Afghanistan in 2003, and in Iraq in 2003:

Wherever I went and young Vietnamese men would look at me I grew scared. There really was no way to tell who was who. You could be in a room with one and not know whether he was really a Charlie or not. It became easy to sense the distrust that must exist in the outlying areas. How could one really fight in the fields and know whether at any time the men beside you were not going to turn tail and train their guns on you? Whom did you begin to trust and where did you draw the line? Another ludicrous aspect of the war. (John Kerry in Brinkley 2003:50)

But even without a common language between them, the villagers seem to know what the Americans have come to do. Silently, turbaned men in long gray tunics open doors in compound walls for five- or six-man groups of helmeted men in desert camouflage. ... All seems accepted: in bitter helplessness against what the Americans are doing or – as the Americans hope – in gratitude for the American defeat of the repressive Taliban. It is impossible for the soldiers to know. Gonzalez speaks of trying to guess the sentiments of the locals not by their smiles but by the firmness of their handshakes. (Bergner 2003:44)

You have enemies but they're ghosts. They hit us and they run. They don't come out and fight us. (in Zaretsky 2003:A4)

This is not a recent development. A French general stationed in Spain in 1810, remarked that "the great difficulty [was] not fighting [the guerrillas] but finding them" (in Tone 1994:105); American soldiers serving in the Philippines in the early 1900s spoke of "chasing a phantom" (May 1991:161); and a British soldier in Malaya recalls: "Somewhere in that gigantic morass were fifty veteran terrorists. How were they to be killed? How were they even to be found?" (Crawford 1958:87).[1] A Pakistani officer in Bangladesh (Salik 1978:103) observed that

---

[1] See also Linn (1989:58); Calder (1984:138;158); Salik (1978:101); Henriksen (1976:397); Meyerson (1970:79); Trinquier (1964:26); Kitson (1960:192).

"the main problem was to isolate the rebels from the innocent people.... It was difficult to distinguish one from the other as all of them looked alike. A rebel carrying a sten gun under his arm could, in emergency, throw his weapon in the field and start working like an innocent farmer." The following exchange between a journalist and an Indian officer in Kashmir captures the identification problem:

I asked him how many terrorists he thought there were.
"Very few, these days," he replied.
Why, then, did the government need to keep half a million men here?
"Because," he replied quietly, "you don't know who they are." (Hilton 2002:73)

These are not mere anecdotes. The CIA estimated that less than 1 percent of nearly 2 million small-unit operations in Vietnam conducted in 1966–8 resulted in contact with the insurgents (Ellsberg 2003:240).[2] Not surprisingly, irregular warfare has been called "war in the shadows" (Asprey 1994) or "phantom" war (Cooper 1979).

As the preceding examples suggest, the identification problem hurts primarily the incumbents: it is their opponents who, being weaker, hide. "It was an extremely one-sided type of warfare," a German officer pointed out about the partisan war in the Soviet Union, "because the German soldier was easily recognizable, and the partisan fighter, because he wore civilian clothes, was not" (in Cooper 1979:89). This explains the difficulty that incumbents have in defeating insurgents, despite their often tremendous advantages in resources. Vietnam is a classic example but far from the only one. In 1965 Peru spent more than $10 million to defeat about one hundred poorly armed guerrillas (M. F. Brown and Fernández 1991:190), and in July 1993 the British domestic intelligence service (MI5) revealed that the greatest part of its budget, "forty-four percent of an undeclared total of many hundreds of millions of pounds, was targeted against [the IRA,] a small, impoverished, working class guerrilla organization of around six hundred fighters with an estimated budget of five million pounds" (Toolis 1997:285).

Yet, insurgents also face an acute identification problem. The populations in the midst of which they hide may turn them in; spies and agents hiding among these populations may also identify them. According to Lucian Pye (1964:177), "The advantages guerrillas and terrorists may possess in opposing the far greater resources of the government can largely be countered if the government has adequate intelligence. At later stages in their insurrection, whatever advantages of mobility, surprise, and *esprit de corps* the guerrillas possess can usually be more than offset if the government has the crucial intelligence at the right moment."

Insurgents are vulnerable if they are identified. Between 1942 and 1944 the French resistance suffered more losses as a result of betrayal within its own

---

[2] Monthly figures for minor operations in Vietnam during 1964 are telling: 59,996 operations for 451 contacts with the Vietcong; 72,794 operations for 406 contacts; 73,726 operations for 491 contacts, and so on (R. Thompson 1966:88). An American officer said "that he had spent the entire year in Vietnam and never seen a single live Vietcong" (Herrington 1997:xv).

ranks than through German action (Laqueur 1998:230). By 1983 the Afghan Communist regime had deployed 1,300 agents in insurgent units, 1,226 along communication lines, 714 in underground political organizations, and 28 in Pakistan (Giustozzi 2000:98). As a result, betrayal becomes a pervasive obsession among insurgents.[3] Insurgent memoirs are replete with an overarching concern about information leaks (e.g., Barnett and Njama 1966:61); conversely, counterinsurgent memoirs (e.g., Aussaresses 2001; Flower 1987) brim with descriptions of thorough penetration of their opponents' organizations – particularly in urban environments.[4]

There are two dimensions to the identification problem: first is the categorical refusal of at least one side, the insurgents, to be reduced to a single identity, that of combatant (Andreopoulos 1994:195). This entails the transformation process that American soldiers fighting the Filipino insurgency in 1900 described as "chameleon act" (May 1991:142–3, 161).[5] Second is the refusal of the surrounding population to identify them to their opponents. Either the people do not know who is really an insurgent, which is sometimes true about spies and clandestine agents; or, much more commonly, they refrain from identifying the insurgent combatants who hide among them – out of diverse motivations, including sympathy and fear. Herein lays the relevance of popular "support."

4.3. SUPPORT

"The battlefield today is no longer restricted," observed a French officer in Algeria (Trinquier 1964:29); "like it or not, the two camps are compelled to make [civilians] participate in combat." The fight is conducted *through* the people; as a Cypriot peasant told the writer Lawrence Durrell (1996:224), it is "like a man who has to hit an opponent through the body of the referee."

It is widely argued that the outcome of irregular war hinges on the behavior of civilians; put otherwise, "civilian" or "popular support" is "the *sine qua*

---

[3] Bouaziz and Mahé (2004:253); J. L. Anderson (2004:176); Bizot (2003:112); Elliott (2003:961); Tucker (2001:87); Portelli (1997:138); Todorov (1996:90); Schroeder (1996:428); Saul and Leys (1995:53); Stubbs (1989:189); Paludan (1981:78). Sometimes, this obsession can lead to excesses. In the Philippines, the Communist New Popular Army launched a "terrifying" purge, killing hundreds of its own members and supporters in 1986–8 because of fears about informing (Jones 1989:265–75).

[4] Identification is not a problem limited to "ideological" wars; it is part and parcel of many (though not all) ethnic civil wars. In many ethnic civil wars armies systematically recruit among their ethnic rivals, fighters switch sides, and civilians collaborate with the army of their ethnic rivals (Kalyvas 2003). At least one political actor (usually the incumbents) seeks to control the "underlying" population of the ethnic rival, rather than exterminate it or remove it. Despite claims positing the impossibility of defection in ethnic (Kaufmann 1996; Ranzato 1994) or even nonethnic conflicts (Zulaika 1988:32), such defection is possible when actively solicited. Defectors do not lose their original ethnic identity but alter it, through the addition of qualifiers such as "moderate," "loyal," "antiextremist," or through their migration to another identity dimension.

[5] Civilian collaborators are equally hard to identify, as Leakey (1954:121) recalls about Kenya: "There is no outward sign by which one can tell whether a man is a Mau Mau supporter or not, for the original practice of making seven cuts on those who were 'initiated' into the movement was very quickly abandoned, because it made recognition by the police too easy."

non of victory" (Trinquier 1964:8). Almost all writers converge in asserting that no insurgent movement can survive without "civilian support," and neither can incumbent victory be achieved without it (Wickham-Crowley 1992:8; Bard O'Neill 1990:70–89). As an IRA man pointed out, "Without the community we were irrelevant. We carried the guns and planted the bombs, but the community fed us, hid us, opened their homes to us, turned a blind eye to our operations" (Collins 1999:225). Even the "Manual for Warfare against Bands" used by German troops during the Second World War made a central point of the fact that "the attitude of the population is of great importance in the fight against bands. Bands cannot continue in existence for any length of time in the midst of a population which entertains good relations with us" (in Heilbrunn 1967:150).

Yet below this unanimity lies extreme confusion, for there are two very different ways of thinking about popular support. One way is to think of it as an *attitude*, *preference*, or *allegiance*, and the other is to emphasize *behavior* or *action*. Obviously, there is a connection between the two, but in an irregular war the gap between attitudes and actions tends to swell; in many ways, this is the main consequence of the war.

Conceptualizing support in attitudinal terms is common. It has been argued that "guerrilla victory depends upon the *loyalties* of civilians in the area of operations," whereas in conventional wars "military operations go on without regard for the hapless civilian population. No one asks it to take sides in the struggle – at any rate not at first, while the battle rages. . . . In revolutionary war . . . the *allegiance* of the population becomes one of the most vital objectives of the whole struggle." (C. Johnson 1962:649; Fall in Trinquier 1964:ix). As a Missouri Unionist argued, "if counties known as *disloyal* would cease to sympathize with treason, and become *earnest* supporters of the Government, guerrilla warfare would soon cease to exist" (in Fellman 1989:91; emphasis added). As there is only a short step between attitudes and ideas, it often is asserted that ideology is central to civil war. In this view, ideology matters more than territory (Angstrom 2001:106); in the crude formulation of an American practitioner, "The only territory you want to hold [in a civil war] is the six inches between the ears of the campesino" (in Siegel and Hackel 1988:119).

The adoption of a primarily attitudinal stance is problematic. Attitudes are unobservable and must somehow be inferred, a hard task when it comes to civil war. A common, yet flawed, solution is to reason backward from the outbreak of the war to its causes, by positing the force of popular beliefs and grievances.[6] Civil wars are evidence of a deep "crisis of legitimacy"; substantial segments of the population (often, just "the people"), this argument goes, are intensely opposed to the regime in place and, consequently, reallocate their support toward rebels; in this sense, civil wars are really "peoples' wars" (Tone 1994:4; C. Schmitt 1992:213; van Creveld 1991:143). The implication is that people actually "choose" what faction to support based on its political and social profile or ideology – as if they were

---

[6] An extension consists in linking support to the outcome of a war: defeats are conveniently ascribed to the dearth of popular support and victories to its abundance.

voting in elections (C. Johnson 1962), and this choice has a tremendous impact on the military conflict: "Military and strategic factors are far less important than popular attitudes in a civil war. If an army is welcomed by the local population, its resources and strength are automatically increased. If, on the other hand, it is unwelcome, its strength is tied up in pacifying and policing the conquered territory" (Brovkin 1994:91).

However, there are good reasons to question the view that the outbreak of a civil war ought to be taken as unproblematic evidence of a deep "crisis of legitimacy" or of massive support in favor of the insurgents. Explanations of rebellion in terms of grievance parallel explanations of regime breakdown in terms of legitimacy; they are, as Adam Przeworski (1991:54–5) points out, either tautological or false; only when organized political forces challenge the sovereign does "political choice become available to isolated individuals." The absence of alternatives often produces collaboration irrespective of the level of popular satisfaction or lack thereof, which may be then wrongly interpreted as a reflection of legitimacy. Moreover, joining a rebellion can be the product of the ongoing war as much as it can be its cause. Stoll (1993:20) is right to observe that "once an armed conflict is underway, the violence exercised by both sides can easily become the most important factor in recruitment. People may join the revolutionary movement less because they share its ideals than to save their lives. . . . Hence, just because an insurgency grows rapidly does not mean that it represents popular aspirations and has broad popular support."

An equally misguided solution to the problem of unobservable attitudes is to derive them uncritically from "revealed" or observed behavior (Sen 1986). Often, the observation that some people collaborate with a political actor is interpreted as evidence of loyalty toward this actor. However, observed behavior is consistent with contradictory attitudes; as a result, it is a poor mechanism of preference revelation (Lichbach 1995:287). In fact, civil wars produce strong incentives for preference falsification (e.g., Calder 1984:155). Clearly, observed behavior is not just an imperfect indicator of preferences, but most probably an inaccurate approximation as well (Kuran 1991).[7] Vietnamese peasants proved particularly adept in this respect:

Both sides recruited military manpower relentlessly, and both sides equally demanded the loyalty of the peasants. Thus, a rice farmer in Hiep Hoa could easily find himself sitting under a banner at midnight, participating in an antigovernment rally during which he might play the role of an outraged and exploited peasant, under the watchful eye of a Communist propaganda cadre. The following morning, the same farmer could send his children to the new, government-built school and then walk to the village office to vote in a local election – this time under the watchful eye of government hamlet chief. The village Vietcong would boast in their report that ". . . So far, 90 percent of the villagers

---

[7] More systematic data can undermine widespread assumptions about preferences, but they are rarely fully reliable or available. The contents of private correspondence opened and read by the Vichy authorities contradicted the assumptions of observers about popular preferences in occupied France: out of 4,352 letters written in December 1943 and mentioning acts that Vichy listed as terrorism in the Montpellier region, 3,976 were hostile to the resistance and only 142 were sympathetic (Kedward 1993:113).

have actively thrown their support to the cause of the revolution." At the same time the Hiep Hoa village chief would inform his superiors that "more than 95 percent of the villagers voted in the recent election, with anti-Communist candidates receiving the near unanimous support of the people." (Herrington 1997:37)

No wonder that careful observers are baffled, like Kevin Toolis (1997:255–6) was in Northern Ireland: "Who can tell the truth in a world filled with double deceptions, handlers, confused loyalties, liars, self-loathing, professional deceivers, disinformation, black propaganda and betrayers? At the end of this journey I began to doubt the motivations of almost everyone I talked to."

This problem of observational equivalence has led to interminable debates, usually contaminated by partisan bias, on how to interpret observed support: on the one hand, those favorable to the rebel side claim that observed civilian collaboration with the rebels reflects genuine support derived from existing grievances and the belief that rebellion is the way to right existing wrongs, and the same observers imply that similar civilian collaboration with the incumbents is instead a result of coercion; on the other hand, those observers siding with the incumbents claim exactly the opposite. For example, arguing that Vietnamese peasants supported the Vietcong rebels because they believed in their program and ideas (e.g., FitzGerald 1989) rather than because they were coerced into supporting them (e.g., Klonis 1972:155) was a key rhetorical weapon in the polarized debate surrounding the U.S. intervention in Vietnam.

No matter how attitudes are inferred, an implication of the focus on attitudinal support is the twin claim that victory requires attitudinal shifts – "hearts and minds" – which can only be achieved through nonviolent persuasion: a "genuine and timely effort to satisfy the grievances of the people" is required since "popular support for the guerrilla is predicated upon the moral alienation of the masses from the existing government" (Ahmad 1970:15); in Robert Thompson's (1966:169) words, "Force of arms alone will not prevail." The main policy implication of this view is that incumbents need to persuade hostile populations to switch their sympathies through programs of political liberalization, economic development, and civic action.[8] However, no matter how deep the beliefs and how powerful the allegiances, they are not the only determinants of behavior. People can be coerced, and violence is used to force people to alter their behavior and behave in ways that may not be consistent with their preferences. As pointed out, election makes a poor analogy for civil war. Even Communist revolutionary doctrine, at the root of the "hearts and minds" approach and best exemplified by Mao's "fish in the sea" dictum, stresses violence much more than is often assumed, when it points out that political power grows out of the barrel of a gun. Participants always recognize that violence plays a key role. In Trinquier's

---

[8] This view has led to a false dichotomy between military and political responses to insurgencies. In fact, the two often go together, since political programs cannot be implemented in "insecure" environments. In Malaya, where the term "hearts and minds" originated, "it became clear that the strategy entailed the use of both the stick and the carrot" (Stubbs 1989:164–5). Conversely, a U.S. officer observed during the 1899–1902 Philippines War: "This business of fighting and civilizing and educating at the same time doesn't mix very well. Peace is needed first" (in Linn 1989:128).

(1964:8) words, civilian "support may be spontaneous, although that is quite rare and probably a temporary condition. If it doesn't exist, it must be secured by every possible means, the most effective of which is terrorism."

The difficulties associated with attitudinal support flow not just from the inference process but also from conceptual problems related to the very motivations that underlie support. For assuming popularity says nothing about how popularity translates into action on the ground. Both joining a rebel army and collaborating with it result from variable and complex sets of heterogeneous and interacting motivations,[9] which are affected by preferences over outcomes, beliefs about outcomes,[10] the behavior of others and the networks into which people are embedded,[11] and security considerations[12] in an environment where chance

---

[9] Barton (1953:141) lists five different kinds of motivations, Maranto and Tuchman (1992:251) eight, and R. Berman (1974:58, 67) twenty-seven!

[10] According to Robert Thompson (1966:170): "Much can be learnt merely from the faces of the population in villages that are visited at regular intervals [by incumbent forces]. Faces which at first are resigned and apathetic, or even sullen, six months or a year later are full of cheerful welcoming smiles. The people know who is winning."

[11] Processes of joining are highly likely to be rooted in network dynamics (Petersen 2001). Stark (1997) shows how social network ties (especially friendship and kin ties) are the best predictors of religious conversion. Insurgents consistently point to the importance of local networks in producing recruitment, based on "the desire of persons to unite with friends, neighbors and kinsmen" (Barnett and Njama 1966:158), and their practice is consistent with this view (Perry 1984:445). Hart's (1999:209) analysis of IRA unit rolls (in 1916–23) shows that brothers constituted between 37 and 58 percent of the battalions he examined. He adds that "the question of personal motivation is oddly absent from most memoirs and memories of the period. Volunteers seem to have regarded their political commitment as completely natural and their motives as self-evident, requiring little reflection.... Veterans are rarely able to recall exactly when and how they joined but they remember vividly how it felt to belong: 'There was a spirit in the air alright.' ... For most IRA men, joining the movement in its early days required little deliberate choice or effort. If you had the right connections or belonged to a certain family or circle of friends you became a Volunteer along with the rest of your crowd. If not, you probably stayed outside or on the fringes" (Hart 1999:203, 220). The list of Colombian guerrillas incarcerated after the Violencia in a Medellín prison was "rife with networks of uncles and nephews, sons and fathers, brothers and cousins" (Roldán 2002:243). Horton (1998:186) found that the former contra combatants she interviewed had an average of five other relatives in the contra army; likewise, the Sandinista rebels had used "multiclass networks of kinship, friendship, and patron-client ties to their own ends" (Horton 1998:69). Paul Berman (1996:66) adds that the country people of Nicaragua "were loyal to their own enormous clans," and this was reflected in patterns of recruitment: "Brothers follow brothers" (P. Berman 1996:78). Goltz (1998:150) found that the Azerbaijani militias of the early 1990s "seemed to be composed more of extended families than soldiers," and Avioutskii and Mili (2003) stress the importance of clan solidarity in rebel recruitment in Chechnya. Examples abound: Nepal (Sengupta 2005c:64), Chechnya (Tishkov 2004:94), Bosnia (Claverie 2002:48), Colombia (Sánchez and Meertens 2001:17; Rubio 1999:102; Pécaut 1996:257), Latin America in general (Wickham-Crowley 1992:152), the Balkans and the Baltics (Petersen 2001), the Congo (Bazenguissa-Ganga 1999a:42), Algeria (Faivre 1994:145), Mozambique from the 1960s to the 1990s (Finnegan 1992:118; Henriksen 1983:96), the Philippines (Kerkvliet 1977:205), Malaya (Stubbs 1989:49), Kenya (Kitson 1960:126), China (Wou 1994:252), and even revolutionary France (Cobb 1972:26).

[12] According to a Dominican guerrilla (in Calder 1984:126), after a Marine captain had threatened his life, he believed that "his only remaining option was to flee into the hills."

and contingency cannot be underestimated.[13] Of course, many fighters are con-scripted or abducted.[14] Additional factors include curiosity and the prospect of excitement and adventure,[15] the lure of danger,[16] the acquisition of a new and more rewarding individual identity or moral worldview,[17] the pleasure of acting as one's own agent,[18] and purely criminal motives.[19] Collaboration may provide access to public goods (such as dispute resolution, or protection against common crime, which explodes when state authority wanes),[20] or individual material bene-fits (including land, lower taxes, higher prices for produce, or debt forgiveness),[21]

[13] A Nicaraguan peasant did not want to become involved in the war, but after encountering by chance some contra rebels in the forest, he gave them food and gradually slipped into more sustained collaboration. As Horton (1998:183) puts it, "once this first step was taken, [he] found it difficult to retreat into neutrality.... Without having made a specific decision to collaborate with the contras, [he] found himself in the role of the contra *correo*. And two years later, in 1983, because of pressures from both State Security and the contras, [he] became a full-fledged combatant with the contras." See also Todorov (1996:94), Fenoglio (1973:60), and Clutterbuck (1966:94) for similar examples.

[14] It is estimated that after the spring of 1942, at least 80 percent of Soviet partisans "joined either unwillingly or because they had no alternative.... The Soviets made no pretense about recruitment for the partisan movement. Compulsion was paramount" (Cooper 1979:71). Even in ethnic civil wars, where individuals are supposed to have extremely strong preferences, participation often results from conscription. Although Somali "warlords could use the language and sentiment of clan to rally allegiance along blood lines [they] built their authority on the power of the gun" (Besteman 1996:590–1). In Bosnia, "many people found themselves carrying a gun whether they liked it or not. If you were of combat age, meaning only that you possessed the strength to fight, kill and possibly survive, then you were conscripted into whichever army represented your denomination, Muslim, Serb or Croat" (Loyd 2001:85). See also Waldman (2003:A1); Seidman (2002:40); Horton (1998:9); Nordstrom (1997:50); Senaratne (1997:99).

[15] Sengupta (2005c:64); Kitson (1960:126).

[16] Tishkov (2004:98).

[17] As a former IRA cadre put it: "At the very least such activity gave a strange edge to my life: I lived each day in a heightened state of alertness. Everything I did, however trivial, could seem meaningful. Life outside the IRA could often feel terribly mundane" (Collins 1999:362). See also Sánchez and Meertens (2001:22); Mahmood (2000:73); Mirzeler and Young (2000:419); McKenna (1998:184); Peters and Richards (1998); Armony (1997:207); Enzensberger (1994:42); Ash (1995:205); Wickham-Crowley (1992:20–1); Ortiz Sarmiento (1990:116); Henriksen (1983:160).

[18] Wood (2003:18).

[19] Criminal motives have long had their place in descriptions of civil war. Consider the following description of the American War of Independence in South Carolina (McCrady 1969:139): "There came with the true patriots a host of false friends and plunderers. And this was true of both sides in this terrible struggle. The outlaw Whig and the outlaw Tory, or rather the outlaws who were pretended Whigs and Tories as the occasion served, were laying waste the country almost as much as those who were fighting for the one side or the other." See also Reig Tapia (1996:583) for the Spanish Civil War. See also Mueller (2004); Silke (1998); Fisher (1997:87); Nordstrom (1997:56–7); Cribb (1991, 1990); Jones (1989); Paul and Demarest (1988); Ash (1988); Henderson (1985).

[20] According to Degregori (1998:135), the most important targets of Sendero in Peru were "abu-sive merchants, cattle thieves, corrupt judges, and drunk husbands." See also Smyth and Fay (2000:123); Rubio (1999:129); Manrique (1998:204); Berlow (1998:95); Senaratne (1997:75); Gallagher (1995:50); Stoll (1993:80); Wickham-Crowley (1991:44); Jones (1989:127); Kheng (1983:148); Kerkvliet (1977:70, 164); Rudebeck (1975:445); Taber (1965:40); Lear (1961:92).

[21] Kedward (1993:96); Stoll (1993:78); Popkin (1979); Race (1973:123–5).

protection against indiscriminate violence from the opposite side,[22] escape from obligations that are seen as more onerous (such as military or labor drafts),[23] acquisition of higher status[24] including what status can be obtained via access to guns,[25] the weight of personal or local disputes,[26] or simply the response to emotions such as anger, moral outrage caused by public humiliation,[27] and the desire to take revenge.[28] Furthermore, support is partially endogenous to the war. This can take many forms, not least of which is the purposeful use of violence to generate support (Snyder 2003), even when and where sympathy for an organization already runs high (Collins 1999:128; 170; Harris 1989:89). Clearly, observed support corresponds to a complex mix of preferences and constraints.

Like the much better-studied motivations for joining the rebels, individual motivations for joining progovernment militias are also heterogeneous and mixed (Rubio 1999; Stoll 1999; Starn 1998; Mackenzie 1997; Cribb 1991).[29] The men

---

[22] Goodwin (2001); see Chapter 5 for a discussion and evidence.

[23] Del Pino (1998:170); Berman (1996:69); Jankowski (1989:123-4); Cooper(1979:25); Race (1973:172).

[24] Collins (1999:164) points out that "in the nationalist community [of Northern Ireland], in republican circles anyway, IRA men have considerable status, and for those Provos who look for sexual advantages from it, there is no shortage of women willing to give more than the time of day to IRA volunteers." When it appeared to be winning, the Chinese Communist revolution "created an unprecedented and unparalleled opportunity for status advancement and social mobility for tens if not hundreds of thousands of persons at both the local and higher levels" (Levine 1987:173). According to Sheehan (1989:177), "there is considerable evidence that many young Vietnamese of peasant origin join the Vietcong because the Communists who have been forced by the nature of their revolution to develop leadership from the countryside, offer them their best hope of avoiding a life on the rung of the ladder where they began – at the bottom." Many young people joined Shining Path in Peru motivated by the "concrete exercise of power in their own localities" (Degregori 1998:130). Todorov (1996:100) tells the story of a Frenchman who worked as an interpreter for the Gestapo and "then discovered that the shame and humiliation he had experienced as an adolescent were soothed by the power he enjoyed in his position with the Gestapo."

[25] Johnson (2001:202); Mirzeler and Young (2000:419); Rubio (1999:115); Finnegan (1992:70); Zulaika (1988:25).

[26] Kalyvas (2003).

[27] Thaxton (1997:308-9) reports that a Chinese peasant cited as his main motivation for joining the Communists the fact that a government officer "kicked over his sweet melon basket and scolded him for daring to sell his 'dirty melons' leaving him to pick up the scattered melons one by one." Humiliation of traditional chiefs by "upstart" village administrators played an important role in Mozambique (Geffray 1990:32). See also T. Brown (2001:42); Horton (1998:106-9); R. Berman (1974:75).

[28] Adams (1994:7) recalls his relationship with a South Vietnamese officer: "I spent many hours talking to Lieutenant Lam. Gradually, he opened up. Late one evening over supper, Lam told me how much he hated the [Vietcong]. They had killed his brother, he said." West (1985:56) describes a South Vietnamese policeman who had tattooed on his chest the words "Kill Communists." The Vietcong had apparently slain his wife and all his children except one. The same policeman was described by a U.S. sergeant in the following terms (in West 1985:160): "Thanh's definitely mean. He hates. He lives only to kill VC."

[29] An analysis of individual causes of joining the French Waffen-SS in Marseille is replete with mixed, even contradictory, motivations. Consider the following statement: "After I'd gambled away my weekly pay my mother berated me and told me that if I didn't recover the money she would send me to my father [from whom she was separated]...unable to find the money, I signed up" (in Jankowski 1989:128-9). Jankowski's is one of the very few studies of motives for joining an armed

who joined the militia in the Philippine island of Negros "cast their lot with the military neither out of ideology nor out of any sense of debt or obligation, but because they had been ambushed or extorted by the NPA, needed work, had been directed to join by their employers, or saw an opportunity to exact revenge against their personal enemies" (Berlow 1998:182). An American officer in Iraq described the motivations of the Sunni commandos fighting on the American side against the insurgents by pointing to their need for a paycheck, their desire for the social status that comes from being members of a professional military, and their yearning for a routine – rather than ideology: "For some, there's definitely a desire to make Iraq better, but for a lot of them, it's just life as they know. For most of them, the cause isn't really that important. They're more used to working in this role.... I think for a lot of them, they couldn't fathom doing something different with their lives" (in Maass 2005:82).

Coercion is often cited as a chief motivation – though this can also be a self-serving claim. "You really didn't have a choice," Mehmet Refiktas, a Kurdish "village guard" in Turkey said. "Asked what happened to the homes of men in his mountain village, Islamkoy, who declined the government's offer, explained, 'Oh, they were burned'" (Vick 2002:A18). David Stoll (1993:128) tells a similar story about Guatemala: "Joining the patrol became a way to protect self, family, and community from the guerrilla contacts that triggered [government] massacres." Indeed, many Guatemalan militiamen were survivors of army massacres (Stoll 1993:162). Security matters in the opposite direction as well: the Portuguese trusted village headmen in Mozambique and gave them weapons because many had been murdered by the rebels and those remaining lived in fear of the same fate (Cann 1997:161).

Economic motivations also matter. Two men who explained why they had joined the pro-Israeli South Lebanese Army: "We were poor. The only work was their army. If you're in the army, you can live. If you are not, you can't" (in Sontag 2000:A1). Turkey pays the 95,000-strong militia it maintains in its Kurdish areas a monthly salary of $115, which is a "valuable sum." Indeed, it was reported that "Turkish officials and foreign diplomats have begun to worry that if these salaries are suddenly cut off and nothing replaces them, some unhappy veterans might grab their weapons and take to the hills" (Kinzer 2000:A8). Economic compensation may also take the form of loot. When the army promised the content of guerrilla storage pits in the outskirts of a Guatemalan town to militiamen who found them, "the race was on, to dig each one up before someone else did" (Stoll 1993:107). Ideology seems to play a minor role for militiamen, probably less than it does for rebels. In fact, militias are often composed of turncoats, either ex-rebels or former supporters of the rebels.[30]

---

organization during a civil war based on contemporary written records; he estimates that the percentage of those whose motives were mixed to be as high as 80 percent (Jankowski 1989:123–4). Almost every single "thick description" that I have read points to a complex and fluid mix of motives. See Tucker (2001:38); Ellis (1999:127); Hammond (1999:260); Horton (1998:6); Faivre (1994:121); Geffray (1990:105–13); Meyerson (1970:95); Barnett and Njama (1966:149).

[30] Berlow (1998:233); Moyar (1997:68); Henriksen (1983:136).

Finally, fear and revenge are important motivations. The fear of insurgents that follows their violence often drives people into militias (e.g., Sengupta 2005a:A3; D. Anderson 2005:73) and revenge is a central motivation, maybe more so for militiamen than for rebels, as suggested by the following examples from Algeria and Chechnya:

Each day when he comes here, Abdurahim (13) (whose family was killed by the Islamists in the village of Haouche Fanir, on May 14, 1997) dreams of joining the patriots. But for his two surviving brothers, who are both militiamen, that seed of revenge is already growing – pointing to a cycle of violence that will be difficult to break. "If I kill 1,000 terrorists, it won't be enough for my one brother," says a brother named Arabah, cradling a gun and wearing a clear-plastic waist pouch stuffed with colorful shotgun shells. "Do I look for revenge? Of course," he says. "Of course." (Peterson 1997a)

Mr. Tovzayev described himself as a fighter against the "bandits" – the rebels – on behalf of Mother Russia. He maintained close ties to the Russian military and was particularly proud of the armored jeep that was presented to him as a gift by Col. Gen. Gennadi N. Troshev, commander of Russian forces in the Northern Caucasus.... [He] spoke of taking up arms against the rebellion in 1995 after a rebel leader, Allaudin Khamzatov, entered his village and assassinated Mr. Tovzayev's father in front of his family. Within three months, he raised a small force of fighters and killed Mr. Khamzatov in an ambush. "This is how this kind of life started – fighting bandits," he said. (Tyler 2001: A8)

Revenge can be triggered by family feuds and local conflicts that become intertwined with the war (Abdi 1997; Leakey 1954:114). The French found that many of the Calabrians who volunteered to join the militia they formed in 1806 "saw the army as an excellent opportunity to settle a long-standing vendetta with some nearby family members" (Finley 1994:29). Often, revenge is exclusively related to the insurgents' past actions (Roldán 2002:258; Linn 1989:54). Because it is possible for rebel agents and sympathizers to hurt, alienate, or humiliate others, incumbents capitalize on discontent with insurgent rule in forming militias in recently "liberated" areas, and the militias' actions are keyed toward revenge. Stephen Ash (1988:155) describes the Unionist militiamen of middle Tennessee as "avenging angels." While the staunchest recruits for the village-based militias formed by the French in their war against the Vietminh were in provinces previously under Vietminh administration (R. Thompson 1966:168). The Algerian men who joined the French army in 1959 complained about the coercion exercised by the FLN rebels, especially the taxes, fines, and the tight control on everyday life that they imposed (Faivre 1994:143; Hamoumou 1993). An NPA commander in the southern Tagalog region of the Philippines "noted that the rise of vigilante groups in some rural barrios of Lopez (Quezon) was due in part to NPA heavy-handedness. The rebel commander recalled there was 'too much taxing' and that 'some of our comrades mistreated some of the people. The opportunity was taken by the military'" (G. Jones 1989:249). Even if such animosities are absent, they can be generated by the very act of militia formation. A U.S. officer reported from the Philippines that "having compromised themselves by collaboration and knowing that they risked guerrilla retaliation, [Filipino defectors] 'seemed most anxious to ferret out all insurrectos in this vicinity'" (in Linn 1989:43–4). The Earl of Carlisle, an envoy of the British government to America in 1778, made the same point about Loyalist militiamen: "In our present condition the only friends we have, or are likely to have, are those who are absolutely ruined for us" (in Shy 1976:186).[31]

Whatever their initial motivations, with time many militiamen develop genuine loyalties, at least to one another. In Cotzal, Guatemala, "an unwanted civil patrol had, paradoxically, become an institution of solidarity" (Stoll 1993:144). Likewise, in Peru "no one imagined that these patrols, too, would turn into a massive movement with an important degree of popular participation and autonomy from the state" (Starn 1998:236).[32]

These complexities of preference formation suggest the need to shift the focus from attitudes to behavior. But understanding support in terms of observed action also entails several problems. First, it is not easy to map behavior during a civil war because data are lacking. Real-time ethnographic observation can partly address this problem (e.g., Sluka 1989), but the limited sample on which it is based and the practical constraints posed by armed combat can defeat the implementation of rigorous research designs (Wood 2003:42). This is why most work relying on retrospective reconstructions is an enterprise fraught with difficulties.

Second, observed support is not dichotomous but can be conceptualized as a continuum that stretches from full association with one political actor to full association with the opposite political actor, while encompassing various shades of association, including neutrality (Petersen 2001:8). This is reflected in distinctions such as those between hard and soft supporters (Sluka 1989:291–4), between passive and active supporters (Bard O'Neill 1990:71–2), between direct and indirect participants and those "caught in the middle" (Kerkvliet 1977:166–7), and between constituents, sympathizers, members, activists, and militants (Lichbach 1995:17). The ethnographer of a Belfast Catholic ghetto widely considered to be a hotbed of insurgent support (Sluka 1989:291) found that "not all the residents who support the guerrillas support them in all of their roles. . . . Many people in Divis support the IRA and INLA in one area or role, while simultaneously condemning them in another." Moreover, observed support is dynamic and relational, hence a person's actions are influenced by others (Petersen 2001).

Third, we must distinguish between reasons for joining an organization and reasons for remaining in it (Molnar 1965:77–82). Students of military history, in particular, have adopted John Lynn's (1984) distinction between initial motivations (why people join an army), sustaining motivation

---

[31] In fact, violence may be used to generate commitment. In Guatemala, to overcome the militiamen's reluctance to kill the first victims, "an officer ordered them to pick executioners by lot. Subsequently, a victim would be tied to a tree and everyone in the patrol ordered to stab him with machetes. Before long, some patrollers were volunteering to kill" (Stoll 1993:107). Note that this explains the form of violence and the perpetrator; the victim could have been picked up as part of a scheme to deter defection.

[32] Two systematic differences in patterns of joining rebel organizations and incumbent militias may be the absence of high risk for first joiners and the absence of ideological indoctrination; both are consistent with an account that would point to the role of the state in assuming many of the costs of militia formation.

(why they stay in despite the cost), and combat motivation (why they fight on the battlefield).[33]

To summarize: inferring preferences from observed behavior is exceedingly difficult; preferences are open to manipulation and falsification; actual behavior is difficult to observe in civil war environments; and even when reliably observed, support is the outcome of a dynamic, shifting, fluid, and often inconsistent confluence of multiple and varying preferences and constraints. This turns the search for one overriding motivation across individuals, time, and space that dominates much of the literature on rebellion into a highly improbable and potentially misleading enterprise. Given the theoretical problems and the state of the empirical record, a sensible solution for a study of violence is to bracket the question of individual motivations and attitudes and to adopt minimal, yet sensible, assumptions about support.

First, it is enough to assume, following Tilly (1978:201), that launching an insurgency and eventually winning requires only "the commitment of a significant part of the population, regardless of motives, to exclusive alternative claims to the control over the government currently exerted by the members of the polity."[34]

Second, it is not necessary to assume stable preferences. There is a dynamic dimension to support, not as an automatic and fixed translation of underlying preferences but as a malleable field of (often strategic) action that corresponds to both preferences and constraints. Indeed, civilians vary the level and the direction of their commitment throughout the war, as suggested by a report written in 1900 by U.S. Major General Elwell S. Otis about the insurgency in the Philippines: "A review of the telegraphic dispatches shows ... that our men were gladly received by the mass of people upon entering the provinces, then later, a portion of the people under insurgent impressment contributed in men and money to drive the Americans out, and finally, that the great majority, gaining confidence, united with our troops to destroy the Tagalo[g]s and the robber bands they directed" (in Linn 1989:29).

Third, this commitment may result from varying combinations of persuasion and coercion. In fact, consistent with J. Scott's (1990; 1985) analysis of peasant attitudes, many accounts of how people collaborate with armed actors point to

---

[33] It is also possible to think of "compounds" that aggregate single motives. Margaret Levi (1997) identifies four models of compliance: habitual obedience, ideological consent, opportunistic obedience, and contingent consent. Contingent consent is a compound that includes the political actor's ability to credibly threaten sanctions, its trustworthiness, the presence of ethical reciprocity between citizens, and the availability of socially provided information. Moreover, even "clean" attitudes, such as willing consent, are compatible with a variety of second-order motivations, which have themselves left a trail of lingering academic debates: class interest (Wolf 1969), narrow individual self-interest (Popkin 1979), or a community's "moral" economy (J. Scott 1976).

[34] A reflection of such an attitude in Vietnam is provided by Sheehan (1989:49–50): "While all of the peasantry in the northern Delta did not sympathize with the guerrillas, the majority either favored the Viet Cong cause or tacitly aided the Communists through the silence of a neutrality that worked against the Saigon government. Whether the neutrality was created by fear of guerrilla terrorism or by sympathy made no practical difference: the Saigon government lacked the cooperation of the peasantry, and cooperation was necessary to suppress the Communist-led intervention."

qualified, cautious, and ambivalent collaboration along the two poles of sympathy and fear. Finnegan (1992:102) recalls a conversation with a Mozambican peasant: "Wouldn't the bandits be recognized and turned over to the police [if they came in town]? The [man] to whom I put this question said, 'Not necessarily. The police are not popular here.' Were the bandits popular, then? 'Not necessarily.'" Consider the point made by a former Vietcong when asked if he joined voluntarily or not: "This is a subtle point. One cannot say that support is voluntary, and one cannot say it is not voluntary" (in Race 1973:129).[35] The ambiguous coexistence of acceptance and fear is perhaps best expressed in Toolis's (1997:68) description of fighters in Northern Ireland: "They were the local thugs turned community warriors. Neither of their respective communities would wholly endorse their action but most ordinary citizens protected them by shutting their eyes and ears. No one, Catholic or Protestant, would have informed on their respective paramilitaries out of communal solidarity and for one other very good reason: if the paramilitaries found out they would have shot the informant in the head."

The coexistence of sympathy and sanctions reflects the mix of persuasion and coercion that political actors typically settle upon once they achieve an acceptable level of control. County Armagh has long been a hotbed of IRA support, yet this is also a place where, as a Catholic man put it, local IRA rule means that "nobody speaks out, because if they speak out, they go down a hole" (in Lavery 2005:A5). Kenneth Matthews, a BBC correspondent who was kidnapped by Greek Communist rebels in 1948 and, as a result, visited rebel-held areas, reached a similar conclusion during his debriefing by British officials after he was released:

In this large stretch of country there are practically no Government forces of any kind nor any functioning officials of the central government.... Throughout the area the rebels exercise simple but effective administrative control.... As regards the feelings of the population in rebel territory, it is clear that Mr. Matthews has a most vivid impression of an almost universal feeling of what he could only describe as "horror" at the situation in which it finds itself. This does not mean that the rebel rule is a terroristic one. Mr. Matthews thinks that if the population thought that the rebel rule had come to stay, most of them would settle down under it more or less, although they would not like it. He did not think that more than 1% of the population could be regarded as really in favour of the rebels.[36]

This last point suggests that deep and unflinching commitment is only required from a few people. These are the "pure, fervent idealists" who occupy a disproportionate position in many journalistic and historical accounts. Yet, an empirical regularity supported by considerable evidence is that only a small minority of people are actively involved in civil wars, either as fighters or active supporters. Lichbach

---

[35] Recruitment of South Vietnamese peasants into the Vietcong army, Richard Berman (1974:198) found, was "neither the spontaneous volunteering often attributed to revolutionary movements nor the conscription of villagers into enforced servitude. Indeed it involved a mixture of coercion and persuasion."

[36] "Notes on Conversation with Mr. Kenneth Matthews on the 1st November, 1948," PRO, FO 371/72217/R1237.

(1995:18) cites extensive evidence in favor of what he dubs the "five percent rule," according to which only about 5 percent of the population is made of active and militant supporters. A study of the percentage of combatants in seven insurgencies between 1940 and 1962 suggests an average of 7 percent can be classified as strong supporters, a combined total for both insurgents and incumbents (Greene 1990:75). This observation is common. The English Civil War "was not simply a struggle between gallant Cavaliers and psalm-singing Roundheads... only a small minority of provincial gentry can be exactly classified in either of these conventional categories" (Everitt 1997:19). In Civil War Missouri, "some clearly identified with one side or the other, maintaining a notion of loyalty of belief and behavior. Many more sought to be disengaged, neutral" (Fellman 1989:xviii). Brian Hall (1994:210) argues that the proportion of people that exhibited intense preferences and violent behavior in the former Yugoslavia was in the range of "one-to-five percent" of the population. In Colombia, only a "tiny minority" of civilians "actively collaborate as committed informers or partisans for the armed groups"; in contrast, the bulk of the civilian population seeks to remain neutral (Fichtl 2004:3).

Even in highly polarized environments and under less dangerous conditions, active participation remains low. Elisabeth Wood (2003) estimates that in the areas of El Salvador she studied, a larger minority (about one-third of the peasants who had not fled these areas) supported the insurgents. During the Spanish Civil War, "only a small minority was unconditionally political and identified with parties and unions.... Even the famous *milicianos*, the volunteer forces that helped to save the Republic when the military rebellion exploded, often had a shaky commitment to the cause" (Seidman 2002:6, 11–12). The total number of fighters in all the Lebanese militias at no time exceeded 30,000, and during fifteen years of war only 90,000 to 100,000 people (close to 3 percent of the population) were ever members of a militia; overall, less than 20 percent of the population was actively involved in supporting one faction or another (Nasr 1990:7). Similar conclusions have been reached about the Bosnian and Chechen wars (Mueller 2004; Claverie 2002:48; Tishkov 1997). Where electoral results are available, they sometimes suggest limited prewar support for very effective insurgents.[37]

Most "ordinary" people appear to display a combination of weak preferences and opportunism, both of which are subject to survival considerations (Chapter 5).[38] Their association with risk-taking minorities tends to be loose and subject to the fortunes of the war and its impact on one's welfare (e.g., Serrano 2002:375; Lison-Tolosana 1983:48). This is the case in both ethnic and nonethnic conflicts,

---

[37] Communist parties in German-occupied Europe are a case in point. There were only 830 Communists in the entire Bosnia Herzegovina at the time of the Axis invasion in April 1941, yet the Communist partisans proved extremely successful there (Hoare 2001:2). Of course, this was true of the Bolsheviks in Russia (Schmemann 1999:208). Insurgents usually start minuscule and grow very quickly. See Berkeley (2001:47); Horton (1998:74); Asprey (1994:537); Stubbs (1989:183); Paget (1967:35); Clutterbuck (1966:5); Barnett and Njama (1966:152); Kitson (1960:126).

[38] Lubkemann (2005:504); Raleigh (2002:140); Schmemann (1999:208); Pyszczynski, Greenberg, and Solomon (1997); Malefakis (1996:26–7); Griffin (1976:137).

as suggested by the following vignettes from the American Revolution, German-occupied Ukraine, and Lebanon:

What emerges from the British record . . . is a picture of the great middle group of Americans. Almost certainly a majority of the population, these were the people who were dubious, afraid, uncertain, indecisive, many of whom felt that there was nothing at stake that could justify involving themselves and their families in extreme hazard and suffering. These are the people lost from sight in the Revolutionary record or dismissed as "the timid." With not even poverty to redeem them, they are also passed over by historians who believe that the inert mass of people in any epoch deserve nothing better than obscurity. These people, however, did count, because they made up a large proportion of a revolutionary republic whose very existence depended on counting. (Shy 1976:215–16)

Taking all of the evidence presented here into account, the following overall conclusion seems tenable: the attitude of the civil populace in this area is best described as docile and malleable. With the exception of the partisans themselves and small numbers of pro-Soviet and pro-German activists who were willing to risk death in order to serve their causes, most people seem to have been willing to obey whichever antagonist appeared most credible at a given time. (T. Anderson 1999:622–3)

Clearly, there were far more victims than perpetrators in the Lebanese civil wars, and most people simply wanted the killing to end. They might have subscribed to patriarchal and kinship values that encouraged ethnic or confessional identity, but unless they were suddenly swept up in both emotion and circumstance they were unlikely to become directly involved in the fighting. (M. Johnson 2001:230)

4.4. FORMS OF COLLABORATION AND DEFECTION

Political actors seek the exclusive and complete collaboration of all civilians. In practice, they are looking for active collaboration from a small number of dedicated supporters, and passive but exclusive collaboration from the population at large; they also seek to prevent civilians from collaborating with their rivals. They also prefer exclusive but incomplete collaboration to nonexclusive collaboration (such as neutrality and hedging); obviously, they prefer a low level of collaboration to no collaboration at all. The minimum core of collaboration is generally *nonbetrayal* to the enemy (Stubbs 1989:2; Leites and Wolf 1970:10). Insofar as civil war tends to be a polarizing process, collaboration and noncollaboration tends to be zero-sum.

The flip side of collaboration is defection, which can be disaggregated into at least three types: noncompliance, informing, and switching sides (Table 4.1); the last two are clearly acts of collaboration with the rival actor, although noncompliance is often construed as such. In this book, I understand defection as active collaboration with the rival actor.

Noncompliance can be public and private, collective and individual; informing is usually private and individual; and switching sides is both individual and collective but usually public. Noncompliance includes actions such as complaining and critiquing, tax evading, shirking, and fleeing. It may be individual or collective (an entire village shirks), private or public. Economic considerations and survival are usually the main motives. While it is the most benign form of noncollaboration, if

TABLE 4.1. *Types of Defection*

Type	Scope	
Noncompliance	Individual and collective	Public and private
Informing	Individual	Private
Switching sides	Individual and collective	Public

left unpunished, noncompliance, may trigger cascades of more serious instances of noncollaboration.

Informing is the act of supplying information about one side to its rival; it is typically a private act that presupposes that information about one side and access to the other are simultaneously possible – something that entails an absence of front lines.[39] While informing indicates some form of association with the political actor to whom information is being directed, it differs from switching sides in that it is usually a private act that requires secrecy. It is also individual rather than collective, and its effectiveness (or damage) tends to be unrelated to the number of informers. In Vietnam, the Vietcong were satisfied when they had one or two secret collaborators in hamlets controlled by the government (Race 1973:147).

Informing matters not just because it provides a direct military advantage (e.g., preventing or facilitating ambushes), but primarily because it solves the identification problem. A positive externality is that knowledge among the population that one side has crucial access to information undermines the population's willingness to collaborate with the other side.

The motivations behind informing, like those behind collaboration in general, are mixed. They may reflect genuine political preferences, expectations of personal gain, private grudges, coercion and blackmail, or survival considerations.[40] And like defection on the whole, informing tends to be responsive to risk. The effective use of violence may successfully deter informing.

Amilcar Cabral, a nationalist leader from Guinea-Bissau, once said that a revolution is like a train journey. At every stop, some people get on, and other people get off (in Finnegan 1992:133). Switching sides is common in civil wars and involves both individuals and entire communities that openly start collaborating with a rival political actor. It is usually a public and visible act: individuals may defect from one army to its rival or entire villages may set up a militia and openly signal that they have defected. Switching is widespread in civil wars; rebel "turncoats" have been used extensively by incumbent forces, and they are usually

---

[39] The failure to provide information one possesses is seen as a consequential act of defection. An officer of the Sandinista army in Nicaragua explained: "What kills directly is the tongue, because if no one tells me that someone is waiting there armed, and I don't notice anything, then I die [in an ambush]" (in Horton 1998:210).

[40] As a Basque man told Zulaika (1988:83), "If you belong to the side of the losers, you have only one possibility of passing to the winners' side – to inform against your friends. In this way you gain power over them, and money."

associated with considerable violence.[41] During the Russian Civil War, entire local revolutionary committees "which had been appointed by the Bolsheviks from among the local people went over to the side of the insurgents"; in fact, "it was not uncommon in central Russia and especially Ukraine that the same individual served in several or all armies, Red, White, and Green" (Brovkin 1994:105, 418). In China, many Communists joined the Nationalist side, especially after losing out in factional conflicts; they were the rebels' worst enemy, "for they knew the guerrillas' ways and were thirsty for revenge" (Benton 1992:475). In Vietnam, "defections from one side to the other occurred frequently as did shifts in the loyalties of villagers" (Berman 1974:31), and the Vietcong "counted defection as one of their greatest problems" (Moyar 1997:250–1). Again, motives vary widely.[42]

Those switching sides provide obvious services: as sources of information, as helpers in getting their former colleagues to defect, and, by the sheer fact of their existence, as propaganda. Ponciano Del Pino (1998:169) also notes that having experienced their former organization from the inside, they are able to overcome the fear that such organizations often invoke in outsiders. Because switching sides is a dramatic and consequential act, the harshest punishment appears to be reserved for those who switch at crucial junctures in the conflict – especially for village leaders or even entire villages. Robert Thompson (1966:25) reports that when the Vietcong regained control over a village that had defected to the government, they seized "the headman and his family, disemboweled his wife in front of him, hacked off his children's arms and legs and then emasculated him."

4.5. THE INSTITUTIONAL SETTING OF COLLABORATION

A rather unexplored aspect of irregular war concerns the institutional context within which interactions between political actors and civilians take place, what I describe as the "meso" level. Sometimes, this interaction is informal. More commonly, however, this process is institutionalized and takes two basic forms: militias and committees. Being armed, militias are typically empowered to use violence directly, whereas committees are not. Political actors rely on both, though incumbents appear to prefer militias and insurgents committees, a preference that may be only due to the availability of weapons.

---

[41] Myers (2005:A4); Hedman (2000:132–3); Bearak (2000); Gossman (2000); Mahmood (2000:83); Clayton (1999:50); McKenna (1998:180–1); Del Pino (1998:169); Zur (1998:106–7); Starn (1998:244); Gacemi (1998); Berlow (1998:182); Moyar (1997:167); Cann (1997:101–2); Swedenburg (1995:156–64, 195); Le Bot (1994:176); Stoll (1993:140); Hamoumou (1993); Cribb (1991:143); Rosenberg (1991:46, 92); Blaufarb and Tanham (1989:63); Flower (1987:115); Crow (1985:170); Calder (1984:158); Henriksen (1983:136); Salik (1978:105); Heilbrunn (1967:69–70); Paget (1967:91–2); Clutterbuck (1966); Kitson (1960).

[42] Among the reasons for defecting from the Vietcong, Moyar (1997:111) includes the following: "disagreements over promotions or demotions, mistreatment of one's family members, accusations about collaboration with the GVN, and animosity between subordinates and superiors."

4.5.1. Militias

Militias are primarily a political rather than a military institution. They are part of a strategy of local rule and state building.[43] As an Algerian argued about the country's militias: "People can't eradicate the terrorists without the army, and the army can't exterminate the terrorists without the people" (in Peterson 1997b). In Guatemala, the main objective of the civil patrols, as militias were known, was "to inform on guerrilla sympathizers in the community" (Carmack 1988b:63). The primary purpose of militias is "population control" (Jones and Molnar 1966:25). While the individual militia members may be focused on defending their villages or families, the fact that they are permanently present in their villages and are operating in places they know well allows incumbents to tap into private information.

Although insurgents rely on local militias (e.g., Geffray 1990; Stubbs 1989:87–8), the term is usually associated with incumbents, who use them as auxiliaries.[44] The various irregular and semiregular groups of anti-rebels, referred to by such diverse names as paramilitaries, militias, death squads, and home, civil, or village guards, are the "opposite" face of the rebels (Zahar 2001; Rubio 1999:20) – "counter-gangs" in Frank Kitson's (1960) formulation. The formation of militias along with the creation of "fortified villages," often described as "local" or "self-defense" programs (Armstrong 1964:30), is an essential part of counterinsurgency efforts (Hedman 2000:133; Barton 1953). Typically, militias are formed at the local (usually village) level, comprise local men (and sometimes women), and their activities are closely tied to their locality.

Militias often reach massive size. It is estimated that by 1985, 1 million rural Guatemalans were involved in patrolling their communities (Warren 1998:89). Militias are also prevalent in ethnic conflicts where states are often able to provoke interethnic defection (Kalyvas 2004). For example, the Indian security services in Kashmir have been successful in getting Muslim militants to switch sides and become "countermilitants" (called "renegades" by the locals and "friendlies" by the government) (Gossman 2000:275). Militias are also a key tool for enforcing occupation. In fact, occupiers are surprised to discover how easy it is to recruit natives and often find that they get more recruits than they have places to fill (e.g., Finley 1994:29).[45]

---

[43] This is visible in their functions. In Guatemala, militias exercised judiciary powers. Whereas before the war, people would go before the local mayor, who served as a judge of first instance, or to a higher-level judge in the provincial capital to settle differences, during the civil war they appealed to local "civil patrol" leaders (S. Davis 1988:29–30).

[44] In this respect, militias in irregular war differ from those in symmetric nonconventional ones, where they often take on an autonomous role.

[45] More than 1 million Soviet citizens fought on the German side and the total number of collaborationists was about double the number of partisans (Klonis 1972:91). In Algeria, more Algerians fought on the French side than against it: "At no time from 1954 to 1962 did the numbers of Algerians fighting with the ALN for independence match the number of Algerians fighting on the French side" (Horne 1987:255). Half of the Portuguese soldiers fighting against independentist rebels in Guinea and two-thirds in Mozambique were natives. By 1974 the independendist rebels had reached a peak of 22,000 men in Angola, as opposed to 61,816 locally recruited troops fighting

Militias can be costly. Although they are formed to engage primarily in "protective violence," they often mete out "predatory" and abusive violence, including extortion.[46] Their reputation for atrocity is well established.[47] They may also cause an escalation in violence because they use their power to fight personal or local conflicts.[48] "Missouri militiamen had a great need to exact revenge against their rebel sympathizing neighbors, and they knew which scores they wished to settle" (Fellman 1989:129). Many cases of abuse were reported from the Kurdish areas of Turkey, where the Turkish government formed progovernment village militias to fight a Kurdish insurgency. In the village of Ugrak, Vick (2002:A18) reports, the state armed the Guclu family, which, by most accounts, "wielded no particular clout until the state made them the law.... The policy had the effect of emptying the village of everyone not named Guclu. The families who left describe being pushed off their land by neighbors who used police powers to commandeer better land and bigger houses." As one of their victims put it, "These people given weapons by the state use the weapons for their own benefit." The village guards, "whom many locals describe as mafias ... do as they please under the color of law, enjoying virtual immunity from prosecution, according to human rights activists and local residents.... Reports of rape at the hands of village guards are rising, and critics describe leaders of prominent clans using guard status to cement their already considerable power, in some cases running smuggling rings unchallenged by state authorities afraid to try to disarm them."

Ironically, the local character of militias that permits the gathering of information so necessary to political actors may also turn them into indiscriminate weapons with counterproductive effects. For example, a British journalist "had no doubt at all," in 1948 Greece, "that the activities of the Right Wing bands ... are responsible for the rebels' strength. He said that recruits are continually coming in and that he saw many arrive himself. He was sure from his conversations with

---

on the Portuguese side, and "there were always more African volunteers for the Portuguese troops than there were openings" (Clayton 1999:51–4; Cann 1997:103–4; Henriksen 1983:60–1).

[46] Trinquier (1964:34) recognizes that in such settings "abuses are always possible." The Confederate rangers created by the Virginia legislature during the American Civil War "used their recognition by the state as a license to steal and murder. They took assumed Unionists from their homes, tried and convicted them on the spot, and meted out whatever punishment struck their fancy. They were not very discriminating in their victims, however, and Confederate sympathizers in the region soon began to ask for protection from their 'protectors'" (Paludan 1981:52). Informers working for the Japanese in the Philippines during World War II would often blackmail people into bribing them by promising nonbetrayal (Lear 1961:27). The same occurs in China (Seybolt 2001:218). In Malaya, "newly recruited officers and sergeants without proper training and a rapidly expanding and poorly supervised rank and file provided fertile ground of corruption. The Emergency made extortion and bribery much easier for those who wished to line their own pockets. If bribes were received there were no arrests, but an uncooperative 'donor' could always be shot as a communist sympathizer" (Stubbs 1989:72).

[47] Roldán (2002:161–2); Zur (1994); Mason and Krane (1989:185); Calder (1984:130); Perry (1984:433); Kerkvliet (1977:196); Shy (1976:187).

[48] The most vivid description in this respect is the one by Paul and Demarest (1988) of the events in the Guatemalan town of San Pedro la Laguna during the civil war. See also Dupuy (1997:158); Fellman (1989:185); Stubbs (1989:72); S. Davis (1988:28); Kerkvliet (1977:196).

them that Right Wing excesses and arbitrary and unjust acts of Government representatives are still rapidly swelling the rebel ranks in the Peloponnese."[49] Because of this tendency, political actors tend to crack down on excesses (e.g., Paul and Demarest 1988).

Because militias threaten insurgents, they quickly become the insurgents' primary targets. Many massacres committed by insurgents take place in villages whose denizens defected by joining newly formed militias (Kalyvas 1999). Hence, even if villagers initially joined the militias under coercion, they may quickly learn to fear and hate the rebels. In Guatemala, Stoll (1993:100) shows, the army relied on this mechanism to solve the problem of trust and prevent militiamen from handing their weapons to the rebels: the militiamen were initially not armed until enough blood had been spilled – militiamen killing guerrillas and vice versa – to confirm that they were on the army's side.[50] Overall, there is a consensus is that, in the end, militias are a rather effective weapon against rebels.[51]

4.5.2. Committees

Local, usually village-based committees handle and screen information for armed actors.[52] Such committees can be found in most settings. In revolutionary France, "vigilance" committees of local patriots "were to be found in every city and town down to most small bourgs, as well as in significant numbers of villages in some areas"; they were "endowed with arrest power and became the lower rung on the ladder of revolutionary repression that led through prison to the revolutionary tribunal and up the steps of the guillotine" (Lucas 1997:33). In revolutionary Russia, Chekas drew the lists of persons to be arrested (Werth 1998:172). During the American Civil War, "vigilance committees" were set up in frontier districts (Ash 1995:123). In Kenya, the Mau Mau insurgents set up local committees that "gave the orders for killings, raids, money collection, and recruitment"

---

[49] "Notes on Conversation with Mr. Kenneth Matthews on the 1st November, 1948," PRO, FO 371/72217/R1237.

[50] Trust is the key issue: as Robert Thompson (1966:136) recommended about Vietnam, "where the people are reliable and can be trusted, then the number of persons armed should be sufficient to defend the hamlet. Where the people are not yet to be trusted, then no one should be armed... There can be no half-way measures where the people are not trusted. This will only lead to treachery and disaster." I was able to find few reports of militiamen collaborating with rebels. Henriksen (1983:159) reports evidence of direct contacts between residents of aldeamentos (strategic hamlets) and insurgents. He adds that "even members of the self-defense militia collaborated with guerrillas, feeding, informing, and occasionally turning firearms over to them." Likewise, it has also been reported that some Chechen pro-Russian militiamen collaborate with the rebels (Nougayrede 2002), while FARC guerrillas appear to have infiltrated progovernmental peasant militias (S. Wilson 2003). The most striking case was investigated by Lacoste-Dujardin (1997), who tells how an Algerian Berber village that was armed by the French joined the FLN on the basis of advice from an anthropologist. It is surprising, however, how unusual these cases seem to be. The problems caused by lack of trust run the other way as well (Race 1973:256).

[51] Richards (1996:171); Blaufarb and Tanham (1989:79); Linn (1989:54); Jones (1989:273–5); Horne (1987:255); Cooper (1979:115); Race (1973:270); Paget (1967:91–2).

[52] Sometimes militias call themselves committees, as in Nepal (Sengupta 2005a). I use the term here to refer to small, information-processing groups rather than armed groups.

(Kitson 1960:45), while in Malaya the British formed similar local "committees of review" that screened civilians arrested during sweeps (Stubbs 1989:74). The Filipino rebels of the NPA relied on committees to determine assassination targets: these committees based their decisions "largely on complaints from sympathizers and rebel intelligence" (G. Jones 1989:249). The same was true in El Salvador (J. L. Anderson 2004:136). Likewise, the South Vietnamese set up "screening committees" consisting of officials at the hamlet, village, and district levels, which reviewed evidence pertaining to the activities of people suspected of collaborating with the Vietcong (Moyar 1997:204). At the same time, the Vietcong set up a vast network of committees beginning at the village level (West 1985:21) in order to ensure "that critical decisions . . . were made by local people, with relatively more flexibility and with some sensitivity to the demands of the particular situation" (Race 1972:164); according to Berman (1974:50), "such a structure placed prime responsibility on low-level cadre." In exchange for their monitoring and information, local agents obtain a valued immanent good: the power to rule over their communities.

Although there is substantial evidence regarding the existence of such committees,[53] we know little about how they actually operate. Perhaps their most important feature is that they often have a role in determining what violence is visited on the locality in which they operate, but how this power is wielded varies. In many cases, these committees have veto power over the use of violence in their community. I return to this issue in Chapters 7 and 8.

4.6. CONCLUSION

This chapter has specified the first part of a theory of irregular war by systematizing well-known but scattered insights about insurgency and introducing a novel conceptualization of sovereignty in irregular war. After raising various problems associated with the concept of "popular support," I discussed identification, the key issue facing political actors. In the following chapter, I keep my focus on collaboration and explore its relationship with control.

---

[53] Fitzpatrick and Gellately (1997); Rosenau (1994:315); Rosenberg (1991:199); Geffray (1990); Gross (1988); Henriksen (1983:148); Clutterbuck (1966:6).

5

A Theory of Irregular War II

Control

Non, décidément, on ne tue pas les mouches à coups de marteau (We definitely don't kill flies with hammers).

Lieutenant Colonel Bigeard, French army, Algeria

This is a political war and it calls for discrimination in killing. The best weapon for killing would be a knife, but I'm afraid we can't do it that way. The worst is an airplane. The next worst is artillery. Barring a knife, the best is a rifle – you know who you're killing.

John Paul Vann, U.S. adviser in Vietnam

This chapter analyzes the relation between collaboration and control and argues that military resources generally trump the population's prewar political and social preferences in spawning control. In turn, control has a decisive impact on the population's collaboration with a political actor. However, the amount of military resources required for the imposition of full and permanent control in a country torn by civil war is enormous and, therefore, typically lacking. This places a premium on the effective use of violence as a key instrument for establishing and maintaining control – and thus for generating collaboration and deterring defection; in turn, effective violence requires discrimination.

5.1. THE ALLOCATION OF COLLABORATION

A robust empirical observation is that the allocation of collaboration among belligerents is closely related to the distribution of control, that is, the extent to which actors are able to establish exclusive rule on a territory. This relationship can be formulated as a hypothesis: the higher the level of control exercised by a political actor in an area, the higher the level of civilian collaboration with this political actor will be.

An immediate concern is the direction of causality. Does control spawn collaboration or is it the other way around? For example, Brovkin (1994:126) observes about the Russian Civil War that "an army of 100,000 could not possibly have taken control of a territory with a population of 40 million people in three months if there had not been a universal resentment of the preceding administration." Likewise, it is claimed that "the most important locational factor" of insurgent base areas "is that political objectives clearly override purely geographic (terrain) advantages" (McColl 1967:156).

There is little doubt that collaboration and control are self-reinforcing. More objectionable, however, is the view that control emerges exclusively from collaboration and never shapes it; similarly objectionable is the "median voter" view of civil war, namely that patterns of control during the course of the war reflect majoritarian preferences, especially as reflected in the prewar period. Indeed, it is not necessarily the case that political majorities enjoy a military advantage over minorities; in fact, the opposite may be true (Massey et al. 1999). The prewar political preferences of the Spanish population, with the partial exception of Catalonia and the Basque country, turned out to be a poor predictor of the distribution of control among Nationalists and Republicans during the first months of the war (Derriennic 2001:168); in Bosnia, the Muslims had a clear numerical advantage but were unable to translate it into a military one. More important, this argument disregards the effects of the war and fails to account for the many instances of preferences that are endogenous to war, as discussed in the previous chapter.

A more encompassing and dynamic hypothesis is that initial patterns of control are predicted by some combination of prewar preferences and existing military resources,[1] but as the war evolves, control is more likely to trump prewar preferences in determining collaboration. Even though collaboration and control are interlinked, it is possible to disaggregate their interaction into a simplified temporal sequence. An example is as follows: at t_1, an insurgent group gains control of a locality through the successful use of military means at t_0, as a result of existing popular preferences, or through a combination of both. As a result, collaboration with that group at t_2 increases. However, the government army may counterattack, chase the insurgents out, and impose its own control through purely military means at t_3. Now, this will spawn collaboration with the army at t_4, even though the population may have had a preference for the insurgents. If the army maintains its control for a long time, the preferences of the population may possibly shift "endogenously" toward the army at t_5.

---

[1] Geffray's (1990:53–4) analysis of the arrival of RENAMO in the Mariri area of the Nampula district in northern Mozambique points to this reinforcing process: the local chief Mahia had been alienated by the policies of the government, hence he welcomed the RENAMO insurgents before they were in a position to protect him; at the same time, however, RENAMO decided to come to this area because of the convergence of favorable geographical features: distance from cities and towns, thick forest, water resources, and proximity of a mountain with many caves. Ultimately, it was the presence of RENAMO that "gave people the military means to place themselves outside the state's scope." In Geffray's (1990:93) words: "Tens of thousands of people moved under the protection of Renamo's weapons in this area . . . outside the range of the Frelimo state. These populations could have never entered in a state of insurrection on their own, without the intervention of an armed force capable to maintain Frelimo's forces at a distance."

This is a process reminiscent of the *cuius regio eius religio* principle, whereby entire populations became Protestant or Catholic following their ruler's choice. Michael Seidman (2002:40) calls the widespread tendency during the Spanish Civil War to side with the camp that dominated the city or region where one lived "geographical loyalty." Finnegan's (1999:50) observation about the dynamics of popular support in Sudan points to the same direction: "People's political views would be highly contingent on the power arrayed around them."

The point is, in short, that although control and collaboration interact, control may trump the political preferences of the population in generating collaboration during the war. This insight is consistent with arguments that stress state capacity (Fearon and Laitin 2003; Coleman 1990:479) and the related observation that insurgencies are likely to develop and acquire civilian support where state control has declined or collapsed (e.g., Del Pino 1998:170; Skocpol 1979).[2] The implication is that prewar popular preferences may be an inaccurate predictor of the distribution of control during the war.[3]

Highlighting the importance of control in no way implies that coercion is the only factor or that popular grievances are irrelevant. Thousands joined the South African–financed RENAMO insurgents in Mozambique because it allowed them to destroy the deeply unpopular new villages created by the Mozambican government. However, they did so only after the insurgents were able to challenge the government and establish local military control, thus shutting out the army (Geffray 1990:39). Popular dissatisfaction with new villages was equally strong in Tanzania, but because no insurgent group challenged the state, this dissatisfaction was not expressed in the context of an insurgency.

Because emphasis on how control may trump prewar preferences and shape collaboration during the war may appear questionable at first sight, I provide a few examples to demonstrate the argument's plausibility before specifying a set of causal mechanisms that translate control into collaboration.

During the Spanish Civil War, many leftists joined right-wing militias (and vice versa) because they found themselves on the wrong part of the front line and wanted to survive (Cenarro 2002:75). Young French men wishing to avoid labor conscription during the Second World War were more likely to join the collaborationist Milice if they lived in the cities, and the Resistance if they lived in

---

[2] James Coleman (1990:479) dubs this "power theory," contrasting it to the "frustration theory." This is particularly visible in the case of weak occupation or colonial administrations and explains the ease with which insurgencies are able to spread. For instance, Cann (1997:21) points out that the insurgency in Angola during the Portuguese colonial rule began in areas where the Portuguese presence was "so sparse that it was physically impossible for [administrators] to maintain anything but the most casual control over their districts." As an American analyst pointed out about the inability of Colombia's military to control the country, "The military can't substitute for the presence of the state" (in Forero 2001:A3). Similar points are made by Evans (1985:211) on Virginia during the American Revolution and Horton (1998:126) on the contras in Nicaragua. Obviously the lack of state presence indicates a key condition for the emergence of insurgencies rather than their timing – why the breakout rather than when. This suggests that joining an insurgency entails lower risks than usually assumed when incumbent forces are absent or very weak (e.g., Degregori 1998:130; Horton 1998:126; Herrington 1997:29).

[3] Elliott (2003:408); Geffray (1990:39); Li (1975:188).

the countryside.[4] Two men explained why they had joined the pro-Israeli South Lebanese Army (SLA) (in Sontag 2000:A1): "We grew up on guns. Guns were muscles. And in this area, the guns were in the hands of the S.L.A."

Practitioners are well aware of this point. Mao Zedong (in Bruno Shaw 1975:209) argued that "the presence of anti-Japanese armed forces" was the first condition for the establishment of a base area. "If there is no armed force or if the armed force is weak," he pointed out, "nothing can be done." A 1968 CIA report from Vietnam (in Moyar 1997:321) observed that "most of the people respond to power and authority, whether that of the Viet Cong or the GVN." A French general described how, following a French military operation in Algeria, in 1959,

The strong rebel zones of Beni Meraï – Babor and Arbaoun-Tamesguida have been seriously dismantled. The rebel elements have either retreated into surrounding sanctuaries or have been broken down into small groups that avoid contact. The rebel political organization, lacking the support of the military apparatus, is partly neutralized and its members are hiding. The logistical infrastructure is deeply disorganized. The population has been freed to a certain extent from the rebel constraint and has begun a clear move back toward our side.... The population's shift is, however, not irreversible; to maintain and accelerate it, we must pursue simultaneously and at every level the destruction of the bands. (in Faivre 1994:148–9)

Ronald Wintrobe (1998:45) identifies two instruments through which a dictator can accumulate power: repression and loyalty. Loyalty can be acquired in a variety of ways, including the provision of material benefits (especially monopoly rents) and ideological appeals. Due to its multilateral dimension, civil war is a context that turns the permanent and stable acquisition of loyalty into a very difficult enterprise. Once the war is underway, war-related resources such as violence tend to replace the provision of material and nonmaterial benefits, inducing individuals, for whom survival is important, to collaborate less with the political actor they prefer and more with the political actor they fear; in other words, the provision of benefits loses out gradually to the effective use of violence. After all, violence is a weapon that is easy to use, yet "promises returns far out of proportion to the amount of time, energy and materials" invested by political actors who rely on it (Thornton 1964:88); and political actors would rather be disliked but feared than liked but not feared when their rival is feared.[5] An American

---

4 Using judicial data, Jankowski (1989:123–4) found that the largest contingent of Miliciens, between a quarter and a third, had signed up to escape labor conscription to Germany, some even as an insurance against receiving a summons, and some the very day they received it. As one of these men put it, "So I joined the Milice to avoid going to Germany, because it was simpler for me, because it allowed me to be close to my [family] and my work. I didn't have all the uncertainty [that would arise from] leaving for an unknown maquis with possible reprisals against my family." The percentage of those who joined out of conviction is estimated by Jankowski to have been close to 5 percent; another 5 percent joined under pressure from family and friends, another 10 percent to take advantage of jobs and privileges, and the rest for multiple reasons.

5 The worse outcome, of course, is being both disliked and not feared. West (1985:157) describes such an instance. Following a failed Vietcong mortar attack against a village, the local police chief "said the story that the Viet Cong had tried to kill the villagers would be known in every hamlet

journalist covering the counterinsurgency in Iraq asked the leader of a unit of Iraqi commandos, Colonel Adnan Thabit, about a local sheik, after the two had met in Samarra and the former had threatened the latter. Adnan replied that "it is not important whether he is with us or against us. We are the authority. We are the government, and everybody must cooperate with us. He is beginning to cooperate with us" (in Maass 2005:56). Richard Nixon's adviser Charles Colson conveyed this insight crudely but clearly: "When you have them by the balls, their hearts and minds will follow" (in Chang 1992:403).

Of course, fear alone does not suffice to sustain rule in the long term (Wintrobe 1998:37; C. Friedrich 1972:60); however, it operates as a first-order condition that makes the production of loyalty possible. Leaving aside the argument that most benefits a political actor is able to deliver will not be sufficient to offset a high risk of violent reprisals at the hands of the rival actor (Mason and Krane 1989:179), one can still note that material benefits become increasingly scarce during civil wars.[6] These wars tend to deplete local economies and thus produce a rise in poverty and a reduction of goods available for distribution; this may turn people away from the political actor with whom they initially sided (Chingono 1996). In response to such shifts, even insurgents may become more coercive vis-à-vis their social base, "alienating the very people whose support they needed most," as Berlow (1998:179) noted in the Philippines: "Villagers would be asked to choose: *pulo ukon polo*, ten pesos or the barrel of the gun." "As the war dragged on," writes David Elliott (2003:348) about Vietnam, "even the poor peasants began to question the benefits of Party membership as compensation for sacrifices. The burdens increased and the rewards decreased." He shows that wealthier peasants fled their villages, in the process freeing land for the Vietcong to redistribute; "but the very insecurity that had made this land available also made it dangerous and unprofitable to cultivate.... Thus the land question diminished in importance, and the daily struggle for survival replaced land as the most critical issue for the rural population" (2003:521). Although the Vietcong used mainly persuasion to recruit followers and fighters between 1957 and 1962, they became more coercive at later stages, when they often relied on an overt and compulsory draft (Berman 1974:50). In Peru, Sendero's sanctions "became increasingly cruel as the years went on" (Del Pino 1998:185). The Rhodesian intelligence chief (Flower 1987:122) describes his government's changing belief "that there had to be less 'carrot' and more 'stick'" as a response to the rebels' increasing brutality. Ideological benefits also lose much of their initial power. The fiercer and longer the conflict, the more likely that "limiting damage" will prevail for individuals over "positive" motivations, such as getting benefits or acting according to ideals (Leites and Wolf 1970:127).

---

the next day. That they had tried and failed was the worst possible combination for them. The villagers had been given the most powerful reason not to like them while not being made to fear them more."

[6] A partial exception may be the local production of illegal goods (such as opium or coca) and primary commodities, especially minerals, which normally would accrue to the central government.

5.2. SURVIVAL

Reporting from German-occupied Greece in 1944, a British officer wrote: "None is ever free from the struggle for existence: everything else is secondary to it."[7] As violence becomes the "main game in town," survival becomes increasingly central for civilians (e.g., Kheng 1983:173). This is particularly true of peasants whose everyday attitude has been described with terms such as "pragmatism," "fatalism," or "resistant adaptation" (Del Pino 1998:178; Herrington 1997:29; Siu 1989:113).[8]

Thucydides (3:83) describes war-torn Corcyra as a place where "everyone had come to the conclusion that it was hopeless to expect a permanent settlement and so, instead of being able to feel confident in others, they devoted their energies to providing against being injured themselves." Fatigue and suffering, the natural consequences of protracted war, effectively undermine preferences and sympathies. Civilians, as Fellman (1989:xviii) nicely puts it, become numb, "separating their consciences from their actions." By 1781 the typical settler of North Carolina, "whatever his initial loyalties, felt a profound need for order and regularity in his daily affairs. For some, the savagery of war begot more savagery, but for most it fueled contrary yearnings for peace and stability" (Ekirch 1985:110). All over the country, people "got angry when British or Hessian or Tory troops misbehaved, but they also grew weary of being bullied by local committees of safety, by corrupt deputy assistant commissaries of supply, and by bands of ragged strangers with guns in their hands calling themselves soldiers of the Revolution" (Shy 1976:13). Survival was similarly a key consideration in the areas affected by the guerrilla war during the American Civil War. As a Tennessee woman wrote in her diary, in 1865 (in Ash 1995:204): "I can see every day people are for themselves and no boddy else.... [M]ost [of the] people have turned out to steal and lied[,] not many that care for any one but themselves." Surveying extensive evidence from Civil War Missouri, Fellman (1989:46, 49) reaches a similar conclusion: "It is my clear impression that there were ... more survivors than heroes – if maintaining loyalty under these circumstances would be the appropriate test of moral probity.... It made more sense to be a living liar than a dead hero, and the stakes were that great." Similar sentiments are expressed in a letter from the Russian region of Saratov that was intercepted by the Cheka in 1921: "The number of arrests is growing in Saratov. Several university professors were arrested. The average inhabitant sits quietly and only curses the Communists, but is so

---

[7] "Woodhouse report on the situation in Greece, January to May 44 (5 July 1944)," PRO, FO 371/43689/R10469.

[8] It has been argued that peasants do not use an economic "maximizing" way of reasoning and that their behavior is irrational as far as land, loans, "fair prices," and income are concerned (Shanin 1975:273). Although this may be true, it does not contradict the fact that when it comes to survival, most peasants, most of the time, prefer to live rather than die and act accordingly. In fact, this claim is consistent with survival-maximizing behavior, which is closer to risk aversion than income maximization. Indeed many studies have found that peasants generally maximize security and minimize risk (Kerkvliet 1977:255). For example, Siu (1989:113) points out that what mattered most for Chinese peasants during the Japanese occupation was "secure livelihood; they hoped at least for political stability and social order, regardless of the slogans the new leaders proposed."

cowardly that when he reads the papers that are posted, his face takes on a loyal expression as if he might see a Bolshevik who might suspect him of disloyalty" (in Raleigh 2002:393).

Compare these examples with behavior in more recent wars. Truman Anderson's (1999:623) detailed account of partisan warfare in the Nazi-occupied Ukraine concludes that "the pragmatic, day-to-day calculus of personal survival played a much more important role than did either pro-German sentiment (rooted in Ukrainian regional hostility to the Soviet regime) or Soviet patriotism." Likewise, the Spanish anti-Franco guerrillas of the 1940s dealt with peasants who "preferred to eat than fight for their freedom, while being favorable to whatever side was in control" (Serrano 2002:374). Even when people have a strong preference for one side over the other, they may find that the circumstances make collaboration exceedingly difficult. In his largely autobiographical novel, the Italian writer Beppe Fenoglio (1973:380) includes the following retort of an Italian peasant to a partisan, following a successful Fascist raid: "We know that you are better than them, we know. But we are afraid, we live in perpetual fear." The internal documents of the Chinese Communist Party suggest that, in contrast to official rhetoric, "the number of willing heroes always decreased precipitously as the risks of martyrdom increased. They repeatedly assert the elusiveness of heroism" (Hartford 1989:112).

By the end of the Biafran War, the majority "of the Biafran people were no longer enthusiastic about the war. What they cared for most was their own 'survival'" (Essien 1987:151). As a Vietnamese journalist remarked: "After twenty years of this war, there is no right cause, no ideal. Neither side can speak in the name of anything in this endless agony. The only right cause that remains is the cause for settling the war urgently" (Chung 1970:xi). "Other than risking death or fleeing from their homes," Nordstrom (1997:52) reports from Mozambique, "the villagers had little option but to meet the demands of each passing group as best they could." "Possibly the most astute observation on the ideology of the violence-afflicted citizens," she adds (1992:266), "came from a young man living in Beira, Mozambique: 'the only ideology the people have is an anti-atrocity ideology.'" As a Chechen woman put it: "Anything but war. I would like to live the rest of my life in peace. I would agree to live on tea and bread. Just anything but war" – a feeling confirmed by a humanitarian worker: "The suffering is so intense and the suffering is not about politics. The vast majority of people we were meeting, they wanted to stay alive; they wanted a life in which their houses weren't bombed and there wasn't chaos and shooting on the street. Politics was not nearly as much on their mind as staying out of harm's way" (Wines 2003:A3; Gall 2001:25). "We need to have peace," said a man from Darfur. "We have suffered too much for this war" (in Polgreen 2005:A3). In sum, the inescapable result is that, like in the Spanish Civil War, "the low reservoirs of popular commitment [are] quickly drained" (Seidman 2002:27).

The combined effect of the reduction in available benefits, the increasing role of violence, and the civilians' orientation toward survival is a situation in which effective threats translate into collaboration. In turn, the effectiveness of threats hinges on control.

5.3. HOW CONTROL SHAPES COLLABORATION

The anecdotal empirical record provides substantial evidence that control spawns collaboration independently of prewar patterns of support. First, there is evidence showing that collaboration follows the *spatial variation* in control. This point was made explicitly by the writer of an economic report of a Greek village: "The whole of this area, being plainsland, was not suited to guerrilla warfare, which adapted itself mostly to mountainous terrain. Besides this, the village was relatively safe due to its nearness to Salonica, a large Army center. The leftist side was rather pronounced but no move was made by anyone so there was no visible result" (Tchobanoglou 1951:1). Consider Shy's analysis (1976:178) of the distribution of British loyalism (Toryism) during the American Revolution:

What appears as we look at places like Peterborough, where Tories are hardly visible, and at other places where Toryism was rampant, is a pattern – not so much an ethnic, religious, or ideological pattern, but a pattern of raw power. Wherever the British and their allies were strong enough to penetrate in force – along the seacoast, in the Hudson, Mohawk, and lower Delaware valleys, in Georgia, the Carolinas, and the transappalachian West – there Toryism flourished. But geographically less exposed areas, if population density made self-defense feasible – most of New England, the Pennsylvania hinterland, and Piedmont Virginia – where the enemy hardly appeared or not at all, there Tories either ran away, kept quiet, even serving in the rebel armies, or occasionally took a brave but hopeless stand against Revolutionary committees and their gunmen.

During the Civil War many Unionist sympathizers in the Appalachian counties of North Carolina ended up supporting the Confederacy: "Because of the influence of secessionists, it was wise to decide that one's sympathies lay with the South. Faced with the presence of Confederate power and the lack of armed organized Federal protection, reasonable men not seeking martyrdom might become southern patriots" (Paludan 1981:64). In the eastern regions of the Dominican Republic, the insurgents controlled the countryside, preventing those "who might have been willing to cooperate with the marines from doing so" (Calder 1984:159). In the occupied regions of the Soviet Union, the Germans initially thought that there was a direct connection between popular dissatisfaction with their rule and the rise of the partisan movement (Cooper 1979:24); however, they eventually realized that this connection was mediated by control. As a Soviet agent noted in 1942, "in those areas where the partisans are not active, the people are against them. In the imagination of the population the partisans are like bandits and robbers" (in Dallin et al. 1964:331). A 1941 Soviet report made the same point: "There are, however, many elements among the population who sympathize with the partisan movement and the Soviet regime. But, since they fear the consequences, they are using utmost caution in their activities" (in Cooper 1979:78). Likewise, Conservative villages in areas controlled by Liberal bands in Colombia during the 1940s were forced to "convert" to Liberalism (and vice versa): the most active Conservatives were killed or fled, and the rest of the population shifted its partisan allegiances (Ortiz Sarmiento 1990:176–7). Robert Thompson (1966:15) observed that support for the Vietcong "greatly expanded" in those areas of the countryside that came under their control. As one of them put it, "There are some, particularly the middle and rich peasants, who do not like the communists, because the communists hurt their interests ... but they don't dare oppose them because, if they oppose the communists, they must go live in a government area. But do they have enough money to go and live in Saigon? Probably not, and so they must be content and remain" (in Race 1973:130). Conversely, Moyar (1997:339) reports that Vietcong cadres serving in areas of heavy U.S. and South Vietnamese activity "defected in large numbers and brought with them great amounts of information," contrary to cadres working in areas of less intense military activity.[9]

Second, there is substantial evidence that collaboration follows the *temporal variation* in control. Gaining control over an area brings collaboration, and losing control of an area brings much of that collaboration to an end. In North Carolina, during the American Revolution, one Revolutionary veteran recalled that the loyalists "gained more confidence and they became more bold, more daring, and more numerous" following the American defeat in Camden in August 1780; in his own militia company, in contrast, only eight members remained "good and true" Whigs – "the rest had joined the Tories" (in Crow 1985:160). The tide shifted once more, until 1781, when Cornwallis's capture "disheartened" the Tories (Crow 1985:160–1). A Union general during the American Civil War found that in Virginia "the majority of people along our track to be reasonably neutral" and noted "the rapid development of loyal sentiments as we progressed with our raid" (in Wills 2001:204).[10] Using a list drawn by the state authorities to assess the political allegiance of villages in the Ille-et-Vilaine in July 1795, Roger Dupuy (1997:194–7) found that their allegiance during the Vendée War is predicted less by their expressed preferences prior to the war (1789–92), and more by the local military balance of power and the village's geographical position – in other words, the extent of control exercised in the area by a political actor. When the counterrevolutionary rebels exploited the military weakness of the republicans and took over the countryside, all neutral villages as well as many staunchly republican villages turned counterrevolutionary. The archival material quoted by Dupuy is replete with remarks about "republican communes" whose "republicanism is diminishing" because of their "geographical position" and the "difficulty of communications," and of villages that will turn counterrevolutionary "if additional forces are not sent in."[11] In fact, the French revolutionary Gracchus Babeuf

---

[9] The spatial relationship between control and support holds beyond civil wars. Kamen (1997:180), for instance, found that one factor accounting for the inability of the Spanish Inquisition to strike fear among most Spanish people was its absence from the majority of localities – "the sheer impossibility of one inquisitor being able with any degree of frequency to visit the vast areas involved."

[10] Wills (2001:204) comments: "For some this loyalty was certainly genuine; for others, any such demonstration need last only as long as the blue-coated soldiers remained in the vicinity."

[11] A couple of examples from this report are worth quoting (Dupuy 1997:194–5): Amanlis: "its patriotism appears to have diminished, its municipality is not corresponding with us anymore; however it is presumably easy to recall [this commune] to the republican principles, but its geographical position and especially the difficulty of communications does not allow us to do so"; Bais: "a large commune which has shown all the energy of patriotism," but "its patriots will be forced to abandon

(1987:120) noted how many republicans began joining the counterrevolutionaries as early as 1797 because of the direction of the war.

At the beginning of the twentieth century, Macedonian villages would change "national camps" and become "Greek" or "Bulgarian" as many times as they were visited by Greek or Bulgarian fighters; a Greek participant referred to one village that kept welcoming both sides by saying that its inhabitants behaved "in a political manner" (Livanios 1999:205). In 1941 a high political cadre of the Chinese Communist army observed that with the removal of the Communist troops, resistance work stopped in the undefended areas, peasant morale plummeted, and local party organizations displayed open hostility toward the military leadership; local Communist soldiers often deserted, circulating stories to justify their flight that further damaged the army's reputation among the population (Hartford 1989:111). A remark by a Soviet partisan in a 1943 letter underscores this point: "When we came here from the Soviet hinterland, the Germans were everywhere and it was not very pleasant. There were many police and other riff-raff who fought side by side with the Germans. The population was also against us. This last year [1943] has brought about perceptible changes. Our partisan area has become large. Now you see no Germans in the rayon centre. This work had to be carried out under difficult conditions; now, however, it has become easier; the population of the whole area stands behind us" (in Cooper 1979:64–5). Susan Freeman (1970:24–5) describes the behavior of a small village near the front lines of the Spanish Civil War:

Valdemora set about the business of survival.... Their approach was to remain aloof when possible and to yield when necessary. This they did as a community. When troops (of both sides), camped in the Sierra, demanded food, the *alcalde* [mayor] assessed all families for equal amounts and sent food into the hills. This is regarded as the only intelligent thing to have done.... In 1936, several individuals in the area who refused troops' demands were killed, and Valdemorans regard them as having wasted their lives for want of a little intelligent realism. As the siege of Madrid continued and the front lines moved away from the Sierra (before the war was one year old), acquiescence to the government in power was life's simple rule, as it had been under both the Monarchy and the Republic.

After the South Vietnamese and U.S. military came to the strongly pro-Vietcong village of My Thuy Phuong, "most of the revolutionary cells died, and the people became divided," a Vietcong rebel pointed out (Trullinger 1994:143). A similar trend was observed elsewhere in Vietnam: prior to January 1960, in the South Vietnamese province of Long An, "a great many people were favorably inclined toward the [Communist] movement but elected not to cooperate overtly because of the risks entailed by the continued government presence.... Yet as the presence of the central government was eliminated, the probability of achieving what the movement promised greatly increased, at the same time as the

their homes," and Bais will turn counterrevolutionary "if additional forces are not sent in." Moyar (1997:301) quotes a Vietcong district-level cadre making a similar point: "These observations of mine made me think that the Front is very active and harmful in quiet areas, while it is weakening there where the GVN [the South Vietnamese military] is active." See also Jon Anderson (2004:140) on El Salvador and Ekirch (1985:114) on revolutionary North Carolina.

risks of involvement greatly decreased" (Race 1973:191). "The people began to draw away from us and to fear our presence, knowing that we would attract government forces and more fighting," recalled a former Vietcong (Herrington 1997:30). Elliott's (2003:1006) massive research on the Mekong Delta confirms this observation: there was "a clear decline in popular support for the revolution that resulted from the loss of physical control." After the United States threw its weight behind the Northern Alliance in Afghanistan, many Taliban switched sides. As one of them explained, "I joined the Taliban because they were stronger. I am joining the Northern Alliance because they are stronger now" (in Filkins 2001: A1).

The obverse of every gain in collaboration that one side experiences with gains in control is the loss of collaboration experienced by the other side along with its loss of control. Del Pino (1998:178) describes how the population of the Ené Valley in Peru "joined" the Shining Path after it took control of the valley in 1988, placing forces at its entrance and exit points. When in 1991 the Peruvian army began to "liberate" the valley and "recuperate" the population, these same peasants joined the local militias in their fight against the rebels. In Kenya, "with the provision of security came a change of conviction, away from some 90 percent general Kikuyu support for Mau Mau's methods (though not necessarily its aims) to support for the government" (Clayton 1999:14). Kerkvliet (1977:237) shows how peasants had to withdraw their support from the Huk rebels in the Philippines because of a shift in control. A related example is the description of the evolution of support in the village of Punta Dumalag located in the Davao area of the Philippines, a reputed Communist stronghold. This village was first organized by Communist cadres in the late 1970s. A clandestine barrio revolutionary organization acted as a shadow government, and most villagers actively participated in the insurgency in a variety of functions. In early 1988, a few months before the writer Gregg Jones's visit, control shifted: the rebels "had been forced to abandon their once impregnable stronghold, and a fiercely anticommunist autocracy led by Alsa Masa [Risen Masses] vigilantes ruled the barrio." Jones found that although the most committed villagers had fled, most villagers remained and "now they too professed allegiance to Alsa Masa. Jones concludes that "if Punta Dumalag residents were secretly unhappy with Alsa Masa, as Davao NDF faithful suggested, it appeared that [they] at least had adjusted to life under the new order" (G. Jones 1989:270–5).

British reports on the Greek Civil War, during its last phase (1946–9), provide a good example of how control shapes collaboration. The following excerpts from these reports to the Foreign Office require no comment:

May 1947. A huge block of nationalist inhabitants in Laconia, although ready and willing to render assistance for the suppression of banditry, fails to find the means to do so. Meanwhile the bandits are intensifying their activity. The nationalists become discouraged and capitulate and in view of the Government's weakness, are giving no assistance to the local authorities.[12]

---

[12] "Greece: Security Situation in the Peloponnese; Sir C. Norton to Mr. Bevin (26 June 1947), Attached Greek Gendarmerie report (16 May 1947)," PRO, FO 371/67006/R8651.

June 1947. As it is, the population of an essentially anti-Communist area are losing confidence in the Government, and is in the mood to capitulate to the Communists for lack of any better alternative.[13]

November 1948. Whilst the majority of the two million inhabitants of the Peloponnese are at heart patriotic and opposed to subjection to Russian communism . . . they are being forced by fear and increasing misery to accept the role of the communist guerrillas in order to survive at all.[14]

February 1949. Civilian morale is steadily on the increase. . . . This is reflected in the greatly increased assistance which is being given by the civilian population to the Army and the Gendarmerie in the collection of intelligence, and the large increase in the number of bandits surrendered. . . . The reaction to the military operations has been what might have been anticipated. For the first few days after the occupation of bandit areas by the troops the attitude of the civilian population was surly and suspicious, but as soon as it was realised that the Government forces had come this time with the intention of remaining, their attitude completely changed – increased cooperation, particularly in the matter of intelligence.[15]

Political actors are obviously well aware that control spawns collaboration. The Vietcong security doctrine made a clear connection between the two: the imposition of control made possible the creation of "a sympathetic environment, that is, an environment (the population) composed of sympathetic and neutral elements, from which the hostile elements have been removed" (Race 1973:146). Likewise, counterinsurgency experts point out that the primary objective of governmental militias is population control so as to deny insurgents "the support of the civilian population" (Jones and Molnar 1966:25).

Forced population removal (often called "resettlement," "population control," or "villagization"), a method used by incumbents in some civil wars, further confirms the endogeneity of collaboration to control.[16] This method, whose use in modern times was pioneered by the British and the United States around the turn of the twentieth century, seeks to deprive insurgents of their population basis; in counterinsurgency parlance, "the population problem . . . may be solved by physical or psychological separation of the two elements: guerrillas and population" (Condit 1961:24).[17] Euphemisms, such as "emptying the tank"

---

[13] "Greece: Security Situation in the Peloponnese; Sir C. Norton to Mr. Bevin (26 June 1947)," PRO, FO 371/67006/R8651.

[14] "Report from Patras (2 November 1948)," PRO, FO 371/72328/R13201.

[15] "Report from the Military Attaché on the Military Situation in the Peloponnese (visit: 18–21 February 1949)," PRO, FO 371/78357/R2293.

[16] Because this method requires extensive resources, it is used primarily by wealthy (or foreign-supported) incumbents, or in times of growth (e.g., Stubbs 1989:113).

[17] The British moved a large part of the Settler South African population into concentration camps during the Boer War (Klonis 1972:53); the U.S. forced thousands of Filipinos into "protected zones," where as many as 11,000 died as a result of malnutrition, poor sanitary conditions, disease, and demoralization (Linn 1989:154–5); similar tactics were used, on a smaller scale, in the Dominican Republic (Calder 1984:xxii). Union troops relied on resettlement in areas prone to guerilla war during the American Civil War (Fellman 1989:95). In the 1950s, the British reintroduced the method of resettlement in fortified villages – both in Malaya and Kenya; the French used it in Algeria during the war of independence, as did the Americans in Vietnam (using British advisers

and "drowning the fish," abound. Despite generating considerable grievances, moving the population into areas where it can be controlled by the incumbents (either in fortified villages or in refugee camps around towns) appears to produce collaboration with the incumbents. Indeed, the forced relocation of peasants in slums surrounding major cities (e.g., in Greece, Vietnam, Turkey) did not seem to generate serious security problems for incumbents. The same peasants who supported the insurgency back in their villages turned quiescent, even though they now had more reasons to complain about the appalling conditions of their new life.[18]

One of the best-researched cases in this respect is the Vietnam War. Summarizing a wealth of surveys and research on the attitudes of refugees, Wiesner (1988) notes that forcible evacuation not only failed to alter peasants' preferences, but it turned many peasants who were resentful of the government for their removal into Vietcong sympathizers. Moreover, it brought Vietcong supporters and cadres into camps located in government-held territory, thus reducing security. As a result, forcible evacuation was criticized by many U.S. officials. However, despite being populated with Vietcong sympathizers (and some cadres), refugee camps never became a security problem for the incumbents. Sympathy did not translate into collaboration with the Vietcong. On the contrary, the Vietcong saw these camps as a threat, as evidenced by the fact that they sometimes bombed them. In fact, when switching from a description of attitudes to that of behavior, the U.S. reports found that most refugees tended to collaborate with the incumbent authorities.[19]

Observers sometimes note this relationship between control and collaboration, but they tend to miss its significance or misinterpret its causal direction. Milton Finley (1994:28–9) notes that the Napoleonic French troops in Calabria were able to recruit local volunteers only from the towns but fails to connect this pattern to the fact that "even nominal French control stopped at the edge of the town; the countryside belonged to the brigands." Consider the following remark about Vietnam made in April 1964 by the American journalist Walter Lippman (in Taber 1965:17): "The truth, which is being obscured from the American people, is that the Saigon government has the allegiance of probably no more than 30 percent of the people and controls (even in the daylight) not much more than a quarter of the [national] territory." It is easy to see the connection between the

---

with experience in Malaya) under the designation "Strategic Hamlet Program," and various colonial, African, and Latin American regimes used it as well – Portugal, Ethiopia, and Guatemala, most notably. Even leftist incumbents, like the Sandinistas of Nicaragua, relied on this method (Horton 1998:229). A recent example of the use of this method is Turkey's evacuation of 1,779 villages and hamlets and 6,153 settlements in the eastern part of the country in the 1990s, in the war against the Kurdish PKK insurgency (Jongerden 2001:80).

[18] John Cann (1997:155) summarizes some of the difficulties in his discussion of the application of the method by the Portuguese in Africa: "Moving people was invariably an emotional process because of their attachment to ancestral lands. Timing was also a large factor, and moving a population after it had been subverted was pointless and generally backfired. Often implemented in a rush, the program experienced unnecessary teething problems that required a sizable amount of time and money to correct."

[19] Wiesner (1988:113, 136–8, 144, 243–4, 357).

similar percentages of allegiance and territorial control that Lippman may have perceived as two unrelated matters.

5.4. CAUSAL PATHS FROM CONTROL TO COLLABORATION

A common causal mechanism that translates control into collaboration is coercion and survival maximization: the imposition of control allows the effective use of violence, thus deterring defection; opponents are identified and flee, are neutralized, or switch sides. The rest of the population complies, while some people may switch their preferences to side with the ruler. Although violence is an important channel though which control spawns collaboration, it is not the only one. I identify six additional mechanisms that translate control into collaboration: shielding, "mechanical ascription," credibility of rule, the provision of benefits, monitoring, and self-reinforcing by-products. By enabling these mechanisms, violence matters indirectly more than directly.

First, as already suggested, the force inherent in control solves collective action problems and deters opposition via coercion. In Tilly's (1992:70) words, "coercion works; those who apply substantial force to their fellows get compliance." Shy's (1976:179) study of individual motivations during the American Revolution confirms "the brutally direct effects on behavior, if not on opinions, of military power." As a Nicaraguan peasant put it, "Those with arms give the orders" (Horton 1998:207).[20] In short, collaboration can be tacit, the product of "no alternative," or "the necessity of the moment." As a resident of the rebel-held "demilitarized zone" in Colombia put it (Forero 2000:A3), "People don't really have the chance to make their own decisions. They don't have a choice. They just go along with this thing."[21] Clearly, combining credible threats of violence with the option to switch sides appears to be very effective. Survival can bend the people's posture (Henriksen 1983:75).[22]

Threats are not the entire story, as indicated by the second mechanism. Control also lowers the cost of collaboration with the established authority by shielding the population from competing sovereignty claims. It does so by providing protection from threats and violence made by the rival actor. "By the early 1780s," writes Roger Ekirch (1985:121) about North Carolina, "a majority of settlers were inclined to support whichever side could ensure a modicum of stability." German reports from occupied Ukraine stressed the vulnerability of potential collaborators to partisan reprisals owing to the absence of any German garrison

---

[20] Note that conscription requires control. Vietcong recruits were more likely to have been conscripted in rebel-controlled areas than in government-controlled ones (R. Berman 1974:69).

[21] See also Horton (1998:136); Kedward (1993:60); Shy (1976:13); Barnett and Njama (1966:151).

[22] Note that the same is true of many ethnic civil wars where incumbents offer the option of collaboration to ethnic minorities. In Punjab, "except for committed [Sikh] guerrillas, defiance was possible only when there was a measure of protection" (Pettigrew 2000:211); in Chechnya, the pro-Russian militia of Ramzan Kadyrov includes rebels who switched sides (Myers 2005:A4). Consequently, ethnic insurgents must also rely on terror (Collins 1999:128), even when they enjoy widespread sympathy among the population (e.g., Herrington 1997:22–3).

in the vicinity. Infrequent German patrols were simply not credible protection, and at that point, some villages had yet to see any German troops at all (T. Anderson 1995). Once the Vietcong were able to control large parts of Long An province in South Vietnam in 1960, "a vastly larger number of people moved into the Party and Party-controlled groups, because the threat of exposure and capture had been greatly reduced by the elimination of the government's 'eyes and ears'" (Race 1973:116). A former Vietcong confirms this point by describing how collaboration in the Mekong village of Ban Long depended on who controlled the larger nearby village of Vinh Kim: "Once Vinh Kim fell under the control of the Front, Ban Long's security would be assured and the tasks of motivating the people (meetings, celebrations, labor recruiting) would be carried out freely and easily. On the other hand, if Vinh Kim was under GVN control, Ban Long would have to pay a lot of attention to safeguarding itself from traitors, keeping secrets, and defending itself" (in Elliott 2003:268).

Third, over time, control produces "mechanical ascription" (Zulaika 1988:32). Long-lasting control spawns robust informational monopolies that socialize populations accordingly. In such circumstances, joining an armed group appears as a natural course of action for many: "In theory, people in the age group to fight have an option of two parties. In practice, with the exception of a few politically sophisticated ones, in rural areas such as Itziar [Basque country, Spain] they simply obeyed the official army's orders" (Zulaika 1988:32). This single option becomes the dominant cultural message and "the undisputed model of heroic activity" for adolescents. "Joining the IRA was not difficult in Meenagh Park," points out Toolis (1997:39); "it was the obvious career move for a young man with time on his hands." He adds: "At the kitchen table, I sat asking the same question over and over again – why had Tony joined the IRA? The logic of the question was unintelligible to the Doris family. In their minds the mere description of life in Coalisland was sufficient to explain why Tony had joined the IRA. My naïve question shook this natural assumption. They searched for ways to explain something that was so obvious it was inexplicable" (1997:40).

In many areas of South Vietnam it was natural for young men to join the Vietcong, which had been the effective government for more than twenty years (Bilton and Sim 1992:57; Meyerson 1970:91). A Taliban defector explained his actions in the following terms: "When the Taliban conquered Afghanistan, all the fighting men in Badakhshan joined them. There was not a single good man in the province from the Northern Alliance" (Filkins and Gall 2001:B2).[23]

The exclusive access to a recruitment pool generates cascades of support because the families of fighters tend to support the armed factions where their

---

[23] For Degregori (1998:131–2) this process results from a "demonstration" rather than a socialization effect – but, in effect, the same mechanism operates. Peruvian youth in the Andes, he points out, were inspired to join the Shining Path, "an organization that was on the rise, prestigious, with a demonstrated effectiveness. Such an organization would empower and transform them. Joining Shining Path had elements of a rite of passage or of initiation into a religious sect: an armed sect." A certain degree of coercion can help. In controlled territories, the fighters' families may act as hostages, to be punished if a fighter deserts (Cooper 1979:74).

younger members are fighting: "For the Chinese who had relatives or friends who had 'gone inside,'" Stubbs (1989:89) notes about Malaya, "there was no question where their allegiance lay." "Whatever her politics," Clutterbuck (1966:93) confirms, "it was no surprise if a mother smuggled food to her son, even though she faced years in jail if caught." As a Nicaraguan farmer told Horton (1998:xiii) about the contras: "Those boys are our sons, our neighbors"; in "rural communities where the contras had already established a foothold." Horton (1998:175) adds, "young men were reluctant to join an army fighting against their neighbors, friends, and even family." Conversely, when the U.S. and the South Vietnamese governments improved their "pacification" efforts and brought more areas under their control, they relied increasingly on local militias, which produced a similar effect (Moyar 1997:313). This is well understood by political actors. The Chinese Communists produced a propaganda verse to that effect:

> If a father gets his son to enlist
> The revolution will take this to heart.
> If a son gets his father to enlist
> He'll be forever revolutionized.
> If an elder brother gets a younger brother to enlist,
> The roots of poverty will soon be excised.
> If a younger sister gets an elder brother to enlist,
> Only then may the roots of wealth reach deep.
> If a younger brother gets an older brother to enlist,
> The Nationalist Army will be smashed to bits.
> If an elder sister gets a younger brother to enlist,
> Victory will soon be ours.
> If a wife persuades her husband to enlist,
> There'll be no worries in the family.
> (Levine 1987:155)

This process explains two oft-noted features of rebel movements: their bulk is usually made up of natives of the region where they operate rather than people who come from other areas to join them (Geffray 1990:39; Barton 1953:70); and, after crossing a certain threshold, tiny groups tend to grow exponentially: Degregori (1998:132) compares the rise of the Shining Path in the Andes during the early 1980s to wildfire. An Algerian woman described to Baya Gacemi (1998:109, 185) the remarkable speed with which her co-villagers first supported the Islamist GIA rebels and, three years later, when the rebels began to be defeated, how they joined the government militia and began informing on the rebels. This initial growth feature is often mistakenly interpreted as proof that these insurgencies articulate very real and widespread popular grievances. Of course, they may, but the point is that exponential growth is observationally equivalent with, and potentially endogenous to, the cascade mechanism.

Fourth, control signals credibility – both the short-term credibility of immediate sanctions, as well as the long-term credibility of benefits and sanctions based on expectations about the outcome of the war. Civilians would rather side with the (expected) winner than the loser.[24] Russian peasants were more inclined to collaborate with the Germans opportunistically while German fortunes seemed favorable and German forces had the upper hand in the partisan war; in contrast, when the Germans were perceived as failing to subdue the partisans, their confidence in the strength of the German army declined and they were more inclined to support or even join the partisans (Hill 2002:43; Cooper 1979:27). U.S. advisers in Vietnam "noticed that rises and declines in the level of Allied military activity tended to produce rises and declines in the rates of Communist desertion in an area" (Moyar 1997:110). In his partly autobiographical novel, Fenoglio (1973:296–7) observes that peasants in the Italian mountains helped the anti-Fascist partisans,

uniquely in exchange of the guarantee that we were going to win, that they would find their harvest, their flocks, their peaceful trade between fairs and markets, once this dirty story of Germans and Fascists had ended once and for all. Now, after the rough [partisan defeat] in Alba, they still had to give, to help, to risk their heads and dwellings, but the victory and the liberation were hazily remote. For months, they helped us smiling and laughing, confidently asking many questions; now they started to help silently, then almost grudgingly, at least with mute complaints, increasingly less mute.

It is often noted that insurgents receive most new recruits after two types of events: indiscriminate incumbent violence against civilians, and successful insurgent engagements against the incumbents.[25] Between 10 and 20 percent of the partisans in 1944 were former collaborators of the Germans; as it became clear that the Germans would lose the war, even more people flocked to the partisans: many were known as "hubbies," Soviet soldiers who had fallen behind, married local girls, and expected to sit out the war, but were eventually compelled to join the partisans (Cooper 1979:70–2). This is why groups trumpet their victories and attempt to hide their defeats (e.g., Tone 1994:109). Obviously, the best indicator that a group is winning the war is a decisive shift in control. The Vietcong popularity in the Hua Nghia province of South Vietnam soared in 1965–6, when many hamlets became virtually off limits to government officials: "At this time, it was not necessary to use threats or terror to obtain" support, a peasant told Herrington (1997:29); "it was given willingly because the people were nearly certain that the future lay with the Communists." Race (1973:39–40) describes how the Vietminh won the support of peasants in Long An province during the war against the French: "The peasantry had *seen* the landlords run, they had *seen* the village councils forced to sleep in outposts and to move in the countryside with armed escorts. As night fell in the countryside, the peasants saw where lay the power of the conflicting sides: the Vietminh slept with the people, the village councils slept with the soldiers in the outposts."

Conversely, when incumbents are able to signal credibly that they will win, many civilians will shift their support away from the rebels and toward them

---

[24] More precisely: few would ever join a side they thought was losing (Hartford 1989:122). See also Manrique (1998:204); Herrington (1997:25); Lichbach (1995:68); Coleman (1990); Sansom (1970:226–7).

[25] Tucker (2001:90); Laqueur (1998:317); Wickham-Crowley (1991:43); Debray (1967).

(Cann 1997:104). In the Philippines, denunciations of actual or suspected insurgents "rose sharply" after the antiguerrilla campaign began to show signs of success (Barton 1953:129). Many Peruvian peasants shifted their support toward the army because "by 1990, most villagers realized that the military was not about to 'collapse before the glorious advances of the people's war,' as the first cadre had promised in 1982" (Starn 1998:229–30). A Pakistani officer who fought in Bangladesh in 1971 recalls that "The Bengalis' behaviour followed the fluctuations in the fate of insurgency operations. They usually sided with the winning party. If our troops were around, the people were apparently with us, but when they were withdrawn, they welcomed their new masters (the [rebel] Mukti Bahini) with full warmth" (Salik 1978:101). In a world where expectations about the outcome matter and where information is mostly local, local control may signal dominance and eventual victory.[26]

Fifth, control makes possible the provision, when available, of all kinds of benefits intended to generate loyalty – "hearts and minds." Under conditions of incomplete or no control, such programs are guaranteed to fail (Harmon 1992; Clutterbuck 1966). As Machiavelli argues in *The Prince*, there can be no good laws where there are no good armies. Insurgents are able to lower or eliminate tenant rents to landlords only where they are able to exercise control (Wood 2003). The Vietcong were able to implement land reform programs where they exercised control rather than in those places where the peasants were more exploited (Elliott 2003:504). In fact, rents to landlords were directly related to the degree of control exercised by the two rivals: the higher the degree of Vietcong control, the lower the rents. The direction of causality ran from control to rents, as peasants living close to major roads and military posts paid much higher rents (Sansom 1970:60–1).

Sixth, control facilitates direct monitoring and population control. Direct monitoring requires better and more extensive administration, which is impossible in the absence of control; in turn, administration reinforces control. Once an area is placed under control, processes such as the registration of inhabitants and the compilation of detailed lists of the population of every locality become possible. The Japanese were able to "detect resistance organization early enough to nip it in the bud" only in areas that the Chinese Communists considered "enemy-occupied" or "weak guerrilla areas" (Hartford 1989:95). In Malaya, the government "extended its administrative net over the population" in the context of its counterinsurgency policy (Stubbs 1989:163); "in areas where the population were reasonably secure and where the methods used by police and military organizations for collecting intelligence were efficient, the greatest amount of information was collected" (Jones and Molnar 1966:29). The rise of the Vietcong reflected a similar process: "First the GVN posts were neutralized, then the intelligence stopped coming. With no intelligence, the larger GVN units were rendered ineffective, and the dangers for GVN agents increased even more" (Elliott 2003:424). A 1942 German report from the occupied Soviet Union made

[26] What is true of civilians is also true of combatants. See Finley (1994:101) and R. Berman (1974:178–9).

this point: "The appointment of reliable mayors and indigenous policemen *in communities recently cleared of partisans* has proved to be an effective device for preventing the formation of new bands in such communities and in the adjacent woods. The mayors and police, in conjunction with German troops in the vicinity and with secret field police and military police detachments, watch closely over the pacified areas, paying particular attention to the registering and screening of all persons newly arrived in the area" (in Cooper 1979:46; emphasis added).

Seventh, control spawns a self-reinforcing dynamic. Because some areas are controlled early on by one political actor, they may develop a reputation of being loyal to this political actor: the Djacovica valley in Kosovo was reputedly pro-KLA, and the villages of the Shamali plain in Afghanistan were perceived as supporting the Northern Alliance. Irrespective of whether this reputation truly reflects a majority preference, it may lead to indiscriminate reprisals (or the expectation thereof), turning potentially accidental or misperceived strongholds into real ones. "Even if it were not true that everyone in the town 'adored' the guerrillas," writes Mary Roldán (2002:243–4) about a Colombian town, "the very fact that the authorities thought so and assumed that the town as a whole could not be trusted, encouraged and reinforced a sense of local identity and collective purpose. This sense of collective involvement enabled local inhabitants to justify having taken up arms against the government." On the Korean island of Chejudo, insurgents were strongest in the villages closest to the mountains; as a result the government forces labeled as enemy territory all areas lying five kilometers from the coast and treated them accordingly (Yoo 2001). In Kenya, Mau Mau instructions included the rule that "warriors were entitled to take by force any foodstuffs in the gardens and livestock concentrated at any Government centers irrespective of whether they belonged to friend or foe" (Barnett and Njama 1966:195). This was the case in the Filipino village of San Ricardo studied by Kerkvliet (1977:166), the Vietnamese village of My Thuy Phuong studied by Trullinger (1994), and the RENAMO-held areas in northern Mozambique studied by Geffray (1990:71).

Such behavior tends to reinforce the association between a political actor and the underlying population. As Dallin et al. (1964:329) point out about the German-occupied Soviet territories, "the survival of the partisans became a prerequisite of [the population's] own survival, since their fate was certain should the Germans reoccupy the area." "Residents in Japanese garrisoned districts [on the island of Leyte, Philippines], particularly the *poblacion* or town center, and the local officials," Lear (1961:27) points out, "came to be branded as ipso facto pro-Japanese." "Lots of guerrillas" a participant recalled, "told me: 'Tacloban people, pro-Jap. They do not fight Jap, they live in Jap town, therefore they pro-Jap. If I catch Tacloban man, I kill him.'" As a result, the inhabitants of Tacloban "did not like the guerrillas. They were afraid of guerrillas, and they had reason" (Lear 1961:28).

Thus, what may have been initially an accident of location may generate new and enduring political identities. Consider the following description of how a small town in northern Spain went from being deeply divided to supporting only one side *once* the civil war began (Lison-Tolosana 1983). The shift resulted from the aggregation of individual strategies of survival maximization after the town found itself in the Nationalist zone; once the local Republican leaders were decimated in the first days of the war, all the young men, irrespective of their family's prewar political affiliation, were drafted into the Nationalist army, fought against the Republic, and "became" Nationalists. This endogenous preference shift was reflected in subsequent patterns of religious practice, where observance serves as a proxy for support for the Nationalist cause: after the Nationalist troops occupied the town, the number of those *not* fulfilling their Easter Duties dropped from 302 in 1936 to 58 in 1937. Initially the result of repression and fear, this shift eventually produced new, real, and enduring identities. Lison-Tolosana (1983:190, 196, 290) was able to establish that, whereas the generation that held power in the town before the civil war was divided between Republicans and Nationalists, the next generation was united and Nationalist. This pattern is confirmed by Freeman's (1970:24) study of a Castilian village that likewise fell under Nationalist control as soon as the war began. Young men were drafted into the Nationalist army, and "their former loyalties are hard to discern today." In contrast, Seidman (2002:38) reports that 80 to 85 percent of wage earners who found themselves in the Republican zone during the Spanish Civil War joined a party or union only after the civil war erupted – and did so for practical rather than ideological motivations. Note that whether villages or towns found themselves in the Nationalist or Republican zone was, for most of them, a matter of accident. These examples are consistent with an interpretation of the Spanish Civil War as shaping preferences rather than just reflecting them.

These new identities may turn ascriptive. As Germaine de Staël (1818:33) remarked, "to kill is not to extirpate ... for the children and the friends of the victims are stronger by their resentments, than those who suffered were by their opinions." Many people branded as kulaks in the Soviet countryside between 1927 and 1935 were not wealthy peasants but rather White army veterans or their relatives (Viola 1993:78). The magnitude of such "genealogical witch-hunts" is suggested by Stalin's 1935 announcement that "sons were no longer responsible for the sins of their fathers" (Viola 1993:80). Hart (1999:294) recounts how, when he was in a pub in Cork County, Ireland, his companions pointed to a middle-aged man and announced, "Here comes the informer now." This man was far too young to have been alive in the 1920s during the Irish Civil War. "Oh yes, I was told afterwards," Hart recounts, "it was his father who had been an informer. They were not sure what he had done to warrant the charge, but 'the informer' was what he had been called behind his back even after, and 'the informer' his son remained." The Chinese Communists institutionalized the identities that emerged from the civil war by developing a nomenclature of "five red types," three of which derived directly from choices made during the civil war: revolutionary cadres, revolutionary soldiers, and dependents of revolutionary martyrs (the two remaining types were workers and poor and lower-middle-class peasants). These categories evolved into ascriptive groups according to the "blood pedigree theory," which was conveyed by couplets such as the following one:

If the father's a hero, the son's a good chap;
If the father's a reactionary, the son's a bad egg.
            (Chang 1992:285; L. White 1989:222)

The relationship between control and collaboration is theoretically significant because it undermines the widespread assumption that joining an insurgent organization is always a highly risky behavior (thus, automatically turning recruitment into a collective action problem). Consider William H. McNeill's (1947:80–1) description of the process of joining the ELAS insurgent army in Greece, for whom the puzzle to be explained is not recruitment but the absence of more recruits:

> In actual fact, a soldier in ELAS lived a good deal better than did the ordinary peasant, and did not have to work with the same drudging toil. He further had the psychological exhilaration of believing himself a hero and the true descendant of the robber klefti who had fought in the War of Independence and were enshrined in the Greek national tradition. Under the circumstances, many a peasant's son found himself irresistibly attracted to the guerrilla life; and an over abundant peasant population made recruitment easy. Fewer came from towns; life was relatively comfortable there, and EAM had other work for townsmen, organizing strikes or serving as propagandists among the more illiterate peasants. From the very beginning the chief factor that limited the number of the guerrillas was lack of weapons.

Given the impact of control on collaboration, it is not surprising that observations about popular support and individual commitment often point to accident, contingency, and chance.[27] Alexander Dallin et al. (1964:336) argue that decisions to side with the Germans or the partisans in the occupied Soviet Union were largely dependent on the "accident of which regime was stronger and happened to control a given area." Lear (1961:237) reached a similar conclusion about the Japanese occupation of the Philippine island of Leyte: "What we are trying to point out by these and other possible examples is that to a large extent chance decreed what motives would be victorious in the inner struggle of competing motives determining whether an individual in Leyte was to be guerrilla or collaborationist." In Greece, "almost half as many young men from [the village of] Kerasia served in the national army as joined the guerrillas. Accidents of call-up and timing probably decided who served in which forces as much or more than ideological conviction. But once committed, one way or the other, a man found it difficult to change sides safely" (McNeill 1978:154). Chris Woodhouse (1948:58–9), the commander of the Allied Military Mission to the Greek Partisans during the country's occupation, describes the "choice" of a Greek peasant:

> He was living in his mountain village in 1942.... [H]e joined the left-wing resistance movement, because it was the first in the neighborhood. (They were on top then, so he was right.)...It happened that he joined the movement which was dominated by the Communists, though he was no Communist: he might as easily have happened in other circumstances to join the Security Battalions formed to fight the Communists, though he would still not have been pro-German. He would not have been a recognisably different individual if things had happened otherwise; but recognisably different things would have befallen him. His fate did not rest in his own hands, but in the chances that brought him into contact with men from above the horizontal line [i.e., outsiders]; *chances that were largely geographical*. If he lived in one part of the mountains, he was more likely to be

---

[27] Loyd (2001:48–50); Tucker (2001:61); Livanios (1999:197); Laqueur (1998:99); Mackenzie (1997); Todorov (1996:94); Chang (1992:449); Henderson (1985:41); McNeill (1947:134).

in contact with the Communist influence first; if in another, with the non-Communist resistance; if in the plains, with the Security Battalions and the collaborating authorities; and so on. (emphasis added)

As this passage suggests, "chance" is another name for a warring party's access to a segment of the population, which, in turn, is largely determined by control. From the preceding discussion, I derive the following proposition:

Proposition 1   The higher the level of control exercised by an actor, the higher the rate of collaboration with this actor – and, inversely, the lower the rate of defection.

5.5. THE DISTRIBUTION OF CONTROL

If collaboration is endogenous to control, then what determines the distribution of control? There are good reasons to think that control hinges largely on military effectiveness; in turn, this type of effectiveness is often (but not always) determined by geography. Because it is improbable that political preferences shape geography, the direction of causality seems obvious. This is not to say that political preferences are irrelevant. As pointed out previously, where political preferences and military resources overlap, as in the case of ethnic minorities that live clustered in isolated and rough terrain, prewar cleavages and geography will likely reinforce each other (Toft 2003). However, where no overlap exists, either because geography is unfavorable (e.g., an ethnic minority that is concentrated in cities) or because a rival actor can effectively muster superior military resources (e.g., a strong incumbent presence in a mountainous ethnic minority enclave), geography will tend to trump popular preferences in producing control.

Control has a clear territorial foundation: rule presupposes a constant and credible armed presence – a fact well understood by practitioners. Mao used to point out that geographical conditions "are an important, not to say the most important, condition for facilitating guerrilla war" (in Benton 200:714); he stressed that without "base areas" it was impossible to sustain guerrilla warfare (in Bruno Shaw 1975:208–9). As an American participant in the Vietnam War realized, control at the microlevel means establishing "suzerainty" over each village (West 1985:191). Armed actors can threaten credible sanctions only where they are able to sustain a military presence; their absence is an open invitation to their rivals. A striking and recurring feature of irregular war is how space shapes control. Towns, plains, key communication lines, and accessible terrain in general tend to be associated with incumbent control, whereas mountains and rugged terrain are generally insurgent strongholds; the location of insurgents is best predicted by variables such as terrain and distance from provincial military bases.[28] The incumbents' presence in remote or inaccessible areas is, at least

---

[28] Kocher (2004); Fearon and Laitin (2003); Hill (2002:44); Shaw (2001:154); Yoo (2001); Zur (1998:82); Tone (1994:13); Tong (1991; 1988); Brustein and Levi (1987); Schofield (1984:315); Crow (1985:129); O'Sullivan (1983); Wolf (1969:292–3); Salik (1978:101). Rough terrain is not synonymous with mountains; plains can sometimes offer an environment favorable to guerrilla

initially, limited to fortified villages and towns, while the insurgents' influence in towns is, at least initially, limited to clandestine organizations. Of course, geography should not simply be understood to mean "terrain." Geffray (1990:53) found that the location of RENAMO bases in Mozambique was a function not just of remoteness and distance from local administrative centers where incumbent forces were garrisoned, but also of proximity to administrative district boundaries. Apparently, RENAMO strategists found that these locations allowed them to benefit from the government's bureaucratic ineptitude, as local authorities tended to reject counterinsurgency jurisdiction when they could.

That military effectiveness as determined by geography generally trumps prewar political and social support in spawning control is best suggested by the following regularity: incumbents tend to control cities, *even* when these cities happen to be the social, religious, or ethnic strongholds of their opponents, whereas the insurgents' strongholds tend to be in inaccessible rural areas, *even* when rural populations are inimical to them.[29]

Insurgents tend to be uniformly weak in cities, although cities are often their prewar strongholds. Observers often note that many big cities in countries in the midst of civil wars look normal and peaceful (e.g., Butaud and Rialland 1998:124). Urban areas are inimical to rebels because it is easier for incumbents to police and monitor the population (Kocher 2004; Trinquier 1964:18; Kitson 1960:78); the collection of information through blackmail and bribes is facilitated because regular contacts between handlers and informers are possible. As a result, urban insurgents are particularly vulnerable to penetration and information leaks, as suggested by the cases of Northern Ireland and Palestine; and once identified, insurgents can be easily defeated by the superior force of incumbents. Urban guerrilla warfare is uncommon – and summarily dismissed by counterinsurgency experts (Blaufarb and Tanham 1989:15–16). As Trinquier (1964:71) puts it, "the most vulnerable part of the enemy organization is in the towns. It is always within the control of the army troops to occupy it, and a police operation . . . can destroy it." Fidel Castro remarked that the city was the "grave of the guerrilla" (Laqueur 1998:xix, 333).[30]

---

war, as suggested by the Vendean "bocage" in France (fields surrounded by tall hedges of bushes, narrow sunken roads, and dispersed villages, hamlets, and farmsteads). Other examples include the thick forests and swamps of Ukraine, Belorussia, and Russia; the rice fields of the Mekong Delta in Vietnam; the swamps and inundated plains of the Henan in China or Malaysia; and the thick orange groves of the Mitidja in Algeria.

[29] In this respect, civil war stands opposite to crime: cities are much more difficult to police for states than rural areas (C. Friedrich 1972:26–7).

[30] From this perspective, the inability of the United States to pacify several Iraqi cities in 2003–5 is a clear indicator of the numerical inadequacy of its military forces. This was eventually acknowledged publicly. A U.S. Marines commander said that "cities like Ramadi and Samarra had been allowed to slip into insurgents' hands largely by default, as the Americans began to concentrate their limited resources on other areas, like protecting the new government and critical pieces of infrastructure. Offensive operations based on intelligence," he added, "were a lower priority" (Filkins 2004:15). American forces were stretched so thin that soldiers even logged scheduled patrols that never took place – known as "ghost patrols" (Packer 2003:72).

The Chinese case is instructive. Mao knew well the dynamics of cities and insurgency: "As for the big cities, the railway stops and the areas in the plains which are strongly garrisoned by the enemy, guerrilla warfare can only extend to the fringes and not right into these places which have relatively stable puppet regimes" (in Bruno Shaw 1975:209). The destruction of the Chinese Communist Party's urban infrastructure was close to total by 1927 (Schran 1976), and even though the Communists were able to return to the cities following the defeat of the Japanese, they had to abandon most of them once again, unable to withstand the pressure from the Kuomintang (Chang 1992:103). Benton (1999:729–30) shows how "armies, not classes, made the Chinese Revolution." He concludes that "class struggle . . . did not well up from below, as a precondition for [the Chinese Communists'] triumph, but was whipped up from above, after they had achieved power by coopting and reorganizing the groups and networks that honeycombed rural China." As a Chinese Communist strategist summarized, "The enemies are the city gods, but we are the village deities" (in Wou 1994:222). The Algerian case offers a test of sorts. During the first half of the 1950s, two nationalist organizations were competing to lead the struggle against the French, the rural-based FLN and the urban based MTLD. Gilbert Meynier (2004:422–3) argues that the FLN prevailed over the MTLD precisely because of its rural connections.

The experience of occupied southern towns during the American Civil War supports this point as well. Garrisoned southern towns, whose citizens lived constantly in the presence and under the thumb of the occupying northern army, were places seething with hostility. On top of their ideological dislike of the Yankees, these towns suffered from unemployment, a severe housing shortage, skyrocketing inflation, and reduced supplies of food, fuel, clothing, medicine, and other basic commodities. As a Union general put it, "The people are suffering for want of almost all the necessaries of life." Naturally, all this further reinforced the existing feelings of bitter hostility vis-à-vis the occupiers. Yet, Ash (1995:82) concludes, "of all the citizens of the occupied South, those in the garrisoned towns posed the least threat to the Federal army, for armed resistance there was out of [the] question." The likelihood of internecine conflict between secessionist majorities and unionist minorities was also greatly reduced because "the secessionists were fundamentally impotent and the Unionists fundamentally invulnerable, thanks to the constant presence of Federal troops" (Ash 1995:122).

The anecdotal evidence is substantial. When the Greek Communist guerrillas attacked the town of Edessa, a known leftist stronghold, they found that the local population failed to assist them, and discovered that the government troops were never threatened from the rear (Vettas 2002:211). In Vietnam, "urban" became a synonym for government-controlled areas (Elliott 2003:1051; Meyerson 1970:16). The Algerian FLN rebels were unable to control any cities and were eventually defeated in Algier's Casbah despite their initial strength there (Aussaresses 2001:41).[31] Although cities in the Portuguese colonies of Africa were critical for the preparation of the insurgency, they did not experience any

---

[31] Rejali (2004b) points out that the French won the battle of Algiers because they were able to destroy the insurgent infrastructure through population control and the recruitment of a large

significant action because the use of informers, curfews, dragnets, and censorship "impaired guerrilla mobilisation" (Henriksen 1976:384). Among the reasons why Biafrans refrained from engaging in guerrilla warfare was the "close concentration of towns" within Biafra and the concomitant absence of "hide-outs" – rather than the absence of a population supporting the independentist cause (Madiebo 1980:105). In El Salvador, state repression deterred opposition in urban areas while intensifying resistance in many rural areas (Stanley 1996:4). In Colombia, "state forces frequently control the centers of larger towns and cities, where municipal government buildings are located," but "the state's authority evaporates" in outlying neighborhoods (Fichtl 2004:3).

Further confirming the importance of military resources in generating control and hence collaboration is the oft-noted propensity of villages located near central roads to collaborate with incumbents. A British officer (Hammond 1993:137) noted that Greek villages that had "the misfortune" to lie "on or near the main roads" of Macedonia tended to collaborate with the German occupation army, the same situation as in Vietnam (Sansom 1970:60–1) and Rhodesia, where such villages were also more susceptible to being labeled "sell-outs" by Zimbabwean guerrillas because "their location close to the roads meant that they were more often visited by soldiers than guerrillas" (Kriger 1992:208).[32] Whereas "modernizing" villages near main roads had been among the first to respond to revolutionary appeals, they were also more likely to be controlled by the government, and "as the risks of political action escalated during the middle and late 1960s, the gap between political attitudes and behavior widened, and many revolutionary sympathizers became inactive when the dangers became too great or, in some cases, adopted a clandestine role so deeply hidden that it often amounted to a temporary cessation of revolutionary activities" (Elliott 2003:589). The availability of external support for insurgents turns the combination of terrain and proximity to borders into a strong predictor of insurgent control.

In pronounced contrast, rural areas tend to be inimical to incumbents, often regardless of their prewar political preferences. A high-ranking American officer serving in the Dominican Republic in 1921, argued that the construction of roads would stifle the insurgency: "A highway would bring the people more in contact with the Capital, thus giving the Central Government an opportunity to control political conditions" (in Calder 1984:164). An examination of both prewar and postwar electoral returns in the Peloponnese region of southern Greece suggests that the Right tended to be stronger in the mountains, and the Center-Left and Left stronger in the plains and towns. Yet, the war reversed this relation. A British agent in occupied Greece reported about the collaborationist Security Battalions that "they have lost their popularity in the mountains but in coastal areas and large towns they are looked upon as the lesser evils."[33]

---

number of informers, not through torture as suggested by Gilles Pontecorvo in his famous film *The Battle of Algiers.*

[32] The same appears to have been the case in the occupied Soviet Union (Cooper 1979:45).

[33] "Second Report of Colonel J. M. Stevens on Present Conditions in Peloponnese (24 June 1944)," PRO, HS 5/669/S6557.

"Rurality" is a proxy for various causal mechanisms, including the ability of combatants to hide without being denounced because of rural norms of solidarity and honor; higher levels of tolerance among rural people to threats of violence; a tradition of rebellion reinforced by norms of reciprocity, which leads to mass participation in antistate activities ranging from contraband and banditry to full-fledged rebellion; and the fact that an economy based on subsistence farming tends to favor armed resistance more than one based on wage labor. Perhaps most important, the dispersion of population settlements in rural environments impedes policing (Kocher 2004); it is easier to enforce a curfew in a town than in a large rural area because taxing and monitoring hundreds or even thousands of hamlets exposes small army detachments to ambush (Tone 1994:13).[34] Hofheinz (1969:76) attributes the realization of "the highest rates of mobilization and participation in Communist politics" in the "rear area base counties" because "of the security provided by terrain and distance." Communist insurgents on the Korean island of Chejudo and in Malaya were linked so closely to the mountains that they came to be known as "mountain," "hill," or "jungle people" (Yoo 2001; Kheng 1983:168). My informants in Greece often referred to the insurgent and incumbent camps using exclusively geographical identifiers: they talked about those "up" and those "down." Even within rural regions, insurgents are more likely to obtain collaboration in the roughest and most remote areas (Horton 1998:126; Nordstrom 1997:99; Escott and Crow 1986:376; Kitson 1960:124).

This insight allows the reinterpretation of some findings that take ideology or ethnicity as the main causal variable of violence. Timothy Gulden (2002) found that in Guatemala more than half of the army killings took place in municipalities in which the Mayas made up between 80 and 90 percent of the population (Mayas make up less than 8 percent of the total population in the country as a whole). Based in part on this finding, he claims that this violence constitutes an instance of genocide. However, these municipalities are mostly rural and located far from centers of government control. They could just as easily have been targeted because they were located in areas of guerrilla presence as because they were Mayan. This raises the issue of endogeneity of grievances: did the guerrillas pick their location based on the presence of Mayan grievances or did they educate the Mayas – who just happened to live in terrain that favored insurgent activity – about their plight? Empirical evidence supplied by Stoll (1993:87) allows a partial separation of the two: the army's repression did not focus on areas where

---

[34] Gambetta (1993:109) finds that the Sicilian countryside is more difficult to police and, therefore, more agreeable to the Mafia than the cities. Not surprisingly, the Mafia is even able to exercise territorial control over some rural areas in Sicily. Tone (1994:162–6) compares the mountainous village of Echauri to the town of Corella, both in the Navarre; he attributes Echauri's insurgent outlook during the French presence to "solid community institutions [that] acted systematically to shelter individuals from the French regime" and Corella's collaborationist behavior to the character of its elites. However, the critical comparison for disentangling the effect of social structure from that of military resources would have been between a village similar to Echauri located just outside a French garrison. If my argument is correct, such a village would have collaborated with the French despite its social structure.

indigenous organizations (and presumably grievances) were strong and guerrillas had little presence, but rather in areas where the guerrillas were trying to organize the peasants despite weak indigenous organizations. In fact, the four areas of greatest government violence *follow* the insurgents' swath as it moved south to cut the Pan-American Highway.

The absence of overlap between prewar and war strongholds is visible where detailed studies are available. The Appalachians, the Cumberlands, and the Ozarks, Beckett (2001:11) notes, saw the rise of Confederate guerrillas during the American Civil War, even though these were the very areas within the Confederacy that most Union sympathizers inhabited. Following their defeat in the cities, the Chinese Communists staged a comeback from backward and isolated "border areas" where the prewar support was minimal if not nonexistent (Schran 1976). The urban populations of the German-occupied Soviet territories were more likely than rural ones to dislike the occupying authorities, partly because of their closer earlier identification with the Soviet regime and partly because of the more miserable conditions of life and work in the towns; yet, as Dallin et al. (1964:335) point out, "paradoxically, the partisan movement was largely a rural phenomenon. Research in a northern Greek region (Antoniou 2001) suggests that the electoral score of the Communist Party in 1936 was a bad predictor of the number of local men who joined the Communist-led resistance in 1942–4; instead, the distance from the town that served as the main base of the incumbent army proved to be an almost perfect predictor: the further away from the incumbent base a village was, the higher the proportion of local men who joined the rebels (prewar preferences appear to account for residual differences between equidistant villages). The French Communist guerrillas were very successful in the rural *département* of Lot, where "communist candidates had stood in only two of the three constituencies in 1936 and had polled only 4,183 votes out of 30,293" (Kedward 1993:131). Elliott (2003:908) reports that the government's bombing and pacification campaign in the Mekong Delta of South Vietnam caused a disjuncture between the Vietcongs' class basis and control zones. The insurgency in El Salvador did not take place in the western departments of Ahuachapán and Sonsonate, homes of a mass peasant rebellion and subsequent massacre in 1932 (as well as of large coffee estates), but began in the isolated and underpopulated departments of Morazan and Chalatenango, which were peopled mostly by smallholders and which provided favorable terrain for organized groups to launch a rebellion (Grenier 1999:84). Likewise, the RENAMO insurgency against the FRELIMO government in Mozambique developed in the same areas where the FRELIMO anticolonial insurgency had been strong; in contrast, areas that supported the Portuguese incumbents during the anticolonial war tended to side with the FRELIMO incumbents during the RENAMO insurgency (Geffray 1990:41). Nordstrom's (1997:98–9) research in the isolated province of Niassa in the same country corroborates this point by demonstrating that RENAMO was able to generate very strong control and collaboration (with minimal violence) in an area that was both isolated and a prewar stronghold of FRELIMO. Geography was a clear proxy for military effectiveness: "As far as I could tell," Nordstrom notes (1997:99), little government "military interest extended to these regions. RENAMO-held zones were essentially left to their own devices."

The Nicaraguan case allows a type of natural experiment, because it is possible to compare the behavior of the Sandinistas in their successive roles as insurgents and, later, as incumbents. This comparison suggests that popular allegiances were largely endogenous to the exercise of territorial control. During the "contra" phase of the war, the (incumbent) Sandinistas firmly controlled the towns but were absent from the mountains: "The only Sandinista presence in the mountains would be a military one" (Horton 1998:137). As a result, people in those areas supported the contras. Many of these mountainous contra zones, however, had supported the Sandinista guerrillas in the 1970s (1998:21–2). The opposite was true of the towns, which were controlled by the (Somozista) incumbents in the first phase of the war and the Sandinista (incumbents) in the second one. In Horton's (1998:21) words, "Hundreds of Sandinista Army soldiers were stationed in the town of Quilalí and as a result the town itself always remained firmly under FSMLN control." The population had no choice but to collaborate with them. In other words, whereas the Sandinistas *qua insurgents* based themselves in inaccessible rural terrain, they found themselves limited to cities when, *qua incumbents*, they faced the contra insurgency. In both cases, however, they obtained the collaboration of the population they ruled.

5.6. CONSTRAINTS ON MILITARY OPTIONS

If it is the case that full and permanent control over an area shapes civilian collaboration, then victory in civil war ought to be primarily a military task entailing the extension of control over the entire territory of a country. This much is conventional wisdom. In the words of a counterinsurgent, "There must be, above all, absolute determination to establish and retain a government police post intact and uncorrupt in every inhabited village. Authority must be re-established patiently, village by village, into the 'liberated' area, dealing with the easiest areas first" (Clutterbuck 1966:176).[35]

Civil wars, however, tend to take place in poor countries and they are protracted and inconclusive (Fearon and Laitin 2003; Fearon 2001). This stalemate reflects the rival actors' inability to establish full control over large areas of the country.[36] Fenoglio's (1973:157) description of the Italian Civil War in 1943–5 is widely applicable: "The partisans were too strong to be attacked on their hills – at least this was the impression they gave; at the same time, they were too weak and

---

[35] This view is, obviously, a reflection of a similar argument that links crime to police presence (C. Friedrich 1972:26).

[36] Long duration in civil war may reflect two different processes. While some areas are "frozen" under the control of one or both actors, others shift back and forth. For example, the Ukrainian capital Kiev changed hands fourteen times in two years during the Russian Civil War (Werth 1998:111; Figes 1996:698). The only "wildly changing detail" in the thick ledgers maintained by UN teams in Sudan "was the column marked 'held by' which described whose fiefdom each village fell from month to month" (Peterson 2000:237).

technically inept to be able to attack and dislodge the fascist garrisons in the towns of the plain."[37]

Once a civil war is on, the military requirements for the establishment and preservation of control over the entire territory of a country are staggering.[38] This general problem, common to foreign occupiers and native sovereigns, is aptly summarized by Toolis (1997:70): "No army can patrol all of the roads all of the time." A military attaché in Mozambique described it as the "big country, small army" problem (in T. Young 1997:150). A South Vietnamese official described it as a puzzle: "[W]e cannot stay with the people all the time. We come and go with operations by day, but we do not have enough strength to protect the people by night. I have yet to figure out how to protect a hamlet with thirty people. From a purely military viewpoint how can it be done? The Vietcong wait and wait, perhaps six months before they attack. We can build for two years, but they can destroy in one night. The person who finds the key to that puzzle has solved the problem" (in Race 1973:135).

Remarks about the numerical inadequacy of incumbent armies are commonplace. Of the counterrevolution in the country's western provinces, a French Republican general reported that the patriots "are so afraid, that we would need an entire garrison to guard every house" (in Dupuy 1997:133). A Union officer stationed in Missouri pointed out in 1863 that it would be impossible to exterminate the Confederate guerrillas "unless the government can afford to send ten soldiers for one guerrilla" (Fellman 1989:126). A British military report about the situation in Ireland in 1920 noted that "the police and military forces are too small to cope" (in Hart 1999:73). A Pakistani officer estimated that in order to successfully face the insurgency in Bangladesh, the Pakistani army would have needed 375,640 men as opposed to its actual force of 41,060 (Salik 1978:101). An American journalist reported that the Mozambican army needed more than a million men just to defend the country's infrastructure from the rebels but could only field thirty thousand (Finnegan 1992:95–6). The Rhodesian intelligence chief realized that demonstrations of force via army sweeps and air force bombings would be ineffective against Zimbabwean rebels because "the people in the rural areas would soon realise that such demonstrations could not be sustained and that a transient military presence could not enforce government policy" (Flower 1987:122). Finally, Forero (2001:A3) reports that in Colombia "the army is simply too small to cover the country. . . . And even when the army has carried out successful offensives, it has often been unable to set up a permanent presence."

A good illustration of this problem is supplied by the German occupation during World War II. The German forces assigned to fight against the various resistance movements were hopelessly inadequate for the task – nowhere more

---

[37] Perpetual war in weak states lacking military resources is averted through the use of indirect rule (Kocher 2004).

[38] Note that in times of peace, states are able to control their territory with much fewer resources that the same task requires from them during times of civil war. This suggests that the emergence of insurgencies cannot be simply accounted for by low levels of state control. Put otherwise, state capacity is a better argument for the dynamics of civil war than it appears to be for its onset.

so than in the Soviet Union. In an area of 43,000 square miles containing more than 1,500 villages and collective farms, the Germans had fewer than 1,700 men available for security duties, of whom only 300 were assigned to active measures against the partisans. In the central Soviet Union, the number of men of all types available for security duties was just 2 for every 3 square miles. "Although Hitler and the military and SS authorities came to understand the necessity of assigning considerable forces to secure the rear area, they were never able to make them available." Not surprisingly, the Germans were able to exercise only limited and very superficial control; vast areas that they simply abandoned quickly came under partisan control. Following a "mopping-up" operation in 1943, the German 221st Security Division reported that "the partisans had the opportunity... of reoccupying their former areas and thus making the success of these operations illusory.... Any removal of troops or a temporary withdrawal of troops from pacified areas resulted in reoccupation by partisans." As a German general put it, "With enough good troops, anything is possible." "The cause of the German failure," Cooper concludes "was both easy to analyse and impossible to rectify; it was simply, lack of troops."[39]

Even the U.S. military, with overwhelming resources in Vietnam, found it hard to overcome this problem: "We come here on an operation, and what does it prove?" remarked a U.S. soldier about a raid in a Vietcong-controlled village, in March 1969. "The VC will be back in control here tonight" (in M. Young 1991:240–1). The American military commander in Vietnam, General West-moreland, was often ridiculed for his incessant demands for more troops, but his defense was not without merit: "I never had the luxury of enough troops to maintain an American, Allied or ARVN presence everywhere all the time. Had I at my disposal virtually unlimited manpower, I could have stationed troops per-manently in every district or province and thus provided an alternative strategy. That would have enabled the troops to get to know people intimately, facilitating the task of identifying the subversives and protecting the others against intimi-dation. Yet to have done that would have required literally millions of men" (in Bilton and Sim 1992:34).[40] The same problem, only more acute, can be seen in American-occupied Iraq. For instance, the 800-men strong Fourth Infantry Division's 1-8 Battalion, based in the area of Balad, in the restive Iraqi province of Anbar, was responsible for nearly 750 square kilometers (Filkins 2005:55). Like-wise, only about 800 soldiers covered the area around the town of Rawa, which is the size of Vermont – and only 300 left their outpost on operations and never all

---

[39] Cooper (1979:45, 143–4, 153–4).

[40] Sheehan (2000:179) confirms this point. The "lack of sufficient American troops to occupy and hold ground when it has been wrested from the Communists," he pointed out, "is one of the major reasons for the extent of damage to civilian life and property." An additional problem is posed by the large proportion of personnel devoted to support in modern armies. Luttwak (2003) estimated that out of the 133,000 American men and women in Iraq, only 56,000 are combat-trained troops available for security duties, while the number of troops on patrol at any one time is no more than 28,000. See as well, Shepherd (2002:351); Tucker (2001:90); Fall (2000:199); Vargas Llosa (1998:137); Fisher (1997:50); Finley (1994:xi, 29); Tone (1994:80, 143–4); Ortiz Sarmiento (1990:132); Ekirch (1985:114); Li (1975:187); Beaufre (1972:66).

at the same time. As a result, "there is only a sporadic American military presence outside the few towns now occupied. Neither the Army nor the Marines maintain any permanent checkpoints" in the main regional road. The dearth of soldiers is critical because, as Colonel Stephen Davis, commander of Marine Regimental Combat Team 2, put it: "You can go through these towns again and again, but you can't get results unless you are there to stay" (in C. Smith 2005:A6).

The difficulty of establishing full and permanent control through sheer numbers puts a premium on the shrewd use and allocation of existing military resources, on resilience, as well as on the ability to claim outside assistance, especially at crucial moments. Limited resources place a premium on the effective use of violence. But what makes violence effective?

5.7. VIOLENCE AND DISCRIMINATION

According to Michael Hechter (1987:162), a key determinant of collaboration is the perceived probability of sanction. Cesare Beccaria pointed out that "the political intent of punishments is to instill fear in other men," while Jeremy Bentham defined deterrence in terms of the "intimidation or terror of the law" (Zimring and Hawkins 1973:75). In its simplest formulation, the theory of deterrence posits that threats can reduce the likelihood that certain actions will be undertaken. In a different formulation, deterrence by punishment is a method of retrospective inference via threats, so that whenever a wrong has been actually committed, the wrongdoer shall incur punishment (Kenny 1907). To Bentham we owe the main hypothesis: "The profit of the crime is the force which urges a man to delinquency: the pain of the punishment is the force employed to restrain him from it. If the first of these forces be the greater the crime will be committed; if the second, the crime will not be committed" (in Zimring and Hawkins 1973:75).

Yet we know that many crimes are committed despite known and credible threats. Katz (1988:12–51) shows that a substantial number of homicides are carried out by people who are indifferent to sanctions; these homicides, which he calls "righteous slaughters," emerge quickly, are fiercely impassioned, and lack premeditation. Bentham's account of deterrence has also been criticized as "mechanical" and based "upon false psychology"; it is argued instead that threats may sometimes generate a desire of noncompliance and that criminal phenomena are completely independent of penal laws. At the same time, it is widely recognized that most people refrain from crime to avoid sanctions. Thus, a reasonable degree of deterrence can be achieved.[41]

When are threats effective? Beccaria (1986:81) argued that sanctions must be public, prompt, necessary, minimal under the given circumstances, proportionate to the crimes, and established by law. Zimring and Hawkins (1973) stress three conditions: threats must be publicly known, persuasive, and personalized. Hechter (1987:151) argues that compliance is more likely when people are

---

[41] In Zimring and Hawkins's (1973:95) formulation, "It appears that the introduction of a threat as a barrier to committing a particular behavior is likely to cause members of a threatened audience to revise attitudes toward the desirability of the behavior."

required to meet highly specific obligations rather than nonspecific ones. These features can be subsumed, to some degree, under the distinction between *selective* (or *discriminate*) violence and *indiscriminate* violence.[42]

Both selective and indiscriminate violence are, in principle, instrumental forms of violence aiming to generate collaboration via deterrence. The distinction is based on the level at which "guilt" (and hence targeting) is determined.[43] Violence is selective when there is an intention to ascertain individual guilt. Because intentions are not always visible (though in many cases indiscriminate violence is publicized by political actors), one way to operationalize this distinction is by noting that selective violence entails personalized targeting, whereas indiscriminate violence implies collective targeting.[44]

In indiscriminate violence, also described by its legal designation, "reprisals," the concept of individual guilt is replaced by the concept of guilt by association: "If such people as are guilty cannot be found," proclaimed the German command in occupied Greece, "those persons must be resorted to, who, without being connected with the actual deed, nevertheless are to be regarded as co-responsible" (in Condit 1961:265–6). The specific rule of association varies and ranges from family to village, region, and nation. The most extreme form of indiscriminate violence is probably the one that selects its victims on the basis of membership in a nation or an ethnic or a religious group; it is often described as "random" violence and its archetypal example is a strain of Nazi terror in parts of occupied Europe. "On more than one occasion in the town of Athens," writes McNeill (1947:57), "a German patrol was sent out to the scene of the death of a German soldier, and there they arrested the first fifty persons who happened to walk down the street, lined them up against a wall and shot them out of hand." German terror in Warsaw during the same period is starkly described by Czeslaw Milosz (1990:90):

Once, in the first year of the War, we were returning from a visit to a mutual friend who lived in the country. As I remember, we were arguing about the choice of a train. We decided against the advice of our host to take a train leaving half an hour later. We arrived in Warsaw and walked along the streets feeling very satisfied with life. It was a beautiful summer morning. We did not know that this day was to be remembered as one of the blackest in the history of our city. Scarcely had I closed the door behind me when I heard shrieks in the street. Looking out the window, I saw that a general man-hunt was on. This was the first man-hunt for Auschwitz. Later millions of Europeans were to be killed there, but at the time this concentration camp was just starting to operate. From the first huge transport of people caught on the streets that day no one, it appears, escaped alive. Alpha

---

[42] Selective violence is personalized, but needs not be public, prompt, or necessary – though it often is; it is certainly minimal and proportionate when compared with indiscriminate violence.

[43] Because what matters is the level at which the targeting takes place, one can talk of violence that discriminates at the individual, local, or national level. However, I use the distinction between selective and indiscriminate violence because it captures the essential differences of targeting at the individual level versus any supra-individual level.

[44] Note that, contrary to widespread perception, selective violence can end up being, and often is, massive in scale. For example, the Vietcong are estimated to have selectively assassinated as many as 50,000 people in a decade and a half (Wickham-Crowley 1990:215).

and I had strolled those streets five minutes before the beginning of the hunt; perhaps his umbrella and his insouciance brought us luck.

Because such threats are completely unpredictable, they produce, at least initially, a paralyzing, turbulent, and irrational fear, scarcely permitting any thought, leading to the atomization of society (E. Walter 1969:25–6; Thornton 1964:81). In a book published in 1947, a group of Greek psychiatrists reported the results of a remarkable study on the effects of German terror on the population of Athens; they found that most people were paralyzed by the daily expectation of an "unpredictable and unknown misfortune" and the "incredible anxiety in front of the unknown which afflicted every individual fate" (Skouras et al. 1947:124–36). As long as the victims have no way to react against such violence, its effect is "to increase compliance with authority among those who feel they may be threatened" (L. White 1989:328). In other words, the population may be pushed into total passivity and political abdication.

Although random violence may work for a dictator (McAuley 1992:50; B. Moore 1954:169–70), it is much less likely to achieve its aims in the midst of a civil war, where the presence of a rival makes defection possible. First, random violence defeats deterrence because it destroys the possibility of anticipation of a forthcoming evil and, hence, the ability to avoid it: it erases the relationship between crime and punishment, thus abolishing the concept of transgression. Its sheer unpredictability makes everyone fear lethal sanctions regardless of their behavior: innocence is irrelevant and compliance is utterly impossible. A German report (in Cooper 1979:27) described the attitude of the average citizen in the occupied areas of the Soviet Union: "If I stay with the Germans, I shall be shot when the Bolsheviks come; if the Bolsheviks don't come, I shall be shot sooner or later by the Germans. Thus, if I stay with the Germans, it means certain death; if I join the partisans, I shall probably save myself." Under such conditions, "abstention ceases to seem a protection. Recruitment of insurgents goes up as risks of passivity and insurgency begin to equalise" (Aron 1966:170). Indeed, Nazi terror in Poland "left the Poles no other alternative but to *ignore* the occupier – either actively, by opposing him, or passively, by behaving as if he did not exist" (Jan Gross 1979:238):

> One would expect that noncompliance with German demands carried such drastic penalties that scarcely anyone would dare to defy them. But full compliance was impossible; terror continued and even intensified with time. The population quickly recognized the new logic of the situation: whether one tried to meet German demands or not, one was equally exposed to violence. . . . It makes no sense, in the context of random punishment, to style one's life according to the possibility of being victimized, any more than it makes sense to orient all of one's everyday acts to the possibility of an accident. (Jan Gross 1979:212)

Second, whereas compliance guarantees no security under conditions of indiscriminate violence, collaboration with the rival faction may both increase one's chances of survival and allow for a sense of normative integrity (Jan Gross 1979:202). In Poland, membership in the resistance made people more prudent and erased the false sense of security that was often fatal to those not involved in it; "conspirators" actively avoided capture by the Germans, while nonconspirators were much less careful in avoiding accidental contacts with the occupiers because they often felt that should they be arrested they would spend a few days in detention and later, once their innocence was established, they would be released. However, this assumption often proved fatal, given that there was little relationship between crime and punishment. "Conspirators" very often had much better identification papers than nonconspirators and, if apprehended, had already prepared satisfactory answers to the typical questions police would ask. When they were caught in a roundup, someone in the network would try to get them out of prison in time, or their families would be given money to bribe the appropriate officials. When threatened with arrest, blackmail, or denunciation, conspirators had vast organizational resources at their disposal: the organization would help them to disappear, find them a new place to live, and give them new employment or new documents (Jan Gross 1979:234–5).

Hence it is possible to argue that indiscriminate violence is of limited value since it decreases the opportunity costs of collaboration with the rival actor. A British counterinsurgent compared indiscriminate violence to "trying to catch fish in a weedy pond by splashing about with a rather widemeshed net as opposed to adopting the tactics of the pike, and lurking quietly in the weeds ready to snatch unsuspecting fish as they swim by" (Paget 1967:110). It is, therefore, possible to formulate the following proposition:

Proposition 2   Indiscriminate violence is counterproductive in civil war.

This proposition is a conjecture. Theoretical work on the related nexus between repression and dissent remains inconclusive (Lichbach 1987:297). Empirically, we lack controlled comparisons of outcomes in the presence and absence of such violence. Little attention has been paid to counterfactuals. For instance, we do not know how many insurgent armed actions would have taken place and how many people would have joined the rebels in the absence of indiscriminate violence. A few detailed studies show that indiscriminate violence was sometimes more successful than generally thought (Hill 2002; Hartford 1989).[45] At the same time, the anecdotal evidence weighs heavily in favor of this proposition. In the following chapter I return to this issue.

In contrast to indiscriminate violence, selective violence personalizes threats; if people are targeted on the basis of their actions, then refraining from such actions guarantees safety. Practitioners and observers agree that selective violence is the most efficient way to deter defection. In Robert Thompson's formulation (1966:25), "Terror is more effective when selective." As an American colonel in

---

[45] A Vietcong cadre argued that indiscriminate shelling by government forces in South Vietnam weakened the insurgency: "From experience, I have realized that the Front is strongest in villages which haven't been shelled and that, on the contrary, it weakens where the shellings happen frequently. To wage Front propaganda and to sow hatred against the GVN, Front cadres need quiet" (in Elliott 2003:767). Elliott concludes that little shelling favors the Vietcong but too much does not, presumably because no protection could be offered.

Vietnam put it, "You really have to use a surgeon's scalpel" (in Race 1973:238); Che Guevara (1998:91) recommended that "assaults and terrorism in indiscriminate form should not be employed." The Vietcong produced many official documents explaining the advantages of selective violence (e.g., Elliott 2003:266).

In practice, the distinction between selective and indiscriminate violence hinges on public perceptions since it is possible to pretend to be selective by indiscriminately targeting isolated individuals. As long as people perceive such violence to be selective, it will have the same effects as selective violence. If people do not perceive it as selective, the results will be the opposite, much like when they perceive selective violence to be indiscriminate. I discuss these issues in detail in Chapter 7.

The choice of whether to use selective or indiscriminate violence is heavily dependent on the quality of information available – one cannot discriminate without the information to discriminate – which itself is heavily dependent on the nature of the sovereignty exercised. Information requires collaboration, which requires a level of control sufficient to reassure those who can supply that collaboration. Although actors are less bound in their ability to perpetrate it, indiscriminate violence is less likely to work under circumstances of fragmented sovereignty. I address these questions in the following chapters.

5.8. CONCLUSION

This chapter has specified a theory of irregular war stressing the role of control in shaping civilian collaboration. A key point is that control – regardless of the "true" preferences of the population – precludes options other than collaboration by creating credible benefits for collaborators and, more importantly, sanctions for defectors. The distribution of control can be shaped by military means, because sufficient military presence raises the credibility of sanctions for defection; at the same time, however, military resources for the establishment of total control are typically lacking. Political actors thus turn to violence, but to be effective, violence must be selective.

The role of sovereignty in shaping the use of selective violence combines with the counterproductive effects of indiscriminate violence to set the remainder of the book's theoretical agenda: first, an account must be provided for the occurrence of indiscriminate violence; second, an analytical treatment of selective violence must be specified. The former is the object of the following chapter, while the latter is addressed in Chapter 7.

6

A Logic of Indiscriminate Violence

Je vois des malheureux, mais, en vérité, je ne puis trouver des coupables.

Stendhal, *L'abbesse de Castro*

We have by our own imprudencies & irregular proceedings made more Enemies than have become so from mere inclination.

General Stephen Drayton, North Carolina, 1781

Look at me – I hadn't wanted to fight, they made me!

A Chechen fighter, after a Russian atrocity

This chapter specifies the logic driving indiscriminate violence. Proposition 2 posits that indiscriminate violence is counterproductive in civil war contexts. If this is so, then why is it observed so often? Addressing this puzzle calls for a theory of indiscriminate violence.[1] I begin by examining how and when indiscriminate violence is observed. Next, I discuss its logic and specify the conditions under which it is counterproductive. I then review four arguments that account for why indiscriminate violence is observed, despite its apparent counterproductivity, including the specious observation of indiscriminate violence because of truncated or misinterpreted data, and its commission as a result of ignorance,

---

[1] This argument applies within the book's scope conditions: it presupposes that at least one actor intends to control the population against which violence is used. Indiscriminate violence may also be used to deport or exterminate particular groups. For example, secessionist insurgents may use indiscriminate violence against ethnic rivals to drive them off the territory they seek to control (e.g., Senaratne 1997:88). The same is the case in instances of "reciprocal extermination." In Lotnik's (1999) account of the Polish-Ukrainian clash of 1943–4, massacres of villagers targeted primarily the rival group. A former Polish partisan, Lotnik (1999:65), recalls his officer's talk on the eve of one of the first massacres: "Don't burn, don't loot. Just shoot young, able-bodied men. If anyone resists, make sure you shoot him before he shoots you. We have to teach them that they cannot take out selected Polish citizens and kill and torture them. We must teach them that they can't get away with that." Such cases are outside the book's scope conditions, which posit civilian compliance as a central goal.

cost, and institutional constraints. I argue that indiscriminate violence emerges, when it does, because it is much cheaper than its selective counterpart. Yet, any "gain" must be counterbalanced by its consequences. Thus, indiscriminate violence is more likely either under a steep imbalance of power between the two actors or where and when resources and information are low. In the absence of a resolution of the conflict, even indiscriminate actors are likely to switch to more selective violence.

6.1. THE INCIDENCE OF INDISCRIMINATE VIOLENCE

Like other forms of violence, indiscriminate violence may be used to achieve a variety of goals, such as exterminating particular groups, displacing people, plundering goods, or demonstrating a group's power and ability to hurt another group. Consistent with this book's scope conditions, my focus in this chapter is on the use of indiscriminate violence to control a population rather than simply to loot, displace, or eliminate it.[2]

Seen from this perspective, indiscriminate violence is, initially at least, a way to come to grips with the identification problem. "A major problem for the Philippine military," writes Berlow (1998:180), "was the one the Americans encountered in Vietnam: They couldn't figure out who the 'fish' were until they started shooting. To be on the safe side, Filipinos, like the Americans in Vietnam, erred on the side of overkill and assumed that anyone was an enemy until proven otherwise."[3]

Distinguishing between indiscriminate and selective violence at the aggregate level is difficult. It is, therefore, close to impossible to estimate the contribution made by each type of violence to the overall fatality count. Indiscriminate violence is much more visible than its selective counterpart and, as such, is thought to be more prevalent (Valentino 2004; Downes 2004). The emphasis on indiscriminate violence often reflects the tendency of many observers to designate as indiscriminate all kinds of extrajudicial killing, including instances of selective violence (e.g., Carlton 1994:1). For example, the killing by Iraqi insurgents of "Iraqi officers, civilians, Iraqi, American and coalition soldiers" is described

---

[2] Recall that this is an ideal-typical distinction. There are several examples of indiscriminate violence that begins as counterinsurgency on the cheap only to evolve into a process of haphazard quasi extermination, such as Darfur (Prunier 2005).

[3] Henderson's (1985:179–80) description of the attitude of the Colombian army during the *Violencia* could apply to almost any case: "The underlying assumption was that every farmer was a 'bandit,' or potentially one, and should be treated as such." As a man from Guatemala told Stoll (1993:97): "All the Ixils of Nebaj, Cotzal, and Chajul they considered guerrillas. They were afraid of their own shadow." According to Gardner (1962:152–3), "the average German soldier [in Greece] became something less than particular about whom he shot or captured. His reasoning was that any man found in the area was either an active guerrilla or in league with the local band. For this reason, German figures for guerrilla casualties were usually much higher than those announced by the *andartes* [Greek partisans]." Young men, in particular, caught in an operation zone in "enemy" territory during a mopping-up operation are particularly likely to be killed. In a letter to their son, the parents of a peasant from the Sarthe described to him in detail how three unarmed friends of his were killed by French Republican soldiers because they began to run when they saw the soldiers coming (Dupuy 1997:182–3).

as indiscriminate (Lins de Albuquerque and Cheng 2005:11). Zulaika (1988:85) writes of the "indiscriminate killings of chivatos (informers) and civil guards carried out by ETA."

The tendency to code all violence as indiscriminate is assisted by the scarcity of information: "The confused, unstable, and dangerous situation," writes Jagath Senaratne (1997:146) about Sri Lanka, "led many to believe that the violence was random and meaningless. The imputations of randomness by some observers (mainly journalists) was a result of the inability to see the many different strands of the violence . . . [and] to disaggregate 'the violence' into its components." Indeed, it is safe to say that rarely is noneliminationist violence totally random. Generally, the victims of indiscriminate violence are selected on the basis of a criterion, usually location. For example, the mass violence perpetrated by the Germans in Athens during the summer of 1944 targeted specific neighborhoods suspected of harboring Communist activity. Furthermore, an important part of this violence targeted specific individuals; neighborhoods were cordoned off, and their inhabitants taken to the central square where local hooded informers would finger individual suspects (I return to this point in section 6.5.1).

We simply do not know what the universe of civil war violence looks like. Nevertheless, descriptions of indiscriminate violence in civil war are numerous enough to suggest that no matter how bad our data, genuinely indiscriminate violence takes place often enough to warrant attention.

6.2. INFORMATION AND INDISCRIMINATE VIOLENCE

The preceding examples suggest that violence is indiscriminate when selection criteria are rough. This is the case when precise information is unavailable. An observable implication is the oft-noted association of indiscriminate violence with incumbents rather than insurgents.[4] Insurgents are almost always the first movers; having eliminated the state's presence in the areas they control, they set up village-based administrations that are able to collect the kind of information that allows them to address the identification problem effectively (Wickham-Crowley 1990:216–17). "While the party had a thousand eyes and a thousand ears," Carlos Iván Degregori (1998:143–4) observes about the Peruvian Shining Path, "the Armed Forces were blind or, rather, color-blind. They saw only black

---

[4] Surveys conducted in Vietnam found that refugees who moved away from their homes because of (indiscriminate) bombardment and ground operations tended to associate these actions with the incumbent regime, while refugees who moved because of (selective) terror and coercion tended to associate them with the insurgents (Wiesner 1988:111). See also Spencer (2000:131); Benton (1999:102–3); Horton (1998:127); Cribb (1991:151); Carmack (1988b:60); Calder (1984:159); Henriksen (1983:118); Armstrong (1964:41); Dallin et al. (1964:328). Linking indiscriminate violence to lack of information is consistent with empirical evidence from the former Yugoslavia and Israel showing that there is much more indiscriminate violence between the same groups when the victimizing group operates outside rather than inside state borders (Ron 2003). Ron provides a different explanation for this pattern, namely that borders have a significant effect on the conduct of war from the perspective of the regime, but the availability of information could be the causal mechanism accounting for the difference.

and white.... They did not perceive nuances; when they saw dark skin, they fired." Likewise, an observer noted that in Indochina "the French destroy at random because they don't have the necessary information" (in Leites and Wolf 1970:109), and a U.S. report (Barton 1953:138) pointed out that "the guerrillas have a more effective intelligence system than their opponents."

Incumbent indiscriminate violence usually takes place in the context of military operations known as "mopping up," "comb," "cordon and search," "search and destroy" or "scorched earth" campaigns that seek to encircle and liquidate insurgents and undercut an insurgency's civilian basis. These campaigns are often dubbed "pacification" campaigns.[5] The result is almost always uniform: indiscriminate violence. A U.S. officer, stationed in the Philippines in the beginning of the twentieth century, pointed out that "we do not know insurrectos and bad men from good ones, so we are often compelled to arrest all alike" (quoted in Linn 1989:139); a Filipino captured this problem when he described the U.S. Army as a "blind giant," powerful enough to destroy the enemy, but unable to find him (quoted in Linn 1989:160). When the U.S. Marines arrived in the province of Segovia in Nicaragua in 1927, they "had no practical way to distinguish between rebel sympathizers, supporters, and soldiers and 'peaceful civilians.' Facing these uncertainties, they opted to wage a brutally violent offensive against Segovian *campesinos* generally" (Schroeder 2000:39). Even pacification campaigns that claim a higher moral ground have resulted in significant indiscriminate violence, as suggested by more recent U.S. counterinsurgencies in Vietnam, Afghanistan, and Iraq (Kalyvas and Kocher 2005).

That indiscriminate violence is related to lack of information (rather than, say, ideology) is confirmed by the fact that insurgents do not shy away from this practice.[6] Insurgents use it when they lack information: against villages that openly support the incumbents by setting up local militias, in areas where their presence is limited (such as urban centers), and after their administrative apparatus has been destroyed, as in Algeria in 1997 (Kalyvas 1999) or Malaya (Clutterbuck 1966:63).

6.3. DETERRENCE AND INDISCRIMINATE VIOLENCE

In 1981, after the Atlacatl Battalion massacred hundreds of villagers in the Salvadoran village of El Mozote, its soldiers carried a green cloth with white letters

---

[5] Unaware of its own irony, a U.S. report in Vietnam pointed out that "areas cannot be pacified if there are no people living in them" (quoted in Wiesner 1988:113). The Japanese used terms such as "operation clean-up" and "operation purification by elimination." Their "three clears" policy (for clearing all grain, draft animals, and people) was termed "three all policy" by their opponents (for "take all, burn all, and kill all"). The Indonesian army coined the term "operation extinction" in East Timor, and the Guatemalan army referred to "operation cinders."

[6] Peterson (2000:220); Horton (1998:167); Manrique (1998:218); Del Pino (1998:163–4, 172); Berlow (1998:197); Richards (1996:181); Swedenburg (1995:153); Shalita (1994:142); De Waal (1991:48); Geffray (1990:214–5); Fellman (1989:25); Horne (1987:221–2); Wiesner (1988:58, 123); West (1985:272); Kheng (1983:65); Rodriguez (1982:33–4); Lewy (1978:276); Paget (1967:93–4); Mallin (1966:60); R. Thompson (1966:25–7); Pye (1956:104); Leakey (1954:101).

that said "If the guerrilla returns to Morazán, the Atlacatl will return to Morazán" (Binford 1996:23). "Even when the Renamo adopted a strategy of mass terror in the mid-1980s," Finnegan (1992:58) points out about Mozambique, "most of its brutalities had discernible motives. Someone was suspected of withholding information, or a village was suspected of withholding food, and the *bandidos* wanted to make sure the neighbors got the message." As these examples suggest, and contrary to much conventional wisdom (e.g., Gurr 1986:51), indiscriminate violence is not necessarily gratuitous, wanton, or solely vengeful; rather, it often aims to deter people from collaborating with the rival actor by *collectively* sanctioning suspected collaborators and those related to them.

The central aim of indiscriminate violence is to shape civilian behavior indirectly through association. "Burn some farms and some big villages in the Morbihan and begin to make some examples," wrote Bonaparte to General Guillaume Brune who, as commander of the army of the West, was getting ready to quash the monarchist rebellion; "it is only by making war terrible," he added, "that the inhabitants themselves will rally against the brigands and will finally feel that their apathy is extremely costly to them" (quoted in Dupuy 1997:158–9). The use of indiscriminate violence against Indian tribes by U.S. troops "raised the hope that severe enough punishment of the group, even though innocent suffered along with the guilty, might produce true group responsibility and end the menace to the frontiers" (Paludan 1981:43). A similar point was made in Missouri during the Civil War: "There will be trouble in Missouri until the Secesh [Secessionists] are *subjugated* and made to know that they are not only powerless, but that any desperate attempts to make trouble here will only bring upon them *certain* destruction and this [certainty] of their condition must not be confined to Soldiers and fighting men, but must extend to non-combatant men *and women*" (in Fellman 1989:201).

A March 1944 public announcement of the Germans in occupied Greece stated that sabotage would be punished with the execution by hanging of three residents of the closest village unless the perpetrators were arrested within forty-eight hours or it was proved that the villagers had actively discouraged sabotage actions. This kind of violence provides a basic incentive for collaboration, namely the prevention of the threatened harm. The Germans' announcement concluded: "Hence the duty of self-preservation of every Greek when learning about sabotage intentions is to warn immediately the closest military authority" (in Zervis 1998:179).

Here is, then, the logic of indiscriminate violence in a nutshell: if the "guilty" cannot be identified and arrested, then violence ought to target innocent people that are *somehow* associated with them. The underlying assumption is that the "innocent" will either force the "guilty" to alter their behavior or the "guilty" will change their course of action when they realize its impact upon "innocent" people they care about – or both. In addition to spreading responsibility, indiscriminate violence also introduces an explicit calculus of comparative sanctions: the targeted population will collaborate with the incumbents because it fears their sanctions more than the rebels'. As a German army order pointed out, "the population must be more frightened of our reprisals than of the partisans" (Heilbrunn 1967:150).

6.4. COUNTERPRODUCTIVE EFFECTS OF INDISCRIMINATE VIOLENCE

Though appalling as a practice, indiscriminate violence is not lacking in logic. Yet few observations seem to enjoy wider currency than the perception – shared by perpetrators, individuals targeted by indiscriminate violence, and outside observers alike – that indiscriminate violence is at best ineffective and at worst counterproductive.

Writing about the Vendée War in 1797, Gracchus Babeuf (1987:119) observed that the violent measures of the Republicans against the Vendean insurgents "were used without discrimination and produced an effect that was completely opposite to what was expected." A Greek guerrilla leader in Ottoman Macedonia at the start of the twentieth century asserted that a judicious balance had to be used in the administration of violence "for indiscriminate killing does harm rather than good and makes more enemies"; another one remarked that "the art is to find who should be punished" (in Livanios 1999:206). "No measure is more self-defeating than collective punishments" argues a classic text of irregular war (Heilbrunn 1967:152). Henriksen (1983:129) affirms that in "revolutionary warfare," "reprisals serve the rebels' cause." He notes (1983:128) that in colonial Mozambique, "again and again, FRELIMO converts pointed to Portuguese acts as *the* prime factor for their decision. Non-Portuguese observers substantiated this assertion." James S. Coleman (1990:501) includes the precept "Do not engage in indiscriminate terror" among the four basic recommendations for action that ought to guide both incumbents and insurgents.

Insurgents are well aware of the features of indiscriminate violence: "The party was correct in its judgment that government doctrine ... would drive additional segments of the population into opposition," a Vietcong document pointed out, "where they would have no alternative but to follow the Party's leadership to obtain protection" (Race 1973:172). Che Guevara went so far as to locate a key mechanism driving peasant support for the rebels precisely in the indiscriminate behavior of incumbents (Wickham-Crowley 1992:139), a point echoed by arguments positing that "along with the organizational catalyst, what is required to convert normally risk-averse peasants into revolutionary soldiers is a high level of indiscriminately targeted repressive violence" (Mason and Krane 1989:176). As Truman Anderson (1995 1:43) concludes, "the primary contribution" of indiscriminate violence to the prosecution of modern wars has actually been to aggravate insurgencies and leave lasting, bitter memories which time does not erase." Arendt (1970:56) must have had indiscriminate violence on her mind when she remarked that "violence can destroy power; it is utterly incapable of creating it."

Perhaps the most striking case for the counterproductive effects of indiscriminate violence is the oft-noted tendency of insurgents to actually welcome incumbent reprisals – or even provoke them by ambushing isolated enemy soldiers close to a village – because such reprisals bring in recruits.[7]

---

[7] Aussaresses (2001:62); Hayden (1999:39, 57); Bennett (1999:143); Keen (1998:21); Senaratne (1997:95); Schofield (1996:246); C. Schmitt (1992:280). International sympathy caused by atrocities represents an additional benefit for insurgents.

The most infamous example of the futility of indiscriminate violence is possibly the Nazi reprisal policy in occupied Europe, aimed at deterring resistance against occupation. Reprisals appear to have been an utter and complete failure: they simply did not stiffle resistance activity and, more importantly, they appear to have actually induced people to join the resistance. "Whatever the purpose of the German policy of reprisals," Condit (1961:268) points out, "it did little to pacify Greece, fight communism, or control the population. In general, the result was just the opposite. Burning villages left many male inhabitants with little place to turn except guerrilla bands. Killing women, children, and old men fed the growing hatred of the Germans and the desire for vengeance."[8] German observers in neighboring Yugoslavia "frankly concluded that rather than deterring resistance, reprisal policy was driving hitherto peaceful and politically indifferent Serbs into the arms of the partisans" (Browning 1990:68). Nazi reprisals produced a similar effect all over occupied Europe (Mazower 1998:179).[9] Japanese reprisals had similar effects in occupied Asia.[10]

The counterproductive effect of indiscriminate violence holds beyond the excessive levels of Nazi and Japanese violence. Consider the following examples from Sudan (Darfur), Guatemala, Vietnam, and Venezuela:

During a week spent traveling on a pickup truck piled high with roughly 15 fighters in the Sudan Liberation Army, or S.L.A., one of Darfur's two rebel groups, one thing stood out as starkly as a full moon over the Sahara: much of the responsibility for the growth of this insurgency lies with the Arab-led government in Khartoum.... Among the foot soldiers of the insurrection, the tactics of the janjaweed [pro-government militia] and government forces have stirred a deep well of anger and distrust and fueled an impulse for redress. To acquaint oneself with the rebels for even a few days is to discover the formula for an insurrection: kill a boy's kin, take a man's cattle, and a rebel is born. "They killed my father, so I joined the S.L.A," is how young Khalid Saleh Banat, [a] 13-year-old, put it. (Sengupta 2004:A1, A8)

Immediately after the Guatemalan army killed about 50 people, including women and children, in the village of La Estancia, forty young men and women left the village to join the guerrillas. (Carmack 1988b:54–5)

"Every time the Army came they made more friends for the V.C." a Vietnamese peasant said about South Vietnamese army raids in his village. (Trullinger 1994:85)

A Venezuelan guerrilla suggested that there was probably a new recruit for every woman raped by government soldiers. (Wickham-Crowley 1990:234)[11]

---

[8] According to historians, reprisals in Greece produced only local and limited aftereffects of intimidation (Hondros 1993:155–6; McNeill 1947:57–8).

[9] Soviet Union (Shepherd 2002; Cooper 1979; Armstrong 1964:30; Dallin et al. 1964:328), Poland (Lotnik 1999:87), Bosnia (Gumz 2001:1037), Italy (Minardi 2002:8; Klinkhammer 1997:83; Collotti 1996:27; Pavone 1994:478), and France (Kedward 1993:190).

[10] China (Lary 2001:109–10; Li 1975:209–10, 231), the Philippines (McCoy 1980:215; Kerkvliet 1977:68), Malaya (Kheng 1983), Burma (Tucker 2001), and Vietnam (Herrington 1997:21).

[11] For general statements, see Rich and Stubbs (1997:7); Andreopoulos (1994:196); Bard O'Neill (1990:80); Molnar (1965:117). Similar observations have been made about the Vendée War (Laqueur 1998:24), the American Revolution in New Jersey (Shy 1976:205–6), South Carolina (Weir 1985:74), and North Carolina (Escott and Crow 1986:393; Crow 1985:145,173);

Yet exactly why and how indiscriminate violence fails remains unspecified. I identify and examine five possible mechanisms: the emotional reactions it provokes, its ambiguous structure of incentives, reverse discrimination, selective incentives for the rivals, and the overestimation by those who use it of the strength of ties between political actors and civilians.[12]

6.4.1. Emotional Reactions and Norms of Fairness

Machiavelli (*The Prince*, III: 19) argued that punishment "should be used with moderation, so as to avoid cause for hatred; for no ruler benefits by making himself odious." Because indiscriminate violence targets people independently of what they did or could have done, it is perceived as deeply unfair. Unfair and immoderate punishment always creates a "bad impression," in the words of a Vietcong cadre (in Elliott 2003:91). Worse, it may trigger an intense emotional

French-occupied Spain (Tone 1994:103); the American Civil War in Missouri, "where the Confederacy gained in popular appeal when Missouri was 'invaded' and occupied by often brutal military forces" (Fellman 1989:11), and in North Carolina during the same period, where "terror did not paralyze guerrillas; it gave them power" (Paludan 1981:101); the Irish Civil War of 1922–3 (Laqueur 1998:180); the U.S. counterinsurgency in the Philippines in 1899–1902 (Linn 1989:85); the Dominican Republic in 1917–22 (Calder 1984:xiv, 123); and Nicaragua in the 1920s, where "the extreme violence of the invading and occupying forces spurred the rapid growth of Sandino's Defending Army (Schroeder 2000:38); the Russian Civil War (Werth 1998:115; Figes 1996:565, 583; Brovkin 1994:201); the Chinese Civil War (Thaxton 1997:308–9; Hua and Thireau 1996:302; Griffin 1976:146); the Soviet reprisals in the Baltic after 1944 (Petersen 2001); anti-Japanese and anticolonial insurrections in Malaya (Stubbs 1989:256; Kheng 1983:24, 65; Kheng 1980:97; R. Thompson 1966:25; Clutterbuck 1966:161; Barton 1953:136); Kenya (D. Anderson 2005:69; 192–3; Paget 1967:29; Barnett and Njama 1966:197), Mozambique (Lubkemann 2005:496; Henriksen 1983:128), and Angola (Cann 1997:28); the Algerian War of Independence (Butaud and Rialland 1998:103); the Colombian *Violencia* in the 1940s (Roldán 2002:209; Ortiz Sarmiento 1990:174; Henderson 1985:143, 180); the Vietnam War (Wiesner 1988:32; Race 1973:197; Klonis 1972:182; Taber 1965:95); Laos in the 1960s (M. Brown 2001:26); the Philippines in the 1950s (Kerkvliet 1977:143; Crozier 1960:217) and more recently (McKenna 1998:156, 191–2; Jones 1989:125); Burma in the 1960s and 1970s (Tucker 2001:43, 90); Cyprus (Paget 1967:29); Cuba (Jones and Molnar 1966:71); Bangladesh in 1971 (Salik 1978:104); El Salvador (J. L. Anderson 2004; Wood 2003; Goodwin 2001; Stanley 1996; Siegel and Hackel 1988:115; Mason and Krane 1989); Cuba and Peru in 1965; Venezuela, Colombia, Guatemala in the 1960s; Nicaragua in the 1970s (Wickham-Crowley 1991:43) and the 1980s (T. Brown 2001:26; Horton 1998:13, 179); Afghanistan in the 1980s (Cordesman and Wagner 1990:185; Barry O'Neill 1990:83); Guatemala in the 1980s (Stoll 1993:15, 119); Peru in the 1980s (Manrique 1998:197; Starn 1998:230; Vargas Llosa 1994:221; Shave 1994:115); Colombia in the 2000s (Semana 2003); Sudan in the 1980s (Keen 1998:22); Liberia (Duyvesteyn 2000:100–1); Algeria in the 1990s (Martinez 1994:104); Sierra Leone in the 1990s (Richards 1996:3–5); Sri Lanka (Senaratne 1997:67; Daniel 1996:170; Barry O'Neill 1990:81); Northern Ireland (Collins 1999:5, 153); Kashmir (Mahmood 2000:78; Mishra 2000); Punjab in the 1980s (Pettigrew 2000:206); the UN intervention in Somalia in the 1990s (Peterson 2000:111); Kosovo (Hayden 1999:37); Chechnya (Gordon 1999a); and the U.S. occupation of Afghanistan (Achakzai 2003) and Iraq (Mahdi and Carroll 2005; Maass 2005:41; Georgy 2003).

[12] Indiscriminate violence also kills people who otherwise may be valuable sources of information. In Kitson's (1960:95) crude formulation: "Although most people felt that Mau Mau were better dead, we preferred them alive. You can't get much information out of a corpse."

reaction (from "ill will" to "moral outrage," "alienation," and "visceral anger"), making people more willing to undertake risky actions.

That indiscriminate violence causes resentment and anger is well documented (e.g., Tishkov 2004:142; Wiesner 1988:366). A Guatemalan peasant told Warren (1998:109) how indiscriminate violence could transform fear into anger: "This was so heavy, so heavy. You were disturbed, you wanted to have some way of defending yourself. The feeling emerged – it wasn't fear but anger. Why do they come persecuting if one is free of faults, if one works honorably? You felt bad, well we all did. Grief but also anger." In turn, anger triggers the desire for action, as one of the earliest theorists of irregular war, J. F. A. Le Mière de Corvey, noted in 1823: civilians normally would not take up arms against regular troops; it was difficult to imagine, for instance, the merchants of Paris constituting them-selves into a fighting force. But this situation might suddenly change if the house of a civilian was destroyed and his wife or children killed (Laqueur 1998:113). The critical mechanism is often the desire for revenge. "As the NPFL came in," the Liberian insurgent leader Charles Taylor told Bill Berkeley (2001:49), "we didn't even have to act. People came to us and said, 'Give me a gun. How can I kill the man who killed my mother?'" A man who was captured by a loyalist band in North Carolina noted in 1781 that the band "consisted of persons who complained of the greatest cruelties, either to their persons or property. Some had been unlawfully Drafted, Others had been whipped and ill-treated, without tryal; Others had their houses burned, and all their property plundered and Barbarous and cruel Murders had been committed in their Neighborhoods" (in Crow 1985:145).

Anger and the desire for revenge produce armed reaction only in the presence of an organization that makes such action possible (Wickham-Crowley 1990:235; R. Thompson 1966:35; Gardner 1962:44). The absence or weakness of organizations leads to passivity or sloppy actions doomed to failure; no matter how outraged, civilians will have no choice but to collaborate with the indiscriminate actor. For example, armed leftist groups in Argentina consciously planned a terror campaign in order to create chaos and unleash indiscriminate violence by the army so as to create massive dissatisfaction and launch a revolutionary process. They were right about the army's ability to terrorize but were also eliminated in the process, and the population had no credible alternative; the Guatemalan rebels, as well as many other insurgents, made a similar miscalculation.

6.4.2. Ambiguous Structure of Incentives

Indiscriminate violence by the incumbent side often fails to generate a clear structure of incentives for noncollaboration with the rebels and may even produce strong incentives for collaboration with them – thus generating defection instead of deterring it. Compliance is almost as unsafe as noncompliance, because the "innocent" can do little to nothing to escape punishment and the "guilty" are no more (and sometimes less) threatened. "The wanton nature of the retaliation – the picking of victims at random," Condit (1961:268) argues, "meant that pro-German Greeks or their relatives suffered as much as anti-German Greeks.

Under these circumstances there was little advantage in being a collaborator [of the Germans].... As the numbers of the homeless and dead grew, the Greek population became simultaneously more terror stricken and more anti-German." In Kenya, it had become dangerous not to admit having taken the Mau Mau oath because "a denial of having taken the oath was often replied [to, by U.K. troops] by a bullet or a club on the head" (Barnett and Njama 1966:130).

Furthermore, indiscriminate violence lacks almost every feature generally considered to be necessary for the effectiveness of sanctions: it is usually late (e.g., Contini 1997), often arbitrary, inconsistent, erratic, and totally disproportionate.[13] Unintelligible and unpredictable violence is likely to arouse unfavorable reaction (Leites and Wolf 1970:109). Inconsistency is shocking, confusing, and may signal weakness (Lichbach 1987:287); it makes one suspect a campaign aimed at mere annihilation, in the face of which chances of survival may seem enhanced through resistance.

These problems are, in large part, a consequence of the fact that usually control fails to follow indiscriminate violence. Indeed, the logic of indiscriminate violence requires that its potential targets be able to prevent its recurrence by denouncing hostile acts planned by the insurgents about which they are supposedly privy. Besides the assumption of information, as discussed in the preceding chapter, this can only work if civilians obtain credible protection from the incumbents; otherwise they will be exposed to insurgent counter-violence. Credible protection requires the establishment of incumbent control. Often, however, incumbents raid an area, kill civilians in reprisal actions, and then depart. Insurgents usually escape unhurt and are quick to return (Binford 1996:25; Geffray 1990:94; Wiesner 1988:128; Dallin et al. 1964:328); they either capitalize on the people's discontent or force collaboration by threatening their own, more credible violence (Sheehan 1989:115). In 1971 Bangladesh, "a Razakar [pro-Pakistani volunteer] from Galimpur in Nawabganj Police Station had gone as a guide with an army column to sweep a rebel hideout. When he returned, he found his three sons killed and a daughter kidnapped" (Salik 1978:105). In 1941 a German officer serving in the Ukraine reasoned: "Were the troops simply to shoot a number of

---

[13] Kedward (1993:181) points out that in occupied France "there was no consistency in the German response to acts of armed Resistance which allows a meaningful correlation between different kinds of maquis action and the incidence of reprisals." In occupied Serbia, the Germans adopted a particularly harsh reprisal policy to quell the resistance: they set the ratio of reprisals to 100 Serbs for each German killed. However, many German commanders fulfilled their quota by drawing from the prisons mainly male Jews, as the "most convenient pool for drawing victims" (Browning 1992:134). Browning (1992:135) adds that in one instance the reprisals resulted in such grotesque absurdities as the predominantly Austrian troops of the 718th division shooting refugee Austrian Jews in Sabac in reprisal for Serbian partisan attacks on the German army. Of all the German officials in Serbia, only one, Turner, seemed to perceive the anomaly, but he consoled himself that "the Jews we had in the camps, after all, they too are Serb nationals, and besides they have to disappear." Todorov (1996) reports a similar case in German-occupied France, with the decision for reprisals taken by French collaborationists. Lomasky (1991:86) describes in a riddle form a more recent but quite parallel absurdity, the May 1972 Lod airport assault: "Q: Why do Japanese commandos fire Czech submachine guns at Puerto Rican passengers departing an Air France flight in an Israeli airport? A: To strike at American Imperialism."

uninvolved residents by way of a reprisal and then simply withdraw, the residents' interest in finding the bandits would be reduced if not completely extinguished, and the danger of further support for the bandits increased" (quoted in T. Anderson 1999:610). In a report sent to his headquarters in April–May 1944, a German field commander in occupied Greece pointed out that the policy of reprisals had no noticeable effect because it did not entail the establishment of permanent control in the areas affected (Zervis 1998:221). This is why counterinsurgency experts (Thompson 1966:114–17) strongly recommend "clear-and-hold" instead of "search-and-clear" operations and warn that when there is no prospect of holding an area that may be cleared, no effort should be made to involve the inhabitants on the side of the government because "it is merely asking them to commit suicide."

6.4.3. Reverse Discrimination

Incumbent indiscriminate violence often produces a reverse discrimination against "non-rebels" and "anti-rebels," who, believing that their "innocence" will shield them, fail to protect themselves effectively. Consider the following example from occupied Italy in 1944: a man from Neviano Arduini, a province of Parma, was waiting for the Germans at his front door. "He was a Fascist, so he welcomed them, when he saw them. They ordered him to show his documents, he got in and came out with his identity card in one hand. He was hardly out, when he was shot in the head and killed. Just so, in front of his children. Then they ordered his wife to cook some eggs and ate them, right there, with the corpse lying on the ground" (Minardi 2002:6).

German reprisals during antiguerrilla campaigns in the Soviet Union frequently victimized pro-German *starostas* (elders) (Armstrong 1964:40). Counterinsurgency sweeps by the British in Kenya tended to grab moderate nationalists, as the much more careful and fearful radical militants fled to the forests (D. Anderson 2005:63). In his detailed investigation of the El Mozote massacre in El Salvador, Binford (1996:115) concludes that the people who were killed by the army "were the least *decidido* ('persuaded,' 'convinced,' but meaning, in this context, 'politically committed').... Prior to the massacre, about 70 percent of the prewar inhabitants of El Mozote left; several dozen of these had enlisted in the ranks of the [insurgent] ERP or supported the government. Those who did none of these things were murdered." A Greek man (Papakonstantinou 1999:313) recalls in his memoirs how he learned, one day, that the Germans would arrest a number of people in his hometown in northern Greece. Having seen the names on the blacklist, he set out to warn these people that their life was in danger and they better run. One of them, a disillusioned former Communist, refused: "I have severed my links to the party, I am not involved in anything right now, why should I flee?" He was arrested and executed, whereas the real communists ran away. Likewise, a Greek villager (Svolos 1990:22) recounts: "One evening the Germans raided our village and caught all the men they found at home. In fact, they found and caught precisely those men who were not associated with [the partisans] and had, thus, no reason to fear. They found and caught them because those who had made up their minds [and were associated with the partisans] used to leave the village at night and sleep outside." An American commander who served in the Dominican Republic summed up this problem in his report (quoted in Calder 1984:154) on concentration camps for the internment of civilians: "As a military measure the concentration was productive of no good results. The good males came in and the bad ones remained out, but were not found."

The result of such actions ought to be obvious. As Stoll puts it in discussing Guatemala (1993:120), "The army was so indiscriminate that I heard of cases where even close family members of EGP [rebels] targets fled to the [EGP] guerrillas for protection, because they were far more selective in defining their enemy."

6.4.4. Selective Incentives for Rivals

Indiscriminate violence allows insurgents to solve collective action problems by turning the protection of the civilian population into a selective incentive. Protection emerges as a good *only* because of indiscriminate violence. As it escalates, so does the value of protection against it. Survival-maximizing civilians will be likely to collaborate with a political actor who credibly offers them protection, when its rival produces only indiscriminate violence. In El Salvador, Cabarrús (1983:195) argued, the power of the revolutionary organization was its ability to provide security for its members. When asked why he joined, a Salvadoran insurgent answered that he "had no choice. . . . It was a matter of survival. Those were the days when *not* to go meant getting killed" (J. L. Anderson 2004:222). A former Muslim rebel in the southern Philippines remarked that he "joined because of the violence created by the Ilaga [Christian fighters]; because there was no place safe during the trouble at that time" (in McKenna 1998:183). In occupied France, "when the acts of reprisals are added to the indiscriminate round-ups and the residue of Vichy collaborationism, the pressure on the population in a multitude of localities to look to the maquis as a place of refuge, or as a receptive and mobilizing organization, was high" (Kedward 1993:190).

Under such circumstances, participation in rebellion entails no collective action problem, but nonparticipation does.[14] What is more, the actor providing protection can decide whether to turn it into a public good available to all or use it as a sanction against particular individuals or communities.[15] The latter option makes indiscriminate violence extremely counterproductive: the decision by insurgents not to protect a village that is unfriendly to them amounts to

---

[14] On this point, see Tone (1994:78), Stoll (1993:20), and Davis (1988:23).

[15] In Japanese-occupied China, the Communists were able to teach peasants how to face Japanese raids following the "run for shelter under enemy attack" *paofan* method. By inducing collective discipline and eliminating free-riding, they were able to turn peasants into a disciplined group; in turn, the peasants won safety, which they could not have achieved on their own (Wou 1994:231). Similar tactics have been used in many places, including such methods as in-site hiding through the building of underground community tunnels (Vietnam), bunkers (Lithuania), or foxholes and caves (Latin America) (Wickham-Crowley 1991:43; Lansdale 1964:85).

exposing it to incumbent violence: in other words, using one's enemies as one's own enforcers.[16]

6.4.5. Overestimating the Strength of Ties between Political Actors and Civilians

Beyond inducing civilians to provide information about hostile activities, the logic of indiscriminate violence assumes civilians to be able to lobby armed actors to decrease the level of their activities. This requires that civilians have access and influence on armed actors and, conversely, armed actors care about civilians. This assumption is reasonable because armed actors depend on their civilian collaborators and wish not to alienate them.

Indeed, there are instances whereby insurgents have reduced or even suspended their activities because of the damage imposed by massive indiscriminate violence on the civilian population. The Norwegian resistance rejected aggressive tactics in 1943 as a result of German indiscriminate violence and justified its decision as follows: "We are convinced that [active assault on the enemy] will bring disasters to the people and the country which will be out of proportion to the military gains, and that it will disrupt and destroy the longer-term work of civil and military preparations which promise to be of the greatest importance to the nation" (quoted in Riste and Nøkleby 1973:68–9).[17] Likewise, there is evidence that insurgents sometimes suspend some of their activities locally because of the negative impact of indiscriminate violence – especially when they are weak (e.g., Fenoglio 1973:166–7). In occupied Greece, British agents reported that reprisals had a negative impact on the popularity of guerrillas, and they were right: an internal Communist document reported that "the people of the village were supporting us, but after its destruction [by the Germans] they began to turn against us."[18] When pressed to extend the struggle in the cities by initiating a total war, Greek partisans objected on the grounds that the expected reprisals would turn the population against them (Mathiopoulos 1980:ix). Furthermore, I was able to uncover, during my research in Greece, a few cases where civilians were successful in lobbying the rebels to suspend their activity and spare their villages from reprisals (e.g., Frangoulis 1988:52).[19]

However, insurgents may also disregard civilian demands, most likely when they come from villages with weak ties to them. The villagers of Malandreni, in the Argolid region of Greece, were told in April 1944 that a German officer would visit them on a set date. Upon learning of this visit, the Communist-led partisans decided to set up an ambush. Fearing German reprisals, the villagers

---

[16] An interesting twist: as a sanction for tax evasion, the Vietcong sent offenders for "reeducation" to hamlets that were shelled by the government army (Elliott 2003:873).

[17] The same logic appears to have led the Cetnik guerrillas in occupied Yugoslavia to tone down their activity.

[18] "Report by Lt. Col. R. P. McMullen on Present Conditions in the Peloponnese," PRO, HS 5/699; "Report about Markopoulo, 13 October 1944," ASKI, KKE 418 24/2/106.

[19] Petersen (2001:196–7) recounts similar incidents in the Lithuanian village of Samogitia during the guerrilla war against the Soviet regime right after the end of World War II.

demanded that the local Communist Party branch intervene with the partisans and have them cancel the ambush. The village party secretary describes the reaction of his regional boss: "Who do you think you are, comrade?" he was told; "A representative of the Germans?" To which he replied: "No, comrade, I just came to compare the benefit [of ambushing the Germans] with its cost, this is why I came." "The Germans burned many other villages," the boss replied, "but these villages joined the partisans" (Nassis n.d.:11). Likewise, when asked to release the hostages he was holding in order to save the town of Saint-Amand from German reprisals in the summer of 1944, the *maquisard* commander François replied: "I couldn't care less about Saint-Amand, the men needed only to go off to the maquis, as we did ourselves" (Todorov 1996:72). Not surprisingly then, civilians often blame the insurgents for incumbent massacres. As one of the inhabitants of the Saint-Amand put it after the *maquisards* fled the town: "On June 7, the maquis ordered the rounds of drinks and, on June 8, it left us the job of paying the check" (Todorov 1996:42–3). He is echoed, sixty years later, by the sheik of the town of Labado in Darfur (Sudan): "We are angry at the SLA because they cause us this bad situation. All of our wealth and our homes are taken, but they run away and don't defend us" (in Polgreen 2005:A3).[20]

Insurgents are usually aware of the risks they force on the civilian population from the outset and are generally unwilling to stop fighting because of them. Yet the absence of information leads incumbents (initially, at least) to overestimate the strength of ties between civilians and insurgents, as suggested by these examples from Civil War Missouri, Malaya, and Ethiopia:

Assuming all Missourians to be enemies, Kansas regiments believed it was their task to suppress them, to strip them of the means of resistance to Union authority as systematically as possible.... For them all Missourians were by nature traitors. (Fellman 1989:35–6)

Every Chinese was a bandit or a potential bandit and there was only one treatment for them, they were to be 'bashed around.' If they would not take a sock in the jaw, a kick in the gut might have the desired result. (Stubbs 1989:73)

We definitely know civilians will get hurt. But, knowing that the people sympathize with the rebels, the order is to bomb everything that moves. (De Waal 1991:123)

In his participant-observation study of a Catholic ghetto in Belfast, Sluka (1989:288–9, 300) described how the use of indiscriminate violence by the incumbents helped form pro-insurgent identities among its civilian targets:

Because of the stereotype that "all" people in Divis either belong to or strongly support the IRA and the INLA, the Security Forces treat them all as guerrilla sympathizers, and the Loyalist paramilitaries consider them all to be legitimate targets for political assassination. This has resulted in turning many who did not support the IRA or INLA before into supporters, sympathizers, and in some cases even members today. One of the best ways to turn politically moderate or apathetic Divis residents into IRA and INLA supporters or

---

[20] Cases of civilians blaming the rebels for having provoked incumbent reprisal violence are provided about German-occupied Italy (Contini 1997; Pavone 1994:482–3) and Greece (Liapis 1994:202–5), Vietnam (Elliott 2003:1135; Wiesner 1988:64), Nicaragua (Horton 1998:168), Guatemala (Debray 1975:331), Peru (M. F. Brown and Fernández 1991:168), civil war Russia (Figes 1996:1098), and German-occupied Soviet Union (T. Anderson 1999:609).

members is for policemen and British soldiers to unjustly harass, intimidate, and brutalize them, and for Loyalist extremists to assassinate members of the community.... Repression of the Catholic population by the Security Forces is enough to generate enough support for the guerrillas to ensure their survival.

6.5. WHY DOES INDISCRIMINATE VIOLENCE OCCUR?

Despite the absence of systematic empirical evidence, it is plausible to claim that the deterrent aim of indiscriminate violence often fails. Confronted with high levels of indiscriminate violence, many people prefer to join the rival actor rather than die a defenseless death. As in the Vendée, where desperate peasants were forced by Republican indiscriminate violence to join the counterrevolutionaries, they prefer to "sell their life at the highest price by defending themselves with vehemence" (Babeuf 1987:120). How are we, then, to account for the frequency with which indiscriminate violence is used?

Most "explanations" of indiscriminate violence focus on the individual level. The combination of weak discipline and strong emotions generates frustration and stress, eventually leading to indiscriminate violence. According to Grossman (1995:179), "The recent loss of friends and beloved leaders in combat can also enable violence on the battlefield.... in many circumstances soldiers react with anger (which is one of the well-known response stages to death and dying), and then the loss of comrades can enable killing.... Revenge killing during a burst of rage has been a recurring theme throughout history, and it needs to be considered in the overall equation of factors that enable killing on the battlefield."

A Guatemalan peasant justified the violence of the army in similar terms (quoted in Warren 1998:100): "When they killed people, it was because they were filled with anger because their fellow soldiers had been cut down in battle." This is particularly true where insurgents avoid open combat, and it is practically impossible to distinguish civilians from rebels (Paludan 1981:94; Li 1975:232); soldiers, this argument goes, will tend to vent their anger by using violence indiscriminately against civilians, especially when they reach the conclusion, as one American loyalist did in 1780, that "every man is a soldier" (Weir 1985:74). Fear is another emotion associated with indiscriminate violence (Fellman 1989:128), as is the pursuit of pleasure (Katz 1988; Leites and Wolf 1970:92–4). Many fighters in Missouri saw the war as a form of hunting (Fellman 1989:176–84); the Rhodesian elite Selous Scouts units attracted "vainglorious extroverts and a few psychopathic killers" (Flower 1987:124). Racist attitudes cannot be discounted either. As Sheehan (1989:110) notes about the South Vietnamese army, most "Saigon officers did not feel any guilt over this butchery and sadism...[T]hey regarded the peasantry as some sort of subspecies. They were not taking human life and destroying human homes. They were exterminating treacherous animals and stamping out their dens."[21] As has been discussed, civil wars offer plenty of

---

[21] John Kerry's remark in his war notes is telling: "The popular view was that somehow 'gooks' just didn't have very much personality – they were ignorant 'slopeheads,' just peasants with no feelings and no hopes." The military command's messages praising his team's killings ended with the words "Good Hunting." Kerry's comment: "Good Hunting? Good Christ – you'd think we were going after deer or something" (in Brinkley 2003:57–8).

opportunities for extortion and blackmail, while exposure to danger and death causes brutalization. These attitudes are compounded by the lack of resources: soldiers forced to live off the land will not shy from indiscriminate violence (De Waal 1991:43). However, although these are plausible individual determinants of indiscriminate violence, they remain unsatisfactory, being silent as they are about collective-level incentives or constraints; it is also unclear whether emotions and attitudes, such as fear, anger, or racism, are the causes, the correlates, or the results of using indiscriminate violence.

The persistence of indiscriminate violence has also prompted speculation that it is an irrational reflection of particular ideologies (Klinkhammer 1997:101) or the result of the "adrenaline of war zones" (Loizos 1988:650); any logic of deterrence is just a "fig leaf" for outright genocide or pure unmitigated acts of revenge on a defenseless population (Paggi 1996). Before resorting to ideological irrationality, however, it makes sense to examine and reject alternative explanations. I review four possible explanations for why indiscriminate violence is being observed: it may be an artifact of truncated data, or reflect ignorance, cost, or institutional constraints.

6.5.1. Artifact

The low visibility of selective violence may lead to a gross overestimation of indiscriminate violence. For one, selective violence is much more widespread than assumed. For instance, the killings by the Germans of persons "denounced as partisans by their fellow villagers" in the area of the Ukraine studied by Truman Anderson (1999:621) cumulatively rivaled two major massacres in that area. More people were killed by Colombian rightist paramilitaries around the town of Dabeiba in an individualized way than were killed in visible massacres (S. Wilson 2002). In my own study in the Argolid region of Greece, I found that civilian fatalities were equally likely to be produced by selective and indiscriminate violence (49.86 percent killed selectively and 50.14 percent indiscriminately), hardly the impression conveyed by the best historical treatment of the events in the region (Meyer 2002), which is replete with instances of indiscriminate violence.

Moreover, many instances of violence may be miscoded as indiscriminate. The 1997 massacres in Algeria targeted specific families and neighborhoods (Kalyvas 1999). The Mau Mau attack against the Kenyan village of Lari in 1953 caused the death of seventy-four men, while another fifty were wounded; this massacre was widely described as indiscriminate. However, David Anderson (2005:127–8) found that it was "far from random in its violence," targeting the families of local chiefs, ex-chiefs, headmen, councilors, and leaders of the local militia; he adds that "the victims had been selected with care, their homesteads identified and singled out.... Neighbours were left unmolested as the gangs went about their business, each attacking group moving systematically between the two or three homesteads for which it had been assigned responsibility." The same is true of several massacres in rural Colombia during the 1950s (Henderson 1985:150). A leader of the men who attacked the Colombian hamlet of El Topacio in May 1952 "knew the place and its people" and strolled from house to house playing a musical instrument, the *tiple*. "On that day, the musician was both judge and jury, for, wherever he paused, the bandits dragged out and shot every man and boy. Ninety-one died in that incident alone." Also in Colombia, the massacre of 140 men and boys from the village of San Pablo in early 1953 seems indiscriminate, until one learns that the victims were all Liberals whose credentials had been "carefully checked to verify affiliation" (Henderson 1985:152).

When the Vietcong attacked a district of Binh Son in 1967, they burned one section of six houses but not the adjacent houses (West 1985:273).[22] Likewise, the homes of about thirty people in the Afghan village of Shakar Daria were burned by the Taliban, but the rest of the village was left untouched (Waldman 2002b:A9). The violence unleashed by the Guatemalan regime in the early 1980s discriminated on the basis of location; one of its notable features was "that neighboring villages fared quite differently: one might be destroyed while another was left untouched, depending on the army's perceived understanding of guerrilla support" (Green 1995:114). Guatemalan villages that were located in areas of high guerrilla activity but "did not have a reputation of being held by guerrillas" were not attacked by the army (Davis 1988:25). When the Serb forces attacked the village of Bukos in Kosovo and "caused the Albanian villagers to flee," they did not touch a similar neighboring village, Novo Selo, probably "because there were no Kosovo Liberation Army guerrillas in the village, residents said" (Gall 1999:A6). The seemingly indiscriminate violence of the Russian Army in Chechnya was not blind: some villages stood "untouched, a reward, Russian officials say, to those who refused to aid the rebels and cooperated with the Russian army" (Gordon 1999b:A1).

Finally, armed actors often refrain from resorting to indiscriminate violence even when they have the ability to exercise it (e.g., McGrath 1997:112), something that usually goes unreported. For example, the Germans often refrained from collective reprisals (Lotnik 1999:61; Pavone 1994:481; Fleischer 1979). As Rana Mitter (2000:180) points out about Manchuria, "The impression given, in other words, is that the Japanese exercised random violence in Manchuria, whereas the evidence suggests that violence was part of a whole repertoire of techniques of coercion, and that co-optation remained their preferred option when available."

In sum, it is likely that the significance of indiscriminate violence is overstated because of a specious reading of available data. This type of violence may be less prevalent than generally thought. Even if this is true, however, one still needs to explain its occurrence.

6.5.2. Ignorance

Robert Thompson (1966:84) reports a joke: "There are only two types of generals in counter-insurgency – those who haven't yet learnt and those who never will!" Most accounts of indiscriminate violence explain it by reference to ignorance and

[22] West (1985:273) also noted the surprising absence of reaction to this pattern: "No one asked why the VC had singled them out."

organizational incompetence. The Vietnam War provides a prime example. For years, the U.S. military leadership failed to grasp the nature of the war (West 1985:256). As a general recalled, "Soon after I arrived in Vietnam it became obvious to me that I had neither a real understanding of the nature of the war nor any clear idea as to how to win it" (quoted in Thayer 1985:3). "Let's go out and kill some Viet Cong, then we can worry about intelligence," quipped a newly arrived general (R. Thompson 1966:84). The absence of front lines proved to be a major cognitive obstacle for officers trained in conventional war. As a result, much of the data generated by the conflict was not properly processed (Thayer 1985:4). Hence, "a theoretical basis for the violence program, consistent both internally and with objective conditions, was never articulated, despite the number of lives it consumed daily. The basis for using violence was a residue of military doctrines developed to deal with friendly military units operating on hostile foreign territory" (Race 1973:227). Several metaphors describe the difficulty that conventional armies have fighting irregular wars, from T. E. Lawrence's quip that irregular war is "messy and slow like eating soup with a knife" to Lieutenant Colonel Bigeard's aphorism ("We don't kill flies with hammers") and to the more recent remark by Lieutenant Colonel Todd McCaffrey in Iraq that fighting a war driven by intelligence with a conventional army is akin to "teaching an elephant to ballet dance" (in Negus 2004:5).

Proximate determinants of this ignorance include undue optimism and lack of preparation, along with the perception that the threat posed by a rebellion is low;[23] fundamental misunderstandings about the nature of irregular war;[24] inadequate organization and training[25] or just sheer professional incompetence and corruption;[26] the military's oft-noted weak institutional memory and lag in learning and updating of war doctrine – a tendency epitomized in the saying that the military fights not the present war but the last one;[27] the prevalence of authoritarian structures within the military;[28] its politicization and/or corruption;[29] and, finally, straight racism.[30] A problem with such explanations is that they seem unable to account for the bewildering variation in levels of indiscriminate violence. For example, in the occupied Soviet Union, the Germans varied the kind and intensity of violence they used considerably.

---

[23] Fall (2000:115); Cann (1997:63); Paget (1967:33).

[24] Harmon (1992:44); Sarkesian (1989:44–5).

[25] Paget (1967:31).

[26] Ellsberg (2003:115); Downie (1998:133); Stubbs (1989:70); Siegel and Hackel (1988:116–17); Leites and Wolf (1970:92–4); Paget (1967:78); Kitson (1960:192).

[27] Downie (1998); Garvin (1991:9); Blaufarb and Tanham (1989:23); Trinquier (1964:61). It appears that the lessons learned in Korea went unheeded in Vietnam, and so did the Vietnam lessons in Central America (Downie 1998:158, 251; Katz 1975:589).

[28] Mason and Krane (1989).

[29] Blaufarb and Tanham (1989:19).

[30] Heer and Naumann (2000); Li (1975:231); Welch (1974:237). An American soldier in Iraq explained an instance of American brutal behavior as follows: "I kind of looked at it as high schoolers picking on freshmen. Us being the seniors; the Iraqis being the freshmen" (in Filkins 2005:92).

Ultimately, ignorance must be qualified as a cause of indiscriminate violence because political actors often seem aware of its deleterious effects from the outset. During the Spanish Civil War, Catalan Republicans warned that indiscriminate violence against opponents in the Republican zone was bringing about a "counter-revolutionary climate in the rearguard" (de la Cueva 1998:360) – yet they did not refrain from using it. After a particularly bloody wave of reprisals in Greece, the German minister plenipotentiary for Southeast Europe, Hermann Neubacher, complained to the military commander of the relevant area: "It is utter insanity to murder babies ... because heavily armed Red bandits billeted themselves, overnight, by force, in their houses, and because they killed two German soldiers near the village. The political effect of this senseless blood bath doubtlessly by far exceeds the effect of all propaganda efforts in our fight against Communism" (quoted in Condit 1961:268).[31] Yet the Germans kept resorting to mass reprisals. The sprawling American counterinsurgency literature of the 1950s and 1960s is replete with warnings about the negative effects of indiscriminate violence – including tens of studies by official or semiofficial outfits such as the Operations Research Office, the Special Operations Research Office, the Counterinsurgency Information Analysis Center, and the Center for Research in Social Systems.[32] The widely distributed "Social Science Research Studies" conducted on various aspects of the Vietnam War argued "that more was being lost in terms of loyalty and respect for the GVN and the Americans than was gained in hurting the VC by bombing and shelling of villages, even where they were VC strongholds and fighting bases" (Wiesner 1988:122–3). These arguments were disseminated and popularized in journals like *Foreign Affairs* (e.g., Lansdale 1964). Indeed the military was well aware in the late 1960s that "the injury or killing of hapless civilians inevitably contributes to the communist cause" (in Bilton and Sim 1992:40). Yet, the U.S. forces indiscriminately shelled and bombed countless South Vietnamese villages for many years. More recently, the Russian army appears to have been aware of the effects of indiscriminate violence in Chechnya, and yet it has largely ignored this information.[33] Hence the question must be restated: why use

---

[31] Klinkhammer (1997:84) and T. Anderson (1995:342) document similar doubts among German officials in Italy and Ukraine.

[32] "Guerrillas may initiate acts of violence in communities that are earnestly cooperating in order to provoke unjust retaliation against these communities. Unjust or misplaced punishment at the hands of the occupying force is vigorously exploited by the guerrillas to gain sympathizers and strengthen their own cause" ("Operations against Guerrilla Forces" quoted in Barton 1953:3). Major studies such as Project Camelot and Project Agile reached similar conclusions (M. F. Brown and Fernández 1991:111, 204). See also Ferguson (1975); Jones and Molnar (1966); Molnar (1965); Gardner (1962); Condit (1961); Barton (1953).

[33] A Russian general pointed out in August 1999 that "there should be no losses among the civilians. To destroy a bandit if he covers himself by a civilian, we must first separate the civilians from the bandit, and then take care of the bandits" (Bohlen 1999:A1). In fact, Russian analysts argued that Chechen rebels might actually seek to provoke indiscriminate violence from the Russian military (Gordon 1999a). Yet, the Russians resorted to indiscriminate violence, which initially united the divided Chechens. Shamil Basayev, the best-known Chechen warlord, sarcastically said that he is "very grateful" to Russia for creating a new sense of unity among his people (*Economist*, 9–15 October 1999). Eventually, the war evolved into a stalemate, where, "paradoxically," the Russian

indiscriminate violence *in the presence* of knowledge about its counterproductive effects? I point to two factors: cost and institutional distortions.

6.5.3. Cost

An overriding consideration in the use of indiscriminate violence is the cost of selective violence.[34] Identifying, locating, and "neutralizing" enemies and their civilian collaborators one by one requires a complex and costly infrastructure. Most incumbents quickly realize that they lack the necessary resources. In a directive sent to the units occupying the Soviet Union, the German Central Command pointed out that "the Commanders must find the means of keeping order within the regions where security is their responsibility, not by demanding more forces, but by applying suitable draconian measures" (quoted in Cooper 1979:143). In short, indiscriminate violence initially appears as a handy substitute for individualized deterrence. Still, the low cost can explain the emergence of indiscriminate violence but not its persistence.

6.5.4. Institutional Distortions

Some cases of indiscriminate violence can be explained as resulting from internal institutional distortions. The Vietnam War provides an excellent illustration. Sheehan (1989) describes how the South Vietnamese military and the U.S. high command in Vietnam administered indiscriminate air and artillery bombardment on peasant hamlets at an estimated cost of about 25,000 civilians killed and 50,000 civilians wounded a year. An American provincial adviser talking about the area under his supervision remarked that "we shot a half-million dollar's worth of howitzer ammunition last month on unobserved targets. Yet the whole provincial budget for information- and intelligence-gathering is $300" (Fall 2000:110). This violence was premised on the theory that it would "terrorize the peasants out of supporting the Viet Cong" (Sheehan 1989:109). Of course, this alienated the population by killing and wounding large numbers of noncombatants and destroying farms and livestock (Taber 1965:95). Sheehan recounts how the U.S. military adviser John Paul Vann denounced the indiscriminate bombing and shelling of the countryside as both cruel and self-defeating. Initially, Vann had found it difficult to believe the utter lack of discrimination with which fighter-bombers and artillery were turned loose; apparently, a single shot from a sniper was enough to call for an air strike or an artillery barrage on the hamlet from which the sniper had fired. A province or district chief could start firing artillery shells in any direction at any hour of the day or night, not even needing an

---

tactics "hardened the resistance," and Chechen fighters were "no longer able to confront Russian troops head-on, but they remain determined to inflict as much pain as possible in the name of Chechen independence" (Myers 2002:A6).

[34] Militaries often quantify this cost. For example, the estimated cost of killing a single rebel in Kenya was £10,000, in Malaya it exceeded $200,000, while in Vietnam it reached $373,000 (Laqueur 1998:379; Paget 1967:101).

unverified report stating that some guerrillas had gathered in a neighboring hamlet. Vann wondered how any American could think that Vietnamese peasants who lost family members and friends and homes would not be mad; in fact, most Vietnamese farmers had an alternative army and government asking for their allegiance and offering them revenge. Vann alerted his superiors to this fact by arguing that the bombing and shelling killed many more civilians than it ever did Vietcong and as a result made new Vietcong. However, he was usually overruled and the hamlets were bombed. As an American Air Force general put it: "The solution in Vietnam is more bombs, more shells, more napalm ... till the other side cracks and gives up" (Sheehan 1989:619).

Why was such a policy allowed to go on? Sheehan argues that the underlying cause was the failure to curb "institutional proclivities." On the one hand, there was competition between different branches within the U.S. military, and the Air Force was quite successful in promoting bombings: it was in the personal interest of the Air Force chief and of his institution to believe that the bombing furthered the war effort, and so he believed it (Sheehan 1989:650). Moreover, processes of learning were undermined by the brief one-year or six-month rotation period for military personnel: as soon as a military adviser began to understand the situation, he had to leave (Meyerson 1970:37).[35] Thus, the American military system does not seem to have encouraged learning. Likewise, South Vietnamese officers saw artillery shelling as an easy way to show that they were aggressive without running the risks of actual "search and destroy" operations. Commanders at all levels who only engaged in shelling could still retain their command and even be promoted, while those who took risks might be relieved if they suffered a setback or sustained heavy losses.[36]

Institutional distortions can be observed in other cases as well. The French revolutionary Bertrand Barère explained the initial failure to put down the rebellion in the Vendée by the "desire for a long war among a large part of the chiefs and administrators" (quoted in Tilly 1964:338). A Pakistani officer (Salik 1978:117) described the situation among his army in Bangladesh: "All the divisional commanders and the brigade commanders, except one major-general and one brigadier, invariably assured General Niazi that, despite their meager resources and heavy odds, they would be able to fulfill the task assigned to them.

---

[35] According to a lieutenant colonel, "The day I got there, that man [his predecessor] was leaving. He had his hat and coat on, threw me the key and said, 'There's the shack. Good Luck. Every day is different around here.' That's all the training I had" (quoted in Katz 1975:591). Snow (1997:106–9) provides an extensive summary of the U.S. mediocre performance in counterinsurgency, central to which is the disdain of a military, high-tech organization for political, low-tech warfare involving civilians. Ellsberg's (2003:185–6) analysis confirms these points.

[36] The South Vietnamese regime encouraged this misallocation of military resources because it was unwilling to commit its military to a full-fledged war; it was primarily concerned instead with preserving its elite troops to protect itself from a coup – as opposed to wasting it in fighting the war. In turn, this calculation could only be sustained because of the perverse effect of the U.S. involvement in Vietnam: the South Vietnamese government assumed that the United States, as the preeminent power in the world, could not afford to let its anti-Communist government fall to Vietcong.

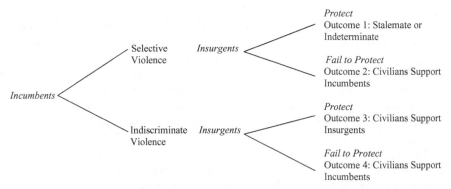

FIGURE 6.1. Civilian Behavior as a Function of Indiscriminate Violence and Protection

'Sir, don't worry about my sector, we will knock the hell out of the enemy when the time comes,' was the refrain at all these briefings. Any comment different from this was taken to imply lack of confidence and professional competence. Nobody wanted to jeopardize his prospects for future promotion."

Again, however, institutional distortions may explain the emergence of indiscriminate violence but not its continuation for a long time in light of inevitable evidence that it is counterproductive.

6.6. ACCOUNTING FOR THE PUZZLE

As I pointed out, the conjecture that indiscriminate violence is counterproductive is not based on systematic empirical research. Because of the inadequacy of data, it makes sense to turn to theory. Assume a setting where incumbents choose whether to use indiscriminate or selective violence, insurgents have the option of protecting civilians from incumbent indiscriminate violence, and civilians collaborate with the political actor who best guarantees their security. In such a setting, civilians will be likely to collaborate with the incumbents if the insurgents fail to protect them, whether incumbents are indiscriminate or selective; they will be likely to side with the insurgents when they are protected by them against indiscriminate incumbents; and the outcome is indeterminate when insurgents protect civilians and incumbents are selective (Figure 6.1).

This analysis yields the following prediction: incumbents can afford to be indifferent about the type of violence they use when insurgents are unable to offer any protection to civilians. Put otherwise, costly discrimination can be dispensed with when insurgents are weak. When this is the case, indiscriminate violence does succeed in paralyzing an unprotected population. When American indiscriminate violence made the Filipino civilians "thoroughly sick of the war," they "were forced to commit themselves to one side"; soon garrison commanders "received civilian delegations who disclosed the location of guerrilla hideouts or denounced members of the infrastructure" (Linn 1989:56–8).

Likewise, most Missourians turned to the Union in their despair, Fellman (1989:78) notes, "not out of a change of faith but as the only possible source of protection." Guatemala provides the paradigmatic case in this respect (Stoll 1999; Le Bot 1994). After the Guatemalan army used massive indiscriminate violence against the population, civilians who had initially collaborated with the rebels were left with no choice but to defect, because the rebels utterly failed to protect the population from massacres (Watanabe 1992:181). As Stoll (1993:6) points out, "while the guerrillas could not be defeated militarily, they were unable to protect their supporters."[37]

Contrasting occupied Greece and Yugoslavia allows for a controlled comparison over both space and time. In October 1941 German troops burned two northern Greek villages, Ano Kerdilia and Kato Kerdilia, and shot all 207 male inhabitants in reprisal for the killing of German soldiers by a fledgling partisan group. The effect was stunning. Immediately after the reprisal, Greek men from surrounding villages were allowed to form militias and set up watch posts around their villages to prevent the partisans from entering and obtaining supplies. In some cases, they even caught a few partisans and handed them over to the Germans, who reported the population's "feelings of hatred toward the rebels" (quoted in Dordanas 1996:91–6). In one case, a partisan was denounced to the Germans (who caught and hanged him) by his cousin's husband (I-1; for list of interviews, see Table A.1 in Appendix A). As a result, "the deterrent effect in northern Greece was swift and resistance faded away in the winter months" (Mazower 1993:87–8). The behavior of the villagers is best explained by their desire to avoid further dreadful German violence. Indeed, a woman I interviewed from a neighboring village (whose uncle was the leader of the partisan group and whose father was among those shot by the Germans) told me that "if the Kerdilia villagers had found my uncle, they would have skinned him alive. 'He was responsible for the massacre,' they said; 'We will find him, we will skin him alive, we will kill him!'" (I-1). This is an instance of effective use of indiscriminate violence in the face of an insurgent group that was extremely weak. A comparison to neighboring Yugoslavia in 1941 and Greece in 1943–4 offers a useful counterpoint: reprisals during this period clearly failed to produce similar effects. The reason is that in both Yugoslavia in 1941 and Greece in 1943–4, an important insurgent infrastructure faced German indiscriminate terror with a strategy that mixed its own selective violence with civilian protection.

In short, indiscriminate violence is likely to be effective when there is a steep imbalance of power between the two actors. Given reasonably strong insurgents, it should be unsustainable, as its counterproductive nature becomes clear. We would, therefore, expect rational incumbents who may initiate indiscriminate violence to muster additional resources and subject whatever institutional distortions they suffer from to the imperatives of their long-term interest. As a conflict waxes on, we should observe a shift toward selective violence, especially among

---

[37] Similar processes are reported about Calabria in 1806–7 (Finley 1994:99), Peru in the 1960s (M. F. Brown and Fernández 1991:140), and Angola in 1961 (Clayton 1999:35–9). The case of Darfur in 2004–5 may fit here, save for the huge international outcry.

incumbents, the ones likely to initiate indiscriminate violence. This insight can be formulated as follows:

Hypothesis 1 Political actors are likely to gradually move from indiscriminate to selective violence.

Anecdotal evidence suggests the plausibility of this hypothesis (for an empirical test see Chapter 9). The transition to more selective forms of violence is particularly striking in the wars fought between German occupiers and European resistance movements during the Second World War. If there is one political actor whose extreme ideological outlook should have clouded its sense of instrumental rationality, clearly it would be the Nazis. They were also fighting a total war and their prospects of victory by 1944 were dim, to say the least. The German military was overstretched and many European countries were occupied by very thin forces. Hence, a policy of indiscriminate violence was overdetermined by both ideological and strategic factors. Yet a closer examination of their practices shows a remarkable and unexpected, if partial, evolution from indiscriminate violence to a mix of selective and indiscriminate violence, wherein the former came to play an increasingly important role.

In Greece, for instance, after a particularly bloody wave of indiscriminate violence in December 1943 that left more than 1,300 Greek villagers dead, German commanders were ordered "to seize the perpetrator himself and take reprisal measures only as a second course, if through reprisal measures the prevention of future attacks is to be expected"; in addition, the authority to order reprisals was removed from lower ranks and moved up to division commanders, who also had to get clearance from the competent administrative territorial commander (Condit 1961:265–6). Although these measures were never fully implemented (and final responsibility for reprisals usually rested with commanders on the spot), this indicated a willingness to change course in the face of the obvious effects of indiscriminate violence. The formation of a Greek auxiliary corps, the Security Battalions, and their explosive growth in the spring and summer of 1944 led to higher levels of discrimination in violence through those troops' access to local information.[38]

A similar process took place elsewhere in occupied Europe (Laqueur 1998:209; Heilbrunn 1967:147, 151; Dallin et al. 1964:327–33), as also occurred among the Japanese in Asia (Hartford 1989; Li 1975:204–9). In Vietnam during the late 1960s and early 1970s, the United States switched from indiscriminate violence to one of the most sophisticated programs of selective violence. In the Phoenix program, the goal was to kill, jail, or intimidate into defection the members of the Vietcong apparatus in the South "person by person" (Adams 1994:178). By 1971 the war was transformed into "one in which whom we killed was far more important than how many we killed" (Herrington 1997:69); a CIA operative claimed that "we had 75 percent of the key [Vietcong] cadres named" (Moyar 1997:146). A similar trend has been documented in El Salvador (Binford 1996:140) and Mozambique

---

[38] Greek memoirs note that, unlike the Germans, the Greek auxiliaries targeted the homes of families whose men were guerrillas or sympathizers (Papandreou 1992:110; Svolos 1990:25).

(Geffray 1990), where many people had been reluctant to leave RENAMO-held places for government-controlled areas because they feared being indiscriminately targeted by government soldiers. More recently, the Russian army became more selective in Chechnya, switching away from *zachistki* or mopping-up raids ("its previously preferred method of hunting down rebels") to targeted disappearances and kidnappings of rebel suspects and the use of a Chechen militia (Gordon 1999c; *Economist* 2003:46). There is considerable evidence documenting similar shifts to higher levels of discrimination in violence in a variety of civil wars.[39]

If this argument is correct, we can explain the relative dearth of indiscriminate violence among insurgents by pointing to their better access to local information. Accordingly, we should expect to see insurgents relying on indiscriminate violence when and where they lack the ability to assess local information. Indeed, there is evidence that they use such violence against groups and places that are opaque to them, such as incumbent-controlled cities; yet even in such cases, they also tend to eventually switch to selective violence.[40] Finally, the argument yields three implications about the incidence of suicide missions. First, insofar as it is a method of indiscriminate violence used to deter civilians (which is not always the case),

---

[39] Such evidence is reported from various conflicts in Macedonia (Livanios 1999:205), the Philippines (McKenna 1998:158–9; Jones 1989:273; Linn 1989:77–8; Kerkvliet 1977:208, 240), China (Wou 1994:127–58), Malaya (Stubbs 1989:252; Pye 1964:177), Zimbabwe (Flower 1987:106–7), Guatemala (Stoll 1993:111, 139–40; Paul and Demarest 1988; Carol Smith 1988; Peralta and Beverly 1980), Peru (Starn 1998:230–8; Rosenberg 1991:207), and Iraq (Maass 2005). Note that the shift toward selective violence was not necessarily one toward correct targeting (Kalyvas and Kocher 2005). I discuss this issue in Chapter 7.

[40] In the course of the Chinese Civil War, the Communist rebels discovered that assassinations of gentry members based solely on their identity forced otherwise rival gentry into a temporary coalition against them; this led to reprisals that were highly effective because gentry members could easily obtain reliable information about whom to target, thus "greatly eroding peasant morale and eventually putting a halt to the Communist peasant movement"; the same applied to grain seizures, which, "although highly appealing to peasants, invariably produced unintended adverse results. They often involved much killing and pillaging. Grain seizure might appeal to poor peasants in one locality, but random violence and killing destroyed villages in other localities and drove settled peasants to the gentry side.... Random violence in fact promoted community cohesion by rallying peasants to the gentry. It also polarized local communities and made it impossible for the communists to expand their movement." As a result, the Communist Party explicitly forbade indiscriminate killing and criticized peasant cadres' perceptions that in conflicts with rival local militias it was normal to kill hundreds of peasants (Wou 1994:123, 142). In fact, the Communists recognized that the "red terror" resulting from "harsh indiscriminate action" was counterproductive and redefined their policy of violence; they were more selective during the Yenan period (1935–41) compared with the earlier Kiangsi Soviet (1924–33): "Rather than sticking stubbornly to past methods, the Communists appeared to learn and experiment" (Griffin 1976:93–4, 146). Likewise, in Malaya the Communist leaders decided that "blind and heated foolhardiness" was to be avoided in the future, while the emphasis was to be on "regulated and moderate methods" (Laqueur 1998:290; R. Thompson 1966:25). In Vietnam, the Communist Party exercised "much tighter control over the procedures for approving executions after 1954, because of the unfavorable consequences of the many careless executions that occurred during the Resistance" (Race 1973:189) and later abandoned the random bombing of urban centers (Fall 2000:111). The Algerian independentist rebels began to more rigorously check denunciations several years after the beginning of the insurgency, in 1957–8 (Hamoumou 1993:203–4).

we may account for its relative scarcity by reference to its counterproductive effects (Kalyvas and Sanchez Cuenca 2005). Second, suicide missions should be observed in places and times where selective violence is extremely difficult or impossible, including areas where control is limited or nonexistent. This is consistent with evidence from Israel/Palestine. Finally, as long as an insurgency is in the ascendant, expanding its territorial control, we should expect it to replace suicide missions with more selective methods.

An important implication of this argument is the following: a major reason why wars of occupation turn into civil wars is that indiscriminate violence is counterproductive. The need for selective violence forces occupiers to rely on local agents, thus driving a wedge within the native population. In contrast, the persistent use of indiscriminate violence points to political actors who are fundamentally weak: this is the case with civil wars in failed states ("symmetric nonconventional wars"), where high levels of indiscriminate violence emerge because no actor has the capacity to set up the sort of administrative infrastructure required by selective violence. In this perspective, the subset of ethnic civil conflicts that display high levels of eliminationist violence could be endogenous to state failure.

The relatively recent spread of international norms against human rights violations has made indiscriminate violence even less desirable for those who use it. It is argued (J. L. Anderson 2004; Greenhill 2003) that weak challengers now have an overwhelming incentive in provoking incumbents into using indiscriminate violence. As recent conflicts in Kosovo and Darfur demonstrate, indiscriminate violence is now likely to attract considerable international negative publicity and even cause external intervention. If this trend continues, we are likely to observe either a decline in the use of indiscriminate violence in irregular wars as incumbents become acutely aware of its costs, or new sophisticated ways for hiding such violence from international scrutiny and ensuring "plausible deniability" (Ron 2000b). Conversely, as incumbent indiscriminate violence ebbs, indiscriminate violence by rebel groups may become more visible.

6.7. CONCLUSION

This chapter has sought to examine the workings of indiscriminate violence when used to generate civilian compliance. A key goal of indiscriminate violence in this context is to shape civilian behavior indirectly through association, and to shift responsibility for hostile actions to a wider group of people. It is likely to emerge when the information necessary for selective violence cannot be obtained with the allocated resources. However, indiscriminate violence seems to be counterproductive, with the exception of situations where there is a high imbalance of power. When violence is indiscriminate, compliance is almost as unsafe as noncompliance, because the "innocent" can do little or nothing to escape punishment and the "guilty" are no more (and sometimes less) threatened. If the rival political actor can provide credible protection against the violence, people will transfer their support. While at first such dynamics may not be clear, or institutional distortions may affect how political actors choose to pursue action on the ground, if a conflict waxes on, we ought to observe a transition toward selective violence as long-term interests begin to win out. Thus, instances of indiscriminate violence may be the product of a lag: political actors appear to engage in it because initially it seems much cheaper than its alternatives; however, they should eventually discern that it is counterproductive and switch to selective violence – the subject of the next chapter.

7

A Theory of Selective Violence

You've got to be on the ground to get the truth.

Lieutenant Colonel Greg Reilly, U.S. Army, Iraq

People talk and people die.

Eamon Collins, former IRA cadre

What kills directly is the tongue.

A Nicaraguan officer

This chapter develops a theory of selective violence as a *joint* process. Political actors operating in a regime of fragmented sovereignty must rely on selective violence to deter defection (i.e., active collaboration with the rival actor), despite lacking the resources for monitoring the population. Selective violence entails the personalization of violence and requires information that is asymmetrically distributed between political actors and individual civilians. Within the institutional context defined by irregular war, violence results from the convergence of two distinct but related processes: the political actors' attempts to deter individual defection, and individuals' decision to provide information to political actors. I supply a political economy of the joint production of violence, formulate a model that captures the key aspects of the theory, and specify a set of empirical predictions.

The argument is as follows. Selective violence presupposes the ability to collect fine-grained information. The most effective way to collect it is to solicit it from individuals, which explains the ubiquity of the practice of denunciation in civil war. Denunciation is central to all civil wars, with the probable exception of a subset of civil wars where no actor attempts to obtain the collaboration of members of groups that allegedly support its rival and where all relevant information is in the public domain, conveyed by visible individual identities. There are two distinct types of denunciation: political and malicious, both of which are accommodated by the theory of selective violence presented here. False denunciations are quite common, as individuals are tempted to settle private and local conflicts. However, false information undermines the very premise of selective violence. Political actors cannot screen all the information they get, but they can mitigate this problem if they generate a credible perception that they are selective in their violence. This perception is conveyed by the presence of local agents, which signals the existence of a network of informants, the related ability of local agents to avoid blatant "mistakes" in targeting, and the clandestine and secret nature of the process of informing for the rival actor. A mix of accurate and erroneous hits is, thus, compatible with a perception of credible selection under these three conditions.

I then turn from political actors to individuals. Although motivations to denounce vary, the constraints faced by denouncers provide a good way to model the process. The key constraint is the likelihood of retaliation against the denouncer via the process of counterdenunciation to the rival actor by the family of the victim. Thus denunciation is a function of the control a political actor has over an area: control affects the likelihood of retaliation against the denouncer because counterdenouncers need access to the rival political actor. The theory predicts that denunciation leading to selective violence will be most likely where one actor exercises dominant but incomplete control. Where actors have total control, they can detect defection directly; this ability is public knowledge, which depresses the levels of defection. Where a political actor's control equals its rival's, no information will be forthcoming. Therefore, selective violence is unlikely where control levels enjoyed by one actor are high and, surprisingly, where the two actors share sovereignty. Put otherwise, the front line in irregular war is likely to be nonviolent. The theory also predicts the location of indiscriminate violence.

7.1. INFORMATION

Information is a key resource in irregular war (Eckstein 1965:158; Pye 1964:177); it is the link connecting one side's strength with the other side's weakness (Crawford 1958:179). It is widely accepted that no insurgency can be defeated unless the incumbents give top priority to and are successful in building an intelligence organization (R. Thompson 1966:84). Intelligence refers not only to "high-level military intelligence on maps, but [to] basic police intelligence at the [opponents'] own grass roots" (Clutterbuck 1966:4). The collection of such intelligence requires an enormous infrastructure: "We have to be everywhere informed," asserted a French officer in Algeria (Trinquier 1964:35); "therefore, we must have a vast intelligence network."

Monitoring is a fundamental problem of rule. As Tocqueville (1988:206) remarked, "the Sovereign can punish immediately any fault he discovers, but he cannot flatter himself into supposing that he sees all the faults he should punish." Indeed, information is as hard to come by as it is essential. As a British officer in Malaya eloquently observed, "We could not bring our military machine to bear without information, and we could not get information without the support of the population, and we could not get the support of the population unless they were free from terrorism, and we could not free them from terrorism until we had sent men to kill the terrorists. So it went round and round – a most complicated combination of vicious circles. The key to breaking these vicious circles remained one thing: information" (Crawford 1958:180–1).

Where does information come from? There are many sources, as suggested by the same officer: "Information came from captured terrorists, who bought their lives with it; from spies; from informers; from every kind of civilian contact and grapevine; from photographs of the jungle; from single footprints in the jungle; from captured documents, weapons, camps, clothes, supplies; from the reports of the jungle-patrols quartering backwards and forwards over the same huge areas" (Crawford 1958:180).

It is possible, nevertheless, to distinguish between three major sources of information: material indices, violent extraction, and consensual provision. Material indices (photographs, captured documents, etc.) require high levels of technical sophistication to obtain, are difficult to interpret, and tend to be of limited value in contested zones. Violent extraction comes in many forms. Intimidation, blackmail, and bribes work better in urban environments, where regular and sustained contacts between handlers and informers are possible, than in rural environments, where such contacts are either impossible or easier to detect. Long detentions, even when feasible, tend to produce false confessions (Rose 2004:134). The "massive screening" of suspects is often counterproductive (Leakey 1954:122). Then, there is torture, for some "a methodological problem, not a moral dilemma" (West 1985:61).

Opinions on torture vary[1] but tend to converge: from Pietro Verri's *Osservazioni sulla tortura* to Hannah Arendt's (1970:50) remark that torture is not a substitute for a "secret police and its net of informers," many authors believe that, besides being immoral, torture is an inefficient way to collect information; they argue that it produces false confessions extorted from victims desperate to save themselves further agony; that it discourages those disaffected with the enemy from turning themselves in and drives into the enemy camp those wrongly submitted to torture; that it signals inability to recruit informers and, hence, an institutional decay that causes sources of human intelligence to dry up; and, that it destroys the long-term use of a source for a doubtful short-term benefit.[2] The Spanish Inquisition rejected as invalid confessions gained under torture, and it turns out that "in statistical terms, it would be correct to say that torture was

[1] Aussaresses (2001) recognizes that the continued use of torture during the Algerian insurgency implies that it worked, yet his book includes more instances of information being gleaned from denunciation than torture. Moyar interviewed a number of U.S. and Vietnamese officials involved in intelligence operations. Some of them testified to the effectiveness of torture, especially during military operations when information was needed for immediate use, while others told him that torture only decreased the quality of intelligence obtained. Most U.S. advisers were not sure if prisoners revealed useful information when tortured. Of those who did think that they knew enough to verify the accuracy of prisoner testimony, a considerable number echoed the claim of American policy makers that torture did not provide any worthwhile intelligence and often yielded false information: "If you put people under physical duress, they'll tell you anything, just to get you to stop hurting them" (Moyar 1997:101–2).

[2] Rejali (2004a); K. Brown (2003:167); G. Thompson (2003); Cann (1997:118); Blaufarb and Tannham (1989:27); Horne (1987:205); *Comisión Nacional sobre la Desaparición de Personas* (1986:61); Clutterbuck (1966:97); Molnar (1965:247).

used infrequently" (Kamen 1998:188). The French reached negative conclusions about its efficiency in Algeria (Rejali 2004b; Crozier 1960:19), as did some American interrogators in Afghanistan (Mackey and Miller 2004). Darius Rejali (2004a) sums up the existing evidence by concluding that "torture during interrogations rarely yields better information than traditional human intelligence." However, hard evidence is not available and it is also true that if torture always failed it would never be used. Nevertheless, it is plausible to argue that the regular use of torture requires a significant infrastructure, that it is difficult to implement in contested rural areas, and that it works in tandem with human intelligence.

The most common, and probably effective, way to access private information is consensual provision. A large body of criminological research shows that the likelihood of solving a crime decreases if the public does not identify suspects to the police (Rejali 2004a). The same is true for civil wars, as in Northern Ireland: "The recruitment of informers has long been the primary British method of gaining intelligence on their republican enemies. Over the centuries informers have been used, with devastating effect, to disrupt and destroy republican rebellions, and despite the electronic hardware of the twentieth century, the Crown's most powerful weapon in the present-day Troubles remained the human informer" (Toolis 1997:194). Indeed, "it is said that informers [within the IRA] supply over two-thirds of all intelligence" to the authorities, who make hundreds of informer recruitment bids per year; during the 1980s, the IRA executed close to forty of its own members that it suspected of being informers (Toolis 1997:212, 193; M. Dillon 1990:283).

Information can be provided by paid informers;[3] however, these are hard to recruit (especially in contested rural areas), expensive to maintain, and easier to spot.[4] A more common practice is denunciation, the casual and undirected provision of information from noncombatants.[5] Denunciation turns the production of selective violence into an outcome jointly produced by political actors and civilians. In this sense, selective violence is a *joint* process.

7.2. DENUNCIATION

Denunciation is a complex social phenomenon that has thus far been little studied (Fitzpatrick and Gellately 1997:1). It is simultaneously surreptitious and shameful. It should not be confused with the practice of "public denunciation" in which

---

[3] The term "informer" generally implies a regular, often paid, relationship to an authority (Fitzpatrick and Gellately 1997:1) – as opposed to the term "informant" or "denouncer." The (British) School of Service Intelligence (Army Intelligence Wing), defines an informant as "any individual who gives information. The term is generally used to describe a casual or undirected source as distinct from an informer, who is normally connected with criminal activities, can be directed and receives payment for his services" (in M. Dillon 1990:283–4).

[4] Eric Schmitt (2003:A20) provides evidence about the difficulties and cost of relying on paid informers in Iraq.

[5] The inverse of denunciation is "recommendation" or "certification." Following the Spanish Civil War, people suspected of having been Republicans could only find jobs if local families of proven loyalty to the regime "certified" them (Aguilar 1996:85). Both denunciation and recommendation are instances of a transfer of private information to political actors.

people assembled in a public meeting accuse a peer (e.g., Madsen 1984:80). Community norms across cultures stigmatize the provision of information to outsiders, but also to insiders, as in Northern Ireland:

The waters cleave and the life of the informer, and their kith and kin, diverges from the tribe. (Toolis 1997:194–5)

To be an informer is to be the "Judas within, the betrayer," and the "lowest of the low." (Smyth and Fay 2000:27)

He ran to the house of a woman who spies on her neighbours for the republican movement, keeping a close eye on happenings offensive to her republican morality. She thinks her association with the IRA gives her clout in the community. In a sense, of course, she is right. But she does not know that behind her back she is loathed and despised. (Collins 1999:3)

These norms are reflected in the variety of pejorative terms invented to describe denouncers: rats, snitches, touts, *soplones*, *chivitos*, *sapos* (toads), *orejas* (ears), ruffians, *mouchards*, and the like. In the West Bank, individuals accused of informing the Israelis have a hard time finding lawyers when they are arrested; often, they are simply murdered, and hospitals have turned away their corpses; in one case, the mother of one informer refused to claim his body. The stigma attached to denunciation makes it almost impossible to find people willing to acknowledge having denounced. "Among my friends some had been with the Reds, such as Luzio and Isasi," said a right-wing Basque villager, "but I was friends with them as before. I never denounced anybody. I have a clean conscience about that at least" (in Zulaika 1988:25). This stigma drives even people who have denounced for "legitimate" political and ideological reasons to keep it concealed. During my fieldwork in Greece, I was unable to find anyone who openly acknowledged having denounced, even though I found several people willing to acknowledge participation in all kinds of unsavory activities and acts of violence.

Thus, denunciation is not easily observable, even ex post. The only exceptions are the salvaged archives of highly bureaucratized organizations that rely on the practice, such as the Catholic Church, the Gestapo, or the Stasi.[6] A good indirect indicator of the presence of denunciation is the generalized suspicion in civil war contexts (e.g., Collins 1999:200; de Staël 1818:125). Consider the following statements:

We live in the middle of spies, the spies are among us like the devil among the Christians. (an Italian peasant in 1944–45, in Fenoglio 1973:386)

Those were the days... of the Whispering Terror. Whispers could bring about death. (a Malayan peasant in the 1940s, in Kheng 1983:141)

The villagers were fearful day and night, and wondered if they had done anything of which they could be accused. (a Vietnamese peasant on his village under Vietcong control, in Elliott 2003:259)

---

[6] It should come as no surprise that almost all studies of denunciation have focused on Nazi Germany and the Soviet Union (Nérard 2004; Joshi 2003; Gellately 1991).

It is often overlooked that the sort of fear that is so pervasive in civil wars is not just generic fear of armed actors but often fear of being denounced by one's own neighbors. During the recent civil war in Algeria, "everyone feared everyone, it was the law of silence. People suspected their neighbors, they were distrustful even within their own families" (Leclère 1997). In Guatemala, "spying and informing became endemic" (Zur 1998:73); fear drove "a wedge of distrust between members of families, between neighbors, among friends. Fear divide[d] communities through suspicion and apprehension, not only of strangers, but of each other" (Green 1995:105). As a provincial Colombian judge put it: "The people stay silent out of fear, because here you can't open your mouth much – if you open your mouth here it will fill with flies" (in Fichtl 2003).

It is possible to distinguish two broad categories of denunciation: those provoked by "political" motives and those by ulterior or personal motives. Denunciation is "political" ("disinterested," "selfless," "loyalty-driven," "pure") when a person denounces someone primarily out of loyalty to a cause or authority.[7] A student who worked for the Vietcong said that he denounced his "friends" because he "looked on these people as the enemy and only wanted to kill them in order to have peace" (Elliott 2003:1099). Of course, private gain (including survival) may flow from the success of the actor to whom one denounces, but the primary motivation is to contribute to this success. Denunciation is "malicious" ("private," "manipulative," "interested") when it is primarily motivated by personal motives unconnected to broader political causes, for example, as payback for personal slights – though such motives can be disguised to appear as political. Sheila Fitzpatrick (1997:117) points out about the Soviet Union that "the motivation is to provoke a state response from which the denouncer would derive some specific benefit or satisfaction. The benefit might be the disgrace of a professional rival or competitor in village politics, the eviction of a neighbor from a crowded communal apartment, the punishment of a former spouse, or the settling of scores with a personal enemy."

The theory of selective violence stresses constraints and is agnostic about the motivations behind denunciation. As such, it accommodates both political and malicious motives. Nevertheless, accounts of malicious denunciation are as pervasive in the descriptive microliterature as they are absent in the theoretical and descriptive macroliteratures; as a result, it is worth examining malicious denunciation closely. I make a few initial observations here and return to this issue in Chapter 10.

Malicious denunciation may originate from individuals, families, village factions, or even entire villages;[8] it may reflect a larger cleavage: for example,

---

[7] A third type may be called "social" denunciation when a person denounces someone because she has transgressed a social norm. For example, Nérard (2004:374) sees denunciation, in a broader sense, as an act of social protest under conditions of authoritarianism, when other channels are closed. Obviously, the boundaries between these types can be fluid.

[8] In some cases, private grievances can be locally collective rather than individual: in revolutionary France, for example, certain villages used the practice of denunciation as a way of removing from the village a perpetual troublemaker or petty thief (Lucas 1997). Similarly, during the Vietnam War, some U.S. advisers opposed the bombing of villages. "They contend that there is something

personal envy can be the individual reflection of a class cleavage, but as long as one *particular* landowner (as opposed to any random landowner) is denounced, malice might also be involved. The same is true when a cleavage-based enmity is mixed with the expectation of private gain, as when one denounces a particular landowner or member of a "rival" political or ethnic group in the hope of acquiring property. Malicious denunciation can spring from preexisting conflicts (a recurring family feud) or it can be triggered by the war itself (revenge or retaliation for a previous action during the war, "counterdenunciation," an attempt to clear one's name by denouncing a neighbor, etc.). The Germans obtained a good deal of information about the resistance from Greeks who had been ill-treated by the partisans (Condit 1961:247) as have the Americans in Iraq (Finer 2005). Although some private denunciations are venal, entailing material benefits (e.g., the property of the denounced person), often the benefit for the denouncer is purely emotional (e.g., pleasure for punishing a despised rival).

Malicious denunciations need not be false, though they often are. One may falsely denounce an adulterous spouse as a spy, but a betrayed spouse may have known all along that her adulterous partner was a spy and only denounced him after she found out about his affair. The Norwegian village of Telavaag was burned to the ground and all its male inhabitants were deported by the Germans after they received correct information that it was used as a transit area for British agents; this information turned out to have come from a woman who found out that she had not received her share of the coffee and other goods brought in by the British agents (Riste and Nökleby 1973:51–2).

Denunciation usually implies a degree of intimacy, since it requires enough familiarity with the denounced person to have information about them. Indeed, a striking aspect of accessing the Securitate files in Romania and the Stasi files in East Germany was the discovery that informers were often associates, friends, even family members (Bran 2002; Garton Ash 1997).

Obviously, false denunciations generate moral hazard issues as CIA officials looking for information about the Vietcong knew:

> The people who identified members of the [Vietcong] shadow government often had many types of non-Communist enemies in their area of operation, particularly if they worked in their native areas. Like most people, they had personal enemies: the men who had insulted their sisters, the men who had stolen their sweethearts, the farmers who had borrowed money from their families and failed to repay it, and even the GVN officials who had beaten their cousins. Family members of these enemies also could be fair game, especially when previous offenses had involved relatives. (Moyar 1997:114)

Denunciation is central to civil war: it is a common (e.g., Franzinelli 2002:197) rather than "a particular twist," as is sometimes thought (e.g., Wickham-Crowley 1990:209). This is why the absence of violence from a community is often explained by reference to the absence of denunciations. John Watanabe

basically wrong with a system by which paid Vietnamese informers can trigger air raids on villages and in which the United States acts primarily as a mechanical arm for the Vietnamese authorities. 'No agent ever calls an airstrike on his own village – it's always somebody else's,' said one American caustically" (Mohr 1966:3).

(1992:182), an anthropologist who worked in Guatemala, observed that "despite the army occupation, almost no one died in Chimbal, in contrast to all the towns around them. When I asked why, many responded that because they were 'good people' – or, more precisely, good 'Christian believers' of whatever persuasion – who had not denounced one another to the army as people had elsewhere."

Because most observers tend to focus on the actual perpetrators of violence and their motivations, they completely miss the fact that the information used to make violence happen may come from civilians, usually closely linked to the victims. Villagers killed in parts of German-occupied Ukraine were executed by German soldiers but "denounced as partisans by their fellow villagers" (T. Anderson 1999:621). The Guatemalan army killed thousands of Maya Indians during the 1980s: however, outside areas targeted for indiscriminate massacres, these were often "people fingered as subversives by local army informers" (Watanabe 1992:181). A Spanish woman explained the assassination of a woman in the town of Zamora during the civil war: "Viloria was a beast. He was paid to kill and he killed my father. He was the one of a group of men who were paid to murder. They shot without knowing who their victims were. 'Kill this one,' the Falangists would say. They would grab them and shoot twenty, thirty, forty, whomever they wanted. But he was not the one to denounce her. He shot her, but the person responsible for her death was he who denounced her. If there had not been denouncers, there would not have been assassins" (in Sender Barayón 1989:145).

It is necessary to distinguish between collaboration/defection and denunciation. Although both actions entail the provision of information to political actors, denunciation only refers to the provision of information about specific individuals, whereas collaboration/defection entails a much broader set of activities, from tax payment to providing information about the military activities of a rival organization. As will become clear, it is possible to collaborate/defect without denouncing, though not vice versa: the act of denunciation is, by its very nature, an act of collaboration/defection. Denunciation is riskier and more consequential than defection, both because of the social stigma attached to it and because it targets specific individuals who are members of the community.

Like any social practice, denunciation can take a variety of forms, ranging from very informal to highly institutionalized. When Iraqi soldiers raided the town of Aleze, north of Baghdad, knocking on doors and searching houses, the American reporter covering the raid noticed that "a corpulent woman whispered to the Iraqi soldiers that her neighbor disliked Americans and spoke of having grenades" (Glanz 2005:A14).[9] Iraqis are also reported to sometimes hand Americans lists of names at checkpoints before driving away (Negus 2004:5). Jon Lee Anderson (2004:140) describes the meeting between a Salvadoran rebel and an informer: "The peasant asks Diego to step aside for a moment, out of earshot. They stand together for a few minutes, the peasant whispering intently, Diego listening and

---

[9] Glanz adds that "a search there turned up nothing, but the Iraqi soldiers were careful to come back and make a show of searching the woman's house as well, so that her neighbor would not suspect that she had spoken up."

nodding. The peasant is a civilian collaborator, giving information about what is happening in the villages that lie ahead."

Denunciation can also be institutionalized. My research in Greece revealed the following procedure: a person denounced someone to a local committee member (or to someone with access to that committee), who brought the case to the committee that discussed the various cases. Committees had three options: they could send all cases to the relevant authority, select among the cases and sent out some, or send none and even veto the use of violence against anyone. Rules and procedures varied but sometimes included a formal vote. For example, when the Germans came to Ermioni in the Argolid, a small town of 2,212, in June 1944, they arrested several men who were accused of membership in EAM, the insurgent organization that had been ruling the town since 1943. An eighty-member assembly was formed to discuss whether fifteen local individuals should be handed over to the Germans or remain in town. The assembly met and decided by secret vote that more than half of them should be deported. This result, however, surprised everyone; a smaller committee was then formed to deliberate further and went to seek advice at the local capital, Kranidi. The Kranidi committee had just discovered that the Germans had, on their own initiative, shot six local men who had been handed to them in a similar fashion and advised the Ermioni men to free all prisoners, as a practical way of preventing any violence that would circumvent their consent. They did this, and everyone was freed (Frangoulis 1988:52–4).[10] This example indicates the complexity of denunciation procedures and the willingness of locals to keep a degree of control on who is handed to outsiders and who is not.

7.3. DENUNCIATION IN ETHNIC CIVIL WARS

In most civil wars, ethnic and nonethnic alike, *initial* information about actual or potential defectors tends to be public. In ethnic civil wars, individual identities are often (though not always)[11] signaled in a variety of publicly visible ways; in turn, these identities may convey (or be perceived as conveying) information about the likelihood of one's future behavior. The same is the case in some nonethnic civil wars, when polarization is pronounced ex ante and where political loyalties are in the public domain.[12] In such environments, no private information is generally needed for violence to be selective. The first burst of violence will often target publicly known local leaders, as in Spain: "In Fuenmayor, when the Civil War broke out in July of 1936, order broke down completely, with predictably tragic results. After securing the town, the paramilitary Guardia Civil, acting in concert with local Rightists, dragged thirty labor leaders down to the municipal cemetery

---

[10] This turned out to be a wise move in retrospect; when the rebels came back to Ermioni, the former prisoners were asked to intercede with the rebels in order to prevent reprisals, which they did.

[11] During the war in Croatia, rival armed groups had to wear ribbons whose colors were changed every day to distinguish friend from enemy (Pervanic 1999:23).

[12] There are many ways to identify "ideological" identities in nonethnic environments (e.g., Figes 1996:665; Rosenberg 1991:41).

and shot them without trial in front of their families. The neighboring town of La Campana, held by the Left at this time, saw a brutal retaliation. The enraged Leftists there herded fifteen members of the landowning class along with the parish priest into the town jail and burned them alive" (Gilmore 1987:44).

Note that, in such environments, the expectation of being targeted based on publicly visible markers of identity will automatically deepen polarization, as individuals coalesce around their respective groups because of security considerations. Following this first round of violence, rival elites will be eliminated, and their "underlying populations" may or may not be given the choice to "surrender" to the rival army. If such an option is not given, these populations are either exterminated or deported, or they may flee.[13] This process produces a front line, and collaboration resembles support during interstate wars. The logic of denunciation has limited application in these settings and applies only to marginal cases of spies and "fifth columnists." If, however, the rival population is given the option to comply, and if some people begin to collaborate with the actor in control, existing identity categories cease to convey information about future behavior (Kalyvas 2004). Such collaboration occurred during the Mau Mau rebellion in Kenya, as described by a British counterinsurgent:

One step of great long-term significance which was made at this time was the decision to form a Kikuyu Home Guard. It was a brave and imaginative move on the part of the Administration to set up, and later to arm, members of the tribe which had given birth to the Mau Mau, and 90 percent of which had taken some form of Mau Mau oath. But it was proved to be a right decision. Within a few months, the Home Guard numbered 10,000, and then rose to 20,000; they fought resolutely against their own tribe, first with spears and pangas, and only later with shotguns and rifles; but together with the Kikuyu Tribal Police, they had by the end of the Emergency killed no less than 4,686 Mau Mau, which amounted to 42 per cent of the total bag.... As a result of their resolute defiance from the start, the rebellion became a civil war within one tribe instead of being a nationalist movement. (Paget 1967:91–2)

---

[13] Mass deportation is different from a decentralized process of segregation, though the two are often difficult to distinguish. Both ethnic and nonethnic civil wars tend to produce segregation. Chamoun (1992:23) recalls how the first months of the civil war in Lebanon led to confessional segregation, "everyone seeking refuge in neighborhoods where his religion was majoritarian." Darby (1990:98) writes that in the Belfast area he studied "more families left their homes, not because they had actually experienced violence, but from anticipation of trouble in the future." This is not restricted to ethnic civil wars. As a man from heavily secessionist Independence, Missouri, wrote to his brother that "All the people are leaving here that are for the Union" (in Fellman 1989:74). In Colombia, villages became politically homogeneous as a result of the civil war because known opponents fled (Sánchez and Meertens 2001:17). When the British occupied Boston, during the American War of Independence, thousands of Patriot supporters and their families fled the city; when the British left in 1776, thousands of Loyalist supporters followed the British troops (Carr 2004). Lear (1961:120) reports that the anti-Japanese guerrillas in the Philippines "encouraged the migration of loyal Filipinos from the enemy-controlled areas to the unoccupied districts." A pro-Japanese administrator reported, "At present there are only 30 families in the poblacion and our efforts to increase the number of returning families meet with little success because guerrilla elements controlling the barrios outside the poblacion are prohibiting or preventing the people to come in, or have contact with the authorities. They threaten to kill, kidnap, punish, or inflict injuries to those who are attached to, and cooperate with, the present regime" (in Lear 1961:208).

In this case, the process of denunciation in ethnic civil wars follows the general lines described in this book.

7.4. IS SELECTIVE VIOLENCE POSSIBLE?

A key paradox of civil war is that it increases the need for monitoring the population while simultaneously undermining the actors' capacity to do so. To address this problem, political actors try to implement decentralization and indirect rule, delegating a measure of power to local committees or militias (Chapter 5). Decentralization produces more local information, but it simultaneously generates problems of moral hazard because inaccurate information leads to indiscriminate violence, causing counterproductive effects. An Afghan villager told U.S. troops that rival tribesmen were falsely claiming that the Taliban were active in the village and added: "Don't make the mistake the Russians made. They had informers and they arrested the wrong people and it turned everyone against them" (in Zucchino 2004:A9). A Guatemalan guerrilla said she joined the guerrillas "to avoid being killed by *envidia* (envy)" – denunciation by a personal enemy to the army (Stoll 1993:136). A village chief in Vietnam pointed out that false denunciations and extortion attempts by corrupt government officials had the same effect: "They would pick you up and then torture you until you had to confess. So a lot of people went over to the Vietcong, even though they didn't like them, because they had no choice. If they had stayed, they would have been arrested" (Race 1973:71–2). Indeed, a key complaint about abuse of power in Vietcong areas was "the killing of people whom the villagers knew to be innocent" (Elliott 2003:944).

Local delegation is a double-edged sword. On the one hand, it makes monitoring possible and, by creating agents who are constantly present on the ground, it facilitates denunciation by providing denouncers with plausible deniability along with an entity to shield them. Because they have access to local information, agents are able to evaluate the accuracy of the denunciations they receive. Colin Lucas (1997:35) suggests that in France, "revolutionary committees in smaller communities did usually seek to ignore or downplay denunciations that were overtly motivated by personal interests and emotions." As a rebel committee member in a Greek village told me, "A young man fell in love with a girl but her brother interfered, so he denounced her brother. He kept telling me that [her brother] was speaking against the organization. I did not listen to him. I was objective and I was able to impose the law here in the village" (I-58). Moreover, local agents facilitate denunciation: by assuming a great part of the responsibility for the violence that follows, they partly shield the denouncer from her act and dilute individual responsibility.

On the other hand, delegation is not a silver bullet against the problem of informational inaccuracy. A particularly brazen case is that of local army agents in a Guatemalan town who intentionally provided misinformation (including the staging of fake battles and the writing of guerrilla graffiti on the walls) in order to manipulate the army into believing that the town was infiltrated by rebels so they could run a criminal protection and extortion racket (Paul and Demarest

1988). Using local authority to settle private feuds takes place even among highly disciplined insurgents, as in Vietnam (Elliott 2003:259). It is simply very hard to monitor local agents, particularly during civil wars, when capacities are stretched thin and there is a lot of pressure to take action.

Political actors are generally aware that many denunciations are false. They know, like the Phoenix operatives did in Vietnam, that often "the distinction between the VC and private enemies became nebulous" (Moyar 1997:115); they dislike the "Hooded Men" system because "of the danger that the men in the hoods might pay off old scores against their enemies" (Kitson 1960:100). In a 1919 letter, Lenin castigated the Cheka of Ekaterinoslav for being a criminal organization that "executed every person they did not like, confiscated, looted, raped, imprisoned, forged money, demanded bribes and then blackmailed those who had been forced to pay bribes, freed those who could pay twenty times more" (in Werth 1998:120). Later on, regional Soviet officials "were well aware that peasants were using mutual denunciation as a tool to pursue village feuds" (Fitzpatrick 1997:107). When the Germans invaded the Soviet Union they were confronted with the same phenomenon. For example, when the 25th Motorized Division entered the territory of Bryansk oblast, it "complained that denunciation was simply rife among the population" (Terry 2005:8).

Sooner or later, political actors discover, as did U.S. officers who fought against Filipino rebels in 1899–1902, that some collaborating mayors "dragged them into local feuds" (Linn 1989:146). As their modern counterparts realized in Iraq, "These people dime each other out like there's no tomorrow" and "out of a hundred tips we've gotten from Iraqi intelligence, one has worked out" (in Packer 2003:71). An American soldier criticized the performance of local Iraqi informers during a military operation in the city of Tal Afar: "We almost never get anything good from them," he said. "I think they just pick people from another tribe or people who owe them money or something" (in Finer 2005:A1). Again in Iraq, Captain John Prior of the U.S. Army realized that "he'd been pulled into a family feud" (Packer 2003:71), a point made colorfully by another officer, Captain Todd Brown:

Yes, that was a Jerry Springer action.... Sometimes that's what we call it when the informant just sends us on a wild-goose chase after guys that have done something to him, kind of a personal vendetta-type deal. So, when it's a personal vendetta, we call it the "Jerry Springer Show" reminiscent of all the – just the funny stuff that goes on in American society. Same thing going on here where it's a personal vendetta, and they just want to – a guy stole his cow or married a girl that he wanted to marry or stole some of his land or property. He's just trying to get back by saying he's a leader of al Qaeda or something like that, and you go on a wild-goose chase with the informant. (CNN, 26 December 2003)

As a result, political actors mistrust their local agents and try to weed out unreliable information. They warn their subordinates, as a Colombian officer did, that to safeguard their independence, they should not allow themselves to be counseled by civilians (Roldán 2002:252). A CIA adviser in Vietnam recalls (in Moyar 1997:122): "There were times when I questioned a name on the blacklist of VCI. 'Is this guy actually VC infrastructure, or is he a political enemy or a business enemy of the province chief or district chief of somebody else?'"[14] During a military operation, a Guatemalan officer warned assembled villagers as follows: "Everyone who did not present themselves today, those who really are guerrillas, bring them to me here. Tied up. But don't bring me innocent people. Don't bring me honorable people. And don't bring me people with whom you have some problem, over a piece of land, over a cow, over a woman, over money, none of that" (in Stoll 1993:102).

However, this is no easy problem to solve, because individuals are generally more practiced at deceiving than at detecting deception (deTurck and Miller 1990). One solution entails devising appeal procedures. The Chinese Communists introduced such procedures but they proved inadequate even during periods of relative stability and had to be suspended during periods of crisis; eventually much of their violence was arbitrary.[15] Moreover, local agents can terrorize individuals who appeal.[16]

Another means of increasing accuracy is to introduce accountability by making the local agents' or the denouncers' identities public. Without the protection provided by anonymity, however, the pool of denouncers and of candidates for positions of local authority would dry up quickly. For example, U.S. commanders had planned to circulate a list of 1,400 people thought to have potential insurgent connections in the town of Tàl Afar in Iraq, seeking verification or denials from local sheiks. "But they decided against it," Oppel (2005a:A8) points out, "because few sheiks would openly affirm or deny the status of insurgent suspects in front of other Iraqis." It is also possible to rotate agents on the assumption that they are less likely to have grudges outside their own turf.[17] Besides the logistical issues entailed in such a method, this solution defeats the logic of delegation, which is

---

[14] The guerrilla leaders in the Japanese-occupied Philippine island of Leyte "sought to bring some approximation to a rule of law in the territory they controlled," meaning that "espionage and collaboration must be discouraged through the judicious application of swift punishment to the guilty. But malice must not be permitted to level false accusations against the innocent, in order that neighbors might conveniently dispose of their personal enemies or improperly acquire their property" (Lear 1961:91).

[15] "Since the responsibility for arrest and investigation, as well as the determination of guilt, were largely vested with one organ, the police, there were no effective checks to avoid unwarranted arrests and punishments" (Griffin 1976:139).

[16] Helen Siu (1989:132) tells the story of a cadre in postrevolutionary China who supported a malicious accusation against a villager and forced him to sell his property in order to pay his accuser. The case was reviewed by a committee that reversed the verdict; it ruled that the villager had been victimized by the "arbitrary, opportunistic accusations of bad elements." This appears to be rather exceptional, however, for civil war contexts. Benjamin Paul and William Demarest (1988) list many cases in which individuals were unable to convince the Guatemalan army that their local agents were running a private racket.

[17] After the inspector general of the Union army visited Missouri in 1864 and realized that "many of the soldiers and their families have suffered from the depredations committed upon them by rebels, and they have their enemies whom they desire to punish, and they are very prone to use their power, which their military positions give them to accomplish unwise purposes," he advocated the use of out-of-state troops who did not have three years' worth of grudges to avenge (Fellman 1989:87). According to a U.S. adviser in Vietnam (in Moyar 1997:222–3), "The police chief and the Special Police chief weren't living up in Phu Yen to pursue a vendetta. If they'd had a vendetta

to save on monitoring costs: nonlocal agents are much less able to collect and assess information compared with local ones.

The most effective solution probably consists of cross-checking denunciations and applying sanctions when they are false. A Gestapo memorandum sent to all headquarters from Berlin in 1941 concerning denunciations among relatives, particularly husband and wives, suggested that denunciation was being used for private ends completely unanticipated by the regime. The memo introduced more thorough rules requiring married denouncers of their wives to answer under oath whether divorce proceedings had already commenced or were contemplated; moreover, the Minister of Justice added that even denunciations eventually resulting in the discovery of a serious crime did not automatically provide grounds for winning a case in a divorce court (Gellately 1991:143, 148–9).[18] More forcefully, the Chinese Communists condemned as traitors those "who falsely accuse others as traitors" (Griffin 1976:173), and the Italian partisans executed people who joined them in order to conduct personal vendettas (Pavone 1994:451). The German occupation army in the Soviet Union arrested and imprisoned false accusers, and in some cases it had them publicly whipped in front of entire villages as a deterrent to future false denunciations (Terry 2005:8). An additional illustration comes from the Japanese-occupied Philippines: "There was a time when a soldier was made drunk by a fellow who . . . wanted to eliminate [the soldier's] barrio lieutenant. The soldier was told that the said barrio official used to receive letters from town. Without investigating further the matter, the soldier looked for the 'Teniente' and shot him cold-bloodedly. Later, when the soldier became sober and perhaps realizing that he had committed a most heinous crime, he fetched in turn the informant and shot him also" (Lear 1961:94).

The empirical record is mixed as to how often and how effectively cross-checking is used. In Peru, a human rights worker remarked that "Sendero always investigates those it kills" (in Rosenau 1994:317). A Phoenix operative in Vietnam claims that "the overwhelming majority of those captured on Phoenix operations were picked up based upon tangible and credible evidence, rather than on the mere say-so of one person motivated by some sort of personal grudge" (Herrington 1997:196), though a U.S. military adviser observed that "falsification of data and targeting of personal enemies did occur, and when discovered usually resulted in some form of disciplinary action" (Moyar 1997:120). The British used a system of multiple hooded informers in Kenya, the idea being that "any genuine terrorist or committee member would be recognized by two or three of them" (Kitson 1960:101).[19] Berlow (1998:247) reports a conversation with an NPA cadre in the Philippines: "'We don't accept demands for retribution from families,' he said, explaining that people often make false accusations to the

---

against anybody, it would have been back home where they came from, not up in Phu Yen. They didn't know anybody up there – that's why the Government had put them there."

[18] However, Nérard (2004:361) found that the cost of false denunciations in Stalin's Soviet Union was low to nonexistent.

[19] Kitson (1960:102) adds that this was "a laborious business and very tiring for the hooded men, especially as the sun came out after a time, making them hot and thirsty."

NPA – just as they do to the military – to try to settle purely personal grudges. 'We have our own policies for meting out penalties, including the death penalty'."

However, effective cross-checking requires a high level of control and an efficient bureaucracy; it is, therefore, very hard to achieve in civil war, when resources are stretched thin, especially in contested zones. The available evidence suggests that authoritarian regimes tend to expand more resources in screening denunciations compared with civil war actors. The Spanish Inquisition often knew when to discriminate between false and true denunciations (Kamen 1998:181), although a villager asserted in the 1480s that "in Castille fifteen hundred people have been burnt through false witness" (Kamen 1998:175). Likewise, James Given (1997:141) reports that one indication of the extent to which individuals attempted to manipulate the inquisition in medieval Languedoc was the frequency with which inquisitors imposed penances on individuals whose chief fault was bearing false witness against the innocent. "Manipulating the inquisition may have given some Languedocians access to a new and unusually effective political resource," he concludes (1997:142); "yet there was always the danger that the inquisitors might discover what was afoot. The price paid by an unlucky schemer for access to this particular resource could be very high."

In contrast, I found very few instances of effective cross-checking in civil wars, particularly outside of zones of full control. Republican militiamen in Spain made no systematic effort to find out whether the denunciations that had led to executions of villagers in a Spanish village were false or malicious (it turns out that they were both) (Harding 1984:75–6). An American officer serving in Iraq remarked that hooded local informants "are the first important step in the process of weeding [the insurgents] out." He added that "You obviously can't just go by what they say because they make plenty of mistakes, but since we don't know these places as well as they do, it helps to have them around" (in Finer 2005:A1). Another officer admitted that he would never get to the bottom of the many contradictory stories told to him by various informers and their victims: "I am not freaking Sherlock Holmes," he exclaimed (in Packer 2003:72).

Instead of cross-checking, political actors turn to "secondary" profiling – secondary in the sense that it takes place once a list of names has been handed in: they look for visible features that may signal loyalty or disloyalty and separate true from false denunciations. The Indian security forces in the Punjab looked for "young Sikh men between the ages of 18 and 40, who have long beards and wear turbans" (Gossman 2000:267). The Nicaraguan contras considered as likely Sandinista supporters rural schoolteachers and health workers (Horton 1998:128) – two professions also targeted by the RENAMO insurgents in Mozambique (Nordstrom 1997:83). The Guatemalan army aimed at teachers, bilingual instructors, catechists, and officers of the cooperatives (Warren 1998:95; Paul and Demarest 1988:125–6). Wealthy Colombians are seen as fair game for insurgents, whereas paramilitaries target labor organizers and human rights workers (Fichtl 2004:5). The Vietcong were particularly suspicious of people who traveled to market towns, where the government was present (Elliott 2003:949–50). Obviously, such profiling is often ineffective. For example, the Languedocian Inquisition failed to screen out false denunciations when the victim was a person who "had offended important members of the local political establishment and thus made himself vulnerable to attack" (Given 1997:147). Furthermore, too much reliance on profiling defeats the basic premise of selective violence. Indeed, it appears that a compromise is made between the demands of selectivity and the limitations on available information. My fieldwork in Greece revealed several cases where profiling was mixed with local information. I found that the mayor of a village was killed by the rebels, probably after being maliciously denounced by the brother of a woman he had falsely promised to marry; as a mayor, he also came into frequent contact with the occupation authorities, a fact that may have tipped the balance against him when the moment of decision came (I-6, I-7).[20]

Ultimately, it is impossible to estimate the proportion of false positives and negatives. Nevertheless, there is evidence that political actors often choose to err in the direction of false positives rather than false negatives. U.S. commanders in the Philippines at the turn of the century drew the consequences of this situation clearly and officially: "To arrest anyone believed to be guilty of giving aid or assistance to the insurrection in any way or of giving food or comfort to the enemies of the government, it is not necessary to wait for sufficient evidence to lead to conviction by a court, but those strongly suspected of complicity with the insurrection may be arrested and confined as a military necessity and may be held as prisoners of war in the discretion of the station commanders until receipt of other orders from higher authority."[21] An Italian partisan formulated the problem in stark terms: "The situation forces us to deal seriously with the problem of spies and denouncers: suspects must be arrested and killed on a minimal evidentiary basis. On the other hand, there is a risk of condemning innocent people: but how is it possible to wait for the proof of the betrayal? From the death or arrest of someone on our side?" (in Franzinelli 2002:204). In Kenya accusations made by others, including hooded informants, needed no corroboration (D. Anderson 2005:203). In Colombia, armed groups "prefer the simple 'justice' of summary executions of suspected collaborators over the convoluted machinations of trials or the awkwardness of taking accused collaborators captive" (Fichtl 2004:5). In 2003 the Colombian government proceeded to arrest hundreds of people in several localities on the basis of just a few denunciations; seventy-four people were arrested in the small town of Cartagena del Chairá on the strength of a single denunciation by a man who many locals accused of malice (Semana 2003).

---

[20] In a sense, profiling reflects the joint production of violence onto the target: those most likely to be turned in are people who happen to both have personal enemies and fit a public profile of disloyalty. This is also an instance of how the master cleavage may shape violence, conditional on local dynamics.

[21] In his description of the Athenian expedition in Sicily, Thucydides (6.53) tells the following story: "After the expedition had set sail, the Athenians had been just as anxious as before to investigate the facts about the mysteries and about the Hermae. Instead of checking up on the characters of their informers, they had regarded everything they were told as grounds for suspicion and on the evidence of complete rogues had arrested and imprisoned some of the best citizens, thinking it better to get to the bottom of things in this way rather than to let any accused person, however good his reputation might be, escape interrogation because of the bad character of the informer."

"Better to kill mistakenly than release mistakenly" went a Vietnamese slogan, popular among some insurgents; for them, "justice was not an abstract ideal, but a tool in the political struggle"; "if it came down to a conflict between the revolution's prestige and abstract notions of justice, it was clear which would prevail" (Elliott 2003:91, 947). A U.S. commander in Iraq remarked about Iraqi counterinsurgents that "if they shoot somebody, I don't think they would have remorse, even if they killed someone who was innocent" (in Maass 2005:47).

Thus, selective violence targets many innocent people. Recounting the violence that took place in his village during the Greek Civil War, the writer of a local history concludes that the killings were caused "somewhat" by the political affiliation of the victims but "more" by the vengeful obsession of their enemies (Kanellopoulos 1981:609). The Phoenix program in Vietnam was often "rooting out the wrong people" (Adams 1994:179; FitzGerald 1989:516), the Huk guerrillas in the Philippines "killed people whom they thought were spies or enemies but were later shown not to be" (Kerkvliet 1977:177), and both the UNITA and the MPLA in Angola executed many innocent people as traitors based on false accusations resulting from personal enmities (Brinkman 2000:15). A local FLN commander in Algeria is said to have caused the execution of as many as 3,000 mainly innocent men and women in his campaign of terror, launched in 1958 and 1959 after the French were able to adroitly foster suspicions amongst the Algerians (Horne 1987:323). In El Salvador, many false denunciations were "enough to seal one's fate, since government forces seldom investigated the charges and 'innocent until proven guilty' was not a principle recognized by the military, security forces, or ORDEN civilian irregulars" (Binford 1996:107; also Wood 2003:96–7). A report about Sri Lanka states that "by taking informers at their word, [security] forces allowed old grudges, land disputes and business rivalries to be bloodily settled" (University of Teachers for Human Rights 1993:38). Joseba Zulaika (1988:99) "found that the solidly established 'facts' about [a presumed informer in the Basque village], such as his traitor role in the events of 1960, were plainly false."[22] Quotas and rewards for "neutralizations" only make this problem more acute (Courtois 1998:21; Moyar 1997:116; Chang 1992:218).

There is some systematic evidence beyond the anecdotal record. Peter Hart (1999:17, 303) extensively researched the archives of the British police and found that among the victims of the IRA in 1916–23 "very few were actual informers. Most were innocent victims." By comparing data on IRA executions and British intelligence, he concludes that the great majority of true informers were never suspected or punished; most of those shot (or denounced, expelled, or burned out of their homes) never informed, and those blacklisted were also usually innocent. In Peru, it was reported that the special antiterrorism courts set up to combat the Sendero insurgency convicted hundreds of people who were later proved to be innocent of aiding rebel groups. By the summer of 2000, 1,089 of these "innocents" were released either by pardon or reversal of their sentences (Krauss 2000:3).

---

[22] Additional instances of false denunciation are reported in Japanese-occupied Malaya (Kheng 1983:144, 180, 181–2), Guatemala (Warren 1998:99), and Sri Lanka (Senaratne 1997:147).

Overall, it is fair to surmise that political actors frequently fail to discriminate between the guilty and the innocent. Shall we then conclude that selective violence is an illusion and that all violence is, in fact, indiscriminate and, ultimately, counterproductive?

Such a conclusion would be erroneous. There is substantial evidence that political actors are successful in generating deterrence via selective violence *in spite of* killing many innocent people. This was clearly the case with the Phoenix program in Vietnam, which is described simultaneously as relatively inaccurate and very effective (Sheehan 1989:116; West 1985:95). The same was true about the IRA. The British authorities concluded in a 1921 intelligence report that the IRA was notoriously inaccurate: "In every case but one the person murdered [by the IRA] had given [them] no information"; at the same time, however, they recognized that, in spite of this, the IRA's war on informers was highly effective (Hart 1999:300). My own research in Greece corroborates this insight: many people were killed selectively but erroneously; yet their deaths were a deterrent, as intended by the perpetrators. In sum, though imperfect, selective violence is effective. But how?

To achieve deterrence, political actors must convince the targeted population that they are able to monitor and sanction their behavior with reasonable accuracy. In other words, they need to cultivate a *perception of credible selection*. They can achieve this goal without being perfectly accurate in their targeting. A mix of accurate and erroneous hits is compatible with a perception of credible selection under three conditions.[23]

First, the very presence of local agents signals the organization's willingness and potential capacity to be selective. Only if the moral hazard problems become excessive do political actors need to intervene; otherwise, the system remains in effect. Political actors advertise their selective capability as being a function of local agency: one of the principal slogans of Shining Path was "the party has a thousand eyes and a thousand ears" (Degregori 1998:143). In this sense, the importance of local agents is based less on what they actually do and more on their very existence. If the public believes that a network of informers is active, they will tend to infer that a victim was guilty (Herrington 1997:39) – or at least they will be too uncertain not to take such a possibility into account, an insight consistent with many observations about the paralyzing effect of the perception that an effective network of informers is active: "No one can be sure who is who" was the expression that described how people felt in Guatemala (Green 1995:105). A man described the situation in Ireland in 1922–3: "Perhaps the most reprehensible things one meets here is what is known as 'Intelligence.' One never knows to whom he is speaking. One never knows who is or who is not an 'Intelligence Officer.' . . . all eyes seem to gaze and all tongues to whisper in suspicion and doubt wherever

---

[23] Obviously, the optimal strategy for political actors is random selection that appears to be selective (I thank Diego Gambetta for pointing this out to me). In practice, this is difficult to achieve; the administrative machinery required to create a credible perception of selection is extremely costly to set up and, once in place, it leads to a mix of correct and erroneous hits rather than purely random targeting.

one happens to go" (in Hart 1999:124). Although violence is often public,[24] there is a certain ambiguity about its true causes. Descriptions of terror consistently include rumors and blacklists compiled in obscurity, as well as "whisperings, innuendos, rumors" about who is on these lists (Green 1995:109; Faivre 1994: 145).

Second, local agents help political actors avoid blatant mistakes, which are easy to spot by the public and create a general perception of consistent mistargeting.[25] As I discussed in the previous chapter, indiscriminate violence produces the highly visible mistargeting of potential or actual sympathizers of the indiscriminate actor, something that can be avoided through local delegation. Political actors do not want people to ask, as they did a local Palestinian leader about the assassination of a suspected collaborator of the Israelis, "Why did you kill this guy? He is innocent" (in Swedenburg 1995:199).[26]

Third, when defection takes place under constraints (i.e., where the rival actor has the upper hand), it is generally a secret activity; people cannot tell whether a particular victim was really a defector or not.[27] In the areas of El Salvador studied by Leigh Binford (1996:112), "the majority of the politically 'undecided' population had no way of knowing whether or not the accusations that the victims [of the army] had collaborated with the guerrillas were merited, since the ERP maintained a low profile there." When uncertain about the victims' innocence or guilt but somewhat persuaded about the organization's credibility, most people tend to infer guilt and alter their behavior accordingly. Consider the following examples from Algeria, Vietnam, Sri Lanka, and Colombia:

When we were hearing that persons X or Y had been found murdered, we said to ourselves: "Who would have believed that they were traitors? But they must have been, since the FLN executed them." (in Hamoumou 1993:157)

[24] They may leave messages on the victims' bodies, occasionally organizing (usually rigged) public trials and public confessions (Kheng 1983:180; Cobb 1972:1921). For example, the Vietcong would pin a "death notice" to the body, which listed the alleged "crimes" of the victim and stated that in the course of committing these crimes, the victim had "amassed many blood debts to the people" and therefore had to be condemned.

[25] Note that the victim's family will not be convinced; however, they will not speak up if it is too dangerous to do so (Hamoumou 1993:157, 174). Plus, claims by a victim's family are not usually seen as being credible.

[26] This is why the option of random selection under the pretense of actual selection cannot work. Note as well that the assassination of individuals who are known to have been victims of malicious denunciation is not necessarily interpreted as an instance of mistargeting since malicious denunciations can also be true.

[27] Even members of the organization targeted by the violence may be unsure of the innocence of some of their colleagues. The degree of secrecy of defection varies depending on additional factors, such as the patterns of past organization. For example, the Japanese noticed that, following their mopping-up campaign, Communist organizations were stronger in Yongqing than in Hejian (both in Central Hebei, China), and this despite the fact that Communist tradition had been much stronger in Hejian. Because organizing in Hejian had started under fairly secure military conditions, Communist activists were known by all villagers; when the Communists were forced out, most local activists could be denounced; in contrast, because the Communist organization in Yongqing was built later and under much less favorable conditions, it included secret organizations that were better able to withstand the Japanese onslaught (Hartford 1989:117).

The VC executed four persons in my village. They explained that these people were paid agents of the Government authorities. Nobody could figure out whether this was true or not. Everybody was afraid. No one dared say anything. (in Mallin 1966:72)

The insurgent JVP succeeded in conveying a "general presumption that, if someone were killed by [them], then s/he had done something which deserved punishment." (M. Moore 1993:628)

There is a widespread belief among the population that victims of the violence had "asked for trouble." Typical comments about people who had been murdered included "*Algo debía*" (He had something on his slate) or "*Es que se habia polarisado*" (He had himself polarized); killings would often be "explained" by designating the victim as a *desintegrado*, a *descompuesto*, a *ladrón* (thief), a *faltón* (someone who hadn't kept his word), a *hablón* (someone who talks too much) or a *desechable* (a disposable person). (G. Martin 2000:181)

In short, the effectiveness of selective violence hinges less on pinpoint accuracy and more on a perception among the population that a process of selection is taking place. The use of local agents is essential in generating this perception and helps explain the apparent paradox of campaigns of selective violence that are highly effective despite failures of accuracy.

7.5. A POLITICAL ECONOMY OF DENUNCIATION

The incidence of denunciation depends on both motivations and constraints. Motivations are plentiful and diverse (Chapter 10); even low levels of social conflict and high levels of solidarity may not prevent denunciations from taking place given the small number of people required to set this process in motion. Constraints are much more effective regulators of denunciation.

The supply of denunciations is subject to a fundamental constraint, namely the likelihood of retaliation faced either by the denouncer or by the local committee that vets denunciations. While the norm-driven loathing often triggered by this act is a potential source of risk for the denouncer, the real risk comes from credible threats of reprisals rather than diffuse feelings of dislike. This dimension, of course, is standard in organized crime: credible threats of retaliation discourage witnesses from testifying (e.g., Butterfield 2005). A similar mechanism can be found in civil war. A Greek villager explained why he refrained from denouncing to the right-wing authorities the leftist villagers who caused the death of his uncle: "There were partisans roaming around the village," he told me; "you did not know what could happen to you" (I-10). A Greek Communist villager (Nikolaidis 1977:55) recalls how he reacted after a Communist guerrilla had a local villager tried by a "popular court" and beat him up: "Do you have any idea how we will suffer because of your kangaroo court? You are leaving but we have to stay here." This process is apparent in the following examples from Kenya, Algeria, Vietnam, and Northern Ireland:

Even when such people are known to "loyalist" Kikuyu living in the towns to be Mau Mau followers, it is not easy for these people to give evidence against them or point them out. If they did so, swift retaliation would follow. (Leakey 1954:121)

The inhabitants will know them, since they suffer terribly from their activities, but will not denounce these agents unless they can do so without risk. Fear of reprisal will always prevent them from communicating to us information they possess.... To succeed, we must never lose sight of the fact that we will receive information only if people can give us information without risk to themselves. (Trinquier 1964:35, 78)

Rule number one was "Never inform the government of Communist activities." In Hiep Hoa, most of the villagers were well aware which families were revolutionary families and who constituted the village's party committee. But no one could be certain of the loyalties of every one of his neighbors.... Virtually every hamlet in Vietnam had at least one clandestine informant who would not hesitate to report to the Vietcong the name of a farmer who warned the Americans about a booby trap. The Vietcong's organization was thus the major device by which the revolution insured the silence of the people – and this silence was sufficient to frustrate our efforts. (Herrington 1997:39)

Thus the major factor in the initial decline of GVN intelligence on the situation in the countryside was a change in the security of the intelligence agents: the GVN lost the ability to protect them. Obviously the risk calculation changed. Given the seriousness of likely reprisals for such activity, those who were in it for the money must have found that it wasn't worth risking their lives. Those who bore grudges against the revolution found that the costs of exacting revenge had escalated dramatically. (Elliott 2003:424)

She lived in the area. She knew who killed her husband, but she couldn't say who killed him, because my brothers all lived there and my father lived in the area, so they would have had to leave the country. They wouldn't have been able to stay. So she couldn't really say anything about who killed him. She saw his killers every day and they used to scare her to make sure she kept her mouth closed. (in Smyth and Fay 2000:23)

The significance of the risk of retaliation as a determinant of denunciation is consistent with psychological studies according to which the relative strength of signs of retaliation inhibit revenge (Bandura 1983); with experimental evidence suggesting that the anticipation of retaliation is, under some circumstances, an effective regulator of aggression (Walters 1966); with sociological studies of rural contexts showing that peasants take seriously into consideration the power of their competitors in deciding whether to challenge them or refrain from doing so (e.g., Hua and Linshan 1996:180–2); and with studies of criminal or quasi-criminal environments demonstrating that credible threats of retaliation by criminals inhibit victims and witnesses from reporting the crime or providing evidence (e.g., Crisp 2000:620) – not to mention numerous casual yet insightful observations in literary texts (e.g., Stendhal 1996:38).

This risk explains why denouncers (as well as informers) seek anonymity. A Russian dictionary defines denunciation as "a secret revelation to government representatives of some kind of illegal activity" (Kozlov 1996). Political actors are often willing to provide anonymity to mitigate the risks of denunciation (Kamen 1998:182; Moyar 1997:74).[28] The figure of the hooded informer fingering the people to be arrested (the infamous *encapuchado* in Latin America) is common across most civil wars.[29] Political actors dislike total anonymity because it is "an open invitation to perjury and malicious testimony" (Kamen 1998:182).

---

[28] An advertisement I saw in the New York subway included the following message: "You don't have to reveal your identity to help solve a violent crime. Call 1-800-577-tips. Rewards up to $2,000."

[29] E.g., D. Anderson (2005:202); Wood (2003:114); Mahmood (2000:83); Zur (1998:80); Stoll (1993:62); Stubbs (1989:44); Kheng (1980:96); Kerkvliet (1977:66); Kitson (1960:100).

However, anonymity is not easy to achieve, especially in small communities. "There were no secrets in a rural Vietnamese hamlet," recalls Stuart Herrington (1997:23). Of a stupid man, Cypriot peasants say: "He thought he could beat his wife, without his neighbors hearing" (Durrell 1996:224). It is often possible to guess the origin of a denunciation, particularly when personal feuds and small communities are concerned (e.g., Butterfield 2005:22; Argenti-Pillen 2003:61-2; Berlow 1998:44).[30] Kevin Andrews (1984:122), who traveled across Greece in 1949, reproduces the following conversation he had in a village:

> "Tell me one thing. The people who burned the houses, the men who killed your sister and her child – what has become of them now?"
> "Become of them now?" He looked at me with Papastavros's same childlike gaze. "Nothing."
> "What do you mean?"
> "They're all there."
> "Still in the village!"
> "Where else would they go?"
> "But does he know who did it?"
> "Of course he does. In a village everything is known."

Petitions to higher authorities written by some victims in Civil War Missouri suggest that victims had guessed the probable identities of their victimizers (Fellman 1989:60); the masked members of a death squad in Guatemala were identified by the relatives of one of their victims (Paul and Demarest 1988:123); rumors about who betrayed Saddam Hussein's sons emerged immediately after they were killed;[31] in one Greek village of my study, the hooded informer who came along with the Germans to finger resistance members was recognized by so many of the villagers who were gathered in the village's central square that he had to take his hood off.

Relatives and friends of a victim of denunciation naturally desire revenge against either the denouncer or the local agents who endorsed the denunciation. Hence, potential denouncers and local committees must take into account the risk of retaliation they face. Unlike revenge in blood feuds, which is direct, retaliation in the context of civil war tends to be mediated. As discussed in Chapter 3, blood feuds are generally ritualistic occurrences regulated by a concrete set of norms about which offenses are subject to retaliation; these norms explain why people are willing to retaliate given the potentially large costs they face (Gould 2003). The unwillingness, in most societies, of the great majority of people to commit violent acts and the absence of revenge can be explained by the absence of blood feud norms.[32] Civil war increases the opportunities for revenge and lowers its costs significantly: a person need not directly bloody her hands.

---

[30] This is the point where feuds and purely political activity diverge: secret informing is much more difficult to detect than malicious denunciations based on personal and local conflicts.

[31] "Host betrayed Saddam's sons," BBC News, 24 July 2003, http://news.bbc.co.uk/1/hi/world/middle_east/3092783.stm.

[32] Consistent with the observation that mass killings are the work of relatively few people (Valentino 2004).

Retaliation takes the form of "counterdenunciation," that is, the denunciation of the initial denouncer to the rival political actor. Just as denouncers may use political actors to carry out their own ends, the family of a denunciation victim may "counterdenounce" the initial denouncer. In short, most people's fundamental dislike for committing violence with their own hands and the political actors' aspiration for monopolizing violence[33] turn counterdenunciation into the main tool for retaliation.

Two conditions must be fulfilled for a counterdenunciation to take place. First, the counterdenouncer must have access to the rival actor (and this actor must have the ability to carry out the reprisal). Access to political actors is asymmetrical, and they are naturally unwilling to endogenize revenge cycles. Second, just as denouncers take into account the risks of retaliation, counterdenouncers must think about counterretaliation.[34] When individuals feel that, even if recognized or revealed as denouncers, the political actor to whom they are denouncing their fellows has the ability to shield them from retaliation, they are more likely to denounce (or counterdenounce);[35] if they worry that in denouncing they are likely to be unprotected and hence face retaliation through counterdenunciation (or if they believe that their denunciation or counterdenunciation is unlikely to be implemented), they are unlikely to denounce.[36]

Although what counts as an acceptable level of protection, given the keenness of the motivating impulse, will vary with individuals' risk tolerance, the baseline answer is that denunciations will be a function of control exercised by political actors. Control also affects the ability of an actor to carry out a reprisal. I integrate this insight into the formal illustration of the theory of selective violence that follows.

7.6. A MODEL OF SELECTIVE VIOLENCE IN CIVIL WAR

I formally illustrate the theory of selective violence and generate predictions about the likelihood of selective and indiscriminate violence across space and about the identity of the perpetrators (whether they are incumbents or insurgents);

---

[33] Kathleen Hartford (1989:114) describes how the Chinese Communist Party placed "traitor-elimination" programs under direct control of the district party committee, not under the village party branch. Assassinations were vetted by the district, and independent revenge killings were not permitted.

[34] Of course, the identity of the counterdenouncer must be equally visible to that of the original denouncer.

[35] I assume that a low probability of being killed does not translate into very large expected costs. In fact, very low probabilities of death could actually make individuals behave as if the expected costs were zero. Substantial experimental evidence suggests that individuals tend to overestimate their chances of success for relatively beneficial actions and to underestimate their chances of success for potentially costly actions (e.g., Mirels 1980; Weinstein 1980; Larwood and Whitaker 1977; Miller and Ross 1975). When I asked several Greek informants why people denounced given a low probability of retaliation, they pointed to the driving habits of many locals who tend to drive very dangerously despite being aware of a low probability that they may suffer an accident.

[36] Denunciation to an actor who is unable to carry out the reprisal is functionally equivalent to be left unprotected by this political actor.

the theory is agnostic about the intensity and timing of the violence. To keep the model simple, I disaggregate it into three distinct but related processes: the individual calculus of defection, the individual calculus of denunciation, and the organizational calculus of violence.

Preferences are straightforward. Political actors maximize territorial control; they seek to "conquer" territory and increase the level of control over the territory they rule. I assume no anarchy; when one actor abandons a territory, the rival actor moves in. Increasing control means obtaining the exclusive collaboration of civilians and eliminating defection, that is, collaboration with the rival actor; this is the main function of selective violence.

The production costs of selective violence are assumed to be inversely related to control; I take the distribution of control at t_0 to be exogenous; once the process has begun, subsequent shifts of control are a function of two factors: first, exogenous military resources that allow an actor to "conquer" territory hitherto controlled by its rival and, second, the use of selective violence in territory that is already "conquered," which increases the degree of collaboration and hence control in the subsequent period t_1 – provided, of course, that the existing balance of power is not exogenously altered by one actor withdrawing forces or the rival actor bringing in additional forces.

Civilians are boundedly rational; they are reward-sensitive and seek to maximize a personal or political utility subject to their likelihood of survival; they also tend to conflate opportunities with their beliefs about opportunities. The model is agnostic about the motives of defection and denunciation: they can be political or personal, expressing ideology, revenge, or spite. However, I assume that denunciations take place locally between people who know each other. I also assume that individuals believe that the level of control exercised where they live is stable. Civilians must make two separate strategic decisions: whether to defect and whether to denounce. Political actors must decide whether to use violence and what kind to employ.

7.6.1. Defection

Consider a distribution of the geographical space into five discrete zones of control, ranging from 1 to 5. Zone 1 is an area of total incumbent control, and zone 5 is an area of total insurgent control. In between lie zones 2, 3, and 4, which are contested areas where control varies as follows: zone 2 is primarily controlled by the incumbents (dominant incumbent control), zone 4 is primarily controlled by the insurgents (dominant insurgent control), and zone 3 is controlled equally by both sides (parity).

Following Proposition 1, I assume that defection (i.e., collaboration with the rival actor) is shaped by the level of control exercised by the competing political actors. If there are k defectors in a village and c is the level of control an organization enjoys in the village, k(c) decreases as c increases. The benefits of defection include the material and/or nonmaterial advantages derived from helping an organization with which one is associated, while the costs of defecting and being caught – prison, torture, death – are steep. If i is the payoff for defecting and u is the cost of the defector being caught, then for the vast majority of people who prize survival $u > i$. The likelihood of being caught will, therefore, condition their willingness to defect given their preferences.

Political actors are willing to pay a premium for collaboration (in the form of more promises, promotion, or material goods) where their capacity to control decreases, even while their ability to deliver this premium decreases with control, as one moves away from zone 3 toward areas of weaker control. In contrast, their capacity to arrest defectors increases with control, as one moves away from zone 3 toward areas of stronger control. A defector is caught either by direct detection or by denunciation. If p is the probability that a defector will either be detected directly or denounced and caught, then the cost of defection is prohibitive where control for the rival actor is total: $pu > (1 - p)i$; p reaches its maximum value under total control and decreases until it reaches zero under the rival actor's total control. Figures 7.1 and 7.2 illustrate the relation between expected cost and benefits for collaboration with incumbents and insurgents respectively (or defection toward incumbents and insurgents) across the five zones of control.

It follows that only martyrs defect under total control (zones 1 and 5), though highly committed individuals defect under dominant control (zones 2, and 4). Defection picks up in zone 3 for both actors and explodes in zones 4 and 5 (toward the insurgents) and 2 and 1 (toward the incumbents) (Figure 7.3). Defection is a problem for incumbents in all zones except zone 1 and for insurgents in all zones except zone 5. Put otherwise, zones 1 and 5 are homogeneous, while zones 2, 3, and 4 are heterogeneous, consistent with their characterization as contested areas.

7.6.2. Denunciation

Consider the following formal illustration of the argument. There are two villagers, A and B; A chooses whether to denounce B or not, and B chooses whether to denounce A or not. Each villager has an exclusive political association with one political organization (villager A with organization A and villager B with organization B); in turn, each organization enjoys a certain level of control; r^A is the degree to which organization A is able to control the village and exclude organization B, and r^B is the degree to which organization B is able to control the village and exclude organization A. Consistent with the preceding discussion in this chapter, the values of r^A and r^B across the five zones of control are as follows: r^A goes up in zones 1 and 2 and down in zones 4 and 5, while r^B goes up in zones 4 and 5 and down in zones 1 and 2; zone 3 is a zone of parity where $r^A = r^B$. The spatial location of each villager (and hence r^A and r^B) is chosen by Nature.

Each villager supplies information to the organization, which carries out assassinations accordingly. I assume that the villagers can only inform the organization with which they are associated and that, once denounced, an individual will be targeted and assassinated by the actor to whom she is denounced with a probability p. Let p^A be the probability that organization A targets and succeeds in assassinating B following a denunciation, and p^B the probability that organization B targets

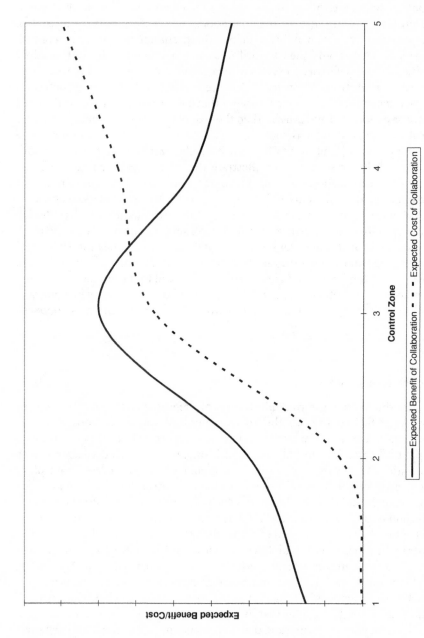

FIGURE 7.1. Payoffs and Expected Cost of Collaboration with (or Defection to) Incumbents

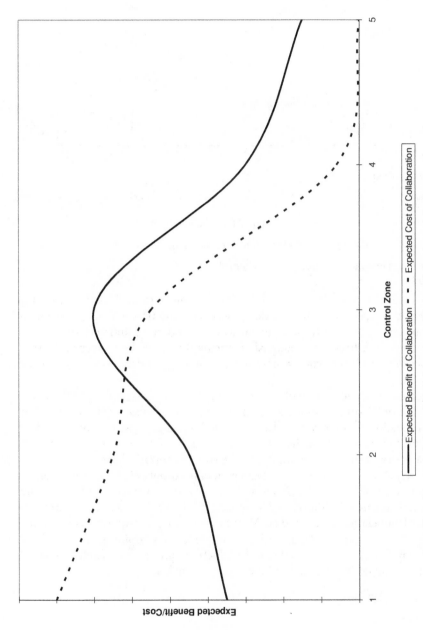

FIGURE 7.2. Payoffs and Expected Cost of Collaboration with (or Defection to) Insurgents

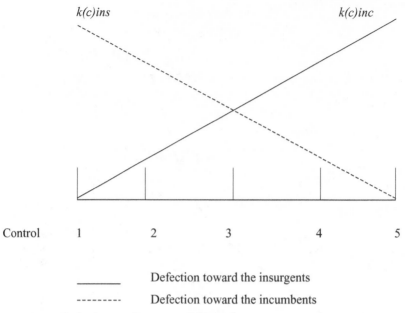

k(c)ins   k(c)inc

Control   1   2   3   4   5

———————   Defection toward the insurgents

----------   Defection toward the incumbents

FIGURE 7.3. Defection as a Function of Control

and succeeds in assassinating A following a denunciation. I assume visibility between the denouncer and the denouncee's family, thus allowing for potential retaliation: the family of a person who is denounced and assassinated has the option of retaliating by counterdenouncing the initial denouncer to the rival organization. Villagers choose between two strategies, denounce (D) and not denounce (N).

Let x be the value to individual A of A's organization's assassinating B and the value to B of B's organization's assassinating A; this is the satisfaction derived by the elimination of a local rival. Let y be the immediate cost to individual A of denouncing B and the immediate cost to individual B of denouncing A, which may consist of detection and sanctioning by the rival organization, which I assume to be death; $y > x$, because one's own death generally far outweighs whatever benefit is derived from a rival's denunciation and death. I assume x and y to be the constant across individuals. In addition to y, suppose q^A is the probability of retaliation via counterdenunciation by individual A's family against B and q^B is the probability of retaliation via counterdenunciation by individual B's family against A; q^A is a decreasing function of r^B, the degree to which organization B is able to control the village and q^B is a decreasing function of r^A, such as:

$$q^A = q^A(r^B)$$
$$q^B = q^B(r^A)$$

Note that these functions are symmetric and that q is convex before zero and concave after zero. The probability of retaliation via counterdenunciation depends on whether the rival organization exercises a monopoly or quasi monopoly of force.

It is, thus, possible to think of r^A and r^B as the extent to which an organization can shield an individual from retaliation by the other side.

There are four possible outcomes: {Denounce, Denounce} or (D,D), {Denounce, Not Denounce} or (D,N), {Not Denounce, Not Denounce} or (N,N), and (Not Denounce, Denounce} or (N,D). The payoffs of each outcome for each player are as follows:

Player A

$$P^A(D,D) = p^A(x - q^B(r^A)y) + p^B(q^A(r^B)x - y)$$

$$P^A(D,N) = p^A(x - q^B(r^A)y)$$

$$P^A(N,N) = 0$$

$$P^A(N,D) = p^A(q^A(r^B)x - y)$$

Player B

$$P^B(D,D) = p^B(x - q^A(r^B)y) + (q^B(r^A)x - y)$$

$$P^B(D,N) = p^B(q^B(r^A)x - y)$$

$$P^B(N,N) = 0$$

$$P^B(N,D) = p^B(x - q^A(r^B)y)$$

The equilibria are the following:

1. (D,D) is an equilibrium when $x \geq q^B(r^A)y$ and $x \geq q^A(r^B)y$ or $x/y \geq \text{Max}[q^B(r^A), q^A(r^B)]$
2. (N,N) is an equilibrium when $x \leq q^B(r^A)y$ and $x \leq q^A(r^B)y$ or $x/y \leq \text{Min}[q^B(r^A), q^A(r^B)]$
3. (D,N) is an equilibrium when $x \geq q^B(r^A)y$ and $x \leq q^A(r^B)y$ or $q^B(r^A) \leq x/y \leq q^A(r^B)y$
4. (N,D) is an equilibrium when $x \leq q^B(r^A)y$ and $x \geq q^A(r^B)y$ or $q^A(r^B) \leq x/y \leq q^B(r^A)y$

Individual A will denounce individual B without B denouncing A (D, N) when r^A is large and r^B is small, that is, when organization A has a monopoly or quasi monopoly of power and organization B cannot protect its supporters. Conversely (N,D) emerges when r^A is small and r^B is large. Given that $x/y < 1$, the mutual nondenunciation equilibrium (N,N) obtains when both organizations are unable to protect their collaborators ($q^A(r^B)$ and $q^B(r^A)$ are high and both r^A and r^B are small); in other words, individuals will refrain from denunciation given a high probability of a very steep cost, in a logic akin to the "mutually assured destruction" of nuclear competition.[37] In contrast, the mutual denunciation equilibrium (D,D) requires both organizations to simultaneously have a capacity to protect

---

[37] The assumption for (N,N) is that that the relationship between y, x, and q is such that at $r = .5$, $x < y * q$.

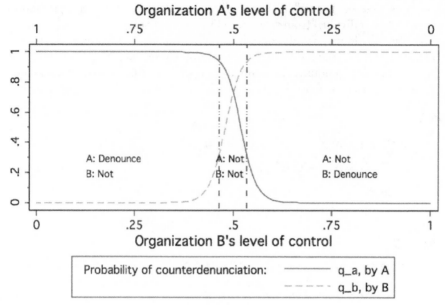

FIGURE 7.4. Individuals' Equilibrium Strategies

their collaborators and prevent retaliation ($q^A(r^B)$ and $q^B(r^A)$ are low, and both r^A and r^B are high); the presence of two strong quasi states at the same time and place is highly unlikely in civil war, where achieving a monopoly of power is the central goal of the rival sides.[38]

A simple simulation using reasonable numerical values for y and x (100 and 33, respectively) shows the distribution of equilibria across the values of r for the two villagers given the values of q (Figure 7.4). Individual A will denounce and individual B will not denounce if organization A enjoys more control compared with organization B, and vice versa. The mutual nondenunciation equilibrium emerges when the two organizations approach parity in control. Given the values of r^A and r^B in the five discrete zones of control, the equilibrium (D,N) should emerge in zones 1 and 2, the equilibrium (N,D) should emerge in zones 4 and 5, and the equilibrium (N,N) should emerge in zone 3 (Figure 7.5). Note that the absence of denunciation from the zone of parity is consistent with the high rates of defection in that zone, as discussed previously.

7.6.3. Violence

I now turn to political actors. Let the benefit of using violence for an actor be b and the cost of violence v. Actors will use violence when b > v and will refrain from using violence when b < v; b includes the consolidation of their control which is

---

[38] Note that (D,D) may also result in nonviolence, as the two sides effectively shield their collaborators from counterdenunciation, but it is unlikely to be the dynamic at work when we see nonviolence occur, as argued previously. In Chapters 8 and 9, I search for direct evidence on the mechanism of nonviolence in zones of parity.

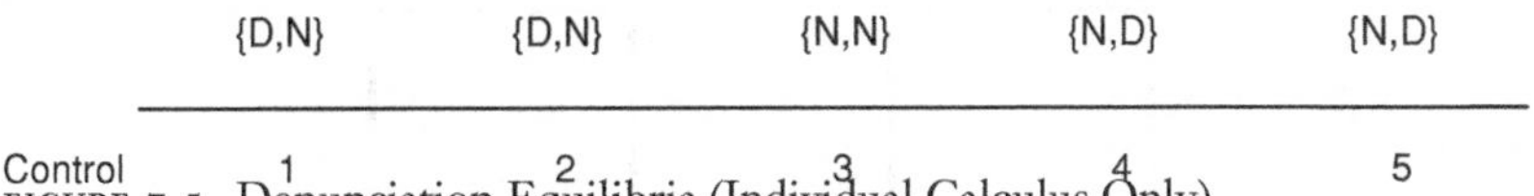

{D,N}	{D,N}	{N,N}	{N,D}	{N,D}
Control 1	2	3	4	5

FIGURE 7.5. Denunciation Equilibria (Individual Calculus Only)

achieved by the elimination of actual defectors and (especially) the deterrence of potential defectors; v captures the potential backfire effect of violence, as those affected by it may, under some conditions, defect toward the rival actor, even though they did not intend to defect prior to the violence; it also includes the alienation effect of violence perceived as being gratuitous, even when few opportunities of defection exist; v is a function of their ability to defect (which depends on access to the competing actor) and the perception that compliance is futile and does not guarantee survival, which depends on the selectivity of violence.

Information about defectors comes either from direct monitoring, when the level of control is high, or from denunciations when control is lower; this is the case because direct monitoring entails a large administrative apparatus that is unavailable when control is challenged, that is, in contested areas. If there are no denunciations, or if denunciations are known to be systematically false, then the cost of violence will exceed its benefit (b < v), hence there will be no violence. An indicator of the overall bias of denunciations is the actors' estimate of the likelihood of defection, k(c). Where the rival actor is absent, defection is unlikely: k(c) = 0; hence most denunciations are likely false.[39] From the discussion of defection it follows that k(c) = 0 for incumbents in zone 1 and for insurgents in zone 5. Therefore, selective violence should not be observed in these zones; selective violence should neither be observed in zone 3 where the theory predicts an absence of denunciations (and, hence, of information) or a local veto to violence due to the fear of counterdenunciation. Figure 7.6 illustrates the predicted relationship between control and violence.

In short, where levels of control are high, there is no defection, no denunciation, and no violence.[40] If violence is observed in zones 1 and 5, it is likely to be indiscriminate violence exercised by the rival actor. Where one actor exercises hegemonic but incomplete control (zones 2 and 4), there will be defections and denunciations; hence political actors have both an incentive and the ability to use selective violence. Finally, in areas of parity (zone 3) there will be much defection but no denunciation. Although the incentive to use violence is high, its cost will be even higher. In the absence of information, using indiscriminate violence in zone 3 could result in mass defection toward the rival actor, hence its low likelihood. Indiscriminate violence should be observed in zones 2 (by insurgents) and 4 (by incumbents), though with lower probability compared to zones 1 and 5, following the conjecture that it is inversely related to the availability of information (Chapter 6). Figure 7.7 provides a depiction of how defection, denunciation, and selective violence are predicted to vary across the five zones of control.

[39] After a few iterations where denunciations are not acted upon, denunciations should cease altogether.

[40] To be more precise, there will be little homicidal violence; violence is likely to take nonhomicidal forms (imprisonment) and be used to achieve goals other than the deterrence of defection (e.g., the punishment of criminals).

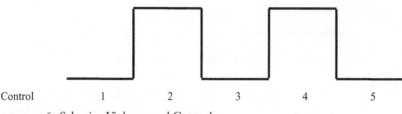

Control   1   2   3   4   5

FIGURE 7.6. Selective Violence and Control

The predictions can be restated as testable hypotheses.

Hypothesis 2 The higher the level of an actor's control, the less likely it is that this actor will resort to violence, selective or indiscriminate. Therefore, no incumbent violence is likely in zone 1 and no insurgent violence is likely in zone 5.

Hypothesis 3 The lower the level of an actor's control, the less likely that this actor will resort to selective violence and the more likely that its violence, if any, will be indiscriminate. Therefore, insurgent violence in zones 1 and 2, if any, is likely be indiscriminate and incumbent violence in zones 4 and 5, if any, is likely be indiscriminate.

Hypothesis 4 Under fragmented control, violence will be exercised primarily by the political actor enjoying an advantage in terms of control: incumbents in zone 2 and insurgents in zone 4.

Hypothesis 5 Parity of control between the actors (zone 3) is likely to produce no selective violence by any of the actors.

These predictions are counterintuitive insofar as neither political actors nor individuals resort to violence where they would like it most. In contrast to Arendt's (1970:56) implication that the highest level of contestation should breed the most violence because this is precisely where "power is in jeopardy," the most contested areas are predicted to be oases of peace in the midst of violence. An additional surprising prediction is that in zone 3, high levels of simultaneous defection toward both sides coexist with low levels of denunciations.[41] In other words, individuals collaborate with both sides but their collaboration excludes denunciation. The prediction about the absence of violence at the very center of the war is interesting in two ways. First, it suggests a complete contrast between symmetric and asymmetric war when it comes to violence. In the ideal type of conventional war, all violence takes place on the front line; in the ideal type of irregular war, the functional equivalent of the front line turns out to be peaceful for civilians. Second, this prediction reflects the theoretical insight about the joint production of violence: selective violence takes place only where and when the

---

[41] Note that even more intuitive predictions such as Hypothesis 2 are far from accepted wisdom; there is an extensive literature that links authoritarian state strength (a functional equivalent of full control) with high levels of violence (e.g., Rummel 1994; Duvall and Stohl 1983:175–6).

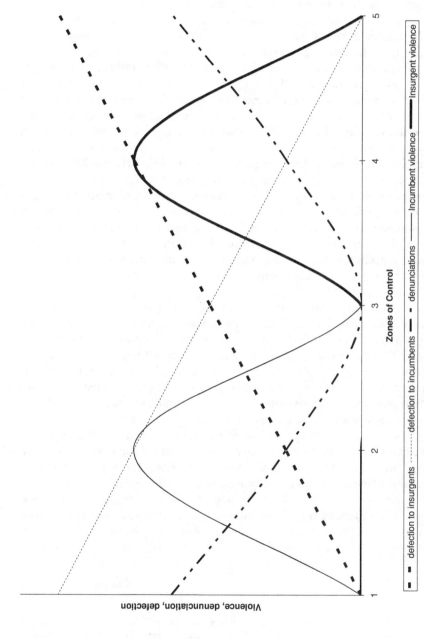

FIGURE 7.7. Predicted Pattern of Selective Violence, Defection, and Denunciation

Zones of Control

Violence, denunciation, defection

- ■ - defection to insurgents .... defection to incumbents ─■─ denunciations ───── Incumbent violence ──── Insurgent violence

205

incentives of local and supralocal actors converge. No violence takes place where political actors alone want it most or where local actors alone are most willing to provide the information necessary for its production.[42] Indeed, individuals will fail to get rid of their enemies where it is safest to denounce.

A key theoretical implication is that the logic of state terror (where power is directly translated to violence) is fundamentally at odds with the logic of civil war violence. The theory also points to the endogeneity of strategies of insurgent violence to the logic of control. For example, when insurgents know that they are unlikely to have an advantage in control, they may adopt a strategy of indiscriminate terrorism – as suggested by the cases of Northern Ireland, the Basque country, and Palestine. Furthermore, the predictions are at odds with the logic of the security dilemma, which posits the emergence of violence through preemption precisely in the most contested areas (zone 3), reasoning that where vulnerability is high every defensive move is likely to be interpreted by the opposite side as an offensive one, hence prompting violence. These predictions also contradict the security version of the technology of warfare thesis, which also sees violence peaking in the most contested areas (zone 3), where the actors are most vulnerable.[43] Likewise, if revenge is Hobbesian behavior, it ought to be observed primarily where authority is more decentralized, that is, zone 3. Finally, if control reflects polarization, the most polarized area should be zone 3, where the population is divided and collaborates with the two rivals. However, exactly the opposite is predicted by the theory.

This theory aims to predict variation in violence within civil wars and should be able to tell us something about cross-national variation in violence? If the theory is correct, the deadliest civil wars will be those where one or more of the following conditions obtain: indiscriminate violence is high; control shifts frequently (zones 2 and 4 dominate); areas of equal distribution of control (zone 3) are limited; and areas of complete control (zones 1 and 5) are limited. Obviously, these patterns are consistent with many types of military interaction. Where indiscriminate violence is high, Chapter 6 suggests that this may be a function of insurgents being threatening but weak, itself a function of the particular geopolitical situation (e.g., an insurgency that seeks to control the state may be seen as more threatening compared with a secessionist one, ceteris paribus). Where control shifts frequently, it may be caused by external intervention at key junctures of the conflict, which allows the side that loses to reclaim territory that was lost. The American and North Vietnamese interventions during the South Vietnamese insurgency are a case in point. An interesting implication is that not all long wars are the same: some long civil wars are stalemates with few control

---

[42] This point resonates with Roldán's (2002:90) observation that in Colombia "violence could not succeed when it was embraced by either a handful of local leaders or the regional government alone."

[43] Recall that the security version of the technology of warfare thesis served as my basis for theoretical development. This is an example of how theoretical predictions can go beyond initial assumptions.

shifts, and hence low violence,[44] whereas other long civil wars may be cases entailing continuous control shifts and, thus, high levels of violence. Obviously, the latter can only be sustained in the presence of high levels of foreign assistance to the rival parties. The multiplicity of competing mechanisms underlying observationally equivalent aggregate outcomes suggests the enormous pitfalls of inductive cross-national studies.

7.7. CAVEATS

Theories simplify, and this one is no exception. Its simplicity constitutes its great strength. Nevertheless, it is worth highlighting these simplifications.

To begin with, the theory exogenizes military decisions concerning the allocation of resources across space and time. The theory also assumes that individuals are good at assessing risk – in this case, they are able to assess the risk of being caught when defecting and the risk of being counterdenounced if denouncing. Yet, there is evidence from psychological experiments that people are not good at assessing risk in general (Kahneman and Tversky 1974). Nonrational concerns cloud or even distort thinking, shorten time horizons, or undermine the instrumental efficiency of behavior. Keep in mind, however, that the urge to survive can be a powerful corrective. Second, the relationship between denunciation and control depicted here is static and assumes a stable strategic environment. Individuals look around, evaluate the level of *present* control exercised by the two rival actors, and if the risk of retaliation is low enough, they denounce. Likewise, political actors care primarily about deterring defection, not about acquiring the peoples' goodwill for future governance. This assumes that individuals ignore the future (the likelihood that control may shift and that they may face retribution) or the past (emotions such as the desire for revenge for the violence that just took place may prove to be so overpowering as to produce a drastic discount in risk assessments).

Without discounting the role of individual expectations and emotions (which I indirectly test for in Chapter 9), it is important to note that individuals tend to underestimate the duration and fluidity of civil wars and hence overestimate their own security, especially in the war's initial stages.[45] During the same period, people are inexperienced and, hence, much more likely to believe the claims of political actors about the stability of their rule. For example, a Mozambican

---

44 This is the case with the regions of El Salvador studied by Wood: late in the war, a stalemate emerged, and there was low violence. At the microlevel, stalemate signals the possibility for individuals to remain neutral (Wood 2003:153).

45 For example, Kerkvliet (1977:165) reports that according to former Philippino Huk rebels "peasants thought the revolt would last only a short time." A former Mau Mau recalls that: "Few realized that the struggle might last two or three years. Most were thinking in terms of a few months" (Barnett and Njama 1966:151). In El Salvador, Binford (1996:112) reports, many peasants "were waiting the situation out and hoping that things would improve. No one – army, ERP combatants, civilians – could have predicted at that time that the Salvadoran civil war would endure for another ten years." Similar observations are made by Joes (2000:73), Upton (1980:275), Escott (1978:171), and Hunt (1974:45).

man recalls that when RENAMO insurgents came to his village in 1984, they organized a meeting and claimed that "Frelimo would never come again and cause trouble" (in Nordstrom 1997:90). The mental transition to a state of civil war takes time: civilians are generally facing a completely novel situation, unlike anything they have known. Moreover, given limitations in the flow of information, many people tend to form expectations about the future based exclusively on local reality. Even when a war has lasted for a long time, people tend to overemphasize the immediate over the long-term future. In his report, a British official who visited northern Greece in 1948, remarked: "I think it would be fair to say that the Western Macedonian peasant, like most people who have to exist in a situation of uncertainty, danger and disaster, is at present living very much on a day-to-day basis, and does not look beyond the immediate future." A BBC correspondent who was kidnapped by the Greek rebels in a different region around the same time stated that the peasants "live in a state of complete uncertainty, able to look only a few weeks ahead."[46] Finally, it is important to stress the geographical fragmentation caused by civil war, whose main product is the fragmentation of information. A Greek observer pointed out in 1944 that the main consequence of the breakdown of communications between the provinces was "the isolation of the inhabitants who have no idea what is going on even in the districts next to them."[47] Therefore, individual decisions are often made on the basis of highly localized information and local developments. The case is easier to make for political actors, whose victory (or survival) is a precondition for the application of any political program.

Finally, I assume only two actors, yet many civil wars give rise to a multiactor context. However, the theory can speak to such contexts as well. War entails a reductionist logic, and very often local environments reduce competition to between only two actors even when the national context is multiactor. Rarely are all actors in a multiactor conflict simultaneously active in every locality of a country and where they are, alliances tend to produce bipolar conflict.

Once again, note that the theory of selective violence is not intended as a complete representation of reality, but as a sensible simplification, a theorical baseline, and a useful tool for the derivation of theorically based empirical predictions. Comparing the actual empirical variation against this baseline allows the specification of the empirical fit of the theory; furthermore, the identification of its empirical failures is particularly productive (Chapter 9).

Nevertheless, the theory can be further refined and expanded. Modeling the very complex military dynamics of the war will help endogenize them into the theory and clarify how different types of war affect violence. In turn, this will allow the derivation of robust hypotheses about the variation of violence across wars, as well as across several types of violence – from organized crime to terrorism and genocide. It is also possible to specify more complex theories that incorporate

---

[46] "Report by Mr. D. S. L. Dodson on a tour of Western Macedonia (26–29 November 1948)," PRO, FO 371/72328/R14275; "Notes on Conversation with Mr. Kenneth Matthews on the 1st November, 1948," PRO, FO 371/72217/R1237.

[47] "General Report on Conditions in Athens," PRO, FO 371/43690.

heterogeneous individual preferences, community structures, and fragmented organizations; additional dimensions of violence (e.g., displacement, hostage taking, imprisonment); a more realistic specification of expectations about the future and learning from the past; and additional parameters (e.g., multiple armed actors, the role of propaganda, modern mass media, diasporas, and transnational networks). Hopefully, this book will help spark a research agenda in these directions.

7.8. CONCLUSION

This chapter has specified a theory of selective violence in civil war as a *joint* process, created by the actions of both political actors and civilians. The key resources around which the process is arrayed are information and violence. Political actors need information in order to be able to target selectively, to distinguish from among the sea of civilians those who are abetting the enemy. Civilians have information, which they provide through denunciation, which can be either political, or, more likely, malicious, in hopes that the violence of the political actors will be directed against those denounced. There is, significantly, a great potential for abuse in such a system, but violence need only be perceived as selective in order to avoid the pitfalls of indiscriminate violence. Denunciation will only occur in such situations in which its benefits, be they psychological or material, outweigh the predicted costs; the most significant cost would be retaliation, quite possibly in the form of a counterdenunciation by the victim or the victim's family to the other political actor. Hence, denunciation will only occur when potential denouncers perceive the political actor as able to protect them from retaliation. This process is modeled in terms of control, with the number of defectors decreasing as control increases and the number of denouncers increasing as control increases. Selective violence can only take place in those areas where control is complete enough for denouncers to denounce, but not so complete that defectors have either fled or simply ceased to be of concern to the political actor. The theory thus predicts that political actors will not use violence where they need it most: it is there that denouncers are most exposed to retaliation, and in the absence of information necessary to make violence selective, no violence is likely to take place.

8

Empirics I

Comparative Evidence

It is difficult to really understand this war here – it is a very complicated thing.

A Mozambican peasant

Then I asked the question to which I had long been seeking an answer:
"Which side, then, has committed more crimes here, the Right or the Left?"
"I can only tell you the side that happens to have most power in one district or another also has the most opportunity to commit them."

Kevin Andrews, *The Flight of Icarus*

In this chapter I focus on control: how to measure it, how it shifts, and how it relates to violence. I then provide broad comparative evidence, a plausibility test and a necessary first step. Chapter 9 supplies a rigorous test in a specific setting.

8.1. MEASURING CONTROL

The most significant empirical challenge is the measurement of control. Control can be defined and measured empirically, using various indicators such as the level of, presence of, and access enjoyed by political actors in a given place and time. Ideally, the perfect indicator of control would reflect "the probability that a certain event or class of events will not occur within a defined area within a defined period of time, for example . . . the probability that the there will be no movement of external hostile individuals within the hamlet area between the hours 1800 and 0600" (Race 1973:277). Because control is such an essential part of civil war, political actors have developed various measures, the most elaborate of which were probably those used by the United States military in Vietnam.[1]

---

[1] These measures of control were initially crude: yellow areas (or areas A) were government-controlled; blue areas (areas B) were disputed; and red areas (areas C) were Vietcong-controlled (R. Thompson 1966:132). Eventually a highly sophisticated and computerized system of measurement

The five-zone measure introduced in the previous chapter is an appropriate instrument for capturing the subtleties of control. Incumbents exercise *full control* in zone 1; they have destroyed most or all insurgent clandestine cells and are able to prevent the rebels from entering or operating with any effectiveness. The population has no access to them. Many cities in civil war settings would fit this description, such as the city of Algiers in the aftermath of the battle of the Casbah. In adjacent zone 2, incumbents exercise *secure but incomplete control*; clandestine insurgent cells are still in operation and the rebels, present in the surrounding area, can make sporadic visits by night. For example, the so-called Passive Wing of the Mau Mau movement in Kenya consisted of clandestine organizations that were formed in areas where control was primarily, but not fully, in the hands of the British and their local allies (Kitson 1960:15–16). In China, the Communists were often able to infiltrate local nationalist militias and turn local officials who were known as "red heart, white skin" (Benton 1989:79).

Conversely, insurgents maintain full control in zone 5 and secure but incomplete control in adjacent zone 4, often referred to as a "semi-liberated area" (e.g., Tucker 2001:144). Zone 5 areas are sometimes known as "base areas" or "liberated areas." There, rebels operate openly with minimum interference from government forces. For instance, the Maoist rebels exercised total sovereignty over vast stretches of Nepal in 2005: "They have instituted a raft of new laws. . . . Legal disputes are adjudicated by a roving people's court. . . . Policing is done by a people's militia." Red flags mark the gates of their capital: "The nearest police station or military post or post office – or indeed any sign of the authority of the Royal Kingdom of Nepal, within whose boundaries this hamlet officially sits – is a three day hike through the hills" (Sengupta 2005c:67). In zone 4 areas, insurgents enjoy prominence: "Outside their so called base areas," Somini Sengupta (2005c:67) notes, "the Maoists don't hold territory for long. But for all practical purposes rural Nepal, apart from the district capitals, is theirs to rule." However, in those areas, they cannot prevent sporadic visits by incumbent forces and must contend with clandestine cells of informers. For example, when the Japanese established themselves in a village during their occupation of China, they sent spies into the surrounding villages that were controlled by rebels (Hartford 1989:99).

Consider the civil war in El Salvador. In what the insurgents designated as *zonas de control*, they exercised full sovereignty: "The army has given up trying

---

was developed. Called Hamlet Evaluation System (HES), it tracked the evolution of control on a regular basis in all 10,000 hamlets of South Vietnam. Measures of control changed over time and the definitive version included five "security" grades ranging from A (best security) to E (worst security), based on the averaging of responses to eighteen questions, plus a sixth category (VC hamlet) (Kalyvas and Kocher 2004; Thayer 1985; HES/70; RG 300 Records of the Office of the Secretary of Defense). In Malaya, the British used blue pins on their maps for villages that came under their control; areas where full control had already been achieved were designated "white areas" (Stubbs 1989; Clutterbuck 1966). In Guatemala the army classified communities according to their supposed guerrilla sympathies using colored pins on maps: green communities were "free of subversion"; red communities were those in enemy hands; pink and yellow communities were those where guerrilla influence was thought to be more ambiguous (Carmack 1988a:xv–xvi). Similar classification schemes are reported about Northern Ireland (Collins 1999:15), Sri Lanka (Lawrence 2000:174), and Colombia (Arnson and Kirk 1993:72) – none of which are in the public domain.

to maintain a fixed presence in the form of garrisons or 'civil defense' militias, nor does it mount civic action programs to win over the people. Army leaders know these are pointless. The *zonas* are the revolution's heartland, where the FMLN exercises complete political authority, and no traces of governmental authority – whether in the form of mayors, or teachers, or health workers – are tolerated" (J. L. Anderson 2004:136–7). Zone 4, or what the insurgents called the *zona de expansión* begins, where the *zona de control* ends. There, Jon Lee Anderson points out (2004:137–9), the rebels didn't feel secure enough to operate as openly as in the *zona de control*. The police posts and army garrisons had all been overrun and the mayors chased out, but the inhabitants were not certain about the strength of the rebels' rule. They had some access to state authorities, present beyond the zone, to whom clandestine informers could have conveyed information about the insurgents; as a result, the insurgents spent "much of their time gathering intelligence, adding to an already impressive dossier on the local civilians."

What distinguishes zones of incomplete control (2 and 4) from zones of full control (1 and 5) is that in the former the population has access, albeit unequal, to both actors. This is not the case in the latter, where the sovereign has a monopoly of force on a daily basis and in pretty much unequivocal fashion. Zone 4 is not within the grasp of the incumbents, but is within their reach – and the converse is true about insurgents and zone 2.

Finally, there is an intermediate area, zone 3, where both actors enjoy equal levels of control. In El Salvador, these areas were designated by the insurgents as the *zonas en disputa*, or contested areas. According to J. L. Anderson's (2004:140) description, "the army still maintains a fixed presence, and government offices remain open, but the guerrillas also claim the loyalty of some of the inhabitants. The FMLN considers these areas to have a 'duality of powers.'" These areas are usually described as places where the government rules by day and the rebels by night (e.g., Livanios 1999:201; Butaud and Rialland 1998:47). "By the day the kishlaks [villages] are ours," observed a Soviet soldier who served in Afghanistan (in Borovik 1991:63) and "by night they are theirs. That's the thing." Such was the situation in certain areas of Namibia: "During the day South African soldiers demonstrate their presence and strength, and at night SWAPO guerrillas turn up" (in Groth 1995:28). A Vietnamese shopkeeper recalled: "The Vietminh were very strong here. The government troops just operated a little bit right around the market, and in the evening they withdrew into the outpost. Then the Vietminh would come up and move around freely" (Race 1973:4). Ellsberg (2003:114) discovered a similar situation in the mid-1960s when he toured rural Vietnam; it was possible to imagine signs that said "GVN traffic on this road only between 7:00 AM and 6:00 PM, at all other hours VC traffic only." Likewise, the village of Mambagaton, in the Philippines was in what the military called an "NPA-infested area," a "Red area," which meant "the Army might claim control in daylight, but at night the terrain belonged to the NPA" (Berlow 1998:33). Sometimes the boundaries of the "night" extend well into the day. During the summer of 2004, in the Iraqi town of Ramadi, the police and national guard kept order until 1:00 P.M., at which point they disappeared from the streets to be replaced by insurgents who controlled the city until daybreak (Huseen and Pelhman 2004).

8.2. HOW CONTROL SHIFTS

Shifts in control are primarily a function of tactical military decisions. First, political actors decide how to allocate scarce military resources (Trinquier 1964:71–2). For example, incumbents may target a group of villages up to then controlled by insurgents (zones 4 or 5); they do so by moving into these villages, "conquering" and occupying them – "clearing and securing" them, in counterinsurgency language (Meyerson 1970:19). Insurgents, who typically lack the military means to defend these villages against frontal assault, flee along with their most prominent local collaborators.[2] However, they may remain in the surrounding area and keep contacts with clandestine cells of collaborators within these villages (i.e., "defectors"); in other words, these villages have moved from zone 4 or 5 to zone 2. Using their newfound control, incumbents begin to collect local information, which they use to exercise selective violence against defectors, in order to eradicate the insurgents' clandestine infrastructure; once they do, and in the absence of insurgent counterattack, these villages move to zone 1 (full incumbent control).[3] I provide a few illustrations.

In the eastern Henan region of China, when the Japanese army moved into areas previously controlled by the Communists, the local insurgent militia either fled, disbanded, or defected, while many local cadres were arrested and killed; many of the "neutral elements" (sympathizers whose relations the party had been cultivating for three years) swiftly changed sides and began collaborating with the Japanese. The revolutionary movement was "put on hold" and survived only as an underground movement (Wou 1994:226). In Malaya, once the government

---

[2] For example, when control of the Colombian town of Dabeiba shifted from the FARC guerrillas to the right-wing paramilitaries, one of the latter told Scott Wilson (2002) that "most FARC supporters left when we arrived, out of fear. They didn't fit." A similar process takes place at the opposite end. A British official reported that when the Greek Communists "conquered" a village, "Most of those who had any reason to fear the Communists, such as the rich and large property owners and those who were known to have actually resisted the Communists with arms or who were "blacklisted" as being strongly opposed to Communism had already fled. Most of those who remained were peasants, small-holders and small shop-keepers. Government officials of all kinds left at an early stage and villages and towns were usually left without leadership or administrative organization" ("Report from Patras Consul (31 May 1949)," PRO, FO 371/78386/R6231). Ellsberg (2003:143–4) provides similar observations from Vietnam. Shelby Tucker (2001:171) reports about the Kachin insurgency in Burma that the insurgent KIA "Seventh Battalion had previously controlled the hills between the Mali Hka and the Kumawng. However, its strength had been depleted to reinforce Pajau Bum, and the Burma Army now patrolled there unchallenged."

[3] The incumbent entry into insurgent-held villages may lead them to start visiting (but not hold) villages hitherto controlled by the insurgents, which then slip from zone 5 to 4. The insurgents will then begin to use selective violence to prevent defections toward the incumbents. The same would be true for villages moving from zone 1 to 2 due to similar incursions by the insurgents.

reoccupied areas it had previously abandoned to the insurgents, "Confidence in the government increased, and a few people were willing to provide information on the local Min Yuen members and guerrilla movements. Using this information, the security forces were able to disrupt the activities of the guerrillas and reduce their effectiveness. This, in turn, induced more people to co-operate with Government officials" (Stubbs 1989:190). Elliott (2003:408) provides a similar description of this process from Vietnam in 1962:

The retaking of Hoi Cu village is described by a [Vietcong] cadre who witnessed this comeback by the Saigon forces. The "GVN had informers in the village who pointed out to them the Front cadres and the stationing points of the Front forces." Using these informers, "The GVN destroyed the Front forces; only five or six Front fighters were left and they had to withdraw to the fields in the back country. There were operations continuously and the people knew that they had all taken part in Front activities one way or another – taking part in demonstrations, beating drums, and so on – therefore, they were all afraid that if they just made the slightest move in support of the Front they would be arrested, beaten up, and jailed.

When the Americans set up a garrison in the northern Iraqi village of Qabr Abed, which was notorious as an insurgent stronghold,[4] they started receiving denunciations, including some from the family of the local insurgent leader, whom they captured. Information via counterdenunciation by a person embittered because this leader had murdered several relatives led to the capture of several dozen insurgent collaborators who were quickly rounded up. After that, the villagers became convinced that the Americans were gaining the upper hand and began providing even more information. In turn, this led many insurgent collaborators to switch sides. One of them, Chief Ali, told Richard A. Oppel (2005b:4) that he threw his lot in with the Americans after they had captured a large number of insurgents. "The American soldiers cleared this area out," he said. Americans were aware that this situation was completely contingent on control: "You always have to tread cautiously, and you can never mistake their hospitality for loyalty." They also knew that the situation could easily backslide: "If you let up at all," one said, "you open the possibility for" a shift in the opposite direction (Oppel 2005b:4).

The last illustration is from the town Tame, in the Colombian province of Arauca (Fichtl 2003). Until 2001 this town was firmly in the grasp of Colombia's two largest guerrilla groups, the Revolutionary Armed Forces of Colombia (FARC) and the National Liberation Army (ELN). The guerrillas levied taxes on local businesses, ranchers, and farmers, and extracted funds from local elected officials still bankrolled by the central government. In 2001 the army along with right-wing paramilitaries moved in; by September 2002 the police contingent had increased its size from 20 to 120 men, and by 2003 the army presence in Tame municipality had reached some 4,000 men, establishing a permanent presence in

---

4 "'It was for the insurgency what the Dominican Republic is to baseball,' said Capt. Kevin Burke, who commands Company C of the First Battalion of the Fifth Infantry Regiment, which oversees Qabr Abed" (Oppel 2005b:1).

the town and flooding the town center with soldiers. Predictably, the situation changed:

Better supplied than the National Police, the soldiers stand guard day and night on Tame's central streets and plaza, at local government offices and at the town's small airport. It is no exaggeration to say that the Colombian soldiers and their Israeli Galil rifles are never out of sight in the town center. They enforce road blocks on some of the streets around the plaza to control traffic, and by night they extend their security cordon to envelope several square blocks in the center of town. In conjunction with the National Police, the army conducts sweeps and patrols of the outlying neighborhoods to check the identity and activities of anyone they don't recognize, to look for stolen vehicles (universally favored for car bombs), and to make their presence felt.

This shift in control forced the insurgents to pull most of their forces out and retreat to the plains and riverine jungles in the rural sector of Tame and deeper into Arauca. The town moved from zone 5 to 2. Then, the paramilitaries launched a campaign of selective violence against suspected guerrilla collaborators, which contributed to a fatality count of more than 300 people in a municipality of about 65,000 people. At the same time, the army began to recruit locally. One program called "Soldado de mi Pueblo," or "Soldier from My Town," inducted locally born and raised men into the military for service in their own communities. One of them said: "We try to get our relatives and friends to bring us information about what the guerrillas are doing. . . . Any remarks or gossip about a kidnapping or a theft or that the guerrillas are going to harass someone, we know in a moment. This is what we do: receive information and pass it to our commanders, so that we can take security measures and counteract what the guerrillas are planning." Faced with their loss of control and local information, the insurgents have tried to resort to indiscriminate violence, though without much success. During his two years in Tame, an army captain said he has deactivated thirty-two explosive devices, four car bombs, and a motorcycle bomb. However, the army lacks the manpower to extend its control outside the town. At its edge, state authority dwindles: guerrilla checkpoints surround the town and control its inbound and outbound traffic. Locals refer to the guerrillas as *los de abajo*, or "the guys down there," just outside town. However, the army and the paramilitaries have been challenging them there as well, relying on indiscriminate violence, such as strafing from helicopters and massacring civilians. If they manage to dislodge the rebels, Tame will move from zone 2 to zone 1.

This process works similarly in the opposite direction, from incumbent to insurgent control. An August 1948 British report from southern Greece describes how several villages slipped from incumbent control and how this shift affected the behavior of the population:

The CHALANDRITSA incident is typical of events in this district during the last six months. A town is attacked by the guerrillas; the gendarmerie force garrisoning it is inadequate; reinforcements are called for but either cannot be supplied or arrive too late or are insufficient in number to deflect the attackers from their objective; the guerrillas establish themselves in the town which has been their principal objective and proceed to loot, forcibly recruit men and abduct a small percentage of the women, harangue the villagers and punish those they know to be working against them. A new town or village falls to the reign of terror. Thereafter villagers are obliged to pay tolls and taxes in kind to the guerrilla administration and to comply exactly with the orders given them. The authority of the Greek government is ended in the district and the inhabitants have no alternative but to serve their new masters.... Once villages have experienced the guerrilla reign of terror they are so afraid of the fate that awaits them if they serve the interests of the Greek Government or its forces that they adopt, at best, a passive role. One encounters more and more the tendency among villagers to refrain from making any adverse comment against the guerrillas or in fact giving any information which might be held against them by the guerrilla fifth-column (soi-disant "self-defenders") of the village and result in punishment when the guerrillas next visit them. In rural communities which are actually at the mercy of the guerrillas or are near to concentrations of the guerrilla forces one detects a manifest reluctance on the part of the inhabitants to say anything at all on the security situation.... Fear is the dominant feature of the lives of the majority of civilians in this district, particularly of those of the rural areas, at the present time.[5]

In fact, the onset of an insurgency follows a "remarkably predictable" course argues Paget (1967:31):

In the unprotected regions that comprise the major portion of the national territory, particularly the vast area of inhabited countryside where police forces are small or nonexistent, terrorist action encounters no opposition at the beginning of a conflict and is most effective. Isolated raids first reveal the existence of a partially organized movement. These attract attention and promote caution among the populace. Then, selective terrorism begins to eliminate lesser persons of influence, petty bureaucrats and various police officials who did not understand the first warnings or were slow to react to them. Administrative cadres are restrained or eliminated. The silence and collusion of the unprotected civilians have been won. Agents of the enemy have a free hand to organize and manipulate the population at will. (Trinquier 1964:18–19)

Insurgents usually show up in areas and times of weak government control. The more extreme the decline or absence of authority in a region, the more the population becomes "virgin territory" for those who would become a "counter-state" or alternative government (Wickham-Crowley 1991:35). Once they establish their authority, they launch an assassination campaign against state representatives. These assassinations perform multiple functions: effectively destroying the state apparatus, signaling strength, and deterring any collaboration with incumbents. A U.S. officer serving in the Philippines from 1899 to 1902 where, according to one estimate, one-quarter of the pro-American Filipinos recorded as assassinated were civil officials, found "all the potential officeholders terrified of being killed and steadfast in their refusal to have anything to do with American civil government"; after a series of insurgent killings, another officer noted bitterly: "It is not likely now that anyone will accept the office of local Presidente at elections set for Sunday night" (Linn 1989:38, 135).[6]

---

[5] "Reports on conditions in Greece. Reports on Visits and Tours Carried Out in Greece," D. P. Reilly, 24 August 1948, PRO, FO 371/72327/ R9844.

[6] There is agreement that "terrorism" is the first active stage of insurgency because it is "the weapon of the weak" (Crozier 1960:160; Paget 1967:28). This does not mean that insurgents are to be blamed for initiating the violence: many civil wars begin in highly repressive and violent regimes.

If the government fails to respond and protect its agents, the villagers begin to collaborate with the insurgents; the village moves to zone 4 (if the army maintains garrisons nearby and exercises pressure by visiting) or zone 5 (if insurgent authority in the wider area expands, governmental presence wanes, the army curtails its visits, and incumbent collaborator clandestine cells are eliminated). It is also possible for shifts to be inconclusive: a village can move from both directions to 3 and remain under divided control. Overall, insurgents are typically the first movers: they dictate the terms of the struggle and impose the tactics to be followed, namely the irregular form of warfare.[7]

An example of this process comes from a Salvadoran village (J. L. Anderson 2004:140, 181–2). First, the rebels targeted a contested village by military means. They sought "to tip the balance of power" in their favor by forcing out military and civil defense posts. Once this aim was achieved, the village entered zone 4. According to J. L. Anderson (2004:212–13), "There are no longer any soldiers stationed in the villages, and most of the collaborators have been killed or forced to flee, but the army can launch a raid anytime from its bases just over the hill. So, wherever the [rebel] group camps for the night, the kids do rotating perimeter watches, and extreme caution is exercised in talking with civilians in order to keep the squad's movements secret." Insurgents then set up new institutions, information starts to flow, and selective violence is used against alleged spies, whose execution leads "directly to the guerrillas' unequivocal control of the hamlet. All remaining active resistance to their authority has ended."

The relation between control and violence exhibits a certain circularity, in the sense that control shifts may trigger violence and that violence may trigger shifts of control. However, careful process tracing and sequential disaggregation take care of endogeneity concerns. In fact, process tracing suggests that a shift in control entails two distinct steps: *initial shift* and *consolidation*. First, tactical military decisions cause control to shift in two directions: from insurgent to incumbent control (from 4 or 5 to 2) and from incumbent to insurgent control (from 2 and 1 to 4). Second, the use of selective violence, *once control has shifted*, triggers a process of consolidation with control moving from 2 to 1 (full incumbent control) and from 4 to 5 (full insurgent control). Hence, in the absence of additional exogenous shifts in military resources, zones 2 and 4 can be thought of as areas in transition; in a sense, they represent a temporal dimension in the process of

---

However, there is a general consensus that, as challengers, insurgents are the "first movers." See D. Anderson (2005:47); Heer (2000:111); Pettigrew (2000:207); Laqueur (1998:27); Horton (1998:75); Senaratne (1997:87, 115–19); Swedenburg (1995:119); Brody (1985:47); Tone (1994:112); Faivre (1994:108); Stoll (1993:64–5); B. Berman and Lonsdale (1992:440); Cribb (1991:162); Geffray (1990:39); Stubbs (1989:45); Kornbluh (1988:14); Horne (1987:135); Flower (1987:121); Cooper (1979:92); Henriksen (1983:119; 1976:382); Race (1973:83); Paget (1967:32); Barnett and Njama (1966:127); Clutterbuck (1966:7–9); Armstrong (1964:40–1); Lear (1961:208); Crozier (1960:161); Leakey (1954:112). This consensus is supported by the empirical observation that there is an initial analytical and geographical discrepancy between the regime's repressive violence on the one hand, and insurgent violence, on the other.

[7] Fellman (1989:131); De Lupis (1987:34); Chaliand (1987:67); Beaufre (1972:61); Paget (1967:33); Taber (1965:19).

control shift. The violence follows the initial shift in control and precedes the consolidation.

As pointed out, the decision to commit resources in order to launch an "invasion" that will trigger a shift in control is taken as exogenous to the theory. It is possible, though, to imagine that local people try to influence a political actor to target their area. Exiles and refugees have always tried to bring in outside actors in order to tip the balance of a local conflict and return to their countries. The story of the Peloponnesian War as told by Thucydides is also a tale of escalation through such lobbying. In practice, however, tactical decisions tend to be taken at the supralocal level due to the scarcity of military resources whose concentration requires coordination; likewise, military operations tend to target entire areas rather than single villages.

In the remaining part of the chapter, I examine each zone of control in detail and check the hypotheses against available anecdotal evidence.

8.3. FULL CONTROL (ZONES 1 AND 5)

Max Weber (1994:310) argued that although violence is "not the normal or sole means used by the state," the relation between the two "is a particularly intimate one"; much of Michel Foucault's work is based on this insight, which is also in line with Hannah Arendt's (1970:56) dictum about the inverse relation between power and violence: "Where the one rules absolutely, the other is absent." As Kate Brown (2003:213) puts it, "personal choice narrow[s] to the eye of a needle." For civilians this translates into a pervasiveness of "surveillance and monitoring," described in Guatemala precisely as *control* (Warren 1998:95). The availability of prisons and the density of monitoring allow the screening of denunciations and the use of forms of repression short of death. This is not to say that coercion is the only means of rule. In fact, zones of full control are the places where one is most likely to encounter a mix of coercion and persuasion.

Although the content and modalities of control are obvious among incumbents, they require some additional discussion for insurgents. Insurgency can best be understood as a process of competitive state building rather than simply an instance of collective action or social contention. Insurgents seek to develop elaborate "counter-states" (Wickham-Crowley 1991) via "political consolidation" (Sánchez 2001:30). State building is the insurgents' central goal and renders organized and sustained rebellion of the kind that takes place in civil wars fundamentally distinct from phenomena such as banditry, mafias, or social movements.[8] Insurgents seek to secure power at the local level, even when they cannot hope to seize the state at the national level. This means conquering and keeping territory – to the extent that this is possible (e.g., Wood 2003:135; Romero 2000:67; Schofield 1984:308). Territories controlled by insurgents are often called

---

[8] "Stationary" bandits who create enduring institutions are state builders (Olson 2000). As Augustine put it, "If by accessions of desperate men this evil [brigandage] grows to such proportions that it holds lands, establishes fixed settlements, seizes upon states and subjugates peoples, it assumes the name of a kingdom" (*On the City of God* IV:iv).

"liberated" or "base" areas. Terms such as shadow government, parallel hierarchy, rebel infrastructure, or alternative government refer precisely to processes of state building.[9] Insurgents engage in statelike activities: they collect taxes, organize policing, administer justice, and conscript fighters. In short, they enjoy a local monopoly on violence, which they use to punish their enemies and sanction noncompliance. In the Canipaco Valley of Central Peru, "Shining Path assumed control and organized every aspect of the inhabitants' daily life. Sendero undertook the administration of justice and played the role of a moralizing force. Shining Path settled marital conflicts, supervised the work of teachers, mediated the relationships between the communeros and those authorities and state functionaries who were not obliged to quit, executed thieves who robbed livestock from the herders and even organized recreation" (Manrique 1998:204).

The Communist insurgency in South Vietnam provides an apt illustration. Based on structures built during the anticolonial uprising against the French (Race 1973:4), the Vietcong were able to establish a highly sophisticated five-level "shadow" administrative infrastructure (nation, region, province, district, and village), run by close to 40,000 full-time employees by the end of 1968. Some areas of South Vietnam had been under rebel control more or less continuously since the end of the Japanese occupation (Schell 2000:208), which explains how the Vietcong were able to turn the career of a party cadre into "one of the standard professions" (Berman 1974:4, 74). Jeffrey Race (1973:199) reports that "one of the striking conclusions from interviewing [Vietcong] defectors is the total absence of the government movement in revolutionary areas for years at a time, except on occasional large-scale sweep operations which had little impact on the Party's local apparatus." According to Paul Berman (1974:4–5), "peasants conscripted into the revolutionary organization became more than soldiers in a temporary fighting force; they potentially became subjects integrated into a new institution founding the basis for a nation-state."

Contrary to widespread perception, state building is not a practice associated solely with leftist insurgency. Many post–Cold War insurgencies (including ethnic ones) develop systems of state rule (Finnegan 1992; Geffray 1990; Linn 1989:40), although the level of sophistication varies from place to place. Insurgent state building is why civil wars are often perceived as "really" being about "a competition in government" (Clutterbuck 1966:57), where individuals face demands from two governments – as in the Philippines during the Huk insurgency (Jones and Molnar 1966:47): "One government was legal, but in these areas had little or no physical control. The insurgent government was illegal, but had partial or complete control and enforcement capability." Hence Robert Thompson's (1966)

---

[9] In the French region of Dordogne, "the population had become irrevocably enmeshed in the networks of alternative power." It became clearer to the authorities "that what was happening was less a total collapse of all authority than a transfer of power from Vichy to the maquisards" (Kedward 1993:97). Similar observations have been made about the Spanish guerrilla war against the French (Tone 1994:6), the Chinese Civil War (Schran 1976), the Mau Mau insurgency in Kenya (Paget 1967:91), past and more recent civil wars in Algeria (Martinez 1998; Peterson 1997a; Faivre 1994:147; Horne 1987:134), Guinea-Bissau (Rudebeck 1975), contra-controlled Nicaragua (Horton1998:127), Sri Lanka (Pfaffenberger 1994:129), and Peru (Rosenau 1994:316).

observation that insurgencies are like icebergs: the fighters are the top, but it is the depth of control below that represents their true strength. This insight has a geographical expression: a well-established yardstick of counterinsurgency experts in Mozambique was that "subversion" (i.e., clandestine rebel organization) preceded the actual fighting by about eighty kilometers (Maier 1974:33).

8.3.1. Violence under Full Control

Because the propensity of defection is largely endogenous to the level of control, full control makes violence redundant: most people are unwilling and largely unable to defect because their access to the rival actor is restricted. Control endows the threat of violence with such credibility as to practically do away with its expression (Tilly 1985:172). In other words, violence is off the equilibrium path. Fear prevails.

If Hypothesis 2 is correct, we should observe limited or no violence by the ruling actor. There is considerable evidence that this is the case (e.g., Wickham-Crowley 1991:50–1). The Japanese tended to kill the inhabitants of hill villages rather than those of the towns they controlled in the Philippine island of Leyte (Lear 1961:214). In Guatemala, the town of San Andrés was tightly controlled by the government forces and did not experience the kind of displacements and massacres that occurred elsewhere in this country (Warren 1998:92–3). Robert Carmack (1988a:xv–xvi) reports that in Guatemala, communities thought to be free of "subversion" by the government were watched by the army but generally left alone and suffered little violence.[10] In Colombia, all actors "use the coercive power of fear to maintain order in their territory, but do not browbeat their subjects on a daily basis" (Fichtl 2004:4). Likewise, there appears to be a correlation between high levels of control and fear. A Human Rights Watch Report about Chechnya notes that "In areas under the effective control of [pro-Russian leader] Ramzan Kadyrov, the fear-stricken atmosphere is astounding" (Myers 2005:A4).

The same appears to be the case for insurgents. "So far as I was able to determine," a British official reported from Greece in 1949, "the Communists did not execute many persons once they had established control."[11] William H. McNeill (1947:156) reports his impression from Greece immediately after the Germans had left: "The Right claimed that EAM's power was based on terror, which in some part it was. Few dissidents dared to raise their voices in the villages and provincial towns in the fall of 1944; and because so few dared, overt acts of terrorism were also few, so that the outward seeming of the country was surprisingly peaceful

---

[10] This pattern can be found in non-civil-war environments. In his classic study of *caciquismo* in a village of southwestern Mexico, Paul Friedrich (1977) found that although *caciques* resort to killing political opponents if necessary, their overwhelming control of the means of violence deters challenges to their authority and minimizes lethal violence. Violence is off the equilibrium path. Of course, the absence of massive lethal violence does not mean the absence of coercion. Mary Roldán (2002:221) found in Colombia an inverse relationship between casualties and high imprisonments: where the former were low, the later were high, and vice versa.

[11] "Consular Reports on Conditions in Greece, Tour Reports by Consular Officers, R 6231, Report from Patras Consul (31 May 1949)," PRO, FO 371/78386.

and calm." Colombian insurgents refrain from the use of mass violence within their zones of control (Sánchez 2001:30). Although contra repression occurred in Nicaragua, "it should be emphasized that in many cases contras did not have to carry out overt violence to maintain control over the communities that formed their social base in the mountains.... The presence of armed men and veiled warnings were often sufficient in themselves to ensure the cooperation of peasants adept at interpreting the realities of military power in their community" (Horton 1998:218). In Vietcong-controlled areas of South Vietnam, peasants complied with the Vietcong, violence was low, and as a cadre put it, "the villagers ... feared the GVN, but they feared it less than they feared the Front" (Elliott 2003:757). Similarly, of the eighty-five families living in the rebel-controlled Filipino village of Barangay Rose in 1988, eighty had at least one member who had joined the rebels. The five remaining families, Gregg Jones (1989:199) was told, "have to follow rules. They don't report to the enemy. They just keep quiet." In fact, in 1985 the rebels executed a local man accused of informing the authorities on rebel activities (i.e., a "defector"). "Long afterward," Jones concludes, this execution "lingered as a powerful reminder to residents: Beyond the matters of livelihood and culture and politics, the revolution held the power of life and death in Barangay Rose."

The evidence is particularly startling in the case of RENAMO in Mozambique, Sendero in Peru, and the GIA in Algeria, three insurgent movements that were notorious for a level of extreme violence often described as random and gratuitous. It turns out that RENAMO was restrained where it enjoyed high levels of control – in the Gorongosa and Zambezia regions, for instance (T. Young 1997:132–3). Carolyn Nordstrom (1997:107) researched an area of north-central Mozambique where "there was little in the way of Frelimo representation," hence RENAMO did not feel that it "had to make examples" by murdering potential FRELIMO supporters. In fact, all the places she documents as being simultaneously held by RENAMO and relatively peaceful were "isolated and removed from Frelimo spheres of influence" (Nordstrom 1997:100). Robert Gersony (1988) reached the same general conclusion: in rural locales where RENAMO soldiers moved freely, instances of brutality, murder, and kidnapping were infrequent.[12] In Peru, Sendero left peasants alone in "liberated zones" such as the Upper Huallaga Valley, where there were no reports of massacres; this fact came as a surprise to many observers, given the violent nature of this organization (Rosenau 1994:317). Likewise the Algerian GIA used little violence in the areas it controlled; it began resorting to mass violence when its control was contested by the army (Kalyvas 1999).[13]

An unobserved implication of the theory is that denunciations will initially abound in zones of full control but will generally be disregarded or will not

---

[12] Gersony (1988) also identified "control areas," places where a RENAMO base was surrounded by both local indigenous and abducted populations. In these places, RENAMO exercised substantial brutality, mainly against the abducted population. This violence, he notes, was extractive rather than terroristic.

[13] Note that the relative absence of violence in strongly controlled areas is often interpreted, when recorded, as an indicator of widespread popular support. The potential spuriousness of this observation should be clear by now.

lead to lethal violence. I could find little specific information, however. One bit comes from Civil War–era Missouri, where such a pattern is reported by Fellman (1989:27); another from Greece, where McNeill (1947:198–9) reports that after the Left lost its local power in a village, "a swarm of informers descended on the Guard commander, accusing the local leftists of all sorts of crimes. Most of these accusations were never acted upon, but a proportion of them resulted in arrests."

An additional implication is that many refugee camps will approximate zone 1 (when access to them is controlled by the incumbents) and zone 5 (when located in areas under insurgent control, especially in neighboring countries that support the insurgents). We should, therefore, observe limited violence in such camps, certainly less compared with camps that are left to their own devices, and of a different form: criminal violence in the latter versus coercive violence in the former. The available evidence points to this direction (Crisp 2000; Prunier 1995; Wiesner 1988). In fact, it is possible to think of the rural displacement strategy component of many counterinsurgency projects as a way to generate areas of zone 1 type by emptying territory and displacing civilians rather than by occupying it.[14]

8.4. NO CONTROL (ZONES 1 AND 5)

A political actor lacks control over areas that are completely controlled by its rival: "no control" is the mirror image of "full control." Deprived of control, the "nonsovereign" is blind and lacks access to people and information. Travel is difficult and fraught with dangers, and locals may never come into contact with representatives of the nonsovereign. This point was clearly conveyed in a report written by a Russian collaborator of the Germans in 1942:

When the peasant faces the problem whether to go with the partisans or with the German troops, unfortunately he must frequently observe that it is impossible to refuse help to the partisans. Indeed, he sees the partisans almost daily, and the Germans very seldom. Even if he wished to fight the partisans wholeheartedly, how should he do this? To throw himself into a direct struggle with them, unarmed as he is, is nonsense. Joining the OD [collaborationist militias] means to deprive his land of the only manpower there is to work and expose his family to annihilation by the partisans. When the peasant follows the activity of the partisans and reports about it to the kommandatura, this fact becomes rapidly known, as almost nothing remains secret in the village, and retribution ensues swiftly. Moreover, the population has convinced itself that its reports [to the Germans] in the overwhelming majority of cases lead to no action whatever. The kommandaturas receive, day after day, reports about the partisans from all parts of the rayon but can react to them in only few instances, because they lack forces. The above state of affairs is extremely dangerous, as it leads to the growth of the partisan movement and hence entails

[14] It is worth researching the variation in the use of population displacement strategies in civil wars. They are, obviously, very expensive to implement properly and when used in the context of a strategy of indiscriminate violence as in Darfur ("counterinsurgency on the cheap"), they may backfire against those who use them (Prunier 2005).

a complete disintegration of the [German] administrative and economic system. (in Dallin et al. 1964:325)[15]

8.4.1. Violence under No Control

Hypothesis 3 states that in the absence of any control, the "nonsovereign" cannot possibly resort to selective violence. When violence is used, it will be indiscriminate. Indeed, a rule of thumb in Colombia during the *Violencia* was that "the most exaggerated and persistent [state] violence occurred in places far removed from effective control by the central government" (Henderson 1985:109). More recently, Colombian insurgents have resorted to terrorist operations and massacres outside their own zones of control (Sánchez 2001:30).

The indiscriminate character of this violence is obvious when it comes to incumbents. When South Vietnamese soldiers killed a peasant in a raid, they told the journalist who witnessed the murder not to be "sentimental. That man undoubtedly was a Viet Cong agent, since these hamlets have been Viet Cong strongholds for years" (Browne 2000:8). As a U.S. Air Force major pointed out, "In the mountains, just about anything that moves is considered to be V.C." (in Schell 2000:214). Elliott (2003:878) found that the hamlet that was shelled most often by the government in an area he studied was the one considered to be the main Vietcong base. Using data collected by human rights organizations, Timothy Gulden (2002) examined the patterns of violence in Guatemala and found that it took different forms in the Mayan highlands and the lowlands. Collective massacres were much more likely to be carried out in the mountains and away from improved roads. Carmack (1988a:xv–xvi) confirms that the Guatemalan army committed the most widespread massacres in so-called red communities, that is, those under insurgent control, where it made no essential distinction between the residents and guerrillas. These examples are consistent with more general findings such as Donald Greer's (1935) classic study showing that the French revolutionary terror targeted the regions where the state faced an internal or external armed challenge, and James Ron's (2003) observation that, in Israel and the former Yugoslavia, violence increased as one moved away from highly controlled areas to contested ones.

Insurgent violence follows a similar pattern. The insurgents in Malaya targeted resettlement centers and towns controlled by the British (Stubbs 1989:105; R. Thompson 1966:25); and the Mozambican FRELIMO mortared and rocketed the "aldeamentos" (government protected villages) on a fairly routine basis during the decolonization struggle (Cann 1997:157). Years later, the RENAMO insurgents committed atrocities against the population – not at random, as often believed, but precisely where the government had a strong base, its assumption being that all civilians there were "affiliated" with FRELIMO (T. Young 1997:132–3); Nordstrom (1997:108) reports cases where RENAMO switched from "leniency" to violence against the same population after that population

---

[15] For similar points, see Hondros (1993:155), Stoll (1993:148), and Cribb (1991:150).

came (against its will) under FRELIMO control. Gersony (1988) designated as RENAMO "destruction areas" those that had some form of governmental presence. The Vietcong resorted to random mortaring and rocketing of places where the South Vietnamese enjoyed control, including refugee camps;[16] the Nicaraguan contras used violence against Sandinista strongholds (Horton 1998:167), the Peruvian Sendero Luminoso against villages that formed militias (Krauss 1999; Del Pino 1998:172, 189; Manrique 1998:218), the RUF in Sierra Leone against villages that formed kamajor militias (Richards 1996:181–2), the ELN in Colombia against villages (such as Carmen de Chucurí) that rose against them (Rubio 1999:120). Note that this applies to both ethnic and nonethnic conflicts. From the wars of decolonization in Africa to the Kurdish insurgency in eastern Turkey, insurgents have consistently targeted their coethnics who collaborate with their enemy, either individually or in the context of militia-building programs.

8.5. CONTESTATION (ZONES 2, 3, AND 4)

A Salvadoran peasant described life in contested areas as akin to being squeezed between the thorn and the sword (*entre la espina y la espada*) (in Binford 1996:100). The life of a Colombian peasant living in a contested zone presents openings for accusations of collaboration with multiple sides: "What did you do in town? Who did you talk to? Were there guerrilla checkpoints on the road? Did you tell the army we had a checkpoint on the road? Do you sell produce to the paramilitaries? Do you sell produce to the guerrillas?" "Of course," Fichtl (2004:4) concludes, "the real question is, does the campesino have a choice?" – a predicament he describes as the "catch-22 of conflicting demands." As a Vietnamese peasant put it, it is like "having one neck bound by two nooses" (in Elliott 2003:258). Colonel J. M. Stevens described the situation of crossing pressures he encountered in occupied Greece, where he operated in 1943–4:

> There are few villages in the PELOPONNESE which have not been visited by Andartes [rebels] and Germans, often three or four times by each. As a general rule the Germans have looted the houses which they have found empty on their drives. The Andartes beat, loot and send off to concentration camps those villagers who stayed behind to protect their property when the Germans came. The result is indescribable misery. . . . village morale is very low, and all the villagers pray for is to be left alone by Andartes, Security Bns., and Germans alike.[17]

Such descriptions recur: people talk of being caught in a "crossfire," "squeezed in the middle," being between "two fires," "opposing fires," "two armies," "two

---

[16] Moyar (1997:307); Wiesner (1988:102, 225–6); West (1985:272); Lewy (1978:276); R. Thompson (1966:27). Wiesner (1988:227, 58) mentions Communist Party Decision No. 9 of 1969, which directed that refugee camps were to be main targets for attack. He also reports an indiscriminate massacre against the village of Dong-Xai in Phuoc Long province, in June 1965 for the same reason.

[17] "Second Report of Colonel J. M. Stevens on Present Conditions in Peloponnese (24 June 1944)," PRO, HS 5/669/S6557.

evils," or "two thorns."[18] The following descriptions, by civilians living in contested areas during five different conflicts (Algeria, Rhodesia-Zimbabwe, Philippines, Namibia, and Afghanistan) all point to the same predicament:

The French army is here, the fellaghi army [insurgents] is here, we are just in the middle. (in Faivre 1994:142–3)

If we report to the Police, the terrorists kill us. If we do not report, the Police suspect us of harbouring terrorists. We just do not know what to do. (in Flower 1987:122)

I think the number one reason is that there is fear of both sides. If you stand up and side with the one group, your life will be in danger. If you side with the other group, again your life will be in danger. If you side with the military, you're afraid of the NPA [New Popular Army]. If you side with the NPA, you're afraid of the military. (in Berlow 1998:202)

In Ovamboland [Northern Namibia], we live between two fires. Either you side with the South Africans or with SWAPO. If SWAPO men come at night, asking for help, and you don't help them, then that means you're on the South African side, and you have to pay with your life. A guerrilla war means a continuous struggle of life and death, day and night. (in Groth 1995:28)

In the daytime, this government is coming to us, and in the nightime the Taliban are coming to us. We are stuck in the middle. (in Sengupta 2005b:A10)

Political actors apply more effort to force people to commit to their side where the incentives for not committing are higher: "In contested areas, where the desire to be left alone was strongest, the GVN and the Communists tried to make [South Vietnamese] peasants help them through a combination of compulsion and persuasion" (Moyar 1997:321). As an American journalist (Kann 2000:409) remarked, "it's a chancy business being a Vietnamese civilian in a 'contested' area." Indeed, from the point of view of the civilian population, the key feature of fragmented sovereignty is a deep sense of uncertainty and danger, nicely conveyed by a Greek man and echoed by an American visitor in Greece and two Guatemalan peasants:

This pseudowar is a bad thing. You don't know how to protect yourself. There is no front line for you to know what to do. You don't know where it'll come from. For example, you walk and you meet someone. How can you tell him who you are? You cannot know who he is, what kind of God he worships. What can you tell him? He might kill you if he doesn't like your answer. That's it. As a result you are scared. There was fear. When they began arresting people, the people slept outside their homes. It was like anarchy. Somebody could kill you and nothing happened, he was accountable to no one. A wild situation. These were bad times. (I-22)

What made the situation intolerable was the fact that the presence of rival armed establishments so close by made the pursuit of ordinary occupations quite impossible. If a man went to the hills to cut wood, the soldiers beat him for consorting with the guerrillas as, in fact, he would have to do so to be able to come and go. But unless the villagers were free

---

[18] Degregori (1998:141–2); Daniel (1996:178–80); Le Bot (1994); Stoll (1993); Fellman (1989:32); S. Davis (1988: 26); Henriksen (1983:133); Chung (1970); Dallin et al. (1964:330); Lear (1961:v).

to use what scanty property they had at their disposal up the mountain, how could they survive at all? Caught thus between the upper and the nether millstone, life in Kerasia was truly desperate. (McNeill 1978:153)

You didn't have security in anything. There was terror at night, great insecurity. You didn't know which group might come to get you. There was fear of both sides. No one had tranquility. (in Warren 1998:93)

The problem was that you never knew what kind of people would turn up, who you were talking to. (in Warren 1998:96)

Life in contested areas means that rumors rule, faith in established categories disappears, the grounds on which everyday trust is built crumbles, and feelings of extreme contingency and vulnerability take over; reality itself becomes divided (Warren 1998:110). As in Northern Ireland, people can be "riddled with deceit, double-dealing, contrived and genuine moves, and sometimes simple methods which are assumed to be complex. Those who are caught between the two sets of players will never know when the rules are being changed or the true nature of the game" (M. Dillon 1990:299). A British visitor in Greece reported about the attitude of the villagers: "They have been under a terrorism of one kind or another for so many years that they do not reason very well, and are easily made the victims of rumours, however wild."[19] Such uncertainty complicates calculations about how to behave. Fellman (1989:xv) describes the prevailing thinking in Missouri during the Civil War: "Which side should you appear to support? . . . Under such peril, how ought you to act? Who *were* they? Who were *you*?" Describing a scene in Vietnam, Kann (2000:409) points out that uncertainty is particularly pronounced after control has just shifted: "An intense pacification program in hamlets at the base of Nui Co To has made modest gains. Most of these hamlets were solidly controlled by the Vietcong seven months ago but now have at least a daytime GVN presence. Driving through these hamlets one is met by sullen stares. 'These people don't know yet if the GVN is here to stay or if the VC are coming back. They haven't decided which way to lean yet, but at least they're debating it for the first time,' says Maj. Fields." A man from Mississippi expressed the same sense of pervasive uncertainty during the Civil War: "We can make no calculations on the future, and need not be surprised at anything a day may bring forth. Truly we are an afflicted people" (in Ash 1995:211).

In sum, contestation makes it difficult for most people to align with a single political actor. This microfoundation undergirds the phenomenon predicted by the theory of high simultaneous defection toward both sides in zones of high contestation, which is typically described as neutrality or fence-sitting, a widespread occurrence in civil war.[20]

Most people prefer neutrality because they are either uncertain which side will be in a position to punish their behavior or they are certain that both sides

---

[19] "Memo: Situation in Greece, February 1948, by Mr. R. Blackbourn (24 February 1948)," PRO, FO 371/72327/R2531.

[20] E.g., Livanios (1999:205); Figes (1996:680); H. Nelson (1980:254); Armstrong (1964:46); Barnett and Njama (1966:135).

would be equally able to do so. Thomas Barrow, a linen-draper in Cheapside, wrote during the English Civil War: "Iff I might butt stand an newtrall I should then be well; for I should . . . butt follow my owne, and not looke after another's business" (in McGrath 1997:91). Fellman's (1989:48) description of the guerrilla war in Missouri is no different: "Loyalty was not the safest and most common presentation of self during this guerrilla war; prevarication was. Frankness and directness led to destruction more often than did reticence and withdrawal." In Trinquier's (1964:31) formulation, "The inhabitants will reject any responsibility that might subject them to the adversary's retaliation." A British report from Greece concluded in the same vein: "Unless there is confidence in the armed forces, and unless the villagers know that help is near at hand if they are attacked, there is little hope that much resistance will be offered, even if weapons are available."[21] Asked which side he supported, a peasant from a village close to Saigon told a Vietcong cadre in 1963: "I do not know, for I follow the will of Heaven. If I do what you say, then the Diem side will arrest me; if I say things against you, then you will arrest me, so I would rather carry both burdens on my shoulders and stand in the middle" (FitzGerald 1989:31). A 1968 CIA report from Vietnam was clear in this respect: "The predominant sentiment . . . is probably one of increasing concern to avoid the hazards of war. . . . Left to themselves [the South Vietnamese] are likely to remain uncommitted and disengaged until the decisive break in the struggle becomes obvious" (in Moyar 1997:321). A Colombian peasant put it in starker terms (in Rubio 1999:205): "*Aquí el que habla, no dura*" (Here the one who talks does not last). Confirming these points is the frequency of individual claims that collaboration was forced (e.g., Tone 1994:134; Fenoglio 1973:53).

For most people, fence-sitting takes the form of passive neutrality and *attentisme*: caught in the crossfire between incumbents and insurgents, with their life on the line, they prefer to remain as uninvolved as possible. "Everyone was waiting to see what would happen" is a sentence that describes the attitude of many peasants during the Chinese Civil War (Hua and Thireau 1996:304). "The populace not unnaturally want to be on the winning side," Julian Paget (1967:35) points out, "and indeed it is very much in their interest that they should be; they therefore try to offend neither side, until they can see which way the struggle looks like going."[22] A report of the Greek military in February 1948 found that rural people "would not fight for the guerrillas nor would they provide the army with information" (H. Jones 1989:52). Local state authorities in contested territory may behave in a similar fashion: "I am neither with the resistance nor with the Americans," the commander of the Iraqi National Guard in the city of Ramadi told Akeel Huseen and Nicolas Pelhman (2004:7).

Civil War Missouri provides an instructive illustration. Most Missourians, Fellman (1989:xviii) found, "sought to be disengaged, neutral." "They were to be whipsawed between the two organized poles of power; in the destruction of the

---

[21] "Report on Volos area," PRO, FO 371/72328/R12508.

[22] Paget (1967:111) adds that when it became evident that the British were gaining the upper hand in Kenya, "the waverers began to jump on to the Government bandwagon."

ensuing guerrilla war, the everyday translation of ideology became the question of which side would enable them best to survive. . . . [They] adopted the same mode of lying [about their involvement] in order to gain as much protection as possible from both sides. . . . If they had a truly free choice, most Missourians would have remained neutral during the war." The Union commander of the state's border districts described the situation he encountered in stark terms: "The worst feature in the country is the cowed and dispirited state of the people. All manhood appears to have gone out of them. Alike in fear of the soldier and the bushwhacker, all they ask is military protection of provost-marshals and the privilege of neutrality."[23]

It is important to stress that fence-sitting, though generally presented as a constant feature of civil war is a variable one, closely associated with the level of contestation. Consider the case of Cabrera, a town of five thousand lying fifty miles southwest of Bogotá in Colombia. In the spring of 2003, the army moved into this town, which had been under rebel rule for years. The rebels fled the town but did not disappear from the surrounding area. Many inhabitants "believe the rebels are simply waiting for the right moment to strike back." "The guerrillas are still up there somewhere," a man said pointing toward the mountains surrounding the town. "If they haven't been killed, then what's to stop them from returning?" The fear of a rebel return was "evident in the reluctance of townspeople to welcome the government forces with open arms. Glancing over his shoulders and refusing to give his name, an elderly man told a reporter: 'There are informers everywhere'" (Housego 2004).

A type of fence-sitting is hedging, that is, helping both sides at the same time. Consider the following contradictory statement by an Afghan man, reported by Gall (2005:A6): "'The people support the Taliban because they don't loot and they respect the women' he said. But he added, 'The whole district wants to help the Americans, because our country is destroyed.'" "To minimize destruction," many people in Civil War Missouri "sought alliances with men of a wide range of loyalties as a form of contingency planning. They wanted friends and protectors in all camps" (Fellman 1989:174). In *Violeucia*-era Colombia some people "carried simultaneously two forms of identification – a Conservative certificate and a Liberal party identity card – that they showed selectively, depending on who was asking" (Roldán 2000:217). In Kenya, some people "endeavoured in very pragmatic fashion to play both sides against the middle, seeking to accommodate Government with one hand and the revolutionary forces with the other" (Barnett and Njama 1966:135). Such "double collaboration" was frequent in Mozambique (Nordstrom 1997:56). Village officials, in particular, are often forced to serve "two masters" and raise taxes for both.[24] In El Salvador, "the same people who helped the guerrillas . . . also cooperated with the army during its frequent operations in the area" (Binford 1996:100). A Vietnamese peasant told how his father, a village deputy chief, had managed things during the war against the French: "My

---

[23] Fellman (1989:xviii, 11, 49, 51, 78).
[24] Hamoumou (1993:166); Jones (1989:236–7); Henriksen (1983:120, 153); Leites and Wolf (1970:43–4); Pike (1966:248); Lear (1961:234); Kitson (1960:206); Leakey (1954:115).

father was a clever man. He whittled the stick at both ends. He did not really like working for the French. . . . [But] he was also friendly with the resistance. He cooperated with them just enough so that they did not want to eliminate him because they were fairly certain that his successor would be worse" (in Herrington 1997:21). During the Chinese Civil War, serving both camps was literally described as "buying insurance" (Chang 1992:158). Particularly risky (and less frequent) is the family strategy of purposefully sending offspring to serve in competing armies. During the English Revolution, "some contemporary cynics argued that these family divisions [between belligerents] were part of a carefully arranged insurance policy, so that whichever side won there would always be someone with influence among the victors to protect the family property from confiscation and dismemberment." (Stone 1972:144).[25]

In a context of parity and stalemate, the manipulation of people's expectations, so as to convince them that the tide is shifting and one side is winning, is a common practice.[26] Indeed, for many authors (e.g., Eckstein 1965:158), the distinctive characteristic of irregular war lies precisely in the combination of violent techniques and "psychological warfare." Gordon Tullock (1987:373) argued that "the real point of the civil war is to convince people that one side or the other is going to win." "If we could make it clear to even the most ignorant villager that we were winning," recalls Oliver Crawford (1958:180) about Malaya, "then information would begin to flow the other way – out to us, instead of back into the jungle"; "in a war in which events were rarely significant in and of themselves," F. J. West (1985:47) concurs, "what counted were the perceptions of people about those events." Hence, political actors make concerted efforts to convince civilians that they are winning, as pointed out by Peruvian and Guatemalan peasants:

They said that Ayacucho was going to be a liberated zone by 1985. A famous illusion that they created among the *muchachos* was, way back in 1981, that by '85 there would be an independent republic. Wouldn't you like to be minister? Wouldn't you like to be a military chief? Be something, no? (in Degregori 1998:130)[27]

The guerrillas said that they were stronger than the army. They said that they were going to bring weapons for the people. Cuba and Nicaragua would help us. In Vietnam, the people had triumphed, and in El Salvador they were about to. . . . [They] advised us not to worry, because each year the movement advances, because we are shooting soldiers by the group, and little by little these soldiers will be finished off, and we will come to triumph in Guatemala. (Stoll 1993:88–9, 149)

Informational cues of all kinds are used, such as the quality of uniforms worn and weapons used. Greek villagers reported that the Communists "were 'grandly' turned out with good uniforms and better equipment than they or the army or the

---

[25] Faivre (1994:123) makes a similar point about Algeria.
[26] Note that even manipulating expectations requires a material basis: "The best propaganda will fall on deaf ears unless it is backed by military successes" (Heilbrunn 1967:36).
[27] Del Pino (1998:184) concurs that the Shining Path in Peru made considerable efforts to portray itself as "invincible and victorious."

gendarmerie had."[28] The Portuguese army in Angola exposed rebel prisoners to "troops in training and demonstrations of firepower [in order to convince them] that the Portuguese would prevail in the struggle" (Cann 1997:118). The organization of military parades and open meetings helped the Vietcong leadership to control the information that reached the rank and file: it stressed battlefield victories, never admitted defeats, and constantly emphasized eventual victory; it also distributed leaflets to peasants stating that the government was going to lose the war, "so it would be better for people to join the victors while they still could" (West 1985:126; Berman 1974). Often military operations serve exclusively psychological goals. The following entries from a Greek Communist partisan's diary illustrate this point:

14 August 1946. We are in [the village of] Glikoneri. Contact with Fotis. In order to trust us, people must see actions.

16 August 1946. Ambush in Nestori. We hit an enemy squad. Two soldiers killed and two wounded.

17 August 1946. We are in Glikoneri. People have begun to think differently. (Papaioannou 1990:160–1)

This technique can be successful, as in colonial Algeria: "All of us believe that the FLN is strong. It makes its presence known when it wants, and always in an efficient manner. When all the [electrical] poles fall at the same time over a distance of two miles, when trees, stone barricades, and trenches suddenly appear to cut off a road and stop car traffic, one has to wonder where this multitude that has spent time and effort has come from and which imperious finger it has obeyed" (Feraoun 2000:59–60).

When such stratagems work, collaboration starts shifting and control follows. Eventually, however, both actors can use these strategies with equal success, thus reinforcing the stalemate. For example, "by demonstrating the continued presence of the party," Soviet partisans in weakly policed areas of Nazi-occupied Ukraine "created the impression that Soviet authority was more real than that of the invader." The Germans, however, responded in kind: they left companies in the areas they were interested in and "made a habit of returning to given villages time and again. This created the impression in the minds of many people that the Germans were in the area to stay, and that made them less fearful of the partisans" (T. Anderson 1999:599, 615). This can be pursued to extreme lengths, as suggested by the following example from a Vietnamese village:

Shortly after the RDs [government agents] left the village, a dozen Viet Cong paddled across the river, entered My Hué, rousted several villagers out of bed and had them tear down a section of the fence.... The PFs [militiamen] gathered some villagers and rebuilt it. A week later the VC gathered some villagers and tore it down. The PFs rebuilt it. The Americans thought the struggle over the fence, which had little tactical value, was silly. Trao, who had opposed the original construction of the fence, recognized the absurdity of

---

[28] "Report of the Third Secretary of the Embassy from His Visit in Levidi, on May 26, 1947, 36 Hours after It was Attacked," PRO, FO 371/67006/R8651.

the contest yet insisted the PFs could not afford to lose since the Viet Cong had decided to make an issue out of it. The PFs had to fight back. (West 1985:206)

In short, the strategy of manipulating expectations to shape collaboration and thus shift control in contested areas is likely to be indeterminate. That leaves violence. There are good reasons to think that contestation sparks an outbidding of violence, as rivals try to tweak the "balance of fear" (Elliott 2003:945) to their advantage. As a counterinsurgency theorist put it, "When two forces are contending for the loyalty of, and control over, the civilian population, the side which uses violent reprisals most aggressively will dominate most of the people, even though their sympathies may lie in the other direction" (Lindsay 1962:268). A Greek participant in the Macedonian guerrilla war at the beginning of the twentieth century observed in an internal document that "it was by the persuasion of the gun" and the shedding of blood that a village "became Greek or Bulgarian"; similarly, a Greek guerrilla chieftain was advised that unless he burned down at least six houses in the village of Strempeno, the peasants would revert to the Bulgarian side (in Livanios 1999:204, 216). "To be credible," concurs a French officer who served in Algeria (Aussaresses 2001:109), "the [French] had to be more terrifying than the [insurgents]." An American officer who fought the Filipino insurgency of 1899–1902, noted that it was essential to "inspire rebellious Asiatics, individually and collectively, with a greater fear of the reigning government than they had of the rebels." He was echoed by another officer, who pointed out that "it is necessary to make the existing state of war and martial law so inconvenient and unprofitable to the people that they will earnestly desire and work for the reestablishment of peace and civil government, and for the purpose of throwing the burden of the war upon the disloyal element" (in Linn 1989:53–4, 153). The British in Malaya argued that they should be recognized as "stronger than the bandits [i.e., the rebels] and [inspire] greater fear" (Stubbs 1989:75). An American officer in Iraq, "echoing the private comments of many American officers," said that the Iraqis seemed to understand only force. "Whoever displays the most strength and authority is the one they are going to obey. They might be bitter, but they obey" (in Filkins 2005:66).

Under such conditions neutrality (even perceived neutrality) does not appear to guarantee survival – it may even undermine it. In Mozambique, both FRE-LIMO and RENAMO soldiers treated those who would not resettle into the zones that were securely under their control as supporters of the other side to be targeted for capture or for death (Lubkemann 2005:497). Many "neutral" Afghans were killed by mujahidin in the Nazian valley south of Jallalabad in the second half of the 1980s, because the fact that their villages were not bombed by the government was deemed sufficient proof that they were collaborating with the government (Giustozzi 2000:126).[29]

Hence the paradox: on the one hand people seem to sometimes manage to duck violence either by fence-sitting or by collaborating with both sides, but on

---

[29] See also Hedman (2000:131); Senaratne (1997:143); Tone (1994:134); Cooper (1979:51); Race (1973:187); Leites and Wolf (1970:128–9).

the other hand, descriptions of life in contested areas sound horrible, and there are clear incentives for political actors to use violence. To resolve this apparent contradiction, it is necessary to distinguish between areas dominated, but not fully controlled, by one actor (zones 2 and 4) and areas equally "shared" by both actors (zone 3). Hypothesis 4 predicts violence by the stronger actor in the former. Fence-sitting and double-dealing should be punished in zones 2 and 4, but not in zone 3, where Hypothesis 5 predicts no violence.

8.5.1. Violence under Dominant Control (Zones 2 and 4)

The theory predicts that simultaneous defection takes place at the very center of the contested area, that is, in zone 3. Instead, the outer boundaries of the contested area, zones 2 and 4, should be places where fence-sitting and hedging are punished severely as acts of defection. However, it is difficult to find evidence that clearly differentiates between zones 2 and 4 on the one hand and zone 3 on the other. Hence the evidence is tentative and indirect. For instance, in the German-occupied Soviet Union, where "by early 1942 the many elements who had sought to escape a choice by simply standing pat were gradually forced to take sides.... Neutralism was the luxury that the occupation did not permit, *at least not in those areas where partisan and antipartisan activities took place*. Sooner or later everyone was exposed to the impact of external forces and had to take his stand on one side or the other" (Dallin et al. 1964:322–4; emphasis added). The observation that fence-sitting is inversely related to the intensity of the war (Herrington 1997:24; Cabarrús 1983:185) also points to control shifts as the "force" behind forced commitment.

Fence-sitting is a risky endeavor, particularly during shifts in control that require extremely subtle microstrategies whereby, as a Vietnamese peasant put it, "if one is too clever, he won't survive; if he is too foolish, he won't survive; the only way to survive is to know when to seem clever and when to seem foolish" (Race 1973:xii). There are many descriptions of the shrinking possibility of neutrality. In Missouri, "the deeper and longer the war, the more the middle ground of neutralism was undercut." A man wrote in a letter that "The times are growing more radical in the border states. This issue is [either] 'the Union, right or wrong,' or sympathy with the rebellion. And men are being forced to show their hands" (Fellman 1989:52). In the Philippine island of Leyte, "with the exception of those adroit enough to straddle the fence, families, in fact whole areas, came to be marked out as either pro- or anti-Japanese" (Lear 1961:27–8). In Kenya, fence-sitting was "frequently vain" (Barnett and Njama 1966:135). Double-dealing can become an "ever dangerous and harsh double-life, filled increasingly with fear, anxiety, suspicion, hunger and brutality" (Barnett and Njama 1966:135). A double-dealing chief in Mozambique was forced to stop, a FRELIMO man said, because "he was afraid. There were two aspects: he was wondering if he was discovered here [i.e., in a FRELIMO area], whether he was going to be killed by us and, on the other hand, he was thinking that if the RENAMO discovered his contacts with the Frelimo, we would also be killed" (in Geffray 1990:74). In Bangladesh, "some prudent fellows kept two sets of flags – Pakistan and Bangla Desh – to hoist on their rooftops to suit the occasion. But it was not a simple matter of hoisting one flag or the other. They suffered heavily if they were found on the wrong side of the fence" (Salik 1978:101). The Chinese Communists punished "insurance buying" harshly (Chang 1992).

In contested zones, neutrality is undermined by several social mechanisms, and is actively (and credibly) discouraged by the stronger political actor.[30] These factors account for what we may call the paradox of polarization: even though few people are actively committed and most people would prefer to stay out of the conflict, most people in those areas end up having to take sides.

First, several social mechanisms work against those seeking to fence-sit. Fence-sitters may be ostracized and pressured to take sides by their peers. Åkerström (1991:57–8) argues that neutrality, the failure to join a crusade and the willingness to declare the conflict irrelevant, is often seen as betrayal by one's peers. "You cannot avoid involvement," an informant told me (I-22); "you are forced to take a side, willingly or not. You can't stay neutral. Since everyone belongs somewhere, how can you say you are neutral?" Moreover, those already committed feel envy and resentment toward the uncommitted, who, they believe, are staying out of the fray only out of convenience and opportunism, letting others suffer and do the fighting.[31] "As for the citizens who held moderate views," Thucydides (3.82) argued, "they were destroyed by both the extreme parties, either for not taking part in the struggle or in envy at the possibility they might survive." Although these social mechanisms are constant across areas, they are activated in zones 2 and 4, where control has tipped in one or the other direction.

Second, political actors feel undermined by fence-sitting, considering it to be equivalent to defection. Neutrality is seen as "passive collaboration with the enemy"; indifference, vacillation, fence-sitting, and any instance of nonconformity are all regarded as tantamount to hostility and betrayal (Guha 1999:200–3). "These 'sitters on the fence' are undoubtedly a severe handicap to those fighting against the Mau Mau," writes a colonialist author (Leakey 1954:115) about Kenya, "for they undoubtedly do not nearly as much as they could to help destroy Mau Mau." In Missouri, "as the war evolved, neither guerrillas nor Unionists permitted neutrality, seeing it as service, however meekly given, to the enemy" (Fellman 1989:51). General J. Franklin Bell, who commanded the U.S. army in a Philippine province during the 1899–1902 insurgency, stated that "neutrality should not be tolerated" (Francisco 1987:17–18). In Ireland, as the conflict escalated "even neutrality could no longer be tolerated. Only people 'in the movement'

---

[30] The weaker actor (insurgents in zone 2 and incumbents in zone 4) have an incentive to encourage fence-sitting as their second-best option (Kedward 1993:85; Hartford 1989:118–19; McColl 1969:624; Barton 1953:141). However, the stronger actor eventually discerns real from simulated pressure and reacts accordingly.

[31] Manrique (1998:204); Horton (1998:234); Åkerström (1991:57–60); Babeuf (1987:120); Cobb (1972:13). Adam Smith (1982:155) made a similar point: "In a nation distracted by faction, there are, no doubt, always a few, though commonly but a very few, who preserve their judgment untainted by the general contagion. They seldom amount to more than, here and there, a solitary individual, without any influence, excluded by his own candour, from the confidence of either party, and who, though he may be one of the wisest, is necessarily, upon that very account, one of the most insignificant men in society. All such people are held in contempt and derision, frequently in detestation, by the furious zealots of both parties."

could be trusted; 'Those who were not for us at the time were against us'" (Hart 1999:80–1). The U.S. Operations Research Office (Barton 1953:v) pointed out that civilian "passivity" is a "guerrilla asset" and recommended that "only active noncooperation...will harm the guerrillas in a serious and lasting way." As a result, political actors actively discourage fence-sitting, along the logic of "those who are not with us are against us." When an army commander in Guatemala charged local leaders with the security of their town, he told them: "This is voluntary, the door is open for anyone who wants to leave. But I tell you one thing. Here there aren't any pinkos. There is just white and red. Either you are with us or you are with them. But if you are with them, you'll die" (in Stoll 1993:106). A Greek informant described to me how he understood this logic: "The partisans told us: 'You are not with us, you do not support us.' You couldn't be neutral. 'No sir,' each organization would tell you; 'You have to straighten up your position so that we know with whom you are. You could be a traitor. How do I know that you will not inform on me? So, you straighten up your position, you say with whom you are, either with us or the others.' There was no trust.... People wanted to be neutral but they wouldn't let them. You had to belong somewhere" (I-22).

Insurgents and incumbents are equally stringent in their respective zones of predominant control. The Soviet partisans in German-occupied Russia "made sure that those not taking sides were aware of the sort of treatment they could expect as 'traitors,' the wartime equivalent of 'enemy of the people,' with the liberation of the occupied territories" (Hill 2002:51). In Algeria, the Islamist guerrillas of the GIA made the same point to the villagers of Sidi Moussa in Algeria in April 1997; their leader traced three circles in the sand before the assembled villagers and told them: "The first circle is us; the second is the *taghout* (the impious power, i.e. the incumbents); the third is the people. We do not accept to hear from you 'we are neither for one camp nor for the other.' You are either with us or against us. You have twenty-four hours to decide." In order to convince them that he was serious, he then killed a villager who was uncooperative (Zerrouky 1997). Even the generally restrained French partisans made a similar point in 1944: they "were particularly prone to be highly judgmental, not just of collaborators but of any section of society unwilling to commit itself to the struggle" (Kedward 1993:158).[32]

Selective violence against defectors in zones 2 and 4 often targets fence-sitters, sometimes in exemplary ways.[33] The anti-Napoleon Spanish guerrilla leader

---

[32] See also J. L. Anderson (2004:139–40); Dupuy (1997:128); Faivre (1994:187); Hamoumou (1993:168); Stoll (1993:120); Barnett and Njama (1966:141).

[33] Political actors may also induce commitment by "compromising" people and exposing them to punishment by their rival, thus forcing them to seek protection under them. The French in Algeria would show up publicly with local Algerian notables so as to expose them to charges of defection; these notables, knowing that they would then be targeted by the FLN rebels for being collaborators of the French, were forced to collaborate with them for protection (Faivre 1994:123; Hamoumou 1993). A U.S. general noted that in the Philippines the only "acceptable and convincing evidence of the real sentiments of either individuals or town councils should be such acts publicly performed as must inevitably commit them irrevocably to the side of the Americans by arousing the animosity and

Mina on one occasion had three mayors hanged because they had not warned him of the presence of enemy units (Laqueur 1998:8). Just before IRA men executed a man in 1921, they told him: "You are a traitor. You are on our side, and you are with them at the same time" (in Hart 1999:15). Consider the following description of how South Vietnamese militiamen treated two peasants who had watched the Vietcong set an ambush near their farm but had said nothing: "For wanting no part of the war, the farmer and his wife received no sympathy or absolution from those who had chosen a side and who risked death. To keep their farm the couple had helped the Viet Cong to kill. The PFs [militias] whipped them until their screams turned to sobs and their minds seemed to have drifted beyond the pain" (West 1985:170).

Invariably, people get the message: "Everyone understood that there can be no waverings: you're either for or against the revolution," wrote a Russian man in his diary in 1919, after witnessing successive waves of Red and White Terror "that struck fear even among those far removed from politics" (in Raleigh 2002:278–9). Most people find themselves in a position where, as a Spaniard puts it, "you had to go with either one or the other side" (in Zulaika 1988:25). In the face of credible sanctions, taking sides can be rational: neutrality attracts the enmity of both sides and the protection of none.[34] According to a Greek proverb: "The solitary sheep ends up being killed either by a wolf or by a knife" (Svolos 1990:60). This is

opposition of the insurgent element" (in Linn 1989:153). In Sierra Leone, enforced participation of young conscripts in atrocities against local leaders was meant to deter them from returning to their village for fear of revenge (Richards 1996:5). Such public acts can take a variety of forms ranging from public denunciation of a fellow citizen to participation in violent action. In Korea, commitment was induced by getting people to sign their names on membership lists or various public petitions (e.g., Yoo 2002:22). In their logical extreme, such acts induce people to think that "if you didn't kill someone, someone was going to kill you" (Hart 1999:11). Moreover, those who commit atrocities are powerfully bonded to those who order them, and to their cause, since only its success can ensure that they will not have to answer for their actions. Violence destroys the possibility of reconciliation with the enemy and becomes a "powerful act of group bonding and criminal enabling" (Grossman 1995:210–11). See also Gourevitch (1998:24); Del Pino (1998: 185–6); Rosenberg (1991:154); Horne (1987:134); R. Thompson (1966:36). The leader of the British mission in occupied Greece, Eddy Myers (1955:73), recalled such an incident: "I learned afterwards that [the partisan leader Aris Velouchiotis] had ... the culprit stripped and publicly beaten in the village square by the newest recruit, a mere boy. It was in this way that he 'blooded' his new adherents."

34 Under conditions of extreme uncertainty and danger, exit becomes a sensible option. An Algerian pharmacist remarked: "It is impossible to work now. One evening three people visited me, they introduced themselves as *moujahidin*. One was wounded and they wanted me to treat him. But if the army saw these people in front of my house, they would have demolished it with explosives, they would have killed me, and they would have thrown my family in the street like dogs. I am not part of this war, I am neither with one nor with the other; this why I left. Because this war is not my business" (in Martinez 1994:56). "If you try to protect yourself [and flee], you lose everything," a Mozambican man told Nordstrom (1997:91); "If you stay, you may keep your possessions and lose your life. There is no sense to this war." Louis Wiesner (1988:109) found that refugee movement in Vietnam was "an adaptive response" of "villagers caught between two equally implacable forces, each of which demanded total commitment, and threatened the people in one or more ways." The peasants of Sello de Oro, in Peru were squeezed by Shining Path pressure from the heights and army pressure from the valley. "This squeeze accelerated the exodus of the villagers of the higher montaña; some remained to live under the power of Shining Path, but others descended to take

conveyed in the following snapshots provided by two peasants from Vietnam and Nicaragua respectively:

I hope that just one side will control us – no matter which one. Living under the control of both sides is too much. (Elliott 2003:144)

There were two paths. You went on their side [the Sandinistas] or you went into the Resistance or you were killed" (Horton 1998:184)

Because descriptions of contested areas typically fail to differentiate between areas of dominant and even control, it is very difficult to find precise evidence about the theory's predictions in the descriptive literature. Consider the following story told by Don Moser (2000:86, 104, 99) about the village of Loc Dien in South Vietnam in 1965. This village of ten thousand was located near the city of Hue and was actually composed of thirteen hamlets. "Beneath the peaceful surface," Moser tells us, "the struggle between the government and the Vietcong goes on night and day. By day most of the village belongs to the government. But the night is a different matter." However, additional information complicates the matter. Moser reports that no Americans were stationed in Loc Dien, that there were no Popular Forces militiamen there, that the leaders of the governmental faction slept outside the village, and that there were only nine soldiers to protect the thirteen hamlets (their leader complained that he "cannot protect the village with his nine men"). The most remote hamlet was under predominant yet incomplete Vietcong control (zone 4); consistent with the theory, the Vietcong exercised selective violence there, and the army indiscriminate violence:

Since the hamlet by the bay is so remote from the village center, V.C. come there frequently, even in the daytime, to take fish from the fishermen, paying them with worthless V.C. money. This year the V.C. have assassinated two men from the hamlet. The place is so

refuge in the valley" (Del Pino 1998:172). Such population movements may cause a process of geographical "squeeze" that may eliminate contested areas for some time and replace them with a "no-man's-land" between territories fully controlled by opposite actors (e.g., Geffray 1990:122–5). Nevertheless, exit is often a nonoption for many people– especially for peasants whose land is their sole livelihood (Binford 1996:112; Ash 1995:123; M. F. Brown and Fernández 1991:127; Hunt 1974:48–9; Lerner 1958:25). "Only enormous fears could fuel flight, and many stayed put, fearing leaving even more than staying," writes Fellman (1989:74) about Missouri. As a Guatemalan man explained: "I haven't done anything wrong, and I don't have any place else to go. Besides who will support my family?" (Annis 1988:168). Indeed, the first people to flee are usually the "most resourceful, both in terms of material wealth and connections" (Zur 1998:87). Surveys conducted during the Vietnam War demonstrate that fleeing was clearly a function of resources, though the relationship is U-shaped: the young, literate, wealthy, skilled, and connected people, but also the most deprived and landless peasants tended to move earlier than not only the old, illiterate, poor, unskilled, and unconnected people, but also the land-owning peasants (Wiesner 1988:109). Moreover, exit can be risky since political actors often consider it to be an act of defection and often inflict reprisals on family members who stay behind (Maier 1995; Wiesner 1988:101; Gage 1984). In El Salvador, the insurgents often discouraged people from leaving the areas they controlled (Binford 1996:114), while in Peru, "Sendero killed people who attempted to escape and even those who simply mentioned escape as a possible alternative. Faced with increasing desertion, Shining Path began to retaliate against the families of deserters. Most who fled the base had family ties, so punishment would fall upon those who stayed behind" (Del Pino 1998:185).

insecure that teachers will not come there as they do to the other hamlets, and many of the children are illiterate. The fishermen have almost as much trouble with the government as with the Vietcong. Elsewhere in the village, the people like the A.R.V.N. soldiers from the battalion and invite them into their houses. . . . When they visit [this] hamlet, they beat up the teenage boys, accusing them of being V.C. and two months ago they killed a respected fisherman merely on suspicion.

Indeed, the available evidence clearly suggests that (undifferentiated) contested zones are sites of considerable violence. In South Carolina during the American Revolution, "both sides were guilty of atrocities, especially during 1781 when neither could really control the countryside" (Weir 1985:74). Dallin et al.'s (1964:330) research on the Soviet Union during the German occupation reaches a similar conclusion: "though life under either German or partisan rule was fairly unpleasant, it was generally secure; to live in the twilight zone exposed a resident to requisitioning by both Germans and partisans, and to reprisals from either (or both) for collaborating with the other; even refusal to work with one granted no immunity from punishment by the other. . . . The net result was that the civilian population in these border areas was worst off, being caught, sometimes literally, between two fires."

Where their control is dominant but not complete, incumbents are responsible for much of the violence. In occupied China, the highest death rates caused by the Japanese were found in the areas immediately adjacent to the Japanese-controlled county towns, rather than inside the towns or in the remote countryside; in the aftermath of the Japanese attack on a Qingfeng County town in early 1938, villagers reported seeing more and more new grave mounds, starting from about five *li* away. The number increased as they came closer to the town, where the Japanese damage was worst. Such a pattern is consistent with Hypothesis 4. The Communist fourth branch army, far removed from these rural towns, enjoyed a comparatively high level of security (Thaxton 1997:208). Likewise, most Japanese destruction in the areas of southern China studied by Helen Siu (1989:97–8) was suffered by peri-urban villages, those located around the towns.[35] A similar pattern is reported about the Japanese-occupied Filipino island of Leyte (Lear 1961:214). In Guatemala, selective violence often took the form of kidnappings by the army; these occurred often, Warren (1998:92) reports, in outlying hamlets where the guerrillas had no permanent presence but passed through as they moved from the coastal regions south of Lake Atitlán to the more active areas north of the lake near Chichicastenango. In Colombia, there was limited violence within the so-called demilitarized zone controlled by the rebels; right-wing violence against alleged guerrilla collaborators took place "just outside the zone," which the rebels did not control but into which they ventured (Forero 2002:A9). After the Colombian army imposed "light" control over a guerrilla stronghold, in January 2004, it carried out arrest sweeps of civilians accused of being guerrilla

---

[35] After a number of massacres, the Japanese troops burned down the peri-urban villages to create a safety zone between themselves and the rural areas. Such zones became known as "the three bare zones" (Siu 1989:97–8).

collaborators (S. Wilson 2004:A14).[36] Likewise, it is reported that as soon as the paramilitaries gained control of the town of Tame, in the same country, they engaged in a process of "selective cleaning": they "went about eliminating those they felt had collaborated with the guerrillas during their reign"; the insurgents, having retreated in outlying areas, responded in kind to maintain their rule. "Killings, reprisal killings, and counter-reprisals have become the order of the day" (Fichtl 2003).

The same pattern, only inverted (i.e., high levels of insurgent violence), is observed where insurgents are dominant but incumbents still have access to the population.

The Iraqi city of Haditha provides a striking illustration. A farming settlement of ninety thousand people by the Euphrates River, it entered zone 4 in 2005. Omer Mahdi and Rory Carroll (2005:1) report that the Islamist rebels "became the sole authority, running the town's security, administration, and communications. A three-hour drive north from Baghdad, under the nose of an American base, it is a miniature Taliban-like state. Insurgents decide who lives and dies, which salaries get paid, what people wear, what they watch and listen to." There is no fighting in Haditha because "there is no one to challenge the Islamists. The police station and municipal offices were destroyed last year and US marines make only fleeting visits every few months." These visits consist of raids to "flush out the rebels." According to the residents, the insurgents withdraw for a few days and return when the Americans leave. There is considerable selective insurgent violence as the rebels carry out executions on Haqlania bridge, the entrance to Haditha. A small crowd usually turns up to watch even though the killings are filmed and made available on DVD in the market the same afternoon. "With so many alleged American agents dying there Haqlania bridge was renamed Agents' bridge. Then a local wag dubbed it Agents' fridge, evoking a mortuary, and that name has stuck."

Considerable anecdotal evidence further supports Hypothesis 4. Race's (1973:114) outline of the pattern of assassinations that took place in Long An province during 1959–60 seems consistent with the hypothesis, and many of the Vietcong killings described by Mallin (1966) appear to have taken place in zone 4, where the Vietcong had a more-or-less permanent presence. Harvey Meyerson (1970:93–4) describes a Mekong Delta village where the Vietcong held enough sway to administer cholera shots to the people while blowing up the house of a suspected government informer, killing his wife and two children. In his comparison of two areas in Peru, one where Shining Path rebels exercised full control (the Canipaco valley) and one where a Shining Path column "visited regularly" but did not stay in (Jarpa), Nelson Manrique (1998:204) found that there was more insurgent coercion in the latter. Elisabeth Wood (2003:155–6) reports that in one area of El Salvador where she conducted research, insurgents (whom the population had to treat as the "local governing authority") were able to locate and kill suspected informers, while the army would kill people indiscriminately during raids.

---

[36] We don't know if these arrests were effective; Scott Wilson (2004:14A) reports that the villagers were skeptical about the army's intention to stay and, as a result, they continued "to heed guerrillas' rules and warnings."

Anderson (2004:194) provides similar evidence from El Salvador. He reports that where insurgents were fully in control (*zonas de control* in El Salvador) justice was administered in a nonarbitrary and limited way. In contrast, "there is less fair play in places such as the expansion zone, where the *compas* [guerrillas] feel less secure. There, more coercive measures are in force." The rebel FMLN could be "extremely ruthless," he adds emphatically (2004:136), "where its political hegemony is threatened." The same pattern of selective insurgent violence in areas of dominant but incomplete rebel control is reported in Burma (Anderson 2004) and Nepal (Sengupta 2005c:67).

Additional evidence can be found in descriptions of erosion of control (i.e., movements from zones 5 to 4 and from 1 to 2). This evidence suggests that violence is particularly likely during erosion. This was the case during the Algerian Civil War (Kalyvas 1999) and the Finnish Civil War: immediately after the Left took power in the town of Huittinen, it killed five people (when the Whites came in, they killed another thirty-seven) (Alapuro 1998). In Malaya, insurgents "began to resort increasingly to violence, extortion, and terrorist tactics" when the British resettlement program started proving successful (Stubbs 1989:123–4; Clutterbuck 1966:63). In Venezuela, there was virtually no guerrilla terror against the peasantry in 1962 and 1963, but when the government started flushing the guerrillas out of their rural strongholds in 1964 and 1965, the insurgents began to kill peasants (Wickham-Crowley 1990:229). The Vietcong terror appears to have increased during the later years of the war when the Vietcong organization had been decimated (Blaufarb and Tanham 1989:9; Berman 1974:50): when the Vietcong had to reassert their challenged authority, in a situation where they themselves were more vulnerable, their sanctions became "swift and terrible" (Elliott 2003:949). Ponciano Del Pino (1998:172) shows how the Shining Path in Peru switched to more coercive tactics after 1984, when contestation replaced full control. In the Philippines, as counterinsurgency became more effective, people were more reluctant to help the rebels who became more violent and made more "mistakes against the people": "The Huks were coercing the very ones they were supposed to protect and alienating those they needed for support" (Kerkvliet 1977:137). The same was the case later with the NPA: as the war deteriorated, it became more violent (Berlow 1998:179). In Colombia, "accusations of civilian collaboration by opposing armed groups – flare up when two or more groups come in contact in a given area, or when land changes hands from one side to another"; the coming of a "new regime" brings with it "the potential for violent purges" (Fichtl 2004:2). According to Fichtl (2004:4) "violence truly explodes when the authority of one of these regimes is challenged by the arrival of another would be ruler." The massacres of civilians that took place during the Algerian Civil War, primarily in 1997, do not appear to support Hypothesis 4 – insofar as the evidence suggests that they were selective massacres carried out by the Islamist rebels in areas where they had just lost control, that is, zone 2 (Kalyvas 1997). These massacres would be in support of Hypothesis 4 if they had been either indiscriminate or perpetrated by the incumbents.

An indirect test of Hypothesis 4 is provided by patterns of violence in "symmetric" civil wars. It is possible to think of areas adjacent to the front lines in these wars as approximating zones 2 and 4: this is where control is more fluid and defection remains a possibility. Evidence from these wars suggests that violence tends to be concentrated in such areas. During the Russian Civil War, "the closer the rebellious area was to the forces of the Whites, just across the front line, the more brutal was the suppression of the internal front;" in fact, the Red Terror was associated with challenges to Bolshevik rule. In Odessa, the lion's share of executions took place in the weeks before the Bolsheviks' departure with eighteen hundred victims executed in Kiev in those last weeks (Brovkin 1994:82; 122; 125); executions increased when the enemy approached (Werth 1998:123–4). Similarly, proximity to the front line appears to be a key predictor of violence in the province of Aragón during the Spanish Civil War (Ledesma 2001:265), while the major massacres against the Italian population in Tuscany took place in zones immediately behind the front line and during the retreat of the German army (Battini and Pezzino 1997:xx; Klinkhammer 1997:19–20). Similar patterns have been observed in Finland (Upton 1980:292), Korea (Yoo 2002:20), Colombia (Forero 2002:A9), and Afghanistan (Waldman 2002b:A9).

Another indirect indicator is the clustering pattern that violence seems to follow in many civil wars. During the anti-British Palestinian rebellion, violence was most pronounced in what the British called "Triangle of Fear" or "Triangle of Terror" in the Jinin-Nablus-Tulkarm district (Swedenburg 1995:xxxii). A similar "Triangle of Death" was reported in Somalia (Besteman 1996:582), Algeria (Kalyvas 1999), and Iraq. The "Triangle" in Algeria was indeed a contested zone, but we do not know whether the "Triangles" elsewhere were equally contested, though available descriptions suggest they were.

Finally, there is some evidence that as an area moves to zone 2 or 4, denunciations increase. After U.S. troops took control of the city of Fallujah in Iraq, they reported that many residents began to cooperate and reveal the locations of weapons caches and suspects (Spinner 2005:A15). In occupied central Russia and Belorussia, the Germans reconquered occupied Soviet territory from the partisans several times (Terry 2005:20–1). In this area, the Wehrmacht was able to pacify newly won territory through the installation of garrisons and the reestablishment of the collaborator police and administration. The Germans were able to do this because the Army Group Center disposed of significantly larger security forces than were typically available in other occupied areas. "The return of German forces," Nicholas Terry points out, "was accompanied by the reappointment of mayors but also often by a wave of renewed denunciations and arrests by the police." Consider, as well, Bruce Calder's (1984:167) description of the Dominican insurgency: "So the [U.S.] marines decided to move into guerrilla-dominated areas and identify these part-time insurgents. Military authorities thought the identification possible because they had developed a large group of informers, including a number of ex-guerrillas, and a new screening process which protected the identity of those who gave information against their neighbors."

8.5.2. Violence under Parity (Zone 3)

According to the theory no information should flow toward the actors in zone 3, and hence no selective violence should take place (Hypothesis 5); also, though defection toward both sides is massive, people do not denounce, and local committees veto violence.

Anecdotal evidence supports Hypothesis 5. The most compelling comes from the contested Vietnamese village of Binh Nghia, where in 1965–7 a detachment of Marines and a local South Vietnamese militia ruled by day while the Vietcong ruled by night. Both sides were able to collect taxes: "Our acting village chief, Mr. Trao," F. J. West recalls (1985:254), "says his opposite number has a list of who should pay and how much." Although the local Vietcong did not dare visit their homes in the village on a regular basis, a former marine who served there (West 1985:5, 219–20) remembers that

> their families were immune from the violence. The relatives and children of both sides were equally vulnerable to reprisals, so no man dared to strike the family of another, lest his own family suffer ten times over.... The PFs [militias] and the Viet Cong had certain rules to their war, understandings which were kept because, and only so long as, they were mutually advantageous. What often has been called accommodation frequently has been nothing more than a precarious balance of power, perceived as such by both sides. Deterrence is a better word than accommodation to describe a situation wherein each side is unwilling to undertake certain acts while the other side retains capability to retaliate in kind.... The ultimate step in escalation – the murder or wholesale slaughter of PF families – was unlikely in Binh Nghia because the VC families acted as hostages. Suong [the leader of the militia] had declared that he would kill ten of their children for each member of a PF family killed. Vulnerability to retaliation set limits on the actions either the PFs or the Viet Cong were willing to take in the struggle for Binh Nghia.

As a result, civilians were not victimized in Bingh Nghia, at least as long as the Marines remained in the village: "It was usually the participants on both sides, not the villagers, who died," concludes West (1985:187).[37] The "phenomenon of unofficial accommodation" between VC and government officials "was something that I would encounter repeatedly as I delved into the realities of the war in Hau Nghia," points out Herrington (1997:21–2) about another part of Vietnam. Ellsberg (2003:127) describes the same phenomenon, while noting the absence of denunciations: "The GVN had pretty good access to the people on many of the days but essentially none of the nights. The VC had good access on some of the days, where there were no GVN troops there, and virtually all the nights. In effect, the GVN 'ruled' by day, and the VC by night. That meant the VC could levy taxes regularly, conduct recruiting, hold indoctrination sessions, and even sleep there many nights. For practical purposes, they lived there; the others wouldn't inform on them, even to the government officials who visited by day, with a guard."

A similar logic seems to have emerged in the village of San Ricardo in the Philippines, during the Huk rebellion. This village, Kerkvliet (1977:163–4) points out, was not in a "liberated area." During the height of the revolt, between 1946 and 1950, threats, counter-threats, fears, and apprehensions frequently led to tacit

---

[37] Also consistent with Hypothesis 5, a CIA case officer who served in Vietnam told Moyar (1997:68) that "many informants were also wary of providing information that would affect people in their village structure. As a result, the [Vietcong] cadres we'd get information on most often were guys from outside of the village coming into the village."

understandings between the two factions that kept their respective armed groups from fighting over harvests. Nordstrom (1997:56) reports that in Mozambique, where people were able to collaborate with both sides, casualties and disorder were kept at a minimum. The town of San Jacinto in Colombia seems to have been located in a similar zone. It went through successive shifts of control from the leftist FARC to the rightist AUC and seemed to have stabilized between the two in the winter of 2002. Scott Wilson (2003) reports that the mayor of this town successfully vetoed the decision of the rightists to massacre suspected leftists. Descriptions of an Iraqi city where there was a balance of forces between state authorities and insurgents during the summer of 2004 coincided with reports of low levels of violence (Huseen and Pelhman 2004:7).[38]

On the negative side, Jay Mallin (1966:56) reports a pattern of Vietcong assassinations and kidnappings in the hamlets of the My Tho area where "the Vietcong are usually no farther away than the nearest clump of trees – just across the road." He does not provide more details, but this could well be an instance of violence in a zone 3 type of area and such violence would contradict Hypothesis 5.

Indirect evidence for the mechanism underlying the absence of violence in zone 3 can be found in the ability of local committees to veto the use of violence by their armed principals. Because political actors depend on local collaboration, they usually abide by the committee's recommendations. Elliott (2003:338) quotes the following account on the relation between the Vietcong and their local village agents:

If there were any questions about problems in the village, or if the district cadres questioned the report of the village Party chapter by mentioning what the villagers had told them, the village Party chapter secretary would say, "Comrade, you don't trust our Party chapter. If you don't trust us, you can disband this Party chapter and set up another one." The district cadres couldn't say anything because the entire village Party chapter was unanimous about the report of the Party chapter secretary, so they just went back to the district and reported to the province level what the village cadres had told them.

The ability of local committees to sometimes veto the use of violence by political actors is confirmed by some additional evidence. In Kenya, many Mau Mau local councils wanted to avoid repressive measures by the security forces, such as "collective fines, the confiscation of livestock, harsh forms of interrogation, arrest and internment in concentration camps"; as a result, they "sought to retain some measure of control over the fighting groups. This was particularly true in Kiambu, where the district council of elders prohibited the killing of loyalists or traitors without council consent and for some time retained their control over the guerrilla units" (Barnett and Njama 1966:155). The mayor of the town of San

---

[38] Stubbs (1989:105–6) reports about a similar area in Malaya: "Even within the new settlements, people had to be very careful. On the one hand there were plenty of communist sympathizers ready to report them to the local Min Yuen or MRLA for co-operating with the police, while on the other hand the Special Branch had taken advantage of the resettlement process to install their own informers who could report on those who were aiding the communists. It was no wonder that so many of the new arrivals in the resettlement centres continued to feel insecure." Unfortunately, he does not provide information about violence.

Jacinto in Colombia refused the request of two rightist paramilitary leaders who approached him with a list of would-be victims, including three town council members, and a request that he allow a large-scale massacre on Christmas eve; as a result, the massacre was averted (S. Wilson 2003). A Vietcong district cadre offered the following assessment on the thirty killings that had taken place in his village between 1960 and 1963: "All death sentences were proposed by the village. Ultimate decisions about them were made by the district, but the district has never rejected any such proposals made by the village, because the district authorities did not know anything. They had to rely on the judgment of the village. *If the village wanted the victims to die they would die, or if it wanted them to live they would live.* Besides, the district also wanted to protect the prestige of the village authorities because they were closer to the scene" (in Elliott 2003:338–9; emphasis added). Pressure from below may cause political actors who lack the ability to break the stalemate through additional resources to eventually stop soliciting denunciations (West 1985:146).

Two testable implications can be derived from Hypothesis 5, although the actual testing of either would be difficult. First, denouncers in zones 2 and 4 should be younger than those of zones 1 and 5 because young people tend to be less risk-averse and denouncing in zones 2 and 4 is riskier. Unfortunately, because so few systematic data are available on the identities of individual denouncers, this implication would be very difficult to test. Second, the absence of denunciations ought to be unrelated to the personal characteristics of denouncers and local agents. It is very common for people to rationalize violence and denunciations as occurring because of the actions of "bad people." For example, in the vast majority of the interviews I conducted in Greece, my informants explained the varying behavior of local agents in terms of personal characteristics: "good, decent, civic-minded" agents blocked false denunciations, whereas "bad" agents used their position to settle accounts or to run rackets. Likewise, in Peru a university student asserted that irresponsible Sendero cadres were the cause of much conflict and violence in his zone and added: "I think that it depends on the zone, in others there were good elements" (in Degregori 1998:154–5). However, although any conflict will involve better and worse elements in different places and at different times, denunciation and violence, and thus the sense that "bad" people are at work, should depend on control. Hypothesis 5 would be strengthened if the empirical evidence were to show that these observations of personal characteristics were endogenous to the particular zone of control – that is, ex post rationalizations of the trouble, or lack thereof, that occurred.

8.6. CONCLUSION

Magnifying the dynamics of a conventional civil war uncovers dynamics that are consistent with the theory of selective violence and the theory's overall predictions. Stephen Ash's (1995) excellent study of the American Civil War in the occupied South, where the geographical situation approximated that of an irregular civil war, is a case in point. The Union occupation, he points out, created in effect not one occupied South but three: the garrisoned towns, whose citizens lived constantly in the presence, and under the thumb, of the Northern army; the Confederate frontier, which federal forces penetrated only sporadically, its citizens at all other times being in the grasp of the Confederacy, whose state authority persisted; and no-man's-land, the zone surrounding the garrisoned towns, which was beyond the pale of Confederate authority and endured frequent Yankee visitations, but did not experience the constant presence of a federal force. These three spheres, Ash found, might well be considered different worlds, so starkly did they delineate distinctive experiences within the occupied South.

We may think of the garrisoned towns as a zone 1, of the Confederate frontier as a zone 4, and of the non-man's-land as combining zones 2 or 3, depending on the federals' degree of penetration. Consistent with Hypothesis 2, garrisoned towns (zone 1) were "islands of order in a sea of violence" despite the bitter hostility toward the Union felt by their inhabitants. At the same time, however, areas strongly garrisoned by the Union army were *also* places where denunciations between neighbors to the Union authorities were a common occurrence, as Fellman (1989:27) found in Missouri. The Confederate frontier (zone 4) was the target of periodical federal raids on missions of seizure and destruction. In other words, it suffered "incumbent" indiscriminate violence. As for the no-man's-land (zones 2 and 3), it was patrolled by Union forces that could project their power at will anywhere within it, and were able to exclude Confederate power and authority from it in some parts (zone 2). Where they had an advantage (zone 2), Unionists were most likely to be violent: it was there that they "most fully gratified their lust for vengeance." Moreover, Unionist violence often exploded "after the Yankees arrived" – that is, after a zone moved to 2. However, federal authority prevailed only when and where Union troops were actually present, and it extended no further "than the range of their muskets and carbines." People lived most of their days in a kind of vacuum of authority, a twilight zone neither Union nor Confederate; they lived in fear, an unremitting sense of anxiety far more unsettling than that which plagued the Confederate frontier, for in no-man's-land the enemy was never far away. Yet, within no-man's-land one could find zones of peace precisely, it turns out, where the power of the Confederates was checked by the presence of the federals. In a few districts where federal raids were frequent, secessionists were restrained by fear of reprisals. "Our Southern friends beseech me not to interfere with the Union men," a Confederate officer wrote from eastern Tennessee while that region was still in Confederate hands, "since [the Unionists] will be certain to report them, and thereby bring down ... retaliation on the part of the Federal troops. ... I have therefore determined not to arrest any Union sympathizers unless known to be aiding and abetting the enemy."

To sum up, this chapter has sought to draw out and evaluate the implications of the theory of selective violence derived in Chapter 7 using evidence from a broad spectrum of civil wars. Shifts in control take place through two processes: initial shifts, which come as political actors make tactical decisions to move military resources in or out of an area, and consolidation, in which actors use selective violence to eliminate defection and take full control of an area. Once control is achieved, violence becomes redundant. Therefore, the higher an actor's level of control, the less likely that actor will use violence. This process works for insurgents as well as incumbents, because insurgency should be understood primarily as a process of alternative state building – insurgent organizations tax, set up administrative structures, and seek to perform government functions for the population they control. Before control is definitively established, defection and denunciation are not the only options pursued by the population. Most attempt to fence-sit, either remaining neutral or seeking to curry favor with both groups simultaneously. Political actors regard fence-sitting as a threat, and try to use violence to punish it and propel the population into their camp. They are more violent where they have more control and more local information, and thus are able to strike effectively. However, because of the threat of retaliation faced by denouncers, there will be no denunciations in zone 3 and hence no selective violence. Evidence from case studies suggests the plausibility of this prediction; Chapter 9 tests it more systematically.

9

Empirics II

Microcomparative Evidence

> We were the ones who directed the partisans. If arrests took place, this meant that we were the denouncers.
>
> Member of rebel local committee, Greece

In this chapter, I test the theory of selective violence and some of its implications primarily against data collected in the Argolid, a region in southern Greece. Taking the village as my unit of analysis, and relying on interviews, judicial archives, and secondary sources, I was able to collect data of high quality and to reconstruct the process of civil war in every locality of this region.

After a description of the research design, I provide background information about the Greek Civil War and the Argolid region along with a short analytic narrative of the civil war in the Argolid. I follow up with descriptive statistics about control, selective violence, and indiscriminate violence and, then, test the theory of selective violence. The results are broadly supportive of the theory. I also discuss the empirical mispredictions. More specifically, the overprediction of violence may be explained by the existence or emergence of a norm of positive reciprocity. Avoiding violence under conditions of stress appears to trigger a norm of positive reciprocity that contributes to the absence of violence in subsequent rounds, even when denunciation is rational. Second, vengeful emotions may explain why the theory sometimes underpredicts violence. Most of the time, revenge tends to take place when the likelihood of retaliation is low. In contrast, the desire for revenge operates as an emotion when it clouds judgment, thus causing an underestimation of risk (Petersen 2002). Acting to take revenge within an unfavorable control zone triggers immediate retaliation – hence the overoccurrence of violence compared with the theory's predictions. I conclude with a battery of out-of-sample tests using data from across Greece, including a replication in an ethnically divided area of the country and the testing of additional implications using data on 136 villages from local histories, ethnographies, agricultural studies, research papers, and additional interviews.

9.1. RESEARCH DESIGN

To overcome the problems discussed in Chapter 2, I adopted a subnational, micro-comparative research design. The general inadequacy of "off-the-shelf" datasets pointed to the need for a "grass-roots" strategy.[1] At the same time, it was also clear that a simple ethnography was inadequate as well. Starting with Tilly's (1964:38) advice to "narrow the focus and step up the magnification," and Przeworski's and Teune's (1970:74) reminder that comparative analysis does not require comparisons between national units, I based my central empirical test on a detailed study of a Greek region, where I reconstructed the process of civil war in each village.[2] By studying the universe of units in one region, I was able to collect detailed and contextualized data of ethnographic quality. Besides producing "thick" insights, this research design allows for a substantial number of observations and extensive empirical variation, precludes sampling on the dependent variable, and permits a high level of control.

The choice of Greece was motivated by practical concerns – the ability to conduct wide-ranging archival and ethnographic research in a rural context. Within Greece, and after conducting pilot studies in four different areas, I selected the prefecture (*nomós*) of Argolid, located in the northeastern part of the Peloponnese peninsula in southern Greece. This choice was dictated primarily by my discovery of an important (and untapped) judicial archive. Using this archive, I was able to construct a dataset including all homicides that occurred during the civil war in every village of the two major counties of the Argolid, an area that in 1940 included sixty-one villages with a total population of 45,086 and two towns with an additional population of 20,050. In most cases I was able to pinpoint the identity of the perpetrator and the victim, the links between perpetrator and victim, the time and location of the homicide, the way it was carried out, the links between this homicide with anterior and subsequent instances of violence, and the justifications (if any) that were given or that can be inferred about it. Appendixes A and B contain a discussion of sources and methodology.

Reconstructing the process of violence in a war that ended in 1949 required an assemblage of multiple sources. Because of the fragmentary character of the sources, I had to proceed as an archaeologist would: "gather discrete and disparate traces of the past and assemble them in order to shed light on the circumstances and background of what we otherwise can only know from a haunted memory" (Geyer 2000:178). I collected the data from three sources: archives; interviews; and published and unpublished memoirs, autobiographies, and local histories. I was able to crosscheck most observations with multiple oral and written sources.

---

[1] I followed Russell Ramsey's (1973:44) advice about Colombia, "The scholar who will walk the terrain of Tolima, or Santander, or Boyacà, interview eye-witnesses, and exhaust local collections of letters and newspapers, will have the basis for a new level of sophistication in violencia scholarship."

[2] I rejected an alternative option, constructing a random sample of localities within a country or across a small number of countries, because of the possibility of cross-checking evidence that only a regional focus can provide.

I also researched some instances of denunciation and explored situations where acts of violence were planned but eventually not carried out.

I then replicated, in less depth, the same research design in the county (*eparchía*) of Almopia, located in northern Greece, in the region of Macedonia, next to the (then) Yugoslav border. The choice of Almopia was dictated by the need to introduce as much contrast to the Argolid as possible in an area of comparable size and ecological variation. Finally, I created a dataset of villages from the entire country using data from additional interviews, two village studies conducted in the late 1940s and early 1950s, and several ethnographies, local histories, and memoirs. I check both theoretical predictions and empirical findings from the Argolid against this "out-of-sample" dataset. Although not a random sample, this makes possible what historians call *mise en serie*, the collection of a large number of observations when it is impossible to collect the universe of cases (Veyne 1996:231). In addition, these data allow me to generate additional test implications and to check further the validity of predictions and findings.

This research design raises the issue of broad generalizability. Bounding the empirical domain, however, is an acceptable trade-off in the study of civil war violence given the state of its theoretical understanding, which remains based on mostly untested conjectures. Although I provided anecdotal evidence from a wide range of civil wars to establish plausibility, my primary empirical objective is to conduct an initial rigorous test of the theory as a first step in a broader research program. My confidence is increased by the fact that the theory was not developed inductively from the data used to test it. Overall, this study fits in a broader trend of recent work that relies on carefully crafted research designs implemented at the microlevel to further our general theoretical and empirical knowledge (e.g., Wilkinson 2004; Posner 2004; Miguel 2004; Wantchekon 2003).

9.2. THE GREEK CIVIL WAR

The Greek Civil War was fought along the left-right cleavage; it was "a bitter and costly internal struggle between two ideologically irreconcilable camps, the Communists and the nationalists" (Nachmani 1993:63). It took place over a period of roughly six years, starting in 1943 during the (primarily) German occupation of Greece and ending with the defeat of the Communist Party of Greece (KKE) in 1949. The war can be divided into three phases. The first one took place during the occupation and immediately after it and included three distinct but related conflicts: first, the resistance organization EAM (National Liberation Front), created and led by the Communist Party in September 1941, and its army ELAS (the National Popular Liberation Army) versus various nationalist resistance organizations, such as EDES (National Democratic Greek League), EKKA (National and Social Liberation), and smaller groups mainly made up of officers of the Greek army; second, EAM/ELAS versus various collaborationist militias, the stronger of which was known as Security Battalions; and, third, EAM/ELAS versus the postoccupation British-backed Greek government in December 1944. This phase ended with the defeat of the Communists. The second phase of the war, in 1945 and 1946, included low-grade and sporadic guerrilla warfare along with sustained persecution of the Left by armed right-wing bands as well as state officials. The third phase was a renewed full-scale Communist insurgency that took place between 1947 and 1949 and ended with the definitive defeat of the Communists.

We lack reliable fatality figures for the entire period, largely because the civil war was intertwined with a foreign occupation. A broad survey of the available evidence reveals the following fatality patterns: during the occupation period, as many as 40,000 civilians may have been killed in reprisal actions or mass executions by the occupying forces, sometimes assisted by local collaborators; the main leftist resistance organization may have also killed close to 15,000 civilians. Up to 2,000 collaborationist militiamen and 4,000 guerrillas (known as *andartes*) were also killed in and after combat. In 1945-6, up to 3,000 civilians were killed mainly by right-wing militias. The last phase of the war claimed the lives of up to 15,000 members of the government army and 20,000 leftist rebels; up to 4,000 civilians were killed by the rebels, while the state executed up to 5,000 leftists, mainly captured guerrillas. This brings the total to approximately 108,000 fatalities for a population of 7,330,000. This account leaves out, obviously, hundreds of thousands who were wounded, displaced, exiled, imprisoned, or otherwise persecuted. More than 1,700 villages were partly or entirely destroyed. The human cost of the Greek Civil War was clearly enormous.

The war was fought primarily as an irregular war with features parallel to many civil wars:

The conflict was dark and murky, a war in the shadows characterised by enemies difficult to define or even to see, and by a search for victory not measurable in territorial terms or human and material loss. The enemy rarely wore uniforms, often fought with confiscated weapons, usually relied upon non-conventional warfare, and nearly always received supplies and shelter from neighboring communist countries. Battlefronts seldom existed, for the guerrillas preferred the terrorist tactics of raiding, pillaging, sniping, and abducting villagers and townspeople into their small but effective force.... The type of war being waged in Greece made it possible for an inferior but motivated army to win by simply avoiding defeat. Patience was the best weapon. A long and frustrating conflict would wear down the morale and determination of disciplined army regulars or it could break the will of civilians and force an end to the war. Victory depended on maintaining the support of the countryside by securing villages through pacification programs while the army encircled and eliminated the guerrillas. (H. Jones 1989:3–4)

9.3. THE ARGOLID: POLITICAL, SOCIAL, AND ECONOMIC BACKGROUND

The prefecture (*nomós*) of Argolid is located in the northeast part of the Peloponnese peninsula in southern Greece (Figures 9.1, 9.2).[3]

The study includes sixty-one villages of the counties of Argos and Nafplía – almost every village in these two counties (see Appendix B for the criteria of

---

[3] This section is based primarily on Karouzou (1995), De Vooys and Piket (1958), and Anagnostopoulos and Gagalis (1938).

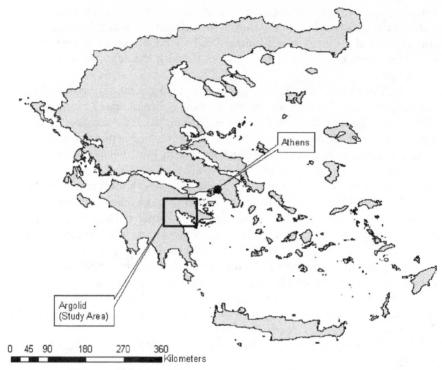

FIGURE 9.1. Greece and the Argolid

inclusion and the full list).[4] The quantitative part of the study excludes the two towns of Nafplio and Argos (see the Appendix for an explanation). Within the Argolid's considerable ecological range, consisting of hills and mountains overlooking a sizable plain, it is possible to distinguish six clusters of inhabitation. First, there is a cluster of fourteen villages located in the "deep plain." In 1940 these were the most prosperous of the villages in the study and were closely connected to the two large towns through a good road network. Their main specialization was wheat production, but during the 1920s and 1930s they had begun to take advantage of their relative proximity to Athens by producing vegetables for the Athenian market. The second cluster includes fifteen villages located in the "outer plain," much less fertile than those of the deep plain. Seven villages of the eastern plain form the third cluster; they were located further to the east, and their economies were similar to those of the outer-plain villages, with the addition

---

[4] In 1940 the Argolid was part of the prefecture of Argolidokorinthia, combining what would later become the separate prefectures of Argolid and Korinthia. The two counties under study included, in 1940, two municipalities (the administrative capital, Nafplio, and the market center, Argos) and fifty-eight "communes" (*koinotites*), of which nineteen included more than one settlement. I excluded the two municipalities, Nafplio and Argos. Surprisingly, the data on violence were much more difficult to collect there. On the one hand, the civil registries were incomplete, and on the other, it was impossible to cross-check these data and supplement them with oral sources due to the size of the towns compared with the size of the villages, as well as their radical transformation since the 1940s.

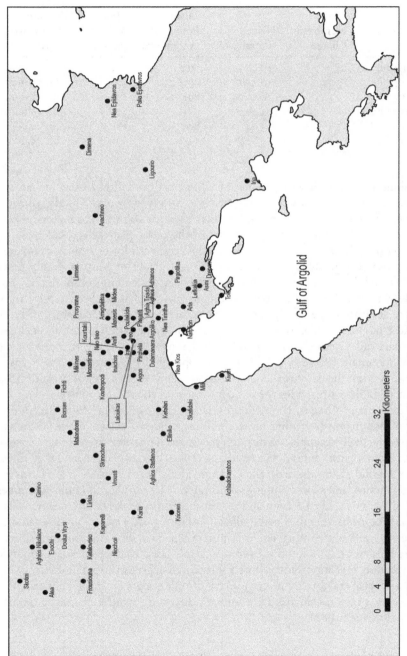

FIGURE 9.2. Villages Studied, Argos and Nafplía Counties, Argolid Prefecture

TABLE 9.1. *Villages: Descriptive Data*

	Number of Villages	Total Population	Mean Population per Village	Mean Altitude (meters)	Mean Distance from Closest Town
Deep plain	14	10,689	764	24	1 hr. 11 min.
Outer plain	15	10,356	690	72	1 hr. 37 min.
Eastern plain	7	6,261	894	103	2 hr. 01 min.
Eastern hills	6	5,704	951	294	3 hr. 25 min.
Western hills	7	5,041	840	317	3 hr. 52 min.
Mountains	13	7,089	545	672	5 hr. 55 min.

of fishing and some olive oil production. The fourth and fifth clusters include the eastern and western hill villages respectively, locally known as "middle villages" (*mesohoria*), which generally lay at altitudes between 100 and 350 meters. These villages had an economy similar to that of the outer-plain villages, relying on farming (mostly wheat and tobacco – a cash crop with lower returns compared with those of vegetables) and livestock. Six villages from Nafplía county make the eastern hills cluster and seven villages from Argos county compose the western hills cluster. Last are thirteen mountain villages that were located in Argos county at altitudes generally exceeding 350 meters. A distinct feature of some of these mountain villages was the presence of fertile farming land in enclosed mountain valleys, which made them somewhat more prosperous than the typical Greek mountain village (see Table B.1 in Appendix B). Plain villages were easily accessible from the two towns, whereas mountain villages were the most difficult to reach. Table 9.1 provides the basic information about these clusters.

Like most of Greece, the Argolid was (and remains) a predominantly rural region, dominated by family farms. The large landed estates of the Ottoman period effectively disappeared through successive land reforms over the course of the late nineteenth century. As a result, most peasants owned the land they tilled. In the Argolid plain, where detailed data are available, there were 5,090 farms for 5,360 families, and sharecropping was limited. The number of landless families there did not exceed 5 percent, and the great majority of the families owned farm property equal to what they could till without hiring extra labor; very few families owned more land than they could farm on their own. The situation was similar in the hills and the mountains.[5] On top of this fairly egalitarian socioeconomic stratification, it is important to note a substantial degree of social mobility, partly due to internal and foreign migration, the prevalence of patronage networks, and the presence of vertical village ties among villagers from different village "strata" (Aschenbrenner 1987).

[5] To provide an example, the hill village of Manesi displayed the following land ownership structure in 1940: ten families owned up to 20 acres (10 percent of the village population), seventy-five families owned from 20 to 40 acres (75 percent of the village population), fifteen families owned between 40 to 100 acres (15 percent of the village population), and there were no landless peasants (De Vooys and Piket 1958).

The Argolid peasants pursued a number of strategies to secure social mobility, including temporary emigration, education, and civil service employment. Children from the poorer hill and mountain villages were much more successful in obtaining secondary education degrees than children from the plain. Despite the individual pursuit of social mobility, the overarching goal was to preserve the family farm. Related to the ideal of defending the family-owned farm was a marked aversion toward wage labor. When a railway line was built in 1885, there were so few locals willing to work that labor had to be imported from outside Greece. In general, Argolid peasants displayed a social profile that could uncontroversially be described as conservative. Urban observers of the time described them as clever, cunning, inhospitable, suspicious toward outsiders, mendacious, noticeably irreligious, and with a low propensity for collective action (Anagnostopoulos and Gagalis 1938: 42–4). At the same time, anthropologists have documented an extensive system of informal cooperation and mutual obligation coinciding, however, with intense competition and conflict (Koster 2000:259).[6]

The absence of class polarization does not imply an absence of conflict. As a British journalist (Capell 1946:212) observed about Greece at the time, "Do you think that a population consisting practically all of small peasantry is without distinction of classes, without envy? But there is the successful peasant and the unsuccessful one, the lucky and the unlucky." Indeed, a great deal of conflict took the form of personal and family quarrels with causes as varied as "the breakdown of former friendships, differences between brothers over inheritance, the flow of disputes which arises from the fragmentation of property and the absence of fencing, the verbal defeat or disparagement of another in public debate, the collapse of negotiations for a marriage" (Campbell and Sherrard 1968:344). In this context, it is not surprising that political differences became enmeshed with personal and family disputes, as in the following example about a dispute between two café owners in the village of Ambéli in Central Greece, supplied by the anthropologist Juliet du Boulay (1974:225):

Although the two men were of different political parties, the quarrel was given its real impetus by the fact that while one family had lost a former high degree of power and prestige, the other was gradually gaining it. This quarrel became further extended when a niece of the left-wing café owner eloped with a man of a family deeply committed to the Right – a situation which developed into a series of lawsuits over land involving witnesses and supporters, and at one time a full-scale row in public when a judge and lawyers were called to the scene itself to try to effect a settlement. Thus a large part of the village was caught up in the division. In this quarrel the significant feature was the accretion, on to the political division, of personal loyalties and interests, and these two factors combined to cause this particular quarrel to become for years one of the chief features of social life in Ambéli.

There was no religious cleavage or ethnic cleavage in the Argolid; like most of the country, its inhabitants were uniformly Christian Orthodox. However, about

---

[6] According to Harold Koster (2000:259), cooperation and competition are complementary since "very close alliances must be maintained with some neighbors as long as hostile relations with others are kept up."

half its population was of Albanian descent, known as *Arvanites*: Christian Orthodox, often bilingual in Greek and *Arvanitika*, conscious of their distinct cultural
identity, yet also with a strong Greek national consciousness. This potential ethnic identity was not politicized during the civil war and is not salient in either
national or local Greek politics. Like elsewhere in Greece, the main political
cleavage on the eve of the Second World War was the republican-monarchist (or
liberal-conservative) split. In most of the Peloponnese, monarchists were dominant, the liberals were weaker but with a significant presence, and the Communist
Party was very weak. This political profile was even more pronounced in Argos
and Nafplía counties, where the combined tally of the three main monarchist
parties in the 1936 elections (the last ones before the advent of the Metaxas dictatorship in the same year) reached 71.3 percent of the vote, while liberal parties
obtained 27.13 percent and the Communists just 0.75 percent. These proportions
were replicated within most villages across the region, suggesting the absence of
deep intraregional cleavages. At the same time, the republican-monarchist cleavage mapped onto subtle microlocal cleavages, mostly based on lineage and kin
(Aschenbrenner 1987).

The Peloponnese was incorporated into the Greek state in 1833, immediately
after independence, and constituted the core of the country. Because of its early
incorporation and the pacification that ensued, it lacked the tradition of banditry
that had survived into the first decades of the twentieth century in some mountainous areas of central and northern Greece. The region also had no tradition
of generalized violence, rebellion, or mass mobilization. In his memoir, a local
leftist leader (Lilis n.d.) bemoans the absence of a tradition of social and political
unrest in the area and recalls only two instances of prewar peasant mobilization,
both extremely localized and short-lived. From this perspective, the case of the
Argolid raises a challenge for theories that associate mobilization, civil war, and
mass violence with generalized grievances and polarization.

9.4. THE CIVIL WAR IN THE ARGOLID

The bulk of the military action took place in 1943–4, when the Argolid was under
German occupation between September 1943 and September 1944 (it had been
occupied by the Italians until September 1943). Although the Argolid again saw
some action in 1948–9, this was limited to the most remote confines and was rather
inconsequential. Thus, in this case, civil war overlapped almost completely with
occupation. Using this setting to test the theory is not a problem because civil
wars associated with occupation are included in my operational definitions. In
fact, such wars place more demands on the theory since it is harder for an occupier
to mimic an incumbent state in terms of collecting local information and winning
local allies. However, the out-of-sample tests in the rest of the country cover the
postoccupation civil war and show that, although the two wars differ in several
dimensions, including geographic location and military tactics, the theory applies
equally well to both. In turn, this result provides an empirical corroboration to
the inclusion of occupation civil wars in the definition.

The first period of the occupation in the Argolid (April 1941–September 1943) was rather calm compared with what was to follow. The occupation authorities relied on the existing administrative structure to run the region; such day-to-day collaboration was both widespread and superficial. Ideologically motivated collaboration was exceptional; no collaborationist party or mass organization was created and the occupation authorities did not encourage processes of mass mobilization on their behalf. A few individuals with linguistic skills served as interpreters, while some notorious local thugs volunteered as guides and inform-ers for the occupying army; they typically used their position to steal, loot, and blackmail, and so were universally despised. While the Italian occupation was broadly resented, violence was relatively limited.[7] Most of the occupying troops were quartered in the two towns of Argos and Nafplio and around a few coastal villages, where they built fortifications in anticipation of an Allied landing that was (mistakenly) expected for the autumn of 1943. The occupation troops visited the plain villages frequently and the hill villages occasionally. They seldom ventured to the mountain villages, which were accessible only with difficulty and lacked strategic value. A letter sent to the representative of the International Red Cross headquartered in the nearby town of Tripolis by the inhabitants of the mountain village of Frousouna, after their village was burned in a German raid in July 1944, speaks volumes about the nature of the occupation up to the summer of 1944: "The saddest thing for the villagers is that they were completely unsuspecting and were surprised by the occupation army because this army and the Security Battalions had never passed through our area and no one here could ever even imagine that such a visit could ever take place since our area is mountainous and away from any transportation route" (in Papakongos 1977:241). The absence of state authority in these areas caused a massive surge of rural banditry, especially cattle thieving.

Although local elites discussed the option of armed resistance, there was no such activity in 1941–2. A few runaway men lived clandestinely in the mountain villages and would skirmish with the occasional Italian patrol. Organized armed resistance in the Greek countryside generally came late, and it came even later in the Peloponnese.[8] Although armed resistance was absent, Communist agitation was not. The Argolid lacked a sustained Communist tradition or presence, but its proximity to Athens made it fertile ground for Communist activities; in addition, the few Communists in the area were extremely active and entrepreneurial.

The first meeting of EAM in the Argolid took place in December 1942, after the Communist Party (KKE) sent a cadre in the region to coordinate local activities. In a January 1943 meeting, a decision was taken to expand the

---

[7] The main victims were villagers hiding weapons or stranded British soldiers who were arrested or, more usually, beaten up. In one instance, in the village of Skinohori, a man died as a result. A few people were jailed, and in the autumn of 1942 some town and village leaders were temporarily deported to Kalavryta in the prefecture of Achaia – including the mayor of Nafplio (HAA/DAN E32/1945).

[8] According to EAM leader Yannis Frangos, in April 1943 "there were only one hundred and fifty andartes in the whole Peloponnese" ("Narrative Account of a Mission to Peloponnese by Capt. P.M. Wand-Tetley, April 1943 to June 1944," PRO, HS 5/699).

still-clandestine EAM organization throughout the region. Using mostly family networks, local clandestine cells were set up in the first half of 1943;[9] however, they did not engage in any significant visible activity.

Guerrilla activity in the northern Peloponnese began in the summer of 1943. First, a group of sixty ELAS guerrillas were dispatched from central Greece to spur the organization's growth. Second, a number of British soldiers parachuted into the area during the same period to set up sabotage groups in anticipation of a possible Allied invasion. They were able to connect quickly with small partisan bands already operating in the mountains and arranged for airdrops of weapons and ammunition. In the Argolid, a group of Greek army officers, fearing preemptive arrest by the Italians, took to the mountains in the summer of 1943 and formed a guerrilla group. However, they were attacked by the stronger Communist guerrillas in August and defeated. Comparable attacks took place across the Peloponnese with similar outcomes; the Communist bands were much better organized and motivated compared with the officers' bands. As a result, the Communists were able to quickly and effectively control all armed resistance activity in the mountains of the Peloponnese.

Up to the end of 1943, there was limited polarization in the region. The quick and early destruction of the officers' guerrilla band had a limited repercussion in the area. The first victims of ELAS in the summer and autumn of 1943 were a few universally despised thuggish collaborators. Similarly, the Argolid authorities were relatively restrained: they occasionally arrested people but stopped short of killing – with two notable exceptions, both toward the end of the year. First, on 4 November 1943, they destroyed the village of Berbati (now Prosymna) as a reprisal for the deaths of three German soldiers in a chance encounter with an ELAS unit from another region that was crossing the area. Four villagers were killed and about one thousand were left homeless. Despite the massive arrest of all the men from surrounding villages (the villagers of Berbati having fled in the mountains), the Germans ended up acceding to the demands of the local Greek notables and refrained from carrying out further reprisals for that incident. Second, a month later, on 3 December, they hanged fifty-two people in the Andritsa railway station as a reprisal for an attack against that station that led to the killing of German soldiers. However, the hostages hanged there were brought from other regions. Elsewhere in the Peloponnese, the German response to the rise of the ELAS was both extremely violent and indiscriminate; in a well-known punitive expedition against the town of Kalavryta and the surrounding villages in northwest Peloponnese, in December 1943 the Germans killed 677 Greek civilians (Meyer 2002). On the other hand, the town of Argos paid a high cost in civilian lives when over 100 people were killed and more than 400 wounded in an Allied bombing gone wrong.

The civil war began in Greece in 1943 with the clash between leftist and rightist resistance organizations; it was vastly magnified in 1944, when EAM clashed with various collaborationist militias (the most prominent of which were known as the

---

[9] For example, the Communist organization in the village of Gerbesi was built around the Lilis, Korilis, and Lekkas families.

Security Battalions or SBs). The civil war in the Argolid can be divided into four time periods that correspond to four major shifts in control.[10] In what follows, I provide a short narrative for each time period.

9.4.1. From September 1943 to 15 May 1944 (t₁)

The capitulation of the Italians in early September 1943 boosted the rebels. As it became apparent that their German successors were unable to police the Argolid with their limited manpower, a power vacuum set in across the entire region, with the partial exception of the two towns of Argos and Nafplio and a few plain and coastal villages. At the same time, many Italian weapons found their way to ELAS (Vazeos 1961:28). By 10 October 1943, the gendarmerie posts in the hills and mountains could no longer be defended, and most gendarmes fled to the towns. The neutralization of the gendarmerie severed the links between villages and towns. EAM, which by this time had formed clandestine local organizations in even the smallest mountain villages, easily filled the vacuum of power in the countryside. A German military report in November 1943 stated that "the Peloponnese must be considered in its entirety a bandit area."[11] Around the same period, a British liaison officer (BLO), J. M. Stevens, reported similar conditions from Central Greece:

Greece to-day forms two separate countries, occupied and unoccupied. In the former, conditions of life vary according as to whether the occupying power is Germany, Italy, or Bulgaria. Unoccupied Greece to-day is as free from Axis interference as England.... Even in the occupied zone the occupation is restricted to certain larger towns, strategically important points and the guarding of vital lines of communication, but there always lurks the danger that Axis troops will visit some outlying village; the Andartes may hamper such expeditions but cannot prevent their occurrence. In the occupied zone, life is uncertain and the freedom movements for self-preservation are underground. In unoccupied Greece, life is free.[12]

A snapshot look at the Argolid in the autumn of 1943 yields the following image: the Communist-controlled EAM was in total control of the Argolid, with the exception of the two large towns and a couple of villages in the plain (where it maintained an active underground organization). It openly ran the villages through newly formed local organizations, which were closely monitored

---

[10] This periodization aims to capture the shifts in control that took place at about the same time for each of the six village groups; in some cases there are slight differences depending on the exact moment of the shift in control.

[11] Information bureau of 117th Jäger-Division, monthly report of 29 November 1943, in Zervis 1998:109.

[12] "Report of Lt.-Col. J. M. Stevens on Present Conditions in CENTRAL GREECE," in Baerentzen (1982:3). This situation was due to three factors, Stevens argued. First, being a mountainous country with few roads in the mountain districts, "Greece is a difficult country to occupy." The effective occupation of the mountainous areas requires large troops and continuous food supply from the plains – easy targets for ambushes. Second, the occupying forces were loathed and received no help from the population. Third, they had "bad intelligence" on the rebels (in Baerentzen 1982:3–5).

by a very small but highly active group of regional cadres that toured the area constantly. By January 1944," Communist Party cells were in place in almost every village and the party itself was growing quickly. EAM collected taxes, provided logistical support for the fighting units of ELAS located in the mountains, controlled all movement by issuing travel permits, policed the villages so effectively that it was able to eradicate cattle thieving, and administered local justice through a network of "peoples' courts." In a matter of a few months, EAM had evolved from a clandestine organization into nothing less than a state (McNeill 1947: 96–7).

An outside observer looking at the Argolid at the end of 1943 would have probably reached the conclusion that this was a staunchly revolutionary area. Indeed, both oral and written sources converge in describing support for EAM during this period as quasi-unanimous.[13] Yet it would be incorrect to deduce from the success of EAM that this steadfastly conservative and monarchist region had turned Communist literally overnight. That a place with no tradition of social conflict or mass mobilization and almost no Communist presence could be swayed in such a quick and overwhelming fashion points to the importance of the twin processes of state collapse and state building as factors in the shaping of individual behavior.

The lightning transformation of small, politically marginal groups into state structures, a feature common in many insurgencies, has often given rise to arguments influenced by retrospective determinism. These arguments hold that for these organizations to have been so successful, they must have reflected deep grievances and expressed popular aspirations. In fact, such arguments reverse the causal path: in the Argolid, mass mobilization clearly followed rather than preceded the establishment of control by EAM, and it was control that spawned collaboration rather than the other way around. Clearly, the population resented the occupation, was very receptive to the nationalist political message expounded by EAM, and was grateful for the provision of tangible public goods, such as order and protection from rural banditry. Yet the establishment of EAM as a state structure would have been impossible without the convergence of three factors. First, the power vacuum along with the disruption of the traditional patronage networks caused by the occupation made it easy for EAM to take over with a very small number of highly dedicated members while lowering the risks of individual collaboration (as I point out later, it was riskier not to collaborate with EAM than to do so). Second, the organizational technology of the Communist Party (its experience in the use of clandestine organization) acted as a multiplier of the party's influence. Finally, the presence in the background of a small but highly visible ELAS fighting force successfully claimed the monopoly of violence in the region and ensured the credibility of its sanctions. This force came from a neighboring area in October 1943 and set up camp in the mountain areas of the Argolid; it carried out several arrests during that time to establish its authority and signal its strength, but avoided more extreme forms of violence. According

[13] E.g., "Report by Lt. Col. R. P. McMullen on Present Conditions in the Peloponnese," PRO, HS 5/699.

to an EAM cadre's memoir (Lilis n.d.:45–6), these arrests created the impression in the villages of the plain that there were hundreds of armed rebels in the mountains, an effect that contributed to the neutralization of all opposition. A parallel process was described in a British report about northern Greece in 1944: "There exists no organized opposition to ELAS in Macedonia. There is the opposition that is whispered furtively behind closed doors, imparted on the streets with swift backward looks, implied by suggestion and innuendo but it is more a helpless and indirected longing for a Deus ex Machina. ELAS are too ruthless to be trifled with, and their powers of arbitrary imprisonment and illegal seizure of goods are unlimited."[14]

Insurgent selective violence was introduced in the region by a specialized group: the Communist Party's death squad organization, OPLA (an acronym standing for Organization for the Protection of Peoples' Fighters). In December 1943, responding to the creation and expansion by the collaborationist government of the Security Battalions, the Communist Party threatened reprisals against those joining or helping them and their families. These directives were communicated to the party's regional branches, which proceeded to disseminate them to local branches. In the Argolid, local meetings about the preemption of collaborationism took place in the autumn of 1943, especially in the villages of the deep and outer plain where the German presence was encroaching on EAM control. Participants in these meetings told me that party cadres handed them a quota of liquidations (usually two or three persons per village) and asked them to supply the names of "reactionaries" and to consent to executions, often formally by signing written documents (e.g., I-12). EAM sought the elimination of influential people who were unwilling to submit to its power and who could shape the behavior of their co-villagers, such as mayors, doctors, or demobilized and noncommissioned officers (NCOs). A British liaison officer reported from the Peloponnese that EAM "were masters of the psychology of the 'exemplary atrocity' . . . they seem to specialise in picking on the one man whose death or disappearance would cause a whole area to continue its more or less docile support for their cause."[15] At the same time, many village committee members used their position to settle personal accounts and local disputes (e.g., I-11; I-12). In other words, violence was jointly produced by party cadres and local civilians.

When names were provided and consent granted, OPLA squads composed of men unknown to the villagers descended at night, met with local guides, abducted the identified persons, and took them to prisoner camps in the mountains. Following interrogation and often torture, most were executed a few days later, usually by having their throat slit. Some were beaten up and sent back to their village, and some were released.

---

[14] "Situation in Greece: Assistance to Greek Resistance Movements," 2 December 1944, PRO, FO 371/43700, R21882.

[15] "Report by Cpl. Buhayar," PRO, HS 5/698. According to another report, "In the Autumn all towns in the PELOPONNESE were subjected to nightly visits by EAM execution squads, mostly directed against Right Wing sympathisers" ("Second Report of Colonel J. M. Stevens on Present Conditions in Peloponnese," PRO, HS 5/699).

This process resulted in the assassination of thirty-seven people, most of whom were killed in January 1944. The epicenter of the violence was the plain: 35 percent of those killed came from villages of the deep plain, 51 percent from villages of the outer plain, and the remaining 14 percent from the rest of the region. These killings achieved their objective of creating an atmosphere of fear and helped consolidate EAM rule. At the same time, this violence created considerable resentment, which, however, could not be expressed given EAM's level of control and the absence of a political alternative. As a BLO observed, the villager "has talked it all out in some dark corner with his brother villagers, he has plotted against and schemed to rid himself of at least the EAM in his village, but he has no gun; so he sits there quietly biting his first finger in that significant way which means 'All right, you are on top for now, but you wait.'"[16] Another one painted a picture of the hill and mountain villages of the Argolid during that period that emphasized the effectiveness of the threat of violence in neutralizing local notables:

As a general rule influential people, i.e. people of good, or better social standing, such as doctors (*not* schoolmasters, who represent the worst element of the mountain population), have had their apparent power and influence very much curtailed by the EAM Gestapo. In actual fact, the influence, especially in the case of doctors, remains ready to be reasserted, provided the EAM do not do away with the person in question. Thus one frequently hears "X is an influential person and we all revere him, but we can say nothing now" etc. Such people are almost invariably opposed to the EAM, though not always overtly. They have their own small circle of Right or Centre political comrades and their time is spent in trying to learn all the crimes of the EAM. They exaggerate and under estimate by turns and altogether present a rather pathetic figure. Some, whose names I give below, have either found a road of compromise with EAM, or else their influence is sufficiently large to prevent the EAM attacking them for fear of popular feeling.[17]

All violence carried out by the insurgents was selective: the victims were chosen, named, and picked up individually. This campaign was facilitated by the absence of the option of counterdenunciation: to have brought in the Germans, an action that was difficult to imagine and even more difficult to plan, would have exposed the counterdenouncers' families to certain and immediate retribution from EAM.

In contrast, the German record for the same period combines both selective and indiscriminate violence: six individuals were killed selectively and sixteen indiscriminately. The selective violence took place in two villages of the outer plain, while the indiscriminate violence was concentrated in the hills (87 percent), the closest rebel-controlled area.

April 1944 was the turning point for the Germans. At that point, the German authorities decided to crack down on EAM organizations in the towns of Argos and Nafplio. By bringing in additional troops they strengthened their presence and were able to tap local sources of information; on 10 April, they arrested several

---

[16] "Report by Lt. Col. R. P. McMullen on Present Conditions in the Peloponnese," PRO, HS 5/699.
[17] "Narrative of Capt P. M. Fraser. Peloponnese July 43–April 44" and "Names of Influential Personnel in Argolido Korinthia," PRO, HS 5/698/S6557.

inhabitants of Nafplio suspected of rebel sympathies and shipped them to a concentration camp they had set up in the nearby town of Korinthos (HAA/EDD Case 336/47).[18] In late April a collaborationist militia, the Third Security Battalion, was organized in Korinthos, and a unit led by a Greek army captain arrived in Nafplio.[19] The Nafplio unit immediately began to recruit locally, eventually reaching a force of about 150 men. Most of these men came from the two towns; many were former gendarmes who were transferred from the moribund gendarmerie to the newly minted militia. Forty men joined from the plain village of Asini, following the lead of one of the Security Battalion leaders who came from that village. The militia was able to effectively seal off both Nafplio and Argos from the rebels and completely destroy the urban EAM organizations. The regional bureau of the Communist Party was cut off from the two towns, the party cadres were forced to flee to the mountains, and several members of EAM defected to the SBs. An EAM cadre confirms in his memoirs that this shift in control led the two towns' population to move away from EAM, causing it "huge damage" (Lilis n.d.: 91–3).[20]

Once control of the towns was consolidated, the Germans and their local allies began to push into the villages of the plain around 10 May; they applied a counterinsurgent strategy that the French would later dub *tache d' huile* (oil spot): they set up several new outposts in and around these villages, increased their patrols, began registering the villagers and checking their identity papers frequently, and imposed a severe curfew. Thus, the villages of the deep and outer plain moved to zone 2.

9.4.2. From 15 May to 31 June 1944 (t_2)

On 19 May, German soldiers and Greek militiamen launched a series of targeted raids in villages of the outer plain suspected of sympathizing with the rebels. Two days later they launched a major raid in the eastern hills, which were viewed as rebel territory. This raid, part of a larger mopping-up operation code-named *Rabe* (Raven), was aimed at annihilating the insurgents in the Korinthia and Argolid regions by cordoning off entire areas at a time and then proceeding to "comb" through them.[21] This was a trying time for the population of the region: the Germans dropped leaflets telling villagers to remain at home and

---

[18] On April 22, eleven individuals among those arrested were shot as a reprisal for an ELAS action (HAA/DAN E32/1945).

[19] "Action Report of the Third Security Battalion of Korinthos," DIS/AEA, 915/B/3.

[20] This is also confirmed by a BLO who noted that EAM violence in the towns of the Peloponnese had become "so bad, that when the Security Bns. first appeared from Athens they were received with great enthusiasm. Even now, town populations consider Security Bns. the lesser of two evils" ("Second Report of Colonel J. M. Stevens on Present Conditions in Peloponnese," PRO, HS 5/699).

[21] It is interesting to note that in preparation for their operation, the German generals Hellmuth Fellmy and Karl Le Suire exchanged a rather heated correspondence about the procedures for reprisals against civilians and the execution of hostages; while expressing the need for selective violence, General Le Suire reserved for himself the right to order any reprisals (Meyer 2002: 397–9).

warning that anyone caught in the fields would be considered a partisan and shot on the spot; at the same time, the rebels ordered the villagers to flee and even threatened anyone staying behind with death, hoping to facilitate their escape and minimize defections. Not trusting the Germans, most people chose to flee. Many of those, including elderly people, women, and children, were shot and killed in the fields (they were reported in German military reports as "killed while trying to escape"). The gratuitous nature of these killings is particularly apparent in several cases involving people who were gunned down just because they happened to be standing outside their houses a few minutes after the 6:00 P.M. curfew (ZSt. V 508 AR 2056/67). Altogether, during this operation 190 people were killed indiscriminately in the two counties of the Argolid I researched, 73 percent of whom came from villages in the eastern hills.[22]

From a purely military viewpoint, operation *Rabe* was a failure. Most rebels, including many of the village cadres, were able to bypass the cordon and reassemble in neighboring regions. However, the villages they ruled had been abandoned. After a few days, most villagers faced starvation and began to return to their homes where they had no choice but to collaborate with the new authority: the Germans and the militiamen. One such case was Heli (now Arachneo), a village in the eastern hills. After having lost twenty-two villagers to this indiscriminate violence, the village was forced, because of its strategic location, to defect and join the Germans. Although many villages defected to the Germans, only a few were asked to contribute men to the collaborationist militia: weapons were limited and strategic location was the main factor for their allocation. In fact, I found several cases of entire villages clamoring for weapons only to face a refusal from the Germans (e.g., I-91; I-117). As the commander of a German unit operating in Greece reported in December 1943, only after German troops posted armed guards, thus establishing security, could the population be influenced against the guerrillas. Otherwise the rebels prevailed and exerted their power unimpeded (Hondros 1993:155). The evidence from the Argolid suggests that he was right: wherever the Germans supplied armed protection, villages collaborated with them.

Why would entire villages join the Germans in the summer of 1944, when it was clear that the war was being won by the Allies? The answer points to the power of local reality over international politics: as the Germans and their local allies chased the rebels from the area, their threats became credible – and for those seeking revenge against the rebels the opportunity appeared safe enough. This was the first time these villagers witnessed such extensive military operations, and they believed that the fleeing partisans had been defeated. This belief is well attested both in my own interviews and in many memoirs, and, together with the threat of collective punishment, was a crucial factor affecting villagers' decisions to defect. A typical interview sentence goes as follows: "People thought that because such a big operation was going on, because the mountains were laden with Germans, that the guerrillas had been destroyed. 'Well,' they said, 'then let's

---

[22] Internal documents of the German army (in Meyer 2002:400) report 235 Greek deaths and 51 arrests in an area stretching beyond the region under study.

join the Germans'" (I-17).[23] As a result, the Argolid went from revolutionary (in April 1944) to largely collaborationist (by late June 1944) even more quickly than it had gone from conservative to revolutionary at the end of 1943.

These collective defections followed a basic pattern. After the Germans and the militiamen arrived in a village, they gathered all the villagers in the central square and offered them a choice: take up arms and join them in the fight against the rebels or suffer collective punishment. The village mayor, in consultation with the most prominent villagers, would typically accept the deal. To induce commitment, the Germans would then request that the villagers deliver to them those EAM sympathizers who had not fled. In some cases, villagers managed to avoid doing this, while in others they did not (or were only too happy to acquiesce). Usually EAM sympathizers would be shot on the spot. The villagers obviously had a limited horizon and were making inferences from the local context, rather than the national or international one (I-18; I-80; I-139; I-209). "The people are hungry for news," wrote a BLO. "I cannot stress too strongly that the ignorance of the villager (and also the townsman, for that matter) is simply staggering."[24]

Altogether, such selective violence by the Germans and their allies cost the lives of fifty-eight villagers. This violence targeted the villages of the eastern hills (31 percent),[25] outer plain (29 percent), deep plain (17 percent), western hills (12 percent), and eastern plain (9 percent), and it consolidated German rule. By the end of June, the Germans and their allies were in control in all of the Argolid except the western hills and the mountains. The rebels and their collaborators were hunted down and denounced to the Germans by local villagers out of fear, revenge, or both. Predictably, the relatives of the victims of EAM were the first to turn against EAM. For instance, my (leftist) informants from the village of Anifi attributed the violence and killings in their village to the four initial executions by EAM that took place during the winter.[26]

The two areas still under rebel control were the mountain and western hill villages; by mid-June, the western hills began receiving visits and occasional raids by the Germans – thus moving from zone 5 to 4. Both individual villagers and EAM cadres were carefully observing what was going on in the eastern hills (Nassis n.d.), and the unprecedented amount of violence frightened both. Many individuals, including EAM sympathizers with connections in the towns, began fleeing there. EAM rule was imploding. At the same time, EAM leaders were horrified by the developments in the rest of the Argolid. As a result, they decided

---

[23] For a description of similar developments in western Macedonia (complicated by ethnic politics), see "Report by a Supporter of EAM on the Development of the Situation in Western Macedonia," PRO, HS 5/234.

[24] "Report by Lt. Col. R. P. McMullen on Present Conditions in the Peloponnese," PRO, HS 5/699.

[25] Selective violence in the eastern hills chronologically followed the indiscriminate violence of the mop-up operation.

[26] Consider the following excerpts from interviews (I-6; I-7; I-8): "Before these [killings] nothing had happened. After this, many things did. This was the first story"; "it all began after this. The village became divided. This is when it became divided"; "Here was the mistake. Had they not killed the four, then there would have been no blood in Anifi"; "Here in our village, listen, if the partisans had not killed the four men, nothing would have happened."

to initiate a new wave of selective violence, which resulted in the killing of fifty-two villagers, mainly in the western hills (69 percent) and a few mountain villages (25 percent) that were exposed to incumbent incursions.

9.4.3. July 1944 (t₃)

After having "pacified" the plain and the eastern hills in June, the Germans and their allies turned their attention to the western hills and the surrounding mountains. On 17 July they launched a big operation to destroy guerrilla bases in the mountains. As soon as the attack was launched, the villagers fled upward toward higher mountains. Geography helped them and the Germans were more restrained this time. As a result, this operation caused few indiscriminate casualties compared with the number in the eastern Argolid, most of them in the mountain villages: 87 percent of the victims of incumbent indiscriminate violence came from these villages.

At the same time, the incumbents were consolidating their control through the use of selective violence; the Germans and the collaborators caused forty-four deaths, more or less evenly distributed across the region. For their part, the insurgents killed more than twice as many people as they struggled against the loss of control. Of their ninety-six killings, 48 percent occurred in the mountain villages and 39 percent in the western hills, the two regions where rebel control was plummeting. It is telling that the partisans executed eighty-seven villagers just before the German raid in July. It is hardly surprising that as soon as the rebels began evacuating the area, the villages of the western hills rose against them; villagers armed with pitchforks and other farming implements attacked the few cadres that had remained behind and either killed them or delivered them to the Germans.

9.4.4. From 26 July to 5 October 1944 (t₄)

By late July 1944 the rapid advance of the Soviet army in the Balkans threatened to completely encircle the Germans in Greece, thus prompting them to evacuate the country. In the Argolid, this process began on 26 July with the evacuation of the mountainous areas that had just been "pacified." In early August the "pacified" hills were abandoned as well, and the occupation army and the collaborationist militia assembled in the towns and its outposts of the deep plain. As soon as the Germans left, armed detachments of partisans began returning, primed for revenge against the villagers who had turned against them. They easily overpowered the mostly unarmed peasants of the western hills and burned their villages; they also attacked the two hill villages of Heli (29 July) and Achladokambos (18 September) that had joined the collaborationist militia, defeating their defenders and subjecting prisoners and civilians alike to indiscriminate violence (106 victims in all). In addition, they selectively killed 69 people, rightly or wrongly accused of having defected (74 percent in the eastern hills). During the same time, incumbent violence fell to insignificant levels.

The Germans evacuated Argos on 19 September, and the Security Battalions surrendered their weapons on 5 October at their bastion of Nafplio. While the spirit of revenge ran high, especially in the two towns and the villages of the outer plain that had been under German control for the entire summer, the EAM organization imposed strict control and forbade acts of revenge.[27] Many arrests took place, but no executions. Although the Argolid remained free from murder, fear was rampant. In November the regional authorities of Nafplía county issued an announcement deploring the flight of people to Athens, allegedly due to rumors about arrests generated by "a small reactionary minority" (HAA/DAN E24/1944).

A final observation concerns the source of the decision to target particular areas for counterinsurgency operations. The available historical evidence suggests very strongly that the locus of the German decision making about when and where to launch their various mop-up operations was at levels of the military hierarchy far above the Argolid (Meyer 2002). In turn, the rebels counterattacked after the Germans left a particular area or decreased their presence substantially. In other words, the application of military resources to particular areas is clearly exogenous to internal developments in these villages and could be explained only in the context of a general (and highly complex) model that would take into account domestic and international military trends.

To conclude this section: it is clearly possible to recount in a cogent way the civil war in the Argolid by relying on the kind of analytic observations about the relation between collaboration, control, and violence that I highlighted in the theoretical section of this book.

9.5. AFTER THE END OF THE OCCUPATION

EAM's transformation into an alternative state in 1943–4 was completed by its transformation into an effective state by October 1944. It unified its sovereignty at the regional level, while at the national level, ministers from EAM joined with the government-in-exile, whose authority did not extend outside Athens, in what was termed a government of National Unity. This government proved stillborn and disagreements over the disarmament of ELAS led to a Communist insurrection in December 1944. ELAS was defeated, and a new government that excluded the Communists took over the country. Following a period of turmoil that included the persecution of former members of EAM, the Communist Party launched a new insurgency in 1946, producing a new round of fighting, which ended with a new and final defeat for the Communists in 1949.

The postwar civil war did not affect the Argolid nearly as much as the civil war during the occupation did. EAM supporters were discriminated against, harassed, and arrested; they were often tormented by people whose chief motivation was revenge; however, murders were rare.[28] Of the EAM members arrested, a few

---

[27] See directive 546/15 of the Secretary of Interior of PEEA (dated 8 September 1944 and signed by Giorgos Siantos), which laid down a conduct code for the newly formed EAM police (Politofylaki) (DAN E27/1944) and a similar directive of the ELAS HQ (dated 24 October 1944) warning against private revenge (ASKI, KKE 418/F30/4/25).

[28] Memoirs of Andreas Kranis, head of Argos Gendarmerie; "Cable from Nauplion," March 2, 1946; "Telegram from Nauplion," March 21, 1946, AMFOGE I, Prefect Reports; "General Report on

were executed, while most had their sentences commuted and served various prison terms. The last inmates were released in 1963 – though some were arrested again, following the 1967 military coup. The Communist rebels of the so-called Democratic Army of Greece were not very active in the Argolid. The first leftist bands appeared in the region during the summer of 1946 and were composed of former EAM members hunted by the authorities. In 1947 new, more centralized, left-wing bands were formed in the mountains of Arcadia, in central Peloponnese, but they seldom came to the Argolid, which remained under firm government control. An aggressive mop-up operation launched in the winter of 1948–9, combined with the evacuation of several mountain villages, a crackdown on suspected rebel collaborators in towns and villages, and an exceptionally harsh winter, led to the total defeat of the insurgents in the Peloponnese. The core of the insurgency in northern Greece was defeated later in that year (Zafiropoulos 1956).

The difference between the two phases of the civil war in the Argolid (1943–4 and 1946–9) can be explained in two ways. One explanation pinpoints the conservative preferences of the peasants along with the alienation caused by the massive leftist violence during the occupation. However, this explanation would fail the comparative test: first, the local collaborationist militiamen were responsible for as massive a level of violence as the Left; second, similarly conservative areas of the Peloponnese as Lakonia and Arcadia experienced much more leftist activity in 1947–9 than did the Argolid, despite high levels of leftist violence during the occupation. The second explanation stresses state capacity. The Greek state, more powerful than the German occupation authorities had ever been, was able to maintain control of the hills and cut off the rebels from the plain. The extent of government control is reflected in the fact that during this period many former EAM guerrillas (including several of my informants) were drafted into the Greek army and fought against some of their former comrades. At the same time, however, the Greek state was not so strong as to be able to control the mountainous areas of the Peloponnese (e.g., in the prefectures of Lakonia and Arcadia) and, particularly, the mountains of central and northern Greece. In other words, the difference in state capacity between the incumbents of 1943–4 and of 1946–9 is reflected in the geographic locus of the two wars: the latter took place in higher altitudes than the former. I return to this observation later in this chapter.

9.6. VIOLENCE: DESCRIPTIVE STATISTICS

Between September 1943 and September 1944, 725 civilians met violent deaths in the 61 villages I studied – 1.61 percent of their total population (Table 9.2).[29] In contrast, only 49 fighters from the Argolid were killed in battles (35 rebels and 14 collaborationist militiamen). Among the individuals killed, 366 (50.48 percent) were killed selectively and 359 (49.52 percent) indiscriminately. The Germans and their allies killed 353 people (48.69 percent), and the insurgents

the Entire Area of Argos," 14 March 1946; "Memorandum from District Board #1 to Central Board, 18 March 1946," AMFOGE I, District Boards.
[29] The overwhelming majority of the victims were men and peasants.

TABLE 9.2. *Basic Descriptive Statistics on Violence*

	Number of Homicides	Percent of Total Violence	Percent of Population
Type of violence			
Selective	366	50.48	0.81
Indiscriminate	359	49.52	0.80
Actor			
Incumbents	353	48.69	0.76
Insurgents	372	51.31	0.83
Time period			
t_1	66	9.10	0.15
t_2	295	40.69	0.65
t_3	168	23.17	0.37
t_4	196	27.03	0.43
Location			
Plains	152	20.97	0.34
Hills	450	62.07	1.00
Mountains	123	16.97	0.27
TOTAL	725		1.61

372 (51.31 percent).[30] According to my tentative estimate, 169 more were killed in the two towns, Argos and Nafplio (0.84 percent of their population);[31] of those, 108 (64 percent) were killed by the incumbents and 61 (36 percent) by the insurgents. Table 9.2 provides a summary of the basic descriptive statistics. Clearly, the violence was predominantly rural, both in absolute and relative terms. The killings peaked between mid-May and June 1944 (t_2), and affected the villages of the hills much more than those of the plains or the mountains. These patterns imply that an analysis that ignored selective in favor of indiscriminate violence and insurgent in favor of incumbent violence (or vice versa) would discard half of the data and bias the analysis.

The spatial distribution of selective and indiscriminate violence throughout the entire period under study and across the two counties of the Argolid is shown in Figures 9.3 and 9.4. Villages that experienced violence are represented by an individual pie chart; size reflects the magnitude of the violence, and color represents the proportional contribution of each political actor to it. Villages with no violence are indicated with a star.

[30] This distribution is an interesting historical finding in and of itself, as the historiographic literature on the occupation and civil war in Greece has underestimated the violence of the Left, emphasizing, to the exclusion of any other factor, its ideological message, alleged popular support, and the disciplined behavior of its followers. I located a classified postwar report to the KKE Politbureau by a regional Communist cadre that mentions "more than 1,200 executions of individuals [by the Communists in the Argolid and Korinthia regions] that we, today, cannot possibly justify at all"; this report also refers to widespread and massive abuses across the Peloponnese (ASKI, KKE 418/F24/2/114).

[31] Thus, the grand total for the two counties of the Argolid is 901 victims.

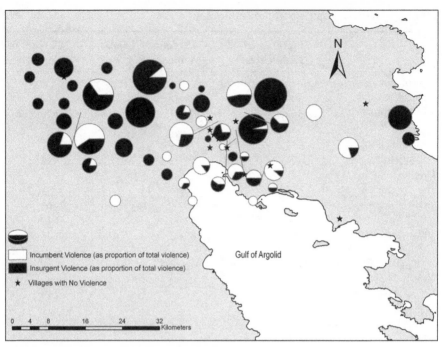

FIGURE 9.3. The Spatial Distribution of Selective Violence, September 1943–September 1944

The main pattern that emerges from a comparison of the two maps in Figures 9.3 and 9.4 is that selective violence was much more evenly distributed than indiscriminate violence, which tends to be more concentrated. Put otherwise, many more villages escaped indiscriminate than selective violence. Although the intensity of violence, selective or indiscriminate, varies widely, the biggest massacres were indiscriminate. Finally, the bulk of indiscriminate violence was produced by the incumbents, which is not the case with selective violence, where insurgents tend to dominate. The underlying data for both types of violence, broken down in three dimensions (actor, location, and time), are displayed in Tables 9.3 and 9.4.

These data suggest the following patterns across the three dimensions of actors, time, and space. First, the overall violence is almost equally divided between incumbents and insurgents. This pattern contradicts a widespread perception, whereby incumbents have a much higher propensity to commit violence against noncombatants; this perception, which is common across many civil wars, dominates both the historiographic literature on the Greek Civil War as well as the local studies of the Argolid, which only or primarily stress the German–collaborationist violence (e.g., G. Margaritis 2000; Papalilis 1981). This underscores the potentially enormous measurement bias afflicting studies that assume that violence is only produced by incumbents and/or rely exclusively on secondary sources, including several large-N cross-sectional studies.

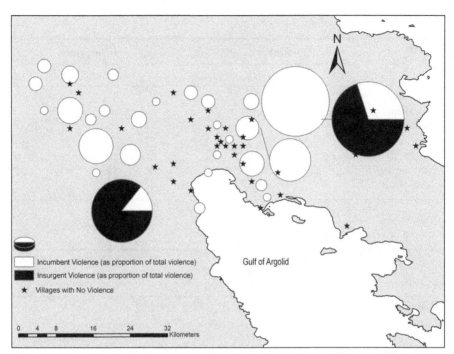

FIGURE 9.4. The Spatial Distribution of Indiscriminate Violence, September 1943–September 1944

Second, the two actors clearly diverge when it comes to the type of violence they use. Insurgent violence is primarily selective (68.55 percent of the time), whereas incumbent violence is the exact opposite (68.56 percent indiscriminate). From a different angle, nearly 70 percent of all selective violence is produced by the insurgents versus 30 percent for the incumbents – and vice versa for indiscriminate violence. This pattern is consistent with the theoretical expectation that discrimination in violence is related to access to local information (Chapter 6): despite their belated reliance on local allies, the Germans had less access to local information compared with the rebels, who enjoyed an extensive local network.

Turning to geographical space, it becomes clear that there is significant variation in the location of violence. The violence is primarily concentrated in the hills, where 62 percent of the total violence is observed (39 percent in the eastern hills and 23 percent in the western hills); the mountain villages experienced 17 percent of the violence, followed by the outer plain (12 percent) and the eastern and deep plain (4 and 5 percent respectively). The impact of the violence becomes clearer when violence is weighted by the village population. The eastern hills stand out, having lost 5.06 percent of their population, followed by the western hills (3.25 percent), the mountains (1.74 percent), the outer plain (.83 percent), the eastern plain (.51 percent), and the deep plain (.32 percent). Note that the violence in the eastern hills is primarily due to indiscriminate violence. Comparing the absolute size of selective violence (number of deaths per village)

TABLE 9.3. *Selective Violence (no. of homicides)*

	Incumbents				Insurgents			
	t1	t2	t3	t4	t1	t2	t3	t4
Deep plain	0	10	7	0	13	0	0	1
Outer plain	9	12	7	0	19	3	6	0
Eastern plain	0	5	4	2	3	0	0	18
Eastern hills	0	18	5	0	0	0	7	51
Western hills	0	7	5	5	1	36	37	0
Mountains	0	1	14	0	1	13	46	0
TOTAL	9	53	42	7	37	52	96	70

TABLE 9.4. *Indiscriminate Violence (no. of homicides)*

	Incumbents				Insurgents			
	t1	t2	t3	t4	t1	t2	t3	t4
Deep plain	0	0	2	1	0	0	0	0
Outer plain	6	21	2	1	0	0	0	0
Eastern hills	5	138	0	0	0	0	0	62
Western hills	9	9	0	0	0	0	0	55
Eastern plain	0	0	0	0	0	0	0	0
Mountains	0	22	26	0	0	0	0	0
TOTAL	20	190	30	2	0	0	0	117

with its relative size (number of deaths per village weighed by village population) produces no change in the patterns (Figures 9.5 and 9.6).[32]

The incumbents were more likely to have been the perpetrators of violence in the deep plain, the eastern hills, and especially the outer plain (35 percent more likely than the insurgents), whereas the insurgents tended to be the violent actors in the eastern plain and especially the western hills (57 percent more likely); the two sides were equally likely to kill in the mountain villages. To an analyst assuming the lowlands to be incumbent strongholds, the mountains to be rebel-controlled, and the hills to be contested areas, assumptions that are *on average* correct, this pattern would suggest a concentration of the violence in areas of contestation and the use of less, but still substantial, violence by the armed actors within their strongholds. However, this geographical interpretation turns out to be erroneous, an error caused by most analysts' lack of an appropriate measure for the level of control and their subsequent inability to correctly capture shifts

---

[32] In the analysis that follows I use absolute rather than weighted numbers of deaths. There are good theoretical reasons for doing so: one death has the same effect in a village of 300 people and a village of 1,000. In any case, given the small variation in the size of villages ($\mu = 739, \sigma^2 = 499.5$), normalized measures are very close to absolute ones.

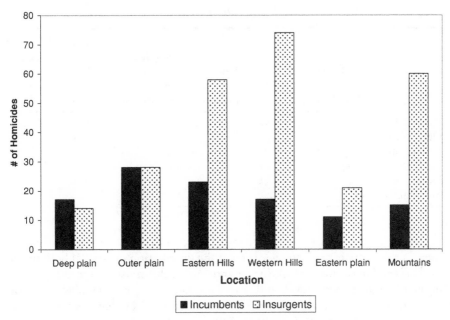

FIGURE 9.5. Selective Violence by Actor and Geographic Location

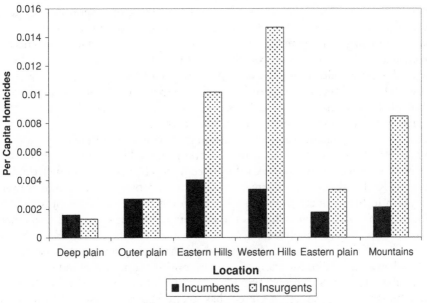

FIGURE 9.6. Selective Violence by Actor and Location (Normalized)

TABLE 9.5. *Conflict Proneness and Civil War Violence*

	Total Violence (no. of homicides)	Total Selective Violence (no. of homicides)	Selective Violence (no. of homicides per 100 inhabitants)	Index of Prewar Litigiousness (no. of trials per capita in 1935–9)
Deep plain	34	31	0.29	0.06
Outer plain	86	56	0.54	0.06
Eastern hills	286	81	1.42	0.08
Western hills	164	91	1.81	0.03
Eastern plain	32	32	0.51	0.09
Mountains	123	75	1.06	0.05

in control. Put otherwise, although control sometimes correlates with geography, there is substantial variation over time in the distribution of control both in the lowlands and in the mountains. In fact, it turns out that most incumbent violence in the lowlands took place when this area was not under full incumbent control; the same is true about the insurgents. This variation is hidden when one looks at the aggregate patterns only. Indeed, the introduction of control washes out the effect of geographical variables, such as altitude and distance from the closest town (discussed later).

From the spatial distribution of the violence, one might be tempted to advance an interpretation that would point either to the villages' prewar political orientation or to some unobserved conflict-inducing characteristics of the most violent clusters of villages. Despite their surface appeal, both interpretations would be problematic. First, there is no correlation between the level of violence and the villages' prewar political orientation; villages who voted for Liberal candidates in prewar elections were no more or less likely to experience violence than villages who voted for Monarchist candidates.[33] Second, the worst-hit villages suffered primarily from indiscriminate violence, and there is no plausible link between prewar conflict proneness and the indiscriminate violence of the Germans during the war. Prewar conflict proneness, in contrast, could be expected to impact selective violence. In the context of Greece, a good proxy for conflict proneness and the breakdown of informal mechanisms of control is the level of prewar litigation in local courts. Consequently, I constructed an index of prewar litigiousness for each village, which is the per capita number of all civil trials that took place in 1935–9, involving at least one inhabitant of the village (N = 2,813). The idea of using this index as a proxy came during interviews: when asked if a village had a reputation for conflict, a typical positive response would stress that its inhabitants kept "suing each other" or "spent a lot of time in courts." In fact, the ethnographic literature on Greece has stressed both the role of litigation as

---

[33] I used as an indicator a dummy variable measuring whether a village had a Conservative or a Liberal majority in the 1933 elections. This is an imperfect indicator. Polling took place in a small number of villages, and it is, therefore, impossible to estimate the exact score for each village.

a common mechanism of conflict resolution (e.g., du Boulay 1974:178) and the pervasive role of lawyers in Greek rural society, as men giving legal advice and attending clients in court, but also as brokers standing between peasants and state authorities (Campbell 1974:242).[34] Hence, it is not surprising to find that, in the Argolid, access to courts was not reserved to the wealthy, or even the well-off – a fact that is also indicated by the high number of trials.[35]

However, an examination of the index shows no correlation between patterns of litigation prior to the war and selective violence during the war. In fact, the most conflict-prone villages (eastern plain) experienced the second-lowest levels of selective violence during the war. In contrast, the least conflict-prone villages (western hills) suffered the worst level of selective violence. In spite of the same level of conflict proneness, the villages of the deep and outer plains experienced divergent rates of violence. Only the villages of the eastern hills display a "matching" level of conflict proneness and civil war violence (Table 9.5). Furthermore, prewar litigiousness fails to predict selective violence at the individual village level as well. The multivariate tests, discussed later, also show that this variable has no effect.

Finally, I turn to the temporal dimension. The general picture is of a slow start, followed by an explosion of violence, and finally a moderate deescalation. The worst period was the second one (t_2), which accounts for 40.69 percent of all the violence, followed by the last one (t_4) (27.03 percent), the third period (t_3) (23.17 percent), and the first one (t_1) (9.10 percent). Disaggregating into type of violence by actor shows that incumbents reduce their indiscriminate violence after t_2, while insurgents rely on it most in t_4 (Figure 9.7).

The evidence is generally consistent with the theoretical expectations about indiscriminate violence, as previously pointed out. At the same time, the readiness of the Germans to resort to mass indiscriminate violence also captures the effect of variables that are explicitly excluded from the theory, such as their ideology, their military weakness in Greece, and the fact that the occupation of Greece was part of a global and total military contest. Evaluating the independent role of these variables requires a comparative analysis across several countries. Nevertheless, the German shift toward more selective violence confirms the importance of the

---

[34] According to Du Boulay (1974:178), the villagers of Ambéli had such frequent recourse to law courts that they had "a reputation of spending most of their time and all of their money there," while the transhumant *Sarakatsani* shepherds studied by Campbell (1974:245) figured "in many court cases."

[35] Regressing the index of prewar litigiousness on altitude and wealth yields a negative correlation (poor and mountainous villages have lower levels of litigation), which, however, is both small and statistically insignificant. It is possible that only wealthy individuals in poor villages used the courts, but the judicial materials I read suggest otherwise, as do my interviews. In the regression analysis, I included an independent variable that interacts control with prewar litigiousness, hypothesizing that prewar conflict may boost violence only under the "right" level of control. This hypothesis is confirmed for two out of the four time periods: in t_1 and particularly t_4, the interaction term is statistically significant with a pronounced effect on violence, while at the same time causing the effect of control to go up. The effect of the interaction term is substantively and statistically insignificant for periods t_2 and t_3. It is, therefore, possible that conditions favoring violence may trigger preexisting conflicts only under locally specific conditions.

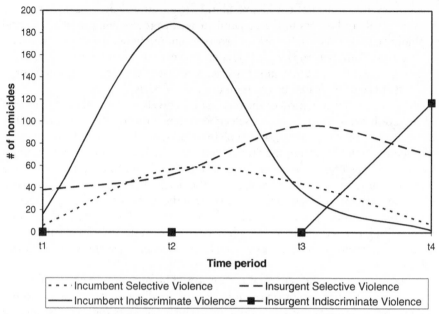

FIGURE 9.7. Temporal Variation of Violence by Actor and Type

dynamics of irregular war in shaping their violence *despite* these more general factors.

Disaggregating by zone of control shows that incumbents target indiscriminately mostly villages located in zone 4. In terms of intensity of violence, however, most of the victims of incumbent indiscriminate violence are inhabitants of villages located in zone 5, that is, in the rebel heartland (Figure 9.8); in other words, large indiscriminate massacres are much more likely in zone 5; although incumbents target villages in the other zones as well, fatalities are low; in fact, the few instances of indiscriminate violence in zones 1, 2, and 3 turn out to have been primarily accidents and mistakes. This pattern is consistent with Hypothesis 3, which posits that political actors tend to use indiscriminate violence where their control level is low. Lastly, consistent with Hypothesis 1 (which posits that indiscriminate political actors are likely to gradually become more selective), the incumbents reduce their indiscriminate violence and switch to more selective violence over time: they are indiscriminate 69 percent of the time in t_1, 78 percent of the time in t_2, 42 percent of the time in t_3, and 22 percent of the time in t_4. The insurgents, however, go from no indiscriminate violence at all during the first three time periods to being indiscriminate 63 percent of the time in the last one. This burst of indiscriminate violence toward the end of the hostilities is inconsistent with my theoretical expectations and points to mechanisms that are explicitly excluded from the theory, such as revenge (I return to this later) or political calculation (the elimination of armed rivals in light of the emerging postwar political situation).

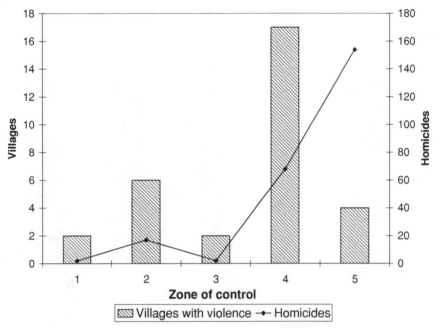

FIGURE 9.8. Frequency and Intensity of Incumbent Indiscriminate Violence

TABLE 9.6. *Mean Scores of Control (village cluster/time period)*

	t_1	t_2	t_3	t_4	Mean Score per Cluster
Deep plain	3.00	2.00	1.00	3.00	2.00
Outer plain	3.73	2.47	1.60	2.47	2.60
Eastern plain	3.86	2.00	1.00	2.29	2.29
Eastern hills	4.80	2.00	1.83	4.00	2.88
Western hills	5.00	3.67	2.83	1.00	3.83
Mountains	5.00	4.71	3.42	4.60	4.38
Mean score per time period[a]	4.06	2.89	1.98	3.12	

[a] Computed on the basis of individual village scores rather than clusters.

9.7. CONTROL: DESCRIPTIVE STATISTICS

I was able to code the shifting levels of control in the Argolid using information about the precise location of the two armies from several sources (the coding protocol is included in Appendix B). Table 9.6 provides the mean scores of control for each group of villages for the four time periods.

The evolution of the conflict in the Argolid can be summarized succinctly by a single metric, the mean score of control for the entire region by time period. Recall that the control index for a given locality varies from 1 (total incumbent

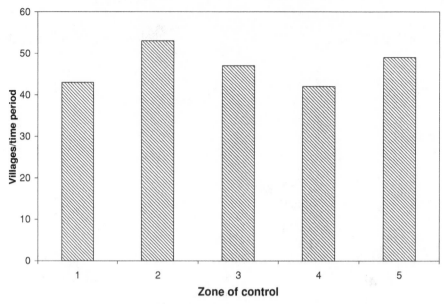

FIGURE 9.9. Distribution of Control across the Argolid (villages–time period)

control) to 5 (total insurgent control). Most of the region was controlled by the insurgents at t_1 (mean control score: 4.06); the incumbents counterattacked successfully in t_2 (mean control score: 2.89) and consolidated their gains in t_3 (mean control score: 1.98), but began retreating in t_4 while still keeping control of the lowlands (mean control score: 3.12). After the Germans left in September 1944 and their local allies either disbanded or left the area, the region's mean control score reached 5.

The impact of geography on control is obvious: as one moves from lowlands to highlands, so does control shift from incumbents to insurgents. Indeed, many of my informants still refer to the two sides in the war by their location: "those below" (*kato*) and "those above" (*pano*). However, a purely geographic interpretation stressing the importance of "rough terrain" at the expense of other factors would hide the considerable temporal variation in the exercise of control and would, therefore, bias the analysis. The Argolid turned out to be a good place to test the theory because all control zones are represented in roughly similar numbers (Figure 9.9).[36]

It is now possible also to examine the patterns of transition in control (Table 9.7; numbers in italics denote villages that stay in the same zone of control).[37] An empirical implication of my discussion about the relation between control and violence is that zones 2 and 4 are transitional areas where control is consolidated

---

[36] The predictions of the theory are, of course, independent of the frequency of particular zones of control.

[37] Since it is not included in the analysis, I leave out the immediate postwar period when all villages came under insurgent control (zone 5).

TABLE 9.7. *Transitions in Control*

	From Zone				
	1	2	3	4	5
To Zone					
1	*38.71*	57.41	0.00	0.00	0.00
2	0.00	12.96	91.67	40.00	21.05
3	48.39	14.81	4.17	5.71	0.00
4	9.68	7.41	0.00	14.29	50.00
5	3.23	1.85	4.17	22.86	28.95
0	0.00	5.56	0.00	17.14	0.00

"endogenously": once selective violence is used, and if we assume no exogenous changes, villages located there should move into zones 1 and 5 respectively. At the same time, control shifts in villages located in zones 1, 3, and 5 should be caused by exogenous shocks, such as new military operations.

It turns out that villages that were controlled in a given time period by the incumbents (zone 1) were almost as likely to shift during the next time period to zone 3 (48.39 percent) or remain in zone 1 (38.71 percent); the massive transition to zone 3 captures the process of gradual withdrawal of the German army in t_4: they were strong enough to maintain their presence in most of the plain but unable to prevent the rebels from coming in almost every night. Villages that were fully controlled by the insurgents display a similar pattern: they were less likely to stay under insurgent rule, and in many places this rule was weakened as a result of incumbent operations (50 percent shifts to zone 4 and 28.95 percent remains in zone 5). Villages where both sides "shared" power (zone 3) were overwhelmingly likely to shift to zone 2 (91.67 percent), again reflecting the military incursion of Germans and SB into insurgent areas in t_2. Finally, villages in zones of predominant but incomplete control (2 and 4) display an interesting pattern. As expected, more than half of the villages in zone 2 moves to zone 1 in the next round (57.41 percent); 12.96 percent remains in zone 2, and 14.81 percent moves to zone 3 instead. In contrast, just 22.86 percent of villages in zone 4 moves to zone 5; 14.29 percent remains in zone 4, while an impressive 40 percent shifts to zone 2.

These patterns can be summarized and interpreted as follows. First, transitions from one extreme of control to the other (zone 1 to 5 or 5 to 1) are almost nonexistent. Clearly, the process of fully shifting from one sovereign to another is gradual, slow, and potentially violent. Second, the process of "endogenous" consolidation of rule (transitions from zone 2 to 1 and 4 to 5) is less prevalent than expected (and is much more pronounced for the incumbents than it is for the insurgents). This pattern captures the specific military situation on the ground, most notably the German summer offensive, which removed the rebels from the area and made possible the consolidation of incumbent control. Related to this trend is the instability of zone 3: most of these villages shift to zone 2. Finally, selective violence seems to "work" better for the incumbents compared with the insurgents: they were able to consolidate their rule at a much higher rate (57.41

percent of villages in zone 2 shifts to zone 1); in contrast, the insurgents failed to achieve a similar result and "lost" most of their villages despite relying on violence (40 percent of villages in zone 4 shifts to zone 2 versus 22.86 percent to zone 5).

This difference captures the effect of exogenous shocks on control, that is, the military dimension of the war during the summer of 1944. As they pushed into the mountains, the Germans and their allies were able to keep the rebels away and consolidate their rule in the newly conquered villages. At the same time, the rebels were fighting what, in retrospect only, turned out to be a rearguard action: violence worked only as long as the incumbents did not push further upward; when they did, selective violence could not prevent their advance – and once they entered in a village, it was their turn to use selective violence in order to consolidate their control. In other words, selective violence is a weapon that enhances and consolidates rule as long as control is not directly challenged by the military actions of one's rival. The use of concentrated military force ("conquest") by one actor trumps the strategic use of violence by the rival actor. However, the problem for military commanders is that this is a limited resource. As soon as the Germans moved their troops out, the rebels returned and their credibility was enhanced by their prior violence combined with the German withdrawal. The case of the Argolid shows that, consistent with the discussion in Chapter 5, irregular war calls for a judicious combination of direct military force and selective violence. Military commanders must display skill in the allocation of their scarce resources: decisions about where and when to move and position troops in order to maximize their impact, and which strategic corridors to block are critical. It follows that "state capacity," a concept that appears in several crossnational studies of civil wars, usually via the per capita GDP proxy (e.g., Fearon and Laitin 2003), would be too crude a measure to use in an analysis of the dynamics of the war, as it would fail to capture what is really the subtle art of making shrewd use of limited military resources.

9.8. QUANTITATIVE EVIDENCE

The most immediate way to evaluate the theory of selective violence is to compare its predictions with the actual observations. Here the importance of the variable for control is most notable, because it clearly qualifies the relation between geography and violence. To begin with, Figure 9.10 suggests a clear relation between selective violence and control – one that was completely hidden in the geographic patterns. Insurgents kill primarily in zone 4 while incumbents kill in zone 2; there is much less violence in zones 1, 3, and 5; the limited selective violence in zones 1 and 5 is caused overwhelmingly by incumbents and insurgents respectively. Interestingly, all of the violence in zone 3 is the result of insurgent action. A different way to depict the relation between control and violence is provided by Figure 9.11, which shows the distribution of violence across zones of control – to be juxtaposed to Figure 7.6, which maps the theory's predictions.

Figure 9.11 is particularly instructive because it shows that, although the violence of the two sides is different in several crucial respects, the overall shape

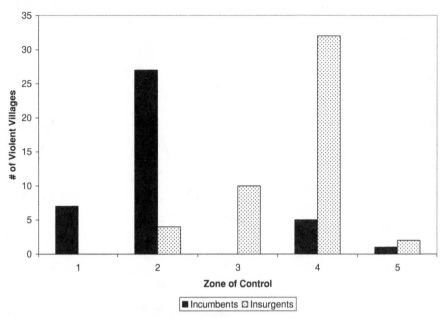

FIGURE 9.10. Selective Violence by Zone of Control and Actor

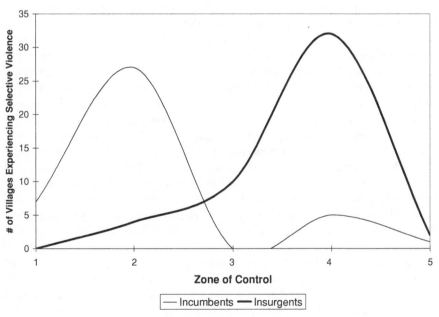

FIGURE 9.11. Distribution of Selective Violence across Control Zones

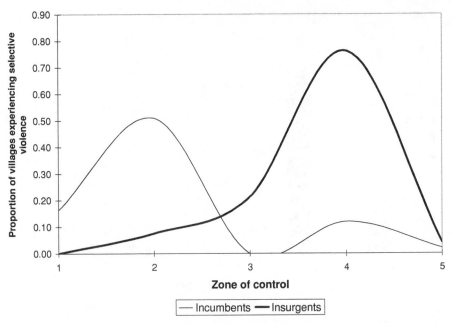

FIGURE 9.12. Proportional Distribution of Selective Violence across Control Zones

is the same. The incumbents tend to target fewer villages in zone 2 than we would expect based on the theory, whereas the insurgents are much more comprehensive in their violence in zone 4; their violence also targets some villages in zone 3. Also, the incumbents are more violent in zone 1 than the insurgents are in zone 5. These patterns reflect the fact that the insurgents had much better access to local information, were more credible in their threats, more persuasive, and were better able to elicit risk-averse behavior from their sympathizers. This pattern is consistent with the identity of the two actors, occupation forces and indigenous resistance. The incumbents were primarily foreigners with relatively few and late ties to the area, whereas the insurgents had been able to build a strong local base. In short, the spatial distribution of violence reflects dimensions that the theory leaves out explicitly (e.g., the political actors' identity, organization, and ideology), yet the theory captures the fundamental logic of the violence. This suggests that the theory is able to subsume the divergent characteristics of armed actors. Put otherwise, while a theory of political actors can elaborate and refine the predictions made by the theory of selective violence, the theory of selective violence is a prerequisite for any theory of political actors.

Figure 9.12 normalizes the distribution, by including the proportion of villages of a given zone of control that experience selective violence; the patterns are unchanged. The overall "fit" of theory's empirical predictions and empirical observations can be seen in Figures 9.13 and 9.14. Though far from perfect, the predictions nevertheless display the posited pattern. Finally, Figures 9.15–9.18 display the relation of control and violence on the map of the Argolid for all four time periods.

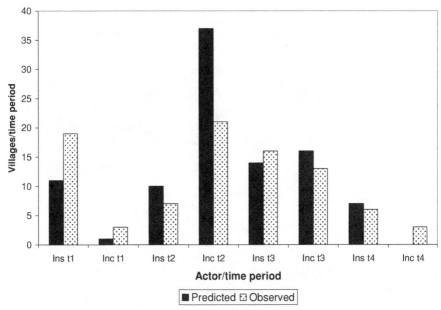

FIGURE 9.13. Predicted versus Observed Violence (Ins = insurgents; Inc = incumbents)

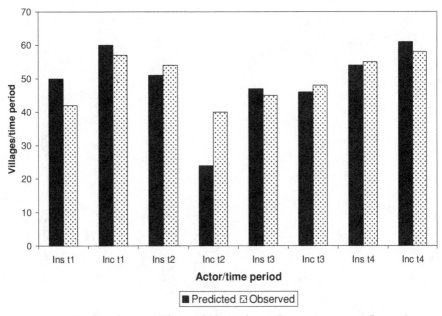

FIGURE 9.14. Predicted versus Observed Nonviolence (Ins = insurgents; Inc = incumbents)

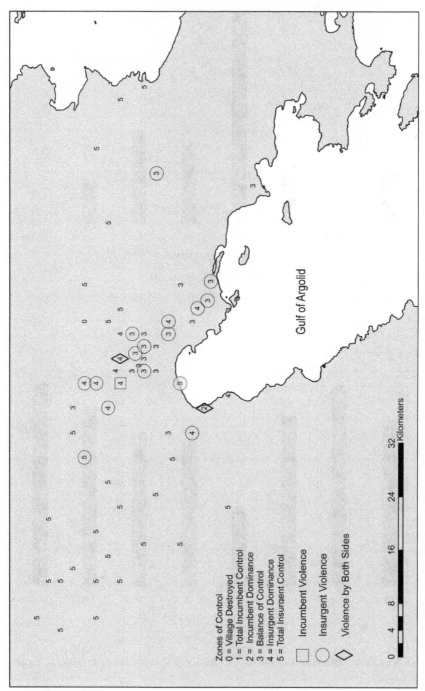

FIGURE 9.15. Violence and Control, September 1943–15 May 1944 (t₁), Argolid, Greece

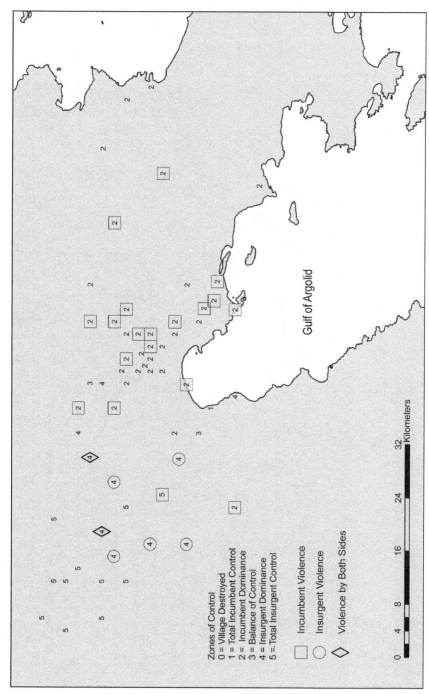

FIGURE 9.16. Violence and Control, 15 May 1944–30 June 1944 (t₂), Argolid, Greece

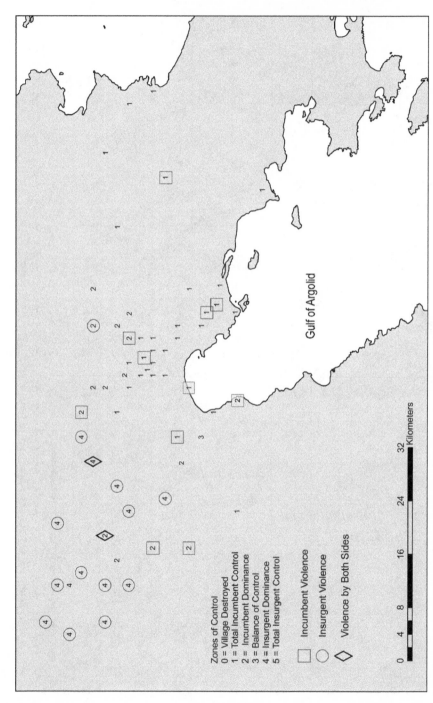

FIGURE 9.17. Violence and Control, 1 July 1944–1 August 1944 (t₃), Argolid, Greece

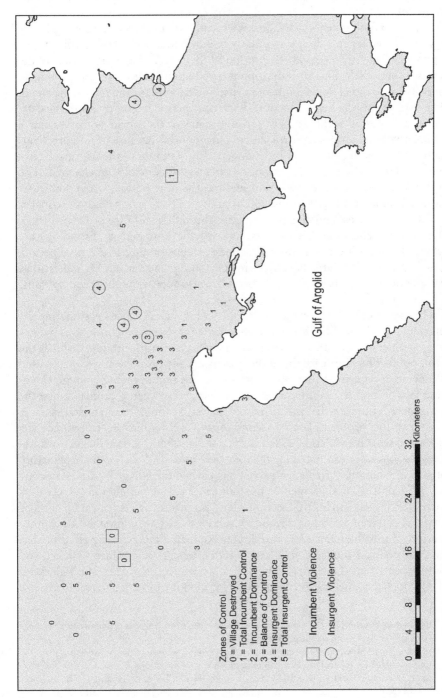

Zones of Control
0 = Village Destroyed
1 = Total Incumbent Control
2 = Incumbent Dominance
3 = Balance of Control
4 = Insurgent Dominance
5 = Total Insurgent Control

☐ Incumbent Violence
◯ Insurgent Violence

Gulf of Argolid

0   4   8   16   24   32
Kilometers

FIGURE 9.18. Violence and Control, 1 August 1944–1 September 1944 (t_4), Argolid, Greece

Up to this point, the testing was essentially bivariate. I now turn to a multi-variate setting to test for the effect of control on selective violence by controlling for a variety of other factors. To address concerns about the possible endogeneity of control to violence, I disaggregated the war into four time periods, thus generating 244 village–time period observations; I then ran regressions on each of the four time periods.[38] This periodization is based on the major exogenous shifts in control: for example, the incumbent push in the outer plain and hills at the end of May 1944 signals the beginning of t_2. Each time period begins on a specific date. A new time period includes three possible states of the world as far as control is concerned: the level of control shifts "exogenously" because of military "conquest"; the level of control shifts "endogenously" because of the use of selective violence during the previous period; or the level of control is unchanged. The level of control remains constant throughout the time period, while homicides always chronologically follow any shift in control. The research design also makes it possible to address endogeneity concerns through qualitative process-tracing. The evidence confirms that violence in a specific time period chronologically follows the imposition of a control regime at the beginning of the time period, though it potentially affects control in the subsequent period. Denunciations, though not directly observable or measurable, also appear to follow control shifts in the predicted way.

The first multivariate test consists of a set of logistic regressions estimating the determinants of the *frequency* of selective violence. I use a dichotomous dependent variable: whether there is violence in a village or not, with one death as the cutoff point. The one death threshold is theoretically justified: if violence is used to generate compliance, then one death meets this requirement given the size of these villages and the density of communications between the inhabitants; the downside, of course, is that this threshold may also capture noise (mistakes, etc.). To address this problem, I ran a second set of OLS regressions to estimate the *intensity* of selective violence, coded as the number of deaths per village. Both sets of regressions were estimated for the four time periods.[39] The main explanatory variable is a dummy variable whose value is 1 when the village is located in zone 2 or 4.[40] Control variables include the following: village population (as recorded in the 1940 census – in log); educational level (measured as the per capita number of village children attending secondary school in 1937–9), intended to capture a variety of possible effects in both directions, including civilizing effects (Elias 1994) or political moderation (Paxson 2002), which may reduce violence and rising expectations (Gurr 1970) or political extremism (Krueger and Maleckova 2002), which may increase it; altitude (logged meters), intended to capture rough

---

[38] This assumes that periods are independent of each other; in reality, this is not always the case. I discuss this in the section on mispredictions.

[39] Logistic estimations could not be obtained for the period t_2 because of the zero-cell problem (the dummy variable for control predicts failure perfectly).

[40] I chose to estimate models for all violence to increase the number of observations. The interpretation of the dummy variable for zones 2 and 4 assumes, of course, that incumbents kill in zone 2 and insurgents in zone 4, which is almost always the case (see the section on mispredictions for a discussion of violence by the "wrong actors"). I also estimated separate models for incumbent and insurgent violence using dummies for zones 2 and 4 respectively, and the results hold.

terrain, which may have a positive effect on violence given that insurgencies are more likely to take place in such areas (Fearon and Laitin 2003; Tong 1988); distance from the closest town (logged travel minutes from the closest town in 1940), intended to capture the geographic ability of the two sides to access a particular locale and provide credible opportunities and sanctions (Tong 1988); litigiousness (the total number of trials in the civil and penal courts of the region during the period 1935–9, logged), intended to capture conflict proneness as well as the absence of social capital, which should reduce violence (Varshney 2002); and a three-scale ordinal GDP proxy, intended to capture wealth and opportunity costs (Collier et al. 2003).[41] Table B.3 in Appendix B lists the independent variables used in multivariate tests. Results are reported in Tables 9.8 and 9.9.

Both sets of regressions confirm the importance of control as a determinant of violence, in precisely the direction hypothesized by the theory.[42] Dominant but incomplete control is consistently an excellent predictor of both the frequency and the intensity of violence. Of the other independent variables used, a few turn out to be relatively significant in some specifications and time periods, but none is consistently significant and their coefficients' sign changes across time periods. These results are robust to all kinds of alternative specifications and resistant to a battery of diagnostic tests.[43] Interestingly, the predictive fit of the theory goes up with the time period, suggesting a tighter match between control and violence. Furthermore, the effect of control on the intensity of violence also goes up with the time period; there is a tenfold increase from t_2 and t_3 to t_4: a move from zones 1, 3, and 5 to zones 2 and 4 causes seven more deaths even though the overall number of selective deaths is about half in t_4 compared with that in t_3. This finding suggests a strong escalatory trend in violence, along with more "calibration" – possibly an instance of learning by the actors. This pattern is consistent with a process of competition between the two actors in trying to increase the credibility of their sanctions. Finally, the data show that in all but a few instances, the actor producing the violence is the one predicted by the theory (e.g., incumbents kill in zones 1 and 2 and insurgents in zones 4 and 5).

Altogether, the empirical analysis provides strong support for all five hypotheses. First, there is a clear decline of incumbent indiscriminate violence along with a rise of selective violence; furthermore, the link between indiscriminate violence and information holds: indiscriminate violence tends to take place where information is low and is used by actors who have restricted access to local information. Second, there is clear decline of selective violence when the level of control goes

[41] The only significant variable that I failed to include is a measure of political polarization. Unfortunately, prewar electoral results are too aggregated to allow a village-level indicator of polarization. However, there was little variation in prewar electoral returns.

[42] With the exception of the model for t_1 in the frequency analysis, which is slightly outside the significance interval (Prob > chi^2 = .151), all other models are significant.

[43] I also estimated negative binomial models and used different combinations of independent variables both logged and nonlogged. In addition, I ran extensive diagnostics to see whether the results were driven by outliers (they are not). Further, there is no time dependence: control in one period does not predict violence in the next one, either alone or in a model that includes control for the same period with violence (control in t_1 predicts violence in t_2, but the effect vanishes when control for the same period is included).

TABLE 9.8. *Frequency of Violence (no. of violent villages per time period): Logistic Regressions*

Dependent Variable: Selective Violence (no. of homicides)	t_1	t_3	t_4
Control zones 2 & 4 (dummy: 1 when control zone is 2 or 4)			
	1.71**	2.25**	4.21***
	(0.85)	(1.22)	(1.27)
	(0.045)	(0.066)	(0.001)
Population (1940) (log)			
	0.81*	0.62	0.77
	(0.49)	(0.58)	(0.73)
	(0.094)	(0.290)	(0.290)
Education level (high school students per capita)			
	0	0.42	0.86
	(0.59)	(0.33)	(0.55)
	(0.997)	(0.212)	(0.111)
Altitude (meters) (log)			
	0.035	0.34	0.16
	(0.30)	(0.33)	(0.70)
	(0.905)	(0.295)	(0.813)
Distance from closest town (in minutes) (log)			
	−0.95	−0.69	0.62
	(0.76)	(0.83)	(2.09)
	(0.213)	(0.407)	(0.765)
Social conflict (court suits per capita 1935–9) (log)			
	0.23	−0.06	0.32
	(0.034)	(0.47)	(0.56)
	(0.487)	(0.897)	(0.560)
GDP proxy (interval variable; wealthiest village = 3)			
	−0.16	−0.63	0.15
	(0.61)	(0.55)	(0.55)
	(0.978)	(0.251)	(0.863)
Constant			
	−1.22	−2.66	0.230
	(4.76)	(4.24)	(9.64)
	(0.797)	(0.530)	(0.88)
Observations	61	61	61
R squared	0.210	0.266	0.378
Prob > chi²	0.151	0.030	0.001

Note: Robust standard errors and *p* values in parentheses. * $p < 0.10$; ** $p < 0.05$; *** $p < 0.01$ (two-tailed test).

up to reach complete sovereignty. Third, there is almost no selective violence in areas where an actor exercises little or no control. Fourth, selective violence tends to emerge under dominant but incomplete control. Fifth, there is little selective violence in areas of parity. In more general terms, these results support the conceptualization of selective violence as a joint process with rational, though

TABLE 9.9. *Intensity of Violence (no. of homicides per time period): OLS Regressions*

Dependent Variable: Selective Violence (no. of homicides)	t_1	t_2	t_3	t_4
Control zones 2 & 4 (dummy: 1 when control zone is 2 or 4)				
	1.29*	3.62***	3.28**	10.06***
	(0.66)	(1.06)	(1.39)	(3.54)
	(0.056)	(0.001)	(0.022)	(0.006)
Population (1940) (log)				
	0.24	1.28**	1.42*	1.05
	(0.22)	(0.59)	(0.73)	(0.81)
	(0.27)	(0.034)	(0.056)	(0.198)
Education level (high school students per capita)				
	−0.11	0.37	0.38	0.52
	(0.21)	(0.52)	(0.42)	(0.46)
	(0.600)	(0.477)	(0.365)	(0.257)
Altitude (meters) (log)				
	−0.22	0.96***	0.63**	0.51
	(0.22)	(0.28)	(0.33)	(0.49)
	(0.335)	(0.001)	(0.044)	(0.298)
Distance from closest town (in minutes) (log)				
	0.36	0.36	−1.47*	0.14
	(0.62)	(0.68)	(0.76)	(0.53)
	(0.561)	(0.597)	(0.066)	(0.789)
Prewar conflict (court suits per capita 1935–9) (log)				
	0.11	−0.67**	−0.47	0.69
	(0.17)	(0.33)	(0.48)	(0.43)
	(0.513)	(0.046)	(0.334)	(0.110)
GDP proxy (interval variable; wealthiest village = 3)				
	0.32	−0.09	−1.13**	0.61
	(0.36)	(0.42)	(0.50)	(0.46)
	(0.379)	(0.815)	(0.028)	(0.192)
Constant	−2.09	−17.65	−3.46	−9.11
	(2.96)	(6.7)	(5.58)	(7.17)
	(0.485)	(0.011)	(0.538)	(0.209)
Observations	61	61	61	61
R squared	0.265	0.372	0.328	0.543
Prob > F	0.0258	0.0172	0.0062	0.1357

Note: Robust standard errors and *p* values in parentheses. * $p < 0.10$; ** $p < 0.05$; *** $p < 0.01$ (two-tailed test).

myopic, actors. Indeed, they suggest that people do tend to make decisions that overestimate the stability of control.

At the same time, the analysis disconfirms a number of alternative theories. Recall that the breakdown thesis predicts a positive relationship between the degree of authority breakdown and the intensity of violence. The data show that, in the Argolid, violence was low where sovereignty was most divided and authority most contested (zone 3); as for indiscriminate violence, actors did not commit it when authority was contested, but when authority was in the hands of the rival actor. The transgression hypothesis is not supported either: even though incumbent troops are more indiscriminate compared with insurgents, they are as violent as the insurgents, in contrast to what this hypothesis would predict. The medievalization variant of the warfare hypothesis, which predicts more violence with less professional troops, similarly fails to find support. Both are damned by the parity in brutality between the insurgents and the incumbents, the first belied by the fact that the rebels killed as much as the incumbents, the second belied by the fact that the incumbents, fielding the more professional troops, killed as much as the insurgents. The absence of violence in zones of equal force also goes against the underlying logic of Roger Gould's (2003) conjecture, namely that conflict and violence are more likely when power between parties is equal.[44] Similarly, the analysis suggests that violence (either selective or indiscriminate) cannot be predicted by levels of social capital or conflict as captured by litigiousness, the level of education and wealth, or the location of the village vis-à-vis towns or rough terrain. Although the failure of rough terrain to act as a predictor of violence does not detract from its potentially predictive value when it comes to the onset of an insurgency, the results do suggest a much more subtle relation between geography and violence. Additionally, although social polarization likely has a role to play in explaining how conflicts evolve, it does a poor job in explaining variation in violence in this particular context. Recall as well that the vulnerability thesis predicts that more violence will be observed where the actors are more vulnerable, while the "security dilemma" predicts that violence will occur as actors strike preemptively at the other's supporters when they find themselves evenly matched or about to be dominated. There is some matter of observational equivalence between these two hypotheses, but in either case the data do not show high levels of violence where control is fragmented but do indicate exactly the opposite. What is more, the evidence suggests that in contrast to the security dilemma conjecture, fear is associated not only with violence but also with the prevention of violence.[45] In short, these results suggest that a security-based theory cannot, on its own, be a theory of violence – but neither can theories of (peaceful) social conflict.

9.9. QUALITATIVE EVIDENCE

In addition to providing the data necessary for the statistical analysis, my research in Greece yielded illustrative examples of the mechanisms posited by the theory at work. The entire corpus of evidence I have collected is too large to be included in this book;[46] instead, I present snapshots from representative villages in each zone.

---

[44] Although the evidence is consistent with an interpretation of this conjecture that stresses uncertainly about the outcome of the conflict. In zone 3, parties know with a high degree of certainty that if they denounce, they will be counterdenounced.

[45] As far as analogies from the study of interstate war go, mutual assured destruction seems a better fit than the security dilemma.

[46] I am presently at work on a book that will highlight this material through a narrative of life during the civil war in Greece.

9.9.1. Zone 5

The village of Tatsi (now Exochi) is an archetypical zone 5 village; located high in the mountains it was so inaccessible to the occupation authorities (the Italians had come only once) that EAM leaders decided to set up their headquarters there. This small village swelled with various officials and dignitaries of the insurgency, along with many partisans. Several houses, including the school, were confiscated and used by the rebels; the villagers were aware that many of these places were used as detention and interrogation centers, and they saw tens of prisoners from the lower villagers brought there on their way to organized concentration camps run by EAM higher up in the mountains – in particular, the notorious monastery of Saint George in the Feneos valley. On occasion, executions took place inside the village and local people were called in to bury the victims. The village was evacuated for a few weeks in late July 1944, during the German mop-up operation in the region, but EAM authorities were quick to return on 3 August, immediately after the Germans left. In spite of the violence that took place in and around this village, no inhabitant was harmed. The presence of the EAM headquarters is most likely the factor that differentiates Tatsi from neighboring mountain villages where the rebels' presence was not as omnipresent and permanent; when, in July 1944, the hill villages were lost to the occupation forces and it looked as if the mountain villages would soon fall as well, the insurgents launched a wave of selective assassinations against people deemed of insufficient loyalty. However, Tatsi was spared.[47]

That Tatsi was not destroyed had nothing to do with the locals being particularly strong and committed EAM supporters; in fact, the irony is that when the Germans entered the village and found it deserted, they did not burn it as they did with some neighboring villages because a Tatsi native who lived in the town of Korinthos and had joined the Security Battalions interceded with them. The villagers participated in various activities and fully complied with the orders of the rebels. "The entire village became involved in EAM," a leftist villager told me (I-71), adding: "What could you do? The rebels asked you to go somewhere for a chore. You replied, 'I will go,' irrespective of whether you wanted to go or not. You could not refuse. They asked for bread? You had to give it to them. They asked for a sheep, a goat? You had to give those to them, what could you do?... Everyone was trying to survive, everyone was trying to forget; you had to pretend to be an idiot. You had to say one thing and its opposite in order to survive."

The absence of violence during the occupation period had longer-term effects as it spilled over the postwar era: although several villagers joined a right-wing paramilitary band in 1946, they did not harm anyone in the village.

---

[47] I have coded Tatsi as a zone 4 village for this period, as my data were not detailed enough to ascertain whether EAM was still present in force, given that all surrounding villages clearly moved to zone 4. The interviews suggest, however, that Tatsi was probably in zone 5 during this period because of the continued presence of the organization's headquarters.

9.9.2. Zone 4

Comparing the experience of Tatsi with that of Malandreni, a village of the western hills, is revealing. Between September 1943 and May 1944, Maladreni was under the undisputed control of EAM (i.e., in zone 5). The partisans moved freely inside the village and did not need to hide. In fact, a group of British agents used the village as their basis in October 1943 to launch a sabotage operation against the Argos airport in the plain.[48] The local EAM leader, Yannis Nassis, reports in his unpublished memoir and confirmed to me in several long interviews (I-78) that during that time several villagers were denounced to the local committee as spies and traitors. For example, one man was arrested by the partisans after being accused of having denounced a number of villagers to the Italians for hiding weapons; it turned out that he had been falsely accused by his sharecropping associate who wanted to keep the farm's crops to himself. The local committee was quite effective in screening these denunciations, but at one point, in April 1944, anonymous denunciations bypassed it and reached the provincial committee. Eventually, an investigation was launched and the accusations were shown to be really, as Nassis recalls, about "olive oil, sheep, etc., the usual stupid stuff." As a result, no one was harmed during that period, an outcome consistent with the theory's predictions.

After the Germans consolidated their control of the two towns of Nafplio and Argos, they turned their attention to the hill villages. The Germans began to visit Malandreni sporadically from mid-April on, but the situation really changed in late May. On 21 May, a small party of Germans raided the village and arrested the local teacher, an EAM cadre, who informed them about the situation in the village and the presence of rebels in it. Using this information, they began to apply pressure on the hill villages. The security enjoyed by the insurgents decreased as the village moved to zone 4. Following the mop-up operations in the eastern hills, many villagers, including scared EAM sympathizers, began fleeing for the relative safety of Argos, which was under solid German and SB control. Given the deteriorating security situation and the rising defections, the EAM regional committee met on 6 and 7 June and asked the Malandreni local committee to request that all villagers who had fled to Argos return to the village. Because EAM rule was not as undisputed as it once was, more villagers fled when this decision was announced. On the afternoon of 9 June, a group of German soldiers and Security Battalion soldiers, accompanied by some of the local men who had fled to Argos, raided Malandreni. They entered the village and caught everyone by surprise. The local EAM leader was shot in the leg but managed to escape. This raid was interpreted by the EAM cadres as evidence that there were informers inside the village. As a result, thirteen villagers, mostly relatives of people who had fled to Argos, were arrested the night of 13 June 1944. They were marched to a concentration camp, where six were released and the remaining seven were executed.

---

[48] "Narrative of Capt P. M. Fraser. Peloponnese July 43–April 44," PRO, HS 5/698/S6557.

The situation remained unstable, however; the Germans and the SBs once again raided the village one day after these arrests and killed four young men from a nearby village who were manning an outpost. EAM responded with more arrests; the obsessive hunt for spies combined with personal feuds generated seventeen more executions in July. Indicative of the arbitrary (and yet selective) nature of the process is the case of a young man named Liakos Dassaklis. His father Christos, a reputed drunkard, had accused him in March or April 1944 of being a German collaborator. At that point, however, his accusations had been screened and rejected. The EAM leader at the time, Yannis Nassis, recalls that he confronted father and son:

> "Sit down," I told him. "What is your problem with Liakos?"
>
> "What is my problem? He doesn't listen to me, he doesn't respect me."
>
> "But you don't mention this in your accusation, you claim that he is collaborating with the Germans."
>
> He began to lose it and [to say] that we must send Liakos "up" [in the EAM-held mountains], that we must teach him how to behave.
>
> "You should be ashamed Christos. Get out of here!" I turned to Liakos: "Listen to me: you listen to your father, otherwise I will keep the denunciation, I will send it up and they will teach you a lesson." He left. It must have been March or April. In July [the partisans] took Liakos up and he never returned. (Nassis n.d.:16)

After the second wave of executions in July, the Germans raided Malandreni one last time and evacuated all villagers to Argos. The great majority followed the Germans to Argos, while a few fled in the guerrilla-held mountains. Several houses were burned down by the two sides and the village stood deserted until the end of the war.

9.9.3. Zone 3

Qualitative evidence is particularly important for zone 3, both for assessing the quantitative evidence and for examining whether the causal mechanism of mutual deterrence is indeed causing the reduction in the levels of violence. In fact, I was able to locate several instances of local committees vetoing the use of violence.[49] Vetoing by local committees because of the high certainty of counterdenunciation and reprisals is a key manifestation of the insecurity of would-be denouncers in zone 3 and points to the mechanism of mutual deterrence. In what follows I provide some illustrations.

The first one is from the village of Boutia (now Ira). I interviewed the leader of the local EAM committee who described to me in detail the strategic situation of the village until late May 1944 (I-212). There were German troops garrisoned ten minutes outside the village; at the same time, the local EAM committee was operating inside the village. Although the village was politically divided, everyone was helping EAM. When I asked him if everyone supported

---

49 Fichti (I-12; I-102), Ira (I-212), Ireo (I-127; I-128), Dalamanara (I-131), Kourtaki (I-124), Panariti (I-81; I-84), Argoliko (I-123), Nea Tirintha (I-86), Pirgela (I-53), Laloukas (I-109), and Poulakida (I-84).

the rebels, he replied that not everyone was a supporter, "but no one spoke up; support was not visible, because when people went to their fields for work they had to supply the rebels with food. They had to do so out of fear. They were afraid that the rebels would come in the village and arrest those who did not collaborate with them." He then went on to describe how at some point an order came from the organization for the arrest of an individual. Apparently, a personal dispute had escalated, the local committee was somehow bypassed, and the denunciation had reached the higher-ups. The local committee then had to arrest that person and take him to the EAM headquarters for interrogation. As the local leader told me, "This man had to be arrested and delivered to the organization, but I thought that if one person is killed from the village, then everyone would start killing everyone else.... The family of the victim would go to the Germans and the Germans would arrest us or send us to Germany or kill us.... The Germans were next door, we had a gun on our temple." The local leader decided to accompany the arrested man to the EAM headquarters and guarantee his innocence. "I decided to do that because I did not like the idea of arrests and killings, but also because we would get into a big dispute and we would kill each other." The story had a positive denouement: the local leader went to the headquarters, vouched for the prisoner, and the village did not fall into a spiral of violence. As another villager put it, "the storm came by, but we stayed dry" (I-213).

A second example comes from the village of Fichti (or Fichtia), an outer plain village that was in zone 3 during the first period. Not only did the rebels come in every night, but the village was the center of active Communist agitation, one of two villages in the area known for its strong Communist organization. However, because the village was located next to the rail line and was home to a train station, it also housed a small German detachment, which did not venture outside its fortified outpost at night. One would have expected such an arrangement to produce mayhem, as rebels and Germans crossed each others' paths. However, the village suffered very few fatalities during the occupation and afterward acquired a reputation as a highly solidaristic place. Indeed, the standard interpretation given by many of its inhabitants, as well as those of surrounding villages, was that the people of Fichtia had been unusually nice to each other. Such an interpretation, however, was challenged by some of my respondents, who recalled several feuds within the village. The village did have relatively low levels of prewar litigiousness, though not as low as one would have expected given its low rates of violence. Several in-depth interviews with two members of the local committee (I-12; I-102) made clear that the village's solidaristic reputation was endogenous to its relatively peaceful behavior during the war and that the fear of mutual denunciations led the otherwise contentious villagers on the path to cooperation.

When the Italians came in, a local man denounced several villagers for hiding weapons, thus creating (or perpetuating) several local grudges. So, when EAM launched its first assassination campaign in the fall of 1943, several denunciations reached its regional representative, Yannis Andreadakis, known by the nickname of Gavos. In a local committee meeting that took place in October 1943, he asked its members to arrest three people who had been denounced as traitors. The reaction was both swift and negative, because the man who had denounced the weapons to the Italians was the first one on the list of those to be arrested and had, as one of my respondents put it, more than "ten first cousins." He recalls having made his argument very forcefully: "Gentlemen, the Germans are in here. We are in the wolf's mouth and we need to be on good terms with them. Germans and camouflaged guerrillas are both walking around here and we have to tread very carefully." Another informant recalled a scene, which works nicely as a metaphor for the experience of those in zone 3, in which a village leader had German soldiers in one room of his house and guerrillas in another one, while keeping them unaware of each other's presence.

A third illustration comes from the village of Panariti, situated in the plain. Apparently, EAM was able to bypass the local organization and arrest six men whom it imprisoned in a local monastery. When the local EAM leader heard about it, he went there to lobby the rebel leaders, some of whom were his own relatives, and managed to fetch them back. His son recalled for me his father's reaction: "We are lost. . . . Unless we go there and snatch them back, the village will splinter and we will all be lost. We must save them by all means" (I-81). His son, one of five children, added that his father was afraid that unless he was able to prevent the executions from taking place he risked losing his children to revenge. Indeed, several of my respondents pointed out that avoiding the initiation of a vicious cycle was a critical concern of local leaders, who would have been the first ones to be targeted by revenge seekers (e.g., I-109).

The mechanism of mutual deterrence comes up in individual accounts as well. A man from the village of Poulakida, located in zone 3 at t_1, told me how his behavior signaled to his local rivals that any attempt to harm his family would be met with immediate retaliation, thus preventing any violence – a threat made credible by the proximity of occupation troops (I-84):

Look. I was a tough guy. . . . They were scared of me. I was dangerous, very dangerous. . . . I didn't act as a human being and they knew it. I behaved like a wild animal. I said, if they do anything I will get there and I will kill them all. I will leave nothing intact. But I was lucky. Nothing happened. They were scared and they were careful. And those up there [the regional leaders] were in contact with them; and they told them, what you are asking us to do will have terrible consequences. We can get his father and his mother and send them up. And then? What will we do then? This guy is ready for anything.

Another man from the village of Lirkia described how his life was spared when he was caught by a right-wing band in the postoccupation period, after his brother had been able to escape (I-60):

They brought me below the pine trees and asked me to wait there. I thought of running away but I was exhausted. I told myself, they will shoot me up here, they will kill me. I waited. They were discussing outside [the right-wing leader's] house. They eventually decided not to kill me. They said: "His brother escaped, what shall we do with this one? Suppose we kill him. What will happen afterwards? His brother will come back, and he will attack us, and our families. What shall we do then?" And they didn't kill me.

Additional direct evidence is available from individual experiences outside the Argolid. A leftist Greek peasant from the Arcadia prefecture in central

Peloponnese recounts in his memoir how in 1948 he escaped death at the hands of an army officer, whom he describes as extremely violent (Antonopoulos 1993:149–51). He was suspected of contacts with the Communist rebels who frequently visited the village because all of his four brothers had joined the rebels and were roaming around the village. The officer and his men beat him, and others, for three consecutive days, hoping to force out of him the location of a cache of weapons. On the third day, a man from a neighboring village, whom Antonopoulos describes as an "arch-murderer and leader of the local right-wing militia," showed up and asked the colonel to stop "hurting these guys." The officer initially refused to listen but the man kept insisting. Eventually the militiaman threatened the colonel: "I don't want to leave my family in the street. If you do something [to these people] you won't leave this place alive, do you hear me?" The dispute ended when another militiaman explained to the colonel that their intervention was not motivated by sympathy toward the leftist peasant, but by the fear of retribution from his brothers: "You will be gone in a couple of days," he told him, "but we will stay here. Who will deal with those guys?" A woman who was present added: "Mr. Colonel, do not kill them, there is an entire nest of them around here; how will we cope later?" The prisoners were promptly freed. A similar story is told by potential perpetrators, members of armed organizations. Recalling his decision not to ambush right-wing men inside his own village, a leftist rebel (Papakonstantinou 1986 2:1071) explains how he was dissuaded by a comrade of his who pointed out that "if we hit them now, tomorrow they will kill your brother's children. Think carefully about what you'll do!" He also tells the story of how pleas from right-wing men in his village spared suspected leftists when a right-wing band came through: "I can hardly describe what was happening in the village. The children and wives of the men who had been apprehended were bellowing and crying and their voices could be heard as far as [the neighboring village of] Likouresi. Most right-wingers of the village began to worry.... They ran right and left. They went to Fanis Tsekeris, the leader of the right-wing band and implored him to kill no one.... He promised them that no one would be killed" (Papakonstantinou 1986 1:196).

In addition to direct evidence, three other explanations commonly given by my respondents or encountered in local histories are consistent with the mechanism posited by the theory. First, several informants credited the presence of German troops near their village for keeping insurgent violence at bay; they argued that German power under some conditions checked the power of the rebels.[50] Second, many informants referred to an informal "contract" between factions to protect each other. Although this observation might point to a process of solidaristic collusion, several respondents also mentioned that the fear of retaliation was the main enforcement mechanism. Finally, almost all informants credited the personal characteristics of a village leader (either committee leader or mayor) for managing the village's fortunes successfully. For example, the absence of violence is attributed in several local histories to the "good character of the local agents [of the insurgents] who prevented the executions from taking

---

[50] See also Avdikos (2002:176) for a similar reference elsewhere in Greece.

place" (Kanellopoulos 1981:609; see also Priovolos 1988; I-169). When I asked my informants to describe exactly what they meant by the term "good charac-ter," they almost invariably used the word "diplomacy": good local leaders were perceived as being great "diplomats," that is, people who knew how to navigate expertly between competing political actors rather than generic "nice people" (e.g., I-22; I-51; I-81; I-102; I-169). This account resonates with the mechanism elaborated in the theory.

Finally, the research design effectively disqualifies alternative interpretations of nonviolence in zone 3. Both the litigiousness index and the fluctuations of control show that villages are not self-selected in zone 3; additionally, there is no significant variation in local practices and institutions of factional accommodation or types of factional and individual interaction in the villages of the Argolid.

9.9.4. Zone 2

Selective violence in villages of zone 2 is, on its face, quite surprising since it requires that individuals denounce their neighbors to the occupation authorities. Yet such denunciations were widespread. Andreas Christopoulos (1946:116), a writer and resident of Argos who recorded his impressions of the occupation in a book published in 1946, recalls the situation in June 1944: "One person goes to the Gestapo offices to tell them that the partisans arrested his family tonight, another person tells them that they burnt down his house, and yet another one that they exterminated his family because he was a reactionary." The main micromecha-nism behind such denunciations was revenge. Many people who joined or aided the collaborationist militia in the summer of 1944 gave me a highly localized narrative, stressing that they did not care who gave them weapons as long as they were able to get them in order to fight back. Fear and pressure were also important motivations. Although these can be seen as self-serving justifications, they are highly plausible and consistent with the available evidence, including the narratives of their local enemies and victims.

The village of Heli (now Arachneo) is a good illustration of how fear and revenge combined to produce denunciations and violence in zone 2. This village was isolated, but strategically located in the middle of a valley in the Arachneo mountain, straddling the mountain paths from Korinthia to the Argolid. Con-trolling this village was essential for the Germans, because it allowed them to reduce the flow of rebels sent by the Sixth ELAS Regiment from the Korinthia mountains into the eastern Argolid. Like most of the surrounding villages, Heli was inhabited by Albanian-speaking peasants and had a reputation of being back-ward. Being deep in rebel-held territory, it was the site of a mass rally organized by EAM in February 1944, at which the partisan units operating in the area and the members of local EAM committees from the entire Argolid took an oath. A local monastery was also used as a detention facility for the people arrested in the plain villages, and a mass execution was carried out there, the night of 13–14 January.

The village leaders of Heli had not been as successful in joining the ranks of the EAM leadership as those of the neighboring village and local rival,

Limnes, equally Albanian-speaking and backward in reputation. This local cleavage produced a process whereby Heli's sheep were constantly confiscated to feed the partisan units, something deeply resented by the Heliots. However, there was nothing they could do other than comply. A few people who tried to voice criticism were arrested by the partisans and badly beaten, though not killed, as the area was considered safe and there was no opportunity for defection.

During the German mop-up operation in May 1944, Heli suffered from mass indiscriminate violence. On 28 May, twenty-two villagers grazing sheep were killed for failing to observe the curfew rule imposed by the Germans. Immediately after that, the Germans came into the village, assembled all the villagers in the central square and threatened to execute them all unless the village defected to them. The village mayor and priest decided to strike a deal with them. The village would be saved, they were told by the Germans, if they used the location of their village to impede the movement of the rebels and if they sent a contingent of local men to join the Nafplio Security Battalion unit. They also thought that this would be a safe move, as the rebels appeared to have been defeated and left the area.

To seal the deal they had to deliver the local EAM committee to the Germans. This they did, delivering five men, whom the Germans shot outside the village. A sixth one, a shop owner from another village who had lived in Heli for a long time and led the local committee, tried to hide. He was caught by villagers and stoned to death in the village. The savage nature of his killing testifies to the resentment that had accumulated in the village against EAM, even though the village had suffered so many deaths by the Germans. During June and July, the village became an anti-EAM stronghold. In several instances the villagers were able to intercept ELAS partisans trying to infiltrate into the Argolid, and in one instance they killed five of them (HAA/EDD 368/1947). Another time they arrested a partisan from Limnes whom they beat very badly but did not kill.

On 29 July the partisans launched a surprise attack against Heli. The Germans had begun to move back to the plain, opening up the hills, and the commander of ELAS along with the Communist commissars decided to punish the traitorous villages of the area. The village could not be defended against the insurgents' superior forces. The insurgents burned several houses and assembled all the inhabitants in the central square. There they discovered that the village leaders had fled, including the mayor and the priest. They took sixty-two villagers captive, including the priest's two daughters, and executed them all a few days later. The partisan from Limnes who had been beaten showed up there as well and killed one of his tormentors publicly (I-11; I-13; I-14; I-15; I-89; I-160).

It is important to point out here that the desire for vengeance operated in a context where collaboration with the occupation authorities was made possible by the rapid shift in control that took place during that time. In other words, the sort of revenge exacted in zone 2 (or zone 4) entails a mechanism that is different from the raw emotion (or passion) of vengeance, which disregards any risk (Elster 1999). To be sure, the desire for revenge burned in the hearts of many people who had been humiliated or abused, or had lost loved ones, especially when that loss had occurred or was assumed to have occurred because of the actions of another local person. However, they had to think carefully about the consequences of their actions. Several informants told me stories of how the dangers of taking revenge tempered their desire to do so (e.g., I-132).

9.9.5. Zone 1

The village of Merzes (now Exostis, part of the village of Aria), is located just outside the town of Nafplio. After Nafplio was brought under German and SB control by the end of May 1944, Merzes quickly followed suit. The Germans had installed an outpost in a tomato paste factory very close to the village and were able to visit freely, while the rebels were chased from the area. Thus, it must have come as a surprise to the inhabitants when a German patrol arrested six villagers on 7 June 1944. The villagers were arrested individually and taken to the Gestapo headquarters in Nafplio where they were accused of being members of EAM and interrogated. However, they were released a few days later, though not without having to pay bribes in the form of "cheese, olive oil, butter, eggs, money, etc." It turns out that they had been denounced by one of their neighbors, Nikolaos Papakonstantinou. What is more, three of the arrested men were his own relatives, including his first cousin. Behind the denunciation was a simple dispute that had taken place in the coffee shop during the previous evening between Papakonstantinou and his cousin, Spyros Filinis. Several men intervened and tried to separate the men, but Papakonstantinou must have felt particularly humiliated, judging from the fact that one of the men he denounced had been laughing at him. Given its location, it must have been clear to the Germans that this village could not have been the site of guerrilla activity and that the denunciation was false, so this story ended without violence (HAA/EDD 16/1947).

9.10. RETURN TO MANESI AND GERBESI

In the introduction of this book, I pointed to the puzzle of the "twin" villages of Manesi and Gerbesi (now Midea) in the Argolid: Gerbesi experienced a vicious insurgent massacre in August 1944 while neighboring Manesi was spared.

When traveling to these villages, it is impossible to miss the dissimilarity of their respective locations despite their proximity. Manesi is located on a low hill that is visible from the plain (at an elevation of 70 meters), whereas Gerbesi is behind the hill and hidden from the plain (at an elevation of 120 meters), on the base of the Arachnaion Mountain, which gives it a large hinterland. To reach Gerbesi, one must leave the plain and venture in an altogether different landscape.

This difference explains why Manesi was located in zone 4 during the first time period and Gerbesi in zone 5. The location of Manesi next to the village of Merbaka (now Aghia Triada), which contained a small German garrison, made it very vulnerable to surprise raids, particularly since the two villages were connected by a road. Reaching Manesi was quick and easy, unlike Gerbesi, where well-placed sentinels using a wire-based telephone network were able to provide enough lead time for guerrillas to hide or escape in the surrounding mountains. This difference in location accounts for the character of the EAM organization in each village; although both villages gave substantial support to the rebels, EAM operated clandestinely in Manesi and openly in Gerbesi, where it even ran its regional printing press.

Despite its unfavorable location in zone 4, however, Manesi did not experience violence in t_1. There were arrests by the insurgents, but they did not result in deaths. Accounts for this outcome vary, but they suggest the intervention of local EAM leaders. At the end of this time period, both villages experienced the full force of German indiscriminate violence. Nine people were killed in Manesi; they were caught violating a German-imposed curfew that forbade villagers from venturing outside their homes after 6:00 P.M. and were shot on the spot; Gerbesi, for its part, lost twenty-nine people, who were killed while trying to escape in the surrounding mountains. Most EAM cadres succeeded in fleeing the attacks; most victims were simple peasants. Indeed, the German raid against Gerbesi in May 1944 was so murderous precisely because the villagers heard that the Germans were coming and tried to flee toward the mountains; the villagers of Manesi had no choice but remain within their village. An EAM member pointed to the logic of control when he told me that the relatively limited indiscriminate violence exercised by the Germans in Manesi was due to the fact that they did not include it in the "dangerous zone. Even though the village had a strong resistance organization, even though more than ten young men had joined the rebels, they considered it to be a hill village, not a mountain village and they, therefore, did not target it" (I-75).

At t_2, both villages entered zone 2. Like everyone else in the area, the villagers had to collaborate with the newly assertive Germans. The EAM organization was destroyed and the rebels were gone, though clandestine cells were in operation according to my informants; the Germans paid frequent visits to both villages. Again, Manesi experienced no selective violence during this period, while one person was killed in Gerbesi. The fatalities experienced by these villages in the previous period may explain the low incumbent violence despite their location in zone 2. I have coded the two villages as remaining in zone 2 at t_3 though they were quite close to being in zone 1. The past presence of large EAM organizations in these two villages and the absence of permanent garrisons contributed to the continuing activity of dormant EAM cells. The Germans were aware of this and kept a close eye on both villages, although they lacked the necessary troops to push these villages into zone 1. While no one was killed in Gerbesi during this time period, five Manesi EAM cadres, who had been caught fleeing during the May mopping-up campaign by the Germans, were shot in reprisal for a rebel attack. Several arrests took place in both villages, and most of the men and women arrested ended up in labor camps in Germany.

In August, the military balance shifted once more. The Germans had begun retreating toward the plain and, on 29 July, the partisans attacked and destroyed the village of Heli, which had been armed by the Germans. In this way, they were able to once again dominate the eastern hill villages. The EAM cadres who had fled in late May came back, local organizations were reconstituted, and most villages crossed into zone 4, as the Germans kept visiting sporadically. The only exception was Manesi, which moved to zone 3 instead. Because of the proximity of Merbaka, Manesi received daily visits by the Germans, as did most villages of the outer plain. In mid-August, EAM implemented large purges in all villages of the eastern hills, in order to liquidate those accused of having collaborated with the Germans during the summer. Several public show trials were staged, and tens of villagers were massacred, including twenty in Gerbesi and twenty-six in neighboring Limnes. These massacres were not limited to men, but encompassed entire families; personal disputes weighed heavily on the selection process. Manesi, however, escaped.

There are three possible explanations for the divergent outcomes in Manesi and Gerbesi. The first one points to different social predispositions between these two villages. Though remarkably similar in many respects, they also diverged in others. For instance, Manesi was much less litigious than Gerbesi; its score on the prewar litigiousness index is about half that of Gerbesi (.08 versus .17). Furthermore, secondary education was emphasized much more in Manesi than Gerbesi: a much larger proportion of Manesi children attended high school compared with the children in any other village of the eastern hills. There are problems with this argument, however. First, the litigiousness index of Manesi is not very different from other eastern hills villages that experienced substantial selective violence, such as Limnes, Amygdalitsa, or Berbati. Second, "social predisposition," at least as measured here, fails to explain the variation in violence across the entire region; an explanation of the difference between these two villages on the basis of social predisposition would be, therefore, ad hoc.

The second explanation would link social predisposition or the personality of local leaders to a practice of positive reciprocity in Manesi. Having avoided violence at t_1 may have primed the villagers to protect each other as the village shifted zones of control. This explanation fits with the narratives of several inhabitants who attribute the outcome to reciprocal protection between the local leaders of the two sides. However, it is inconsistent with evidence about local conflicts and denunciations taking place during the same period. For example, a young man defected from EAM in June and joined the Security Battalions because of a dispute with another young man who was a leading cadre of EAM's youth organization. Because the cadre felt that the other man had insulted his sister, he had the first man beaten up badly. As a result, when the latter defected to the SBs, he denounced eight people from the village who were sent to labor camps in Germany (I-75).

The last explanation points to control. Unlike Gerbesi, Manesi was located in zone 3 at t_4. As a result, local EAM leaders had strong incentives to prevent any violence that could quickly backfire on them. In fact, the way in which the massacre was avoided in Manesi is quite telling. Manesi was included in the EAM's plan to purge all the villages of the eastern hills. A list of names had reached the organization, apparently from local lower-level cadres. In mid-August an OPLA squad came to the village to arrest these people. As soon as it arrived, however, local leaders rang the church bells to signal that the Germans were coming in, thus causing the OPLA men to flee. The potential victims were then able to escape, and no one was harmed. Note that whereas EAM felt safe enough to stage a mass rally in Gerbesi, bringing in hundreds of people from the surrounding area to taunt the victims, it could not implement its planned arrests in Manesi. This narrow escape from violence goes a long way to explain why right-wing regional chieftains spared the village from reprisals in the postwar period, unlike what happened in Gerbesi (I-21). In short, although it is impossible to exclude the personal characteristics of the local EAM leaders in Manesi from an explanation of its nonviolence, it is clear that these characteristics operated, if at all, along with the logic of control.

9.11. MISPREDICTIONS

Although the theory does very well in predicting the spatial distribution of violence, it also fails in a number of instances. The research design allows for the analysis of mispredicted cases. By asking why the theory failed and why a particular village did not behave as predicted by the theory, it is possible to uncover the causal mechanisms at work with much more precision. Recall three caveats I pinpointed in Chapter 7: the absence of the past in the decisions of individuals; the absence of the future; and the independence of village–time units. Exploring the mispredictions allows for the incorporation of these dimensions in the analysis.

Because the theory takes rational and instrumental action as its baseline, explicitly excluding noninstrumental motives, the comparison of its predictions with the actual observations provides some clues as to how much work is done by rationalist assumptions and where it is appropriate to look to alternative motives. The analysis suggests that, although a significant part of the violence can be accounted for by a theory with rationalist foundations, two types of noninstrumental mechanisms that are explicitly excluded from the theory may play a residual but nevertheless important role, namely norms and emotions (Elster 1999).[51]

There are three significant clusters of mispredictions, one relating to the insurgents (underpredicted violence at t_1) and two relating to the incumbents (overpredicted violence at t_2 and t_3). During the winter of 1943–4 (t_1), the insurgents killed people in more villages than the theory predicts they should have, while during May, June, and July 1944 (t_2 and t_3), the incumbents killed people in fewer villages than the theory predicts.[52] In what follows, I look at two groups of atypically violent villages (located in zone 3 at t_1 and zone 1 at t_3) and one group of atypically nonviolent villages (located in zone 2 at t_2). I compare these villages to those correctly predicted by the theory and trace their behavior during

---

[51] It is worth noting here that the research design allows for the identification of the role of norms and emotions through specific observable implications of the theory rather than via the more conventional way of positing the existence of norms and emotions and then affirming, with more or less plausibility, their presence in an ex post facto way.

[52] The theory predicts insurgent violence in eleven villages in t_1 and incumbent violence in thirty seven villages in t_2; the actual observations are of nineteen and twenty-two villages, respectively.

preceding and subsequent time periods. I conclude by examining cases where the actor perpetrating the violence is not the one predicted by the theory.

9.11.1. Atypical Violence I (Zone 3, t_1)

Of the twenty-one villages located in zone 3 during t_1, nine experienced violence, contrary to the theoretical expectations. Five cases turn out to be assassinations either of individuals who engaged in transgressive behavior that was universally condemned in the village, or of marginal people who lacked local clout and thus could be eliminated easily.[53] For instance, a woman from the village of Drepano was killed for having an affair with a German soldier (I-153). These assassinations provide an indirect confirmation of the mutual deterrence causal mechanism. The victims were people who could not credibly threaten retaliation, either because their family was weak or there was no family – and hence no access to the rival actor – or because their family was unwilling to counterdenounce because of their transgressive behavior. Of the remaining four cases, one was an internal settling of accounts between leftists, and three are real deviations from the theory: the targeting of an army officer's entire family, of a village mayor, and of a village doctor – all people with clout and the capacity to threaten credible retaliation.[54] I was unable to collect enough information about the case of the officer's family.[55] In the case of the doctor, it is clear that the village committee was bypassed. Although the local insurgent leader visited the insurgent headquarters and pleaded repeatedly and tenaciously with the rebels to spare the doctor, he failed to persuade them for reasons that remain unknown (I-211). As for the village mayor, he was denounced by an employee who bypassed the local committee and used his personal connections with a rebel leader (I-119; I-120; I-121; I-122). As expected, these four cases of denunciation in zone 3 triggered revenge and caused an escalation of violence in subsequent time periods – thus confirming that counterdenunciation is indeed off the equilibrium path.

In short, no single mechanism explains atypical violence in zone 3 at t_1: norms of transgression, social weakness, and intense dislike may have led to excess violence. Yet these mispredictions provide indirect confirmation of the causal mechanisms posited by the theory.

---

[53] Nea Tyrintha, Nea Kios, Pirghela, Asini, and Drepano. I found similar evidence from the village of Nea Zoi in northern Greece. This plain village was close to a German base but received nightly visits from the rebels. The only person killed by the rebels was a person who came to the village in 1941 and had no local connections. My informant was also not from the village but had married there during the war. He would have been killed by the rebels, he told me, because of a dismissive statement he made, if not for his wife's relatives: "I was not from the village, but my wife's relatives protected me" (I-163).

[54] In, respectively, Poulakida, Ireo, Aghia Triada, and Ligourio.

[55] I interviewed a daughter of this officer, who refused to tell me who had denounced her family and why, though she asserted that she knew. She claimed that she did not want to taint co-villagers after all these years. This was also one of the very few cases in which an informant refused to be tape-recorded.

9.11.2. Atypical Violence II (Zone 1, t_3)

Zone 1 in t_3 (the peak of incumbent control) includes thirty villages. The theory predicts that villages where control had been consolidated should not have experienced further homicidal violence. Indeed, most villages (twenty-four) did not experience any violence, exactly as predicted. Six villages, however, did.[56] It turns out that five out of these six villages had been in zone 3 in t_1 *and* four of them had been atypically violent during that period. In t_2, all these villages moved to zone 2 and experienced violence, as expected. In t_3, they moved to zone 1. Unlike in the other villages, however, violence did not stop. This excessive violence points to a path-dependent effect in the form of a vicious cycle. Villages that were initially more violent than expected experienced more violence later on, even when their level of control primed them for nonviolence. The qualitative evidence from these villages suggests that some people kept pushing for violence, most likely because they blamed their victims for having initiated violence in the first place. It seems that initiating violence in a context where surrounding villages did not called for extra punishment later on.[57] The individual motivation is revenge, tinted with a sense of transgression. In fact, I found several accounts of people expressing wonder and admiration at instances of individuals foregoing the option of revenge (e.g., Dalianis 1998:152). N. Katevatis (n.d.:77) recounts the following story. In 1944, a group of ELAS men under the command of a neighbor came to his family's house to search it, without hurting his mother who lived there; he adds:

> Forty years later in Athens, I learned that [my former neighbor] had an accident and was taken to a hospital. I immediately went there, told him who I was, put myself at his disposal, and offered him any help he might have needed. . . . I stressed that my visit was due to the fact that although he could have hurt my mother forty years earlier, he had instead been kind to her. I am not sure if he realized what I was saying: although gratitude results from past good deeds, my debt to him was of a negative nature, flowing from the fact that he did not behave badly even though he could have done so.

9.11.3. Atypical Nonviolence (Zone 2, t_2)

Twenty-one villages were located in zone 3 during t_1. Of those villages, twelve did not experience violence, as predicted by the theory, but nine did. All twenty-one villages then shifted to zone 2 in t_2. Of the nine atypically violent villages, six experienced violence in the next round under zone 2 as predicted, and three did not. However, contrary to the theoretical expectations, of the twelve villages that had no violence in t_1, only three experienced violence during t_2. This pattern suggests another path-dependent effect, but a virtuous one this time. The absence of violence in the first time period appears to have helped suppress violence in

---

[56] Ligourio, Nea Kios, Asini, Ireo, Kefalari, Lefkakia.

[57] Unfortunately, I could not find out how these people were able to persuade the incumbents to carry out these extra assassinations in zone 1 villages where the danger of defection was minimal. One possibility is that they pointed to the extra deaths that took place at t_1 in order to claim that the local insurgent sympathizers were unusually hardcore – which justified a tougher crackdown.

the following one, in spite of the effect of control. This effect is related to this particular type of transition, originating from zone 3.[58] Why were zone 3 villages that escaped violence less likely to experience more violence in the following round *despite* conditions that favored it – when villages that did not experience violence in zones 1 or 5 were much more likely to suffer from violence under similar conditions?

A possible mechanism is as follows. Being in zone 3 subjected villages to intense stress due to pressures for denunciation and counterdenunciation coming from both sides. Even though it was rational not to engage in violence under such conditions, the experience of escaping unscathed may well have triggered a norm of reciprocity, whereby people who had the option to denounce under favorable conditions in subsequent rounds refrained from it. Forgoing an advantage would then set off an obligation of reciprocity, and so on. In other words, the (rational) mechanism of mutual deterrence that prevented violence in the first round may have activated a noninstrumental mechanism in the subsequent round.[59]

It could be argued that what is going on is simply a rational strategy of tit-for-tat, which is unleashed once someone abstains from using violence, provided that in the following time period people realize the "iterated" nature of the process. It would still be necessary, however, to explain the behavior of the first movers. Moreover, this argument cannot differentiate the villages in question from those that shifted to violence-prone zones of control from zones 1 or 5 instead of zone 3; most of these villages were nonviolent but not atypically so.

There is additional evidence in favor of the reciprocity mechanism. There were eleven villages located in zone 4 at t_1; they moved into three different zones in t_2: seven moved to zone 2, two to zone 3, and two remained in zone 4. This variation in control transitions was caused by the dynamics of the war, namely the location of the German incursion. Of the seven villages that moved to zone 2, five experienced violence, as expected. Four out of these five villages had experienced violence in the previous round and one had not. On the other hand, the two villages that did not experience violence in t_1 did not experience violence in t_2 either, that is, they were atypically nonviolent in two consecutive periods (Manesi and Neo Ireo). I found that in both villages there had been arrests by the insurgents in t_1, but executions were prevented by local agents of the rebels,

---

[58] Regressing the violence of a time period on the violence of its antecedent one yields no significant effect.

[59] Even the three villages that did experience violence in t_2 while avoiding it in t_1 (Fichti, Panariti, and Tolo) resemble the nonviolent villages. Their violence seems to be idiosyncratic compared with that of the violence in the other zone 2 villages. The one person from Fichti executed by the Germans was a young man who was involved in killings during the previous period in the neighboring village of Anifi and was denounced by an inhabitant of that village (I-102; I-143; HAA/EDD 333/47). In Panariti, a member of EAM was arrested by Security Battalion forces from another village, although he was not killed because of the forceful intervention of village leaders; eventually however, he committed suicide while in prison (I-109; I-81; HAA/EDD 93/46). Finally, the violence in Tolo was related to a feud from the neighboring village of Drepano and involved the daughter of a man from that village who had married in Tolo (I-153).

most likely for idiosyncratic reasons (I-127; I-128; I-75). When things turned around and rebel authority was replaced by incumbent power, their local rivals reciprocated by protecting the local agents of the rebels. Like the villages moving from zone 3 to zone 2 without suffering violence, the experience of these villages suggests the possible role of a virtuous cycle based on the norm of reciprocity – in a slightly different variation: avoiding violence under an unfavorable initial set of circumstances appears to prime future nonviolence.

The question, then, is what accounts for the initial nonviolence in these villages? Although I cannot completely exclude the impact of some unobserved variable, I was unable to uncover any structural village characteristics that would predict the initial emergence of nonviolence (or violence). For instance, the litigiousness index does not point to any particular predisposition, and neither does my reading of the history and socioeconomic background of each of those villages. In other words, there is not much to suggest the endogeneity of unusually virtuous or vicious cycles to preexisting social conditions.

Generally, the qualitative evidence strongly suggests that people were well aware of the importance of preventing initial acts of violence so as to avoid spirals of violence. An insurgent agent argued in his memoir that he was able to prevent violence in his village by making sure it was never initiated: "I knew," he points out, "that if someone started killing it would go on without end" (Priovolos 1988:8). At the same time, however, people clearly overestimated the stability of the control regime they lived under. This may seem surprising in retrospect, but the interview material clearly suggests that many people thought that rebel rule in the winter of 1943–4 or the German counterattack in the summer 1944 was a long-term trend. The qualitative evidence also includes several instances of public and highly symbolic announcements of individuals forgoing revenge (e.g., I-22; I-24; Dalianis 1998:163). McNeill (1978:145) describes how violence ended in one of the villages he visited: "The mayor of the village of Methoni, a committed man of the right, asked the gendarmes to release two village boys who had been arrested after returning from serving with the guerrillas. He did so despite the fact that his own son had been killed in the war; and when the gendarmes decided to release the two suspects this sealed the political reconciliation within the village effectively and lastingly." What is interesting about this particular example is that the mayor's action came after the defeat of the rebels and the end of the war; therefore, it could not be based on an expectation of gain from future iterations or be a rational tit-for-tat strategy.

Finally, the qualitative evidence is chock-full with local interpretations that stress the role of obligation and gratitude. Stelios Perrakis (2006:116) provides an example from an interview he conducted in Manesi:

"In our village [local leftist leader Meidanis] was the one responsible for keeping the peace among the villagers and avoiding any persecutions of political opponents when the Left held the power. The Right appreciated this and, in their turn, refrained from any reprisals after the war. There were also no judicial actions against the Left since there had been no executions of reactionaries in our village." I pointed out that this was a far cry from what had happened in Gerbesi, just a few kilometers further along the road, and they agreed. Manesi was, indeed, a rare instance of an Argolid village that had been spared the fratricidal struggle that left so many scars elsewhere. Meidanis' relatives had … only praise for the rightwing elements of their own village who had sheltered them from overzealous officials or rightwingers from elsewhere, out of gratitude for what the Left under Meidanis' leadership had done during the war.

It is telling in this respect, that a right-wing man, who did not hesitate to give me a detailed account of how he victimized several leftists in the area, singled out Manesi as a village where he refrained from attacking anyone because he considered the behavior of his political rivals to have been exemplary (I-21).[60] Although this interpretation may be an ex post rationalization, it points to an important mechanism and should be taken seriously.

In general, instances of atypical nonviolence show that civil wars do not only foster vicious cycles of violence but also virtuous cycles of nonviolence. These virtuous cycles often become "institutionalized" into an ethos of solidarity, which is typically assumed, after the end of the war, to have predated it. By and large, the data suggest that atypical village behavior, both violent and nonviolent, is path-dependent and largely endogenous to the war.

9.11.4. Wrong Actors

In a few instances, the theory mispredicts the actor producing the selective violence observed.[61] These include raids by an insurgent unit during the peak of incumbent control (zone 1); although these originated in neighboring Arkadia, the unit members were from the Argolid and were able to move in an otherwise hostile environment using their local knowledge. Some of the incumbent cases are also instances of similar types of raids (Malandreni in t_2). Other cases signal the role of revenge as an emotion, when action is undertaken without any concern for risk. The Greek expression about the mental state of people who fall prey to vengeful emotions is that their "blood is boiling." Here I discuss three cases where emotions led to violent action under unfavorable control: Aghios Stefanos in t_1, Anifi in t_1, and Lirkia in t_2 – all cases where incumbent selective violence takes place in areas controlled, predominantly or fully, by the insurgents.

The role of revenge as an emotion is particularly visible in the case of Aghios Stefanos, a village located in the mountains and under solid rebel control. On 12 June, villagers captured the local EAM leader, Thanassis S. Michalopoulos, and handed him over to the Germans. The ringleader was his own cousin, Vassilis, who, along with the other villagers, had been alienated by Michalopoulos's use of local power to confiscate goods and threaten people. This action was taken in complete disregard of the consequences. Indeed, the following day, EAM men

---

[60] This also suggests the complementary character of revenge (i.e., negative and positive reciprocity). This man displayed absolutely no regret when recounting the various abuses he committed against his local rivals; the one moment in his interview when he flinched was when he recalled a man whose execution by firing squad he had worked to achieve in 1949 before learning that this man had previously helped his family; he kept reiterating his genuine regret about having transgressed the norm of positive reciprocity.

[61] There are four cases of incumbent violence in zone 4 (Anifi in t_1, Lirkia and Malandreni in t_2, and Malandreni in t_3), one case of incumbent violence in zone 5 (Aghios Stefanos in t_2), and four cases of insurgent violence in zone 2 (Mili in t_1, Lirkia, Berbati, Monastiraki in t_3).

arrested seven people, including Vassilis Michalopoulos. Three were executed publicly in the neighboring village of Karia on 13 June and three more a few days later. Vassilis himself was stoned to death in a public execution in the village of Kefalovriso during a mass rally attended by hundreds of villagers on 6 July (HAA/EDD 51/1945; 8/1947; I-9; I-79; I-91).

The effects of revenge can also be seen in the village of Lirkia in the western hills. Lirkia was solidly in EAM hands during the winter of 1943–4; there was no public dissension, and no violence was used. Despite this apparent tranquillity, not all of the villagers were happy with the state of things. As spring came, this unhappiness began to manifest itself. In April, the local EAM leader, a teacher named Panayotis Stathis, defied the wishes of EAM and ran in the elections to represent the area in the national meeting of the Political Committee of National Liberation (PEEA), EAM's attempt to set up a de facto government in Greece. After Stathis was elected, the Communist Party had to cancel the elections to force him out. This minor insubordination combined with the German mop-up operations in May to create a deterioration of the security situation in Lirkia. A German raid took place on 21 May. On 6 June, EAM arrested the local priest, Panayotis Papageorgiou, and his daughter to put pressure on his brother, a pro-German doctor in Argos whose wife also happened to be German. On 15 June, Stathis, Thanasis Karas, a local doctor described by the local BLO as "one of the most influential men in the ARGOLID, the most influential in the INACHOS valley,"[62] and two more men were arrested and taken to the EAM headquarters in Tatsi. There were two more arrests on 16 June, including Karas's wife, following the doctor's confession under torture of the existence of an imaginary ring of spies (I-79). The doctor was murdered that night. In the middle of all this, an EAM leader from the town of Argos with family connections in Lirkia stopped in the village on his way back from the PEEA meeting in central Greece. The young man's name was Iason Boukouras, and he was the son of a prominent Argos doctor. Apparently, some villager intent on revenge leaked this information to the arrested priest's son, Petros Papageorgiou, who was in Argos. Papageorgiou reported this information to the Germans who raided the village on 18 June. While the Germans surrounded the village, Boukouras tried to hide but was found, and Papageorgiou identified him publicly. Immediately, a German officer shot him. Papageorgiou's actions can be explained as the result of raw emotion, since his father and sister were EAM hostages and the village was under EAM control. Indeed, he paid the price. The next day, ELAS partisans returned to the village with the priest and his daughter in tow. After burying Boukouras, the partisans executed both. According to my respondents, just before his death the desperate priest called his son a "patricide and a fratricide" for his actions (HAA/EDD 242/1945; 15/1946; 334/1947; I-60).

The final example comes from the village of Anifi, a village of the outer plain that was in zone 4 during t_1. Anifi contained one of the region's most active EAM

---

[62] "Narrative of Capt P. M. Fraser. Peloponnese July 43–April 44" and "Names of Influential Personnel in Argolido Korinthia," PRO, HS 5/698/S6557.

cells and was a hotbed of insurgent political activity. In addition, several local men had joined the guerrillas. However, the village was also located close to the village of Merbaka (now Aghia Triada), which housed a small German outpost. In January 1944 EAM assassinated four villagers in Anifi, including the mayor. The assassinations helped to consolidate EAM control, although the village's proximity to the German outpost continued to impede the movements of the rebels. Yet, despite the proximity of the German outpost, no information flowed from the locals to the Germans until April 1944. On Palm Sunday, 9 April, the Germans conducted a major raid in Anifi. In the days leading up to the raid, the Germans had adopted a more aggressive stance, including bringing additional troops into the Argolid. On the previous day they had carried out a mass of targeted arrests in Nafplio, effectively decapitating the rebel organization in that town. The raid in Anifi proceeded with the Germans searching the houses and assembling all male inhabitants in the village center. For the first time, they had managed to obtain intelligence about the village. Indeed, they were accompanied by a hooded informer who proceeded to identify all local EAM cadres. Several men were arrested, including some important local leaders, and a young man was shot while trying to escape in the fields surrounding the village (he died of his wounds a few days later). Later in April, two senior leaders were shot in the concentration camp that the Germans had set up in Korinthos. The identity of the hooded man points directly to the motivation behind the denunciation to the Germans: he was a close relative of one of the men that EAM had assassinated in January. In fact, he was recognized by several villagers.[63] His decision to denounce the EAM cadres to the Germans was very risky, as the Germans had no control of Anifi and did not plan the raid with the goal to occupy it. They targeted it for a raid earlier than most other villages of the outer plain and eastern hills, including some that had a reputation of being more Communist, because of actionable intelligence; and they were able to obtain it because of the desire for revenge that was bred by the EAM assassinations. Unlike the previous two cases, however, this denunciation did not provoke retaliation, for reasons that remain unclear. German control was established sometime after these killings, when the Germans launched their large-scale mop-up operation across the region.[64] Eventually, they installed a small outpost in the village, consolidated their control, and provoked additional defections as several local men, some previously EAM members, joined the SBs.

To sum up, these three examples are vivid instances of how emotions may cloud judgment and lead to violence under conditions where rational assessment would preclude violence.

---

[63] According to my informants, someone snatched the hood off his head; according to some others, after having been recognized, he defiantly took his hood off himself.

[64] Not immediately, though. The absence of retaliation during this transition period may have been caused by the arrest of some local EAM men from Anifi who may have acted as hostages. Hostage taking was a somewhat limited practice in the Argolid that backfired most of the time, but sometimes it appears to have contained violence, as in the case of Lefkakia (I-54; I-88).

9.12. A REPLICATION: ALMOPIA

To increase the validity of the microcomparative test, I replicated my study in the region of Almopia, in northern Greece. Similar in size and ecological range, Almopia differed from the Argolid in terms of strategic location and ethnic composition. Although I did not conduct a study of depth similar to that of the Argolid, I was able to trace the main patterns of control and violence.

The district of Almopia, part of the prefecture of Pella, includes three kinds of terrain: plains, hills, and mountains. Its population of about thirty thousand in 1940 was almost all rural, distributed in forty-six villages, whose average size was close to six hundred, and one town. The history of the area reflects that of the broader region. Before its incorporation into the Greek state in 1913, Almopia was part of the Ottoman Empire. It was inhabited by Christian and Muslim peasants, mostly tenant farmers in large farms (*cifliks*) owned by Muslim landlords. The main languages spoken in the area were Turkish, a local Slavic language close to Bulgarian and contemporary Macedonian, Greek (mostly in the district's single town, Karatzova or Aridaia), and Vlach (a language close to Romanian spoken by the pastoralist Vlachs). Greek was the language of trade; the vast majority of the Christian population in the area (and the majority of Muslims who were of Slavic extraction) spoke the local Slav Macedonian. Until the late nineteenth century, religion provided the basis for the identification of the population, an institutional reflection of the *millet* system, which served as the foundation of Ottoman rule and spelled out the privileges and obligations of each religious community. However, the Christian population was divided by the rise of competing nationalisms during the late nineteenth century. Throughout Macedonia, competing agents of Greece, Serbia, Romania, and Bulgaria fought a shadow war in order to acquire the loyalty of Macedonia's mostly rural Christian population. The most intense conflict, which took the form of guerrilla war waged between competing bands, took place between Greece and Bulgaria. The ethnic cleavage found an appropriate ideological reflection in religion: the formation of an independent Bulgarian church (the Exarchate) challenged the membership monopoly of the Greek Orthodox Patriarchate of Constantinople (Istanbul) over the Christian population of the Ottoman possessions in Europe. Gradually, choosing the Patriarchate or the Exarchate became equivalent to picking a national identity and eventually becoming Greek or Bulgarian. This decision was often induced by violence (used by competing guerrilla bands) and reinforced by schooling through a concerted school-building effort made by the various Balkan states. Although this cleavage sometimes divided families, it ultimately produced new national identities that elicited loyalties so strong that two generations were enough to erase any memory of this initial "choice" (Karakasidou 1997; Danforth 1995).

Following the Balkan Wars of 1912–13, the region of Macedonia was divided into three parts; the largest was incorporated into the Greek state, with the two smaller parts going to Bulgaria and Serbia. These wars, fought with considerable ferocity, produced numerous atrocities and considerable ethnic cleansing (Carnegie Endowment for International Peace 1993). Although ethnic diversity decreased considerably following the Balkan Wars, Macedonia maintained a substantial degree of both religious and ethnic diversity. However, religious diversity in Greek Macedonia was destroyed in the wake of Turkey's defeat of Greece in their war of 1920–2 and the "exchange of populations" that followed. The Muslims left, and a wave of Christian refugees from Anatolia settled in their villages. Nevertheless, the region retained a multiethnic character, with the 1928 census listing 40 percent of the population as "Slavophones," 6 percent as Vlachs, and 54 percent as "refugees" (from Asia Minor).

The new settlers spoke a variety of languages, including Greek, Pontic, and Turkish, and were far from a unified population. Their arrival provoked intense competition along ethnic lines, spurred by the distribution of Muslim lands. Many of the local Slav Macedonian tenant farmers saw the lands they were hoping to acquire carved into smaller plots to accommodate the settlers. As a result, a "simple peasant population that was traditionally distrustful of all outsiders, particularly Greeks" (Rossos 1997:70), found even more reason to mistrust the refugees, whom they also perceived as foreigners. In turn, the refugees saw the Slav Macedonians as non-Greeks, speaking a language akin to that of an enemy of Greece, Bulgaria. Having been uprooted once, the settlers feared the prospect of new territorial changes and new population movements (Marantzidis 2001).

There is considerable evidence that these two groups – which spoke different languages, viewed each other with suspicion, did not intermarry, tended to identify with different nation-states, and competed for local resources – developed a pronounced hostility toward one another (Marantzidis 2001; Koliopoulos 1999; Yannisopoulou 1998). During the interwar years, substantial pro-Bulgarian activity in Almopia, including some guerrilla activity during the 1920s, met with repression by the Greek authorities. The Metaxas dictatorship's (1936–40) policy of forced linguistic assimilation of the Slav Macedonian populations increased the resentment of the Slavophone population in Almopia.

During Greece's occupation by German, Italian, and Bulgarian forces (1941–4), northern Greece witnessed a violent civil war greatly informed by ethnic polarization (Koliopoulos 1999; Kofos 1993). In the prefecture of Pella, as well as neighboring prefectures, mostly in western Macedonia, many Slav Macedonians joined a pro-Bulgarian militia, known as *komitadji* (a name harking back to the Macedonian guerrilla war of the late nineteenth and early twentieth centuries), even though the area was not occupied by the Bulgarian army. For its part, the Bulgarian army carried out an extensive program of ethnic cleansing and resettlement, expelling Greek populations from the areas of eastern Macedonia it occupied. The 1942–3 arrival in western Macedonia of these refugees greatly increased tensions between ethnic groups. These tensions exploded into civil war and violence during the occupation, and continued during the 1946–9 period. This civil war was informed by a patchwork of fluid nonethnic and ethnic motives and symbols often hiding below the master cleavage of left versus right. For example, the battles between the Communist partisans (ELAS) and collaborators (Greek National Army – EES) often turn out to be, on closer examination, *also* instances of conflict between Slav Macedonians and Turkish-speaking Greek settlers (Marantzidis 2001).

After the end of the occupation and the demobilization of the Communist partisans (1945–6), the reconstructed Greek state persecuted leftists and Slav Macedonians alike. Trials of collaborators were used as an opportunity for ethnically motivated persecution as well as the pursuit of all kinds of local feuds. As a result, many Slav Macedonians, both those who had participated in EAM but also many who saw action in the various collaborationist militias, fled across the border into the Republic of Macedonia, newly formed as part of socialist Yugoslavia. Whereas during the occupation many Slav Macedonians had claimed a Bulgarian identity and collaborated with the Bulgarian troops, many now claimed a Macedonian identity and looked up to Tito's Yugoslavia; many among them joined an independence movement (NOF) and a unit known as the First Aegean Brigade. Both organizations were closely allied with Yugoslav Macedonia's Communist authorities, who themselves maintained complex ties with the Greek Communists. At the mass level, there was a growing overlap between the Slavophone linguistic identity, the Slav Macedonian (or Macedonian) ethnic identity, and the propensity to side with the Communist Left in 1946–9. Although the overlap was not complete, with a significant minority of Slav Macedonians siding with the Greek government,[65] it is clear nonetheless that most Slav Macedonians either collaborated with or openly fought with the Greek Communist rebels between 1946 and 1949 – 85 percent according to one estimate (Rossos 1997:63). Conversely, many Greek settlers, especially in mixed villages, supported the Greek Right, even though they had been ardent supporters of the Liberal Party during the interwar period (Marantzidis 2001).

In short, although the Greek Civil War in Macedonia was by no means an ethnic war, it took on a pronounced ethnic character. The Slav Macedonians "made a significant, indeed a critical contribution to the communist side during the Civil War in Greece"; they bore the brunt of the war, since they inhabited the regions of Macedonia where the heaviest fighting took place. Their participation in the ranks of the rebel army was very high, "far out of proportion to their relatively low number in the total population of Greece at the time.... Their estimated representation in the DSE [the "Democratic Army of Greece," as the Communist rebel army was known] ranged from more than a quarter in April 1947 to more than two-thirds in mid-1949." By 1948 the Communist Party "had become almost totally dependent on the relatively small, mainly Macedonian-populated areas it held in central and western Macedonia." Importantly, however, the nature of the Slav Macedonians' participation in the Greek Civil War (at least at the elite level) was nationalist rather than Communist. The Communists were convenient allies in a struggle that was supposed to lead to secession from Greece and a merger with the Yugoslav Republic of Macedonia. For the NOF "it was primarily a national struggle, a battle for the national liberation of the

---

[65] These "Greekophile or assimilated Macedonians" were "derisively" called *Grkomani* by the militant Slav Macedonians (Rossos 1997:63), who frequently targeted them for raids. A Greek official, on the other hand, distinguished between *Slavophones* and *Slavophrones* ("Notes on Tour from Salonica to Verroia, Edessa and Kaimaksalan, September 11th and 12th, 1948," PRO FO 371/72327).

Macedonians in Aegean Macedonia" (Rossos 1997: 42, 43–4, 64, 42). Yet, despite this acute ethnic polarization, the homicidal violence against civilians in Almopia was much lower than I expected it to be – certainly lower than in the Argolid – during both the 1943-4 period and the 1946-9 period.

Because of its geographical outlook (an isolated region removed from vital communication axes), Almopia presented little interest to the occupation authorities, who effectively abandoned it. As a result, Communist partisans acquired effective control of the area from 1943 on. Many villagers saw occupation troops only once or twice during the entire period. The partisans executed some "reactionary" elements, but these executions remained rather limited (thirty to forty cases at most). Around eighty people were killed in an indiscriminate fashion during one mop-up operation conducted by German and Bulgarian troops in early 1944. No village experienced complete destruction and the population exhibited few signs of political division despite the prior ethnic and political polarization – something reflected in the interviews I conducted: most people do not remember this period as one of civil war. Having no choice but to support the group with an undisputed local sovereignty, EAM, the population did so in a unitary fashion. In the terms of the theory of selective violence, Almopia began as predominantly zone 5 with some villages in zone 4; it then moved (and remained) in zone 5. Consistent with the theory, the zone 4 villages, where security was more of a concern and where selective assassinations by EAM took place, tended to be in the lowlands, closest to the main road that linked the region with Pella's capital, the town of Edessa.

In a way, Almopia can be thought of as a counterfactual Argolid: had the occupation in Argolid ended in April 1944, there would have been no difference between the two areas in spite of the variation in the level of ethnic polarization. Location, which turned Almopia into an EAM safe haven, explains why violence was limited.[66] Neighboring areas (such as the neighboring district of Peonia in the prefecture of Kilkis or the prefectures of Kastoria and Kozani) experienced considerable levels of civil war violence despite a similar social and ethnic profile, mainly because of their strategic importance to the occupiers, who contested the territory.

Following the end of the occupation and the demobilization of the partisans in 1945, Almopia underwent a process similar to that of the rest of Greece: the reconstructed Greek state and bands of right-wing irregulars, mostly from neighboring areas, harassed and terrorized suspected leftists as well as many Slav Macedonians. Although "low-intensity" violence was considerable (many people were arrested and jailed, many were beaten up, property was looted, and some people fled across the border in order to escape), the homicide rate remained low. At the same time, an important realignment took place. Many people, mostly refugees, who had supported (actively or passively) the partisans during the occupation period switched sides and became right-wingers and royalists. Motivations

---

[66] Marantzidis (1997:158) reports a similar finding from the deeply divided villages of Georgianoi and Lefkopetra in the Imathia prefecture of northern Greece. The full control exercised by EAM during the occupation prevented their intense local cleavage from being articulated.

varied, but shifting expectations about who the eventual winner was going to be were key. In other words, Almopia moved into zone 1.

In 1946 the Communist Party launched its insurgency. Armed bands of partisans who had been training in Yugoslavia crossed the border and began harassing the gendarmerie stations, killing mayors, and mobilizing villagers. Its location on the border with Yugoslavia put Almopia at the front line of this civil war. Most Slav Macedonian villages, located in the eastern part of the district, contributed significant numbers of men to the insurgent Communist "Democratic Army." The fatalities in this period were substantial: some villages lost sixty to seventy men each. Yet, the great majority of fatalities were battlefield related. Very few civilians were killed during this period. Even though the Greek army regularly shelled some Slav Macedonian villages, and in one case the rebels raided a refugee village and murdered thirty-nine civilians in the single worst massacre of the war in this area, the violence against civilians in Almopia was limited compared with that of Southern Greece in 1943–4. In fact, the ratio of fighters to civilians killed in the Argolid and Almopia was almost the inverse.

Two factors related to the conduct of the war (and unrelated to the nature of cleavages) explain the difference between the Argolid and Almopia. First, over the course of 1948, the Greek army emptied most villages in Almopia in line with the traditional counterinsurgency method of separating the rebels from the population. Most villagers either left the area altogether or went to a refugee camp set up in the town of Aridaia. Some villagers, sympathetic to the rebel cause, crossed the border into Yugoslavia. As a result, after 1948 there were few potential civilian victims in rural Almopia. Second, starting in 1946, but especially in 1947 and 1948, most able-bodied men (as well as many women) were drafted into various military and paramilitary groups on both sides. This extensive militarization shifted violence from the civilian to the military sphere.

Although these factors help account for the low levels of violence against civilians, they still fail to fully explain the relatively low levels of violence against civilians *before* the evacuation of the villages and the mass conscription of men. My research suggests that, consistent with the theory, the low levels of violence were mainly due to the distribution of control among political actors in 1946–8. Most villages were located in areas that were equally accessible to both sides, that is, zone 3 areas. The army and the police visited the villages on a daily basis but could not prevent the rebels from coming in every night. In fact, it is this inability that led the army to its decision to evacuate all civilians to the town of Aridaia. In turn, the army was constrained by the presence of an international border: the rebels enjoyed a safe haven in Yugoslavia, a feature of the civil war in Almopia that gave them a tremendous advantage. What makes the case of Almopia particularly interesting is that ethnic polarization was trumped by the logic of control – an issue I explore in depth elsewhere (Kalyvas 2004).

9.13. OUT-OF-SAMPLE TESTS IN GREECE

In this section I examine village data from across Greece to ascertain if patterns of violence are consistent with the predictions of the theory. I use several sources:

first, a study of 13 villages conducted in 1951–2 by the Near East Foundation; second, a study of 5 villages conducted in 1947 by the historian William H. McNeill; third, data from 136 villages culled from ethnographic studies and local (mostly single village) histories, as well as interviews I conducted outside the Argolid. Though not a random sample of Greek villages, these data cover most of Greece and provide a general sense of the rural wartime experience across the country during the entire 1943–9 period (Table B.4 in Appendix B). Because the motivations of the writers and their sources are very diverse, no single bias dominates.

Besides allowing me to assess the extent to which the Argolid is representative of the rest of Greece, these tests allow me to evaluate whether patterns of violence match patterns of control across these villages in a way that is consistent with the theory. I do so both through a close examination of the evidence and by testing an additional observable implication of the theory: selective violence in 1943–4 should be observed in lower altitudes than selective violence in 1946–9. As pointed out earlier in this chapter, a key difference between the occupation and the postwar period was the state capacity of the incumbents. Unlike the Germans, who were only interested in and capable of controlling the main towns, roads, and railways and were willing to relinquish control of the mountainous hinterland to the rebels, the postwar Greek state was able to challenge the rebels directly in their strongholds. As a result, total incumbent control was generally uncommon even in the lowlands during the occupation, as was total insurgent control even in the highlands during the postwar period. Put otherwise, time serves as a proxy for the presence of incumbents in higher terrain and underlies the correlation between terrain and fragmented sovereignty. Because the theory predicts lower selective violence against civilians in zones of total control, we should observe a clustering of nonviolent villages in the highlands during the 1943–4 period (when they were likely to be fully controlled by the insurgents) and in the lowlands during the 1947–9 period (when they were likely to be fully controlled by the incumbents).[67] From an analytical perspective, the intermediate period of 1945–6 is closer to the occupation period, as the Greek state remained weak and left the field open to right- and left-wing irregular bands.

In short, low altitude should correlate with higher levels of selective violence in 1943–6 and with lower levels in 1947–9. Likewise, altitude should predict the timing of the internal division of villages. Local histories of lowland villages should tell a story of polarization and division during the occupation, and local histories of highland villages should locate the beginning of polarization during the postoccupation period. I would also expect highland areas that were contested between competing insurgent organizations during the occupation to resemble their lowland counterparts during the same period and exhibit selective violence. Finally, indiscriminate incumbent violence in 1943–4 should be more likely in villages located in higher ground: if my account of indiscriminate violence is

---

[67] Zone 3 should also be located in a lower altitude during the occupation (and vice versa). However, judging from the Argolid where most zone 3 villages shifted from or to zone 2 or 4, the (nonviolent) effect of zone 3 is likely to remain unobserved in the absence of a disaggregated measure of control.

TABLE 9.10. *A Typology of Greek Villages*

| | Selective Violence in 1947–9 | |
	No	Yes
Selective violence in 1943–6		
No	Type 1	Type 3
Yes	Type 2	Type 4

TABLE 9.11. *Descriptive Statistics*

Village Type	Frequency	Percent	Median Altitude (meters)	σ^2
1	26	19.12	420	321.6
2	36	26.47	125	310.4
3	55	40.44	730	283.1
4	19	13.97	460	393.5

correct, incumbents ought to indiscriminately target those villages under total rebel control. To structure the discussion of the patterns of violence across these villages, I distinguish between four types of villages based on the incidence of selective violence (Table 9.10).

Type 1 includes villages that remained nonviolent throughout the war; type 2 includes villages that experienced substantial selective violence during the occupation phase of the civil war (1943–4) with some lingering violence immediately thereafter (1945–6), before the authority of the Greek state could be fully reasserted, but no selective violence after 1946; type 3 includes villages that experienced either no violence at all or only indiscriminate violence during the occupation but suffered selective violence after 1946. Finally, type 4 includes villages that experienced selective violence during both periods. Because I am interested in the selective violence against civilians rather than battlefield violence, I coded only civilian homicides. To be consistent with the theoretical expectations, type 2 villages should be located in lower altitudes than type 3 villages. There is no clear geographical expectation for type 1 and 4 villages as there are multiple configurations of control compatible with them. Type 1 villages ought to be those that were either fully controlled by either side or in zone 3 throughout the entire decade, while type 4 villages should be those that were contested during both periods.[68] Figure 9.19 is a scatterplot of village type by altitude and population, while Table 9.11 summarizes the data on all 136 villages.

The findings support the posited relation between altitude and the timing of violence. Villages that experienced selective violence in 1943–6 (type 2) have a

---

[68] In classifying villages into these four types, I used a less stringent threshold than what I used in the Argolid study (one homicide per village); information is often lacking and my goal is to capture the broad patterns of violence.

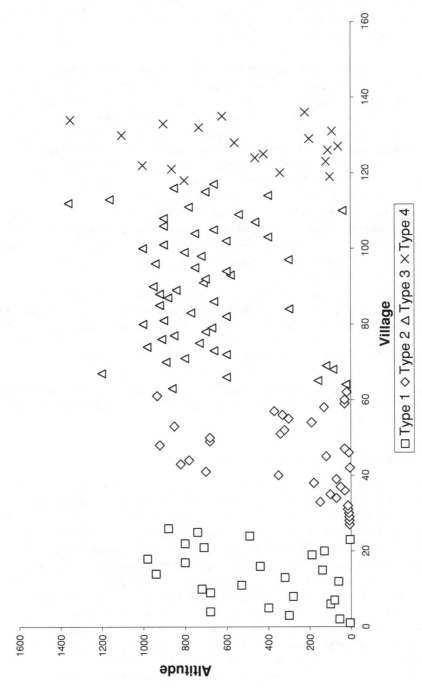

FIGURE 9.19. Village Type and Altitude

much lower median altitude than those that experienced selective violence in 1946–9 (type 3): 125 meters versus 730 meters. Unlike these two types, continuously peaceful and violent villages tend to display much less clustering in terms of altitude: their standard deviations are higher compared with those of type 2 and 3 villages.

This pattern also indicates that the Argolid, an area with primarily type 2 villages, is not representative of Greece as a whole (as indicated by its comparison with Almopia), but neither is it an outlier; in fact, the levels of differentiation induced by the war are such that it would be impossible to find a region that is representative of the entire country. It would be fair to say that the Argolid is representative of areas that experienced significant violence during the occupation period but remained relatively nonviolent in the following period, that is, type 2 areas. Irrespective of how representative the Argolid is, this test underlines the capacity of the theory of selective violence to explain both intraregional and interregional variation. The same argument that explains variation in selective violence inside the Argolid in 1943–4 can account for variation in the rest of the country across time periods. This further confirms the point made earlier that even though political actors differ across a variety of dimensions, their violence follows similar patterns.

Two additional empirical implications are also confirmed. First, the dynamics of violence among competing insurgent organizations during the occupation period generated dynamics that were similar to those produced by the interaction between incumbents and insurgents, though the overall intensity of violence is somewhat lower (Filos 2000). Second, type 3 villages were targeted more often by German indiscriminate violence during the occupation period than type 2 villages. In the following section, I examine in a more direct way the consistency of the theory with the patterns of control and violence that emerge from this body of evidence.

9.13.1. The Near East Foundation Study

Under contract from the U.S. Economic Cooperation Administration, the Near East Foundation produced a study of thirteen villages for the Greek Ministry of Agriculture in 1951–2. This study encompassed the entire ecological range of continental Greece, though irrigated lowland villages were overrepresented for reasons having to do with rural development priorities. This study was undertaken as a way to rationalize subsidies to agricultural production in the immediate postwar period (Sanders 1953). The villages studied are all located in central and northern Greece, thus providing a nice counterbalance to the Peloponnese. The study consists of thirteen "social surveys," that is, short reports of twelve to fifteen pages each that cover the history, social structure, and economy of the villages, with an emphasis on agricultural practices, while providing suggestions for improvement. They all include a short overview of the impact of the occupation and the civil war.[69] There is more longitudinal variation here than in the

---

[69] As far as I know, this study was never published and its results were not reported publicly.

Argolid study, because the study covers the entire civil war period until 1949. In terms of control, mountain villages approximate type 3, hill villages type 2, and plain villages are either type 1 or 2. The variation in the violence of plain villages is probably explained by the dynamics of control specific to the regions in which these villages are located. The study's identification of considerable social and political variation among plain villages with similar experiences of violence suggests that control trumps both political conflict and social structure in explaining the incidence of violence.

Consistent with the theoretical expectations, mountain villages were much more involved in the resistance against the occupation than hill or plain villages. Of the three mountain villages included in the study, two were not physically occupied at all; these zone 5 villages collaborated with the insurgents, and some men became partisan fighters; one village suffered an indiscriminate German attack that killed five villagers. In contrast, the third mountain village looks like a zone 1 village: it was physically occupied mainly by the Italians, who used repression to control it, though short of killing. During the postwar period, all three mountain villages became contested territory in which the insurgents had the upper hand but lacked full control (zone 4). Initially, they used selective violence successfully to move them to zone 5. The period of rebel ascendancy was of short duration, however, as the Greek army was able to evacuate the villagers to the towns it controlled.

The two hill villages included in the study were under Bulgarian occupation. One did not suffer selective violence, while the other did: twenty-three families fled and ten villagers were killed; no details are provided, however. There was no selective violence there in 1946–9, as both villages were controlled by pro-government local militias. According to the author of the study, the location of the second village near the plain of Serres "helped ward off the guerrillas."

Finally, the eight plain villages display a range of variation. In the first phase of the war, five of them were under one or another form of German control. At least one of these villages is reported to have been physically occupied by the Germans, while the others ranged between zone 1 and zone 2. In terms of violence, one of these five villages experienced no violence at all during the occupation, in two villages the Germans arrested and deported several villagers but killed no one, whereas the last two villages suffered seven and nine deaths, respectively, at the hands of either the Germans or the collaborationists. An interesting piece of information comes from one of these villages, Anthili, where German "terror was greatest when the underground movement headed by EAM began to infiltrate the village," indicating a village of zone 2. In short, the picture in these five villages is one of either nonhomicidal violence or selective violence that contrasts sharply with the indiscriminate violence experienced by the mountain villages and matches the experience of the Argolid lowland. The control situation in the remaining three plain villages is complicated by the fact that two competing insurgent organizations, EAM and the non-Communist National Democratic Greek League (EDES), were vying for control over them. As expected, each of these three villages experienced some degree of selective violence. In one village,

EDES killed a man, in another EAM killed four, and in the last there were killings but neither the number nor the perpetrator was recorded. Again, this pattern suggests that violence appears to follow a similar dynamic whether the war pits occupiers against natives, collaborationist militiamen against resistant fighters, or resistant fighters against each other. During the second phase of the war, six out of these eight plain villages experienced some nonhomicidal violence (arrests) or no violence at all.[70] One of the remaining villages saw two men killed by the incumbents, while the other suffered a devastating attack by the rebels, in which forty individuals were abducted; of those, twenty-six managed to escape and return, and fourteen were killed (no information is provided to allow the classification of this violence into selective or indiscriminate).[71] The reports are very clear about the cause of the relative absence of violence in the majority of the plain villages: their location made them inaccessible to the rebels. Given the great range of variation in indicators for some alternative explanations, including social divisions over land ownership (Evinohori), political loyalties and affiliations (Kymina), and ethnic polarization (Kalohori), the by-and-large uniform behavior of the plain villages confirms the importance of control. Finally, there seems to be no path-dependent effect among these villages: villages that experienced violence during the occupation were as likely to be nonviolent during 1947–9 as villages that experienced no violence.

Overall the data contained in the NEF study are consistent with the predictions of the theory. Three features are worth stressing. First, the comparison between the first and second phase of the civil war clearly shows that geography is a better proxy for military resources rather than for social structure. Villages that were "peaceful" during the first period became violent during the second, and vice versa; what changed was the dynamics of the war, not their social or political profile. Second, when control and geography diverge, control clearly trumps geography: it is telling that the single mountain village that was incumbent controlled behaved very much like incumbent villages in the plain. Finally, contested villages show similar patterns of violence whether they were contested by the insurgents and the occupiers, by rival insurgent organizations, or by the insurgents and the Greek state.

9.13.2. McNeill Study

The distinguished American historian William H. McNeill spent considerable time in Greece after 1944 fulfilling various diplomatic functions. He has written extensively on several aspects of the Greek Civil War. In one of his books, *The Metamorphosis of Modern Greece*, he reports on five villages that he visited repeatedly over a period stretching for more than forty years – four of them beginning

---

[70] Several men were killed in some of these villages as soldiers in the army, in battles against the rebels away from their villages. In one village (Anthili), twenty-two men joined the rebels in 1947–9.

[71] This village (Nea Nikomidia) was the only one in the plain that experienced no violence at all during the occupation. Unfortunately, the report contains very little additional information. In any case, I coded it as type 3 – it is one of the outliers of this type.

in 1947, in the midst of the war (Table B.4 in Appendix B).[72] Again plain villages are overrepresented, with three, versus one hill village and one mountain village. Three of the villages are in northern Greece, one is in southern Greece, and one is in central Greece. McNeill's insights are invaluable, with the richness of participant observation funneled through the analytical mind of a great historian. His findings are consistent with the theoretical expectations.[73]

The first village McNeill reports about is Methoni, a plain village located just under Mount Olympus in north-central Greece, which approximates type 3 (i.e., nonviolent during the occupation, but violent afterward). The population included native Greeks and Greek refugees from Anatolia; following the 1927 land reform, every family farmed equal farm plots, leaving little basis for class divisions. Though a lowland village, it was controlled by EAM during the occupation because its location was not strategically attractive to the occupiers (zone 5). Hence, like the Almopia plain villages, this was a village where the effect of geography can be disentangled from that of control. Predictably, about twenty local young men joined ELAS. During the war, McNeill reports, opinion within the village was about evenly divided between families that sympathized with EAM and others who distrusted the leftists. However, the dominance of EAM suppressed the expression of dissent. As expected, the repression fell short of homicidal violence. The situation changed in 1945, when EAM dominance was replaced with a "precarious" dominance of the right, during which leftist elements roamed the mountains. When McNeill visited in 1947, he found that "only a few villagers ever committed themselves irrevocably to one side or the other, by carrying arms or acting in some public leadership position either for or against EAM. The majority remained passive, hoping to avoid being singled out as an enemy by one party or the other." He noticed widespread distrust: "No one was sure of his neighbor," and "fear was close at hand all the time." In other words, the situation was approximating that of zone 2, with armed men patrolling the village "keeping a wary eye on known or suspected leftists," and rebels nearby but unable to enter the village on a regular basis. After a successful guerrilla raid, some fifteen persons from the village were arrested by the army, "on suspicion of having helped the guerrillas reach their goal; one of them was executed." This use of selective violence helped tip the village into zone 1. There was no more violence in Methoni after the guerrilla band was forced to leave the area.

The second village McNeill visited was Old Corinth, in the Korinthia prefecture of the Peloponnese, north of the Argolid. A clearly type 2 village, it was unusual in its sharp class polarization: about one-fifth of the village population was landless and had been strong EAM supporters during the occupation. This village most closely matches the experience of the outer plain villages of the Argolid. There was significant selective violence on both sides, and McNeill alludes to shifts in control. As in the Argolid, however, the village's location eliminated the prospect of guerrilla warfare after 1945. Lacking high mountains and being close

---

[72] He also writes about a sixth village, but provides almost no information about the civil war.
[73] References in the discussion come from McNeill (1978:138–205).

to Athens, the area of Old Corinth was not propitious for guerrilla war and, as a result, the village's acute social polarization could not find an outlet in insurgent action during the second phase of the civil war. As a result, the total domination of the Right brought an end to homicidal violence.

Kerasia, a hill village on Mount Pelion, in north-central Greece, was the third village studied by McNeill. The village had two sections, one in the upper part of the mountain (Upper Kerasia), where the villagers spent their summers grazing their sheep, and one in the low hills (Lower Kerasia), where they wintered. During the occupation it was firmly under EAM control and the villagers, for the most part, sympathized with EAM. Many young men joined the guerrillas, and the upper village was destroyed in an indiscriminate German reprisal. In 1945 the village came under the dominance of the Right (zone 1). "Even the professed and vocal leftists of the village," McNeill reports, "freely admitted that they voted for the return of the king in September 1946 (after [a] rightist raid) just to keep out of trouble." In late 1946, however, a leftist insurgent band was formed in the mountain, and the village shifted to zone 3. The upper village became a guerrilla encampment, and the lower village "found itself in the intersecting position of falling by day within the jurisdiction of a Greek army detachment stationed at Kanalia, some three or four miles out into the plain; whereas at night the guerrillas came down from the heights above and took control of the community." A covert but effective rebel committee structure was set up to assess and gather contributions from individual families for the insurgents' support. During this period there were beatings and house burnings on both sides. However, there was no deadly violence. Soon after McNeill left, in March 1947, the village was evacuated by the Greek army and its inhabitants moved to a refugee camp near Volos. Although they hated the refugee camp, these predominantly leftist villagers complied readily with the authorities. "Everyone knew that any obvious shift in the balance of forces could soon result in the melting away of the mass of followers from either side," notes McNeill, and this is precisely what happened.

The mountain village of Kota in northern Greece was firmly under insurgent control (zone 5) when McNeill visited (he does not provide any information about the occupation period, which probably did not affect this village). During his visit the village faced an acute food crisis and starvation loomed. According to McNeill, "since neither Greek nationalism nor Communist revolution offered any sort of practical solution to their difficulties, political ideology was at a low ebb. The two guerrilla soldiers were apolitical and illiterate, less interested in abstract causes than in posing for a photograph, glaring at the camera fiercely amidst an array of bandoliers and guns." No violence is reported, but McNeill was unable to collect much information.

The study's last village is Lofiskos, a type 1 village in the plain of Thessaly, in central Greece. McNeill first visited in the 1950s, so his description is much less precise. He notes the village's radical bent, inherited from the days of struggle against a Greek landlord: "EAM's line, accusing the rich of collaboration, probably struck a sympathetic chord in the minds of most villagers. But political commitment was tepid, one way or the other, and the restoration of Athens' authority in the spring of 1945 created no particular problems either." There was no guerrilla band nearby, "thus the war and its hardships passed Lofiscos by, leaving remarkably little residue in anyone's memory at the time I first began asking questions of the inhabitants." In other words, control trumped political preferences in shaping behavior. Overall, McNeill's five visit reports are consistent with my theoretical expectations.

9.13.3. Ethnographies and Local Histories

In this section, I review some village ethnographies and local histories that provide enough detail to allow for an assessment of how the theory accounts for variation accross the entire country.[74] Though hardly a systematic test, this additional out-of-sample test provides additional support for the theory.

Twenty-six villages in the sample (19.1 percent) can be classified as type 1; they did not experience any homicidal violence throughout the 1940s. They include plain villages controlled by the incumbents in both periods of the civil war; hill and mountain villages controlled by the insurgents during the occupation and the incumbents during the second period; mountain villages that were evacuated before they experienced any violence; villages that experienced a combination of full control and parity; and villages that deviate from the theory, where mutual protection trumped the incentives for denunciation.

Overall, I found relatively few detailed accounts of the events that took place in these villages, not entirely surprising since nonviolence typically makes for a nonstory. An inhabitant of Eleohori, a hill village that was controlled by the Germans because the train line passed through it, told me that the village escaped "because we had the Germans inside the village. The train was here, so the Germans were here. The Germans did not come to hurt us" (I-25). The same was true for villages controlled by the insurgents. An informant from the mountain village of Kerasia (800 meters; in the Achaia prefecture of the Peloponnese) explained to me why his village escaped violence during the 1947–9 period: "The rebels were totally dominant, there was no army around here, and the people did what they were told by the rebels" (I-51). One type 1 village for which there is a detailed account is Fourtzi in the Messinia prefecture of the Peloponnese (Balta 2002). Insurgents controlled this hill village during the occupation; some villagers genuinely preferred and supported EAM, while some joined because they had no choice. When asked, a villager told Nasi Balta (2002:180): "Yes, I did not agree [with EAM] but I was law-abiding, and at the time the law of EAM was dominant everywhere, the area was controlled by EAM." During this period, some people were arrested, but no one was killed. Following the end of the occupation, a local right-wing chieftain who was responsible for several atrocities in the region spared Fourtzi because of kinship ties with several local families,

---

[74] A few village names are pseudonyms, following the practice of some anthropologists to disguise the true names of their field sites.

thus preempting the vicious cycle of violence and counterviolence that took place in several surrounding villages. At the same time, the testimonies point to the development of a norm of reciprocal protection between rival villagers. Balta (2002:187) concludes her study stating that "ideology comes ex post to provide a name, give shape, and justify choices which may contain an ideological element but are due to more complex causes; very often, ideology necessarily follows, as in the case of many EAM supporters who joined the communist party after having been persecuted as fellow-travelers.... Many people found themselves on one or the other side because their family had been 'colored' in a certain way, or because its members were persecuted even though they themselves had not participated in politics."

Thirty-six villages in the sample approximate type 2 (26.5 percent); these villages experienced substantial violence during the occupation phase of the civil war (1943–4) but limited or no violence thereafter. These villages, which underwent several control shifts during the occupation period, are mainly located in the plains and hills. Most villages of the Argolid would be included here.

An unusually detailed study of a type 2 village was conducted by the anthropologist Stanley Aschenbrenner (1987) in the village of Karpofora, a plain village in the Messinia prefecture of the Peloponnese. This small village experienced twenty-three deaths – eighteen during the occupation and five in the immediate postwar period. According to the villagers, once begun, the violence there became a vicious cycle of action and reaction that could not be broken; these actions, they said, seemed senseless to them in retrospect. Aschenbrenner documents eight control shifts from zone 2 to zone 4 and back in 1943–4. He also was able to map the exact local cleavage that informed loyalties and violence, namely a factional divide between coalitions of families.

Most of the type 2 villages came under total or incomplete incumbent control early after the end of the occupation, in 1945; they were brought firmly under incumbent control after 1946 and experienced little violence thereafter. At the same time, there is a small cluster of type 2 villages located in higher elevations. The majority of these villages is located in the Peloponnese where the rebels were very weak during the 1947–9 war, hence the nonviolence during that period. In addition, some evidence exists indicating a process of learning that helped to turn the experience of violence during the occupation into local preemptive peace deals later (a mechanism that is close to mutual deterrence but diverges from it). I was able to locate some evidence of preemptive peace deals in some villages of the Argolid mountains where violence could have erupted in 1947–9 but did not. As the leader of a local insurgent committee in the village of Lirkia told me: "At that point the [right-wing] mayor of the village was Dimitris Kolovos, but I had approved him first. When he was offered the post, he called me up and told me that he was going to accept only if I approved of it. I told him to go ahead and accept. Things are not going well, I said, and the bad times are going to come back, so at least let's protect the village to prevent what happened during the occupation. We made a deal. And we kept it" (I-60). Another village leader, from the village of Karia, described a similar process and concluded: "We were wiser; we knew; we learned" (I-117).[75]

In addition to these thirty-six villages, several regional studies provide evidence that a similar pattern of violence could be observed in broader regions, such as the plain of Thessaloniki in northern Greece (Glaveris 1998), the plain of Kozani, also in northern Greece (Georgiadis 2004; Kallianiotis 2002, 2001), several areas of western and eastern Macedonia (Marantzidis 2001), and the hills and mountains of Korinthia in the Peloponnese (Rigas 1998; Balafoutas 1981; Bouyoukos 1973).

Type 3 villages are the most common in the sample, possibly a reflection of selection bias in the local history literature.[76] The fifty-five villages in the sample (40.4 percent) experienced either no violence at all or only indiscriminate violence during the occupation period, but suffered extensive selective violence during the last phase of the civil war. Most of these villages are located in higher altitudes where the insurgents had an overwhelming advantage during the occupation (zone 5) period but lost it when challenged by the Greek state. This depressed their violent potential during the occupation but failed to do so during the postwar period, while also contributing to incumbent violence.

For example, the village of Ambéli in the island of Evia, in central Greece, is an instance where "the village split naturally into Left and Right, with some of the Left helping the Communists out of sympathy, those of the Right out of fear – neither however, at any rate in the beginning, aware of the real political movements in which they were so disastrously taking part" (du Boulay 1974:237). After the end of the war, however, insurgent rule waned only to reappear in 1947; these control shifts were associated with high levels of selective violence. Another such village is Lia in the Epirus mountain of Mourgana, next to the Albanian border, the home of the journalist Nicholas Gage, who later told the story of his family in an international best seller, *Eleni* (1984). Lia experienced relatively little violence during the occupation; a collaborator of the Italians was killed, some villagers were beaten up in the context of the internecine struggle between EAM and EDES, and many houses were burned down during a German raid in April 1944. The village was eventually brought under firm EAM control, and the population collaborated with the insurgents. Hearing of the renewed fighting in 1946–7 by the reformed rebel army in nearby Macedonia, the villagers of Lia discussed them "like reports of a local team's victories in a distant country" (1984:157). The village soon came under renewed insurgent control, but in the

---

[75] These deals were possible in a context where one of the parties, the rebels in this case, was too weak to pressure its local representatives, but still represented a substantial threat, especially given their past reputation.

[76] This bias may operate in a number of ways: people from villages that underwent violence during a period tainted by collaboration with the occupation may have been less willing to write about it; villages that experienced a longer insurgent presence could have become more sympathetic toward the rebels and, therefore, people were more willing to tell the story of the defeated side; or mountain villages being poorer were more likely to produce teachers, the primary authors of village histories, who were also likely to sympathize with the rebels.

spring and summer of 1948 the army pressure grew so great that a group of villagers fled the village for the safety of government-held areas in July 1948. The rebels reacted by ordering the execution of five villagers. This episode became the tragic conclusion of Gage's book, whose mother did not manage to flee and was executed for arranging her family's escape.

Most villages of the mountainous region of Evritania in central Greece were type 3. The strategic importance of this area being limited, the occupiers mostly left it unmolested; the villages were never physically occupied (Collard 1989:101). The Italians initially, and the Germans later, launched occasional mop-up raids, but were uninterested in establishing a permanent presence. Although most villagers were royalist in the prewar period, they collaborated with the insurgents during the occupation because they were the only authority. In fact, the area became known as a stronghold of EAM, which was able to develop into a fully operational state – one that was much more effective and "dense" than the prewar Greek state had been (Woodhouse 1948). Its short-lived "government," the Political Committee of National Liberation, was headquartered in an Evritania village. Overall, there was little selective violence during that period beyond occasional arrests and a few public executions that conveyed the message that EAM was the new authority. The population complied on the basis of the kinds of motivations described in Chapter 5.

Evritania became polarized after the end of the occupation, when the Greek government began to reassert its authority by persecuting people who had collaborated with EAM. As a result, when the Communists launched a new insurgency in 1947, they found willing supporters among those who had been mistreated and were eager for revenge. A new round of violence followed against perceived right-wingers, and the region was engulfed in a process of contestation, with the insurgents asserting their control over most of the area before being defeated in 1949.

An unusually detailed unpublished memoir by Ioannis G. Kolimenos highlights the key events of the period in the village of Dafni, in Evritania.[77] He provides a description of life in his village, stressing the tension between norms of solidarity and the frequent disputes between individuals and villages. Dafni was raided a few times by Italian troops but escaped destruction and indiscriminate violence. The author describes how he was initially forced to join EAM's political organization, being one of the few educated men of the village, and how he became a true supporter with time. The rebels only needed to beat up a few people to establish their authority, he recalls, but did not have to kill because everyone complied, begrudgingly or not. However, the balance of power shifted in 1945, and it was then the Right's the turn to impose its rule. The villagers complied with the new authorities, and the village was able to escape from the abuses of the right-wing bands that terrorized the region. However, things changed again in 1947, with the Communist insurgency. Kolimenos recalls the celebration of Easter 1947 as the last instance of a harmonious communal celebration.

---

[77] I am grateful to Dimitri Kastritsis for sharing this memoir with me.

The spread of the insurgency and the inability of the army to maintain control of the mountain villages forced the leaders of the village right-wing faction to move to the capital of Evritania, the town of Karpenisi, but many villagers stayed behind. At that point, the village was split both politically and geographically. The rebels resurrected their local organization and reasserted their authority in the village, but could not prevent the army from visiting the village. Starting in May 1947, they killed seven people whom they accused of being informers for the army, thus fanning the hatred between the two sides. The author, by then the local leader of the Left, describes how he was accused by the rebels of hedging and how he was pressured to denounce his right-wing neighbors, even though he had reached a modus vivendi with them – an instance of how local deals that could potentially foster norms of reciprocity can be undermined under unfavorable conditions of control (here zone 4). In July 1948 the army raided the area, assisted by local militias composed of village "exiles," the men who had left earlier for Karpenisi. During this raid, the militia massacred fifteen men and women accused of collaborating with the rebels. Kolimenos provides a detailed account of this massacre with an emphasis on its entirely local character, which included killings between close relatives. He was lucky to escape just before the army arrived, and this apparently saved his wife's life after she was captured by the militia, since her captors would have to fear his future retaliation if they killed her. Seven months later, in February 1949, the rebels attacked Karpenisi, defeated the army, and occupied the town for a short time. Thirteen right-wing villagers, including several women, were either killed during the battle or executed after it ended. The army counterattacked soon after, and the war ended that same year with the defeat of the rebels. The author was arrested, served two years in prison, and returned to the village where he was subjected to petty harassment by his local rivals. The description of the events in Dafni matches most descriptions of type 2 villages – both in memoirs (e.g., Nassis's description of the events in Malandreni in the Argolid) or by ethnographers (e.g., Aschenbrenner's description of Karpofora). The only differences are that the violence in Dafni occurred in 1947-9 whereas the violence in Malandreni took place in 1943-4 and the incumbents were different actors. Carbon-copy descriptions exist for several villages of Evritania, including Aghia Triada, Petralona, Domiani, Vraha, Kleistos, Fourna, Hohlia, Papparousi, Dytiki Fragista, Kastania, Helidona, and Marathea, all of which suffered tens of deaths in the post-1947 period (Hunter 2003; Sakkas 2000; Zevgaras 1999; Vrana 1999; Triantafyllis 1997). Regional studies of the Karditsa-Domokos and Agrafa-Karditsa areas of central Greece by Magopoulos (1998; 1990) confirm this pattern. Several villages in the mountains of Messinia, Arkadia, and Achaia in the Peloponnese also underwent similar violence. At the same time, it is possible to find a few villages in Evritania that were able to escape most of the violence during the same period; these include Aghios Haralambos (Sakkas 2000:202), Chryso (Koutelos 1999), and Koryschades (Sarris 1998). Unfortunately, details are scant how these villages were able to escape violence, but the few references suggest local deals involving mechanisms of reciprocity under unfavorable conditions of control.

Finally, the nineteen type 4 villages (14 percent of the sample) include both mountain villages that experienced internecine violence between insurgent organizations during the occupation before becoming contested between incumbents and insurgents in 1947–9, and hill villages that, for various reasons mostly related to location, were contested in both periods. The mountainous village of Mesohora (800 meters) in central Greece is an example of the first instance and the hill village of Skala (100 meters) in the southern Peloponnese is an example of the second.

The diverse experiences of all these villages have shaped the memories of their inhabitants in predictable ways. Those who lived in villages that underwent violence primarily during the occupation describe this period as the "real civil war," which was worse compared with the postwar civil war (e.g., Papandreou 1992:94). In contrast, the "social memory" of the inhabitants of villages that experienced violence primarily during the postwar period stresses their experience during 1947–9 at the expense of the occupation period, the memory of which remained positive (Collard 1989:93–4). Likewise, the moment when their community became polarized and "broke down" is placed by the former in the occupation period and the latter in the postwar period.

9.14. CONCLUSION

The theory of selective violence identifies subnational and even subregional variation in the distribution of control as crucial; thus, testing the theory requires data collected at the subnational level. Because of the dearth of such data, I have used a dataset I collected in a Greek region by traveling to each village in the sample, talking to the inhabitants, and cross-checking their statements with information from local, national, and international archives. Although the data are from Greece, there is nothing uniquely Greek about the patterns of violence and nonviolence it reveals. The theory of selective violence is shown to be robust to several different tests. On the one hand, dominant but incomplete control did indeed lead to violence both cross-sectionally and across time: areas largely but not totally controlled by one warring group (zones 2 and 4) were significantly more likely to see selective homicidal violence than villages in which control was either complete or completely fragmented; and as patterns of control in villages shifted, the pattern of violence in those villages tended to shift as the theory predicts. In addition, areas where control was equally shared by rival armed factions were, for the most, surprisingly nonviolent, despite strong pressures for denunciation.

At the same time that the evidence offers support for the theory of selective violence, the data undercut several popular alternative hypotheses, finding, for example, little evidence that fear, breakdown, lack of discipline, ideology, or prewar social and political polarization can account for the observed patterns of violence and nonviolence.

Like any theory of human behavior, the theory of selective violence does not correctly predict all cases. In many ways, these mispredictions are the best proof of the value of a well-specified theory: being able to ask why a place is more or less violent than should generally be expected is a powerful tool for grasping the causal mechanisms at work, while providing opportunities to observe the workings of important noninstrumental mechanisms such as emotions and norms. Beyond this, additional testing in diverse settings should contribute to further theoretical development on this front. Initial results from ongoing research using detailed microlevel data from Vietnam (Kalyvas and Kocher 2004) and Colombia (Salamanca Núñez 2005; Chacón 2003) are broadly consistent with the theory.

10

Intimacy

"And let's not yet say whether war works evil or good," I said, "but only this much, that we have in its turn found the origin of war – in those things whose presence in cities most of all produces evils both private and public."

Plato, *The Republic*

I should not return to Uyo, for my people were after my blood.

Jeremiah Mose Essien, *In the Shadow of Death: Personal Recollections of Events during the Nigerian Civil War*

All the terrible things come from inside the village, not from outside.

A Greek villager

After he had confronted his old friend and neighbor Sir Ralph Hopton, Sir William Waller called the English Civil War a "warr without an Enemie" (quoted in McGrath 1997:91). For him, the real enemy could only be foreign and unfamiliar.

Civil war fails to supply such enemies, for it is mostly an intimate war taking place "on home ground against the home-grown" (Donagan 1994:1137). Even when civil war supplies foreign enemies, as is the case with occupation and foreign intervention, the foreigners acquire local allies who tend to focalize the antagonism of their local rivals.

Intimacy is essential rather than incidental to civil war: it defines "civil war in its most basic sense" (Ash 1995:125); it is a "fratricidal" war "against our selves, our brothers," as the English Civil War was described by contemporary participants (Donagan 1994:1166); it divides families, pitting brothers and sisters, parents and children, against each other (e.g., S. Dillon 1991:xiii; West 1985:132). In the Guatemalan village she studied, Judith Zur (1998:72) was told that "brother fought brother, sons fought their fathers, killings occurred between spouses and fear (*miedo*) caused pregnant women to miscarry. The end of the world, as foretold in the Bible, had arrived."[1] As a participant pointed out, not without some irony, "At least, we know whom we kill" (quoted in Bouthoul 1970:448). In short, civil war is barbaric also *because* it is the war of neighbor against neighbor, friend against friend (Montherlant 1965).

The intimate character of violence in civil war is puzzling only because we tend to assume the inherent goodness of intimate relations (e.g., Toolis 1997:3; Bailey 1996). The word *neighbor* evokes mutual concern and even obligation, as in the biblical injunction to love one's neighbor (Tymowski 2002:298). Jan Gross (2001) called his study of the massacre of the Jewish people of Jedwabne in the hands of their Polish co-villagers *Neighbors* precisely to underscore this point. No wonder, then, that we are both shocked and fascinated by civil war violence. In proclaiming his wish "to understand how neighbors are turned into enemies, how people who once had a lot in common end up having nothing in common but war," Ignatieff (1998:35, 46) highlights his puzzlement: "The transformation of brothers into enemies has puzzled the human imagination at least since Genesis. For Genesis begins the story of mankind not with a murder between strangers, but between brothers. It is precisely because the difference between them is so slight that the roots of the crime remain so mysterious."

It is generally thought that people are reluctant to exercise violence against those whom they know; acquaintance, it is believed, tends to decrease ferocity (van Creveld 1991:137). It is easier, Sudhir Kakar (1996:29) notes, "to kill men who are strangers, to obliterate faces which have not smiled on one in recognition, and to burn houses which have never welcomed one as a guest." "There is no man," concurs Madame de Staël (1818:116), "not even the most criminal, whom we can detest when we know him, as we do when he is only delineated to us." Traditionally, warfare has edged toward barbarization when the enemies were infidels, outsiders, and "savages" (Howard 1994); indeed, parties to civil wars

---

[1] Fratricide is used more as a metaphor for the intimacy of violence than as an actual description. Thucydides' account of the civil war in Corcyra includes a reference to "fathers [who] killed their sons" (3.81). Horowitz (1985:184) notes how ethnic conflict is often articulated in a "sibling idiom." Actual cases of close relatives fighting against each other tend to be rather unusual. Nevertheless, there are a few examples. The Chissano brothers were in opposite camps during Mozambique's war of independence. Joaquim Chissano was a high-ranked leader of the rebel group FRELIMO, who went on to become this country's president, while his brother served as a lieutenant in the Portuguese army (Henriksen 1983:107). A South Vietnamese lieutenant colonel, Tran Ngoc Chau, had a brother who was a North Vietnamese intelligence officer of the same rank (Ellsberg 2003:116); Pavone (1994:267) mentions a similar case from the Italian resistance, and Zur (1998:88) reports several instances of women's brothers being involved in the murder of their husbands. A few of my informants in Greece told me about internal divisions in their family (e.g., I-33), though not about actual violence between family members. Often, this is the result of contingency rather than of a conscious choice. In Cambodia, "each family in the liberated zone was required to provide one son to the Revolution Army; but General Lon Nol's army offered each new recruit a salary equivalent to the loss of earnings from two sons, so brother would find himself armed against brother" (Bizot 2003:146). For all their ghastly violence, civil wars do not sever irrevocably the bonds they strain so horribly. Many fighters in the Lebanese civil war "had been friends with their enemies on the other side of the line, and many would become friends again once the war was over" (M. Johnson 2001:125).

engage in sustained efforts to portray their enemy as a foreigner, an outsider, an "other." In his famous experiments, Stanley Milgram (1974) found that decreasing the distance between victimizer and victim significantly reduced the likelihood of obedience-driven violence. Indeed, armies have made considerable efforts to increase the psychological distance between their soldiers and their potential targets in order to facilitate killing (Grossman 1995).[2]

At the same time, however, there is massive criminological evidence suggesting that criminal homicide is often intimate. A large part of nonpredatory common murder implicates relatives, friends, or at least acquaintances, and the relationship between victims and assailants is horizontal: people tend to kill their mates, friends, and acquaintances rather than their bosses (Katz 1988:21–2).[3] Hence the following paradox. On the one hand, political violence and criminal violence are generally considered to be opposite phenomena lying at either end of a spectrum: political violence is thought to be impersonal, public, and collective, whereas criminal violence is largely personal, private, and intimate (Decker 1993; Black 1993, 1976). Yet, on the other hand, selective violence in civil wars exhibits a surprising similarity to criminal violence: it is often intimate and private. The theory of selective violence entails an interpretation of the intimate character of violence in civil war that also solves this paradox.

This chapter examines the implications of the theory of selective violence for the oft-noted intimate character of violence in civil wars. The theory suggests a set of counterintuitive implications, which depart from prevailing views that stress either the effects of ideological or identity-based polarization and hatred, or the consequences of random and anomic violence. Rather than just signaling the politicization of private life, the theory suggests, intimate violence also reflects exactly the opposite process: the privatization of politics.

Although the theory of selective violence accounts for the political actors' demand of information and predicts *where* individuals will denounce or refrain from denouncing, it is agnostic about *why* individuals respond to demands for information by denouncing. I begin with a discussion of denunciation and suggest that it constitutes a key microfoundation of intimate violence. I discuss the sociology of denunciation and provide evidence about its frequently malicious and private character. Because malicious denunciation is closely associated with dense face-to-face environments, it can be viewed as the dark face of social capital. It has often been suggested that deep divisions, such as ethnic polarization, override the norms of neighborliness (Banton 2000:495; Bringa 1995). I argue instead that violence is often a reflection rather than a transgression of neighborliness – though a perverse one. I close with a discussion of several testable

---

[2] Even when violence does erupt between intimates, it tends not to escalate and remains individual: the degree of intimacy between the alleged offender and the victim appears to be inversely related to the likelihood of a subsequent lynching (in the United States), even after controlling for the offender's race (Senechal de la Roche 2001:131–2).

[3] In the United States, in 2002, 43 percent of all murder victims were related to or acquainted with their assailants; 14 percent of victims were murdered by strangers, while 43 percent of victims had an unknown relationship to their murderer (U.S. Department of Justice, Bureau of Justice Statistics, http://www.ojp.usdoj.gov/bjs/cvict_c.htm).

implications about denunciations in institutional settings other than that of civil war, including democratic and authoritarian regimes.

10.1. INTIMATE VIOLENCE

Despite claims that violence "between social actors who lived in the same local worlds and knew or thought they knew each other . . . seems to belong to a new moment in history" (Das and Kleinman 2000:1), intimate violence has been the central feature of civil war for a very long time. "Fratricide," lamented in the biblical story of Abel and Cain or *The Mahabharata*, turns civil war into a despicable phenomenon at least since Thucydides' *History of the Peloponnesian War* and Lucan's *Bellum Civile*. More than anything else, intimacy is the attribute that sets interstate war apart from civil war. Whereas in interstate wars, physical proximity and ease of aggression tend to be inversely related, violence in civil war is frequently exercised among people who share membership in a legally recognized or "imagined" community (a sovereign unit or a nation) and/or everyday ties of social and spatial interaction, such as neighborhood, friendship, kinship, even family.

There is a diachronic consensus that intimacy is the feature that endows civil war with its particularly abhorrent character (e.g., Faivre 1994:225).[4] A Northern Irish Catholic woman tells how her brother-in-law was killed in 1975: "That was really awful, when he was killed, because it was his own people, and people he knew really well that walked into the house and shot him" (quoted in Smyth and Fay 2000:23). Plato's distinction between war and faction (his equivalents of foreign war and civil war) was made in terms of what he saw as the unnatural character of civil war:

The name faction is applied to the hatred of one's own, war to the hatred of the alien. . . . when Greeks fight with barbarians and barbarians with Greeks, we'll assert they are at war and are enemies by nature and this hatred must be called war; while when Greeks do any such things to Greeks, we'll say that they are by nature friends, but in this case Greece is sick and factious, and this kind of hatred must be called faction. . . . [If a faction] occurs and a city is split, if each side wastes the fields and burns the houses of the others, it

---

[4] There is disagreement about the normative implications of "intimate" violence. On the one hand, Tina Rosenberg (1991:8) argues that this kind of violence is "more evil" than purposeless, random, individual violence of the criminal kind, but she does not explain why. Chateaubriand strikes a note of disagreement: he noted that it was horrible when close neighbors of a community "lay waste each other's property and stain each other's home with blood," yet he wondered whether it is "really that much more humane to massacre a German peasant whom you do not know and with whom you never exchanged a word, whom you rob and kill without remorse, and whose wives and daughters you dishonor with a clear conscience simply because *c'est la guerre*?" Instead, he argued that "civil wars are less unjust and revolting as well more natural than foreign wars" (quoted in Mayer 2000:5–6). Along the same lines, Italo Calvino (1995) wrote a short story in which a man named Luigi volunteers for the army because he wants to find and kill his personal enemy, Alberto. He is, therefore, upset when told that he is supposed to be killing enemies in general rather than particular enemies. For him, enmity cannot be an abstraction: it is infinitely worse, he reasons, to kill people he does not know and who never harmed him. Nevertheless, Luigi ends up killing a lot of people during the war and wins many medals, but fails to encounter Alberto. He does find him, however, after the war, kills him, and as a result is tried and hanged.

seems that the faction is a wicked thing and that the members of neither side are lovers of their city. For, otherwise, they would never have dared to ravage their nurse and mother.[5] (*The Republic* 470d)

For Plato, then, violence between Greeks (and even more between citizens of the same *polis*) is fundamentally unnatural: it is "a domestic war, one within the family" leading to violence that is akin to the tasting "of kindred blood with unholy tongue and mouth" (*The Republic* 521a, 565e). "The war against another country is a beautiful one," recalled a veteran of the Spanish Civil War (quoted in Zulaika 1988:26), "but that war against one another... that is a hard thing. Nobody who hasn't experienced it knows what it's like." Here lies the essence of Antoine de Saint-Exupéry's (1936) aphorism: "A civil war is not a war, but a disease. The enemy is internal. One almost fights against oneself. And this is undoubtedly why this war take this terrible form. There are more executions than battles." Indeed, epidemic and illness have been privileged metaphors for civil war since fifth-century Greece (Price 2001:28–30).

This perception recurs, even though the civil wars to which they refer are separated by time, distance, and type. An officer who fought in the American War of Independence asserted in 1781 that "civil wars are always attended with something horrid. The bare idea of Friend against Friend & nearest Relatives in armed opposition shocks human nature!" During the same conflict, a Hessian officer made a similar observation: "Presently this country is the scene of the most cruel events. Neighbors are on opposite sides, children are against their fathers;" while a historian described the situation in backcountry Virginia as one in which "suspicion, fear, and anger were rampant. Neighbor informed on neighbor" (Crow 1985:147; Evans 1985:193; Shy 1976:15). Tzvetan Todorov (1996:94) describes the dilemmas faced by French *maquisards* in executing captured collaborationist militiamen in central France during the summer of 1944: "In many cases, guards and detainees have had frequent association since childhood, attended school together, and dated the same girls." Often, close ties turn out to be a liability, with threats more likely to come from neighbors than from strangers. A Spanish man recalls how his mother was arrested and executed by local acquaintances: "She came home thinking that because she knew everyone there would be no problems, and instead went to her downfall not knowing why" (Sender Barayón 1989:124). In this sense, a civil war is not only a war without enemies, as William Waller remarked about the English Civil War, but also a war where the enemy is everywhere, including one's most intimate surroundings – as Thomas Hobbes asserted about the same conflict.

Intimacy is not restricted to "ideological" civil wars. Violence in ethnic wars is often intimate, both within and across ethnic boundaries. Consider Toolis's (1997:3) description of the assassination of Judge William Doyle by the IRA:

[He] was also the enemy within. He was a Catholic on a Protestant/Unionist judicial bench which asserted the authority of the British Government.... Someone in the congregation

---

[5] Plato (471a–c) then moves on to recommend for Greeks that "as Greeks, they won't ravage Greece or burn houses, nor will they agree that in any city all are their enemies – men, women, and children." He suggests that this be given as a law to the guardians of the Republic.

at St. Brigid's had recognized him and told the IRA, and they came on the right Sunday to kill him. There was an awful Irish intimacy about his death, murdered at Mass in front of the congregation, fingered by someone who was part of that congregation. The IRA did not need to travel to kill Doyle. Their supporters were already there in St. Brigid's, also dressed in suits and Sunday best on the Malone Road, hidden amongst the smiling schoolgirl choir or walking back down the aisle slyly staring after Holy Communion.

The Lari massacre carried out by Mau Mau insurgents in Kenya in 1953 was a "communal" affair between neighbors, closely linked with local factional politics and personal animosities and steeped into a broader conflict about land; this massacre contributed to the transformation of the nationalist insurgency into a civil war among the Kikuyu of Kenya (D. Anderson 2005:119–80). Basque "terrorism" in the small Basque village of Itziar was also a deeply local affair. All six victims of political assassinations carried out by the ETA between 1975 and 1980 were Basque, five of them either villagers or married to villagers: "Carlos and Martin, leaders of the opposing factions, were milk brothers and confidants. The civil guard Benito and José Mari, whom he arrested, each married the daughter of a local restaurateur" (Zulaika 1988:86, 97). The war between Ukrainians and Poles in the Soviet borderlands during the Second World War was "often personal, fought between neighbors and family members. They skirmished for this village, that bend in the river, this church yard" (K. Brown 2003:222). In the wars of the former Yugoslavia, violence among people who knew each other was widespread – though much violence was also exercised by bands of paramilitaries and thugs unknown to the people they victimized (Mueller 2004; Ron 2000a). "Men on either side of the front line once were neighbors.... Before the war, they had been to the same schools, worked in the same garage, went with the same girls" (Ignatieff 1998:34). A Serbian elementary school teacher in Croat-controlled Mostar had her apartment looted by a group of men that included one of her former students (Human Rights Watch 1992:333); a Bosnian Muslim who was interned in a concentration camp suffered at the hands of Serb classmates and neighbors (Pervanic 1999:xviii); many women were raped by men who had been their neighbors, even their friends (Gutman 1993:68–73), and in massacres such as that of Slovinje, "there was a great deal of familiarity between the persecutors and the persecuted" (Bearak 1999a:A3). Catherine Dale (1997:81) tells the story of a woman whose Abkhaz relatives fought against her Georgian relatives during the 1992 Abkhaz-Georgian war. For this woman "and many others, the war was not a political battle for sovereignty, but a highly personal, bloody contest among neighbours and family members" – a description that also applies to the war between Armenians and Azerbaijanis over Nagorno Karabakh (Goltz 1998:78).[6]

---

[6] Intimacy can also be a feature of violence in pogroms, riots, and genocides. In Rwanda the perpetrators of the 1994 genocide included "neighbors, schoolmates, colleagues, sometimes friends, even in-laws" (Gourevitch 1998:18; André and Platteau 1998:39–40); many survivors could name their victimizers (Vidal 1996:358); the Jews of Jedwabne, Poland, in 1941, were killed by their Polish neighbors (Jan Gross 2001:121).

There is, obviously, a close connection between the intimate character of violence and the local dimension of civil war. In places where both sides vied for local control, the American Civil War was "a struggle of neighbor against neighbor, for guerrillas and Unionists were both deeply rooted in their community. Guerrillas knew of Unionists from local gossip or personal knowledge; frequently, in fact, they were longtime acquaintances of their Unionist victims" (Ash 1995:125). The Irish Revolution and Civil War was "an intimate war, played out within homes and neighborhoods, often between people who knew each other" (Hart 1999:18). The Spanish Civil War unleashed passions that were "local, fought out by neighbors in each and every town and village.... People today still mumble about whose father killed whose uncle, whose uncle betrayed whose father: these are vivid memories that die slowly" (Gilmore 1987:44–5); a Spanish woman described her brother's assassin as someone who "was from Canfranc where I lived, where my father was Director of Customs. His family had a bakery and every day he brought our bread" (Sender Barayón 1989:155). The Vietnam War was also "a highly personal, parochial, and bitter war, a war waged in a world so small a man could walk from one end of it to the other in an hour, a war not between faceless enemies but between men who knew each other only too well" (West 1985:xv). The JVP insurgency in Sri Lanka was a process that "permeated the capillary relations of everyday interaction: your political opponents would be neighbors usually, kin often, former friends sometimes" (Spencer 2000:134).

The theory of selective violence specifies the link that connects the intimacy of the violence and the local dimension of civil war: selective violence requires local information which, in turn, tends to come from denunciations motivated by personal conflicts.

10.2. WHY DENOUNCE? A SOCIOLOGY OF DENUNCIATION

Following the theory, most individuals participate in the production of violence indirectly, via denunciation. Selective violence results from the *joint action* of local and supralocal actors, insiders and outsiders, civilians and political actors. It is the outcome of an *exchange* between them and entails, therefore, an intimate relation between denouncer and denouncee.[7] In other words, denunciation is the most obvious place for exploring the sources of intimate violence in civil war. A key theoretical implication is that joint violence is likely to be intimate and that intimacy will likely (though not necessarily) reflect private and local concerns. The following section provides a theory accounting for the supply of denunciation, along with anecdotal empirical support – the only available.

Practices of denunciation, like all social practices, display widely varying patterns. It is reasonable to surmise that different social and political environments produce different rates of conflict and hence denunciation (Lucas 1997). Conflictual environments should be *ceteris paribus* more prone to denunciation than solidaristic ones. However, it is extremely difficult to determine ex post the

---

7 In Stalin's Soviet Union and in Nazi Germany, denunciations involving people who did not know each other were extremely rare (Nérard 2004:338; Joshi 2003:xv).

direction of causality between denunciation and conflict. Furthermore, systematic empirical data on denunciations are rarely available.

Nevertheless, the anecdotal record suggests that the supply of denunciation never seems to fail to satisfy demand, given a situation where the actor seeking denunciations has a level of credible control. Furthermore, malice seems pervasive. Thucydides was probably the first author to link malicious denunciation and civil war. In his description of civil strife in Corcyra, he mentions that some people "were accused of conspiring to overthrow the democracy, but in fact men were often killed on grounds of personal hatred or else by their debtors because of the money that they owed" (3.81). The same observation has been made countless times since. For example, Paul Jankowski (1989:134) reports dozens of cases from German-occupied Marseille: from the illiterate woman who joined the Fascist PPF and "promptly threatened to denounce anyone in the neighborhood who annoyed her," to the unemployed man "who had his brother-in-law deported after quarreling with him."

Dislike and envy are pervasive;[8] interpersonal conflict is bound to occur in any society (Worchel 1974:110). Far from being dysfunctional, conflict is essential to group formation and maintenance (Coser 1956; Simmel 1955). Everyday interpersonal conflict tends to remain nonviolent. The anthropologist David Gilmore (1987) shows how petty disputes in a Spanish village are directed into nonviolent forms of abuse (such as gossiping, name-calling, insulting and other verbal abuse, ritual conflict, general contentiousness, etc.) and perform a socially beneficial function; such conflict not only fails to harm social relations, but reinforces social bonds. Even the desire for vengeance typically fails to induce violent action. Fantasies of revenge for all kinds of petty everyday conflicts appear to be widespread across all eras and societies (Frijda 1994:264), but they are rarely enacted – even less enacted in a homicidal fashion.[9] Thomas Schelling (1991:19) notes that there must be a million people living within the public transportation radius of his home who could burn down his house with impunity and a dollar's worth of gasoline, or could kidnap his children as they played in the street, and, although he would be willing to pay much to forestall such easily accomplished damage, he is puzzled by the fact that he has never been targeted. Whether it is due, as Schelling claims, to the difficulty

---

[8] As a Hollywood entrepreneur put it, "I think Hollywood's long knives are out for everybody. That's sort of a way of life out there. If somebody's held in high esteem, based on, you know, hits, or something like that, then five minutes later everybody's got a knife out for them. It's the way of life" (quoted in Auletta 2002:81).

[9] Violent revenge is a central theme of Hollywood movies: "In real life," a film critic points out, "Americans would rather sue than shoot. But on screen we want our revenge, the bloodier the better" (A. Scott 2004:24). According to a study conducted by Nico Frijda (1994:264), 46 percent of the respondents admitted to remembering at least one vengeful instance. He also cites (1994:264–8) recent studies that indicate that in everyday life vivid thoughts of revenge are felt, and some enacted, for motives such as erotic unfaithfulness, indiscretions, small slights, being cheated, having one's bicycle stolen, and the like. These fantasies have a virulent quality and are often remarkably violent, including impulses toward the physical destruction of objects, images of stabbing the offender, or wishing that he or she be killed or tumble into great misery. Violence springing from jealousy is, according to him, a paradigmatic indicator of revenge.

of translating this action into concrete benefits, to internal moral restraints, to fear of sanctions, or just to stupidity or smallness of soul as Friedrich Nietzche argued,[10] the fact remains that there is a surprising scarcity of violence relative to its actual desire and a pronounced discrepancy between vengeful desires and vengeful acts.

Denunciation in civil war turns common disputes into violence. To begin with, the practice of denunciation exists to some degree in all organized societies (Fitzpatrick and Gellately 1997:13), though it is really at home under authoritarianism. In East Germany, one of the best researched cases, informing for the Stasi was so widespread that "the dichotomy between victims and perpetrators did not stand up" (Gellately 1997:209). As Anne Thurston (1990:167–8) recalls: "In 1980, when the Cultural Revolution had ended and an American teacher in China had occasion to teach her class on the Ten Commandments, there was one commandment her students simply did not understand: 'Thou shalt not bear false witness against thy neighbor.' Products of the Cultural Revolution, they had grown up steeped in false witness. They had never learned it might be wrong."

In fact, political actors are often surprised and overwhelmed by the response they receive when they solicit denunciations. In April 1934 Nazi bureaucrats expressed their surprise about the quantity of denunciations that was coming their way, especially false charges; they noted that they had reached "altogether unacceptable proportions." Even Hitler, in 1933, complained: "We are living at present in a sea of denunciations and human meanness" (Gellately 1997:206; Connelly 1997:183, 177; Gellately 1991:135–43). As the German army conquered Soviet territory in 1941, it kept receiving hundreds of reports fingering partisans in outlying villages (Terry 2005:9). A French officer who served in Algeria recalls that he found it very easy to obtain a steady flow of denunciations (Aussaresses 2001:33). Americans in Iraq were delighted to discover in the winter of 2003 that "ordinary Iraqi citizens now produce so much information that [Americans] must prioritize the raids they stage to arrest former Hussein loyalists" (Loeb 2003:A14). At some point, they even set up a telephone hotline for denunciations.

However, what political actors take time to realize is that many denunciations are malicious, and a significant proportion false. In Iraq, Americans realized, as an officer put it, that "these people dime each other out like there's no tomorrow" (in Packer 2003:71). Said an Iraqi man: "It is just like under Saddam. We are still under the cup of a neighbor or a jealous person. Then, it was enough to know a Baathist in order to send someone to prison. Now, we can just call a cell number. Isn't this progress?" (in Ourdan 2004:2). Clearly, the demand for denunciation translates often trivial private dislikes into violence; it is a time when, in Richard Cobb's (1972:60) words, public disaster provides the opportunity for private profit.

Ordinary people are liable to ignore "moral self-sanctions" and engage in activities that further their self-interest but injure others even under everyday

---

[10] Nietzsche, as Baier (1991:45) puts it, thought that only stupidity or smallness of soul could explain why women did not use their allowed rule of the kitchen to poison their masters.

"normal" circumstances (Bandura 1990:162), but the immense majority stop short of homicidal violence. By exchanging violence for denunciations, political actors assume the considerable moral and practical costs of ridding people of their personal enemies: they encourage people to spy on each other (e.g., De Waal 1991:119), replace sanctions with impunity,[11] provide a comforting illusion of anonymity,[12] supply "a rationale for more drastic acts than would have been possible in peace" (Freeman 1979:164),[13] trigger a number of "psychosocial mechanisms of moral disengagement" (Bandura 1990:162),[14] cultivate self-deception,[15] and, perhaps most importantly, undertake the execution of the act of violence.[16] Altogether, political actors shield denouncers from the crime they cause since "it is relatively easy to hurt others when their suffering is not visible and when causal actions are physically and temporally remote from their effects" (Bandura 1990:177).

In short, denunciation represents a new means to satisfy a long-repressed grudge or provide a decisive advantage in previously restrained contests. In this way, the possibility of violence increases its desire, to paraphrase Stendhal; as Hannah Arendt (1963:134) put it, these are situations in which evil almost loses the quality of temptation. General Stephen Drayton, who fought against the

---

[11] In the Spanish Civil War, Juan Peiró, an anarchist activist, made an "eloquent and candid attack" on those who have killed "because they could kill with impunity" (Thomas 1986:277–8). During the American Civil War, a western Tennessee man observed that "all, all, are more or less demoralized & do things, [that] a few years ago, they would have scorned the idea of doing" (quoted in Ash 1995:204).

[12] In its effort to destroy the insurgency in the Dominican Republic, the United States developed a "screening process which protected the identity of those who gave information against their neighbors" (Calder 1984:167). More recently, and outside civil wars: a website that makes possible anonymous emails with "virtual curses," including virtual voodoo dolls and curses such as "This is the end of you" sends 2,000 to 3,000 curses daily (J. Cohen 2000:G1).

[13] Denunciation is proclaimed to serve a higher cause: nation, class, or religion. According to Eamon Collins (1999:3), a former IRA operative, "Republicanism gives political legitimacy to the age-old pastime of spying on one's neighbours, turning neighborhood vendettas into noble struggles."

[14] Mechanisms of moral disengagement include euphemistic language, displacement and/or diffusion of responsibility (thus obscuring the link between conduct and consequences), disregard for or distortion of the consequences of action, and group decision making, "which enables otherwise considerate people to behave inhumanely, because no single person feels responsible for policies arrived at collectively. When everyone is responsible, no one is really responsible" (Bandura 1990:170–7; Gurr 1975:101). Also, by presenting a decision on aggregate targets as definitive ("we will kill five people from the village"), they make it easier for individuals to decide *who* these five people will be.

[15] Working-class wives in Nazi Germany thought that by denouncing their husbands as Communists to the Gestapo, they would get them to "be educated" in a work or concentration camp. Joshi (2002:433), who reports this fact, observes that "given the kind of ruthless persecution to which communists were subjected, it is all the more remarkable that the women thought this way."

[16] The following example comes from the Philippines. After his father-in-law was killed in a dispute about the theft of a *carabao*, a man considered taking revenge against his killer. At this time, he was approached by the Communist NPA (quoted in Jones 1989:289): "I told them about my father-in-law's death, and they told me to forget my revenge because the NPA will take care of the problem. The NPA had received other complaints about the same person. When I heard about the death of this person, I was glad I didn't have to kill my fellow man. I was impressed by the NPA. After several months, I joined them."

British during the American Revolution, pointed to this in 1781, when he wondered about the situation in North Carolina: "Who is safe where prejudice, envy, or Malice may prevail in the breast of a bad man; are not the best liable to be called an Enemy & treated as such?" (in Crow 1985:147). Binford (1996:107) notes that in El Salvador "No one was immune from the violence. An argument with a neighbor, a conflict over a debt, or an insult made under the influence of *güaro* might lead the aggrieved party to tell a soldier, a guardsman, or a government official that person X or Y was engaging in suspicious behavior." Consider the following excerpt from an interview I conducted in Greece (I-10):

> There were many personal disputes in the village, but people did not have the opportunity to kill before the war. Nobody sang the glory of killing then. It was boiling inside them.... The worst human instincts came up with the civil war. In the subconscious of everyone there was jealousy, there was envy.... The villager's psychology is peculiar. He envies the people who move ahead of him. Obviously, he does not express his envy, he cannot, there is no reason he would, but it is there, boiling inside him. When society is disorganized, he has the opportunity to punish without being seen; it is not a public trial where you need to call up witnesses or something like that.... And they had the opportunity to call [their personal enemy] a traitor and they could kill him without this person being a traitor or anything.... You could be called a traitor for nothing. Our life was agonizing. Could you escape here in the village? You could not.

It is obviously impossible to know with exactitude what type of motivation prevails. Theoretically, there is reason to think that denunciation is primarily private and malicious rather than political. The provision of group control is subject to the free-rider problem: control is necessary for group solidarity (and solidarity enables the production of nonexcludable joint goods), yet free-riding is the best strategy for rational individuals; it follows that mutual control (or monitoring through denunciation) will not appear unless it provides individual benefits (Hechter 1987).[17] Although ideology may be thought of as a personal benefit, nonideological concerns are rife, especially in rural areas.

Evidence from studies of police work, a very different context from civil war, shows that the motivations of police informers typically include "fear, insecurity, revenge, envy, remorse, money" (Wilensky 1967:67–8).[18] Beyond this, the little systematic evidence available is to be found in the archives of authoritarian regimes (for which there are better records than for civil wars), and appear to confirm the ubiquitous character of malice. Summarizing extensive research in the Spanish archives of the Inquisition, Henry Kamen (1998:175) reports that "petty denunciations were the rule rather than the exception," while James Given (1997:141–65) provides extensive evidence to show that manipulation of the

---

[17] Fehr and Gächter (2002) provide experimental data showing that people are willing to punish free-riders even at a cost to themselves; if this is the case, group control may not be subject to the free-rider dilemma. However, control in situations where communities are divided may still provide openings for private benefits.

[18] As a late nineteenth-century edition of Larousse put it, "even today, the most precious discoveries of the police are due not to overt or secret agents but to anonymous denunciations which arrive every day at Rue de Jérusalem, products of vengeance of betrayed women and friends or jealous parents" (quoted in Fitzpatrick and Gellately 1997:14).

Inquisition was a central aspect of how this institution operated in medieval Languedoc. Denunciation was pervasive in the context of the highly localized medieval institutions: "Efforts to manipulate governing institutions like the inquisition were unique neither to the inquisition nor to Languedoc. Wherever the records allow us to examine the workings of medieval governing institutions, which were under construction during this period, we discover people busily at work influencing and exploiting them for their own ends. Manipulation of these organizations for purposes other than those for which they had been created was perhaps more the rule than the exception" (1997:163). Comparing levels of repression between the late 1960s and the early 1970s in China, Jung Chang (1992:488) points to malice as the main motivation behind denunciations. The contributors to the first (and, so far, sole) comparative treatment of denunciation "encountered comparatively few cases where denunciations seemed to be motivated by genuine ideological fervor" (Fitzpatrick and Gellately 1997:10).

The study of the Düsseldorf Gestapo files by Reinhard Mann shows that a plurality of cases was used to resolve private conflicts.[19] Robert Gellately (1991:151) also found that "spite informers" were of far greater significance in generating cases for the Gestapo than paid informers and that "there were extremely few charges that were laid clearly for the 'right' [i.e., political] reasons." As a policeman told a woman under investigation, "[Y]ou have no idea how many denunciations we must cope with at headquarters! And it is our duty to check each and every one of them, even if most turn out to be malicious suspicions or backbiting" (in Gellately 1991:72). A Nazi district leader "clearly felt uncomfortable with the overpoliticization of private matters" and complained that, "We cannot become involved in purely family matters." The management of the Deutsche Bank tried to combat the problem by announcing that it was not interested in "stories about the intimate lives of its employees," while the minister of the interior asked local authorities to take steps to curb the rapid expansion of all denunciations, "too many of which were based merely on conflicts with neighbours" (Gellately 1991:134, 146). Local Gestapo officials occasionally published reminders in the press that it was not the "complaint bureau for personal spitefulness or even of base denunciations." In her study of denunciation in Germany, Vandana Joshi (2003:xv) omits so-called loyalty denouncers because "such cases were rare to find. The evidence found in the files," she adds, "mainly points towards instrumental denunciations." She concludes (2003:xi) that "If the Gestapo derived its strength from the co-operation of the masses, clearly, the masses did not do it with the sole intention of rooting out the enemies of the state." No wonder, then, that postwar definitions of denunciation in Germany associate it with malice (Joshi 2003:9).

---

[19] At least 26 percent of all cases began with information voluntarily provided to the police by individual citizens (more if one takes into account those provided to other organizations); further, his study shows that 37 percent of these denunciations were attempts to resolve private conflicts and 24 percent were motivated by loyalty to the regime (no motive could be discovered for 39 percent of the cases). Gellately remarks that "these statistics suggest that the important ingredient in the terror system – denunciation – was usually determined by private interests and employed for instrumental reasons never intended by the regime" (Gellately 1991:134, 146).

Individual testimonies provide similar insights about insurgent organizations. Consider, for instance, the following recollection by an IRA operative:

After a while, one aspect of my encounters with people and their complaints began to depress me. I realized that a lot of people, often not even republicans, would seek the help of Sinn Fein in order to draw on the threat of IRA muscle – so they hoped – in solving their disputes. At times I felt as if people were treating me as a Mafia godfather. One former work colleague asked me if I could sort out his son-in-law. Apparently the latter was beating up his wife, my former colleague's daughter. I said that it was none of Sinn Fein's business. Then my former colleague said: "Yes, it is. That man is never out of the police station. I am sure he's an informer." I said that he was making a very serious allegation. I said that if the IRA were to investigate it and find it to be groundless then they would come looking for the person who made the allegation. Unfortunately, the allegation that so-and-so was an informer (was 'never out of the police station') became one that I heard regularly from people who wanted extreme violence done to their neighbours. (Collins 1999:229)

Stephen Lubkemann, who conducted extensive field research in Mozambique, including tens of in-depth life-history interviews, reports (2005:498) that accounts of malicious denunciation were "typical rather than exceptional." My own sense, both from my fieldwork in Greece and from reading a broad array of secondary accounts of many different wars, supports the predominance of malice in denunciation. The evidence is anecdotal yet massive and seems to transcend history, geography, and types of civil war.[20] It is indeed striking that the frequently

[20] Evidence about the private content of "political" violence, including malicious denunciation, turns up in in-depth studies of such diverse conflicts as the 1640–60 war in Ireland (Clifton 1999:113), the American Revolution (Selesky 1994:77; Escott and Crow 1986:393), the French counterrevolution (J.-C. Martin 1994:40–4; Lucas 1983; Cobb 1972), the Calabrian uprising against the Napoleonic armies (Finley 1994:28–9), the Risorgimento in southern Italy (Pezzino 1994:62), the American Civil War in frontier states (Fisher 1997:63 – eastern Tennessee; Ash 1995:183 – Virginia; Fellman 1989:60 – Missouri; Paludan 1981:77 – North Carolina), the Russian Revolution and Civil War (Werth 1998:118, 174; Figes 1996:525, 535), the Finnish Civil War (Upton 1980:519), the Irish Revolution of 1916–23 (Hart 1999:15), the Sandinista insurrection in Nicaragua during the 1920s (Schroeder 2000:34, 38; Horton 1998:32), the guerrilla war in the Dominican Republic in 1917– 22 (Calder 1984:xvii), the Spanish Civil War (Cenarro 2002:79–80; Moreno 1999:309; Abella 1996:455; Sender Barayón 1989; Thomas 1986:277–8; Harding 1984; Freeman 1979), the Chinese Revolution and Civil War (Thaxton 1997:290; Chan et al. 1992:28; Marks 1984:244) including the Cultural Revolution (Chang 1992; Madsen 1984:91), the Greek Civil War (Gerolymatos 2004; Ward 1992:217–20), the civil conflicts that took place in Nazi-occupied Europe, including France (Sweets 1994:235), Poland (Paczkowski 1999:311), Belorussia (Terry 2005:8; Heer 2000:97), Ukraine (T. Anderson 1999:616), and Yugoslavia (Djilas 1980:78), the Greek Civil War (Xanthakou 1998:12), civil wars in Japanese-occupied Asia including Malaya (Kheng 1983:178) and the Philippines (Rodriguez 1982:x; Lear 1961:94, 105), anticolonial revolts, such as the Mau Mau insurrection in Kenya (D. Anderson 2005:176, 204; Berman and Lonsdale 1992:446, 453), the Algerian War of Independence (Faivre 1994; Hamoumou 1993) and the ongoing civil war in Algeria (Kalyvas 1999; Gacemi 1998; Abdi 1997), the Palestinian rebellion of 1936–9 (Swedenburg 1995) and the Palestinian intifada (Haberman 1991), the mass killings in Indonesia in 1965–6 (Cribb 1990:28), the various stages of the Vietnam War (Elliott 2003:259; Moyar 1997:71; Bilton and Sim 1992:89; M. Young 1991:213; Blaufarb and Tanham 1989; Race 1973:12, 71; Hosmer 1970:61; Crozier 1960:94), civil wars in Latin America, such as Guatemala (Stoll 1993; S. Davis 1988; Paul and Demarest 1988; Ebel 1988), Venezuela (Wickham-Crowley 1992:143), Colombia

petty motives behind much violence in civil wars are simultaneously ubiquitous and marginalized in the macrolevel literature. The following section is intended to provide a sense of the sweeping geographic and historical range of malicious denunciation.

10.3. THE RANGE OF MALICIOUS DENUNCIATION

Malicious denunciations are common in all kinds of societies, including those that are sharply polarized in terms of class (Stoll 1999; Binford 1996; G. Wilson 1970), religion (McKenna 1998:181; Chamoun 1992:24), and ethnicity (Collins 1999:229; Pervanic 1999; Hamoumou 1993; Haberman 1991; Jan Gross 1988). They have also been observed in a wide range of civil wars. Consider the following vignettes.

10.3.1. "Classic" Civil Wars

A federal officer (quoted in Fellman 1989:63) concluded in 1863 that "many of the [Unionist] soldiers [in Warsaw, Missouri] are in the neighborhood of their homes, and all have private wrongs to avenge, and it is plain to see the effect." The same was true in east Tennessee, where "many selfish motives, including greed, revenge, fear, and personal spite, also influenced this struggle" (Fisher 1997:63). A Tennessee resident wrote in her diary about some of her neighbors that "private grudges of years standing, are brought to light & revenge is considered sweet" (in Ash 1995:204). "Settling scores with real and imaginary opponents became the essence of politics," writes Vladimir Brovkin (1994:419) about the Russian Civil War. Both White and Red Terrors were often arbitrary (Brovkin 1994:226): "Flimsy definitions of what constituted 'Bolshevism' generated all kinds of settling accounts, denunciations, and total disregard for legal procedures." Orlando Figes (1996:535) recounts how "many of the early victims of the Red Terror had been arrested on the basis of no more than a single denunciation by some personal enemy." "People informed to protect themselves, out of jealousy, out of spite, to free up a room in a communal apartment" (Schmemann 1999:259). "Just local stuff," is how a Russian memoirist explained his arrest during the Stalinist purges (Grigorenko 1982:85). In Ireland, "Many IRA and other witnesses have reported cases of people being falsely accused of informing out of 'local spite,' because of some feud or grievance. A large number of killings seem to have had an

from the 1940s to the present (Jones 2000; Wickham-Crowley 1992:146; Henderson 1985:128), El Salvador (Wood 2003:114; Binford 1996:106–7; Wickham-Crowley 1992:260), Nicaragua (Horton 1998:217), and Peru (Starn 1998:244; Manrique 1998:204–5), the Philippines in the 1980s (Berlow 1998:182; Jones 1989:127, 289), Lebanon in the 1970s and 1980s (Mouro 1999:19; Makdisi 1990:86; Randal 1983:81), Uganda (Kannyo 2000:167–8, 172), Mozambique in the 1960s and 1970s (Henriksen 1983:97) and the 1980s and 1990s (Nordstrom 1997:83; T. Young 1997:132; Geffray 1990:56–7), Angola in the 1980s and 1990s (Brinkman 2000:15), Zimbabwe (Kriger 1992), the Punjab in India (Pettigrew 2000:210), Sri Lanka (Argenti-Pillen 2003; Spencer 2000:131; Senaratne 1997:143), Sierra Leone (Richards 1996:8), Sudan (Jok and Hutchinson 1999:134), and the U.S. occupation of Iraq (Finer 2005; Packer 2003:71).

agrarian subtext," Peter Hart points out, and adds (1999:299–300, 306): "The typical informer [in the Irish Civil War (1922–3)] was not someone with a cause but rather someone with a grudge, a grievance, or with people or property to protect. Others saw the opportunity for gain or to settle old scores. . . . People were often denounced by informers for the same sorts of personal reasons for which people were denounced as informers. Much of what passed for 'intelligence' in Cork was little more than 'fear or malice.'" A British officer charged with investigating suspected Nazi collaborators after the end of the Second World War in Greece recalls: "In a situation where the German departure had left a vacuum which the communists threatened to fill and where those who had been fence-sitting during the Occupation were now scrambling for seats on the bandwagon, the time was ripe for the settlement of private scores. Denunciation became the insidious weapons of attack. Whether the charge be one of collaboration or communism, it made little difference, for each was equally damaging. . . . Denunciation, therefore, became the ideal means of settling many irrelevant private grudges and vendettas" (Ward 1992:217).

10.3.2. Anticolonial Revolts

Andrew Elliott, a Royal officer and lieutenant governor of British-controlled New York during the American Revolution, warned that "a destructive war" would be counterproductive and would simply fill British prisons with victims of what he called "private revenge" (Shy 1976:189). In his account of the Palestinian revolt of 1936–9, Ted Swedenburg (1995:155) reports many stories "of men falsely accused of treason by their adversaries, who were motivated by personal or family reasons, and how those wrongly charged were executed on the order of rebel commanders." He reports (1995:119) that, though it was supposed to be a rebellion against the British, "many executions of accused traitors were in fact the work of local Arab notables . . . who used to allege that a particular person with whom they had a personal grudge was a traitor, arrange to have him killed, and then ensure that blame for the slaughter was pinned on [rebel chieftain] Abû Durra." "Denunciation was jealousy" is how an Algerian peasant described the situation in Algeria in the late 1950s (in Hamoumou 1993:199). In East Timor, a FRETILIN Central Committee edict stated that "various FRETILIN delegates in the Maubisse area have taken advantage of the present situation to exact personal vengeance, in the name of FRETILIN, and have been tempted to exploit the people" (Jolliffe 1978:135).

10.3.3. Civil War during Occupation

Paul Jankowski provides the following account of denunciations in Nazi-occupied France:

The villains of casual private collaboration . . . were the *corbeaux*, the denouncers. Malice was their only motive. First came zealots denouncing complete strangers, overheard uttering Gaullist, communist or anti-German views – there was often a reward for turning them in. Then came neighbours, landlords and tenants denouncing one another, then spouses and lovers, employers and employees, finally business colleagues and associates. Ostensibly these turned each other in for listening to the BBC, for harbouring *réfractaires* or foreign Jews, for voicing Gaullist or communist views, for hiding arms, but *nearly always* a more prosaic grievance lay behind the loathing letter to the SD [German Secret Police]: a dispute over rent, a bad marriage, a rivalry at work, or simple jealously: "[The only reason] I was arrested was because my neighbours in the quartier had ill-feelings towards me because I had the nicest vegetable garden." (1989:133; emphasis added)

10.3.4. "Cold War" Insurgencies

In Malaya, "some members of the police force were not above reporting people as suspects for personal reasons" (Stubbs 1989:74), while in Vietnam "there were an awful lot of vendettas being carried out with Phoenix license," a U.S. intelligence officer recalls (quoted in M. Young 1991:213). In Sri Lanka, "the prosecution of the JVP often got bound up with the common feuds and envy of Sinhalese rural life. Seeing an opportunity for revenge or to vent jealousies, [Sinhalese] villagers were accusing their enemies of JVP sympathies, which was enough to bring down the wrath of government forces" (McGowan 1992:221). In Guatemala, "denunciations often involved private vendettas or political feuds rather than revolutionary activism: as one Chimalteco official said.... '(People) died from fights over women, over land, (even) over religion'" (Watanabe 1992:181); people "could act on personal animosities and envy by denouncing fellow townspeople to either side. Vengeance in this situation became tantamount to a death sentence," Warren observes (1998:99) about the same country. She quotes two peasants: "I believe some took advantage of the situation, some people who had personal differences. They used the opportunity to complain about others. There was much violence and many deaths because of this.... Because of envy, there were personal differences over something.... The most painful thing was that many died because of vengeance, because of envy. Just because a person was there, someone got bothered because he was doing all right. So he would go and say, 'This man is with the guerrillas.'"

10.3.5. "Ethnic Conflict"

In Liberia, "the search for national enemies became inseparable from the search for personal enemies.... In this guise, there was a great deal of settling of scores" (Ellis 1999:117). "Land disputes, family quarrels and related rifts between friends and even relatives claimed victims all over the place" (Brehun 1991:67). In Sri Lanka, denunciations motivated by personal grudges took place both along and within ethnic lines. A young Tamil "was being paid to finger LTTE suspects, but in reality he was using his newfound power to vent a lifetime of grudges" (McGowan 1992:242–3).

10.3.6. Motives

Participants in civil wars confirm these observations. Almost all the examples of denunciation supplied by Paul Aussaresses, a French officer who served as head intelligence officer during the Algerian insurgency, center on private motivations: "Denunciations began to flow in. In the countryside, many *douars* [villages] were in principle hostile to the FLN. Besides the desire to live in peace, they also had private reasons, grudges, usually disputes about women." Aussaresses (2001:40, 118) adds that during the battle of Algiers, "denunciations were often meant to fulfill personal grudges." These remarks are also consistent with many observations pointing to the trivial character of most denunciations.

It is further possible to distinguish between various motives of malicious denunciations. Local factionalism is a frequent one – consistent with the salience of local cleavages in civil war (see Chapter 11). Consider the following example from south China during the Japanese occupation (Siu 1989:103). Chen Chulin of Tianma Xiang township had a quarrel with the Ye brothers of the neighboring Tianlu Xiang township. Because the most powerful bosses of Tianma were on good terms with the collaborator government in the town of Huicheng, they falsely denounced Tianlu for harboring Chinese troops. As a result, the collaborator government sent soldiers who looted houses and raped women.[21] Warren (1998:99) points to similar dynamics in Guatemala: "In San Andrés, the process was felt to be driven by ethnic and individualized hatred; in other towns, existing factions or emerging power brokers turned on each other, which lead to widespread killings."

Interpersonal conflict, such as professional rivalry, feuds between neighbors, family quarrels, disputes between spouses, and romantic rivalries, are the other major cause of malicious denunciation.

Denunciations motivated by the entire cycle of relations between men and women (romantic rivalries, conflict between lovers, spouses, and ex-spouses) are exceedingly common.[22] After all, disputes arising between lovers and spouses can be very nasty even under normal conditions.[23] Romantic rivalries are particularly prone to violence and are exacerbated by the fact that civil war empowers young people.[24] A South Vietnamese colonel told Mark Moyar (1997:116) about the

---

[21] The story did not end there. The Ye brothers reacted by mobilizing the outraged villagers and ambushing and killing the soldiers. In retaliation, the Japanese military bombed Tianlu and then razed it. In the wake of the bombing, Tianma villagers went to Tianlu and looted it, even to the point of carting off bricks and bridges. Most of Tianlu's four thousand residents fled, and only half of them ever returned.

[22] Terry (2005:8); Elliott (2003:1244); Aussaresses (2001:40); Pettigrew (2000:210); Swedenburg (1995:167); Madsen (1990:184).

[23] "Petty vengeances manifest themselves at a time when one partner may be ambivalent about the sale of property. I remember visiting a pretty Sussex cottage and was astounded by the blatant honesty of the husband when he showed my wife and me around. He had no hesitation in pointing out damp spots, the unsafe electrical wiring, the impossibility of getting out of the lane in anything but a mildest winter" (Mackwood 2002:13).

[24] In his study of the Shining Path in Peru, Degregori (1998:134) points out that the rural youth that joined the insurgency were not disengaged "from the tightly woven networks of kinship and

Provincial Reconnaissance Units: "If they saw a beautiful girl, they tried to be her boyfriend. If they got turned down, then they accused her of being a VCI [a member of the Vietcong Infrastructure]."[25] Similar instances have emerged elsewhere. For example, in the West Bank, "it emerged that a so-called collaborator [of the Israelis] who was killed recently had been having an affair with the wife of the man who killed him" (Haberman 2001:A1). Romantic rivalries in rural environments may also be closely intertwined with family strategies. Paul and Demarest's (1988) in-depth study of a death squad in the small town of San Pedro la Laguna in Guatemala is chock-full of similar examples. Particular cases include the abduction of a man as retaliation for having married a woman who was formerly the wife of a death squad member, and the denunciation by a woman of a man as a "subversive" because, in fact, "he had stolen her daughter-in-law's affections." Sender Barayón (1989), the U.S.-raised son of a woman who was executed by the Nationalists during the Spanish Civil War, researched the circumstances of his mother's death in the town of Zamora and discovered that she was killed by a former romantic suitor whom she had rejected previously (after being denounced by her in-laws, who coveted her part in the family inheritance!).[26]

Denunciations between spouses (and ex-spouses) got so far out of hand in Nazi Germany that in 1941 the Gestapo headquarters in Berlin sent a letter to all local Gestapo posts in which they requested that special attention be paid to denunciations between relatives – particularly married couples (Gellately 1991:148). Indeed, Joshi (2002:427–9) found that the majority of denunciations that the Düsseldorf Gestapo received from women against their husbands were filed by women who had also filed divorce suits; she also found denunciations of men by wives who were involved with other men and for whom denunciation was "the best and quickest means of getting rid of their husbands." Domestic abuse and battering also led many women to denounce their husbands as being leftists, in order to bring the situation under control (Joshi 2002:421–2). Likewise, *Pravda* deplored malicious denunciations from angry ex-spouses (Fitzpatrick 1997:104). A French counterinsurgent in Algeria (Aussaresses 2001:119–20) recalls how, during the first days of the battle of Algiers, he received a visit from a Muslim woman who denounced her husband, a rebel: "In fact, she wanted to get rid of him and had set her conditions: she would exchange her information for a warranty

community relations, with their own dynamic of reciprocities, grudges, hatreds, and preferences, in which they had been immersed. As a result, the youthful representatives of the new power were frequently dragged into inter- and intra-communal disputes."

[25] Though not a denunciation per se, the following case from El Salvador fits this trend. A guerrilla squad leader was assassinated by a local guerrilla commander after the former's girlfriend left him for the latter. The assassination was motivated by fear that the squad leader may have betrayed the guerrilla encampment out of spite. Philippe Bourgois (2001:21–2) who reports this story adds that "romantic jealously results in comrades-in-arms killing one another over mere suspicions."

[26] "Magdalena nodded. 'Viloria. He courted Amparo at one time. He fell in love with her. But Amparo told him, 'No!' I gasped in amazement. 'What?' 'That's what happened,' her husband concurred. 'That's history.' What a grotesque twist! Viloria was doing more than following orders. He was avenging himself on the woman who had resisted his advances. Unbelievable!" (Sender Barayón 1989:164).

of widowship." A captain in the South African Security Police named Michael Bellingan "tried to justify murdering his wife in 1991 on the grounds that she was allegedly going to leak information about the Security Branch" (Gottschalk 2000:246).[27]

Likewise, fights between relatives are common and include both intergenerational disputes and quarrels between siblings, cousins, and in-laws. David Stoll (1999) generated a great deal of controversy when he showed that the victimization suffered by the family of the Nobel-prize winning Guatemalan activist Rigoberta Menchu was not just the result of an ideologically motivated class conflict, as she had argued, but also the outcome of a feud between in-laws. An anthropologist who studied a Greek village points out that "it is said that one man joined the Communists with the express intention of killing a rival inheritor of his father's" (du Boulay 1974:239). Lubkemann (2005:498) reports the case of a man in Mozambique who after being a successful migrant was able to start several grinding mills; this caused intense jealousy on the part of his older brothers who had not been as successful in their own migratory careers. Even though he was a RENAMO sympathizer and had moved to an area controlled by the insurgents, his brothers convinced RENAMO troops that he was taking grain into the villages and giving it to government soldiers; as a result, he was shot by RENAMO troops. Intrafamily competition can be particularly acute in polygamic settings. In Mozambique, one of two junior wives of a man interviewed by Lubkemann (2005:498) reported to government soldiers that the son of a rival co-wife was about to join RENAMO. As a result, the rival wife and her children were forcibly removed and the son in question was detained and died later under interrogation.

Denunciations that spring up from disputes between neighbors are commonplace as well. A badly timed curse was enough to turn a *muzhik* into a kulak, and then to labor camp, in revolutionary Russia (Schmemann 1999:269). An Algerian villager recalls that in the wake of the conclusion of the war many murders of alleged collaborators of the French resulted in fact from "settling accounts between families that had nothing to do with the War of Algeria. You stole a sheep from me in the past, you took a blanket from me . . ." (quoted in Faivre 1994:202). When the Namibian rebel organization SWAPO launched a campaign of terror among refugees all over the world, the "fear of being denounced by personal enemies or even neighbours became general throughout the exiled community" (Saul and Leys 1995:56). In his investigation of the civil war in Guatemala's Ixil country, Stoll (1993:98) found that "many of the deaths came out of personal quarrels, when small-town enemies denounced each other as subversives or army informers. One woman is said to have charged vengeance-seekers money to take denunciations of their enemies to the army – until the army realized what she was doing and took her away too." An American academic (Forment 2000:5) who spent nearly two years living in Ayahualulco in Veracruz, Mexico, at a time of social agitation and guerrilla activity could not help but notice these dynamics

---

[27] Joshi (2002:422) quotes a woman's denunciation, which, after a detailed accusation of her husband for all kinds of domestic abuse, concludes: "And now the main point: he is left-oriented."

and report them in the acknowledgments section of his dissertation (which is on an entirely different topic): "Ayahualulco was not, fortunately, regarded a hot-spot, although fall-out from the campaign reached us as well and made daily life difficult and, at times, even risky. PRI bosses led a witch-hunt against anyone in the region who was against the ruling party. Friends and neighbors in several communities took advantage of the situation to settle family feuds, accusing each other of supporting or engaging in subversive activities."

Professional rivalry is another recurring cause for denunciation. During the Spanish Civil War, in the village of Ibieca in Aragon, a carpenter named Joaquín Murillo was executed by anarchist militiamen; his execution, Susan Harding's fieldwork revealed (1984:75), "had little to do with either war or revolution, according to one of his neighbors, who said that Murillo was denounced by a fellow carpenter out of rivalry." A woman from Madrid said that "her father, a blacksmith, had not even been interested in politics; he had been executed, she insisted, because another blacksmith, who had influence with the local Falange, had wanted his business" (Kolbert 2003:66). Eleni Papadaki, a famous Greek actress who was executed by the Communists in December 1944, was apparently denounced by an older rival who was the leading theater actress until Papadaki dethroned her (Gerolymatos 2004:167). The denial of a promotion caused a customs employee in Northern Ireland to inform on his boss, leading to his assassination by the IRA (Collins 1999:21). The gangster Jean Grimaldi was killed by the German police in occupied Marseille after his local rivals deceived the Germans into believing that he was a leading resistance member (Jankowski 1989:117). During the Cultural Revolution in China, many people were accused by their colleagues as counterrevolutionaries "but were really the object of their colleagues' jealousy" (Chang 1992:328). A subtype of professional rivalry concerns the desire to obtain a job. The two daughters of the Conservative mayor of a Colombian town during the *Violencia* were public school teachers who had gained their appointments by falsely accusing the two teachers before them of being party traitors (Roldán 2002:215).

Often, denunciations involve the kind of relationships that can generate much dislike in everyday life without resulting in homicidal violence. For example, judges are often targeted for revenge by those who have been convicted by them (e.g., Thomas 1986:276). The teacher-student relationship is, likewise, the source of many denunciations. When Mao launched the Cultural Revolution, he encouraged students to turn against their teachers. "In practically every school in China," Chang (1992:284) recalls, "teachers were abused and beaten, sometimes fatally. Some schoolchildren set up prisons in which teachers were tortured"; she describes meetings in her school, where students beat up their teachers as class enemies. They were "accused of all sorts of outlandish crimes; but they were really there because . . . some pupils had grudges against them" (Chang 1992:293). In Lebanon, the onset of the civil war in 1976 meant that "many students" at the American University of Beirut "began harassing and even threatening members of the administration and faculty over differences in political affiliation and, more dangerously, over dissatisfaction with the grades they received" (Mouro 1999:19). Likewise, during the civil war in Liberia, one could cause the death of "the teacher who flunked him" (Ellis 1999:117).[28] Such dynamics appear in other situations involving everyday power dynamics and the bitterness they can engender. Hugh Thomas (1986:278) cites the case of an ex-sacristan who was active on the Republican side killing priests in 1936 (in 1939, when the tide turned against the Republicans, he denounced his fellow murderers and busied himself killing Republicans).

Denunciations of lenders by borrowers are also quite common, as during the Spanish Civil War (Ledesma 2004:288; Reig Tapia 1996:580; Thomas 1986:274). In the village of Qian Foji in China during the Chinese Civil War, a wealthy peasant returned to his village, which he had fled when a Kuomintang army raided it in 1947, and informed the Kuomintang troops of his uncle's Communist membership. Ralph Thaxton (1997:290) notes that he had been previously "asked to return back interest to local borrowers including his uncle." A U.S. adviser in Vietnam (quoted in Moyar 1997:293) recalled such a case: "One guy who was a source of information about the VC relieved his family of three generations of debt. He turned in phony reports fingering as Viet Cong people his family owed money to."

Particularly disturbing is the recurring observation about the lack of proportion between the nature of the offense and the size of the sanction caused by the denunciation (Gellately 1997:206; Fitzpatrick 1997:108; Gellately 1991: 147–51). For example, in the village of Arrow Rock in central Missouri during the American Civil War, a woman appealed to the provost marshal for the release of her husband, who had been accused by his brother-in-law of being a guerrilla collaborator when in fact "he fell out in a settlement and came near fighting and . . . being a coward was afraid that my husband would whip him some day for his abuse – so he thought that the best way for him to do was to go to Huntsville and swere fauls against my Husband" (quoted in Fellman 1989:60). During the Russian Civil War, a man was arrested after a denunciation that was provoked by a petty squabble over his place in the queue outside the Moscow Opera (Figes 1996:643). An IRA operative recalls how some people denounced their neighbors as informers over issues such as "damage to bushes, dents in cars, loud music" (Collins 1999:229).

The ubiquitous character of malicious denunciation is consistent with the theory of selective violence, and especially the notion of joint violence. Furthermore, the focus on the dynamics of denunciation allows an understanding of civil war violence as a process taking place *because* of human aversion to undertaking homicidal violence – as opposed to the widespread Hobbesian view positing that violence in civil war reflects the fundamentally violent nature of human beings. People are generally repelled by the prospect of acting violently, and so they will not, unless someone else handles the gory details while shielding them.

---

[28] Teachers are not always on the receiving end, though as partisan actors their motivations have not been so obviously malicious. A Bosnian Muslim inmate in a Serb concentration camp recalls about his interrogators: "My teachers of yesterday were my judges of today. Back then they had decided what grades I should get – now they were deciding whether I should live or die" (Pervanic 1999:134).

Rather than an indicator of Hobbesian anomie, denunciation-related violence is, like the violence of blood feuds, a negative by-product of mechanisms of social control; an outgrowth of dense social interaction rather than the result of random societal breakdown and chaotic anarchy – an indicator of "passion," and perverse "overhumanization," rather than dehumanization. The understanding of violence afforded by the analysis of denunciation is also at odds with the Schmittian view of mass political violence as resulting from impersonal hatred of the political enemy. In contrast, civil war appears often to pit individuals against each other not only as generic members of competing groups but also as specific individuals motivated by private enmity.

Besides being potentially lethal, denunciation is highly ironic. It suggests that rather than just politicizing private life, civil war also works the other way around: it privatizes politics. Civil war *transforms* often trivial and petty conflicts and grievances into lethal violence; once used, this violence becomes endowed with a political meaning that may be quickly naturalized into new collective identities. It is not unusual for the trivial origins of these new identities to be lost in the fog of memory or reconstructed according to the new politics fostered by the war – making their retrospective reconstruction very difficult. This should not prevent us from detecting their importance.

10.4. THE DARK FACE OF SOCIAL CAPITAL: THE SOCIAL BASIS OF MALICIOUS DENUNCIATION

Malicious denunciation is closely related to interpersonal conflict in contexts of "organic" solidarity: small-scale, face-to-face social settings, where people develop dense interpersonal interactions, living and working together in daily mutual dependency, rivalry, and love. These include tight-knit neighborhoods, villages and small towns, apartment buildings,[29] family businesses,[30] and work environments (including academic departments).[31] Surprisingly, ethnically homogeneous and socially egalitarian settings that lack deep ethnic, religious, or class divisions appear not to be as adverse to denunciation, as one would expect.[32] Indeed, denunciation is often horizontal. For instance, a recurrent motive of

---

[29] Lobbia (1999:49).

[30] Less than a third of family businesses in the United States will continue to be family owned in the next generation, partly because of conflicts that arise when family members are in business together (Ellin 2001:C1).

[31] After a strike crippled British Airways in the summer of 2005, the company set up a confidential phone line, "encouraging employees who participated to identify employees and union members who instigated the walkouts" (Timmons 2005:C3). Fitzpatrick (1997:108) reports a case from the Soviet Union in which the wife of a biologist denounced a colleague of her husband's as "a pitiful scientific pigmy, a plagiarist and compiler."

[32] Egalitarian environments may exist within unequal societies. Consider, for example, a village of Peruvian peons, a township of Indians in Guatemala, a group of industrial workers, or the inmates of a concentration camp. Of course, vertical and horizontal conflicts may coexist within the same community. Redfield's (1989:134) study of the village of Tepoztlán in Guatemala uncovered that "differences between rich and poor lead to serious dislikes and distrusts; and especially that within many families there are many kinds of frustrations, suspicions, and sufferings."

denunciations, jealousy induced by "romantic competition," is conditional on a high degree of social egalitarianism, since competition over the same person is generally impossible for people belonging to different castes or rigidly stratified classes and closed ethnic groups. A study of 5,422 cases of denunciation in Nazi Germany shows that it was primarily horizontal ("denouncers belonged to the same social milieu as the denounced") rather than vertical (the "humbly stationed in life" denouncing their social superiors) (in Gellately 1991:144). Likewise, most violence resulting from denunciations in the Soviet Union was generated not between but within class lines, by warring kolkhoz factions (Fitzpatrick 1994:254).[33] Prisons and concentration camps are environments prone to informing among inmates (Lloyd 1999; Overy 1997:231).[34] In short, denunciation parallels nonpredatory common murder, which tends to occur between intimates and equals.

The link between malicious denunciation and small-scale, face-to-face social settings is shocking because we tend to positively rate such environments – as reflected in the literature on social capital, broadly understood as dense networks of social contact and exchange. In this respect, the practice of denunciation may be thought of as the dark face of social capital. This interpretation helps make sense of the paradox of the explosion of violence in social contexts characterized by high levels of contact, exchange, and even interpersonal trust (e.g., Finnegan 1992:99). In fact, sociologists, anthropologists, and historians have long noted that environments rich in social capital, including small villages with their "supreme intimacy," can also breed less visible but nevertheless intense interpersonal conflict (e.g., Figes 1996:90; Zulaika 1988:97). In a parallel fashion, the civic-minded German bourgeois turn out to have been particularly prone to denounce each other (Gellately 1991:146).

According to Hans Magnus Enzensberger (1994:12), "the original target of our hatred was probably always our neighbour." Though vague, this insight does point to two key causal mechanisms, both of which are consistent with Leon Festinger's "social comparison theory," according to which humans evaluate themselves not so much by objective standards as by comparison with people around them: relatively homogeneous, tight-knit, and egalitarian social settings may be prone to high levels of denunciation for two distinct reasons: symmetry and concentration.

10.4.1. Symmetry

After the U.S.-supported Northern Alliance moved against the Taliban in 2001, a Taliban commander agreed to surrender his troops; when he realized, however,

---

[33] However, Fitzpatrick (1997:103) also found that denunciation between family members was rare. This, though, seems to exclude spouses or ex-spouses, who denounced each other in both prerevolutionary Russia (Burds 1997:66) and the Soviet Union (Fitzpatrick 1997:104).

[34] Bizot (2003:201) describes the situation among the people who sought refuge from the Khmer Rouge in the French Embassy in Phnom Penh: "Within a few days, our campus had become a breeding ground for all the basest instincts: theft, jealousy, selfishness, aggression. Old quarrels between clans and families resurfaced, without anyone knowing what they were originally about."

that he would have to hand in his weapons to a Northern Alliance commander who was a fellow Pasthun and his own cousin, he reneged. "He'd hand over his weapons to a Tajik," but not to a Pashtun. "That would be too humiliating," reported Elizabeth Rubin (2001). This example suggests that status equality (or symmetry) does not prevent interpersonal conflict – quite the opposite.

Symmetric contexts foster denunciation, via the mechanisms of fear of status loss and envy. Social hierarchies in symmetric environments tend to be fluid (people are ranked in relation to others in terms of subtle gradations) and open to modification (unlike with castes or rigid strata). Competition for status ("face" or "honor") is open, daily, and intense; it generates humiliation, shaming, and "loss of face" – usually experienced as among the worst things that can happen to a person.[35] It is well known that challenges to honor originate from parties of equal rank (Barry O'Neill 1999), and that egalitarian peasant societies tend to be associated with a culture of honor (M. Johnson 2001:67) or "face," which submits individual behavior to constant and exacting social judgment (Hua and Thireau 1996). Martin Yang's (1945:167–72) analysis of conflicts in a Chinese village shows how loss of face makes sense only in the context of symmetric relations since interpersonal conflicts are threatening among peers:

If the insulting person is only a plain peasant or one who has been considered ignorant or mean, a cultured man does not lose face at all, because people will say that the trouble is caused by the peasant's ignorance and is not the other's fault, and if the latter remains impervious to the taunt, he will win great praise from the villagers for being too great to quarrel with a mean person, or so kind that he can forgive another's ignorance. Inequality of social status can nullify the fearing of loss of face in another way. When a plain villager is scolded or injured by a gentleman, he may resent it but he will not lose face.[36]

Because slight personal losses of face often signal (or even amount to) losses of social power that demand redress, they spur denunciation when such an opportunity arises.

More generally, Georg Simmel (1955:43–4) argued that similarity breeds intense conflict and that people who have many common features often do one another worse wrong than complete strangers do. For Simmel, even the slightest

---

35 Loss of face means losing prestige, being insulted, or being made to feel embarrassment before a group (Yang 1945:167). The interviews I conducted in Greece are full of cases of humiliation generating a desire for revenge and driving action – from denunciation to joining an army. In one interview (I-91), a right-wing man who had been imprisoned by leftist partisans and then fought against them told me how he came close to switching sides after being humiliated by a gendarme: "If there was a rebel organization around then," he told me, "even one rebel, I would have gone over to them. I would have joined them just to kill these gendarmes." In Vietnam, "an individual has a pathological fear of offending other people and of losing face"; "loss of face often resulted in murder or suicide" (R. Berman 1974:43, 41).

36 When one of two equally popular professors is refused by the other in some request, Yang adds (1945:167–72), the former will have lost face, but if a student is similarly treated by a professor, the student does not suffer loss of face. The worst conflicts, he points out, are produced when an upper-class family is attacked with bad words or violent actions by another family of similar social status. Like denunciations, these attacks typically concern what we would consider minor issues: a villager purposely reveals some secret of his neighbor before a public meeting or intentionally poses difficult questions to another person at a meeting.

antagonism among similar people "has a relative significance quite other than that between strangers, who count with all kinds of mutual differences to begin with. Hence the family conflicts over which people profoundly in agreement sometimes break up." Both Donald Horowitz (1985:182) and Michael Ignatieff (1998:48–53) draw on Freud's "narcissism of minor differences" to explain the intimate aspect of ethnic violence. Freud began from the observation that, in intimate groupings (friendships, marriage, relations between parents and children), feelings of hostility coexist with feelings of affinity, and he reached the conclusion that the closer the relation between human groups, the more hostile they are likely to be toward each other. In Freud's words (quoted in Ignatieff 1998:59), "Of two neighboring towns each is the other's most jealous rival; every little canton looks down upon the others with contempt. Closely related races keep one another at arm's length; the South German cannot endure the North German, the Englishman casts every kind of aspersion upon the Scot, the Spaniard despises the Portuguese." In the same vein, Adam Smith (1982:229–30) remarked that "national prejudices and hatreds seldom extend beyond neighbouring nations," while in his review of violent practices in ancient Greece, André Bernand (1999:273) concludes that "the narrower the space of loot and crime, the stronger the hatred." The violent potential of symmetric relations has also been stressed by students of international conflict. Writing in 1602, William Fulbecke pointed out that war emerges from "controversies" between two "princes of equal power" (in Hale 1971:7). Recently, Roger Gould (2003) demonstrated that trivial interpersonal disputes can escalate into violence when they involve peers in relatively symmetric relations because of ambiguity about relative social rank.

Envy is another mechanism that triggers interpersonal conflict in symmetric contexts. Intimacy does not prevent envy. In fact, the people we envy most tend to be those closest to us. "You will envy more a colleague of yours who makes a thousand dollars more a year," notes Aaron Ben-Ze'ev, "than you will a C.E.O. who makes a million dollars more than you" (in St. John 2002:A17). The psychologist Daniel Nettle points out that a wealthy man is basically anyone who earns £100 more than his wife's sister's husband (in Persaud 2005:W3). David Hume's remark that the source of envy and malice lies in comparisons with others (in Frijda 1994:280), Alexis de Tocqueville's (1933:185–6) observation that greater equality tends to produce envious comparisons (as they become more equal, individuals find their decreasing but easily comparable inequality harder to bear), and Jon Elster's (1999) remark that envy presupposes the belief that "it could have been me," thus driving resentment – all converge in linking relative symmetry and denunciation via envy.[37] Indeed, recent psychological studies show that wellbeing is largely determined by whom people compare themselves with rather than what they objectively have and that the reference group of such comparisons are equals, such as neighbors, work colleagues, and family. This insight explains why school reunions famously provoke all sorts of competitive instincts

---

[37] This is reflected in a well-worn joke from the Soviet era, about a peasant who complains that his neighbor has a cow and he does not. "So you also want a cow?" "No, I want you to take his away" (Schmemann 1999:34).

and envy (Persaud 2005:W3). From envy to denunciation there is only a step, as a Guatemalan peasant told Stoll (1993:143): "There's a lot of *envidia* here in Cotzal.... So that if guerrillas show up, the envious are capable of telling them, he's an informer for an army. Or of telling the army that he spoke with a guerrilla. This is why so many people died here."

10.4.2. Concentration

Concentration refers to the dense overlap of social interaction in small and closed settings. Such environments are highly interdependent. Small-scale "moral communities" characterized by density of network ties combine vulnerability (from interpersonal competition and the associated insecurity) with mutual dependence in a context characterized by repeated interaction. Highly elaborate mechanisms of social control, coupled with full information about the likely outcome of conflicts, contain and regulate interpersonal conflict (Gilmore 1987). "As in any small town," writes Watanabe (1992:ix) about his Guatemalan field site, "disputes and animosities abounded, yet these remained largely of personal rather than political import."

The existence of institutions that defuse conflicts has often led observers to interpret such dense environments as being solidaristic (e.g., Petersen 2001; Skocpol 1979). However, anthropologists have pointed to their fundamentally dual nature: they are conflictual *and* solidaristic.[38] After describing the intense internecine violence of a Basque village that resulted in a number of locally instigated murders, Zulaika (1988:98) describes it as a place where he never saw "an actual fight or public verbal insults between two adults. A rowdy argument in a bar creates extreme tension among those present and is therefore much disliked."[39]

Close observers note that high attachment and loyalty to one's village coexists with heightened suspicion toward non-kin members; that profound and intense attachment to family accompanies mutual suspicion and intense intrafamily

---

[38] The two faces of dense environments are not always captured by the same researcher. One anthropologist described the villagers of Tepoztlán in Guatemala as "a relatively homogeneous, isolated, smoothly functioning and well-integrated society made up of a contented and well adjusted people," skipping over issues of "poverty, economic problems, and political schisms," and emphasizing its "cooperative and unifying factors." Another anthropologist, however, described the same village in a way that stressed "the underlying individualism of Tepoztecan institutions and character, the lack of cooperation, the tensions between the villagers within the municipio, the schisms within the village, and the pervading quality of fear, envy, and distrust" (see Redfield 1989:134).

[39] This duality is also visible during periods of open conflict. Zulaika (1988:96–7) tells the story of the kidnapping by the Basque ETA of a (Basque) industrialist in 1986. Both the industrialist and one of the kidnappers were from the same village, Itziar. When the industrialist was freed, the local kidnapper was killed. The former extended his best regards to the latter's mother, who reciprocated with greetings to his wife. Zulaika points out that "the exchange was as sincere and normal as it would have been in any casual situation. During the days of captivity this 'normalcy' had been clouded by the antagonistic roles they had been led to play in a plot neither could fully master; but now they were again friendly co-villagers."

competition, such as pronounced sibling rivalry;[40] that the centrality of friendship in people's lives is not exclusive of intense competition between friends;[41]
and that a profusion of ideals and mechanisms for avoiding interpersonal conflict coincides with high levels of interpersonal conflict about trivial and petty
matters – but also with a considerable capacity for overcoming the deep wounds
such conflict can cause. In short, these environments tend to be simultaneously
close-knit and intensely competitive, outwardly unified and internally divided,
"familistic" but also conflictual. In his study of a southern Spanish village, David
Gilmore (1987:3) found that underlying all peer relations in this tight-knit, face-
to-face community was an "intensely powerful emotional substructure normally
concealed.... In private, in the depths of their feelings, family seemed arrayed
against family, and man seemed poised against man; and the intensity of distrust
and the passion of envy [was] always hidden darkly beneath the bright veneer of
showy amiability ... this dark substratum of emotional tension affects the life of
the community in powerful ways, as powerfully and pervasively as class polarization and politics."

Concentration causes interpersonal conflict through two mechanisms: first,
the number of interactions between the same individuals is high, hence the higher
likelihood that interpersonal conflicts and grievances will emerge.[42] Conflicts
in dense environments tend to be intense, Simmel (1955:44–5) has suggested,
because the depth of relations between persons in intimate relationships who
quarrel causes "not a single contact, not a single word, not a single activity or pain"
to remain isolated. It is no coincidence that name-calling, character assassination,
and gossip (which Roland Barthes [1977:169] aptly called "murder by language")
are prevalent in dense social environments.

Second, dense contexts entail the presence of an audience for every interaction. The higher the number, and the greater the density of interactions among
the members of a group, the greater the opportunity to directly observe each
other's behavior (Gambetta 1993:168; Hechter 1987:154). The opinions of peers
carry tremendous weight and often determine self-worth. As a Chinese villager
points out, in a village, "face is difficult to obtain. People are observing you from
the day of your birth" (Hua and Thireau 1996:127). According to Yang (1945:
167–8), "loss of face means losing prestige, being insulted, or being made to feel
embarrassment *before a group*. ... The question of losing or not losing face is based

---

[40] Anthropologists report that while sibling solidarity is usually touted as an ideal by Mediterranean
peasants, it is often directly contradicted by open and violent animosity among brothers (Gilmore
1987:43).

[41] Richard Berman (1974:43) notes that, in Vietnam, "friendships between males are of intense quality
akin to a love relationship within which emotion, loyalty, solidarity, complete trust, equality, and
lack of concern over status are the ideals. In a very real sense, the friend becomes a brother, a
member of one's primary group. Yet, these friendships are rare in Vietnamese society and, thus,
may be more a fantasy wish than a reality." As a Spaniard told Gilmore (1987:6): "Damn them,
the worst enemies of all are your friends."

[42] This is clearly the case with extended families that combine many households under the same
roof. Such cohabitation "gives rise to many apparent or potential troubles in the family, breeding
jealousy, suspicion, misunderstanding, resentment, and selfish anxiety" (Yang 1945:239).

on anticipation of the effect upon a third person or party. Therefore, the village streets or public gatherings are places where one is in danger of losing face."[43] Indeed, as Joseph Epstein (2002) suggests, snobbery can only be local; people may be amused by the excesses of rock-star taste but are snippy about their neighbor's tastes.[44] In short, dense communities fit the Spanish adage "small village, big hell."

Clearly, dense egalitarian environments can simultaneously be deeply satisfying, because of the human closeness they generate, and deeply unsettling, because of the competitive dynamics they unleash. The intimate character of violence in civil war is in many ways a faithful reflection of the character of these contexts. This connection has not escaped a few careful observers who gesture toward the surprising connection between gossip and violence. As Fellman (1989:38) points out, "the horror of guerrilla war [in Missouri] lay in part in its turning a normally disputatious rural society, filled with verbal abuse, occasional physical fights, and endless law suits, into the locale of war of all against all." Perhaps an ideal illustration of this point is the "vigilance committee" set up in 1863 by Unionists in Andrew County in northwest Missouri to determine which citizens were "obnoxious" and order them out of the county (Fellman 1989:54). Hart (1999:314–15) concludes his analysis of the violence in the Irish Revolution and Civil War in a similar fashion:

Beneath the welter of pretexts and suspicions, beneath its official rhetoric of courts martial and convictions, the IRA were tapping a deep vein of communal prejudice and gossip: about grabbers, black Protestants and Masonic conspiracies, dirty tinkers and corner boys, fly-boys and fast women, the Jews at No. 4 and the disorderly house at No. 30. This sort of talk was normally confined to pubs, kitchens, and crossroads. What the revolution did was to take it from behind closed doors and squinting.... Revolution had turned these people and their families into strangers, and their neighbours into enemies.

---

[43] Yang (1945:168–9) argues that loss of face requires an intermediate level of social distance. If the observer of the loss of face is intimate with one or both of the opposing parties, the defeated or insulted party does not feel that he has lost face, or at least the feeling will be negligible. The problem becomes more serious when social distance extends outside the family to the neighborhood, to the village, and even beyond. But beyond a certain distance, this factor declines in significance because loss of face is irrelevant when the other is a complete stranger: "When a man lives in a completely strange society, there is no problem of face, no matter what kind of mistakes he may make, because nobody knows him.... That is why a person who always behaves well in his local community may act very differently in a big city." Yang also points to additional factors as well, such as social sanction (some issues matter, others do not), the consciousness of one's own prestige (the more conscious one is of his status, the stronger is his fear of losing face), and age (middle-aged people are more vulnerable to loss of face).

[44] Jean-Jacques Rousseau (1964:149) argued that the origins of inequality are to be found in such local interactions: "Each one began to look at the others and to want to be looked at himself, and public esteem had a value. The one who sang or danced the best, the handsomest, the strongest, the most adroit, or the most eloquent became the most highly considered; and that was the first step toward inequality and, at the same time, toward vice. From these first preferences were born on the one hand, vanity and contempt, on the other shame and envy; and the fermentation caused by these new leavens eventually produced compounds fatal to happiness and innocence."

Arendt (1970:55) remarked that terror causes atomization, which is then "maintained and intensified through the ubiquity of the informer, who can be literally omnipresent because he no longer is merely a professional agent in the pay of the police but potentially every person one comes into contact with." True, if one takes into consideration that dense social interaction can, surprisingly, underlie atomization and that informers are particularly likely to emerge in dense social environments.

10.5. VARYING THE INSTITUTIONAL SETTING OF DENUNCIATION

The theory of selective violence would be strengthened if it generated interesting and plausible implications outside its empirical domain. First, we should be able to locate practices of denunciation in dense face-to-face environments even in peaceful democratic contexts, because the mechanisms driving the supply of denunciation should be present in reduced form, even when the demand for denunciations is low or marginal. Second, we should be able to explain the omnipresence of denunciation in authoritarian regimes in a way that is consistent with the theory. Third, we should be able to account for variation in levels of violence across authoritarian regimes.

Denunciation is a marginal practice in democracies, where there are strong norms against it. However, despite its marginality, denunciation is not absent. For example, when the American state of Georgia decided to restrict outdoor watering for the fifteen-county Atlanta region in the summer of 2000, it encouraged people to report those neighbors guilty of illegal watering as "water criminals" (Firestone 2000:A16). More ominously, the FBI received thousands of denunciations following the September 11th attacks (Moss 2003:A1); there were 365,000 leads by 20 October 2001 and 435,000 by late November (Van Natta 2001:B1; A. Davis et al. 2001:A1) – and they contained many malicious denunciations. According to a spokesman for the Chicago FBI, "There are more men in jail right now because an ex-wife or an ex-girlfriend decided to rat them out" (in A. Davis et al. 2001:A1).

The theory suggests an additional reason for this relative scarcity: democracies tend to emerge in highly developed and urbanized societies that foster atomized lives and anonymous relationships. An additional testable implication is that exceptionally dense, small-scale, or non-atomized poor areas in rich democracies and poor democracies (which are more likely than their rich counterparts to be rural) should experience higher levels of denunciation.

Police rely routinely on denunciatory "tips" to solve and control crime in poor neighborhoods (e.g., Goldberg 1999:A18). The post–September 11 arrest of four immigrants of Middle Eastern origin in Evansville, Indiana, had "apparently been brought about by a lovers' falling out in which a woman tipped the police that one of the nine had talked threateningly of suicide" (Clines 2001:B7). Likewise the arrest of Abdrezak Besseghir, a Paris airport baggage handler of Algerian origin found with weapons and explosives in his car, turned out to be the result of a plot by his in-laws to frame him (Craig Smith 2003:A4). Electricity theft in New

York is often denounced by "jilted lovers, disgruntled former employees, prying neighbors" (Urbina 2004:A1). In short, malicious denunciation correlates with intimacy, even in democracies.

Short of denunciation, we should also be able to observe high levels of inter-personal competition (and, potentially, conflict) in the most symmetric and con-centrated environments. In contrast, atomized social environments should be less prone to interpersonal competition. Indeed, a sociological study of the Ameri-can suburb concludes that it is a social context dominated by "nonconfrontation, toleration, and avoidance," which undermines "quarreling, violence, mediation, adjudication" (Baumgartner 1988:vi). Yet, when disputes take place there, they are more likely between those next-door neighbors who do interact with each other (e.g., Shattuck 2000:F1). For example, small-town America, where the overlap between working and living arrangements is much higher, displays more com-petitive features.[45] The same is true of high schools and work environments, where both daily interaction and interpersonal competition abound. In explain-ing why "the most horrifying" school violence has been at suburban, middle-class, homogeneous schools, the principal of such a school in Arizona hinted to this logic: "In big cities, there are lots of places where kids make connections, where they have pieces of their lives. But in a place like this, we're pretty much it" (in Lewin 1999). Even though composed of relative social equals, these schools are divided into tens of competitive "cliques" that generate intense competition. "Assisted-living communities" (expensive alternatives to nursing homes) are also places where "friendships are intense and so are rivalries. Everybody knows every-body else's business" (Jane Gross 2005:1).[46] Disputes among tenants, between tenants and landlords, and among owners of condominium apartments in New York City have a reputation for being particularly vicious – more so than, say, in Los Angeles where social relations tend to be less dense.[47] Professional and workplace environments that entail dense daily interaction are also notorious for their vicious politics (MacGregor Serven 2002) and "the lengths that people go to extract retribution for mundane infractions" (Urbina 2005:35), including actual denunciation to the authorities for various regulatory violations motivated by spite and revenge (Rasenberger 2005). The special genre of self-help books

---

[45] William Glaberson (2001:A13) reports that "Even in the biggest cities, drug investigations are often built on betrayal. But in a small community like Columbus [Montana], the duplicity has a special power, as spouses, friends and business acquaintances turn on one another. In a place where almost everyone knows almost everyone else, the waves from a big case can wash over an entire town."

[46] "Except for the traffic jam of wheelchairs and walkers," Jane Gross (2005:1) observes, "the dining room at the Atria assisted living community here might as well be a high school cafeteria."

[47] It was reported that the hot market for rental housing has sent New York landlords of rent-regulated buildings "prying into tenants' paper trails, hiring private investigators to videotape their comings and goings, even making deals with neighbors to spy on each other." If an owner believes a tenant is not living in an apartment as his primary residence or is subletting, he can be evicted. As the president of the city's largest landlord lobby put it: "The stakes are much higher not only because of the market, but because of the vacancy allowance. If you can prove your case, there's value there." See Lobbia (1999:49).

providing advice on office politics includes one bearing the telling title *Cain &
Abel at Work*. Malice also plays a big role in the more rarefied literary (James
2003:13) and academic worlds. Frijda (1994:285) tells that he personally knows
"of someone who blocked the professional promotion of a man because the latter's friend had once, in his view, slighted him, and later actually admitted to have
done so out of spite."

Unlike in democracies, denunciations are much more common in authoritarian regimes where demand for information is high (Jan Gross 2001; Fitzpatrick
and Gellately 1997).[48] Authoritarian regimes resemble zones of full control in
civil war: we should, therefore, observe both high levels of denunciation and low
levels of violence. The omnipresence of denunciations under authoritarianism
is well established empirically. In fact, the bulk of the studies of denunciation
have been produced by scholars of authoritarianism. These studies all point to its
intimate and malicious character. Writing about the Spanish Inquisition, Kamen
(1998:175, 177) notes:

> The fear set in train by the early Inquisition cannot be doubted. But fear of the tri-
> bunal was not the principal spur. The systems of justice prevailing at that time in Europe
> relied overwhelmingly on the collaboration of the community. And it was the testimony
> of the community – of, that is, neighbours, relatives, enemies – that the accused most
> dreaded.... Fear of neigbours, rather than of the Inquisition, was on this premise the
> first – and constant – concern of those denounced.... The Inquisition became a useful
> weapon for paying off old scores.... The records of the Inquisition are full of instances
> where neighbours denounced neighbours, friends denounced friends, and members of the
> same family denounced each other.

Both Fitzpatrick and Gellately's (1997) comparative overview of denunciation
in modern European dictatorships and Jan Gross's (1988:118–19) study of the
Soviet occupation of western Ukraine and western Belorussia in 1939 emphasize
similar features. As soon as Germany came under the Nazis, Gellately (1991:139)
points out, "Nazi types took advantage of the novel situation to settle accounts
with old enemies, and 'ordinary' citizens were not above capitalizing on the opportunity to get rid of business competitors through allegations that led to arrest and
internment." It is estimated that during the German occupation, the French wrote
between 3 and 5 million unsolicited letters of denunciation, most of them signed,
while the Stasi relied on information provided by millions of "ordinary citizens"
who were not members of the secret police but who collaborated on a regular
basis (Fitzpatrick and Gellately 1997).

The practice of denunciation under authoritarianism further undermines the
idea that impersonal polarization forms a necessary basis for intimate violence
in civil war. Indeed, the politicization of life, as occurs under extreme forms
of authoritarianism, results in the privatization of politics. This is not because
political passions penetrate everyone but rather because the extreme politicization

---

[48] Violence is often produced jointly in the context of riots, state terror, and genocide. In Sri Lanka,
the anti-Tamil riots "gave some Sinhala businessmen the opportunity to wipe out their competitors,
enabled some landlords to get rid of unwanted tenants, and so on" (Tambiah 1996:97). Similar
evidence has emerged in Rwanda (Straus 2004; André and Platteau 1998).

of life creates opportunities to use denunciation for personal gains. Fitzpatrick and Gellately (1997:11) emphasize this point:

Because of the totalitarian state's exceptional willingness to receive denunciations from its citizens and to act upon them, that state's formidable powers were in effect put at the disposal of individual citizens. If you have a private enemy, why not denounce him to the police as a Jew or Trotskyite? Then the Gestapo or the NKVD would take him away to a concentration camp, and your problem would be solved.... This kind of manipulative denunciation was extremely common in both societies. Class enemies were denounced in Stalin's Soviet Union by neighbors who coveted their apartments; Jews were denounced by neighbors in Nazi Germany for the same purpose, and with similar success.

Jan Gross (2001:4) argues that the essence of the regimes that encouraged and thrived on denunciation was "the institutionalization of resentment." In his study of the Soviet occupation of western Ukraine and western Belorussia in 1939, Gross (1988:117–20) found that the new power apparatus was "motivated by *particular* interests, like avenging personal wrongs, assuaging hunger, or satisfying greed." His description of the occupation is telling: "Soviet authorities conducted searches and arrests... directly in response to denunciations by neighbors who had personal accounts to square"; "accusations, denunciations, and personal animosities could lead to arrest at any moment. People were officially encouraged to bring accusations and denunciations"; "whoever had a grudge against somebody else, an old feud, who had another as a grain of salt in the eye – he had a stage to show his skills, there was a cocked ear, willing to listen." He describes this process as akin to the privatization of the instruments of coercion and the state itself, which "was franchised, as it were, to local individuals, who used their power to pursue their private interests and settle scores; the pursuit of private interests became the principal method of carrying out official duties and establishing authority." Jun Jing (1996:87) shows how, during the Chinese Cultural Revolution, the intimacy of violence resulted from the intermixing of political and private concerns:

A notable characteristic of the Maoist campaigns that ravaged the Chinese countryside was the close link between political victims and their tormentors. Rural society was not a passive universe helplessly rocked by political campaigns launched from above. What the political campaigns did was to unlock a Pandora's box, pushing the local agents of the state into the hunt for concrete targets at the grassroots levels, in pursuit of the "perpetual revolution" envisioned by Mao. At the center of thousands of villages were local collaborators trying to manipulate these campaigns to their own advantage. In many cases, they were motivated by long-standing hostility between individuals, families, or local factions. More often than not, their victims were neighbors, childhood playmates, or even immediate relatives by blood or marriage.

Likewise, Jung Chang (1992:495–6) locates the source of much violence perpetrated during the Cultural Revolution with Mao's mobilization of envy and resentment. Local committees "usually contained retired men and old housewives, and some of them became notorious for minding other people's business and throwing their weight around" (Chang 1992:265). In her family history, she shows eloquently how the politicization of private life ultimately leads to the privatization of politics (1992:134, 184):

> The Communists had embarked on a radical reorganization not just of institutions, but of people's lives, especially the lives of those who had "joined the revolution." The idea was that everything personal was political; in fact, henceforth nothing was supposed to be regarded as "personal" or private. Pettiness was validated by being labeled "political," and meetings became the forum by which the Communists channeled all sorts of personal animosities.... In each campaign everyone in the category which had been designated as the target by Peking came under some degree of scrutiny, mostly from their workmates and neighbors rather than the police. This was a key invention of Mao's – to involve the entire population in the machinery of control. Few wrongdoers, according to the regime's criteria, could escape the watchful eyes of the people, especially in a society with an age-old concierge mentality. But the "efficiency" was acquired at a tremendous price: because the campaigns operated on very vague criteria, and because of personal vendettas, and even gossip, many innocent people were condemned.[49]

Finally, the theory also suggests a testable implication accounting for variation in the levels of joint violence across authoritarian regimes: the spiraling of mass violence may be caused by competition among several institutions seeking denunciations. If these institutions check each other, then violence should be low (mimicking the logic of mutual deterrence that prevails in zone 3). If, however, these institutions can compete against each other for denunciations (in a situation mimicking zones 2 and 4), we should observe a spiral of violence. Descriptions of the mass terror in the Soviet Union and China suggest that this is a plausible hypothesis.

10.6. CONCLUSION

A Chechen man recalled his experience of the war in Chechnya in the following terms: "I began to understand that war isn't always brought to us from outside. War, death, ruin – those horrors are right under our feet, so close to us that a man can sink into the abyss at any time.... We all tread on a thin crust, as it were, and might at any moment plunge through into the depths" (in Tishkov 2004:145). This statement provides a fitting conclusion to this chapter, for intimate violence in civil war is, as I suggested, often related to interpersonal and local disputes (it is "right under our feet, so close to us ... ") rather than impersonal abstract hatred. Yet this statement should be interpreted less as a mere endorsement of the Hobbesian view of human nature as fundamentally violent under conditions of insecurity, and more as an observation about the power of the practice of denunciation as spurred by interpersonal competition. For intimate violence signals less a process of politicization of individual life and more a

---

[49] Chang (1992:173) provides the following personal example: "My mother was also horrified to hear that my grandmother had been denounced – by her own sister-in-law, Yu-lin's wife. She had long felt put upon by my grandmother, as she had to do the hard work around the house, while my grandmother ran it as its mistress. The Communists had urged everyone to speak up about 'oppression and exploitation,' so Mrs. Yu-lin's grudges were given a political framework."

process of pervasive privatization of politics; less a transgression of social ties and more their full, though perverse, expression. The key mechanism, suggested by the theory, is malicious denunciation. The evidence of malicious denunciation in symmetric and concentrated environments further undermines the view of intimate violence as an exclusive outcome of deep divisions – though such violence can eventually transform interpersonal hatreds into impersonal ones.

This chapter has provided a theoretical account of the nature and causes of intimate violence in civil war, one derived from the theory of selective violence and its focus on the joint production of violence. This account helps solve a key puzzle: political violence is supposed to stand at the exact opposite pole of criminal violence, yet both share a critical common feature: intimacy. In doing so, this chapter reconciles two separate research programs long perceived to be incompatible with each other: one focusing on small-scale interpersonal violence (exemplified by Gould 2003) and one focusing on large-scale political violence. By alluding to a process through which the grand issues of the conflict and the actual dynamics on the ground connect to each other (or fail to), this chapter also lays the foundation for the next and final chapter, which elaborates the theoretical implications of this disjunction.

11

Cleavage and Agency

It's a complicated war.

William Finnegan, *A Complicated War*

Neither side necessarily acted on principle. It was the old case of tweedle-dum and tweedle-dee – naked rivalry for the spoils of local office. Between factions in some municipalities, a long enmity had existed. It was only to be expected that if the faction in office found itself ranged on the side of collaboration, the faction out of office would loudly condemn its adversary and proclaim its devotion to resistance.

Elmer Lear, *The Japanese Occupation of the Philippines, Leyte, 1941–1945*

Up to this point, my focus has been on how armed actors use violence as an instrument of coercion. Although violence aims primarily to deter defection, it also serves additional goals and generates several externalities. In this chapter, I explore an additional dimension of violence: its role as a resource for mobilization at the local level. Examining how actors at the center are linked with action on the ground, and how cleavages as elocuted in national-level discourse are connected with local conflicts that often have little in common with them, brings up some important implications for our general understanding of civil wars.

I begin with an oft-noted but poorly understood puzzle: conflicts and violence "on the ground" often seem more related to local issues rather than the "master cleavage" that drives the civil war at the national level. This is the case despite the fact that local cleavages are usually framed in the discursive terminology of the master cleavage. This disjunction raises the question of agency for a variety of processes that occur in civil war. Does agency – for recruitment, for violence, for identity formation, for each of the other processes that attend and contribute to the upheaval of civil war – lie primarily in the private or the public sphere?

A key insight from the discussion of denunciation in the previous chapter is that individuals and local communities involved in the war tend to take advantage of the prevailing situation to settle private and local conflicts whose relation to the grand causes of the war or the goals of the belligerents is often tenuous. Under normal circumstances, these conflicts are regulated and do not result in violent conflict. We hardly think of them as connected to political violence in general and civil war in particular. This disjunction can be elucidated once it is recognized that the loci of agency spawned by civil war are inherently multiple – hence the confusing diversity and ambiguity of motives and identities observed. In other words, the fusion and interaction between dynamics at the center and the periphery are fundamental rather than incidental to civil war, a matter of essence rather than noise.

The theory of selective violence, through its insight about the joint production of violence, provides a key missing link between the public and private spheres, and between master cleavages and local cleavages. Civil war can be analyzed as a process that transforms the political actors' quest for victory and power, and the local or individual actors' quest for personal and local advantage into a joint process of violence. This book proposes, as an implication of the theory of selective violence, an alternative basis for the linkage between elite and ground dynamics: *alliance*. Alliance entails a transaction between supralocal and local actors, whereby the former supply the latter with external muscle, thus allowing them to win decisive local advantage; in exchange, supralocal actors recruit and motivate supporters at the local level. Viewed from this perspective, violence is a key selective benefit that produces collective action and support on the ground. Several theoretical implications follow.

First, the locus of agency in civil war is simultaneously located at different levels of aggregation: the center, the region, the village, and so on. Second, identity labels should be treated with caution: actors in civil war cannot be treated as if they were unitary. Labels coined at the center may be misleading when generalized down to the local level; hence, individual motivations cannot be inferred from group identity. Third, the assumption of individual interchangeability that underlies the concept of "group conflict" and "collective violence" should be treated as a variable rather than a constant. Finally, the theory implies that debates about the "true" cause or type of a civil war may be ultimately unsolvable and counterproductive. In sum, the study of civil war requires a clear specification of the relevant level of analysis and, ultimately, it must integrate all levels. Only such specification respects the complexity of the phenomenon while making it theoretically and empirically tractable. Put succinctly, the bridge between the conceptual and positive enterprises sketched in the introduction lies in the proper conceptual disaggregation of the process of civil war.

The focus on local cleavages completes and extends the theory of selective violence by fully specifying the logic of local participation in the production of violence; it also suggests the importance of local cleavages for the more general processes of state collapse and state formation.

11.1. CENTER AND PERIPHERY

Civil wars are typically described, classified, and understood on the basis of what is perceived to be their overarching cleavage dimension: thus, we speak of ideological, ethnic, religious, or class wars and we designate political actors in ethnic civil wars as ethnic actors, the violence of ethnic wars as ethnic violence, and so on. Yet, such framing turns out to be much trickier than it seems. Are the insurgents in Iraq Baathist activists, Sunni separatists, Islamic jihadists, or Iraqi nationalists? Were the clashes between Dayaks, Malays, and Madurese in West Kalimantan, Indonesia, about religion or ethnicity (Davidson 2003)? Was Algeria's civil war about religion or class (Freeman 1994:14)? Are Ivory Coast rebels mutinous soldiers hungry for power, champions of a marginalized sector of society, or foreign mercenaries in the pay of the country's regional rivals (Wax 2002:A30)? Were the Afghans who rose against the Soviet occupation a seemingly "monolithic horde of freedom fighters," or a bunch of ethnic and tribal militias motivated by greed and power (Bearak 1999b)? Who are the Taliban? Pashtun tribesmen disguised as Islamist fundamentalists, or Islamist fundamentalists who happen to be Pashtuns? Are the Chechen rebels nationalists, Islamists, transnational terrorists, or common criminals? Is the Chechen War a secessionist conflict, a religious war, or something much more complicated, such as a "tangle of clan rivalries, ethnic hatred and blood debts" (Mydans 2003:A6)? And who was Jesse James? A common criminal, or the last rebel of the American Civil War (Stiles 2002)?

Classifying civil wars often feels like unwrapping Russian dolls: one layer of interpretation yields to another in an endless and irresolvable quest for a "real" nature that presumably lies hidden underneath. Thus it is often argued that an ideological civil war is really about ethnicity, or that an ethnic war is really about greed and looting, and so on. This is not a recent trend. Writing in 1623, Emeric Crucé argued that, to the purely secular causes of war, "one could add religion, if experience had not made known that this serves most often as a pretext" (in Hale 1971:9).

Because of the analytical dominance of national-level cleavages, grassroots dynamics are often perceived merely as their local manifestation. Likewise, local actors are seen only as local replicas of central actors. As a result, local dynamics and actors tend to be dismissed. However, on-the-ground descriptions of civil wars typically convey a perplexing and confusing world, entailing a mix of all sorts of motives that makes it difficult to neatly link the forces driving violence on the ground to the war's stated motives and goals. Such descriptions suggest that a real disjunction between issues, identities, and motives at the local and national levels often exists. A perusal of the reports filed by election observers in Greece in 1946 yields a consistent and permanent sense of confusion about the true motives of the violence and the mystifying mix of political, local, or personal elements:

It would be difficult to determine whether these [killings] were purely of a political nature or of a feud character. One incident which took place in Verria which was brought to my attention was of the latter variety.

Quite often the reason behind the incident is personal rather than political, but party lines are definitively followed in some of the incidents. Much of the bad personal feelings are a result of conduct of members of the ELAS during the Civil War; and since many of these ELAS men are now members of the EAM coalition, the Royalists are using their position in power to vent their feelings on these members of EAM.

In some cases these family vendettas go even further back than the 1944–45 incidents. In at least one case a recent fight had its cause in a murder which happened as the result of a love quarrel in 1942. Sometimes, too, the fights have been provoked by women whose husbands were killed by ELAS. Although these women have no real political axe to grind, their feuds are irresistibly drawn into the political arena by virtue of their being the wives of Rightists. It is extremely difficult to draw the dividing line between family vendettas and political persecutions.

Many cases are feudistic rather than political.

There were outbreaks of violence in various parts of the district during the period of observation. On the island of Kephalonia at least eight people were murdered by a group of Rightist banditi. There were attacks on EAMite members which were wholly or partly political in many villages during the month preceding the election. In the extreme north where there are villages of EAMite sentiment, there were attacks on the Right by the Left. The whole of this region has throughout history resorted to violence occasionally, and while during recent years this violence has tended to draw a line between political parties, much of it is really of feud or vendetta character. . . . Accustomed as they are to the institution of the feud and the vendetta, the villagers on the whole are determined not only to prevent a return of the horrors of 1943 and 1944, but also to revenge themselves on the ELAS leaders whom they consider responsible for the excesses.[1]

Narrative accounts of civil wars that are sensitive to this proliferation of motives point to a process whereby the national is often subverted by the local. As in many other places, the occupation of the Philippines by the Japanese during the Second World War generated both a resistance movement and a civil war, as some Filipinos sided with the Japanese. In his research on the Western Visayas, Alfred McCoy (1980) found that although the country underwent successive radical political changes between 1941 and 1946 (including a U.S. Commonwealth democracy, a Japanese Military Administration, and national independence), provincial and municipal political leaders kept fighting parochial factional struggles with their local rivals. The region's competing factions, he points out, were not insensitive to the larger events emanating from Manila and beyond; in fact, they adapted quickly to each successive regime in an effort to use its resources to their own advantage and to the detriment of rivals: costume and casting directors changed constantly, but actors and dialogue remained the same. While the context shifted and factions and their alliances split and realigned, peer rivals remained in constant diametric opposition and, in so doing, defined the meaning of increasingly nominal party labels or categories such as "guerrilla" or "collaborator." The conflict's violence was directly related to these peer conflicts. McCoy's detailed investigation of the assassination of eight prominent men in Iloilo province in 1942 revealed that, without exception, each of these assassinations originated in prewar electoral conflicts between rival municipal factions for control of

[1] Respectively: "Unofficial Observations Made on a Visit to Salonika," 14 March 1946, AMFOGE I, District Boards; "Joint Report on Khalkidhiki," 28 March 1946, AMFOGE I, Complaints and Investigations; "Memorandum from District Board, Salonika to Central Board, Athens," 29 March 1946, AMFOGE I, Complaints and Investigations; "Daily Summary of Reports and Observations, from District No. 5 to Central Board," 30 March 1946, AMFOGE I, District Boards; "Report for District No. 4, Patras," AMFOGE I, District Boards.

mayoral and council posts. He concludes that wartime factional disputes were not imposed on Iloilo from above but sprang spontaneously from the lowest level of the provincial political system. Elmer Lear's (1961) research in the island of Leyte confirms this conclusion; he found that the Filipino guerrillas recruited their supporters from the political faction that had lost the last election prior to the war, while the winners were drafted into serving the Japanese occupiers.

Lest one is tempted to discount this example as minor or marginal, consider the way in which the French Revolution was articulated outside Paris. It turns out that the cleavages informing this classic ideological conflict were often highly local. The Revolution provided a language for the expression of all sorts of conflicts, Colin Lucas (1983) argues. For example, the spatial reorganization of the provinces of the old regime into a modern hierarchy of administrative regions led to an unparalleled strife among towns. Ted Margadant (1992) shows that beneath the changing political rhetoric of the period one could find a conflict between rival towns: smaller versus bigger, administrative versus commercial, departmental capitals versus outlying towns; in short, parochial concerns mapped onto national cleavages. Among the staunchest supporters of the French Revolution in the provinces were the leaders of small- and medium-sized towns, who instrumentally appropriated concepts such as equality and ideas such as the hatred of aristocracy to obtain administrative privileges for their towns, including their designation as district seats. Margadant shows how a focus on this competition explains political alignments during the Revolution better than class differences. Richard Cobb (1972:123) provides the following snapshot of the formation of allegiances during the French Revolution:

> It was a question of chance, of local power groups, of where one stood in the queue, of at what stage ambitions had been satisfied, of how to leap-frog over those in front. This is where external events could be easily exploited; the Paris political labels, when stuck on provincial backs, could mean something quite different.... The labels might not even come from Paris; they could be of more local origin. In the Loire, "federalism" was brought in from the outside, by groups of armed men riding in from Lyon. But the experience of "federalism" and the subsequent repression directed against those who had collaborated with it, enabled one power group – of almost exactly the same social standing and wealth, to oust another in those towns that had been most affected by the crisis.

The same impressions echo through David Stoll's (1993:259) description of Guatemala and William Finnegan's (1992:71, 214) description of Mozambique:

> When outsiders look at Ixil country, they tend to see it in terms of a titanic political struggle between Left and Right. But for most Nebajenos, these are categories imposed by external forces on a situation they perceive rather differently. Class and ethnic divisions that seem obvious to outsiders are, for Nebajenos, crosscut by family and community ties. Because of their wealth of local knowledge, Nebajenos are intimately aware of the opacity and confusion of local politics, far more so than interpreters from afar.... What seem clear consequences of national and international developments to cosmopolitan observers are, for local people, wrapped in all the ambiguity of local life.[2]

---

[2] Furthermore, Stoll (1993:68, 76) shows how the first Ixil Indians who collaborated with the rebels in Guatemala "were not impoverished seasonal plantation laborers, as [rebel] strategists seem to

I heard about an area where the pattern of allegiances was a checkerboard: each clan chose to work with the side that its nearest neighbor and traditional rival had not chosen, so as to be armed against that rival. Larger regional and ethnic rivalries inevitably came into play, as did smaller intrafamily disputes, and this escalating spiral of strife only swelled Renamo's ranks.... The threat hanging over [the town of] Ribangue [by Renamo rebels] sounded like an Appalachian family feud or an inner-city gang fight.

Thus, the recent journalistic discovery that Afghanistan is "a world where local rivalries and global aims seem to feed off each other" and where "politics are intensely local, with many warlords swapping sides in alliances of convenience that have shifted with the changing fortunes of the 22 years of war that began with the Soviet invasion in 1979,"[3] is not unique to Afghanistan, but rather the latest instance of a recurring pattern. For example, writing about the civil war in a Chinese county, Keith Schoppa (2001:175) concludes that, "whereas one might see the struggles in Shaoxing county as civil war, pitting Japanese and puppet troops against both the Guomindang and Communist troops, in reality there was no strong demarcation between the 'sides': united fronts formed and disintegrated and formed again between forces that were presumably antagonistic." Likewise Lubkemann (2005) shows how wartime violence "was significantly shaped by local-level tensions and micropolitical goals, defined and operating at the community and even family level." He demonstrates how the inhabitants of the district he studied "managed to appropriate the means of violence of the government and the insurgents...in the puruist of local social struggles whose dynamics were defined by culturally distinct logics. By and large," he concludes, "these micro-political objectives were entirely unrelated to the contest for state power."

Actors operating at the national level often miscode such dynamics. Parisian revolutionaries either failed to grasp the complex dynamics of the civil war that erupted in the French South in 1790–1 between the towns of Avignon and Carpentras, which was less about ideas and programs and more about settling local accounts, or they did not want to acknowledge them. Robespierre, for instance, did not hesitate to frame the conflict along the lines of the national cleavage (J.-C. Martin 1998: 95–6, 121; Skinner 1995: 143).

The inherent ambiguity of local-level dynamics parallels in many ways the distinction between "objective" structures and "subjective" actions.[4] The anecdotal

---

have expected. Instead, they were prominent men from San Juan Cotzal, relatively well-situated merchants and labor contractors, who wished to enlist the guerrillas in the bitter political feuds of their town." Conversely, their local enemies "who had disgraced themselves in office and were being defeated in elections could now denounce their opponents to the army."

[3] Local factions in Afghanistan have accused each other of being "Taliban" or "Al Qaeda" so as to have their rivals bombed by the U.S. Air Force (Bergner 2003:44; Waldman 2002a:A15). Similar instances have been reported in U.S.-occupied Iraq among local factions and tribes (Graham 2005; Oppel 2005a; Clover 2003).

[4] It is possible to think of a person's envy as an individual manifestation of class conflict (e.g., Harding 1984), or the other way around, of a person's participation in abstract class struggle as an individual alibi for the expression of her subjective individual envy. Cribb (1990, 28) makes a somewhat similar claim when he argues about the violence that took place in Indonesia in 1965–6, that

evidence, from a wide variety of civil wars, is impressive in this respect; indeed, it would hardly be an exaggeration to say that references to a disjunction between dynamics in the center and the periphery are present in almost every descriptive account of civil war (Kalyvas 2003).[5]

Local cleavages can aggregate in misleading ways. For example, a conflict classified as class-based may aggregate local dynamics whereby wealthy peasants support one political actor in one region and its rival in a neighboring region or village (Geffray 1990; Cabarrús 1983; Hofheinz 1969); or wealthy merchants are targeted both by class-conscious revolutionary peasants and poor right-wing death squad members (Paul and Demarest 1988:128, 150); the same Hindu caste could be at war with the British in one region and fighting with them in another (Guha 1999:331), and so on. Sets of diverse and occasionally overlapping regional and local cleavages, such as socioeconomic, factional, lineage, clan, tribal, gender, or age cleavages, combine to produce fluid (and even shifting) allegiances that may misleadingly appear to be uniform from a highly aggregate perspective; vertical relationships and ties (patron-client, community, neighborhood, parish, corporation, faction, clan, or kin) interact with, crosscut, and often trump "horizontal" nationwide cleavages such as class and ethnicity. Personal relationships, individual political and religious preferences, and rural perceptions of honor and obligation frequently play an autonomous role. Michael Seidman (2002:6) argues that Spaniards, while aware of their class identity, "used class organizations – whether parties or unions – for their own individual purposes.... Kin and intimates could successfully compete for loyalties with class and gender." Gregor Benton (1999:168) shows how the Chinese Communist "New Fourth Army" succeeded in allying with "people in the war who would not naturally be seen as their allies. They created these alliances in ways that had little to do with Communism as normally conceived and that relied greatly on the exploitation of ties of friendship, kinship, provenance, schooling, and the like.... Such reliance became systematic and even normative." Lynn Horton (1998:69) reports how the leftist Sandinista rebels in Nicaragua, "pragmatically recognizing that 'a finquero [wealthy farmer] can recruit a colono, a poor peasant, but a poor peasant can never recruit a finquero,' would first win over a finquero and then give that producer the autonomy to build his own network of collaborators, which generally included his extended family and his workers and colonos."[6]

---

killings motivated by private grudges were political since they took place in a charged atmosphere where "very little was non-political in one sense or other, and grudges fell into that broader pattern of social polarization." Still, it is both valuable and possible to disentangle the two analytically.

[5] Zucchino (2004:A9); Roldán (2002:251, 206, 212); Seybolt (2001:202); Peterson (2000:207); Romero (2000:53); Ellis (1999:128–9); Zur (1998:114); Vargas Llosa (1998:113); Howell (1997:315); Dalrymple (1997:253); Schroeder (1996:424, 431); P. Berman (1996:65); Hua and Thireau (1996:270–1); Kedward (1993:152–3); Cribb (1990:24–7); Fellman (1989:90); Crow (1985:162); Freeman (1979:164); Shy (1976:206).

[6] Similar evidence is provided by Lubkemann (2005); Ledesma (2004); Davidson (2003); Chung Kunsik (in Yoo 2002:5); M. Johnson (2001); Schoppa (2001:178); Cahen (2000:173); Bax (2000:29); Pettigrew (2000:206); Romero (2000:53); Schroeder (2000:39–40); Bazenguissa-Ganga (1999b:356); Hart (1999:177); Berlow (1998:180); Horton (1998:14); McKenna (1998:162);

In short, group interests often turn out to be "localistic and region-specific";[7] individual motives are not necessarily informed by impersonal cleavage-related grievances but often by local and personal conflicts.[8] The considerable and oft-noted "local ecological variation" of civil war (Perry 1984:440) and its "federal" character (Levine 1987:129) point to the significance of local cleavages, even for societies that are sharply polarized in terms of class (Cenarro 2002:72; Stoll 1999; Gould 1995), religion (Dean 2000:81; Fawaz 1994), and ethnicity (Richards 1996:6; Hamoumou 1993; Jan Gross 1988).

All of this is consistent with the observation that civil wars are "welters of complex struggles" (Harding 1984:59) rather than simple binary conflicts neatly arrayed along a single-issue dimension. In this sense, civil wars can be understood as processes that provide a medium for a variety of grievances to be realized within the space of the greater conflict, particularly through violence. An understanding of civil war dynamics as substantially shaped by local cleavages is also fully consistent with recurring observations and insights suggesting that master cleavages often fail to account for the nature of the conflict and its violence (e.g., Roldán 2002; Dean 2000; Duyvesteyn 2000); that violence is either incompletely related or totally unrelated to the dominant discourse of the war (e.g., Varshney 2001; O'Leary and McGarry 1993); that patterns of democratization at the local level are a powerful determinant on the likelihood of rebellion (Trejo 2004:332); and that civil wars are imperfect, multilayered, and fluid aggregations of highly complex, partially overlapping, diverse, and localized civil wars with pronounced differences from region to region and valley to valley, reflecting the rupture of authority into "thousands of fragments and micro-powers of local character" (Ledesma 2001:258) and into "very localized, often fluid spheres of influence" (Fichtl 2004:2).[9] In other words, civil wars are made up of a "mosaic of discrete miniwars" (Berkeley 2001:151).

This body of evidence is, finally, consistent with the more general observation that the introduction of national electoral politics exacerbates local factionalism (J. Scott 1977a:141), and that local politics are not just (or primarily) the local reflection of national politics but that, instead, party labels are appropriated within the village to serve ends that often have only local significance and little or nothing to do with the parties as national institutions, in a process that has been described as "parochialization" (J. Scott 1977c:221). In his analysis of local

Starn (1998:235); Nordstrom (1997:48); Hart (1997:143); Besteman (1996); Figes (1996:525–6); Tambiah (1996:23); Groth (1995:91); Brovkin (1994:8–9); Stoll (1993:149); Kriger (1992:8); May (1991:40–8); Geffray (1990:31, 92); Lipman (1990:75); Linn (1989:56, 66); Jones (1989:124); L. White (1989:307); Collier (1987:13); Henderson (1985:42, 63); Perry (1984:445, 1980:250); Calder (1984:121); Hinton (1984:527); Marks (1984:264); Cabarrús (1983:185–97); McCoy (1980:198–9); Fiennes (1975:133); Hynt (1974:12–20).

[7] Tishkov (2004:15); Keen (1998:53); T. Young (1997:138–42); Chingono (1996:16); Berry (1994:xvii); Wou (1994:378); J.-C. Martin (1994:40–4); Wickham-Crowley (1992:131); Tilly (1964:305); Lear (1961:109); Barton (1953:12).

[8] E.g., Bouaziz and Mahé (2004:253–4); Mydans (1999); McKenna (1998); Swedenburg (1995); Tone (1994); Yoon (1992); Paul and Demarest (1988); Lucas (1983); Kheng (1983; 1980); Freeman (1979).

[9] K. Brown (2003:222); Loyd (2001:179); Hoare (2001:1); M. Johnson (2001:124); Burg and Shoup (1999:138); Nordstrom (1997:47); Dale (1997:81); Pécaut (1996:266); Finnegan (1992:71).

politics in Sri Lanka, Jonathan Spencer (1990:12, 80, 184) shows that "villagers did not simply have politics thrust upon them; rather they appropriated politics and used them for their own purposes;" he adds that "people were not necessarily enemies because they were in different parties; more often they had ended up in different parties because they were enemies." In turn, "at least part of the apparent ideological and sociological incoherence of political party allegiance" can be traced to the fact that politics provides a means of expressing local conflicts: "It is possible to see a great part of village politics as little more than the dressing up of domestic disputes in the trappings of party political competition, exploiting the public expectation of trouble which accompanies party politics in order to settle private scores in the idiom of public affairs. Party politics are established so firmly in Sri Lanka, in part because of their elective affinity with those divided or dividing communities which otherwise lack an everyday idiom in which to characterize their own disunity: politics provide just such an idiom."

The significance of local cleavages helps explain two recurring features of civil wars: their very quick initial expansion (wildfire is a typical metaphor) and their tendency to ground to a standstill (e.g., Geffray 1990:67).[10] Furthermore, a focus on local cleavages raises questions about concepts such as "group conflict" or "group violence" (or ethnic conflict and ethnic violence, and so on), which presuppose the complete interchangeability of individuals, either as participants and perpetrators or as targets. "Group conflict" makes sense only if group members are fully substitutable for each other (Kelly 2000:5; Loizos 1988). If targets of violence are selected along lines that go beyond group attributes, then violence cannot be described as simply ethnic, class, or some similar category. Often, the master cleavage establishes a baseline that determines what the relevant groups are, but a secondary selection criterion based on individual characteristics unrelated to group identity determines who is targeted, violating the assumption of the interchangeability of individuals. Intergroup victimization motivated by looting among neighbors is common (e.g., Toolis 1997:100; Dale 1997). "The East Tyrone Brigade [of the IRA] were not an army but a band, a company of latter-day woodkernes, of ordinary farmworkers, mechanics, tractor drivers, the unemployed, the odd school-teacher, inheritors of the dispossession, who gathered together to kill *particular known enemies* like Edward Gibson, Thomas Jameson and Harry Henry. The IRA were not waging a war but a sporadic assassination campaign in the tiny rural communities of Tyrone to attack the enemy in their midst" (Toolis 1997: 81–2; emphasis added).[11] Because the class cleavage

---

[10] Given the relationship between control and support discussed in Chapter 7, local cleavages are likely to play the most important role in the early stages of a civil war and in contested areas, where rival actors lack sufficient manpower to establish control. At the same time, the advantages that local cleavages hold for political actors are likely to decay over time, as they become obstacles to the establishment of control. The local cleavages that survive tend to be increasingly absorbed into the dominant ideological discourse and cleavage structure. This process, however, can take a very long time.

[11] Also in Northern Ireland, the violence between the neighboring villages of Coagh and Ardboe, which took the lives of thirty men (from a total population of just over a thousand people) in the space of three years in the late eighties and early nineties, was not simply violence between the Catholic IRA and the Protestant UVF, but also a "bitter vendetta" and the "freshest cycle

defined the relevant group identities in Republican Barcelona during the Spanish Civil War, concierges, maids, and domestic personnel in well-to-do neighborhoods could victimize the middle-class families residing in the buildings where they worked (De Foxà 1993:291–2). Yet, as a resident of Barcelona told me, concierges often handpicked their individual victims based on the additional criterion of personal dislike: not all bourgeois were alike.

Individualized selection may take place even under the extreme circumstances of ethnic cleansing and genocide. Members of households who owned large land properties in Rwanda had a higher chance of dying violently in 1994–2000, meaning that "apart from ethnicity, other regularities can be observed in the killing process" (Verwimp 2003:438). Catherine André and Jean-Philippe Platteau (1998:40) found that the Rwandan genocide "provided a unique opportunity to settle scores or to reshuffle land properties, even among Hutu villagers."[12] The description by a former prisoner of the violence inflicted by Serb guards on Muslim inmates in the notorious Omarska camp in Bosnia provides many such instances (Pervanic 1999:120, 156–7). On one occasion, a Serb guard came in at night and insulted a prisoner who, as a judge, had fined him for a traffic offense in the late 1970s! In another instance,

Sakib Pervanic, a thirty-two-year-old from my village, "disappeared" because of an old grudge against his father. Sakib's father, Mustafa, had had business deals with Rade Gruban – but over the years they had failed to settle some business debts. Rade owned a couple of small grocery shops also selling home appliances. One of the shops was in my village. The business was going well and he decided to expand it through bulk sales of cement, but he did not have the necessary storage space. Mustafa lent him a part of his basement for this purpose, but they could not agree on the amount of the rent. As a result, Mustafa refused to pay Rade for some appliances he had purchased on credit. Rade now wanted revenge – but Mustafa was in the Trnopolje camp. It saved him, but not his son.

Jan Gross's (1988:42) observation about the violence that erupted in western Poland during the Soviet occupation of 1939 captures the individual aspects of group violence particularly well: "Yet, much as the violence represented an explosion of combined ethnic, religious, and nationalist conflict, I am nevertheless struck by its intimacy. More often than not, victims and executioners knew each other personally. Even after several years, survivors could still name names. Definitively, people took this opportunity to get even for *personal* injuries of the past" (emphasis added).

---

of a blood feud" that pitted these *particular* two villages against each other. In other words, the nature of the violence in this area cannot be understood by simple reference to the religious cleavage in Northern Ireland but requires knowledge about the local cleavage between Coagh and Ardboe (Toolis 1997:35). Likewise, the violence along Shiite-Sunni lines in south Iraq following the American invasion of 2003 could be disaggregated into competition between *specific* Shiite and Sunni clans (Andrews 2003).

[12] The assassination of a Tutsi woman during the genocide, in the Rwandan village they studied, cannot be reduced to a "purely racial act," André and Platteau (1998:40–1) argue, because she was disliked for a variety of reasons: she was an outsider, having come to the village from another region; she had inherited a relatively large plot of land from her husband, although she was his fourth wife; and she was involved in many land disputes.

Although ubiquitous in the descriptive literature, these dynamics are completely overlooked by macrolevel studies of civil wars, both historical and theoretical.[13] Instead, most accounts infer local and individual identities and actions directly from the war's master cleavage. Researchers sensitive to the grassroots report these dynamics and are able to disentangle "the reality from the ideologically structured appearances" (Prunier 2005:4), but generally fail to theorize them. A starting point in this direction is to sketch a few broad distinctions. Local cleavages may be preexisting or war-induced; they may align neatly with central cleavages or subvert them; and they may be consistent over time or more fluid and random.

First, local cleavages may be preexisting as opposed to war-induced. In the first case, the war activates existing fault lines, while in the second one, it creates new ones. When prewar local cleavages have already been politicized and grafted onto the national structure of cleavages, their autonomy and visibility *qua* local cleavages are diminished; even then, however, the master cleavage may not erase them. In the most extreme cases, local cleavages lose all autonomy and turn into mere local manifestations of the central cleavage. However, this process may also work the other way around: a central cleavage may branch out into local cleavages that remain active even after the central cleavage has died. This seems to have been the case in Colombia, where the ideological cleavage of Liberals and Conservatives spawned residential segregation and governed intermarriage patterns long after it lost its salience (Henderson 1985).

Often, preexisting local cleavages are not fully grafted onto the master cleavage – which increases their visibility. Thus, the conflict between Royalists and Parliamentarians during the English Civil War in Leicestershire was also a conflict between the Hastings and the Grey families that "went back to personal feuds of far longer standing than the Civil War, in fact to their rivalry for the control of the country since the mid-sixteenth century. For these two families, the Rebellion was, at one level, simply a further stage in the long drawn-out battle for local dominion" (Everitt 1997:24). More generally, it is argued that in the context of the English Civil War "local grievances became the medium through which many national concerns were perceived, while the issues and labels of national debate were used to clothe the continuing local political struggles" (Howell 1997:324). The Protestant-Catholic violence that erupted in southeastern France during the French Revolution was not simply religious violence; rather, it pitted particular families with a track record of past feuding against each other: the Lanteiris against the Labastine in Chamborigaud, the Bossier against the Roux in Vauvert, and the Roussel against the Devaulx in Bagnols. Likewise, "family and faction dictated the course of the IRA split in units all over Ireland" during the civil war: "Once again, it was the Brennans against the Barretts in Clare, the Hanniganites against the Manahanites in east Limerick, and the Sweeneys versus the O'Donnells in Donegal as all the old feuds were reignited." The Liberal-Conservative clash in Colombia "frequently grew out of long-standing family feuds. Liberal Urregos, for instance, joined Franco, while their long-time

---

[13] The rare exceptions include J.-C. Martin (2002:57 and 1994:62) and Ranzato (1994:22).

enemies, the Cossios and Montoyas from Caicedo, made up the ranks of the police and Conservative contrachusma [bands] in nearby towns." More recently, the war between the pro-Baath Iraqi Kurd *jash* militia and Iraqi Kurdish rebels was also a conflict between the Sourchi and the Barzani families; on a lower level of aggregation and the opposite side of the border, in Eastern Turkey, the war between ethnic Kurds and the Turkish state in the village of Ugrak was a war between the Guclu, the Tanguner, and the Tekin families, all ethnic Kurds.[14]

Additionally, war may generate new local cleavages because power shifts at the local level upset existing delicate arrangements. As in medieval Japan, "armed contests over political jurisdiction within the community of would-be governors gave way to brutal family quarrels, agrarian rebellion, clashes between religious sectarians, ferocious dissension over commercial privileges and indebtedness to moneylenders" (Berry 1994:7). After Shining Path rebels appointed new village leaders, "the guerrilla column would leave, without realizing that it had left behind a hornet's nest of contradictions that could not be resolved. The imposition of these new authorities generated initial resentments and the first peasant allies of the armed forces, 'informers' (*soplones*) in the senderista terminology" (Degregori 1998:135). In the central Peruvian valley of Canipaco, the population enjoyed a "kind of honeymoon" with Shining Path, which ended when a dispute erupted between two communities over the distribution of lands previously usurped by haciendas – a description suggesting the absence of prior cleavage between these communities: "The participation of armed Shining Path cadres on the side of one of the communities in a massive confrontation against a confederation of rival communities provoked a rupture with the latter, who decided to turn over two senderista cadres they had captured in the scuffle to the authorities in Huancayo. This action provoked Shining Path reprisals, which culminated in the execution of thirteen peasant leaders. The victims were kidnapped from their communities and assassinated in the central plaza of Chongos Alto" (Manrique 1998:204–5). Among the most potent cleavages produced by civil wars is the generational one: rebels (but also incumbents) often recruit young people, who then proceed to repress their villages' elders.[15]

Finally, local cleavages may even subvert central ones, causing factional conflicts within supposedly unified political camps. During the Japanese occupation in Western Visayas, Philippines, members of the same political faction on opposite sides cooperated closely with each other, while members of opposite factions, within the resistance and the Japanese-sponsored government, respectively,

---

[14] Respectively: Lewis (1978:133); Hart (1999:265–6); Roldán (2002:243); Chivers (2003:A8); Vick (2002:A18).

[15] Many observers have noted the emphasis that insurgent movements place on recruiting young people (e.g., Pike 1966:287), but few have noted that this produces a generational cleavage between the newly empowered youth and the dispossessed elders (exceptions include D. Anderson 2005:67; Hart 1999; Degregori 1998:134; Figes 1996; 1989; Kriger 1992; L. White 1989:295–302). Note that this cleavage may be caused by incumbent-sponsored militias as well. For example, the South Vietnamese government made an important mistake with the strategic hamlet program: by strongly emphasizing the Republican Youth, it created seeds of conflict within the community between the youth and the traditional elders (R. Thompson 1966:126).

fought bitterly against each other (McCoy 1980:205-6). Likewise, kin-based conflicts in some rural communities in El Salvador caused important divisions within
political factions (Cabarrús 1983:189).

In short, local cleavages matter. Although these cleavages are not the only
mechanism producing allegiance and violence, they appear to have a substantial
impact on the distribution of allegiances as well as the targets and intensity of
violence. Of course, the evidence can only be anecdotal, since we lack systematic
studies of the dynamics of civil wars at the local level, as well as empirical measures
of local cleavages.[16] Although it is impossible to ascertain at this point the relative
weight of local cleavages within and across wars, it is necessary to acknowledge
the significance of this phenomenon as a precondition for its systematic study.

11.2. *KTO KOVO?* THE LOCUS OF AGENCY

The phenomenon of malicious denunciation and the significance of local cleavages both raise the question of agency: if individual agents can manipulate their
principals to serve their own agendas, where does the locus of agency lie?

The interstices of political and private violence allow considerable space for
manipulation, something noted by participants and observers alike. For example,
the French troops sent by Napoleon to suppress the 1807 rebellion in Calabria
noticed that the local people were hijacking their war. The local volunteers who
joined the Civic Guards had a "tendency to pursue local vendettas quite apart
from the war effort. There is much evidence that the desire to settle a long-
standing feud with a local rival family was a strong impetus for joining the Civic
Guards. On several occasions local town dwellers asked the French to allow them
to execute Calabrian prisoners who happened to be members of a rival family or
from a rival town" (Finley 1994:73). The question of agency has obvious moral
implications; yet it is also an empirical puzzle. Gage, the author of the book about
his mother's execution during the Greek Civil War cited earlier, sets this question
as his central theme (Gage 1984:19):

> As I drove toward the central square, I kept hearing over the sound of the car's engine a
> phrase that my sister and my father had repeated a hundred times: "*Tin fagane i horiani*" –
> "It was the villagers who devoured her." To my family, the Communist guerrillas like Katis
> were an impersonal act of God, unleashed on our village by war, like a plague. It was our
> neighbors whom they held responsible for my mother's death; the villagers who whispered
> secrets to the security police and testified against her at the trial. This was something I
> had to resolve: perhaps the villagers really were more culpable for her death than the men
> who passed the sentence and fired the bullets. I wondered if something about my mother
> incited the people of Lia to offer her up like a sacrificial lamb. Or perhaps the villagers
> had only been manipulated by the guerrillas, who exploited their moral weaknesses, petty
> jealousies and fears, because the guerrillas wanted my mother killed for some political
> purpose. What was the real reason she was executed?

Disentangling the political from the private dimension of violence is a recurrent quandary for observers of civil wars and generates considerable confusion

---

[16] The Ethnolinguistic Fractionalization Index (ELF) obviously does not capture local cleavages.

among them. "What in one document looks like a clear case of civil war between Whig and Tory," John Shy (1976:191) remarks about an incident that took place during the American Revolution, "becomes in another a messy affair in which political commitment and revolutionary emotion are less in evidence than personal prudence and blatant criminality." Hence the question: where does the locus of agency lie? This question can be succinctly expressed in Lenin's formulation: *Kto kovo? –* Who is using whom?

Prevailing perceptions are informed by two competing interpretive frames, typically juxtaposed dichotomously – most recently as "greed and grievance" (Collier and Hoeffler 2002) or "supply-side and objective causes." The first is Hobbesian in inspiration, stressing an ontology of civil wars characterized by the breakdown of authority and subsequent anarchy. In this view, civil wars encourage the privatization of violence, bringing to the fore in a virtually random fashion all sorts of motivations in a "war of all against all." This thesis informs some popular understandings of ethnic civil wars (Mueller 2004; Posen 1993) and so-called new wars, which are allegedly motivated by greed and loot (Kaldor 1999; Keen 1998). The other frame, which we may call Schmittian, entails an ontology of civil wars based on abstract group loyalties and beliefs, whereby the political enemy becomes a private adversary only by virtue of a prior collective and impersonal enmity. The impersonal and abstract enmity that Carl Schmitt thought was the essential feature of politics (C. Schmitt 1976) echoes Rousseau's perception of war as a matter not of the relationship of "man to man," but only that between "State and State." Individuals, claimed Rousseau, were only enemies by accident, not as individuals but as soldiers (De Lupis 1987:4). In contrast to the Hobbesian thesis, which prioritizes the private sphere to the exclusion of the political one, the Schmittian one stresses the fundamentally political nature of civil wars and its attendant processes; it informs interpretations of traditional "ideological" or "revolutionary" civil wars (Ranzato 1994; Bobbio 1992; Payne 1987), as well as arguments about ethnic civil wars and "intercommunal violence" that stress strong beliefs, group enmity, and cultural antipathy (Varshney 2003; Horowitz 1985). Rather than posit a dichotomy between greed and grievance, the discussion so far points instead to the interaction between political and private identities and actions.

It should be clear by now that the Schmittian view can be misleading because the violence of civil wars is not necessarily externally imposed upon unsuspecting and, therefore, innocent civilians. Many detailed descriptions of violence suggest the presence of a substantial degree of local input in the production of violence. Rather than violence always being imposed upon communities by outsiders, this evidence suggests that it can grow from dynamics within the community. George Collier's (1987:162–3) description of right-wing violence during the Spanish Civil War is paradigmatic in terms of how violence may be both produced and interpreted:

Villagers clearly attribute major responsibility for the Falangist retribution to outsiders. Although they were guided by Inocencio Moreno, it was Falangists from outside the town who accompanied occupying forces, organized townfolk into squadrons for drills and manhunts, and directed the repression. The mass execution followed higher orders that gave local authorities a quota of people to kill. The Civil Guard, all outsiders, were instrumental in the arrests and executions; one captain is blamed for ten deaths.... Yet the Falangists had their sympathizers, outsiders their collaborators, within the town. Only villagers could have identified the fathers and brothers of leading Socialist and militant youth for Falangists to round up for the first mass execution. Outside authorities invited and usually acted on the denunciations of villagers; only two "witnesses" were needed to back up one of these accusations. The rightists appointed to the Town Council and court were the ones who drew up the lists of those to be killed when orders to fill a quota came from higher up. Villagers, some of them alive today, summoned fellow townfolk to headquarters and helped in the manhunts. Survivors remember these acts as discretionary acts, even though they were ordered from above. Villagers felt that the executions would not have happened at all in Los Olivos if the rightists had interceded on behalf of other villagers. They cite the example of Los Marines, a nearby town where reportedly no executions took place because leading families interceded every time a villager was arrested.

The presence of local input in acts of violence is pervasive in microlevel studies and descriptions. When Federal forces invaded central Arkansas in 1863, a delegation of Unionists from Pine Bluff went to meet them and escort them to their town. On arriving in Pine Bluff, the troops proceeded to ransack the homes of rebel sympathizers and as one resident noted, "They knew every ones name & where they lived" (in Ash 1995:127). By examining written testimonies of the civil war that took place in Nicaragua during the 1920s, Schroeder (2000:35) found that victims and assailants were usually well acquainted; most eyewitnesses could identify a dozen or more gang members by face and by name, pointing to one of the most striking aspects of the violence, its local roots: "These were neighbors butchering neighbors." In his postwar trial, Lieutenant General Takeo Ito, a Japanese commander in Papua New Guinea, told the judges that "the lists for executions were compiled in this way. Information would be given to a Japanese soldier by a native that some person was a spy and had contacted Australian soldiers" (in H. Nelson 1980:253).[17] In Guatemala, "at the same time Maya agricultural communities were caught in a frightening national crisis over which they had no control, it was increasingly apparent that both the army and the guerrillas depended on local contacts for information. Thus, part of the world out of control, part of the insecurity and violence Trixanos suffered, was locally authored" (Warren 1998:99). Local Serbs participated in the massacre of about forty ethnic Albanians in the village of Slovinje in Kosovo; according to a witness, "When the army came, our own Serbs put on masks and joined in the butchery. They knew who to single out. They knew who had money" (Bearak 1999a:A3). A Basque peasant woman, whose family suffered at the hands of the nationalists during the Spanish Civil War, summarizes it best: "It wasn't Franco who harmed us, but people from here – the village" (Zulaika 1988:21).

The reliance of political actors on local information is typically conveyed by the widespread use of "name lists" or "blacklists" in processes of violence, as

---

[17] Ito added that the arrested person would be ill-treated, forcing him to denounce others, thus causing the lists to grow.

suggested by an archetypal report from Colombia: "At least eight peasants were killed in the northern village of San Roque in what the police said they suspected was a right-wing paramilitary attack. Gunmen killed four members of a family at a gas station, then stormed into the homes of four farm workers and opened fire after checking their identities against a list they carried, the police said. The area is also a frequent stage for leftist rebel attacks" (J. Moore 1999:A10).[18]

Local participation is compatible with all sorts of motives, ranging from the most ideological to the most opportunistic. As with malice in the case of individual denunciations, settling local and private scores emerges as a key motivation in the context of local dynamics. Often, acts of violence, which on the surface (and to outsiders) appear to be generated by abstract political motivations, turn out, on closer examination, to be "caused not by politics but by personal hatreds, vendettas, and envy" (Harding 1984:75). Thucydides (3.81) argued that personally motivated crime masked by political pretext is one of the essential features of civil war, while, Niccolò Machiavelli describes a situation in which politically motivated riots offered a pretext for private violence.[19] Tocqueville (1988:17) made a similar observation when he argued that "private interest, which always plays the greatest part in political passions, is . . . skillfully concealed beneath the veil of public interest." In her study of Guatemala, Kay Warren (1998:98) describes the hidden local and private underpinnings of a murder which seemed political and impersonal as its "deeper message." The same is the case with malice in the process of denunciation, about which Sheila Fitzpatrick (1994:255) observes that, while it "can be seen in 'top down' terms as a state control mechanism and a means of monitoring public opinion . . . there is also a possible 'bottom up' interpretation of the function of denunciation: if the state used this practice to control its citizens, individual citizens could also use it for the purpose of manipulating the state." This realization produces interesting statements, as when Thaxton (1997:275) reports that in occupied China, "Yang's puppet regime exerted its own interest over that of its Japanese masters."[20] Again, private motives tend to be miscoded at the macrolevel, as Brass (1997) has nicely shown; they are overlooked because

---

[18] The use of name lists is exceedingly common in civil wars. They have been used, among other places, during the guerrilla war in Navarre (Tone 1994:113), the American Civil War (Ash 1995:183; Fellman 1989:61), the Russian Civil War (Werth 1998:79, 117), the Spanish Civil War (Ledesma 2001:260), Malaya (Kheng 1980:96), Italy (Franzinelli 2002:204; Fenoglio 1973:47, 194), the Colombian *Violencia* (Roldán 2002:162), Algeria (Faivre 1994:145; Hamoumou 1993:199), Vietnam (Herrington 1997:13; Wiesner 1988:162; Hosmer 1970:7, 29), Angola (Mair 1995), Liberia (Ellis 1995:186), Guatemala (Stoll 1993; Carmack 1988b:53; Paul and Demarest 1988), Punjab (Rosenberg 1991:46; Arnson and Kirk 1993:79), Sri Lanka (Argenti-Pillen 2003:65), Rwanda (Berkeley 2002:3), Sierra Leone (Richards 1996:8), Congo-Brazzaville (Bazenguissa-Ganga 1999a:46). Rumors stating that name lists have been compiled are also prevalent (Kaufmann 2001:3).

[19] "And many citizens, to avenge private injuries, led them to the houses of their enemies; for it was enough that a single voice shout out in the midst of the multitude, 'to so-and-so's house,' or that he who held the standard in his hands turn toward it" (*Florentine Histories* 3.15).

[20] As Ken Flower (1987:262), the chief of Rhodesian intelligence, said about the RENAMO insurgency in Mozambique: "I began to wonder whether we had created a monster that was beyond control."

of the lack of a theoretical framework that would give them a place in the study of civil war, and conflict more generally. The fact that local cleavages are typically articulated in the language of the war's master cleavage has reinforced this tendency.[21] The claim here is not that all "political violence" is privately motivated but, rather, that there is a pronounced tendency to interpret and code all violence taking place in civil wars as purely and only political.

All these examples would appear to lend support to the Hobbesian frame. As opposed to the group polarization and action suggested by Schmitt, this frame envisions civil war as a decentralized process that produces anomic and random violence (e.g., Roldán 2002:211). Both the war and its violence are depoliticized and privatized: the political is subsumed by the private. Civil war provides a mere pretext, a costume in which to clothe the pursuit of private conflicts; it just disguises private and local motivations as political ones. Thus, accounts that stress the microlevel and local aspect of violence in civil war do so in explicit contrast to arguments that point to the political and strategic dimensions of this violence (e.g., Lubkemann 2005:494–5). Civil wars are therefore reduced to simple aggregations of private feuds and local conflicts – much as Homer often described war as an aggregation of duels (Bernand 1999:90); they are "feuds writ large" (Loizos 1988). Noticing widespread criminal activity in the midst of recent civil wars (and ignoring its prevalence in idealized older ones), some observers (e.g., Kaldor 1999; Keen 1998; Ignatieff 1998; Enzensberger 1994) have concluded that we face a new type of war, motivated by greed rather than grievance – a criminal rather than a political phenomenon.

However, the Hobbesian view can be as misleading as the Schmittian one: whereas the latter ignores the private sphere, the former disregards the public one. Hobbesian interpretations of violence overlook the context in which action unfolds. As I have pointed out, local conflicts and private grudges are present in many places at many times but do not usually erupt into violence – and this is the case even within civil war.[22] Claims of widespread criminality should be equally qualified.[23] In other words, the private is rarely fully independent of the political. As a Manchester Parliamentarian remarked, the "private and particular

[21] The story of Aristogiton and Harmodius as told by Thucydides (6:54–9), and the post-mortem vagaries of Pavlik Morozov, the Soviet boy martyr who denounced his kulak father and was killed by his uncles in revenge in September 1932 (Fitzpatrick 1994:255–6), are probably the most suggestive in this respect.

[22] For example, Watanabe (1992:ix–x) found that although personal and local disputes and animosities abounded in the small Guatemalan town he studied, they did not result in violence: "Even during the worst months of the Guatemalan army's counterinsurgency campaign in 1982–3, the town refused to succumb to the self-serving recriminations, power-mongering, and murder that infected all its neighbors."

[23] Partisan and ethnic gangs are sometimes color-blind and extort everyone equally. This happened in Zvornik, Bosnia, where a Serb paramilitary group called "Yellow Wasps" extorted well-to-do Serbs (Ron 2000b:297). More often, however, they discriminate along cleavage lines. The gangsters of Jakarta who joined the Indonesian insurrection against the Dutch "blended brigandage with patriotism" by plundering only those whose skin was too light (Chinese, Eurasians, and Europeans) or too dark (Ambonese and Timorese) (Cribb 1991:52). The Georgian robbers who looted Sukhumi in 1992 often asked first for the nationality of the intended victims and proceeded only when they were Abkhaz (Dale 1997:87). Likewise, the Colombian *Violencia* "became an

interests are wrapped up in the Publique, not so much publique in private" (in Blackwood 1997:276). The South African Truth and Reconciliation Commission made a similar point when it argued that the apartheid state pursed a policy "to manipulate social, ethnic and other divisions with the intention of mobilising one group against another" (in Pigou 2001:226). Although the South Vietnamese village of Binh Nghia displayed a "lukewarm attitude toward the Viet Cong" because the local Communist movement had originated across the river, in the Phu Long hamlets, this hostility was actively cultivated by external actors:

The hostility between the Phu Longs and Binh Nghia was generations old, focused on a feud over fishing rights. It was natural that the Phu Longs assumed economic as well as political power when the Viet Cong were on the rise and this was done at the direct expense of fishermen from Binh Nghia. So later when the Viet Cong came across the river to spread the gospel, there were many in Binh Nghia who resented them and any cause they represented. *The police chiefs had fed this resentment with money and had built a spy network.* (West 1985:146–7; emphasis added)

Indeed, Paul and Demarest's detailed description of the operation of a death squad in a small town of Guatemala – showing how a group of individuals was vested by the army with exceptional power, which they used in pursuit of "money, liquor, and sex," vengeance, or local power – concludes with a note of caution (1988:153):

It may be tempting to blame the outbreak of violence in San Pedro on social divisiveness and the settling of old scores, but the temptation should be resisted. Religious competition and vigorous political infighting were features of San Pedro life for decades before 1980 without producing violence. The same can be said for interpersonal antagonisms. They arose in the past and were settled by means short of murder. What disrupted the peace in San Pedro was not the presence of differences and divisions, but the army's recruitment of agents and spies that had the effect of exploiting these cleavages.[24]

11.3. ALLIANCE

Positing a strict dichotomy between the political and the private (or the center and the periphery) is misleading. Demonstrating the omnipresence of local and private conflicts cannot be used to reject the importance of political and strategic dimensions in civil wars, very much like the emphasis on these dimensions cannot possibly hide the significance of local and private conflicts.

Local and private conflicts explode into violence neither because civil war is an instance of Hobbesian anarchy nor as a result of the designs and manipulations

umbrella under which every variety of criminality could be found. As the depredations of men under arms grew even more ghastly, it became clear that large numbers of psychopaths and common bandits had joined those who claimed to be fighting to maintain their political principles." Yet, Henderson (1985:149–50) found that "the political motive was usually present no matter how heinous the crime. Conservative and Liberal violentos avoided murdering campesinos who were clearly of their political affiliation."

[24] Kheng (1980:117), Siu (1989:103, 115), and Argenti-Pillen (2003) make similar points about Japanese-occupied Malaya, Japanese-occupied China, and Sri Lanka.

of supralocal actors. What matters, instead, is the interaction between the political and the private spheres. José Luis Ledesma (2001:260, 267) argues correctly that the decentralized and localized nature of the Republican violence during the Spanish Civil War does not mean that it was an instance of spontaneous and anarchical violence by uncontrolled actors, as is usually assumed by historians of the Spanish Civil War. Warren (1998:99) is also right when she describes the violence of the Guatemalan civil war as *double-edged*, as are Michael Schroeder (2000:29) – who observes that violence in Nicaragua during the 1920s "was deeply rooted in local social relations and was at once political and personal, . . . and based on intersecting relations of family, community, party, ethnicity, and class" – and Joshi (2002:435), who concludes her study of denunciations to the Gestapo in Nazi Germany by stating that "the private/public dichotomy was not just being dismantled from above but also from below. The public/political did not remain isolated from the private/domestic/personal. Therefore, the 'big world' of politics did not stand over and above the 'small world' of the family. The two became inextricably intertwined." Likewise, Richard Cobb (1972:56, 90) describes in detail several instances of violence during the French Revolution as situations created by people putting their "private violence to public use." "While the distinction between violence motivated by political ends and violence originating in personal grievances is not unimportant," Noel Fisher (1997:63) writes about the Civil War in east Tennessee, "the participants did not always separate the two." A 1944 letter from occupied Greece nicely conveys this interaction: "Jason, son of P.," the letter states, served the Italians on his island so well that the Italians "carried out all his desires" (in Mazower 1993:xv). Stanley Aschenbrenner (1987:116) describes the civil war in a Greek village as "a sequence of action and reaction that needed no outside energy to continue, though it was of course exploited by outside agents." The description of Afonso Gonçalves's murder in September 1999 in East Timor is almost paradigmatic of this process of interaction. Gonçalves was not killed just for the pro-independence views he held, but also because of a family feud related to a niece who eloped, despite family resistance, with a pro-Indonesia militiaman. A year later, during the terror that engulfed East Timor in the wake of the referendum, members of the militiaman's family came to Gonçalves' house and killed him. This murder, Seth Mydans (1999) concludes, was "as personal as it was political."

The social science literature uses the concept of "cleavage" to refer to the link between actors at the center and action on the ground. To a great extent, the existence of master and local cleavages as separate impulses is not problematized. However, "What one needs to know is the manner in which the local issues, local perceptions, and local problems shaped and informed the national perspective . . . and conversely how that sense of generality, which is so integral a part of the national perspective, was transferred and perhaps translated back into the framework and language of local politics" (Howell 1997:309). Possible connections between center and periphery include common preferences rooted in preexisting identities (Horowitz 1985; Lipset and Rokkan 1967), centralized organization (Kalyvas 1996; Bartolini and Mair 1990), fear contingent on identity (Posen 1993), and coordination around focal points (Chwe 2001; Hardin 1995).

Although each of these mechanisms has its merits, they are inconsistent (or not fully consistent) with the observed disjunction between center and periphery. Alternatively, a mechanism that links center and periphery and is consistent with the observed disjunction can be described as "alliance."

Alliance entails a process of convergence of interests via a transaction between supralocal and local actors, whereby the former supply the latter with external muscle, thus allowing them to win decisive advantage over local rivals; in exchange, supralocal actors are able to tap into local networks and generate mobilization. A great deal of action in civil war is, therefore, *simultaneously* decentralized *and* linked to the wider conflict. Thus civil war is (also) a process that connects the collective actors' quest for power and the local actors' quest for local advantage. Put otherwise, violence can also be a selective benefit that produces local mobilization via alliance.

Alliance is for everyone involved a means rather than a goal (Clastres 1999).[25] Political actors external to the community play a critical role in the conversion of local and private conflicts into violence because they provide incentives without which local actors would be unable or unwilling to undertake violence. At the same time, local actors make a conscious decision to ally with outsiders. Civil war can thus be viewed as an interface. This insight goes back to Thucydides (3:82), who argued that "in peacetime there would have been no excuse and no desire for the calling [of external allies] in, but in time of war, when each party could always count upon an alliance that would do harm to its opponents and at the same time strengthen its own position, it became a natural thing for anyone who wanted a change in government to call in help from outside." Machiavelli's *Florentine Histories* is full of similar insights. In Mozambique, RENAMO insurgents were able to garner local support only where traditional leaders with popular followings were willing to make alliances with them (Roesch 1990:25). In Sri Lanka, Jonathan Spencer (1990:184) observes, "if politics provide a necessary medium for the working out of local disputes and grievances, they do so by appeal to forces and powers outside the local community." The popularity of Liberal guerrillas and Conservative counterguerrillas in Colombia during the early 1950s can be attributed to the fact that "they enabled certain local factions to take revenge on the opposition with impunity and to use the threat of terror to obtain real advantages" (Roldán 2002:206). Disputes among peasant families over water and land, as well as local political power, led to violence in El Salvador because "they tried to resolve them using their political groups" (Cabarrús 1983:189).

Determining when and how such alliances occur calls for fine-grained research. For instance, a recurring pattern is that losers in local conflicts are more likely to move first and, hence, be the first ones to ally with outside forces. If this is true, civil war is particularly destabilizing since it supplies new opportunities to losers in local power conflicts who are seeking an opportunity for *revanche*. This is consistent with several observations: the first to collaborate with the Japanese

---

[25] Jan Gross (2001:4) argues that the purposeful activation and exploitation of "every conceivable cleavage in society" is the essence of totalitarianism. In civil wars, however, the activation of local cleavages typically appears to be more of a means and less of a goal than Gross implies.

occupiers in China sometimes included "those who had failed in politics and teaching" (Lary 2001:111); local leaders who had been marginalized by the government were highly likely to join the RENAMO insurgency in Mozambique (Geffray 1990); losers in local land or chieftaincy disputes sometimes sided with the insurgents in Sierra Leone to secure revenge (Richards 1996:8); embittered and resentful people were used as local agents by the Khmer Rouge in Cambodia (Bizot 2003:44); and German wives were far more likely to denounce their husbands to the Gestapo than the other way around (Joshi 2002). Sometimes, it is a matter of who shows up first. In a Guatemalan town, the losers in local elections allied with the army rather than the insurgents (Stoll 1993:76). It is difficult to convey this insight better than the man who, after the Union army entered Madison County in Alabama, announced his intention to kill his local rival and then "get some of the Union soldiers and take everything out of [his] house and burn the whole place up.... He has been a big fellow for a long time, but now is my time to bring him down" (in Ash 1995:128).

From this perspective, "master" cleavages can be understood as simultaneously symbolic and material formations that simplify, streamline, and incorporate a bewildering variety of local conflicts – a view compatible with the way outside observers, such as historians, rely on a "master narrative" as a means of "emplotment" – to tell a straight, compelling story out of many complex ones (Ricoeur 1984). The concept of alliance allows us to reintroduce complexity, albeit in a theoretically tractable way. Civil wars are concatenations of multiple and often disparate local cleavages, more or less loosely arrayed around the master cleavage. For example, Olivier Roy (1999) interprets the Islamist-conservative cleavage of the 1992 civil war in Tajikistan in terms of what he calls *mahalgera'y* or localism. He disaggregates that civil war's master cleavage (religion) into a number of disparate conflicts along multiple dimensions, such as region, profession, position within the state apparatus, and ethnicity.[26] Predictably, it is easier to discern these dynamics in recent civil wars that lack the sort of modular discourses provided by the Cold War. But the available evidence suggests the commonality of these dynamics; perceived differences between post–Cold War conflicts and previous civil wars may be attributable more to the demise of readily available conceptual categories caused by the end of the Cold War than the fundamentally different nature of pre–Cold War civil wars (Kalyvas 2001). Likewise, the fact that ethnic or religious local cleavages are generally easier for outside observers to spot than factional ones may also cause a bias in reporting, coding, and interpreting evidence.

The mechanism of alliance points to a critical dilemma for both central and local actors. On the one hand, central actors must mobilize at the local level – even when their ideological agenda is opposed to localism. For example, Gregor Benton (1999) masterfully demonstrates how the Chinese Communists were able

---

[26] The "islamo-democratic faction" included regional, professional, and ethnic groups such as the Gharmi (from the Karategin area), the Pamiris (from the Gorno-Badakhshan area), and intellectuals (from the Pendjikent area), whereas the "conservative faction" was composed of Leninabadis from the Leninabad area, Koulabis from Koulab, Hissaris from Hissar, and ethnic Ouzbeks (O. Roy 1999:222–5). Salibi (1988) provides a similar analysis of the Lebanese Civil War.

to penetrate local society along particularistic ties rather than through abstract ideological appeals.[27] Central actors realize that their universalistic appeals often fail to produce the desired local mobilization, as such appeals often are not heeded or even understood. At the same time, they must also transcend particularism and localism, because, as James Scott (1977c:222) puts it, "within every great tradition rebellion with mass support there is also a little tradition revolt that threatens to usurp that rebellion for its parochial ends."

Localism is what distinguished traditional peasant jacqueries from modern insurgencies and crippled the former. Friedrich Engels argued that the peasant rebels of the German Peasant War of 1525 "never overstepped the boundaries of social relations and local outlook" and "were confined to their local horizon"; he castigated their "stubborn provincialism," and "appalling narrow-mindedness," qualities he described as "always inevitable among the peasant masses," which ultimately ruined their revolt. Trotsky argued that "local cretinism is history's curse on all peasant riots," and Mao criticized localism in peasant guerrilla units, "which are frequently preoccupied with local considerations to the neglect of the general interest" (in Guha 1999:278–9). Hence, central actors try relentlessly (though to varying degrees) to absorb local cleavages into the master cleavage. At the same time, local actors resist their absorption into centralized and hierarchical structures. Though instrumentally tied to the master cleavage, they strive to remain distinct and maintain a degree of autonomy. "The peasantry has sorely tried the patience of archbishops and commissars alike," notes James Scott (1977b:1). The history of many insurgent movements is a tale of the tension between these conflicting goals.[28] Seen from this perspective, civil war is a process of political and administrative "normalization," and state building can be seen as an externality of civil war.

The relevance of alliance as a mechanism that brings local cleavages into the master cleavage of a conflict is twofold: first, it allows for a theoretical understanding of civil war that incorporates rather than ignores the puzzle of the disjunction between center and periphery and the extensive ambiguity that surrounds this process. Second, it turns the center-periphery interface into a central issue and forces us to think more precisely about the modalities linking distinct actors and motivations. Recognizing the existence of a concatenation of multiple and disparate local cleavages allows the exploration of the relation between central and local cleavages – a possibility precluded by the prevailing understanding of cleavage.

---

[27] The Chinese and Vietnamese Communists constitute a clear example in this respect (Benton 1999; Huan and Thireau 1996; Hunt 1974:12), as well as African anticolonial insurgencies (e.g., Finnegan 1992:116–17).

[28] Chinese Communist documents show that Red Army troops refused to fight guerrilla wars in the "white zones," preferring to remain in the "red zones," where they could lead quiet and tranquil lives, with local residents serving them as sentries. This tendency was known as parochialism (*difang zhuyi*) (Wou 1994:140). Donald Raleigh (2002:74–108) documents how the Soviet regime used purges, among other instruments, to destroy the independence of regional and local party organizations. Local actors in Macedonia sometimes pushed for more violence than was acceptable to central actors (Livanios 1999:206), and so on.

Surrogate warfare in international politics has a long history, from the days of the Roman Empire (Shaw 2001:155) to the Cold War. Yet we have failed to conceptualize civil war as a proliferation and aggregation of surrogate wars. It is now possible to reconcile within the same analytical frame motivations that are thought to be contradictory, without bundling them – such as strategic action by political actors and opportunistic action by local groups and individuals. The theoretical advantage of alliance is that it allows for multiple rather than unitary actors, agency located in *both* center and periphery rather than only in either one, and a variety of preferences and identities as opposed to a common and overarching one. A key methodological implication is that careful disaggregation must precede macro-interpretation. In a different formulation, we cannot get at the micromechanisms from the analysis of macrovariables.

Empirically, alliance is consistent with the intimate and often malicious nature of selective violence, the endogeneity of cleavages to the war, and the limited visibility of local cleavages after the war. Once a war has ended, the master narrative of the conflict provides a handy way ex post facto to simplify, streamline, and ultimately erase the war's complexities, contradictions, and ambiguities. An interesting implication is that what differentiates premodern rebellions and modern insurgencies is the absence of urban elites and their discourse in the former. Furthermore, many so-called postmodern (or "symmetric nonconventional") insurgencies also appear to lack a connection with articulate urban elites. Alliance is also consistent with the finding that a country's per capita gross domestic product is inversely correlated with the onset of civil war: since education correlates with GDP and ideological messages require education, we would expect alternatives to ideological mobilization, such as local cleavages, to be prevalent in civil wars.

The claim here is that alliance is one mechanism, not the only one; it certainly is, however, the most overlooked mechanism of cleavage formation and articulation; and as already pointed out, recognizing the role of local cleavages in no way implies abandoning the study of national-level dynamics and master cleavages. The focus on interaction requires a careful analysis of both. If I stress the local dimension, it is only because it has been so overlooked.

Paying attention to local cleavages is necessary for achieving a closer fit between macrolevel and microlevel theory and interpreting cross-national findings about macrovariables, such as the onset, duration, and termination of civil wars. For instance, one of the most robust predictors of civil war onset, per capita gross domestic product (Fearon and Laitin 2003; Collier and Hoeffler 1999), could be capturing the effect of local cleavages: poor, nonmodernized states never penetrated their periphery effectively, thus failing to reduce the salience of local cleavages (Lipset and Rokkan 1967) and leaving such cleavages as a resource for rebels to access.

11.4. CONCLUSION

A key implication of the theory of selective violence for our understanding of civil wars is that the current insistence on a Hobbesian-Schmittian dichotomy can be greatly misleading. First, and counter to Schmitt, actions in civil wars, including "political violence," are not necessarily political and do not always reflect deep ideological polarization. Identities and actions cannot be reduced to decisions taken by the belligerent organizations, to the discourses that are produced at the center, and to the ideologies derived from the war's master cleavage. Hence, an approach positing unitary actors, inferring the dynamics of identity and action exclusively from the master cleavage and framing civil wars in binary terms is misleading; instead, local cleavages and intracommunity dynamics must be incorporated into theories of civil war, as illustrated by the theory of selective violence. Second, and counter to Hobbes, civil war cannot be reduced to a mere mechanism that opens up the floodgates to random and anarchical private violence. Private violence is generally constrained by the logics of alliance and control – that is, by national elites and supralocal actors. Civil war fosters a process of interaction between actors with distinct identities and interests. It is the convergence between local motives and supralocal imperatives that endows civil war with its intimate character and leads to joint violence that straddles the divide between the political and the private, the collective and the individual.

Conclusion

Μόχθος δ᾽ ἐκ μόχθων ᾄσσει (Misfortunes follow from misfortunes).

Euripides, *Iphigenia in Tauris*

This book has marshaled theory and evidence to demonstrate that there is logic to violence in civil war and that violence against civilians cannot be reduced to opaque madness. Shakespeare and Goethe had the right intuition: There is logic in madness and hell has its laws. The popularity of the assumption that violence is impenetrable has contributed to a proliferation of hand-waving explanations for violence emphasizing collective emotions, ideologies, and cultures that have low explanatory power. At the same time, the logic of violence in civil war turns out to be very different from widespread but rather tautological interpretations positing that violence is used because "it pays." Such views confuse the rationality of choices with the optimality of outcomes, and derive the former from the latter and vice versa.

Instead, the goal of this book has been to specify exactly if, how, when, where, and for whom violence "pays." Simply put, indiscriminate violence is an informational shortcut that may backfire on those who use it; selective violence is jointly produced by political actors seeking information and individual civilians trying to avoid the worst – but also grabbing what opportunities their predicament affords them. In both instances, violence is never a simple reflection of the optimal strategy of its users; its profoundly interactive character defeats simple maximization logics while producing surprising outcomes, such as the relative nonviolence of the "front lines" of civil war.

At a more abstract level, I asked why civil wars produce violence that tends to assume simultaneously a highly brutal and a deeply intimate character. Is violence a reflection of human nature, as argued by Thucydides and Hobbes? Or is it an expression of deep political divisions that turn individuals into lethal enemies, as Schmitt alluded? Such questions are pitched at too high a level of generality, and this book does not address them directly; however, it does provide theoretical insights and empirical evidence that question the exclusive link between civil war violence and either cruel predisposition or intense political passions.

The overwhelming focus on the metaphors of anarchy and polarization has caused us to overlook a critical dimension of civil wars: the fact that they provide powerful incentives for the production of "indirect" violence by "ordinary" civilians. For the many people who are not naturally bloodthirsty and abhor direct involvement in violence, civil war offers irresistible opportunities to harm everyday enemies. It is this banality of violence, to paraphrase Hannah Arendt, that gives civil wars a great deal of their appalling connotation.

Rather than just politicizing private life, civil war works the other way around as well: it privatizes politics. Civil war often transforms local and personal grievances into lethal violence; once it occurs, this violence becomes endowed with a political meaning that may be quickly naturalized into new and enduring identities. Typically, the trivial origins of these new identities are lost in the fog of memory or reconstructed according to the new politics fostered by the war.

Two general implications follow. First, there should be no fundamental difference in aversion to direct violence or willingness to harm one's neighbors between the people of countries that experience civil wars and the people of those that do not. Second, war is a transformative phenomenon,[1] and civil war even more so. The advent of war transforms individual preferences, choices, behavior, and identities – and the main way in which civil war exercises its transformative function is through violence. In other words, there are several ways in which violence works as an independent variable. This insight is hardly new, yet it is surprising how little it has influenced recent research on civil wars.

Most recent work on civil wars consists of large-N studies of onset, duration, and termination of civil wars. Unlike this valuable work, I have studied the dynamics of violence once civil wars begin; and unlike this book, these theories have close to nothing to say about violence; they treat it as an automatic outcome of war, unworthy of study in its own right. This is a consequential neglect related to the larger issue of current practices in political science regarding the causal status of preferences, strategies, and identities.

Still, there are some implications to be derived from this book for extant theories of civil war. First, that civil wars are highly "endogenous" processes is often ignored. Collective and individual preferences, strategies, values, and identities are continuously shaped and reshaped in the course of a war. Popular loyalty, disloyalty, and support cannot be assumed as exogenous and fixed. Hence, theories that assume actors and preferences to be frozen in their prewar manifestations, and rely on this assumption to explain various aspects of civil wars, such as their onset, duration, or termination, will be biased. This bias is reinforced by the tendency to deduce prewar actors, preferences, and identities from "master narratives" of civil war. To be sure, such narratives simplify the complexity of civil wars.[2] However, the fact that civil wars are state-building processes means that

---

[1] A point eloquently made by, among others, George Kennan (1951).

[2] This is why pervasive nonethnic motives behind much violence in "ethnic" wars, such as robbery and the takeover of neighbors' apartments, tend to be disregarded, and ethnicity becomes "the

their "master narratives" are likely to be contaminated by the war's outcome: they will be distorted, and their ambiguities and contradictions will be erased.[3] Often the hegemony of such narratives is so powerful that even researchers who collect detailed accounts tend to disregard or downplay their findings because they do not fit into existing frames. For example, the observation that a great deal of violence flows from private disputes has been profusely reported and simultaneously marginalized. As a result, theories of civil war onset based on these accounts are likely to derive their causes from their outcomes.

Second, individuals are simply absent from current theories of civil wars. When they are not aggregated into groups ("the Serbs," "the people") whose actions are directed by others, they are portrayed as the victims of violence. There is a tendency to see violence as being externally imposed on unsuspecting and, therefore, innocent civilians – a perspective reinforced by the discourse of human rights and echoed in instrumentalist theories of ethnic conflict according to which individuals are perpetually manipulated by politicians. In short, individuals tend to be seen as objects rather than subjects of the violence. This perspective is succinctly expressed in various sayings about proverbial ants caught between fighting elephants or buffaloes. However, individuals cannot be treated simply as passive, manipulated, or invisible actors; instead, they often manipulate central actors into helping them fight their own conflicts. In short, they must be explicitly incorporated into theories of civil war in ways that reflect the complexity of their participation.

Third, much work neglects the fact that there is no necessary overlap between the micro- and the macrolevels. The current emphasis on the macrolevel implies that "on-the-ground" dynamics are perceived as a rather irrelevant local manifestation of the macrolevel. Local actors are seen as local replicas of central actors, and studying them is justified only on grounds of local history or antiquarian interest. This neglect has several causes: a division of labor separating the tasks of collecting evidence at the microlevel and interpreting macrodynamics; an epistemic preference that marginalizes the particular; and the interpretation of microlevel dynamics in the language of the master cleavage. The result is a view of political actors as unitary and a derivation of individual motives from the decisions of elites along the "modular" themes of religion, ethnicity, or class. However, the disjunction between central and local cleavages raises serious doubts about the validity of such inferences. In other words, violence in an "ethnic" or "class war" is not automatically or necessarily ethnic or class violence. This is not to say that ethnic, religious, or class allegiances are false or irrelevant, but, rather, that their effect varies considerably across time and space within the same civil

---

primary category with which people on the ground narrate and comprehend the war's violence" (Dale 1997:91).

[3] In fact, academic studies often share with "official historiographies" the tendency to erase troubling internal divisions, "class fissures, acts of treachery, or peasant initiatives that were independent of elite control" and to smooth over "the past's jagged edges" (Swedenburg 1995:21; Kedward 1993:160).

war, and that their consolidation is often the outcome rather than the cause of violence.

The process of inferring on-the-ground dynamics from the macrolevel will likely generate biased inferences, in a way that parallels the well-known problem of ecological fallacy. To be sure, grass roots are messy. This "local messiness" can be overlooked if the only goal is a simplified macrohistorical account intended for a broad audience; however, the rigorous theoretical and empirical analysis of civil war is impossible in the absence of close attention to microlevel dynamics. Likewise, it is incorrect to explain the behavior of individuals by reference only to the actions of elites or vague "groups." The relation between individuals and elites is variable in time and space. It follows that theories of civil war must incorporate a multilevel analysis, simultaneously accounting for the interaction between rival elites, between elites and the population, and among individuals. Failing to do so will distort the analysis and miss the mechanisms that mediate between opportunities and constraints at the center and the periphery.

The frequent misinterpretation of microlevel dynamics has contributed to the production of microfoundations that are either untested (i.e., "stylized") or false; it has also led to overly aggregate conceptualizations of variables that are typically vulnerable to problems of observational equivalence. For example, per capita GDP is consistent with several mechanisms of civil war onset; state capacity is consistent with many types of resource allocation; despite what is often averred, individual motivations for joining rebel movements are rarely just a manifestation of "grievance" or an expression of "greed" – and joining often entails no collective action problem at all; anarchy is typically the wrong metaphor for the situation on the ground; fear need not lead to violence; elite decisions are far from the single cause of violence; the source of control is not necessarily to be found in popular preferences; and so on. Put otherwise, conceptualizations and microfoundations must emerge from careful empirical research rather than dubious stylized facts.

In addition to being necessary for properly understanding civil wars, the focus on the endogenous dynamics of civil war points to potential policy implications that do not hinge exclusively on an analysis of prewar politics. Reducing violence requires as much local action as action at the center. At least in the short and medium term, tinkering with local control could be a more efficient way to achieve peace and stability than investing in mass attitudinal shift. From this perspective, the incorporation of an operational measure of control ought to become a priority for peacekeeping and peacebuilding operations. The allocation of troops and, especially, administrative resources should be based on a clear understanding of the local balance of control. Conversely, encroaching on the local control of an armed actor with no mandate or ability to protect civilian "defectors" aggressively may cause serious harm. Likewise, since selective violence is jointly produced, peacekeepers ought to approach civilians as agents and take their behavior into account when designing peacebuilding strategies. And since civilians are often active yet indirect perpetrators of violence, coming to terms with past violence becomes a much more complicated issue than it already is.[4]

Focusing on the endogenous dynamics of civil war has methodological implications as well. Chief among these is the importance of disaggregation, at the level of both theory and empirical investigation. For example, asking what causes a civil war is not the same as asking what causes violence within a civil war; the study of the formation of new armed groups is not the same as the study of the recruitment of people by already formed armed groups, and so on. Generating robust intuitions about microfoundations and testing them with reliable data ought to be a prerequisite for research at the macrolevel. There is much we can learn by appreciating the "messiness" of civil wars, and subnational research designs can be very useful in that respect.

The inherent complexity of civil war also makes methodological eclecticism productive, as this book has sought to show. While macro-oriented researchers have ignored local complexity, researchers attuned to the grass roots consistently fail to systematize and theorize the local dynamics they report. This book demonstrates that abstract analytical theories can shed light on evidence thought to be trivial or parochial; it stresses the theoretical import of evidence deemed "marginal" on the basis of prevailing frames of understanding and calls for its incorporation into theoretical work; it suggests ways in which ethnographic evidence can be harnessed to address well-defined empirical implications of abstract theories, and shows that it can be combined with several tools, including statistical analysis; it calls for collecting data both on aggregate outcomes and actual processes; and it demonstrates the necessity and possibility of submitting the hypothesized mechanisms connecting independent and dependent variables to direct test, rather than just positing or assuming away links.

A few years ago, I presented some of my findings to a Greek audience, which, blinded by partisan bias, was unwilling to accept the fact that Greek resistance fighters had killed many innocent Greek civilians. A local public intellectual rose angrily to tell me he felt disturbed by my talk; he then asked me what the "true motives" of my research were. In writing this book, I have been driven by intellectual curiosity about a particularly disturbing and opaque facet of human behavior. This book will have achieved its goal if it succeeds in inspiring a research program geared toward the rigorous analysis of the microdynamics of civil wars. However, if it happens to contribute to the effort of decreasing the violence of civil wars, it will have accomplished much more than I ever set out to do, or than I could reasonably hope for.

---

[4] An intriguing implication regarding the reintegration of combatants in their communities is as follows: insofar as they may have information about who denounced whom, their return may prove contentious, exacerbate local conflict, and destabilize communities. This is an aspect that has not been addressed in studies of demobilization and reintegration. I thank to Ana Arjona for pointing this out to me.

Appendix A: Data Sources

Archives are often of limited value in the study of civil war violence, since much of the violence simply goes unrecorded (Klinkhammer 1997:xi; Roy 1994:5). The archives of developing countries (where most civil wars take place) are usually run-down or poorly maintained. Several Greek archives, for instance, are either inaccessible or in poor condition.[1] I had the good fortune to locate a major archival source: the judicial archives for the criminal courts of the entire eastern Peloponnese.[2] Although the archive was uncatalogued at the time that I did my research, it contains records from all the courts of the eastern Peloponnese of criminal trials that took place after 1945. Between 80 and 90 percent of criminal trials between 1945 and 1950 dealt with either wartime crimes by the Communist-led resistance (which made up the bulk of these trials) or with postwar crimes committed by right-wing militias. The archive also contains the records of the Special Court of Collaborators (*Eidikon dikastirion dosilogon*) for the Argolid, a tribunal set up to try individuals accused of collaboration with the occupation authorities. Most files include extensive summaries of the trials; a substantial number, however, contain the entire trial files, which include the relevant indictments, depositions and affidavits, and interrogation records, as well as supplemental materials such as police records, newspapers, letters, and photographs.

The major problem in using judicial evidence lies in its inherent biases. Justice in postwar Greece was biased against the Left (Delaportas 1978). As in many other post-civil-war settings, a victor's justice prevailed (e.g., Auman 1984:91);

---

[1] According to a historian of Greece, "The state of Greece's archives is a national disgrace . . . sustained research into the wartime period is almost impossible on the basis of Greek archives alone" (Mazower 1993:423). Most archival material related to the civil war, including tens of thousands of police files, was destroyed in 1989 to celebrate the national reconciliation symbolized by the formation of a right-wing–Communist coalition cabinet.

[2] Initially located at the Court of Appeals of Nafplio, these archives were transferred in 1998 to the Historical Archive of the Argolid. I also used the municipal archives of the town of Nafplio.

"hearsay and guilt by association" (Fellman 1989:47) were in many cases the main evidence. Prosecution witnesses often exaggerated the guilt of those charged, implicated innocent people, and exonerated their own actions. All participants, defendants, plaintiffs, and witnesses had an incentive to testify in ways that maximized the extraction of favorable outcomes. The testimony of the defendants is often exculpatory and mendacious, misrepresenting motivations, deemphasizing commitment to political causes, repenting, and so on.[3]

Despite their flaws, judicial sources are an important source. They require careful sifting and weighing. Because lies and misrepresentations tend to be "patterned," it is possible to see through them.[4] Cross-checking with other sources is essential. When evaluated critically, judicial sources provide a thick description of violent events and actors, including detailed chronologies. Often, they are the only source.[5] Frequently, they include extensive memoranda written by defendants that provide useful counterpoints to the arguments of the prosecution. Even flaws can be useful: the types of arguments admitted in court are in themselves precious pieces of information. For example, a recurring argument made by defendants was that one could not possibly be implicated in the death of a person because one did not know him or her personally, which suggests a crucial and credible but unstated assumption that a great deal of violence was exercised among people who knew each other. Michael Schroeder (1996:409) found that "in spite of their spare, sterile language," judicial sources in Nicaragua "are extraordinary documents [that] provide a view of rural politics that is rarely seen or even perceived by outside observers." This was also my experience.

In short, judicial sources are not mere recitations of crimes and verdicts, but rather include very rich material that allows subtle interpretation. This is why they are a critical tool for historians (Hobsbawm 2001:xvii). In fact, they have been used with success in a number of studies that have dealt with both political violence (e.g., D. Anderson 2005; Joshi 2003; Jan Gross 2001; Della Porta 1995; Browning 1992; Gellately 1991; Ortiz Sarmiento 1990; Fellman 1989; Jankowski 1989; Lucas 1983; McCoy 1980; Cobb 1972), as well as rural criminal violence (Gould 2003; Gambetta 1993).

In addition to the judicial archives, I consulted the archives of the Greek Communist Party and the Greek army – both of which are incomplete and became

---

3 Fellman (1989:49–50) found that in Civil War Missouri, "When they were arrested and interrogated by Union authorities, most guerrillas and guerrilla sympathizers lied about their involvement. The formula for denying or downplaying involvement was to claim that one had been coerced and threatened into giving aid or had been involuntarily conscripted into guerrilla service.... Playing dumb, minimizing involvement, denying that they gave out information on Union activities, insisting that failure to comply with guerrilla demands was overridden by guerrilla robbery, stressing the fear of destruction, and all the while professing active loyalty to the Union were standard defense ploys."

4 Jankowski (1989:173–4) provides a useful set of practical rules on cross-checking the content of declared motivations. He warns that there is "a margin of error in the collective analysis of motivations, making conclusions reliable only if the patterns and the numbers are sufficiently loud and clear for confidence. Otherwise, conclusions must be qualified."

5 Discussing the available sources on Nazi-occupied Poland, Jan Gross (1979:44) points out that "no history of the period would ever be written if one insisted on using only materials of irreproachable veracity."

available only recently, but contain useful information about the Argolid. I also examined the archives of both the British Foreign Office and the Special Operations Executive, located in the Public Records Office in London. Both institutions took a keen interest in Greek affairs because Greece was considered to lie within the British sphere of influence. In fact, reports of SOE operatives in the Argolid during 1943–4 complement other local sources. I also studied the detailed reports of the Allied Mission for Observing the Greek Elections (AMFOGE). Finally, I made limited use of German military and military justice archival material that focuses on the military situation in the Argolid.

A.2. ORAL SOURCES

Maurice Halbwachs (1968) observed that in periods of national crisis, national history is directly connected with personal history. What is more, personal history captures many aspects that are usually left out of official reports and national histories. Historians, Ramón Sender Barayón (1989:115) points out about the Spanish Civil War, "have chronicled the glorious combats. But it was the anguish of families which enshrined the true saga of humanity." By capturing such personal aspects of conflict, oral recollections act as a necessary corrective to the urban bias. Accordingly, they constitute a major source for this book. I spent ten months in the Argolid between 1997 and 1999;[6] moreover, in 2000, I conducted three additional months of fieldwork in Almopia (combined with archival research in the criminal court of Thessaloniki). Altogether, I conducted 215 taped interviews, of which 116 were with residents of the Argolid, 35 with residents of Almopia, and the remainder with people from other parts of Greece. Figure A.1 shows photographs I took of some of the respondents. Table A.1 includes a complete list of the interviewees, their place of origin, and a short description.

In addition, I conducted several formal but untaped interviews and found myself in countless informal conversations about the civil war. The interviews were open-ended, in-depth, structured household conversations that lasted between one and four hours; I also conducted some small-group discussions, usually in a public setting (coffee shops and public squares). I approached informants through "snowball sampling," whereby initial contacts suggest new ones. Given the sensitive nature of the issue, I never attempted an interview without a prior introduction or recommendation by a relative or friend of the informant.

It is important to stress here that I did not restrict myself to "victims." While my informants do not constitute a representative sample, they do include (in the case of the Argolid) every knowledgeable person I was able to identify and interview during my fieldwork (with a half century having passed since the end of the civil war, most participants are no longer alive). Every single village of the region is represented. I interviewed both women and men, active participants (in various capabilities: low-level and middle-level political and military cadres, soldiers,

---

[6] Summer 1997 (three months); winter 1998 (two months); summer 1998 (three months); and summer 1999 (two months).

FIGURE A.I. Respondents from Thiriopetra, Almopia; Tseria, Messinia; and Prosimni, Argolid

TABLE A.I. *Interviews*

Number of Interview	Interviewee's Place of Origin	Interviewee's Short Description
1	Efkarpia, Serres	Peasant; husband was DSE guerrilla
2	Aghia Triada, Imathia	Father, brothers, and sisters were DSE guerrillas
3	Platanorevma Servion, Kozani	ELAS & DSE guerrilla
4	Midea, Argolid	EAM regional cadre
5	Midea, Argolid	Husband was ELAS guerrilla
6	Anifi, Argolid	Brother was ELAS guerrilla
7	Anifi, Argolid	EAM local cadre
8	Anifi, Argolid	Son of EAM regional leader
9	Vrousti, Argolid	Peasant; association with SB
10	Evandro, Arkadia	Peasant
11	Koutsopodi, Argolid	Peasant; EAM member
12	Fichtia, Argolid	Local EAM cadre
13	Cheli, Argolid	Peasant
14	Cheli, Argolid	Peasant
15	Cheli, Argolid	Peasant
16	Cheli, Argolid	Peasant
17	Cheli, Argolid	Shepherd
18	Asini, Argolid	Peasant
19	Limnes, Argolid	Peasant
20	Aghios Andrianos, Argolid	Peasant; right-wing activist
21	Midea, Argolid	Peasant
22	Eleochori, Arkadia	Peasant; EAM sympathizer
23	Eleochori, Arkadia	Student
24	Eleochori, Arkadia	Peasant
25	Eleochori, Arkadia	Peasant
26	Kastri, Arkadia	Peasant; EAM sympathizer
27	Kastri, Arkadia	Peasant
28	Kastri, Arkadia	SB cadre
29	Kastri, Arkadia	ELAS guerrilla, then SB soldier
30	Kastri, Arkadia	EAM regional cadre
31	Kastri, Arkadia	Peasant
32	Nikiti, Chalkidiki	Peasant; local militia member
33	Nikiti, Chalkidiki	DSE officer
34	Kosmas, Arkadia	Daughter of EAM regional leader
35	Kastri, Arkadia	Army officer
36	Kastri, Arkadia	Peasant
37	Kastri, Arkadia	Peasant
38	Kastri, Arkadia	Peasant
39	Tseria, Messinia	ELAS guerrilla
40	Tseria, Messinia	Peasant; EAM/DSE collaborator
41	Kambos Avias, Messinia	EAM collaborator; right-wing band conscript
42	Malta, Messinia	Right-wing band conscript

(continued)

TABLE A.1 *(continued)*

Number of Interview	Interviewee's Place of Origin	Interviewee's Short Description
43	Vromovrisi, Messinia	Student
44	Kopanaki, Messinia	Peasant
45	Handrinos, Messinia	Peasant
46	Malandreni, Messinia	Peasant
47	Leonidio, Korinthia	Peasant
48	Gralista, Karditsa	Peasant
49	Neos Pyrgos, Evia	Merchant
50	Tatari, Karditsa	Student
51	Kerasia, Achaia	Student
52	Malandreni, Argolid	ELAS guerrilla
53	Pirgela, Argolid	EAM sympathizer
54	Lefkakia, Argolid	SB soldier
55	Argos, Argolid	KKE member
56	Kranidi, Argolid	Peasant
57	Kranidi, Argolid	Peasant, EAM sympathizer
58	Mikines, Argolid	EAM village leader
59	Achladokambos, Argolid	Peasant
60	Lirkia, Argolid	EAM collaborator
61	Kapareli, Argolid	Peasant
62	Irakleio/Argos, Korinthia/Argolid	Peasant; son of SB collaborator
63	Skinochori, Argolid	Peasant
64	Korakovouni, Arkadia	Peasant; EAM youth member
65	Kalivia, Korinthia	Peasant
66	Douka, Argolid	Shepherd
67	Skotini, Argolid	DSE guerrilla
68	Kalivia, Korinthia	Peasant
69	Kalivia, Korinthia	EAM sympathizer
70	Prosymna, Argolid	ELAS guerrilla
71	Tatsi, Argolid	Peasant
72	Monastiraki, Argolid	Right-wing band leader
73	Monastiraki, Argolid	Peasant
74	Monastiraki, Argolid	Peasant
75	Manesi, Argolid	EAM youth member; son of EAM village leader
76	Aghios Andrianos, Argolid	Peasant
77	Manesi, Argolid	ELAS/DSE guerrilla
78	Malandreni, Argolid	EAM village leader, KKE member
79	Kapareli, Argolid	EAM village leader
80	Asini, Argolid	Peasant
81	Panariti, Argolid	Son of EAM village leader
82	Poulakida, Argolid	ELAS/DSE guerrilla
83	Pournaria, Arkadia	DSE guerrilla
84	Poulakida, Argolid	KKE member, then dissident; SB collaborator
85	Argos, Argolid	Right-wing band leader

Number of Interview	Interviewee's Place of Origin	Interviewee's Short Description
86	Nea Tirintha, Argolid	Peasant
87	Nafplio, Argolid	Student
88	Lefkakia, Argolid	Peasant
89	Cheli, Argolid	Right-wing band leader
90	Athikia, Korinthia	Peasant
91	Karia, Argolid	EAM/KKE cadre
92	Midea, Argolid	OPLA member
93	Midea, Argolid	Peasants (collective)
94	Iraklio, Korinthia	Gendarme
95	Methochi, Argolid	Peasant
96	Methochi, Argolid	Peasant
97	Methochi, Argolid	Peasant
98	Stemnitsa, Arkadia	Peasant
99	Frousiouna, Argolid	EAM local cadre
100	Frousiouna, Argolid	ELAS guerrilla
101	Kefalovriso, Argolid	Peasant
102	Fichtia, Argolid	EAM local cadre
103	Borsa, Argolid	Peasant
104	Midea, Argolid	Peasant; sister of OPLA leader
105	Amigdalitsa, Argolid	ELAS/DSE guerrilla
106	Amigdalitsa, Argolid	Peasant
107	Inachos, Argolid	ELAS guerrilla
108	Anifi, Argolid	Peasant
109	Lalouka, Argolid	EAM collaborator; brother was DSE guerrilla
110	Limnes, Argolid	Peasant
111	Ireo, Argolid	Peasant
112	Tristrato/Inachos, Argolid	Peasant
113	Achladokambos, Argolid	Student
114	Achladokambos, Argolid	Local SB leader
115	Tristrato/Inachos, Argolid	EAM village leader; National Army soldier
116	Skinochori, Argolid	Peasant
117	Karia, Argolid	EAM local cadre
118	Niochori, Argolid	Peasant
119	Aghia Triada, Argolid	Peasant
120	Aghia Triada, Argolid	Peasant
121	Aghia Triada, Argolid	Peasant
122	Aghia Triada, Argolid	Peasant
123	Argoliko, Argolid	Elite soldier
124	Kourtaki, Argolid	EAM local cadre
125	Manesi/Kourtaki, Argolid	EAM collaborator
126	Nea Kios, Argolid	EAM local cadre
127	Neo Ireo, Argolid	Peasant
128	Neo Ireo, Argolid	Peasant
129	Skafidaki, Argolid	Peasant
130	Prosymna, Argolid	Peasant

(continued)

TABLE A.1 *(continued)*

Number of Interview	Interviewee's Place of Origin	Interviewee's Short Description
131	Dalamanara, Argolid	Peasant
132	Monastiraki, Argolid	Peasant
133	Nemea, Korinthia	Peasant
134	Aghios Nikolaos/Platani, Argolid	Peasant
135	Aghios Nikolaos/Platani, Argolid	Peasant
136	Nea Epidavros, Argolid	Peasant
137	Nea Epidavros, Argolid	Peasant
138	Nea Epidavros, Argolid	Peasant
139	Asini, Argolid	SB regional military commander
140	Miloi, Argolid	EAM collaborator
141	Pirgela, Argolid	Peasant
142	Anifi, Argolid	Peasant
143	Anifi, Argolid	Peasant
144	Gimno, Argolid	Peasant
145	Krioneri/Kefalari, Argolid	Peasant
146	Krioneri/Kefalari, Argolid	Peasant
147	Elliniko/Krioneri, Argolid	Peasant
148	Krioneri/Zonga, Argolid	Peasant
149	Partheni, Arkadia	ELAS/DSE guerrilla
150	Arachovitsa-Chochlia, Evritania	Peasant
151	Mavronoros, Ioannina	Peasant
152	Nifi, Kefalonia	Daughter of EAM local cadre
153	Drepano, Argolid	Son of EAM village leader
154	Kiveri, Argolid	EAM village leader
155	Kiveri, Argolid	Peasant
156	Kiveri, Argolid	Peasant
157	Nemea, Korinthia	EAM cadre
158	Riza, Korinthia	OPLA squad leader
159	Alonakia, Kozani	Peasant, then gendarme
160	Cheli, Argolid	SB soldier
161	Aghios Stefanos, Argolid	Peasant
162	Gimno, Argolid	Peasant
163	Nea Zoi, Imathia	Peasant
164	Velvendo, Kozani	Student
165	Thessaloniki	Gendarme
166	Thessaloniki	Housewife
167	Omali, Kozani	Peasant
168	Omali, Kozani	Peasant
169	Glykokerasia, Kozani	Peasant; local militia member
170	Velvendo, Kozani	Student
171	Korrisos, Kastoria	EAM local cadre
172	Stavrochori, Kilkis	Peasant
173	Foustani, Almopia	Peasant

Number of Interview	Interviewee's Place of Origin	Interviewee's Short Description
174	Kostantia, Almopia	Peasant
175	Thiriopetra, Almopia	Peasant
176	Notia, Almopia	ELAS & DSE guerrilla
177	Exaplatanos, Almopia	Peasant
178	Thiriopetra, Almopia	SB fighter, then local militia member
179	Ida, Almopia	Peasants; soldiers of ELAS Macedonian battalion
180	Perikleia, Almopia	Peasant
181	Orma, Almopia	Peasant
182	Chrisi, Almopia	Peasant
183	Theodoraki, Almopia	Peasant
184	Milia, Almopia	Peasant
185	Archaggelos, Almopia	Peasant
186	Polykarpi, Almopia	Peasant
187	Filoteia, Almopia	Peasant
188	Rizochori, Almopia	Peasant
189	Xifiani, Almopia	EAM cadre
190	Xifiani, Almopia	Peasant
191	Xifiani, Almopia	EAM cadre
192	Aridaia, Almopia	EAM collaborator
193	Tsakoi, Almopia	EAM collaborator
194	Chrysa, Almopia	DSE guerrilla
195	Aloro, Almopia	ELAS guerrilla
196	Niochori, Almopia	Peasant
197	Niochori, Almopia	EAM cadre; ELAS guerrilla
198	Vorino, Almopia	Local militia member; village leader
199	Neromylos, Almopia	Peasant
200	Prodromos, Almopia	EAM collaborator
201	Dorothea, Almopia	Peasant
202	Aridaia, Almopia	Merchant
203	Sossandra, Almopia	Peasant
204	Sossandra, Almopia	EAM village cadre
205	Milia, Promachoi, Almopia	Peasant
206	Promachoi, Almopia	Peasant
207	Promachoi, Almopia	Peasant
208	Nafplio, Argolid	City dweller
209	Asini, Argolid	Peasant
210	Nafplio, Argolid	Merchant
211	Ligourio, Argolid	Peasant
212	Boutia (Ira), Argolid	EAM village leader
213	Boutia (Ira), Argolid	Peasant
214	Nafplio, Argolid	OPLA squad member
215	Nafplio, Argolid	Daughter of EAM leader

collaborators of various shades) and nonactive participants, mostly peasants; I also interviewed perpetrators, victims, (often the two properties coincided in the same person), their relatives, and bystanders; finally, I talked to leftists, rightists, and a few politically uncommitted people, as well as people who shifted political identities over time.[7]

Like other researchers (Smyth and Fay 2000:3), I found people more than willing to share their painful experiences. A key advantage was being simultaneously an "insider" and an "outsider." As an insider (being Greek), I was able to empathize with my informants and be welcomed by them as a credible interlocutor,[8] while being able to detect most (I think!) verbal and nonverbal "stratagems" they used[9] and to probe their recollections. As an outsider with no family connections to their village or area, I was perceived as a kind of third party, untainted by local feuds.[10]

Most historians agree that oral sources can be problematic: they are a slippery source (Hobsbawm 2001:xi), and "it is a rule among historians, and a good one, to place greater reliance on contemporary sources than on recollections produced years later, after memory has been reprocessed and refigured" (Novick 1999:106). Indeed, recollections, particularly of violent and politically charged events, are distorted by their confusing nature (Vargas Llosa 1998:101), by time, and by several complex psychological and cognitive processes (Goldberg 2003), including the tendency to fill in the lack of information with commonsensical narratives (Mendelsohn 2002:55). Recollections can also severely compress time (M. F. Brown and Fernández 1991:118), are often influenced by subsequent events, and can be biased by partisanship, embellishment, and vindication. Most importantly, political actors and the post-civil-war state actively try to shape collective memories in ways consistent with their objectives. Memories are also affected by the context in which they are transformed from individually held recollections into narratives shared with a researcher, in a specific context. In short, oral recollections can be self-contradictory, incomplete, and biased. The researcher faces many challenges. How does one know that informants actually believe what they say or say what they believe? What should one do when informants give conflicting renditions of the same event or when an individual makes contradictory statements? Does one treat all individual viewpoints and actions as equally important? As summarized by Giovanni Contini (1997:17), "it is difficult to

---

7 Thaxton (1997: xvi–xvii) acknowledges that 75 percent of his informants were Communist peasant activists or sympathizers (none appears to have been a KMT sympathizer). Conversely, many studies of the Vietnam War (e.g., R. Berman 1974) are exclusively based on interviews with former rebels, prisoners, and defectors.

8 Carol Swain (1993:229), a political scientist, reports that several black congressmen in the U.S. would not have talked the way they did to her if she were white.

9 As a Bosnian villager warned Tone Bringa (1995:xvi), "Always remember that people do one thing, say another, and think a third."

10 One man who insisted on seeing me although he was sick and confined to bed told me that he felt his conversation to be like a (religious) confession (I-30). This man admitted, apparently for the first time, that he had informed on a friend. He added that he felt a sense of relief for speaking out. Indeed, Horton (1998:316) stresses the "cathartic" aspect of some of the interviews she conducted in Nicaragua and connects them to her "outsider" status.

distinguish facts from interpretations in a narrative, to isolate the distortion from its meaning; one risks accepting in an uncritical way the anachronisms, the inversions of temporal and subject sequences, the condensation of many events into one and the omission of particular events."

These problems are exacerbated when the issue is past violence. For example, a central problem in interviews with victims (and perpetrators) of violence is what Antonius Robben (1996) has termed "seduction," the conscious and unconscious ways in which interviewees influence the interviewer's understanding. Although some researchers do not perceive this to be an issue,[11] it clearly raises some serious problems. Because the use of oral recollections is unusual in political science, I review these problems in more detail.

A.2.1. Time

Time matters: memories grow thin. The Greek Civil War ended fifty years ago and this has undoubtedly affected the memories of survivors. Most informants had a difficult time or were incapable of remembering exact dates;[12] their recollections were selective and prone to telescoping, and their narration was nonlinear. I was able to address most of these problems through my parallel use of written sources about the same events.

Less obviously, in addition to eroding memory and bringing the deaths of many potential informers, time can also be an important advantage. In Chapter 2, I discussed some of the problems of fieldwork in a war context. After a civil war, political repression may severely restrict what people are free to say about the conflict. Fear affects the willingness of people to talk about their experiences (Brinkman 2000:2; M. F. Brown and Fernández 1991:9; Cribb 1990:3), and supporters of the defeated side have no choice but silence (Juliá 1999:37–8). Jun Jing (1996:55–6) found that interviews in a Chinese province "proved far more difficult than expected.... they were marked by evasions and silences. The oral narratives of the village's political history were frustratingly fragmentary. In fact, village informants were reluctant to talk about the political campaigns prior to the Cultural Revolution because [they] still cannot be criticized."[13] This can go on for years. During the first half of the 1990s, it was still a serious crime in Indonesia to have any link with the Communist Party, "so that few people wish to discuss the [massacres of 1965] openly, still less to admit any deep knowledge of the party" (Robinson 1995:xii). Silence is not just a matter of external repression. Denial may set in: people know what not to know (Suárez-Orozco 1990:367). The anthropologist Kay Warren (1998:93, 110) found that although Guatemalan peasants were willing to talk about the civil war, they were reluctant

---

[11] Marie Smyth and Marie-Therese Fay (2000:2) state that: "We perceived ourselves as instruments, through which the interviewee's account could be documented."

[12] In fact, "the informant who remembers dates is a rare find" (B. Allen and Montell 1981:26).

[13] Jing (1996:56) adds that his respondents often resorted to a "'vindictive strategy' in which they frequently protested that they had been wrongly labeled as enemies of the people, rather than question the premises of the persecution. Some tried to convince the listener that they had been framed when they were classified as counterrevolutionaries."

to discuss it in detail; "silence and denial" and "carefully crafted ambiguity" were dominant. Memories of violence are so unpleasant that they might be repressed by those who experienced them (Kheng 1983:xiv). The leftist writer Ramón Sender, who came to the United States after the Spanish Civil War, refused to talk to his son about his wife's death at the hands of the rebels (Sender Barayón 1989). Caution is a typical reaction of people who have lived in civil wars when asked to describe their experience (e.g., Horton 1998:206). In his study of a Greek village, the anthropologist Stanley Aschenbrenner (1987:106) found that the villagers' references to the civil war were characterized by a stance of suppression and "studied avoidance." It took Aschenbrenner a tremendous amount of patience and much time (seventy months of fieldwork during a period of fourteen years) to piece together the puzzle of the war in the village he studied.[14]

When silence is no problem, passions may kick in. Susan Freeman (1979:164) reports that during her research in a town in northern Spain she found the "snarl of relationships and motivation . . . difficult to untangle, especially because many of the hostilities are still active and still have their political colorings." Lynn Horton (1998:315) points out that one of the major difficulties of her fieldwork in Nicaragua was the postwar polarization of peasant communities. McNeill (1978:148) described his 1947 visit in the village of Old Corinth in the Peloponnese: "Several wartime deaths among the villagers [of Old Corinth], some inflicted by the Germans, some by ELAS [the leftist rebels], exacerbated political tensions. But it was impossible to get a clear picture of what had happened within the village because the rival versions as told by supporters of the different factions were wildly discrepant."

In the Greek case, the political situation was such that interviews about the civil war could only be conducted with relative ease after the end of the 1980s. The repression against the Greek Left lasted well until the early 1960s. The Communist Party was outlawed. Thousands of its supporters fled to Soviet bloc countries and many others were imprisoned or deported from their localities into internal exile. A right-wing military coup in 1967 extended the repression until the dictatorship fell in 1974. The 1981 victory of the socialist party (PASOK) brought with it high levels of political polarization, largely based in civil war memories (Kalyvas 1997). For example, during the 1980s the main space of (male) socialization in villages, the coffee shop, became segregated along partisan lines. As a result, fieldwork on the civil war in rural areas was extremely difficult. Only during the 1990s did political passions decline, thus providing an opening for research.

Public perceptions of the Greek Civil War are highly stereotypical as a result of historical narratives developed by urban intellectuals with little understanding of, or interest in, rural Greece. These public narratives did away with complexities and ambiguities in favor of a set of simplified and streamlined versions of the past that are generally closely associated with either the Right or the Left. Although these narratives marginalized the private and local dimensions of

---

[14] The French anthropologist Marie-Élisabeth Handman (1983:42–3) had an even more difficult experience doing research on the same period: although she conducted fieldwork in a Greek village between 1973 and 1978, she was only able to gather very elliptical information.

individual memories, they did not destroy them. In fact, I discovered that public and private narratives coexisted in most people.[15] When first queried, my informants would invoke public narratives that emphasized elite politics, including snippets of diplomatic history; however, when asked to speak about specific local stories, they quickly switched to a very different narrative, one that gave central position to ambiguity.[16] The familiarity with the details of local history that I derived from my archival work proved essential in triggering the private and local memories of my respondents.

A.2.2. Bias

Time wears down political passions, but it does not erase them. The animosities produced by the Russian Civil War became an important factor in fueling violence during the collectivization period in the Soviet Union (Viola 1993:74). Robben (1995:94) observes that "any research on political violence runs into too many skeletons to handle, too many closets to inspect. Aside from deliberate lies, half-truths, and unfounded accusations – many of which are impossible to trace or verify – there is a lot of malicious gossip and character assassination." I realized during fieldwork that most informants still felt very strongly about the civil war. While intermarriage between left-wing and right-wing families has now become quite common (Aschenbrenner 1987), a development suggesting that the civil war cleavage has lost its saliency among new generations, many older people from across the political divide still refuse to speak or socialize with one other.[17]

It is also natural for many people to supply interpretations that stress the positive role they played and suppress the negative aspects of their actions.[18] "I

---

[15] In contrast to Primo Levi (1988:24), who observed that "a memory evoked too often, and expressed in the form of a story, tends to become fixed in a stereotype . . . crystallized, perfected, adorned, installing itself in the place of the raw memory and growing at its expense."

[16] Paludan (1981:xii) reports his experience from researching the American Civil War in a community of North Carolina: "When people in the valley talk about the Civil War, they care little about the conflict of cultures or the breakdown of politics or the wave of modernization. The war to them means the murder of their great-grandfathers and great-uncles and cousins. It means the time when Granny Franklin had to watch soldiers burn down her house and kill her three sons who were hiding there and what she did after the war when one of her brothers murdered one of the soldiers involved." However, Brinkman (2000:5) found that the Angolan refugees whom she interviewed prioritized a "national history" frame over a local one. Urvashi Butalia (2000:12) reports that the narratives of violence she collected from victims of the Partition of India were gendered: men emphasized broader political issues, while women focused on the everyday details of life. My interviews were likewise gendered, with the proviso that if specifically asked, men were also willing to talk about local aspects of the conflict.

[17] A woman I interviewed in 1998 told me that a couple of days before the interview she met a village man with whom she had not talked since 1944, when her brother had ordered this man's entire family killed. This man, whom I had interviewed in 1997, approached her in the village square and told her that it did not make sense for them not to speak to each other anymore since they were not going to live for much longer (I-104).

[18] For instance, Swedenborg (1995:24-6) found that the Palestinian villagers he interviewed about the uprising of 1936-9 "balked at relating stories about rebels' involvement in activities like assassination, robbery, or clan feuds. Another taboo area concerned the existence as well as rebel treatment

want to tell you this," an informant warned me: "In the villages you visit, the war hasn't ended yet. The people who lived through it are still fighting against each other and [the information you get] depends on whom you talk to" (I-143). All this is compounded by the fact that many acts of violence are shrouded in secret: though suspicion is rife, it is not always known who ordered what, who carried out a particular action, or what was the reason behind an action. Like a criminal investigation, research on violence is confronted with *Rashomon*-like multiple versions of the same events and contradictory clues. There is a tendency to brush aside such issues. For instance, Smyth and Fay (2000:4) argue that since no "singular truth" exists, researchers should only record accounts: "Whether such presentation is less true than another version is not a judgment we are equipped or prepared to make. We all tell ourselves stories about events that are compatible with our image of ourselves and tend to mask our culpability or failings. It should not surprise us that interviewees do likewise." While not without some valid underlying insights, such an attitude is problematic. Insofar as the goal is to reconstruct events, however complex or multifaceted, bias has to be taken into account and minimized. This is a challenging obstacle for research on attitudes and intentions, but my primary goal was to reconstruct the course of specific events.

History is often remembered in personal, family, and local terms, and placing aspects of violence discussed in interviews within a particularistic context produced individual accounts that varied far less from each other than I initially expected. In fact, there was generally consensus about the basic set of events (e.g., who got killed, by whom, when, where). Surprisingly, there was also considerable "bipartisan" agreement about the interpretation of particular acts of violence (e.g., whether a certain killing was "fair" or "unfair," whether it resulted from past feuds or not).[19] Cross-checking (and cross-interviewing – i.e., returning to the same informant with more information) also proved very helpful. Moreover, the variations of a story can be extremely useful since they underline the points of contention. As a rule, I gave extra weight to "intramural criticism": critical remarks about the actions of one's own political faction (there was far more of it than I expected). Some informants who turned out to have been implicated in acts of violence reacted with silence or evasion to some questions; others, however,

---

of traitors and spies. As with most peasant insurgencies, the rebels of 1936–9 frequently meted out harsh punishment to those known to be traitors to the cause and spies for the enemy.... Perhaps more significant in this regard was the desire not to tarnish the luster of this central national symbol and forerunner of today's liberation movement.... Even villagers who acknowledged that robberies, assassinations, or land sales occurred during the revolt were frequently vague on the details. Others claimed that such things happened only in other places, never in *their* village or *their* district." Another version of this attitude is to fault the enemy for all atrocities, even resorting to elaborate conspiracy theories.

[19] In her investigation of a communal riot in Bangladesh, Beth Roy (1994:99) likewise found that "reports of the initial quarrel had a similar quality; people unselfconsciously told the tale from their own point of view. When it came to accounts of the riots itself, however, the stories agreed more closely. To be sure, accounts tilted toward descriptions of one side or the other as being the more aggressive. But they concurred in important respects."

were surprisingly blunt and open in their willingness to acknowledge their role in acts of violence.

Although I did not reveal my own political preferences during the interviews (the general assumption being that no one can be politically neutral),[20] I tried to send out the appropriate political signals. For example, I adapted my vocabulary to my informants: when talking to left-wing informants I told them I was conducting a study of the "resistance," a term that, along with "civil war," was best avoided with right-wing informants.[21] Typically, during a round of interviews, I approached only people from one side of the political spectrum; I spoke to their local opponents in future rounds, later on. Once people got to know me well, they were generally willing to accept the fact that I was on talking terms with both groups.[22] Because I "entered" three networks (right-wing and left-wing – plus an amorphous "middle ground") that were largely independent of each other (the probability of being referred to a right-winger by a left-winger was generally low), I was able to cross-check information across partisan networks. Furthermore, I ran additional checks both across spatial and partisan boundaries. People were generally well informed about the surrounding villages (though surprisingly misinformed or not informed at all about the rest of the region). Whenever possible, I conducted repeat interviews with the same person after I had obtained new information from additional sources. I also made it a point to stay after the formal end of the interview, when I would often be invited for lunch or dinner; generally my informants felt they knew me better after the interview and the discussion would veer toward their family, their work, and other personal topics. These conversations increased my understanding of my informants: their values, their outlook on life, their fears, their regrets. An advantage of going through these informal sessions was gleaning additional information about the civil war and making much better sense of it; often important information would emerge as an aside to other matters considered more important. I met some informants more than ten times over the four years in which I was conducting research and developed friendships with them and their families.[23] Finally, conducting a high number of interviews about the same topic and in the same area allowed me to develop a stronger feel for plausibility and, hence, reliability.[24]

---

[20] Sluka (1989:2) reports the following Belfast joke: A Belfaster asks an American tourist his religion. "I'm an atheist," replies the quick-thinking American. "Ah, but are ye a Catholic atheist or a Protestant atheist?" responds the Belfaster.

[21] Many right-wingers still refer to the civil war as the "bandit war," the term used officially by the Right.

[22] While news travels fast in villages, the level of political segregation among survivors remains substantial, and this allowed me to establish a relationship of trust with one group before I contacted their local opponents, who often had little or no knowledge of my prior contacts in their village. Sometimes, of course, this got me into trouble, as my previous informants thought I was betraying them.

[23] These relations sometimes acquired a transatlantic feel, since many had family in New York. An additional by-product of this process, I should hasten to add, was my unrelenting targeting as a marriage prospect, even transnationally!

[24] My experience matches Lear's (1961:vii) description of the process of his research in the Philippines: "Now I commenced to systematize the congerie of facts I had been collecting. A pattern began to

A.2.3. Memory

Personal memory is, as Eric Hobsbawm (1988:18) has observed, a remarkably slippery medium for preserving facts. It is less a recording than a selection mechanism – and one subject to continuous change. Collective memory expresses and defines identity; hence, it is likely to marginalize or even suppress events that do not fit with it. Individual memory is reconfigured and reshaped continuously in the course of one's life. Information gained from later readings of a defining event and stories of others tend to stylize and transform individual memories this event, often in ways that are not conscious. Memories at t3 of an event y that took place at t1 may be influenced by events at t2. For instance, Contini (1997) shows how the local memory of the 1944 Nazi massacre of 212 inhabitants in the Tuscan villages of Civitella Val di Chiana, La Cornia, and San Pancrazo (ostensibly in retaliation for the killing of three German soldiers by partisans), after which the villagers blamed the leftist partisans for having provoked the Nazi reprisals, was largely shaped by both interwar and postwar Italian politics. The effect of intervening events ("t2") is likely to be more pronounced when these events are heavy in significance. Swedenburg (1995:xxvi–xxvii) found that what was particularly remarkable about the Palestinians he interviewed regarding the uprising of 1936–9 "was the degree to which their sense of history was overdetermined by the current situation. In particular, popular views tended to be couched within a contemporary nationalist idiom.... Old Palestinian men were keenly aware that they were engaged in a struggle over the very legitimacy of their national existence, and many felt that to portray their history as fractured might sully a national reputation that was under constant assault. So they usually took care to protect the Palestinian image and project a history of national history and propriety."

Even when the intention is not to protect a past image, the memory of violence is hard to countenance in the time of peace. Alessandro Portelli (1997:138) reports that former Italian partisans found it difficult, "in the time of memory and recollection, to reconcile the immediate necessity and the state of mind of the time with their present values and feelings, to reconcile the memory of violence, hatred, and excess with the ideals of democracy and civilized society (which, to further complicate things, are the ideals they were fighting for in the first place)."

In short, memories are contested fields of meaning that are amenable to a multiplicity of political and cultural expressions and interpretations, and they lend themselves to continuous modifications, manipulations, and reinventions; they can be better indicators of current (or recent) political and social developments

emerge of significant relationships, constituting a framework for further accessions of information and a tool of inquiry during interviews. I knew what to ask, what to look for. I had worked out a time sequence of significant temporal intervals during the Occupation.... With this perspective, I became better equipped to make discerning judgments, recognizing when my informant was garbling the record for reasons of self-glorification or defamation of his opponents. In the privacy of my own thought, I was able to put certain questions to the data I had amassed, intended as hypotheses to explain wartime developments on the Island. These hypotheses underwent further modification as further interviews and the gradual accumulation of written materials punctured some of the notions I had been entertaining."

than the past events they purport to describe. A related issue stems from the fact that memories are not just available for the taking; they have to be collected through the medium of narrative, which affects the information provided. The act of having one's memories recorded can "contaminate" them because it provides the opportunity for relatively obscure narrators to be canonized in public discourse; it is a public speech act by people who rarely have the opportunity to speak publicly (Gilsenan 1999:111; Portelli 1997:161). As Beth Roy (1994:5) discovered, "It is true that the stories I heard in that Bangladeshi village were not about 'what happened' (itself a questionable concept). What I heard was how people *saw* what happened, or, rather how people *remembered* what they saw, or, rather how they *talked* about what they remembered, or, rather, how they talked to *me* about what they remembered – or rather, what I *heard* people say to me about what they remembered."

Clearly, the construction of individual and collective memories as well as the individual narratives and the official discourse of violence are rich social phenomena fully deserving to be turned into primary objects of study (Portelli 1997; Gilsenan 1996; Aguilar 1996; Robben 1995). Indeed, some researchers argue explicitly that memories themselves are more interesting objects of investigation than the facts they refer to (Contini 1997:17; Swedenburg 1995:xxvi). Portelli (1997:128) focuses precisely on distortions of facts in oral recollections as hints about the work of memory, imagination, and interpretation.[25] Some go as far as to assert that they are less concerned with whether "facts" are real than with the politics of their interpretation and representation (Taussig 1987:xiii).

I must remind the reader here that my primary goal in this book was the study of the *actual* violence – as opposed to its memories, representations, and narratives. This is feasible despite the problems inherent in oral sources. Although it is true that memories are biased, it is also the case that violent events are so traumatic that they remain vivid in people's minds (Green 1995:115; Gilmore 1987:44). Memory is particularly attuned to events that took place in the context of family and community: the civil war was not an abstract conflict but one that marked the life of most people, most often in a dramatic way. Indeed, I found that memories of the civil war among many informants were vigorous, flush with detail and substance.[26] My research was greatly facilitated by the fact that violence is quite tangible: my specific queries about who got killed in a village, when, how, by whom, and under what circumstances produced specific answers most of the time.[27]

---

[25] "Let me repeat: this is not a true account. But let me also repeat: this is why it is important" (Portelli 1997:136).

[26] Often, informants would tell me that they could not remember what they had for dinner the previous evening and would then go on to provide an amazing wealth of information about what happened to them fifty years ago – down to the tiniest details.

[27] I noticed during pilot interviews that people responded to general and vague inquiries (e.g., "did the people in the region support the rebels?" or "what did the people think about the violence?") by being either vague or highly partisan (or both), whereas when asked specific and contextualized questions (e.g., "who was killed in your village?"), they became far more specific and impartial. They became even more specific when I referred to detailed information about these acts of violence gathered from other interviews and archives.

This tangibility is why oral sources have been used successfully to investigate civil wars and rebellions (Vervenioti 2003; McKenna 1998; Thaxton 1997; Kedward 1993), as well as periods of civil turmoil and repression (Jing 1996; Chan, Madsen, and Unger 1992). Oral sources are a key tool for the capture of dynamics on the ground (Fraser 1993). As a historian of the French resistance points out, "Oral testimony, even fifty years after the event, suggests hypotheses, provides personal details, reveals local colour, facilitates insights, and preserves individuality in a way that historians cannot easily afford to ignore" (Kedward 1993:vii).

By combining oral sources with written sources from the period in question, I was able to introduce a powerful check that allowed me to gauge the general reliability of each oral source. This was possible because the regional focus of my study allowed me to collect written and oral information about the same set of events and people.[28] Generally, I found that the recollections were consistent with the archival sources (and vice versa). In H. R. Kedward's (1993:viii) formulation, "realities are fractured and pluralized, but they are rarely eclipsed." In fact, these two types of sources complemented each other nicely. On the one hand, judicial files provided a host of details, together with linearity and chronology. On the other hand, oral histories provided additional perspectives and depth, while revealing the "hidden transcripts" (J. Scott 1990) or "unauthorized narratives" (McKenna 1998:183) that informed many of the events contained in the judicial files, in addition to providing a nuanced and empirically grounded understanding of both substantive issues (e.g., perceptions about the costs of joining the rebels) and theoretical ones (e.g., perceptions of costs and benefits of a number of actions). For example, the interviews allowed me both to gauge the villagers' attitudes toward risk and to figure out the way to operationalize risk in the theoretical analysis.[29]

Indeed, the practice of relying exclusively on archival sources in order to infer motivations is at least as fraught with dangers as relying on oral recollections. For instance, historians of the Greek Civil War infer individual motivations for joining one side or the other exclusively either from reports by British agents who often had only a scant understanding of the local context in which they did their tour of duty, or from self-serving memoirs of participants.

A.3. MEMOIRS, AUTOBIOGRAPHIES, LOCAL HISTORIES

In addition to interviews and archival evidence, I also availed myself of several published and unpublished memoirs, autobiographies, and local histories. Such

---

[28] In some cases I interviewed people whose affidavits and depositions from fifty years ago I had just retrieved from the judicial archives. Kerkvliet's (1977) study of the Huk rebellion in the Philippines and Truman Anderson's (1999) study of partisan warfare in the Ukraine in 1941–2 are examples of studies that combine a local or regional focus with oral sources and archival research.

[29] The analysis of individual decisions hinges on an understanding of the context in which they take place. As Richards (1996:xxii) points out about Sierra Leone, "insurgents in Sierra Leone treat the forest, the history of resource struggles taking place within forests, and the character of forest social institutions, as a 'spur' to a series of practical judgments about the risks and benefits of political action based on violence. Remove the forest from the picture (or ignore it) and the rationality disappears."

documents generally require caution since they can be highly biased; the great majority of the authors are self-serving and motivated by partisan concerns. These authors tend to forget "nonconformist truths" and substitute rhetoric for reality (Veyne 1996:256–7). For example, the memoir of a former Communist cadre in the Argolid (Papalilis 1980) almost fails to mention his side's widespread use of violence against its enemies. However, the chief importance of these accounts lies in the archetypal material they contain rather than in the factual veracity of particular details (Kakar 1996:30). Additionally, casual observations and throwaway remarks that are adjunct to the author's central point, including random but revealing comments, indirect references, passing assertions, and even private gossip, can provide substantial payoffs. They are "residual" narratives, "relatively untouched, unrevised, and unincorporated by national ideological apparatuses. . . . Standing 'outside' or 'adjacent' to national histories, they were often recounted unselfconsciously" (Swedenburg 1995:111). Surprisingly, some of these memoirs, especially the unpublished ones written by ordinary people who thought their experiences were worth recounting to a restricted circle of family and friends, turned out to be extremely insightful and candid about a large range of controversial issues.

Appendix B: Coding Protocols

The Argolid (a distinct part, in 1940, of the Argolidokorinthia prefecture) is sub-divided into three counties: Argos, Nafplía, and Ermionidotrizinía. To recall, I studied the counties of Argos and Nafplía, which in 1940 included two munic-ipalities (the administrative capital, Nafplio, and the market center, Argos) and fifty-eight "communes" (*koinotites*) (of which nineteen included more than one settlement). The total number of "villages" studied is sixty-one. I arrived at this number in the following way. First, I included all communes save two, Tracheia and Adami, which are located in the extreme east of Nafplía county and are closely connected with the villages of Ermionidotrizinia. Second, I counted as villages all hamlets that lacked administrative autonomy if their population exceeded 200 people. There were seven exceptions to this rule. On the one hand, I included one hamlet with a population of less than 200 (Amigdalitsa) on grounds of distance and relative political independence; on the other hand, I excluded four hamlets with a population of (slightly) more than 200 (Houtaleika, Aghios Dimitrios, Sterna, and Kalamaki) on similar grounds: they were, then, organic parts of the commune's central village, under which I subsumed them. Table B.1 provides basic descriptive data for all villages, Table B.2 provides information about the six ecological clusters, and Table B.3 lists the independent variables of the villages used in multivariate tests. Finally, Table B.4 provides a list of the out-of-sample test villages from across Greece used to check the validity of the sample from the Argolid.

I excluded from the quantitative analysis the two towns, Argos and Nafplio, because it turned out to be much more difficult to reconstruct events at the microlevel in the towns than it was in the villages. Unlike the villages, the towns have changed enormously since 1949, making the coding for control on a neigh-borhood basis, as would have been appropriate, almost impossible. Furthermore, it is very difficult to ascertain the level of control with precision given urban

TABLE B.1. *Villages Included in the Argolid Study*

Name[a]	County	Altitude (meters)	Population (1940 census)	Number of Victims
Achladokambos	Argos	479	1,926	67
Aghia Triada (Merbaka)	Nafplía	30	1,165	5
Aghios Adrianos (Katsigri)	Nafplía	80	1,114	12
Aghios Nikolaos	Argos	760	244	14
Aghios Stefanos	Argos	700	325	15
Alea (Boyati)	Argos	280	705	6
Amigdalitsa (Bardi)	Nafplía	200	114	8
Anifi	Nafplía	30	936	14
Arachneo (Heli)	Nafplía	600	1,930	92
Argoliko (Koutsi)	Nafplía	20	704	0
Aria	Nafplía	40	654	0
Asini	Nafplía	50	1,171	10
Borsas	Argos	230	168	1
Dalamanara	Argos	10	767	1
Dimena	Nafplía	190	254	0
Douka Vrysi	Argos	480	245	3
Drepano	Nafplía	20	1,532	2
Elliniko	Argos	250	349	3
Exochi (Tatsi)	Argos	760	232	0
Fichti	Argos	100	751	5
Frousiouna	Argos	760	437	4
Gimno	Argos	430	691	5
Inachos (Passa)	Argos	40	574	3
Ira (Boutia)	Argos	18	494	0
Ireo (Honika)	Argos	25	252	8
Iria	Nafplía	20	292	0
Kaparelli	Argos	380	387	17
Karia	Argos	700	1,930	42
Kefalari	Argos	20	409	2
Kefalovriso (Pano Belesi)	Argos	750	445	14
Kiveri	Argos	40	769	4
Kourtaki	Argos	15	371	0
Koutsopodi	Argos	40	1,600	5
Krioneri	Argos	960	244	6
Laloukas	Argos	14	559	0
Lefkakia (Spaitsikou)	Nafplía	40	759	8
Ligourio	Nafplía	370	1,491	10
Limnes	Argos	520	1,555	104
Lirkia (Belesi)	Argos	250	1,102	25
Malandreni	Argos	300	883	29
Manesis	Nafplía	70	602	9
Midea (Gerbesi)	Nafplía	120	470	50
Mikines (Harvati)	Argos	110	342	4

(continued)

TABLE B.1 *(continued)*

Name[a]	County	Altitude (meters)	Population (1940 census)	Number of Victims
Mili	Argos	15	438	3
Monastiraki (Priftiani)	Argos	90	284	7
Nea Epidavros (Piada)	Nafplía	100	1,327	14
Nea Kios	Argos	10	1,899	8
Nea Tirintha (Kofini)	Nafplía	30	1,686	2
Neo Ireo (Avdibei)	Argos	30	470	1
Niochori	Argos	700	250	6
Palia Epidavros	Nafplía	370	761	4
Panariti	Nafplía	45	556	1
Pirghela	Argos	15	578	1
Pirgiotika	Nafplía	120	201	0
Poulakida	Nafplía	45	595	6
Prosymna (Berbati)	Argos	250	979	19
Skafidaki	Argos	50	598	3
Skinochori	Argos	260	575	25
Skotini	Argos	690	890	7
Tolo	Nafplía	10	604	2
Vrousti	Argos	660	451	6

[a] The old names, still in local use, are in parenthesis.

TABLE B.2. *Ecological Clusters*

Cluster	Villages
Deep plain	Aghia Triada, Argoliko, Aria, Dalamanara, Ira, Ireo, Kefalari, Kourtaki, Laloukas, Nea Kios, Nea Tirintha, Panariti, Pirghela, Poulakida
Outer plain	Anifi, Asini, Elliniko, Fichti, Inachos, Mikines, Neo Ireo, Aghios Adrianos, Kiveri, Koutsopodi, Lefkakia, Mili, Panariti, Pirgiotika, Poulakida, Monastiraki, Skafidaki
Eastern hills	Amigdalitsa, Prosymna, Midea, Arachneo, Limnes, Manesis
Western hills	Achladokambos, Borsas, Kaparelli, Lirkia, Malandreni, Skinochori.
Eastern plain	Dimena, Drepano, Iria, Nea Epidavros, Palia Epidavros, Ligourio, Tolo
Mountains	Aghios Nikolaos, Aghios Stefanos, Alea, Douka Vrysi, Frousiouna, Gimno, Karia, Kefalovriso, Krioneri, Niochori, Skotini, Exochi, Vrousti

density and neighborhood boundary fluidity. Nevertheless, I was able to estimate a tentative fatality rate for both towns, relying mostly on their incomplete civil registries; I also incorporated the events that took place in the two towns in the narrative. The overall patterns of violence in the two towns is generally consistent with the theory, and their exclusion from the analysis does not bias the results.

TABLE B.3. *Independent Variables*

Variable	Range	Source
Control zones 2 & 4 (dummy: 1 when control zone is 2 or 4)		Own coding using material from the Historical Archive of the Argolid (HAA) and interviews
Population (1940)	Mean: 739 Min: 114 Max: 1,930	Population census (1940)
Education level (secondary school students per capita)	Mean: .66 Min: 0 Max: 3.7	School archives, Argos and Nafplio high school records, Historical Archive of the Argolid (HAA)
Altitude (meters)	Mean: 238 Min: 10 Max: 960	Miliarakis 1886; Stamatelatos and Vamva-Stamatelatou 2001
Distance from closest town	Mean: 2 hr. 50 min. Min: 15 min. Max: 8 hr. 30 min.	Miliarakis 1886; Anagnostopoulos and Gagalis 1938
Prewar conflict: per capita court cases (1935–9)	Mean: .06 Min: .01 Max:.24	Archives of the Civil Courts of Nafplio, Historical Archive of the Argolid (HAA)
GDP proxy (interval variable; wealthiest village = 3)		Own coding based on Anagnostopoulos and Gagalis 1938

B.2. CIVILIANS

It is well known that civil war blurs the line between combatants and non-combatants and that these identities can be interchangeable. In the words of a former Filipino guerrilla, "We were peasants by day and guerrillas by night" (Kerkvliet 1977:70). Joseph Clémenceau's (1909:8) description of the rebel fighters in the Vendée is a precursor to dozens of similar descriptions from more recent civil wars: "After the action, whether victors or vanquished, they went back home, took care of their usual tasks, in fields or shops, always ready to fight." Clearly, no unequivocal and fixed dividing line between combatants and noncombatants exists. There is no easy solution to this problem, given that collaboration with armed parties is both widespread and very often coerced. Since my goal is not to ascertain legal or moral responsibility but to explain a large part of the violence that takes place outside the battlefield, I have chosen a broad definition of noncombatants as individuals who are not full-time armed members of a faction. This definition covers collaborators of various stripes, part-time fighters killed outside armed action, and unarmed prisoners.

TABLE B.4. *Villages Surveyed across Greece*

Name	Altitude (meters)	Population (1940)	Prefecture	Location in Greece	Source
Palaioxari	660	454	Fokida	Center	Andreopoulou 1999
Karpofora	100	195	Messinia	South	Aschenbrenner 1987
Paleohori	300	200	Thesprotia	North	Ballios 1999
Fourtzi	300	461	Messinia	South	Balta 2002
Mesohora	800	541	Trikala	Center	Baroutas 1998
Pournia	900	438	Ioannina	North	Christidis 1991
Kalapodi	350	837	Fthiotida	Center	Dalianis 1998
Greveniti	980	796	Ioannina	North	Damianakos 1996
Pouri	400	846	Magnisia	Center	Diamantakos 1997
Christianoi	400	372	Messinia	South	Dimitropoulos n.d.
Farsa	120	498	Kefalonia	West	Drakatos 1999
Ambeli	600	144	Evia	Center	du Boulay 1974
Fourka	1,360	808	Ioannina	North	Exarchos 1987
Agnanta	660	829	Arta	North	Filos 1991
Lia	660	787	Thesprotia	North	Gage 1984
Alona	1,000	991	Florina	North	Gali 1999
Rodohori	730	258	Kozani	North	Gavanas 1999
Parakalamos	400	1,454	Ioannina	North	Gogos 1995
Livadi	1,160	3,199	Larisa	Center	Goumas 1973
Rendina	900	1,786	Karditsa	Center	Haidas 1999
Kapsas	700	1,170	Arkadia	South	Halkiopoulos 2000
Athani	340	737	Lefkada	West	Halkiopoulos 2000
Krioneri	680	326	Messinia	South	Hunter 2003
Kastania Ditiki	950	656	Evritania	Center	Hunter 2003
Frangista	710	785	Evritania	Center	Hunter 2003
Papparousi	700	391	Evritania	Center	Hunter 2003
Zaravina	580	415	Ioannina	North	Hunter 2003
Evandro	680	175	Arkadia	South	I-10
Nemea	320	4,247	Korinthia	South	I-133; I-157
Partheni	680	1,439	Arkadia	South	I-149
Mavronoros	900	317	Ioannina	North	I-151
Alonakia	710	592	Kozani	North	I-159
Nea Zoi	130	344	Pella	North	I-163
Velvendo	420	3,614	Kozani	North	I-164; I-170
Omali	780	387	Kozani	North	I-167; I-168
Glikokerasia	800	125	Kozani	North	I-169
Stavrohori	110	3,108	Kilkis	North	I-172
Eleftherohori	60	332	Kilkis	North	I-172

Name	Altitude (meters)	Population (1940)	Prefecture	Location in Greece	Source
Eleohori	530	836	Arkadia	South	I-22; I-24; I-25
Kastri	920	1,868	Arkadia	South	I-26; I-27; I-28; I-29; I-35; I-36; I-37
Platanorevma	490	242	Kozani	North	I-3
Nikiti	40	1,738	Halkidiki	North	I-32; I-33
Tseria	600	360	Messinia	South	I-39; I-40
Kambos Avias	300	553	Messinia	South	I-41
Malta	330	226	Messinia	South	I-42
Vromovrisi	370	65	Messinia	South	I-43
Kopanaki	190	953	Messinia	South	I-44
Handrinos	320	1,007	Messinia	South	I-45
Gralista	560	1,045	Karditsa	Center	I-48
Neos Pyrgos	5	1,247	Evia	Center	I-49
Zoodochos Pigi	190	447	Larisa	Center	I-50
Kerasia	800	122	Achaia	South	I-51
Lehouri	980	453	Achaia	South	I-51
Livartzi	932	850	Achaia	South	I-51
Iraklio	340	534	Korinthia	South	I-62; I-112
Korakovouni	60	642	Arkadia	South	I-64
Kalivia	850	1,073	Korinthia	South	I-65; I-68; I-69
Assiros	180	1,635	Thessaloniki	North	Karakasidou 1997
Aghia	200	2,910	Larisa	Center	Kardaras 1982
Merkada	850	531	Fthiotis	Center	Katsoyannos 1994
Elafotopos	1,100	391	Ioannina	North	Kikopoulos 1991
Dafni	600	550	Evritania	Center	Kolimenos n.d.
Artemisio	680	1,143	Arkadia	South	Koutelos 1999
Chryso	720	487	Evritania	Center	Koutelos 1999
Simiades	720	447	Arkadia	South	Koutelos 1999
Kremmydi	280	153	Kefalonia	West	Kremidas 1999
Aghios Vassilios	670	460	Arkadia	Center	Latsis 1991
Aghios Georgios	120	532	Magnisia	North	Liapis 1994
Nimfeo	1,350	929	Florina	North	Loustas 1988
Gardiki	1,000	1,183	Fthiotida	Center	Maloukos 1992
Amigdalia	620	1,013	Fokida	Center	Manetas 1996
Mantamados	140	2,839	Lesvos	East	Marantzidis 1997
Georgianoi	440	398	Imathia	North	Marantzidis 1997
Gerania	460	464	Larisa	Center	Marantzidis 1997

(continued)

TABLE B.4 *(continued)*

Name	Altitude (meters)	Population (1940)	Prefecture	Location in Greece	Source
Skala	100	1,054	Messinia	South	T. Margaritis 1995
Lofiskos	56	114	Larisa	Center	McNeill 1978
Palaia Korinthos	70	1,389	Korinthia	South	McNeill 1978
Methoni	85	791	Pieria	North	McNeill 1978
Kerasia	120	295	Magnisia	North	McNeill 1978
Kotas	890	586	Florina	North	McNeill 1978
Mesenikola	700	1,450	Karditsa	Center	Militsis 1997
Arbounas	700	222	Achaia	South	Nasiopoulos 1996
Psathotopi	6	322	Arta	North	NEF
Kalohori	7	1,373	Thessaloniki	North	NEF
Anthili	8	1,463	Fthiotis	Center	NEF
Kymina	8	2,175	Thessaloniki	North	NEF
Neohori	10	2,421	Etoloakarnania	Center	NEF
Gouria	15	880	Etoloakarnania	Center	NEF
Evinohori	15	590	Etoloakarnania	Center	NEF
Vamvakia	150	539	Serres	North	NEF
Moussounitsa	860	339	Fokida	Center	NEF
Nea Nikomidia	25	841	Imathia	North	NEF
Dafnon	160	1,490	Xanthi	North	NEF
Tsoukka	600	1,024	Fthiotis	Center	NEF
Kotyli	1,200	57	Kastoria	North	NEF
Athira	30	1,542	Pella	North	Nikolaidis 1977
Mesia	30	433	Kilkis	North	Nikolaidis 1977
Aghios Petros	30	1,435	Kilkis	North	Nikolaidis 1977
Distrato	1,000	1,033	Ioannina	North	Nikou-Stolou 1999
Krestena	100	3,154	Ilia	South	Notias 1999
Kardamila	80	2,837	Chios	East	Notias 1999
Spilia	820	394	Kozani	North	Notias 1999
Arna	780	874	Lakonia	South	Notias 1999
Morfi	860	329	Kozani	North	Notias 1999
Lehovo	900	1,477	Florina	North	Oikonomou 1976
Paloumba	740	461	Arkadia	South	Papachristou 1994
Harokopio	130	1,080	Messinia	South	Pasagiotis 1998
Inoi	730	900	Kastoria	North	Pelagidis 1996
Spetses	20	3,612	Pireas	South	Perrakis 2004
Petrina	220	942	Lakonia	South	Poulimenakos 1989
Elos	5	1,141	Lakonia	South	Rouvelas 1999
Aghios Haralambos	880	295	Evritania	Center	Sakkas 2000

Name	Altitude (meters)	Population (1940)	Prefecture	Location in Greece	Source
Aghia Triada	770	773	Evritania	Center	Sakkas 2000
Petralona	297	900	Evritania	Center	Sakkas 2000
Domiani	660	698	Evritania	Center	Sakkas 2000
Vraha	880	857	Evritania	Center	Sakkas 2000
Fourna	840	1,591	Evritania	Center	Sakkas 2000
Hohlia	920	357	Evritania	Center	Sakkas 2000; I-150
Kleistos	920	1,489	Evritania	Center	Sakkas 2000; Zevgaras 1999
Koryschades	940	380	Evritania	Center	Sarris 1998
Koskinas	70	263	Ilia	South	Skaltsas 1994
Theodoriana	940	1,410	Arta	North	Skoutelas 1994
Karoplesi	910	820	Karditsa	Center	Souflas 1991
Sami	10	912	Kefalonia	West	Spathis 1999
Athamanio	750	602	Arta	North	Stasinos 2000
Vamvakou	800	837	Lakonia	South	Stavropoulos 1989
Komboti	90	1,822	Arta	North	Tatsiopoulos 1971
Helidona	600	265	Evritania	Center	Triantafyllis 1997
Ziaka	900	830	Grevena	Center	van Boeschoten 1997
Moshopotamos	460	1,807	Pieria	North	Varmazis 2002
Zevgolatio	30	2,552	Korinthia	South	Velentza 1999
Ambelofyto	50	1,000	Serres	North	Vermeulen 1993
Kertezi	850	1,442	Achaia	South	Voryllas 1994
Achladia	540	355	Trikala	Center	Vourlas 1992
Marathea	800	534	Evritania	Center	Vrana 1999

B.3. HOMICIDES

As explained in Chapter 1, I focus on homicides. No complete list of homicides exists for the Argolid. I based the coding primarily on information from court records and village civil registries; I cross-checked it with lists of victims compiled by Antonopoulos (1964), Papalilis (1980), and names culled from local histories, memoirs, monuments, graves in cemeteries, and my own interviews. I entered a homicide in the dataset if it was present at least in the court records, the civil registries, or the list compiled by Antonopoulos from official sources. I made two adjustments to this dataset: first, I excluded thirteen deaths in five villages (Inachos, Ira, Lefkakia, Poulakida, and Krioneri) that were unintentional (arrests carried out with an explicit intention not to kill, and deaths caused by accidents). Second, I coded five deaths in a single village (Ireo) that did not actually take place: these people were slated for execution but escaped at the last moment. These adjustments do not alter the coding of a village as either violent or nonviolent, or alter it in ways that contradict, rather than confirming, my predictions (e.g., Ireo is coded as zone 3 in t_1 when the planned executions would have taken place).[1]

B.4. TYPE OF VIOLENCE

The main distinction in categorizing type of violence is between selective and indiscriminate violence. I coded a homicide as being selective when there was evidence of individualized selection. This includes the use of a name list, the visible use of an informer, an arrest following an identity check, or arrests associated with interrogations. Because procedures and name lists used by the two sides are not available, it is impossible to be completely certain about the selectiveness of the process, but the indirect evidence tended to be strong. When my investigation generated no evidence of individualized selection or when there was evidence of selection on the basis of a collective criterion, I coded a homicide as indiscriminate. For example, the Germans often issued declarations before their raids, stating that their violence was going to be indiscriminate. A judicial investigation conducted by German military justice in the 1960s for the May–June 1944 mop-up operations (ZSt. V 508 AR 2056/67 (Argos)) corroborates oral recollections and Greek postwar trial evidence about the purely indiscriminate character of some of the killings, which included random strafing of people fleeing in the fields and the massacre of villagers or prisoners without any prior selection. I also coded as indiscriminate violence various incidents such as shootings at checkpoints. To be precise, my coding captured the *public perception* of selective or indiscriminate violence, which is consistent with the theory.

As an example, take the village of Anifi, which I described briefly in Chapter 9. In April 1944 the Germans raided the village and used a hooded informer to arrest several men whom they later shot. This is an instance of selective violence. In May of the same year, the Germans instituted a curfew and announced that anyone caught outside his or her house after 6 P.M. would be shot on the spot. Four men were sitting outside their house talking when a German car drove by; a German soldier lowered the window and shot and killed them all (I-108). This is an instance of indiscriminate violence.

A few cases were more difficult to adjudicate. There were some cases of individual arrests and assassinations for which I lacked information about name lists, informers, or similar evidence. My informants almost always had a story about who denounced whom, but these could clearly be ex post facto. I usually relied on all the information I had collected about the village in order to decide how to code such cases. For example, the Germans shot three men on 21 May 1944, in the village of Passa (now Inachos). Twenty men were chosen from all the assembled males, and three of those were shot. One was a local EAM cadre and two were not

---

[1] Descriptive accuracy requires that the total number of the rebels' victims be reduced to 367 from 372.

members of the organization. My initial interviews did not allow me to adjudicate with a reasonable degree of confidence whether these killings were selective or indiscriminate, although an informant mentioned that these three men had been denounced. I then interviewed a local EAM cadre from a neighboring village who gave a great deal of detail about this event and named the alleged denouncer (I-115). It also turned out, from another interview, that German soldiers were roaming in the village the evening before, checking identity papers and looking at a list with photographs (I-107). I, thus, decided to code these homicides as instances of selective violence; if anything, the interviews suggested that they were widely perceived as being selective.

B.5. CONTROL

I used the following protocol to code for control.

Zone 1: Incumbent combatants permanently garrisoned in the village or within a one-hour radius; incumbent combatants and administrators operate freely during all times of day and night; no insurgent activity reported; insurgent clandestine organizations never set up or completely destroyed.

Zone 2: Incumbent combatants permanently garrisoned in the village or within a one-hour radius; incumbent combatants and administrators operate freely during all times of day and night; insurgent clandestine organizations operate inside the village; clandestine meetings take place; sporadic visits at night by insurgent combatants.

Zone 3: Incumbent combatants permanently garrisoned in the village or within a one-hour radius, but do not move freely at night; incumbent administrators usually do not sleep in their homes; insurgent organizers are active; meetings take place regularly at night; regular visits by insurgent combatants at night.

Zone 4: Insurgent combatants permanently garrisoned in the village or nearby; insurgent combatants and administrators operate freely during all times of day and night; incumbent clandestine organizations operate inside the village, and/or clandestine meetings take place, and/or sporadic visits by incumbent combatants.

Zone 5: Insurgent combatants permanently garrisoned in the village or nearby; insurgent combatants and administrators operate freely during all times of day and night; no incumbent activity reported; incumbent clandestine organizations never set up or completely destroyed.

0: Village completely destroyed and/or abandoned.

The relevant information was culled from both oral and written sources (court records; Greek, British, and German military records; and local histories). Because of the relatively short duration of the war and its restricted territorial scope, the interview material and the written sources tend to match each other. When the material was contradictory or inconclusive, I coded the village as being in the same control zone with its closest neighbor. In most instances, there was a high correlation in the control measures among the villages in each of the six ecological clusters. Villages in the same region shifted control at roughly the same time and mostly in the same direction. It is worth noting that this is not an instance of spatial autocorrelation, but of the same treatment being administered to a set of units. There are some exceptions to this trend, mostly due to particularities. For example, all of the eastern hill villages in t_4 are coded as being in zone 4, except two: Arachneo (Heli) is in zone 5 and Manesi is in zone 3. Arachneo, the most isolated of these villages, had been raided and conquered by the rebels, who executed all the rivals they could lay their hands on while causing the rest to flee; Manesi was a ten-minute drive from the village of Aghia Triada, which was garrisoned by the Germans who visited on a quasi-daily basis. Likewise, Fichti is coded as being in zone 3 in t_1, unlike most surrounding villages that were in zone 4, because the presence of a train station led the Germans to install a small unit in the village.

Appendix C: Timeline of Conflicts

Peloponnesian War, 431–404 B.C.

English Civil War, 1642–51

American Revolutionary War, 1775–83

French Revolution, 1789–99

France, Vendée War, 1793–6

Spain, Peninsular War, 1808–14

American Civil War, 1861–5

Filipino insurgency against U.S. occupation, 1888–1902

Mexican Revolution and subsequent violence, 1910–28

Dominican Republic insurgency against U.S. occupation, 1916–24

Russian Revolution and Civil War, 1917–21

Finnish Civil War, January–May 1918

Irish Revolution and Civil War, 1916–23

Chinese Civil War (including insurgency against Japanese occupation), 1926–49

Nicaraguan Civil War, 1927–33

Palestinian uprising, 1936–9

Spanish Civil War, 1936–9

Malayan insurgency against Japanese occupation and against the British, 1941–5; 1950–60

Philippines, insurgency against Japanese occupation and Huk rebellion, 1941–51

Greek Civil War (including resistance against German occupation), 1943–9

Burma, Kachin and Karen insurgencies, 1948–93

Colombian *Violencia*, 1948–58

Kenya, Mau Mau insurgency, 1952–60

Korean War, 1950–3

Algeria, War of Independence, 1954–62

Vietnam War, 1957–75

Angola, War of Independence and Civil War, 1961–91

Guatemalan Civil War, 1961–6

Mozambique, War of Independence and Civil War, 1962–92

Guinea-Bissau Civil War, 1962–74

Indonesia, anti-Communist massacres, 1965–6

Colombian Civil War, 1966–

China, Cultural Revolution 1966–9

Spain, Basque seccessionist campaign, 1968–

Zimbabwe/Rhodesia, War of Independence and Civil War, 1966–79

Namibia, War of Independence, 1966–89

Nigeria, Biafran War, 1967–70

Cambodian Civil War, 1970–5; 1992–8

Northern Ireland Seccessionist Campaign, 1968–94

Bangladesh, War of Independence, 1971

Philippines insurgency, 1972–2001

Lebanese Civil War, 1975–90

East Timor insurgency against Indonesian occupation, 1975–99

Ethiopian Civil War, 1974–91

El Salvador Civil War, 1979–91

Afghanistan, insurgency against Soviet occupation and Civil War, 1979–2001

Uganda, various civil wars, 1986–95

Peru, Shining Path insurgency, 1980–

Nicaraguan Civil War, 1981–90

Sudan, various civil wars, 1983–

Sri Lanka, JVP insurgency and Tamil insurgency, 1983–

Turkey, Kurdish insurgency, 1983–99

India, Sikh insurgency, 1984–94

Palestine/Israel, First Intifada, 1987–93; Second Intifada, 2000–

Armenians and Azerbaijan, war over Nagorno Karabakh, 1988 (no settlement reached)

Liberian Civil War, 1989–96

Sierra Leone, Civil War, 1991–2002

Somali Civil War, 1991–

Algerian Civil War, 1992–

Georgia, Abkhaz insurgency, 1992–3

Bosnian Civil War, 1992–5

Chechen Civil War, 1994–6; 1999–

Congo-Brazzaville War, 1997–

Kosovo, Civil War, 1999

Indonesia, Dayaks versus Madurese of West Kalimantan, 2001–2

Afghanistan, insurgency against U.S. occupation, 2001–

Iraq, insurgency against U.S. occupation, 2003–

References

1 Primary and Unpublished Sources

1.1 Archives

Archive of Contemporary Social History (Αρχεία Σύγχρονης Κοινωνικής Ιστορίας) (ASKI), Athens
  Arhive of the Communist Party of Greece (KKE)
Directorate of Army History (Διεύθυνση Ιστορίας Στρατού) (DIS), Athens
  Archive of National Resistance (1941–4) (AEA)
Eric Gray Newspaper Collection, Christ Church Library, Oxford
Historical Archive of the Argolid (Ιστορικό Αρχείο Αργολίδας) (HAA), Nafplio
  Municipal Archives of Nafplio (Δημοτικό Αρχείο Ναυπλίου) (DAN)
  Nafplio Three-member (*Trimeles*) Court of Appeals (Indictment Files) (ATEN) (DIK. 1.2.2)
  Nafplion Five-member (*Pentameles*) Court of Appeals (Minutes-Decisions) (APEN) (DIK. 1.4.2)
  Nafplion Criminal Court (Indictment Files) (AKN) (DIK. 1.5.1)
  Nafplion Criminal Court (Minutes-Decisions) (AKN) (DIK. 1.5.2)
  Tripolis Criminal Court (Indictment Files) (AKT) (DIK. 1.6.1)
  Tripolis Criminal Court (Minutes-Decisions) (AKT) (DIK. 1.6.2)
  Sparta Criminal Court (Indictment Files) (AKS) (DIK. 1.9.1)
  Sparta Criminal Court of (Minutes-Decisions) (AKS) (DIK. 1.9.2)
  Gytheion Criminal Court (Indictment Files) (AKG) (DIK. 1.12.1)
  Gytheion Criminal Court (Minutes-Decisions) (AKG) (DIK. 1.12.2)
  Special Court of Collaborators (Ειδικόν Δικαστήριον Δοσιλόγων) (EDD) (DIK. 1.16.1)
National Archives and Records Administration (NARA), Washington D.C.
  Allied Mission for Observing the Greek Elections (AMFOGE I and II), Retired Lot Files of NEA/GTI, Lot M-72, 62 A 624
  General Records of the Department of State, Decimal File 1945–9
Near East Foundation, New York
  Village Social Organization in Greece
Public Records Office (PRO), Kew Gardens
  Foreign Office Records (FO series)

Special Operations Executive Records (HS series)
Zentrale Stelle der Landesjustizverwaltungen (ZSt.), Ludwigsburg
    V 508 AR 2056/67 (Argos)

1.2 Unpublished Memoirs

Harisis Asimopoulos, Velvendo, Kozani
Kiriakos Dimitropoulos, Christianoi, Messinia
Petros S. Hasapis, Kiveri, Argolid
Efthimios Katsoyannos, Kleisto, Evritania
Ioannis G. Kolimenos, Dafni, Evritania
Panayotis Kondylis, Ancient Olympia, Ilia
Andreas Kranis, Argos, Argolid
Panayotis Lilis, Midea, Argolid
Yannis Nassis, Malandreni, Argolid
Dimitris Oikonomou, Heli, Argolid
Ioannis Petrou, Didyma, Argolid
Anastasios Rodopoulos, Neochori, Aridaia
Thanasis Siaterlis, Poulakida, Argolid
Giorgos Stamatiou, Spetses, Argosaronikos
Petros E. Tavoulareas, Tseria, Messinia

1.3 Student Research Papers (Village Histories)

Angeliki Andreopoulou, University of Athens, 1999
Vassiliki Ballios, New York University, 1999
Gerasimos Drakatos, University of Athens, 1999
Sofia Gali, University of Athens, 1999
Thomas Haidas, University of Athens, 1999
Olga Halkiopoulos, New York University, 2000
Dorothea Hunter, University of Chicago, 2003
Kali Koutelos, New York University, 1999
Evangelia Kremidas, New York University, 1999
Katerina Nikou-Stolou, University of Athens, 1999
Carol Notias, New York University, 1999
Helen Rouvelas, New York University, 1999
Evangelos Spathis, University of Athens, 1999
Ioanna Velentza, University of Athens, 1999
Elsa A. Vrana, University of Athens, 1999
Ioanna Zevgaras, New York University, 1999

2 Greece and the Greek Civil War

2.1 General

Andrews, Kevin. 1984. *The Flight of Ikaros*. London: Penguin.
Antoniou, Giorgos. 2001. The Importance of Interwar Communism in the Spread of the
    Resistance Movement (EAM). Unpublished paper, European University Institute.
Antonopoulos, Kosmas E. 1964. *Ethniki Antistasis 1941–1945* [National Resistance, 1941–
    1945]. 3 vols. Athens.

Baerentzen, Lars. 1982. *British Reports on Greece 1943–44 by J. M. Stevens, C. M. Woodhouse and D. J. Wallace*. Copenhagen: Museum Tusculanum Press.

Campbell, John, and Philip Sherrard. 1968. *Modern Greece*. New York: Praeger.

Capell, Richard. 1946. *Simiomata: A Greek Note Book, 1944–1945*. London: MacDonald.

Close, David H. 1995. *The Origins of the Greek Civil War*. London: Longman.

Condit, D. M. 1961. *Case Study in Guerrilla War: Greece during World War II*. Washington, D.C.: Special Operations Research Office, American University.

Danforth, Loring M. 1995. *Macedonian Conflict: Ethnic Nationalism in a Transnational World*. Princeton, N.J.: Princeton University Press.

Delaportas, Pavlos G. 1978. *To simiomatario enos Pilatou* [The notebook of a Pilatus]. Athens: Themelio.

Dordanas, Efstratios N. 1996. *I periochi tis Thessalonikis kai tis evriteris Makedonias kato apo ti Germaniki katochi, 1941–1943* [The Thessaloniki and wider Macedonia are under German occupation, 1941–1943]. Unpublished paper, Department of History, Aristoteleian University of Thessaloniki.

Fleischer, Hagen. 1979. Antipoina ton germanikon dinameon katochis stin Ellada 1941–1944 [Reprisals of the German occupation forces in Greece, 1941–1944]. *Mnimon* 7:182–95.

Gardner, Hugh H. 1962. *Guerrilla and Counterguerrilla Warfare in Greece, 1941–1945*. Washington, D.C.: Office of the Chief of Military History, Department of the Army.

Gerolymatos, André. 2004. *Red Acropolis, Black Terror: The Greek Civil War and the Origins of Soviet-American Rivalry, 1943–1949*. New York: Basic Books.

Gerolymatos, André. 1984. The Role of the Greek Officer Corps in the Resistance. *Journal of the Hellenic Diaspora* 11, 3:69–79.

Hammond, N. G. L. 1993. *The Allied Military Mission and the Resistance in Western Macedonia*. Thessaloniki: Institute for Balkan Studies.

Hondros, John L. 1993. *Occupation and Resistance: The Greek Agony, 1941–1944*. New York: Pella.

Jones, Howard. 1989. *"A New Kind of War": America's Global Strategy and the Truman Doctrine in Greece*. New York: Oxford University Press.

Kalyvas, Stathis N. 2000. Red Terror: Leftist Violence during the Occupation. In Mark Mazower (ed.), *After the War Was Over: Reconstructing Family, State, and Nation in Greece, 1944–1960*, 142–83. Princeton, N.J.: Princeton University Press.

Kalyvas, Stathis N. 1997. Polarization in Greek Politics: PASOK's First Four Years, 1981–1985. *Journal of the Hellenic Diaspora* 23, 1:83–104.

Karakasidou, Anastasia N. 1997. *Fields of Wheat, Hills of Blood: Passages to Nationhood in Greek Macedonia, 1870–1990*. Chicago: University of Chicago Press.

Kofos, Evangelos. 1993. *Nationalism and Communism in Macedonia: Civil Conflict, Politics of Mutation, National Identity*. New Rochelle, N.Y.: A. D. Caratzas.

Koliopoulos, Ioannis S. 1999. *Plundered Loyalties: Axis Occupation and Civil Strife in Greek West Macedonia, 1941–1949*. London: Hurst.

Marantzidis, Nikos. 2001. *Yasasin Millet, Zito to Ethnos. Prosfygia, katohi kai emfylios: Ethnotiki taftotita kai politiki symperifora stous tourkofonous elinorthodoxous tou Dytikou Pontou* [Yasasin Millet, long live the nation: Uprooting, occupation, and civil war: Ethnic identity and political behavior in the Turkish-Speaking Greek-Orthodox of Western Pontos]. Irakleio: University Press of Crete.

Marantzidis, Nikos. 1997. *Mikres Mosches: Politiki kai eklogiki analisi tis parousias tou kommounismou ston Elladiko agrotiko choro* [Little Moscows: A political and electoral analysis of the communist presence in the Greek rural space]. Athens: Papazissis.

Margaritis, Giorgos. 2000. *Istoria tou Emfyliou Polemou* [History of the Civil War]. 2 vols. Athens: Vivliorama.

Mathiopoulos, Vasos. 1980. *I Elliniki Antistasi (1941–1944) kai oi "Symmchoi"* [The Greek Resistance and the "Allies"]. Athens: Papazissis.

McNeill, William H. 1978. *The Metamorphosis of Greece since World War II*. Oxford: Blackwell.

McNeill, William H. 1947. *The Greek Dilemma: War and Aftermath*. Philadelphia: J. B. Lippincott.

Mazower, Marc. 1993. *Inside Hitler's Greece: The Experience of the Occupation, 1941–1944*. New Haven: Yale University Press.

Mazower, Mark. 1992. Military Violence and National Socialist Values: The Wehrmacht in Greece, 1941–1944. *Past and Present* 134:129–58.

Meyer, H. F. 2002. *Von Wien nach Kalavryta. Die blutige Spur der 117. Jäger-Division durch Serbien und Griechenland*. Moehnesee: Bibliopolis.

Meyer, H. F. 1995. *Missing in Greece: Destinies in the Greek Freedom Fight, 1941–1944*. London: Minerva.

Myers, E. C. W. 1955. *Greek Entaglement*. London: Hart-Davies.

Nachmani, Amikam. 1993. Guerrillas at Bay. The Rise and Fall of the Greek Democratic Army: The Military Dimension. Civil War in Greece: 1946–1949. *Journal of Modern Hellenism* 9:63–95.

Rossos, Andrew. 1997. Incompatible Allies: Greek Communism and Macedonian Nationalism in the Civil War in Greece, 1943–1949. *Journal of Modern History* 69, 1:42–76.

Skouras, F., A. Hadjidimos, A. Kaloutsis, and G. Papadimitriou. 1947. *I psichopathologia tis pinas, tou fovou kai tou agxous: Nevroseis kai psichonevroseis* [The psychopathology of hunger, fear, and anxiety: Neuroses and psychoneuroses]. Athens.

Vervenioti, Tasoula. 2003. *Diplo vivlio. I afigisi tis Stamatias Barbatsi* [Double book: The narrative of Stamatia Barbatsi]. Athens: Vivliorama.

Voigt, F. A. 1949. *The Greek Sedition*. London: Hollis and Carter.

Ward, Michael. 1992. *Greek Assignments. SOE 1943–1948 UNSCOB*. Athens: Lycabettus Press.

Woodhouse, C. 1948. *Apple of Discord: A Survey of Recent Greek Politics in Their International Setting*. London: Hutchinson.

Zafiropoulos, D. 1956. *O Antisymmoriakos agon, 1945–1949* [The anti-bandit struggle, 1945–1949]. Athens.

2.2 Local Studies and Local Memoirs

Antonopoulos, Antonis. 1993. *Mnimes enos andarti tou ELAS* [Recollections of an ELAS guerrilla]. Athens: Alfeios.

Aschenbrenner, Stanley. 1987. The Civil War from the Perspective of a Messenian Village. In Lars Baerentzen, J. O. Iatrides, and O. L. Smith (eds.), *Studies on the History of the Greek Civil War, 1945–9*, 105–25. Copenhagen: Museum Tusculanum Press.

Avdikos, Evangelos Gr. 2002. *Halase to horios mas halase* [Our village is ruined]. Alexandroupoli.

Balafoutas, Yannis. 1981. *Apo ton promachona tis Stimangas* [From the bastion of Stimanga]. Athens.

Balta, Nasi. 2002. "Tote me ta 'hitika' den kotages na peis oute t' onoma sou." Martiries gia ton emfylio se ena chorio tis Pylias. ["Then with the 'hitika' you didn't even dare to say what your name was." Testimonies about the civil war in a village of

Pylia]. In Ilias Nikolakopoulos, Alkis Rigos, and Grigoris Psallidas (eds.), *O Emfylios Polemos. Apo ti Varkiza sto Grammo, Fevrouarios 1945–Avgoustos 1949* [The Civil War: From Varkiza to Grammos, February 1945–August 1949], 176–87. Athens: Themelio.

Baroutas, Kostas G. 1998. *Mesochora*. Athens: Irodotos.

Campbell, J. K. 1974. *Honour, Family, and Patronage: A Study of Institutions and Moral Values in a Greek Mountain Community*. New York: Oxford University Press.

Christidis, Christodoulos I. 1991. *Pournia Konitsis-Ioanninon*. Athens.

Collard, Anna. 1989. Investigating "Social Memory" in a Greek Context. In E. Tonkin, M. McDonald, and M. Chapman (eds.), *History and Ethnicity*, 89-103. London: Routledge.

Dalianis, Anastasios I. 1998. *Iampolis, Valtetsi, Kalapodi*. Athens: Arsenidis.

Damianakos, Stathis. 1996. *Le paysan grec. Défis et adaptations face à la société moderne*. Paris: L'Harmattan.

Diamantakos, Nikos. 1997. *To Pouri*. Volos: Koinotita Pouriou.

du Boulay, Janet. 1974. *Portrait of a Greek Mountain Village*. Oxford: Oxford University Press.

Exarchos, Christos G. 1987. *I Fourka Ipirou*. Thessaloniki.

Filos, Stefanos. 2000. *Ta Tzoumerkohoria*. Athens.

Filos, Stefanos. 1991. *Agnanta Artas*. Athens: Adelfotis Agnantiton Athinas.

Gage, Nicholas. 1984. *Eleni*. New York: Ballantine Books.

Gavanas, Dimtrios G. 1999. *Rodohori Voiou*. Thessaloniki.

Georgiadis, Georgios. 2004. O Emfylios Polemos stis Vorioanatoliki Eordea (1943–1949) [The civil war in Northeast Eordea]. Unpublished paper.

Glaveris, Theodoros Ath. 1998. *O kambos tis Thessalonikis*. Thessaloniki.

Gogos, Andreas K. 1995. *Parakalamos*. Athens: Dodoni.

Goumas, Eleftherios. 1973. *Livadi*. Livadi.

Handman, Marie-Élisabeth. 1983. *La violence et la ruse: Hommes et femmes dans un village grec*. Aix-en-Provence: Édisud.

Hartomatsidis, Pavlos Ch. 1989. *Pontoirakleia Kilkis, 1924–1984*. Thessaloniki.

Kallianiotis, Thanasis. 2002. Oi protoi andartes sta Ventzia, 1942–1943 [The first rebels in Ventzia, 1942–1943]. Unpublished paper.

Kallianiotis, Thanasis. 2001. I OPLA tou Tsiartsamba, 1941–1949. Unpublished paper.

Kardaras, Takis G. 1982. *Mnimes sto diava mias zois* [Memories in the course of a life]. Athens.

Katevatis, N. n.d. *Anamniseis apo tin Katohi stin Zakintho kai i megali apogoitefsis* [Reminiscences from the occupation in Zakynthos and the great disappointment]. Athens.

Katsogiannos, Stelios. 1994. *I agnosti alitheia gia ton ELAS* [The unknown truth about ELAS]. Athens.

Kikopoulos, Menelaos St. 1991. *Elafotopos (Tservari)*. Ioannina.

Latsis, Vaggelis P. 1991. *Oi antartes tou Parnona* [The guerrillas of Parnon]. Athens: Forma.

Liapis, Kostas. 1994. *O "megalos" Ai-Giorgis tou Piliou*. Volos.

Loustas, Nikolaos Arg. 1988. *I Istoria tou Nimfeou-Neveskas Florinis*. Thessaloniki.

Magopoulos, Nikos V. 1998. *Agonistes ton Karditsiotikon Agrafon kai tou kambou 1940–1950* [Fighters from the Agrafa part of Karditsa and the plain, 1940–1950]. Karditsa.

Magopoulos, Nikos V. 1990. *Genia agonon kai thision. 33 choria Karditsas-Domokou stin Antistasi* [Generation of struggles and sacrifices: 33 villages of Karditsa and Domokos in the Resistance]. Athens.

Maloukos, Konstantinos I. 1992. *Enthimimata katochika kai antistasiaka* [Recollections from the occupation and the resistance]. Thessaloniki.

Mandas, Georgios I. E. (or Hondros). 1996. *Apomnimonevmata apo to 1876 os to 1966* [Memoirs from 1876 to 1966]. Tripoli.

Manetas, Athanasios Th. 1996. *Plessa-Amygdalia*. Athens.

Margaritis, Thodoros. 1995. *I Skala Messinias*. Athens: Vivliogonia.

Militsis, Christos M. 1997. *Agrafa. Karditsa, Mesenikola kai ta choria tou teos dimou Nevropolis* [Agrafa. Karditsa, Mesenikola and the villages of the former municipality of Nevropolis]. Karditsa.

Nasiopoulos, Andreas Ath. 1996. *O Arbounas*. Athens: Paraskinio.

Nikolaidis, Kostas. 1977. *I alithia gia tin Ethniki Antistasi* [The truth about the National Resistance]. Thessaloniki.

Oikonomou, Pantelis. 1976. *To Lehovo*. Thessaloniki.

Papachristou, Giannis D. 1994. *Tou Paloumba kai oi Paloumbaioi*. Tripoli: Fylla.

Papaioannou, Achilleas. 1990. *Giorgis Giannoulis: I thriliki morfi tou Grammou. To agnosto imerologio tou* [Giorgis Giannoulis: Grammos' legendary figure; His unknown diary]. Athens: Glaros.

Papakongos, Kostis. 1977. *Archeio Person. Katochika documenta tou DES Peloponnisou* [Person archive: Documents from the International Red Cross Office in the Peloponnese during the occupation]. Athens: Papazissis.

Papakonstantinou, Konstantinos (Belás). 1986. *I nekri merarchia* [The dead regiment]. 2 vols. Athens: Alfeios.

Papakonstantinou, Michalis. 1999. *To chroniko tis megalis nichtas* [The chronicle of the long night]. Athens: Estia.

Papandreou, Andreas K. 1992. *Odoiporiko sta dyskola chronia* [Journey during the hard years]. Kavala.

Papasteriopoulos, Ilias. 1965. *O Morias sta opla* [Morias in arms]. 4 vols. Athens: Erevna kai Kritiki tis Neoellinikis Istorias.

Pasagiotis, Nikos P. 1998. *Anamniseis* [Recollections]. Athens.

Pelagidis, Stathis. 1996. *I Inoi tis Kastorias*. Thessaloniki: Community of Inoi.

Poulimenakos, Aris G. 1989. *I Petrina*. Athens.

Priovolos, Kaisar. 1988. *Imoun Ipefthinos* [I was responsible]. Athens.

Sakkas, John. 2000. The Civil War in Evrytania. In Mark Mazower (ed.), *After the War Was Over: Reconstructing Family, State, and Nation in Greece, 1944–1960*, 186–209. Princeton, N.J.: Princeton University Press.

Sanders, Irwin T. 1953. Village Social Organization in Greece. *Rural Sociology* 18, 1–4:366–75.

Sarris, Konstantinos A. 1998. *Chroniko Koryschadon* [A chronicle of Koryshades]. Athens: Vasilopoulos.

Skaltsas, Panagiotis D. 1994. *Stis ochthes tou Kladeou* [On the of banks of Kladeos]. Athens.

Skoutelas, Rigas-Giorgos S. 1994. *Theodoriana Artas*. Athens: Kinotis Theodorianon.

Souflas, Kosmas. 1991. *Peninta palikaria* [Fifty young men]. Athens.

Stamatelatos, Michail, and Fotini Vamva-Stamatelatou. 2001. *Epitomo Geographiko Lexiko tis Ellados* [Geographical dictionary of Greece]. Athens: Ermis.

Stasinos, Kostas G. 2000. *To Athamanio ton Tzoumerkon*. Athens.

Stavropoulos, Nikos Ch. 1989. *I Vamvakou*. Athens: Sokolis.

Svolos, Alexandros. 1990. *Andartis sta vouna tou Moria. Odoiporiko (1947–49)* [Guerrilla in the mountains of Morias: A journey (1947–49)]. Athens.

Tatsiopoulos, Lambros A. 1971. *To Komboti Artis*. Ioannina.

Tchobanoglou, Marie. 1951. A Macedonian Village. Prepared under the direction of William J. Tudor. Unpublished Paper, Near East Foundation.

Triantafyllis, Kostas N. 1997. *Me nychia kai me dontia* [Tooth and nail]. Athens.

van Boeschoten, Riki. 1997. *Anapoda chronia. Sillogiki mnimi kai istoria sto Ziaka Grevenon (1900–1950)* [Hapless Years: Collective Memory and History in Ziakas, Grevena (1900–1950)]. Athens: Plethron.

Varmazis, Nikos D. 2002. *Dyskola Chronia stin Pieria* [Difficult years in Pieria]. Katerini: Mati.

Vermeulen, Hans. 1993. To varos tou parelthontos. I exousia ton kapetaneon sto xorio tou Kain kai tou Avel [The weight of the past: The power of the capetans in Cain's and Abel's village]. In E. Papataxiarchis and Th. Paradellis (eds.), *Anthropologia kai parelthon: simvoles stin koinoniki istoria tis neoteris Elladas* [Anthropology and past: A contribution to the social history of Modern Greece], 113–33. Athens: Alexandria.

Vettas, Yannis. 2002. *I machi tis Edessas* [The battle of Edessa]. Thessaloniki: Erodios.

Vourlas, Fotios St. 1992. *Mnimes kai didagmata. Emfylios dihasmos (1944–1949)* [Memories and lessons: Civil strife (1944–1949)]. Achladia.

Voryllas, Andreas Ch. 1994. *Kertezi*. Athens: Paraskinio.

Xanthakou, Margarita. 1998. Violence en trois temps: Vendetta, guerre civile et désordre nouveau dans une région grecque. Unpublished paper.

Yannisopoulou, Maria. 1998. I anthropologiki proseggisi. Almopia: parelthon, paron kai mellon [The anthropological approach: Almopia: Past, present, and future]. In National Center of Social Research, *Makedonia kai Valkania: xenophobia kai anaptyxi* [Macedonia and the Balkans: Xenophobia and development], 330–426. Athens: Alexandria.

Zervis, Nikos I. 1998. *I Germaniki katochi sti Messinia* [The German Occupation in Messinia]. Kalamata.

2.3 North Peloponnese (Including the Argolid)

Anagnostopoulos, Ioannis Sp. 1961. *I istoria tou Achladokambou* [The history of Achladokambos]. Athens.

Anagnostopoulos, N. N., and G. Gagalis., 1938. *I Argoliki Pedias* [The plain of Argolid]. Athens.

Barelos, Panayotis. 1983. *Skotini 17 Iouli 1944* [Skotini, 17 July 1944]. Skotini.

Binardopoulos, Yannis, Lambis Roupas, and Thodoris Chliapas. 1987. I Egialia stin katochi kai tin antistasi [Egialia during the occupation and the resistance]. Athens.

Bouyoukos, Takis. 1973. *I Feneos ana tous aiones* [Feneos throughout the centuries]. Athens.

Christopoulos, Andreas Ch. 1946. *Oi Italogermanoi stin Argolida* [The Italians and Germans in the Argolid]. Nafplion: Tipografion Efimeridos Sintagma.

Danousis, Kostas. 1994. Opuscula Argiva XIII. *Anagennisi* 321:4–13.

De Vooys, A. C., and J. J. C. A. Piket. 1958. Geographical Analysis of Two Villages in the Peloponnesos. *Tijdschrift van het Koninklijk Nederlandsch Aardrijkskundig Genootschap* 75, 1:31–55.

Frangoulis, Apostolos Ch. 1988. *Imerologio Ethnikis Antistasis Ermionis* [National Resistance diary of Ermioni]. Piraeus.

Kanellopoulos, Georgios A. 1981. *Istoria kai laografia ths Anatolikis Egialias-Kalavryton* [History and folklore of eastern Egialia and Kalavryta]. Athens.

Karouzou, Evi. 1995. Cultures maraîchères dans la Méditerranée: Les transformations de la plaine et la société argolique, 1860–1910. Ph.D. dissertation, European University Institute, Florence.

Koster, Harold A. 2000. Neighbors and Pastures: Reciprocity and Access to Pasture. In Susan Buck Sutton (ed.), *Contingent Countryside: Settlement, Economy, and Land Use in the Southern Argolid Since 1700*, 241–61. Stanford, Calif.: Stanford University Press.

Ladas, Vasilis. 2002. Oi Andartes tis Thalassas [Sea guerrillas]. Athens.

Miliarakis, Antonios. 1886. *Geographia politiki, nea kai archaia, tou nomou Argolidos kai Korinthias* [Political geography, modern and ancient, of the prefecture of Argolid and Korinthia]. Athens.

Panagopoulos, Andreas M. 1981. *Istoria tou choriou Malandreniou Argous* [History of the village Malandreni of Argos].

Papalilis, Giorgos. 1981. *I Ethniki Antistasi stin Argolida* [The National Resistance in Argolis]. Argos: Anagennisi.

Perrakis, Stelios. 2006. *Plaka Beach*. Madison, N.J.: Fairleigh Dickinson University Press.

Perrakis, Stelios. 2004. Collaboration as Revenge: Evidence from a Local Study in the Eastern Argolid. Unpublished paper.

Rigas, Dimitris. 1998. *Martyrologio. Ta thimata tis Korinthias* [List of martyrs: The victims of Korinthia]. Loutraki.

Spanos, Dimtris. 1990. *Istoria tis Karias Argolidos* [History of Karia, Argolid]. Thessaloniki.

Vazeos, Emmanouil. 1961. *Ta agnosta paraskinia tis Ethnikis Antistaseos eis tin Peloponnison* [The unknown back-stage of the National Resistance in the Peloponnese]. Korinthos.

3 General Secondary Sources

Abdi, Nidam. 1997. C'est devenu une guerre de tribus. *Libération*, 24 September.

Abella, Rafael. 1996. La vida cotidiana. In Edward Malefakis (ed.), *La Guerra de España (1936–1939)*, 451–79. Madrid: Taurus.

Achakzai, Saeed Ali. 2003. US Troops Provoke Anger, Fear in Afghan Villages. *Reuters*, 23 August. http://www.reuters.com, storyID=3326254.

Adams, Sam. 1994. *War of Numbers: An Intelligence Memoir*. South Royalton: Steerforth Press.

Aguilar Fernández, Paloma. 1996. *Memoria y olvido de la Guerra Civil Española*. Madrid: Alianza Editorial.

Åkerström, Malin. 1991. *Betrayals and Betrayers: The Sociology of Treachery*. New Brunswick, N.J.: Transaction.

Alapuro, Risto. 2002. Violence in the Finnish Civil War of 1918 and Its Legacy in a Local Perspective. Paper presented at the Workshop on "Civil Wars and Political Violence in 20th Century Europe," European University Institute, Florence 18–20 April.

Alapuro, Risto. 1998. Artisans and Revolution in a Finnish Country Town. In Michael P. Hanagan, Leslie Page Moch, and Wayne Brake (eds.), *Challenging Authority: The Historical Study of Contentious Politics*, 73–88. Minneapolis: University of Minnesota Press.

Allen, Barbara, and William Lynwood Montell. 1981. *From Memory to History: Using Oral Sources in Local Historical Research*. Nashville, Tenn.: American Association for State and Local History.

Allen, Tim. 1999. Perceiving Contemporary Wars. In Tim Allen and Jean Seaton (eds.), *The Media of Conflict: War Reporting and Representations of Ethnic Violence*, 11–42. London: Zed Books.

Allen, Tim. 1989. Violence and Moral Knowledge: Observing Social Trauma in Sudan and Uganda. *Cambridge Anthropology* 13, 2:45–67.

Allen, Tim, and Jean Seaton. 1999. Introduction. In Tim Allen and Jean Seaton (eds.), *The Media of Conflict: War Reporting and Representations of Ethnic Violence*, 1–7. London: Zed Books.

Anderson, David. 2005. *Histories of the Hanged: The Dirty War in Kenya and the End of Empire*. New York: W. W. Norton.

Anderson, Jon Lee. 2004. *Guerrilla: Journeys in the Insurgent World*. New York: Penguin.

Anderson, Scott. 2004. How Did Darfur Happen? *New York Times Magazine*, 17 October, 49–63.

Anderson, Truman. 1999. Incident at Baranivka: German Reprisals and the Soviet Partisan Movement in Ukraine, October–December 1941. *Journal of Modern History*, 71:585–623.

Anderson, Truman. 1995. The Conduct of Reprisals by the German Army of Occupation in the Southern USSR, 1941–1943. 2 vols. Ph.D. dissertation, University of Chicago.

André, Catherine, and Jean-Philippe Platteau. 1998. Land Relations under Unbearable Stress: Rwanda Caught in the Malthusian Trap. *Journal of Economic Behavior and Organization* 34, 1:1–47.

Andreopoulos, George J. 1994. The Age of National Liberation Movements. In Michael Howard, George J. Andreopoulos, and Mark R. Shulman (eds.), *The Laws of War: Constraints on Warfare in the Western World*, 191–213. New Haven: Yale University Press.

Andrews, Edmund L. 2003. Once Feared, a Southern Iraqi Clan Finds Itself Hunted. *New York Times*, 15 June, 10.

Angstrom, Jan. 2001. Towards a Typology of Internal Armed Conflict: Synthesizing a Decade of Conceptual Turmoil. *Civil Wars* 4, 3:93–116.

Annis, Sheldon. 1988. Story from a Peaceful Town: San Antonio Aguas Calientes. In Robert M. Carmack (ed.), *Harvest of Violence: The Maya Indians and the Guatemalan Crisis*, 155–73. Norman: University of Oklahoma Press.

Appadurai, Arjun. 1996. *Modernity at Large: Cultural Dimensions of Modernization*. Minneapolis: University of Minnesota Press.

Apter, David E. 1997. Political Violence in Analytical Perspective. In David Apter (ed.), *The Legitimization of Violence*, 1–32. New York: New York University Press.

Arendt, Hannah. 1973. *The Origins of Totalitarianism*. New York: Harcourt, Brace, Jovanovich.

Arendt, Hannah. 1970. *On Violence*. New York: Harcourt, Brace and World.

Arendt, Hannah. 1963. *Eichmann in Jerusalem: A Report on the Banality of Evil*. New York: Viking.

Argenti-Pillen, Alex. 2003. *Masking Terror: How Women Contain Violence in Southern Sri Lanka*. Philadelphia: University of Pennsylvania Press.

Armony, Ariel C. 1997. The Former Contras. In Thomas W. Walker (ed.), *Nicaragua without Illusions*, 203–18. Wilmington, Del.: Scholarly Resources.

Armstrong, John A. 1964. Introduction. In John A. Armstrong (ed.), *Soviet Partisans in World War II*, 3–70. Madison: University of Wisconsin Press.

Arnson, Cynthia J., and Robin Kirk. 1993. *State of War*. New York: Human Rights Watch/Americas.

Aron, Raymond. 1966. *Peace and War*. London: Weidenfeld & Nicolson.

Ash, Stephen V. 1995. *When the Yankees Came: Conflict and Chaos in the Occupied South, 1861–1865*. Chapel Hill: University of North Carolina Press.

Ash, Stephen V. 1988. *Middle Tennessee Society Transformed, 1860–1870: War and Peace in the Upper South*. Baton Rouge: Louisiana State University.

Asprey, Robert B. 1994. *War in the Shadows: The Guerrilla in History*. New York: Morrow.

Auletta, Ken. 2002. Beauty and the Beast. *New Yorker*, 16 December 2002, 65–81.

Auman, William T. 1984. Neighbor against Neighbor: The Inner Civil War in the Randolph County Area of Confederate North Carolina. *North Carolina Historical Review* 61, 1:59–92.

Aussaresses, Paul. 2001. *Services spéciaux. Algérie 1955–1957*. Paris: Perrin.

Avioutskii, Viatcheslav, and Hayder Mili. 2003. The Geopolitics of Separatism: Genesis of Chechen Field Commanders. *Central Asia and the Caucasus* 2, 20:7–14.

Azam, Paul, and Anke Hoeffler. 2002. Violence against Civilians in Civil Wars: Looting or Terror? *Journal of Peace Research* 39, 4:461–85.

Babeuf, Gracchus. 1987. *La guerre de la Vendée et le système de dépopulation*. Edited by Reynald Secher and Jean-Joël Brégeon. Paris: Tallandier.

Baier, Annette C. 1991. Violent Demonstrations. In R. G. Frey and Christopher W. Morris (eds.), *Violence, Terrorism, and Justice*, 33–58. Cambridge: Cambridge University Press.

Bailey, F. G. 1996. *The Civility of Indifference: On Domesticating Ethnicity*. Ithaca: Cornell University Press.

Baker, Peter. 2002. GIs Battle "Ghosts" in Afghanistan. Search for Elusive Enemy Frustrates Americans. *Washington Post*, May 16, A1.

Bandura, Albert. 1990. Mechanisms of Moral Disengagement. In Walter Reich (ed.), *Origins of Terrorism: Psychologies, Ideologies, Theologies, States of Mind*, 161–91. Cambridge: Cambridge University Press.

Bandura, Albert. 1983. Psychological Mechanisms of Aggression. In R. G. Green and E. I. Donnerstein (eds.), *Aggression: Theoretical and Empirical Reviews*, 1–40. New York: Academic Press.

Banton, Michael. 2000. Ethnic Conflict. *Sociology* 34, 3:481–98.

Barnett, Donald, and Karari Njama. 1966. *Mau Mau from Within: Autobiography and Analysis of Kenya's Peasant Revolt*. Letchworth: MacGibbon and Kee.

Barnstone, Willis. 1995. *Sunday Morning in Fascist Spain: A European Memoir, 1948–1953*. Carbondale: Southern Illinois University Press.

Barrett, David P. 2001. Introduction: Occupied China and the Limits of Accommodation. In David P. Barrett and Larry N. Shyu (eds.), *Chinese Collaboration with Japan, 1932–1945: The Limits of Accommodation*, 1–17. Stanford, Calif.: Stanford University Press.

Barth, Fredrik. 1994. Enduring and Emerging Issues in the Analysis of Ethnicity. In Hans Vermeulen and Cora Govers (eds.), *The Anthropology of Ethnicity: Beyond "Ethnic Groups and Boundaries,"* 11–32. Amsterdam: Het Spinhuis.

Barthes, Roland. 1977. *Roland Barthes*. New York: Hill and Wang.

Bartolini, Stefano, and Peter Mair. 1990. *Identity, Competition, and Electoral Availability: The Stabilization of European Electorates, 1885–1985*. Cambridge: Cambridge University Press.

Barton, Fred H. 1953. *Salient Operational Aspects of Paramilitary Warfare in Three Asian Areas*. ORO-T-228. Chevy Chase, Md.: Operations Research Office.

Bartov, Omer. 1992. *Hitler's Army: Soldiers, Nazis, and War in the Third Reich*. New York: Oxford University Press.

Bass, Gary Jonathan. 2000. *Stay the Hand of Vengeance: The Politics of War Crimes Tribunals*. Princeton, N.J.: Princeton University Press.

Bates, Robert H. 1999. Ethnicity, Capital Formation, and Conflict. Paper prepared for a conference sponsored by the Social Capital Initiative of the World Bank, 15–16 June, Washington, D.C.

Battini, Michele, and Paolo Pezzino. 1997. *Guerra ai civili: Occupazione tedesca e politica del massacro, Toscana 1944*. Venice: Marsilio.

Bauer, Yehuda. 2000. *Rethinking the Holocaust*. New Haven: Yale University Press.

Baumgartner, M. P. 1988. *The Moral Order of a Suburb*. New York: Oxford University Press.

Bax, Mart. 2000. Warlords, Priests and the Politics of Ethnic Cleansing: A Case Study from Rural Bosnia Hercegovina. *Ethnic and Racial Studies* 23, 1:16–36.

Bayly, C. A. 1988. "Rallying around the Subaltern." Review of the Writings of the Subaltern School. *Journal of Peasant Studies* 16, 1:110–20.

Bazenguissa-Ganga, Rémy. 1999a. The Spread of Political Violence in Congo-Brazzaville. *African Affairs* 98, 390:37–54.

Bazenguissa-Ganga, Rémy. 1999b. Les Ninja, les Cobra et les Zoulou crèvent l'écran à Brazzaville: Le rôle des medias et la construction des identités de violence politique. *Canadian Journal of African Studies* 33, 2–3:329–61.

BBC News. 2002. Egypt Feud Ends in Carnage. 10 August. http://news.bbc.co.uk/1/hi/world/middle-east/2185164.stm.

Bearak, Barry. 2000. A Kashmiri Mystery. *New York Times Magazine*, 31 December, 26–36.

Bearak, Barry. 1999a. Kosovo Town's Tale of Betrayal and Massacre. *New York Times*, 6 May, A3.

Bearak, Barry. 1999b. Afghan "Lion" Fights Taliban with Rifle and Fax Machine. *New York Times*, 9 November, A1.

Beaufre, André. 1972. *La guerre révolutionnaire. Les formes nouvelles de la guerre*. Paris: Fayard.

Beccaria, Cesare. 1986[1764]. *On Crimes and Punishments*. Translated from Italian by David Young. Indianapolis: Hackett.

Beckett, Ian F. W. 2001. *Modern Insurgencies and Counter-Insurgencies: Guerrillas and Their Opponents since 1750*. London: Routledge.

Belluck, Pam. 2001. On a Sworn Mission Seeking Pretenders to Military Heroism. *New York Times*, 10 August, A1.

Benini, Aldo A., and Lawrence H. Moulton. 2004. Civilian Victims in an Asymmetrical Conflict: Operation Enduring Freedom, Afghanistan. *Journal of Peace Research* 41, 4:403–22.

Bennett, Rab. 1999. *Under the Shadow of the Swastika: The Moral Dilemmas of Resistance and Collaboration in Hitler's Europe*. New York: New York University Press.

Benton, Gregor. 1999. *New Fourth Army: Communist Resistance along the Yangtze and the Huai, 1938–1941*. Berkeley: University of California Press.

Benton, Gregor. 1992. *Mountain Fire: The Red Army's Three-Year War in South China, 1934–1938*. Berkeley: University of California Press.

Benton, Gregor. 1989. Communist Guerrilla Bases in Southeast China after the Start of the Long March. In Kathleen Hartford and Steven M. Goldstein (eds.), *Single Sparks: China's Rural Revolutions*, 62–91. Armonk, N.Y.: M. E. Sharpe.

Bergner, Daniel. 2003. Where the Enemy Is Everywhere and Nowhere. *New York Times Magazine*, 20 July, 38–44.

Berkeley, Bill. 2001. *The Graves Are Not Yet Full: Race, Tribe, and Power in the Heart of Africa*. New York: Basic Books.

Berlow, Alan. 1998. *Dead Season: A Story of Murder and Revenge*. New York: Vintage.

Berman, Bruce, and John Lonsdale. 1992. *Unhappy Valley: Conflict in Kenya and Africa*. Oxford: James Currey.

Berman, Paul. 1996. In Search of Ben Linder's Killers. *New Yorker*, 23 September 1996, 58–81.

Berman, Richard. 1974. *Revolutionary Organization: Institution-Building within the People's Liberation Armed Forces.* Lexington, Mass.: D. C. Heath.

Bernand, André. 1999. *Guerre et violence dans la Grèce antique.* Paris: Hachette.

Berry, Mary Elizabeth. 1994. *The Culture of Civil War in Kyoto.* Berkeley: University of California Press.

Besteman, Catherine. 1996. Violent Politics and the Politics of Violence: The Dissolution of the Somali Nation-State. *American Ethnologist* 23, 3:579–96.

Bigeard, Marcel-Maurice. 1995. *Ma guerre d'Algérie.* Paris: Hachette/Carrère.

Bilton, Michael, and Kevin Sim. 1992. *Four Hours in My Lai.* New York: Penguin.

Binford, Leigh. 1996. *The El Mozote Massacre: Anthropology and Human Rights.* Tucson: University of Arizona Press.

Bizot, François. 2003. *The Gate.* New York: Knopf.

Black, Donald J. 1993. *The Social Structure of Right and Wrong.* San Diego: Academic Press.

Black, Donald J. 1976. *The Behavior of Law.* New York: Academic Press.

Black-Michaud, Jacob. 1975. *Cohesive Force: Feud in the Mediterranean and the Middle East.* New York: St. Martin's Press.

Blackwood, B. G. 1997. Parties and Issues in the Civil War in Lancashire and East Anglia. In R. C. Richardson (ed.), *The English Civil Wars: Local Aspects,* 261–85. Phoenix Mill: Sutton.

Blaufarb, Douglas S., and George K. Tanham. 1989. *Who Will Win? A Key to the Puzzle of Revolutionary War.* New York: Crane Russak.

Bobbio, Norberto. 1992. Guerra Civile? *Teoria Politica* 1–2:297–307.

Boehm, Christopher. 1984. *Blood Revenge: The Enactment and Management of Conflict in Montenegro and Other Societies.* Philadelphia: University of Pennsylvania Press.

Bohlen, Celestine. 1999. Russia Troops Are in New Battle with Separatists in the Caucasus. *New York Times,* 9 August, A1.

Borovik, Artyom. 1991. *The Hidden War: A Russian Journalist's Account of the Soviet War in Afghanistan.* London: Faber and Faber.

Bosch Sánchez, Aurora. 1983. *Ugetistas y libertarios. Guerra civil y revolución en el pais valenciano, 1936–1939.* Valencia: Instituto Alfons el Magnanim.

Boswell, Laird. 1998. *Rural Communism in France, 1920–1939.* Ithaca: Cornell University Press.

Bouaziz, Moula, and Alain Mahé. 2004. La Grande Kabylie durant la guerre d'Indépendance algerienne. In Mohammed Harbi and Benjamin Stora (eds.), *La guerre d'Algerie. 1954–2004, la fin de l'amnésie,* 227–65. Paris: Robert Laffont.

Boudon, Raymond. 1988. The Logic of Relative Frustration. In Michael Taylor (ed.), *Rationality and Revolution,* 245–67. Cambridge: Cambridge University.

Bougarel, Xavier. 1996. *Bosnie, anatomie d' un conflit.* Paris: La Découverte.

Bourdieu, Pierre. 1977. *Outline of a Theory of Practice.* Cambridge: Cambridge University Press.

Bourgois, Philippe. 2001. The Power of Violence in War and Peace: Post-Cold War Lessons from El Salvador. *Ethnography* 2, 1:5–34.

Bouthoul, Gaston. 1970. *Traité de polémologie. Sociologie des guerres.* Paris: Payot.

Bran, Mirel. 2002. Dona Cornea: Dans le miroir de la Securitate. *Le Monde,* 8 October, 14.

Brass, Paul R. 1997. *Theft of an Idol: Text and Context in the Representation of Collective Violence.* Princeton, N.J.: Princeton University Press.

Braud, Philippe. 1999. Violence symbolique, violence physique. Éléments de la problématisation. In Jean Hannoyer (ed.), *Guerres civiles: Economies de la violence, dimensions de la civilité,* 33–45. Paris: Karthala-Cermoc.

Brehun, Leonard. 1991. *Liberia: The War of Horror*. Accra: Adwinsa Publications.

Bringa, Tone. 1995. *Being Muslim the Bosnian Way: Identity and Community in a Central Bosnian Village*. Princeton, N.J.: Princeton University Press.

Brinkley, Douglas. 2003. Tour of Duty: John Kerry in Vietnam. *Atlantic Monthly*, December, 47–60.

Brinkman, Inge. 2000. Ways of Death: Accounts of Terror from Angolan Refugees in Namibia. *Africa* 70, 1:1–23.

Brody, Reed. 1985. *Contra Terror in Nicaragua: Report of a Fact-Finding Mission, September 1984–January 1985*. Boston: South End Press.

Brovkin, Vladimir N. 1994. *Behind the Front Lines of the Civil War*. Princeton, N.J.: Princeton University Press.

Brown, Kate. 2003. *A Biography of No Place: From Ethnic Borderland to Soviet Heartland*. Cambridge, Mass.: Harvard University Press.

Brown, Mervyn. 2001. *War in Shangri-La: A Memoir of Civil War in Laos*. London: Radcliffe Press.

Brown, Michael F., and Eduardo Fernández. 1991. *War of Shadows: The Struggle for Utopia in the Peruvian Amazon*. Berkeley: University of California Press.

Brown, Timothy C. 2001. *The Real Contra War: Highlander Peasant Resistance in Nicaragua*. Norman: University of Oklahoma Press.

Browne, Malcolm W. 2000. Paddy War. In *Reporting Vietnam: American Journalism, 1959–1975*, 3–10. New York: Library of America.

Browning, Christopher R. 1998. *Ordinary Men: Reserve Police Battalion 101 and the Final Solution in Poland*. New York: HarperCollins.

Browning, Christopher R. 1992. *The Path to Genocide: Essays on Launching the Final Solution*. Cambridge: Cambridge University Press.

Browning, Christopher R. 1990. Germans and Serbs: The Emergence of Nazi Antipartisan Policies in 1941. In Michael Berenbaum (ed.), *A Mosaic of Victims: Non-Jews Persecuted and Murdered by the Nazis*, 64–73. New York: New York University Press.

Brubaker, Rogers, and David D. Laitin. 1998. Ethnic and Nationalist Violence. *Annual Review of Sociology* 24: 423–52.

Brustein, William, and Margaret Levi. 1987. The Geography of Rebellion: Rulers, Rebels, and Regions, 1500 to 1700. *Theory and Society* 16:467–95.

Buoye, Thomas. 1990. Economic Change and Rural Violence: Homicides Related to Disputes over Property Rights in Guangdong during the Eighteenth Century. *Peasant Studies* 17, 4:233–59.

Burds, Jeffrey. 1997. A Culture of Denunciation: Peasant Labor Migration and Religious Anathematization in Rural Russia, 1860–1905. In Sheila Fitzpatrick and Robert Gellately (eds.), *Accusatory Practices: Denunciation in Modern European History, 1789–1989*, 40–72. Chicago: University of Chicago Press.

Burg, Steven L., and Paul S. Shoup. 1999. *The War in Bosnia-Herzegovina: Ethnic Conflict and International Intervention*. Armonk, N.Y.: M. E. Sharp.

Buruma, Ian. 2002. The Blood Lust of Identity. *New York Review of Books*, 11 April, 12–14.

Butalia, Urvashi. 2000. *The Other Side of Silence: Voices from the Partition of India*. Durham: Duke University Press.

Butaud, Christian, and Marina Rialland. 1998. *Le blé en feu: Algérie, années 50*. Paris: Editions du Reflet.

Butterfield, Fox. 2005. Guns and Jeers Used by Gangs to Buy Silence. *New York Times*, 16 January, A1.

Byrne, Hugh. 1996. *El Salvador's Civil War: A Study of Revolution*. Boulder, Colo.: Lynne Rienner.

Cabarrús, Carlos Rafael. 1983. *Génesis de una revolución: Análisis del surgimiento y desarrollo de la organización campesina en El Salvador*. Hidalgo: Ediciones de la Casa Chata.

Cahen, Michel. 2000. Nationalism and Ethnicities: Lessons from Mozambique. In Einar Braathen, Morten Bøås, and Gjermund Sæther (eds.), *Ethnicity Kills? The Politics of War, Peace and Ethnicity in SubSaharan Africa*, 163–87. London: Macmillan.

Calder, Bruce J. 1984. *The Impact of Intervention: The Dominican Republic during the U.S. Occupation of 1916–1924*. Austin: University of Texas Press.

Calvino, Italo. 1995. *Numbers in the Dark and Other Stories*. Translated by Tim Parks. London: Jonathan Cape.

Cann, John P. 1997. *Counterinsurgency in Africa: The Portuguese Way of War, 1961–1974*. Westport, Conn.: Greenwood Press.

Carlton, Eric. 1994. *Massacres: An Historical Perspective*. Aldershot: Scolar Press.

Carmack, Robert M. 1988a. Editor's Preface to the First Edition. In Robert M. Carmack (ed.), *Harvest of Violence: The Maya Indians and the Guatemalan Crisis*, ix–xvii. Norman: University of Oklahoma Press.

Carmack, Robert M. 1988b. The Story of Santa Cruz Quiché. In Robert M. Carmack (ed.), *Harvest of Violence: The Maya Indians and the Guatemalan Crisis*, 39–69. Norman: University of Oklahoma Press.

Carnegie Endowment for International Peace. 1993[1913]. *The Other Balkan Wars: A 1913 Carnegie Endowment Inquiry in Restrospect*. Washington D.C.: Carnegie Endowment for International Peace.

Carpenter, Charli R. 2003. "Women and Children First": Gender, Norms, and Humanitarian Evacuation in the Balkans, 1991–95. *International Organization* 57:661–94.

Carr, Jaqueline Barbara. 2004. *After the Siege: A Social History of Boston, 1775–1800*. Boston: Northeastern University Press.

Casanova, Julián. 1985. *Anarquismo y revolución social en la socieadad aragonesa, 1936–1938*. Madrid: Siglo XXI.

Casas de la Vega, Rafael. 1994. *El Terror: Madrid 1936; Investigación histórica y catálogo historico de víctimas identificadas*. Madrid: Editorial Fénix.

Cela, Camilo José. 1992. *Mazurka for Two Dead Men*. New York: New Directions.

Cenarro, Ángela. 2002. Matar, vigilar y delatar: La quiebra de la sociedad civil durante la guerra y la posguerra en España (1936–1948). *Historia Social* 44:65–86.

Chacón Barrero, Mario. 2003. *Dinámica y determinantes de la violencia durante "La Violencia": Una aproximacion desde la econometria espacial*. Unpublished paper, Universidad de los Andes.

Chaliand, Gérard. 1987. *Terrorism: From Popular Struggle to Media Spectacle*. London: Saqi Books.

Chalk, Frank, and Kurt Jonassohn. 1990. *The History and Sociology of Genocide: Analyses and Case Studies*. New Haven: Yale University Press.

Chamoun, Tracy. 1992. *Au nom du père*. Paris: J.-C. Lattès.

Chan, Anita, Richard Madsen, and Jonathan Unger. 1992. *Chen Village: Under Mao and Deng*. Berkeley: University of California Press.

Chandrasekaran, Rajiv. 2004. Violence in Iraq Belies Claims of Calm, Data Show. *Washington Post*, 26 September, A1.

Chang, Jung. 1992. *Wild Swans: Three Daughters of China*. New York: Doubleday.

Che Guevara, Ernesto. 1998 [1961]. *Guerrilla Warfare*. Lincoln: University of Nebraska Press.

Chingono, Mark F. 1996. *The State, Violence, and Development: The Political Economy of War in Mozambique, 1975–1992*. Aldershot: Avebury.

Chivers, C. J. 2003. Feud between Kurdish Clans Creates Its Own War. *New York Times*, 24 February, A8.

Chung, Ly Qui. 1970. *Between Two Fires: The Unheard Voices of Vietnam*. New York: Praeger.

Chwe, Michael Suk-Young. 2001. *Rational Ritual: Culture, Coordination, and Common Knowledge*. Princeton, N.J.: Princeton University Press.

Clastres, Pierre. 1999. *Archéologie de la violence*. Paris: Editions de l'Aube.

Clausewitz, Carl von. 1976. *On War*. Edited and translated by Peter Paret and Michael Howard. Princeton, N.J.: Princeton University Press.

Claverie, Elisabeth. 2002. Apparition de la Vierge et "retour" des disparus. La constitution d'une identité à Medjugorje (Bosnie-Herzégovine). *Terrain* 38:41–54.

Clayton, Anthony. 1999. *Frontiersmen: Warfare in Africa since 1950*. London: UCL Press.

Clémenceau, Joseph. 1909. *Histoire de la guerre de Vendée (1793–1815)*. Paris: Nouvelle Librairie Nationale.

Clifton, Robin. 1999. "An Indiscriminate Blackness"? Massacre, Counter-Massacre, and Ethnic Cleansing in Ireland, 1640–1660. In Mark Levene and Penny Roberts (eds.), *The Massacre in History*, 107–26. New York: Berghahn Books.

Clines, Francis X. 2001. Harsh Civics Lesson for Immigrants. *New York Times*, 11 November, B7.

Clover, Charles. 2003. Pro-Saddam "Fighters" or Feuding Neighbours? *Financial Times*, 14–15 June, 7.

Clutterbuck, Richard L. 1966. *The Long Long War: Counterinsurgency in Malaya and Vietnam*. New York: Praeger.

CNN. 2003. Inside the Hunt for Iraqi Insurgents. *Paula Zahn Now*, aired 26 December, http://www.cnn.com/TRANSCRIPTS/0312/26/pzn.00.html.

Cobb, Richard. 1972. *Reactions to the French Revolution*. London: Oxford University Press.

Cohen, Joyce. 2000. Revenge among the Nerds. *New York Times*, 24 August, G1.

Cohen, Roger. 1994. A UN Aid Says Plight of Gorazde Is Exaggerated. *New York Times*, 30 April, A3.

Coleman, James S. 1990. *Foundations of Social Theory*. Cambridge, Mass.: Belknap Press.

Collier, George A. 1987. *Socialists of Rural Andalusia: Unacknowledged Revolutionaries of the Second Republic*. Stanford, Calif.: Stanford University Press.

Collier, Paul, V. L. Elliott, Håvard Hegre, Anke Hoeffler, Marta Reynal-Querol, and Nicholas Sambanis. 2003. *Breaking the Conflict Trap: Civil War and Development Policy*. Washington, D.C.: World Bank and Oxford University Press.

Collier, Paul, and Anke Hoeffler. 1999. Justice-Seeking and Loot-Seeking in Civil War. Unpublished paper, World Bank.

Collins, Eamon (with Mick McGovern). 1999. *Killing Rage*. New York: Granta Books.

Collotti, Enzo. 1996. Occupazione e guerra totale nell'Italia 1943–1945. In Tristano Matta (ed.), *Un percorso della memoria: Guida ai luoghi della violenza nazista e fascista in Italia*, 11–35. Trieste: Electa.

Comisión Nacional sobre la Desaparición de Personas. 1986. *Nunca Más: The Report of the Argentine National Commission on the Disappeared*. New York: Farrar Straus Giroux.

Connelly, John. 1997. The Uses of *Volksgemeinschaft*: Letters to the NSDAP Kreisleitung Eisenach, 1939–1940. In Sheila Fitzpatrick and Robert Gellately (eds.), *Accusatory Practices: Denunciation in Modern European History, 1789–1989*, 153–84. Chicago: University of Chicago Press.

Contini, Giovanni. 1997. *La memoria divisa*. Milan: Rizzoli.

Converse, Philip E. 1964. The Nature of Belief Systems in Mass Publics. In David E. Apter (ed.), *Ideology and Discontent*, 206–61. New York: Free Press.

Cooper, Matthew. 1979. *The Nazi War against Soviet Partisans, 1941–1944*. New York: Stein and Day.

Cordesman, Anthony H., and Abraham R. Wagner. 1990. *The Lessons of Modern War*. Vol. 3: *The Afghan and Falklands Conflicts*. Boulder, Colo.: Westview Press.

Coser, Lewis A. 1956. *The Functions of Social Conflict*. New York: Free Press.

Coster, Will. 1999. Massacre and Codes of Conduct in the English Civil War. In Mark Levene and Penny Roberts (eds.), *The Massacre in History*, 89–105. New York: Berghahn Books.

Courtois, Stéphane. 1998. Les crimes du communisme. In Stéphane Courtois, Nicolas Werth, Jean-Louis Panné, Andrzej Paczkowski, Karel Bartosek, and Jean-Louis Margolin, *Le livre noir du communisme: Crimes, terreur, répression*, 5–38. Paris: Laffont.

Cranna, Michael (ed.). 1994. *The True Cost of Conflict*. New York: New Press.

Crawford, Oliver. 1958. *The Door Marked Malaya*. London: Rupert Hart-Davis.

Crenshaw, Martha. 1995. The Effectiveness of Terrorism in the Algerian War. In Martha Crenshaw (ed.), *Terrorism in Context*, 473–513. University Park: Pennsylvania State University Press.

Cribb, Robert. 1991. *Gangsters and Revolutionaries: The Jakarta People's Militia and the Indonesian Revolution, 1945–1949*. Honolulu: University of Hawaii Press.

Cribb, Robert. 1990. Introduction: Problems in the Historiography of the Killings in Indonesia. In Robert Cribb (ed.), *The Indonesian Killings of 1965–1966: Studies from Java and Bali*, 1–43. Monash University: Centre of Southeast Asian Studies.

Crisp, Jeff. 2000. A State of Insecurity: The Political Economy of Violence in Kenya's Refugee Camps. *African Affairs* 99:601–32.

Crouzet, Denis. 1990. *Les guerriers de dieu: La violence au temps des troubles de religion (vers 1525–vers 1610)*. 2 vols. Seyssel: Champ Vallon.

Crow, Jeffrey J. 1985. Liberty Men and Loyalists: Disorder and Disaffection in the North Carolina Backcountry. In Ronald Hoffman, Thad W. Tate, and Peter J. Albert (eds.), *An Uncivil War: The Southern Backcountry during the American Revolution*, 125–78. Charlottesville: University Press of Virginia.

Crozier, Brian. 1960. *The Rebels: A Study of Postwar Insurrections*. Boston: Beacon Press.

Dale, Catherine. 1997. The Dynamics and Challenges of Ethnic Cleansing: The Georgia-Abkhazia Case. *Refugee Survey Quarterly* 16, 3:77–109.

Dallin, Alexander, Ralph Mavrogordato, and Wilhelm Moll. 1964. Partisan Psychological Warfare and Popular Attitudes. In John A. Armstrong (ed.), *Soviet Partisans in World War II*, 197–337. Madison: University of Wisconsin Press.

Dalrymple, William. 1997. *From the Holy Mountain: A Journey among the Christians of the Middle East*. New York: Henry Holt.

Daniel, E. Valentine. 1996. *Charred Lullabies: Chapters in an Anthropology of Violence*. Princeton, N.J.: Princeton University Press.

Danner, Mark. 1994. *The Massacre of El Mozote*. New York: Vintage.

Darby, John. 1990. Intimidation and Interaction in a Small Belfast Community: The Water and the Fish. In John Darby, Nicholas Dodge, and A. C. Hepburn (eds.), *Political Violence: Ireland in a Comparative Perspective*, 83–102. Ottawa: University of Ottawa Press.

Das, Veena, and Arthur Kleinman. 2000. Introduction. In Veena Das, Arthur Kleinman, Mamphela Ramphele, and Pamela Reynolds (eds.), *Violence and Subjectivity*, 1–18. Berkeley: University of California Press.

Davenport, Christian, and Patrick Ball. 2002. Implications of Source Selection in the Case of the Guatemalan State Terror. *Journal of Conflict Resolution* 46, 3:427–50.

David, Steven R. 1997. Internal War: Causes and Cures. *World Politics* 49, 4:552–76.

Davidson, Jamie S. 2003. The Politics of Violence on an Indonesian Periphery. *South East Asia Research* 11, 1:59–90.

Davies, Rees. 2003. The Medieval State: The Tyranny of a Concept? *Journal of Historical Sociology* 16, 2:280–300.

Davis, Ann, Maureen Tkacik, and Andrea Petersen. 2001. A Nation of Tipsters Answers FBI's Call in War on Terrorism. *Wall Street Journal*, 21 November, A1, A8.

Davis, Shelton H. 1988. Introduction: Sowing the Seeds of Violence. In Robert M. Carmack (ed.), *Harvest of Violence: The Maya Indians and the Guatemalan Crisis*, 3–36. Norman: University of Oklahoma Press.

Dealey, Sam. 2004. Misreading the Truth in Sudan. *New York Times*, 8 August, WK11.

Dean, Roger. 2000. Rethinking the Civil War in Sudan. *Civil Wars* 3, 1:71–91.

De Baecque, Antoine. 2002. Apprivoiser une histoire déchaînée: Dix ans de travaux historiques sur la Terreur. *Annales HSS* 57, 2:851–65.

Debray, Régis. 1967. *Revolution in the Revolution? Armed Struggle and Political Struggle in Latin America*. New York: Grove Press.

Debray, Régis (in collaboration with Ricardo Ramirez). 1975. Guatemala. In Regis Debray (ed.), *Las pruebas de fuego*, 249–324. Mexico: Siglo Veintiuno Editores.

Decker, Scott H. 1993. Exploring Victim-Offender Relationships in Homicide: The Role of Individual and Event Characteristics. *Justice Quarterly* 10:585–612.

De Figueiredo, Rui J. P., Jr., and Barry R. Weingast. 1999. The Rationality of Fear: Political Opportunism and Ethnic Conflict. In Barbara F. Walter and Jack Snyder (eds.), *Civil Wars, Insecurity, and Intervention*, 261–302. New York: Columbia University Press.

De Foxà, Agustín. 1993. *Madrid de Corte a Checa*. Barcelona: Planeta.

Degregori, Carlos Iván. 1998. Harvesting Storms: Peasant *Rondas* and the Defeat of Sendero Luminoso in Ayacucho. In Steve J. Stern (ed.), *Shining and Other Paths: War and Society in Peru, 1980–1995*, 128–57. Durham: Duke University Press.

de la Cueva, Julio. 1998. Religious Persecution, Anticlerical Tradition, and Revolution: On Atrocities against the Clergy during the Spanish Civil War. *Journal of Contemporary History* 33, 3:355–69.

Della Porta, Donatella. 1995. *Social Movements, Political Violence, and the State: A Comparative Analysis of Italy and Germany*. Cambridge: Cambridge University Press.

Del Pino, H. Ponciano. 1998. Family, Culture, and "Revolution": Everyday Life with Sendero Luminoso. In Steve J. Stern (ed.), *Shining and Other Paths: War and Society in Peru, 1980–1995*, 158–92. Durham: Duke University Press.

De Lupis, Ingrid Detter. 1987. *The Law of War*. Cambridge: Cambridge University Press.

DeNardo, J. N. 1985. *Power in Numbers*. Princeton, N.J.: Princeton University Press.

Derriennic, Jean-Pierre. 2001. *Les guerres civiles*. Paris: Presses de Sciences Po.

De Staël, Germaine. 1979 [1798]. *Des circonstances actuelles qui peuvent terminer la révolution et des principes qui doivent fonder la république en France*. Critical edition by Lucia Omacini. Geneva: Librairie Droz.

De Staël, Germaine. 1818. *Considerations on the Principal Events of the French Revolution*. London: Baldwin, Cradock, and Joy.

deTurck, M. A., and G. R. Miller. 1990. Training Observers to Detect Deception: Effects of Self-Monitoring and Rehearsal. *Human Communication Research* 16, 4:603–20.

De Waal, Alexander. 1991. *Evil Days: Thirty Years of War and Famine in Ethiopia*. New York: Human Rights Watch.

Díaz-Balart, Mirta Núñez, and Antonio Rojas Friend. 1997. *Consejo de guerra: Los fusilamientos en el Madrid de la posguerra (1939–1945)*. Madrid: Compañía Literaria.

Dillon, Martin. 1990. *The Dirty War: Covert Strategies and Tactics Used in Political Conflicts*. New York: Routledge.

Dillon, Sam. 1991. *Commandos: The CIA and Nicaragua's Contra Rebels*. New York: Henry Holt.

Dion, Douglas. 1997. Competition and Ethnic Conflict: Artifactual? *Journal of Conflict Resolution* 41:5, 638–48.

Djilas, Milovan. 1980. *Tito: The Story from Inside*. New York: Harcourt Brace Jovanovich.

Donagan, Barbara. 1994. Atrocity, War Crime, and Treason in the English Civil War. *American Historical Review* 99, 4:1137–66.

Downes, Alexander B. 2004. Drastic Measures: Why Civilians Are Victimized in War. Ph.D. dissertation, University of Chicago.

Downie, Richard Duncan. 1998. *Learning from Conflict: The U.S. Military in Vietnam, El Salvador, and the Drug War*. Westport, Conn.: Praeger.

Dulić, Tomislav. 2004. Tito's Slaughterhouse: A Critical Analysis of Rummel's Work on Democide. *Journal of Peace Research* 41, 1:85–102.

Dupuy, Roger. 1997. *Les chouans*. Paris: Hachette.

Durkheim, Emile. 1951 [1897]. *Suicide: A Study in Sociology*. New York: Free Press.

Durkheim, Emile. 1938 [1895]. *The Rules of Sociological Method*. New York: Free Press.

Durrell, Lawrence. 1996 [1957]. *Bitter Lemons*. New York: Marlowe.

Duvall, Raymond, and Michael Stohl. 1983. Governance by Terror. In Michael Stohl (ed.), *The Politics of Terrorism*, 179–219. New York: Marcel Dekker.

Duyvesteyn, Isabelle. 2000. Contemporary War: Ethnic Conflict, Resource Conflict, or Something Else? *Civil Wars* 3, 1:92–116.

Dwyer, Jim. 2001. Memories of the Louima Case: 1 Meeting, 4 Trained Observers. *New York Times*, 19 August, 14.

Earle, Timothy. 1997. *How Chiefs Come to Power: The Political Economy in Prehistory*. Stanford, Calif.: Stanford University Press.

Ebel, Roland H. 1988. When Indians Take Power: Conflict and Consensus in San Juan Ostuncalco. In Robert M. Carmack (ed.), *Harvest of Violence: The Maya Indians and the Guatemalan Crisis*, 174–91. Norman: University of Oklahoma Press.

Echandía, Camilo. 1999. *Conflicto armado y las manifestaciones de violencia en las regiones de Colombia*. Santafé de Bogotá: Presidencia de la República de Colombia, Oficina del Alto Comisionado para la Paz, Oberservatorio de Violencia.

Eckhardt, William. 1989. Civilian Deaths in Wartime. *Bulletin of Peace Proposals* 20, 1: 89–98.

Eckstein, Harry. 1965. On the Etiology of Internal Wars. *History and Theory* 4, 2:133–63.

Economist. 2003. Far from Normal. An Impending Referendum Will Bring Neither Peace nor Security. 22 March, 46.

Ekirch, A. Roger. 1985. Whig Authority and Public Order in Backcountry North Carolina, 1776–1783. In Ronald Hoffman, Thad W. Tate, and Peter J. Albert (eds.), *An Uncivil War: The Southern Backcountry during the American Revolution*, 99–124. Charlottesville: University Press of Virginia.

Elias, Norbert. 1994. *The Civilizing Process*. Translated by Edmund Jephcott. Oxford: Blackwell.

Ellin, Abby. 2001. Family Conflicts That Can Bring a Business Down. *New York Times*, 29 August, C1.

Elliott, David W. P. 2003. *The Vietnamese War: Revolution and Social Change in the Mekong Delta, 1930–1975*. 2 vols. Armonk, N.Y.: M. E. Sharpe.

Ellis, Stephen. 1999. *The Mask of Anarchy: The Destruction of Liberia and the Religious Dimension of an African Civil War*. New York: New York University Press.

Ellis, Stephen. 1995. Liberia 1989–1994: A Study of Ethnic and Spiritual Violence. *African Affairs* 94, 375:165–97.

Ellsberg, Daniel. 2003. *Secrets: A Memoir of Vietnam and the Pentagon Papers*. New York: Penguin.

Ellul, Jacques. 1969. *Violence: Reflections from a Christian Perspective*. New York: Seabury Press.

Elster, Jon. 1999. *Alchemies of the Mind*. Cambridge: Cambridge University Press.

Enzensberger, Hans Magnus. 1994. *Civil Wars: From L.A. to Bosnia*. New York: New Press.

Epstein, Joseph. 2002. *Snobbery: The American Version*. New York: Houghton Mifflin.

Ermakoff, Ivan. 2001. Ideological Challenge, Strategies of Action, and Regime Breakdown. Unpublished paper, Department of Sociology, University of Wisconsin-Madison.

Escott, Paul D. 1978. *After Secession: Jefferson Davis and the Failure of Confederate Nationalism*. Baton Rouge: Louisiana State University Press.

Escott, Paul D., and Jeffrey J. Crow. 1986. The Social Order and Violent Disorder: An Analysis of North Carolina in the Revolution and the Civil War. *Journal of Southern History* 52, 3:373–402.

Essien, Jeremiah Moses. 1987. *In the Shadow of Death: Personal Recollections of Events during the Nigerian Civil War*. Ibadan: Heineman.

Esteban, J., and D. Ray. 1994. On the Measurement of Polarization. *Econometrica* 62: 819–52.

Estrada i Planell, Gemma. 1995. *La Guerra Civil al Bruc*. Barcelona: Publicacions de l'Abadia de Montserrat.

Evans, Emory G. 1985. Trouble in the Backcountry: Disaffection in Southwest Virginia during the American Revolution. In Ronald Hoffman, Thad W. Tate, and Peter J. Albert (eds.), *An Uncivil War: The Southern Backcountry during the American Revolution*, 179–212. Charlottesville: University Press of Virginia.

Everitt, Alan. 1997. The Local Community and the Great Rebellion. In R. C. Richardson (ed.), *The English Civil Wars: Local Aspects*, 15–36. Phoenix Mill: Sutton.

Faivre, Maurice. 1994. *Un village de Harkis*. Paris: L'Harmattan.

Fall, Bernard B. 2000. Vietnam Blitz: A Report on the Impersonal War. In *Reporting Vietnam: American Journalism, 1959–1975*, 106–17. New York: Library of America.

Falla, Ricardo. 1994. *Massacres in the Jungle: Ixcan, Guatemala, 1975–1982*. Boulder, Colo.: Westview Press.

Fawaz, Leila Tarazi. 1994. *An Occasion for War: Civil Conflict in Lebanon and Damascus in 1860*. Berkeley: University of California Press.

Fearon, James D., and David D. Laitin. 2003. Ethnicity, Insurgency, and Civil War. *American Political Science Review* 97, 1:75–86.

Fearon, James D., and David D. Laitin. 2000. Violence and the Social Construction of Ethnic Identity. *International Organization* 54, 4:845–77.

Fehr, Ernst, and Simon Gächter. 2002. Altruistic Punishment in Humans. *Nature* 415: 137–40.

Fein, Helen. 1993. *Genocide: A Sociological Perspective*. London: Sage.

Fein, Helen. 1979. *Accounting for Genocide: National Responses and Jewish Victimization during the Holocaust*. Chicago: University of Chicago Press.

Feldman, Arnold S. 1964. Violence and Volatility: The Likelihood of Revolution. In Harry Eckstein (ed.), *Internal War: Problems and Approaches*, 111–29. New York: Free Press.

Fellman, Michael. 1989. *Inside War: The Guerrilla Conflict in Missouri during the American Civil War*. New York: Oxford University Press.

Fenoglio, Beppe. 1973. *La guerre sur les collines*. Paris: Gallimard.

Feraoun, Mouloud. 2000. *Journal 1955–1962: Reflections on the French-Algerian War*. Lincoln: University of Nebraska Press.

Ferguson, A. Thomas, Jr.. 1975. Sources for the Study of Revolutionary Guerrilla War-
    fare. In Sam C. Sarkesian (ed.), *Revolutionary Guerrilla Warfare*, 617–23. Chicago:
    Precedent Publishing.
Fichtl, Eric. 2004. The Ambiguous Nature of "Collaboration" in Colombia. *Colombia
    Journal Online*, March. http://www.colombiajournal.org/colombia181.htm.
Fichtl, Eric. 2003. Araucan Nightmare: Life and Death in Tame. *Colombia Journal Online*,
    August. http://www.colombiajournal.org/araucan_nightmare.htm.
Fiennes, Ranulph. 1975. *Where Soldiers Fear to Tread*. London: Hodder and Stoughton.
Figes, Orlando. 1996. *A People's Tragedy: The Russian Revolution, 1891–1924*. New York:
    Penguin.
Figes, Orlando. 1989. *Peasant Russia, Civil War: The Volga Countryside in Revolution (1917–
    1921)*. Oxford: Clarendon Press.
Filkins, Dexter. 2005. The Fall of the Warrior King. *New York Times Magazine*, 23 October,
    52–177.
Filkins, Dexter. 2004. US Plans Year-End Drive to Take Iraqi Rebel Areas. *New York Times*,
    19 September, 1.
Filkins, Dexter. 2001. Surrender of Taliban Begins at Final Northern Stronghold. *New
    York Times*, 25 November, A1.
Filkins, Dexter (with Carlotta Gall). 2001. Fierce Fighting at Kunduz Undercuts Surren-
    der Deal. *New York Times*, 23 November, B2.
Finer, Jonathan. 2005. Informants Decide Fate of Iraqi Detainees. U.S. Military Relies
    on Guidance of "Sources" in Tall Afar. *Washington Post*, 13 September, A1.
Finley, Milton. 1994. *The Most Monstrous of Wars: The Napoleonic Guerrilla War in Southern
    Italy, 1806–1811*. Columbia: University of South Carolina Press.
Finnegan, William. 1999. The Invisible War. *New Yorker*, 25 January.
Finnegan, William. 1992. *A Complicated War: The Harrowing of Mozambique*. Berkeley:
    University of California Press.
Firestone, David. 2000. Booming Atlanta Saps Water as Drought Wilts Georgia. *New York
    Times*, 15 June, A16.
Fisher, Noel C. 1997. *War at Every Door: Partisan Politics and Guerrilla Violence in East
    Tennessee, 1860–1869*. Chapel Hill: University of North Carolina Press.
FitzGerald, Frances. 1989. *Fire in the Lake: The Vietnamese and the Americans in Vietnam*.
    New York: Vintage Books.
Fitzpatrick, Sheila. 1997. Signals from Below: Soviet Letters of Denunciation of the 1930s.
    In Sheila Fitzpatrick and Robert Gellately (eds.), *Accusatory Practices: Denunciation in
    Modern European History, 1789–1989*, 85–120. Chicago: University of Chicago Press.
Fitzpatrick, Sheila. 1994. *Stalin's Peasants: Resistance and Survival in the Russian Village after
    Collectivization*. New York: Oxford University Press.
Fitzpatrick, Sheila, and Robert Gellately. 1997. Introduction to the Practices of Denun-
    ciation in Modern European History. In Sheila Fitzpatrick and Robert Gellately
    (eds.), *Accusatory Practices: Denunciation in Modern European History, 1789–1989*, 1–21.
    Chicago: University of Chicago Press.
Flower, Ken. 1987. *Serving Secretly: An Intelligence Chief on Record; Rhodesia into Zimbabwe,
    1964–1981*. London: John Murray.
Forero, Juan. 2002. Colombian Troops Move on Rebel Zone as Talks Fail. *New York Times*,
    11 January, A9.
Forero, Juan. 2001. Colombia's Army Rebuilds and Challenges Rebels. *New York Times*,
    2 September, A3.
Forero, Juan. 2000. Rebel-Held Zone in Colombia Fears End of Truce. *New York Times*,
    16 December, A3.

Forment, Carlos A. 2000. *Democracy in Latin America: Civic Selfhood and Public Life in Postcolonial Mexico and Peru*. Unpublished paper.

Foucault, Michel. 1977. *Discipline and Punish: The Birth of the Prison*. New York: Pantheon Books.

Franzinelli, Mimmo. 2002. *Delatori. Spie e confidenti anonimi: L'arma segreta del regime fascista*. Milan: Mondadori.

Fraser, Ronald. 1993. La historia oral como historia desde abajo. *Ayer* 12:79–92.

Freeman, Simon. 1994. Learning the Fundamental Lessons of Religious Conviction. *Scotsman*, 28 December, 14.

Freeman, Susan Tax. 1979. *The Pasiegos: Spaniards in No Man's Land*. Chicago: University of Chicago Press.

Freeman, Susan Tax. 1970. *Neighbors: The Social Contract in a Castilian Hamlet*. Chicago: University of Chicago Press.

Friedrich, Carl J. 1972. *The Pathology of Politics: Violence, Betrayal, Corruption, Secrecy, and Propaganda*. New York: Harper & Row.

Friedrich, Paul. 1977. *Agrarian Revolt in a Mexican Village*. Chicago: University of Chicago Press.

Frijda, Nico H. 1994. The Lex Talionis: On Vengeance. In Stephanie H. M. Van Goozen, Nanne E. Van de Poll, and Joseph Sergeant (eds.), *Emotions: Essays on Emotion Theory*, 263–89. Hillsdale, N.J.: Lawrence Erlbaum Associates.

Furet, François. 1981. *Interpreting the French Revolution*. Cambridge: Cambridge University Press.

Gacemi, Baya. 1998. *Moi, Nadia, femme d'un émir du GIA*. Paris: Éditions du Seuil.

Gall, Carlotta. 2005. Despite Years of U.S. Pressure, Taliban Fight On in Jagged Hills. *New York Times*, 4 June, A1, A6.

Gall, Carlotta. 2001. The Way We Live Now: Questions for Kenneth Gluck; Home Free. *New York Times Magazine*, 11 March, 25.

Gall, Carlotta. 1999. Villagers Hope Kosovo Peace Arrives before the War. *New York Times*, 15 March, A6.

Gallagher, A. M. 1995. Policing Northern Ireland: Attitudinal Evidence. In Alan O'Day (ed.), *Terrorism's Laboratory: The Case of Northern Ireland*, 47–58. Aldershot: Dartmouth.

Galtung, Johan. 1975. *Peace: Research, Education, Action*. Copenhagen: Christian Ejlers.

Gambetta, Diego. 1993. *The Sicilian Mafia: The Business of Private Protection*. Cambridge, Mass: Harvard University Press.

Garton Ash, Timothy. 1997. *The File: A Personal History*. New York: Random House.

Garvin, John R. 1991. Uncomfortable Wars: Toward a New Paradigm. In Max G. Manwaring (ed.), *Uncomfortable Wars: Toward a New Paradigm of Low Intensity Conflict*, 9–28. Boulder, Colo.: Westview Press.

Gawande, Atul. 2001. Under Suspicion. The Fugitive Science of Criminal Justice. *New Yorker*, 8 January, 50–3.

Geffray, Christian. 1990. *La cause des armes au Mozambique: Anthropologie d'une guerre civile*. Paris: Karthala.

Gellately, Robert. 1997. Denunciations in Twentieth-Century Germany: Aspects of Self-Policing in the Third Reich and the German Democratic Republic. In Sheila Fitzpatrick and Robert Gellately (eds.), *Accusatory Practices: Denunciation in Modern European History, 1789–1989*, 185–221. Chicago: University of Chicago Press.

Gellately, Robert. 1991. *The Gestapo and German Society: Enforcing Racial Policy, 1933–1945*. Oxford: Oxford University Press.

Genschel, Philipp, and Klaus Schlichte. 1998. Civil War as a Chronic Condition. *Law and State*, 58:107–23.

Georgy, Michael. 2003. Iraqi Tribal Revenge Fuels Falluja's Anti-U.S. Rage. *Reuters*, 6 November. http://www.reuters.com, storyID = 3766606.

Gersony, Robert. 1988. Summary of Mozambican Refugee Accounts of Principally Conflict-Related Experience in Mozambique. Report submitted to Ambassador Jonathon Moore, Director, Bureau for Refugees Program and Dr. Chester Crocker, Assistant Secretary of African Affairs, Washington, D.C., April.

Getty, J. Arch, and Roberta T. Manning. 1993. Introduction. In J. Arch Getty and Roberta T. Manning (eds.), *Stalinist Terror: New Perspectives*, 1–20. Cambridge: Cambridge University Press.

Geyer, Michael. 2000. Civitella della Chiana on 29 June 1944. The Reconstruction of a German "Measure." In Hannes Heer and Klaus Naumann (eds.), *War of Extermination: The German Military in World War II, 1941–1944*, 175–216. New York: Berghahn Books.

Gilbert, Daniel T., and Patrick S. Malone. 1995. The Correspondence Bias. *Psychological Bulletin* 117, 1:21–38.

Gillespie, Richard. 1995. Political Violence in Argentina: Guerrillas, Terrorists, and *Carapintadas*. In Martha Crenshaw (ed.), *Terrorism in Context*, 211–48. University Park: Pennsylvania State University Press.

Gilmore, David D. 1987. *Aggression and Community: Paradoxes of Andalusian Culture*. New Haven: Yale University Press.

Gilsenan, Michael. 1999. Problems in the Analysis of Violence. In Jean Hannoyer (ed.), *Guerres civiles: Economies de la violence, dimensions de la civilité*, 105–22. Paris: Karthala-Cermoc.

Gilsenan, Michael. 1996. *Lords of the Lebanese Marches: Violence and Narrative in an Arab Society*. London: I. B. Tauris.

Girard, René. 1977. *Violence and the Sacred*. Baltimore: Johns Hopkins University Press.

Giustozzi, Antonio. 2000. *War, Politics, and Society in Afghanistan, 1978–1992*. Washington, D.C.: Georgetown University Press.

Glaberson, William. 2001. A Tale of Betrayals Unfolds in a Montana Drug Trial. *New York Times*, 14 May, A13.

Glanz, James. 2005. New Iraqi Soldiers Gain Ground but Face Pitfalls. *New York Times*, 6 April, A14.

Given, James B. 1997. *Inquisition and Medieval Society: Power, Discipline, and Resistance in Languedoc*. Ithaca: Cornell University Press.

Goldberg, Carey. 2003. Studies Say Old Memories Can Be Lost. *Boston Globe*, 30 December, A1.

Goldberg, Carey. 1999. Court Ruling Sets Guides on Use of Informers. *New York Times*, 16 September, A18.

Goldhagen, Daniel. 1996. *Hitler's Willing Executioners: Ordinary Germans and the Holocaust*. New York: Alfred A. Knopf.

Goldstein, Robert Justin. 1992. The Limitations of Using Quantitative Data in Studying Human Rights Abuses. In Thomas B. Jabine and Richard P. Claude (eds.), *Human Rights and Statistics: Getting the Record Straight*, 35–61. Philadelphia: University of Pennsylvania Press.

Goltz, Thomas. 1998. *Azerbaijan Diary: A Rogue Reporter's Adventures in an Oil-Rich, War Torn, Post-Soviet Republic*. Armonk, N.Y.: M. E. Sharpe.

Goodwin, Jeff. 2001. *No Other Way Out: States and Revolutionary Movements, 1945–1991*. Cambridge: Cambridge University Press.

Goodwin, Jeff. 1999. *Are Rebels Opportunists? Political Opportunities and the Emergence of Political Contention*. Unpublished paper.

Gordon, Michael R. 2000a. Chechen Rebels Swim in Friendly Waters to Nip Russians. *New York Times*, 12 January, A3.

Gordon, Michael R. 2000b. Russia Takes Chechen Town, but Can It Keep It? *New York Times*, 14 January, A4.

Gordon, Michael R. 1999a. Russian Generals See Victory Near in Caucasus Clash. *New York Times*, 16 August, A1.

Gordon, Michael R. 1999b. Russia Uses a Sledgehammer in Chechnya War This Time. *New York Times*, 8 December, A1.

Gordon, Michael R. 1999c. Chechens Say They Were Shot at in Safe Corridor. *New York Times*, 17 December, A1.

Gossman, Patricia. 2000. India's Secret Armies. In Bruce B. Campbell and Arthur D. Brenner (eds.), *Death Squads in Global Perspective: Murder with Deniability*, 261–86. New York: St. Martin's Press.

Gottschalk, Keith. 2000. National, Ethnic, and Religious Identity Conflict. In Bruce B. Campbell and Arthur D. Brenner (eds.), *Death Squads in Global Perspective: Murder with Deniability*, 229–59. New York: St. Martin's Press.

Gould, Roger. 2003. *Collision of Wills. How Ambiguity about Social Rank Breeds Conflict*. Chicago: University of Chicago Press.

Gould, Roger. 1995. *Insurgent Identities: Class, Community, and Protest in Paris from 1848 to the Commune*. Chicago: University of Chicago Press.

Gourevitch, Philip. 1998. *We Wish to Inform You That Tomorrow We Will Be Killed with Our Families: Stories from Rwanda*. New York: Farrar, Straus, and Giroux.

Graham, Patrick . 2005. The Message from the Sunni Heartland. *New York Times*, 22 May, WK3.

Green, Linda. 1995. Living in a State of Fear. In Carolyn Nordstrom and Antonius C. G. M. Robben (eds.), *Fieldwork under Fire: Contemporary Studies of Violence and Survival*, 105–27. Berkeley: University of California Press.

Greenberg, Joel. 2001. As Violence Erupts, Barak and Sharon Agree on Unity Guidelines *New York Times*, 13 February, A1, A8.

Greene, Thomas H. 1990. *Comparative Revolutionary Movements: Search for Theory and Justice*. Englewood Cliffs, N.J.: Prentice-Hall.

Greenhill, Kelly M. 2003. The Use of Refugees as Political and Military Weapons in the Kosovo Conflict. In Raju G. C. Thomas (ed.), *Yugoslavia Unraveled: Sovereignty, Self-Determination, and Intervention*, 205–42. Lanham, Md.: Lexington Books/Rowman and Littlefield.

Greer, Donald. 1935. *The Incidence of the Terror during the French Revolution: A Statistical Interpretation*. Cambridge, Mass.: Harvard University Press.

Grenier, Yvon. 1999. *The Emergence of Insurgency in El Salvador: Ideology and Political Will*. Pittsburgh: University of Pittsburgh Press.

Griffin, Patricia E. 1976. *The Chinese Communist Treatment of Counterrevolutionaries: 1924–1949*. Princeton, N.J.; Princeton University Press.

Grigorenko, Petro G. 1982. *Memoirs*. New York: Norton.

Gross, Jan T. 2001. *Neighbors: The Destruction of the Jewish Community in Jedwabne, Poland*. Princeton, N.J.: Princeton University Press.

Gross, Jan T. 1988. *Revolution from Abroad: The Soviet Conquest of Poland's Western Ukraine and Western Belorussia*. Princeton, N.J.: Princeton University Press.

Gross, Jan T. 1979. *Polish Society under German Occupation: The Generalgouvernement, 1939–1944*. Princeton, N.J.: Princeton University Press.

Gross, Jane. 2005. Under One Roof, Aging Together Yet Alone. *New York Times*, 30 January, 1.

Grossman, Dave. 1995. *On Killing: The Psychological Cost of Learning to Kill in War and Society*. Boston: Little, Brown.

Groth, Siegfried. 1995. *Namibia – The Wall of Silence: The Dark Days of the Liberation Struggle*. Wuppertal: Peter Hammer Verlag.

Grotius, Hugo. 1925[1625]. *De Jure Belli Ac Pacis*. Translated by Francis W. Kelsey, with the collaboration of Arthur E. R. Boak, Henry A. Sanders, Jesse S. Reeves, and Herbert F. Wright. Oxford: Clarendon Press, 1925.

Guelke, Adrian. 1995. *The Age of Terrorism and the International Political System*. New York: St. Martin's Press.

Guha, Ranajit. 1999. *Elementary Aspects of Peasant Insurgency in Colonial India*. Durham: Duke University Press.

Gulden, Timothy R. 2002. Spatial and Temporal Patterns in Civil Violence: Guatemala, 1977–1986. Working Paper No. 26. Wasington, D.C.: CSED.

Gumz, Jonathan E. 2001. *Wehrmacht* Perceptions of Mass Violence in Croatia, 1941–1942. *Historical Journal* 44, 4:1015–38.

Gunther, John. 1949. *Behind the Curtain*. New York: Harper.

Gurr, Ted R. 1986. The Political Origins of State Violence and Terror: A Theoretical Analysis. In Michael Stohl and George Lopez (eds.), *Government Violence and Repression: An Agenda for Research*, 45–72. New York: Greenwood Press.

Gurr, Ted R. 1980. *Handbook of Political Conflict*. New York: Free Press.

Gurr, Ted R. 1975. Psychological Factors in Civil Violence. In Sam C. Sarkesian (ed.), *Revolutionary Guerrilla Warfare*, 75–114. Chicago: Precedent Publishing.

Gurr, Ted R. 1970. *Why Men Rebel*. Princeton, N.J.: Princeton University Press.

Gutman, Roy. 1993. *A Witness to Genocide: The First Inside Account of the Horrors of "Ethnic Cleansing" in Bosnia*. Shaftesbury, Dorset: Element Books.

Haberman, Clyde. 2001. Arab Fury Rising at Enemy Within. *New York Times*, 7 August, A1.

Haberman, Clyde. 1991. After Four Years, Intifada Still Smolders. *New York Times*, 9 December, A11.

Halbwachs, Maurice. 1968. *La mémoire collective*. Paris: PUF.

Hale, J. R. 1971. Sixteenth-Century Explanations of War and Violence. *Past and Present* 51:3–26.

Hall, Brian. 1994. *The Impossible Country: A Journey through the Last Days of Yugoslavia*. New York: Penguin.

Hamilton-Merritt, Jane. 1993. *Tragic Mountains: The Hmong, the Americans, and the Secret Wars for Laos, 1942–1992*. Bloomington: Indiana University Press.

Hammond, Jenny. 1999. *Fire from the Ashes: A Chronicle of the Revolution in Tigray, Ethiopia, 1975–1991*. Lawrenceville, N.J.: Red Sea Press.

Hamoumou, Mohand. 1993. *Et ils sont devenus Harkis*. Paris: Fayard.

Harbom, Lotta, and Peter Wallensteen. 2005. Armed Conflict and Its International Dimensions, 1946–2004. *Journal of Peace Research* 42, 5:623–35.

Hardin, Russell. 1995. *One for All: The Logic of Group Conflict*. Princeton, N.J.: Princeton University Press.

Harding, Susan F. 1984. *Remaking Ibieca: Rural Life in Aragon under Franco*. Chapel Hill: University of North Carolina Press.

Harff, Barbara. 2003. No Lessons Learned from the Holocaust? Assessing Risks of Genocide and Political Mass Murder since 1955. *American Political Science Review* 97, 1: 57–73.

Harkavy, Robert E., and Stephanie G. Neuman. 2001. *Warfare and the Third World*. New York: Palgrave.

Harmon, Christopher C. 1992. Illustrations of "Learning" in Counterinsurgency. *Comparative Strategy* 11, 1:29–48.

Harris, Rosemary. 1989. Anthropological Views on "Violence" in Northern Ireland. In Yonah Alexander and Alan O'Day (eds.), *Ireland's Terrorist Trauma: Interdisciplinary Perspectives*, 75–100. New York: St. Martin's Press.

Hart, Peter. 1999. *The I.R.A. and Its Enemies: Violence and Community in Cork, 1916–1923*. New York: Clarendon Press.

Hart, Peter. 1997. The Geography of Revolution in Ireland, 1917–1923. *Past & Present* 155:142–55.

Hartford, Katherine. 1989. Repression and Communist Success: The Case of Jin-Cha-Ji, 1938–1943. In Kathleen Hartford and Steven M. Goldstein (eds.), *Single Sparks: China's Rural Revolutions*, 92–127. Armonk, N.Y.: M. E. Sharpe.

Hayden, William. 1999. The Kosovo Conflict: The Strategic Use of Displacement and the Obstacle to International Protection. *Civil Wars* 2, 1:35–68.

Hechter, Michael. 1987. *Principles of Group Solidarity*. Berkeley: University of California Press.

Hedges, Chris. 2003. *War Is a Force That Gives Us Meaning*. New York: Anchor Books.

Hedges, Chris. 1997. War Crime "Victims" Are Alive, Embarrassing Bosnia. *International Herald Tribune*, 3 March.

Hedman, Eva-Lotta. 2000. State of Siege: Political Violence and Vigilante Mobilization in the Philippines. In Bruce B. Campbell and Arthur D. Brenner (eds.), *Death Squads in Global Perspective: Murder with Deniability*, 125–51. New York: St. Martin's Press.

Heer, Hannes. 2000. The Logic of the War of Extermination: The Wermacht and the Anti-Partisan War. In Hannes Heer and Klaus Naumann (eds.), *War of Extermination: The German Military in World War II, 1941–1944*, 92–126. New York: Berghahn Books.

Heer, Hannes, and Klaus Naumann. 2000. Introduction. In Hannes Heer and Klaus Naumann (eds.), *War of Extermination: The German Military in World War II, 1941–1944*, 1–12. New York: Berghahn Books.

Heilbrunn, Otto. 1967. *Partisan Warfare*. New York: Praeger.

Henderson, James D. 1985. *When Colombia Bled: A History of the Violencia in Tolima*. Tuscaloosa: University of Alabama Press.

Henriksen, Thomas H. 1983. *Revolution and Counterrevolution: Mozambique's War of Independence, 1964–1974*. Wesport, Conn.: Greenwood Press.

Henriksen, Thomas H. 1976. People's War in Angola, Mozambique, and Guinea-Bissau. *Journal of Modern African Studies* 14, 3:377–99.

Héritier, Françoise (ed.). 1996. *De la violence*. Paris: Odile Jacob.

Herrington, Stuart A. 1997. *Stalking the Vietcong: Inside Operation Phoenix: A Personal Account*. Novato, Calif.: Presidio Press.

Hill, Alexander. 2002. The Partisan War in North-West Russia, 1941–44: A Re-examination. *Journal of Strategic Studies* 25, 3:37–55.

Hilton, Isabel. 2002. Between the Mountains. *New Yorker*, 11 March, 64–75.

Hinton, William. 1984. *Shenfan: The Continuing Revolution in a Chinese Village*. New York: Vintage Books.

Hoare, Marko. 2001. The Partisans in Bosnia-Herzegovina, 1941–1946. Unpublished paper.

Hobbes, Thomas. 1968 [1651]. *Leviathan*. Edited by C. B. Macpherson. Harmondsworth: Penguin.

Hobsbawm, E. J. 2001. Foreword. In Gonzalo Sánchez and Donny Meertens, *Bandits, Peasants, and Politics: The Case of "La Violencia" in Colombia*, ix–xii. Austin: University of Texas Press.

Hobsbawm, E. J. 1997. *On History*. New York: New Press.

Hobsbawm, E. J. 1988. History from Below – Some Reflections. In Frederick Krantz (ed.), *History from Below: Studies in Popular Protest and Popular Ideology*, 13–27. Oxford: Blackwell.

Hodson, Randy, Dušco Seculić, and Garth Massey. 1994. National Tolerance in the Former Yugoslavia. *American Journal of Sociology* 99:1535–58.

Hofheinz, Roy, Jr. 1969. The Ecology of Chinese Communist Success: Rural Influence Patterns, 1923–45. In Doak Barnett (ed.), *Chinese Communist Politics in Action*, 3–77. Seattle: University of Washington Press.

Holsti, Kalevi J. 1996. *The State, War, and the State of War*. Cambridge: Cambridge University Press.

Horne, Alistair. 1987. *A Savage War of Peace: Algeria, 1954–1962*. New York: Penguin Books.

Horowitz, Donald L. 2001. *The Deadly Ethnic Riot*. Berkeley: University of California Press.

Horowitz, Donald L. 1985. *Ethnic Groups in Conflict*. Berkeley: University of California Press.

Horton, Lynn. 1998. *Peasants in Arms: War and Peace in the Mountains of Nicaragua, 1979–1984*. Athens: Ohio University Center for International Studies.

Hosmer, Stephen T. 1970. *Viet Cong Repression and Its Implications for the Future*. Lexington, Mass.: D.C. Heath.

Housego, Kim. 2004. Colombian Towns Fear a Rebel Resurgence. http://archive.wn.com/2004/03/10/1400/colombiapost/.

Hovil, Lucy, and Eric Werker. 2005. Portrait of a Failed Rebellion. An Account of Rational, Sub-optimal Violence in Western Uganda. *Rationality and Society* 17, 1:5–34.

Howard, Michael. 1994. Constraints on Warfare. In Michael Howard, George J. Andreopoulos, and Mark R. Shulman (eds.), *The Laws of War: Constraints on Warfare in the Western World*, 1–11. New Haven: Yale University Press.

Howell, Roger, Jr. 1997. Newcastle and the Nation: The Seventeenth-Century Experience. In R. C. Richardson (ed.), *The English Civil Wars: Local Aspects*, 309–29. Phoenix Mill: Sutton.

Hua, Linshan, and Isabelle Thireau. 1996. *Enquête sociologique sur la Chine, 1911–1949*. Paris: Presses Universitaires de France.

Hull, Isabel V. 2004. Instant Degeneration: Systemic Radicalization in German Warfare in the First Months of World War I. Unpublished paper.

Human Rights Watch. 1992. *War Crimes in Bosnia-Hercegovina: A Helsinki Watch Report*. Vol. 1. New York: Human Rights Watch.

Hunt, David. 1974. Villagers at War: The National Liberation Front in My Tho Provinces, 1965–1967. *Radical America* 8, 1–2:3–184.

Huseen, Akeel, and Nicolas Pelhman. 2004. Rebels' Writ Runs Large across the Troublesome Sunni Triangle. *Financial Times*, 30 July, 7.

Ignatieff, Michael. 1998. *The Warrior's Honor: Ethnic War and the Modern Conscience*. New York: Henry Holt.

Jacoby, Susan. 1983. *Wild Justice: The Evolution of Revenge*. New York: Harper & Row.

James, Clive. 2003. The Good of a Bad Review. *New York Times*, 7 September, 13.

Jankowski, Paul. 1989. *Communism and Collaboration: Simon Sabiani and Politics in Marseille, 1919–1944*. New Haven: Yale University Press.

Jing, Jun. 1996. *The Temple of Memories: History, Power, and Morality in a Chinese Village.* Stanford, Calif.: Stanford University Press.

Johnson, Chalmers. 1968. The Third Generation of Guerrilla Warfare. *Asian Survey* 8, 6:435–47.

Johnson, Chalmers. 1962. Civilian Loyalties and Guerrilla Conflict. *World Politics* 14, 4:646–61.

Johnson, Michael. 2001. *All Honourable Men: The Social Origins of War in Lebanon.* London: I. B. Tauris.

Jok, Madut, and Sharon Elaine Hutchinson. 1999. Sudan's Prolonged Second Civil War and the Militarization of Nuer and Dinka Ethnic Identities. *African Studies Review* 42, 2:125–45.

Jolliffe, Jill. 1978. *East Timor: Nationalism and Colonialism.* St. Lucia, Queensland: University of Queensland Press.

Jonassohn, Kurt (with Karin Solveig Björnson). 1998. *Genocide and Gross Human Rights Violations in Comparative Perspective.* New Brunswick, N.J.: Transaction.

Jones, Adrian H., and Andrew R. Molnar. 1966. *Internal Defense against Insurgency: Six Cases.* Washington, D.C.: Center for Research in Social Systems.

Jones, Gregg R. 1989. *Red Revolution: Inside the Philippine Guerrilla Movement.* Boulder, Colo.: Westview Press.

Jones, James C. 2000. We're Targeting a Colombia We Don't Fully Understand. *Washington Post*, April 2.

Jongerden, Joost. 2001. Resettlement and Reconstruction of Identity: The Case of the Kurds in Turkey. *Global Review of Ethnopolitics* 1, 1:80–6.

Joshi, Vandana. 2003. *Gender and Power in the Third Reich: Female Denouncers and the Gestapo (1933–1945).* Houndmills: Palgrave Macmillan.

Joshi, Vandana. 2002. The "Private" Became "Public": Wives as Denouncers in the Third Reich. *Journal of Contemporary History* 37, 3:419–35.

Jouanna, Arlette. 1998. Saint-Barthélemy. In Arlette Jouanna, Jacqueline Boucher, Dominique Biloghi, and Guy Le Thiec, *Histoire et dictionnaire des guerres de religion*, 1262–4. Paris: Laffont.

Juliá, Santos. 2000. Introducción: Violencia política en España. Fin de una larga historia? In Santos Juliá (ed.), *Violencia política en la España del Siglo XX*, 11–23. Madrid: Taurus.

Juliá, Santos. 1999. De "guerra contra el invasor" a "guerra fratricida." In Santos Juliá (ed.), *Víctimas de la guerra civi*, 11–54. Madrid: Temas de Hoy.

Kahneman, Daniel, and Amos Tversky. 1974. Judgment under Uncertainty: Heuristics and Biases. *Science* 185:1124–31.

Kakar, Sudhir. 1996. *The Colors of Violence: Cultural Identities, Religion, and Conflict.* Chicago: University of Chicago Press.

Kaldor, Mary. 1999. *New and Old Wars: Organized Violence in a Global Era.* Stanford, Calif.: Stanford University Press.

Kalyvas, Stathis N. 2004. Ethnicity and Civil War Violence: Micro-level Empirical Findings and Macro-level Hypotheses. Unpublished paper.

Kalyvas, Stathis N. 2003. The Ontology of "Political Violence:" Action and Identity in Civil Wars. *Perspectives on Politics* 1, 3:475–94.

Kalyvas, Stathis N. 2001. "New" and "Old" Civil Wars: A Valid Distinction? *World Politics* 54, 1:99–118.

Kalyvas, Stathis N. 1999. Wanton and Senseless? The Logic of Massacres in Algeria. *Rationality and Society* 11, 3:243–85.

Kalyvas, Stathis N. 1996. *The Rise of Christian Democracy in Europe.* Ithaca: Cornell University Press.

Kalyvas, Stathis N., and Matthew Kocher. 2005. Il modello Vietnam in Iraq. *Il Manifesto*, 21 June, 5.

Kalyvas, Stathis N., and Matthew Kocher. 2004. Violence and Control in Vietnam: An Analysis of the Hamlet Evaluation System (HES). Unpublished paper.

Kalyvas, Stathis N., and Nicholas Sambanis. 2005. Bosnia's Civil War: Origins and Violence Dynamics. In Paul Collier and Nicholas Sambanis (eds.), *Understanding Civil War: Evidence and Analysis*, 2:191-229. Washington, D.C: World Bank.

Kalyvas, Stathis N., and Ignacio Sanchez-Cuenca. 2005. The Absence of Suicide Missions. In Diego Gambetta (ed.), *Making Sense of Suicide Missions*, 209-32. Oxford: Oxford University Press.

Kamen, Henry. 1998. *The Spanish Inquisition: A Historical Revision*. New Haven: Yale University Press.

Kann, Peter R. 2000. A Long, Leisurely Drive through Mekong Delta Tells Much of the War. In *Reporting Vietnam: American Journalism, 1959-1975*, 401-12. New York: Library of America.

Kannyo, Edward. 2000. State Terrorism and Death Squads in Uganda (1971-79). In Bruce B. Campbell and Arthur D. Brenner (eds.), *Death Squads in Global Perspective: Murder with Deniability*, 153-79. New York: St. Martin's Press.

Katz, Amrom. 1975. An Approach to Future Wars of National Liberation. In Sam C. Sarkesian (ed.), *Revolutionary Guerrilla Warfare*, 587-601. Chicago: Precedent Publishing.

Katz, Jack. 1988. *Seductions of Crime: A Chilling Exploration of the Criminal Mind – from Juvenile Delinquency to Cold-blooded Murder*. New York: BasicBooks.

Kaufman, Stuart J. 2001. *Modern Hatreds: The Symbolic Politics of Ethnic War*. Ithaca: Cornell University Press.

Kaufmann, Chaim. 1996. Possible and Impossible Solutions to Ethnic Civil Wars. *International Security* 20, 4:136-75.

Keane, John. 1996. *Reflections on Violence*. London: Verso.

Kedward, H. R. 1993. *In Search of the Maquis: Rural Resistance in Southern France 1942-1944*. Oxford: Oxford University Press.

Keen, David. 1998. The Economic Functions of Violence in Civil Wars. *Adelphi Paper*, 320.

Keiser, Lincoln. 1991. *Friend by Day, Enemy by Night: Organized Vengeance in a Kohistani Community*. Fort Worth: Holt, Rinehart and Winston.

Kelly, Raymond C. 2000. *Warless Societies and the Origin of War*. Ann Arbor: University of Michigan Press.

Kennan, George F. 1951. *American Diplomacy, 1900-1950*. Chicago: University of Chicago Press.

Kenney, George. 1995. The Bosnia Calculation. *New York Times Magazine*, 23 April, 42-3.

Kenny, C. S. 1929. *Outlines of Criminal Law, Based on Lectures Delivered in the University of Cambridge*. 13th ed. Cambridge: Cambridge University Press.

Kenny, C. S. 1907. *Outlines of Criminal Law*. Revised and adapted for American scholars, by James H. Webb. New York: Macmillan.

Kerkvliet, Benedict J. 1977. *The Huk Rebellion: A Study of Peasant Revolt in the Philippines*. Berkeley: University of California Press.

Khan, Amadu Wurie. 1998. Journalism and Armed Conflict in Africa: The Civil War in Sierra Leone. *Review of African Political Economy* 78:585-97.

Kheng, Cheah Boon. 1983. *Red Star over Malaya: Resistance and Social Conflict during and after the Japanese Occupation of Malaya, 1941-1946*. Singapore: Singapore University Press.

Kheng, Cheah Boon. 1980. The Social Impact of the Japanese Occupation of Malaya (1942–1945). In Alfred W. McCoy (ed.), *Southeast Asia under Japanese Occupation*, 91–123. New Haven: Yale University Southeast Asia Studies.

Kinzer, Stephen. 2000. In Kurdish Turkey, Problems of Peace. *New York Times*, 11 May, A8.

Kitson, Frank. 1960. *Gangs and Counter-Gangs*. London: Barrie and Rockliff.

Klinkhammer, Lutz. 1997. *Stragi Naziste in Italia: La guerra contro i civili (1943–1944)*. Rome: Donzelli.

Klonis, N. I. 1972. *Guerrilla Warfare: Analysis and Projections*. New York: Robert Speller & Sons.

Knight, Jonathan. 2003. Statistical Model Leaves Peru Counting the Cost of the Civil War. *Nature* 425, 6.

Kocher, Matthew. 2004. Human Ecology and Civil War. Ph.D. dissertation, University of Chicago.

Kolbert, Elizabeth. 2003. Looking for Lorca. *New Yorker*, 22–9 December, 64–75.

Kornbluh, Peter. 1988. Nicaragua: U.S. Proinsurgency Warfare against the Sandinistas. In Michael T. Klare and Peter Kornbluh (eds.), *Low-Intensity Warfare: Counterinsurgency, Proinsurgency, and Antiterrorism in the Eighties*, 136–57. New York: Pantheon Books.

Kozlov, Vladimir A. 1996. Denunciation and Its Functions in Soviet Governance: A Study of Denunciations and Their Bureaucratic Handling from Soviet Police Archives, 1944–1953. *Journal of Modern History* 68:867–98.

Krauss, Clifford. 2000. Peru "Innocents" Get Back Lives. *International Herald Tribune*, 18 July, 3.

Krauss, Clifford. 1999. A Revolution Peru's Rebels Didn't Intend. *New York Times*, 29 August.

Kriger, Norma. 1992. *Zimbabwe's Guerrilla War: Peasant Voices*. Cambridge: Cambridge University Press.

Krueger, Alan, and Jitka Maleckova. 2002. Education, Poverty, Political Violence, and Terrorism: Is There a Causal Connection? NBER Working Paper No. 9074. Cambridge, Mass.

Kuran, Timur. 1991. Now Out of Never: The Element of Surprise in the Eastern European Revolution of 1989. *World Politics* 44:7–48.

Kuromiya, Hiroaki. 1993. Stalinist Terror in the Donbas: A Note. In J. Arch Getty and Roberta T. Manning (eds.), *Stalinist Terror: New Perspectives*, 215–22. Cambridge: Cambridge University Press.

Lacey, Mark. 2005. The Mournful Math of Darfur: The Dead Don't Add Up. *New York Times*, 18 May, A4.

Lacoste-Dujardin, Camille. 1997. *Opération "Oiseau bleu": Des Kabyles, des ethnologues et la guerre en Algérie*. Paris: Découverte.

Laitin, David. 2001. Secessionist Rebellion in the Former Soviet Union. *Comparative Political Studies* 34, 8:839–61.

Lansdale, Edward G. 1964. Viet Nam: Do We Understand Revolution? *Foreign Affairs* 43, 1:75–86.

Laqueur, Walter. 1998. *Guerrilla Warfare: A Historical and Critical Study*. New Brunswick, N.J.: Transaction.

Larwood, L., and W. Whitaker. 1977. Managerial Myopia: Self-Serving Biases in Organisational Planning. *Journal of Applied Psychology* 62:194–8.

Lary, Diana. 2001. A Ravaged Place: The Devastation of the Xuzhou Region, 1938. In Diana Lary and Stephen McKinnon (eds.), *Scars of War: The Impact of Warfare on Modern China*, 98–116. Vancouver: UBC Press.

Last, Murray. 2000. Reconciliation and Memory in Postwar Nigeria. In Veena Das, Arthur Kleinman, Mamphela Ramphele, and Pamela Reynolds (eds.), *Violence and Subjectivity*, 315–32. Berkeley: University of California Press.

Lavery, Brian. 2005. Families in Northern Ireland Break Silence about Killings. *New York Times*, 14 March, A5.

Lawrence, Pamela. 2000. Violence, Suffering, Amman: The Work of Oracles in Sri Lanka's Eastern War Zone. In Veena Das, Arthur Kleinman, Mamphela Ramphele, and Pamela Reynolds (eds.), *Violence and Subjectivity*, 171–204. Berkeley: University of California Press.

Leakey, Louis Seymour Bazett. 1954. *Deafeating Mau Mau*. London: Methuen.

Lear, Elmer. 1961. The Japanese Occupation of the Philippines, Leyte, 1941–1945. Data Paper No. 42, Southeast Asia Program, Department of Far Eastern Studies. Cornell University, Ithaca, N.Y.

Le Bot, Yvon. 1994. Violence, communauté et territoire. In Denis-Constant Martin (ed.), *Cartes d'identité: Comment dit-on "nous" en politique?*, 163–83. Paris: Presses de la Fondation Nationale des Sciences Politiques.

Lebrun, Guy. 1998. *Le lieutenant aux pieds nus. Conchinchine 1952–1954*. Paris: Éditions France-Empire.

Leclère, Thierry. 1997. Raïs, retour sur un massacre. *Télérama*, 2493, 22 October, 10–16.

Ledesma, José Luis. 2004. *Los días de llamas de la revolución. Violencia y política en la retaguardia de Zaragoza durante la guerra civil*. Zaragoza: Institución "Fernando el Católico."

Ledesma, José Luis. 2001. Espacios de poder, violencia y revolución: Una perspectiva política de la represión en el Aragón republicano durante la guerra civil. In Antonio Morales Moya (ed.), *El difícil camino a la democracia*, 249–68. Madrid: Sociedad Estatal España Nuevo Milenio.

Leiden, Carl, and Karl M. Schmitt. 1968. *The Politics of Violence: Revolution in the Modern World*. Englewood Cliffs, N.J.: Prentice-Hall.

Leites, Nathan, and Charles Wolf Jr. 1970. *Rebellion and Authority: An Analytic Essay on Insurgent Conflicts*. Chicago: Markham.

Le Pape, Marc. 1999. L'exportation des massacres du Rwanda au Congo-Zaire. Paper presented at the Conference on the Political Uses of Massacres, CERI, Paris, 16 November.

Lerner, Daniel. 1958. *The Passing of Traditional Society: Modernizing the Middle East*. New York: Free Press.

Levene, Mark. 1999. Introduction. In Mark Levene and Penny Roberts (eds.), *The Massacre in History*, 1–38. New York: Berghahn Books.

Levi, Margaret. 1997. *Consent, Dissent, and Patriotism*. Cambridge: Cambridge University Press.

Levi, Primo. 1988. *The Drowned and the Saved*. Translated by Raymond Rosenthal. New York: Summit Books.

Levine, Steven I. 1987. *Anvil of Victory: The Communist Revolution in Manchouria, 1945–1948*. New York: Columbia University Press.

Lewin, Tamar. 1999. Arizona High School Provides Glimpses inside Cliques' Divisive Webs. *New York Times*, 2 May 1999.

Lewis, Gwynne. 1978. *The Second Vendée*. Oxford: Oxford University Press.

Lewy, Guenter. 1978. *America in Vietnam*. New York: Oxford University Press.

Leys, Colin, and John S. Saul. 1995. Introduction. In Colin Leys and John S. Saul, *Namibia's Liberation Struggle: The Two-Edged Sword*, 1–18. Athens: Ohio University Press.

Li, Lincoln. 1975. *The Japanese Army in North China, 1937–1941: Problems of Political and Economic Control*. Tokyo: Oxford University Press.

Lichbach, Mark Irving. 1995. *The Rebel's Dilemma*. Ann Arbor: University of Michigan Press.

Lichbach, Mark Irving. 1987. Deterrence or Escalation? The Puzzle of Aggregate Studies of Repression and Dissent. *Journal of Conflict Resolution* 31, 2:266–97.

Licklider, Roy. 1998. Early Returns: Results of the First Wave of Statistical Studies of Civil War Termination. *Civil Wars* 1, 3:121–32.

Lindsay, Franklin A. 1962. Unconventional Warfare. *Foreign Affairs* 40, 2:264–74.

Linn, Brian McAllister. 1989. *The U.S. Army and Counterinsurgency in the Philippine War, 1899–1902*. Chapel Hill: University of North Carolina Press.

Lins de Albuquerque, Adriana, and Alicia Cheng. 2005. 14 Days in Iraq. *New York Times*, 16 January, 11.

Lipman, Jonathan N. 1990. Ethnic Violence in Modern China: Hans and Huis in Gansu, 1781–1929. In Jonathan N. Lipman and Stevan Harrell (eds.), *Violence in China: Essays in Culture and Counterculture*, 65–86. Albany: State University of New York Press.

Lipset, Seymour M., and Stein Rokkan. 1967. "Cleavage Structures, Party Systems, and Voter Alignments: An Introduction." In Seymour M. Lipset and Stein Rokkan (eds.), *Party Systems and Voter Alignments: Cross-National Perspectives*, 1–64. New York: Free Press.

Lison-Tolosana, Carmelo. 1983. *Belmonte de los Caballeros: Anthropology and History in an Aragonese Community*. Princeton, N.J., Princeton University Press.

Livanios, Dimitris. 1999. "Conquering the Souls": Nationalism and Greek Guerrilla Warfare in Ottoman Macedonia, 1904–1908. *Byzantine and Modern Greek Studies* 23: 195–221.

Lloyd, John. 1999. The Russian Devolution. *New York Times Magazine*, 15 August 1999, 34–45.

Lobbia, J. A. 1999. Your Landlord's Dick. *Village Voice*, 3 August, 49.

Loeb, Vernon. 2003. Bagdhad Army Chief Says Bombings Obscure Progress. *Washington Post*, 29 October, A14.

Loizos, Peter. 1999. A Duty of Care? Three Granada Television Films Concerned with War. In Tim Allen and Jean Seaton (eds.), *The Media of Conflict: War Reporting and Representations of Ethnic Violence*, 102–24. London: Zed Books.

Loizos, Peter. 1988. Intercommunal Killing in Cyprus. *Man*, 23:639–53.

Lopez, George A., and Michael Stohl. 1992. Problems of Concept and Measurement in the Study of Human Rights. In Thomas B. Jabine and Richard P. Claude (eds.), *Human Rights and Statistics: Getting the Record Straight*, 216–34. Philadelphia: University of Pennsylvania Press.

Lotnik, Waldemar. 1999. *Nine Lives: Ethnic Conflict in the Polish-Ukrainian Borderlands*. London: Serif.

Louie, Richard. 1964. The Incidence of the Terror: A Critique of a Statistical Interpretation. *French Historical Studies* 3, 3:379–89.

Loyd, Anthony. 2001. *My War Gone By, I Miss It So*. New York: Penguin.

Lubkemann, Stephen C. 2005. Migratory Coping in Wartime Mozambique: An Anthropology of Violence and Displacement in "Fragmented Wars." *Journal of Peace Research* 42, 4:493–508.

Lucan. 1985. *Bellum civile IX*. Introduction and notes by David P. Kubiak. Bryn Mawr, Pa.: Thomas Library, Bryn Mawr College.

Lucas, Colin. 1997. The Theory and the Practice of Denunciation in the French Revolution. In Sheila Fitzpatrick and Robert Gellately (eds.), *Accusatory Practices:*

Denunciation in Modern European History, 1789–1989, 22–39. Chicago: University of Chicago Press.

Lucas, Colin. 1983. Themes in Southern Violence after 9 Thermidor. In Gwynne Lewis and Colin Lucas (eds.), *Beyond the Terror: Essays in French Regional and Social History, 1794–1815*, 152–94. Cambridge: Cambridge University Press.

Luttwak, Edward N. 2003. So Few Soldiers, So Much to Do. *New York Times*, 4 November, A25.

Luttwak, Edward N. 1995. Great-Powerless Days. *Times Literary Supplement*, June 16.

Lynn, John. 1984. *The Bayonets of the Republic: Motivation and Tactics in the Army of Revolutionary France*. Urbana: University of Illinois Press.

Maass, Peter. 2005. The Way of the Commandos. *New York Times Magazine*, 1 May, 38–83.

MacGregor Serven, Lawrence B. 2002. *The End of Office Politics as Usual: A Complete Strategy for Creating a More Productive and Profitable Organization*. New York: Amacom.

Machiavelli, Niccolò. 2003[1513]. *The Prince*. Translated by George Bull. London: Penguin.

Machiavelli, Niccolò. 1988[1532]. *Florentine Histories*. Translated by Laura F. Banfield and Harvey C. Mansfield, Jr. Princeton, N.J.: Princeton University Press.

Mackenzie, S. P. 1997. *Revolutionary Armies in the Modern Era: A Revisionist Approach*. London: Routledge.

Mackey, Chris, and Greg Miller. 2004. *The Interrogators. Task Force 500 and America's Secret War Against Al Qaeda*. New York: Back Bay Books.

Mackwood, Neil. 2002. Breaking Up Can Be So Hard to Sell. *Financial Times*, 19–20 October, 13.

Madiebo, Alexander A. 1980. *The Nigerian Revolution and the Biafran War*. Enugu: Fourth Dimension Publishing.

Madsen, Richard. 1990. The Politics of Revenge in Rural China during the Cultural Revolution. In Jonathan N. Lipman and Stevan Harrell (eds.), *Violence in China: Essays in Culture and Counterculture*, 175–201. Albany: State University of New York Press.

Madsen, Richard. 1984. *Morality and Power in a Chinese Village*. Berkeley: University of California Press.

Magalhães, Eduardo. 1996. Civil Wars. In Frank N. Magill (ed.), *International Encyclopedia of Government and Politics*, 225–8. Chicago: Fitzroy Dearborn.

Mahdi, Omer, and Rory Carroll. 2005. Under US Noses, Brutal Insurgents Rule Sunni Citadel. *Guardian*, 22 August, 1.

Mahmood, Cynthia Keppley. 2000. Trials by Fire: Dynamics of Terror in Punjab and Kasmir. In Jeffrey A. Sluka (ed.), *Death Squad: The Anthropology of State Terror*, 70–90. Philadelphia: University of Pennsylvania Press.

Maier, F. X. 1974. *Revolution and Terrorism in Mozambique*. New York: American African Affairs Association.

Maier, Karl. 1995. A Fragile Peace. *Africa Report* 40: 22–7.

Makdisi, Jean Said. 1990. *Beirut Fragments: A War Memoir*. New York: Persea Books.

Malcolm, Noel. 1998. The Roots of Bosnian Horror Lie Not So Deep. *New York Times*, 19 October.

Malefakis, Edward. 1996. Aspectos históricos y teóricos de la guerra. In Edward Malefakis (ed.), *La guerra de España (1936–1939)*, 11–47. Madrid: Taurus.

Mallin, Jay. 1966. *Terror in Viet Nam*. Princeton, N.J.: Van Nostrand.

Manrique, Nelson. 1998. The War for the Central Sierra. In Steve J. Stern (ed.), *Shining and Other Paths: War and Society in Peru, 1980–1995*, 193–223. Durham: Duke University Press.

Maranto, Robert, and Paula S. Tuchman. 1992. Knowing the Rational Peasant: The Creation of Rival Incentive Structures in Vietnam. *Journal of Peace Research* 29, 3: 249–64.

Margadant, Ted W. 1992. *Urban Rivalries in the French Revolution.* Princeton, N.J.: Princeton University Press.

Margolin, Jean-Louis. 1999. L'armé, le Parti, les milices: Indonesie, 1965, et après. Paper presented at the Conference on the Political Uses of Massacres, CERI, Paris, 16 November.

Marks, Robert. 1984. *Rural Revolution in South China: Peasants and the Making of History in Haifeng County, 1570–1930.* Madison: University of Wisconsin Press.

Marshall, S. L. A. 1947. *Men against Fire.* New York: William Morrow.

Martin, Gerard. 2000. The "Tradition of Violence" in Colombia: Material and Symbolic Aspects. In Goran Aijmer and Jon Abbink (eds.), *Meanings of Violence,* 101–91. New York: Berg.

Martin, Jean-Clément. 2002. Dans la guerre civile tout est permis. *L'Histoire* 267:56–9.

Martin, Jean-Clément. 1998. *Contre-Révolution, Révolution et Nation en France, 1789–1799.* Paris: Éditions du Seuil.

Martin, Jean-Clément. 1995. Guerre civile et modernité: Le cas de la Révolution. In Jean-Clément Martin (ed.), *La guerre civile entre histoire et mémoire,* 57–64. Nantes: Ouest Éditions.

Martin, Jean-Clément. 1994. Rivoluzione francese e guerra civile. In Gabriele Ranzato (ed.), *Guerre fratricide: Le guerre civili in età contemporanea,* 27–85. Turin: Bollati Boringhieri.

Martinez, Luis. 1998. *La guerre civile en Algérie.* Paris: Karthala.

Martinez, Luis. 1994. Les Eucalyptus, banlieue d'Alger dans la guerre civile: Les facteurs de la mobilisation islamiste. In G. Kepel (ed.), *Exils et royaumes,* 89–104. Paris: Presses de la FNSP.

Mason, T. David, and Dale A. Krane. 1989. The Political Economy of Death Squads: Toward a Theory of the Impact of State-Sanctioned Terror. *International Studies Quarterly* 33:175–98.

Massey, Garth, Randy Hodson, and Dušco Seculić. 1999. Ethnic Enclaves and Intolerance: The Case of Yugoslavia. *Social Forces* 78, 2:669–91.

May, Glenn Anthony. 1991. *Battle for Batangas: A Philippine Province at War.* New Haven: Yale University Press.

Mayer, Arno J. 2000. *The Furies: Violence and Terror in the French and Russian Revolutions.* Princeton, N.J.: Princeton University Press.

Mazower, Mark. 1998. *Dark Continent: Europe's Twentieth Century.* London: Allen Lane.

McAuley, Mary. 1992. *Soviet Politics, 1917–1991.* Oxford: Oxford University Press.

McColl, Robert W. 1969. The Insurgent State: Territorial Bases of Revolution. *Annals of the Association of American Geographers* 59, 4:613–31.

McColl, Robert W. 1967. A Political Geography of Revolution: China, Vietnam, and Thailand. *Journal of Conflict Resolution* 11, 2:153–67.

McCoubrey, Hilaire, and Nigel D. White. 1995. *International Organizations and Civil Wars.* Aldershot: Dartmouth.

McCoy, Alfred W. 1980. "Politics by Other Means": World War II in the Western Visayas, Philippines. In Alfred W. McCoy (ed.), *Southeast Asia under Japanese Occupation,* 191–245. New Haven: Yale University Southeast Asia Studies.

McCrady, Edward. 1969. *The History of South Carolina in the Revolution, 1780–1783*. New York: Paladin.

McGowan, William. 1992. *Only Man Is Vile: The Tragedy of Sri Lanka*. New York: Farrar, Straus, and Giroux.

McGrath, Patrick. 1997. Bristol and the Civil War. In R. C. Richardson (ed.), *The English Civil Wars: Local Aspects*, 91–128. Phoenix Mill: Sutton.

McKenna, Thomas M. 1998. *Muslim Rulers and Rebels: Everyday Politics and Armed Separatism in the Southern Philippines*. Berkeley: University of California Press.

Mendelsohn, Daniel. 2002. What Happened to Uncle Shmiel? *New York Times Magazine*, 14 July, 24–55.

Merrill, John. 1989. *Korea: The Peninsular Origins of the War*. Newark: University of Delaware Press.

Meyerson, Harvey. 1970. *Vinh Long*. Boston: Houghton Mifflin.

Meynier, Gilbert. 2004. Le PPA-MTLD et le FLN-ALN, étude comparée. In Mohammed Harbi and Benjamin Stora (eds.), *La guerre d'Algérie, 1954–2004, la fin de l'amnésie*, 417–50. Paris: Robert Laffont.

Meynier, Gilbert, and Pierre Vidal-Naquet. 1999. Le sens d'une agression. *Le Monde*, 1 December.

Miall, Hugh. 1992. *The Peacemakers: Peaceful Settlement of Disputes since 1945*. New York: St. Martin's.

Miguel, Edward. 2004. Tribe or Nation? Nation Building and Public Goods in Kenya versus Tanzania. *World Politics* 56, 3:327–62.

Milgram, Stanley. 1974. *Obedience to Authority: An Experimental View*. New York: Harper & Row.

Miller, D. T., and M. Ross. 1975. Self-Serving Biases in Attribution of Causality: Fact or Fiction? *Psychological Bulletin* 82:213–25.

Miller, William Ian. 1990. *Bloodtaking and Peacemaking: Feud, Law, and Society in Saga Iceland*. Chicago: University of Chicago Press.

Milosz, Czeslaw. 1990. *The Captive Mind*. New York: Vintage.

Minardi, Marco. 2002. War in the Mountains: Community Ties and Civil War in Central Italy. Paper presented at the Workshop on "Civil Wars and Political Violence in 20th Century Europe," European University Institute, Florence 18–20 April.

Mirels, H. L. 1980. The Avowal of Responsibility for Good and Bad Outcomes: The Effects of Generalized Self-Serving Biases. *Personality and Social Psychology Bulletin* 6, 299–306.

Mirzeler, Mustafa, and Crawford Young. 2000. Pastoral Politics in the Northeast Periphery in Uganda: AK-47 as Change Agent. *Journal of Modern African Studies* 38, 3: 407–29.

Mishra, Pankaj. 2000. Pride and Blood in Kashmir. *New York Times*, 22 March.

Mitchell, Christopher, Michael Stohl, David Carleton, and George A. Lopez. 1986. State Terrorism: Issues of Concept and Measurement. In Michael Stohl and George A. Lopez (eds.), *Government Violence and Repression: An Agenda for Research*, 1–25. Westport, Conn.: Greenwood Press.

Mitchell, Edward J. 1968. Inequality and Insurgency: A Statistical Study of South Vietnam. *World Politics* 20, 3:421–38.

Mitter, Rana. 2000. *The Manchurian Myth: Nationalism, Resistance, and Collaboration in Modern China*. Berkeley: University of California Press.

Mohr, Charles. 1966. Questions on U.S. Raids: Many Feel Johnson Should Have Asked about Political Merit of Hamlet Attacks. *New York Times*, 16 August 1966, 3.

Molnar, Andrew R. 1965. *Human Factors Considerations of Undergrounds in Insurgencies.* Washington, D.C.: Special Operations Research Office.

Montaigne, Michel de. 1991. *The Complete Essays.* Translated by M. A. Screech. London: Penguin.

Montherlant, Henry de. 1965. *La guerre civile.* Paris: Gallimard.

Moore, Barrington. 1966. *Social Origins of Dictatorship and Democracy: Lord and Peasant in the Making of the Modern World.* Boston: Beacon Press.

Moore, Barrington. 1954. *Terror and Progress: USSR.* Cambridge, Mass.: Harvard University Press.

Moore, Jeanne. 1999. World Briefing. *New York Times,* 19 August, A10.

Moore, M. 1993. Thoroughly Modern Revolutionaries: The JVP in Sri Lanka. *Modern Asian Studies* 27, 3:593–642.

Moore, Robert Ian. 1987. *The Formation of a Persecuting Society.* Oxford: Blackwell.

Moreno, Francisco. 1999. La represión en la posguerra. In Santos Juliá (ed.), *Víctimas de la guerra civil,* 277–405. Madrid: Temas de Hoy.

Moser, Don. 2000. Eight Dedicated Men Marked for Death. In *Reporting Vietnam: American Journalism, 1959–1975,* 84–105. New York: Library of America.

Moss, Michael. 2003. False Terrorist Tips to the FBI Uproot Lives of Suspects. *New York Times,* 19 June, A1.

Mouro, Gladys. 1999. *An American Nurse amidst Chaos.* Beirut: American University of Beirut.

Moyar, Mark. 1997. *Phoenix and the Birds of Prey: The CIA's Secret Campaign to Destroy the Viet Cong.* Annapolis, Md.: Naval Institute Press.

Mueller, John. 2004. *The Remnants of War.* Ithaca: Cornell University Press, 2004.

Münkler, Herfried. 2002. *Uber den Krieg. Stationen der Kriegsgeschichte im Spiegel ihrer theoretischen Reflexion.* Weilerswist: Velbrück Wissenschaft.

Murshed, S. Mansoob, and Scott Gates. 2005. Spatial-Horizontal Inequality and the Maoist Insurgency in Nepal. *Review of Development Economics* 9, 1:121–34.

Mydans, Seth. 2003. Russia's Chechen Plan: Pick a Leader and Leave. *New York Times,* 18 September, A6.

Mydans, Seth. 1999. East Timor Family's Terror: Trapped at Home by Gunmen. *New York Times,* 27 September, A1.

Myers, Steven Lee. 2005. Even Chechnya's Dream Street Is a Dead End. *New York Times,* 23 March, A4.

Myers, Steven Lee. 2002. Chechen Rebels in Limbo Vow Endless Resistance. *New York Times,* 23 August, A6.

Nabulsi, Karma. 2001. Evolving Conceptions of Civilians and Belligerents: One Hundred Years after the Hague Peace Conferences. In Simon Chesterman (ed.), *Civilians in War,* 9–24. Boulder, Colo.: Lynne Riener.

Nabulsi, Karma. 1999. *Traditions of War: Occupation, Resistance, and the Law.* Oxford: Oxford University Press.

Nagengast, Carole. 1994. Violence, Terror, and the Crisis of the State. *Annual Review of Anthropology* 23:109–36.

Nahoum-Grappe, Véronique. 1996. L'usage politique de la cruauté: L'épuration ethnique (ex-Yougoslavie, 1991–1995). In Françoise Héritier (ed.), *De la violence,* 273–323. Paris: Odile Jacob.

Nasr, Salim. 1990. Lebanon's War: Is the End in Sight? *Middle East Report,* No. 162, 4–8, 30.

Negus, Steve. 2004. US Squares Up to Long Guerrilla War in Iraq. *Financial Times,* 27–8 November, 5.

Nelson, Hank. 1980. *Taim Bilong Pait*: The Impact of the Second World War on Papua New Guinea. In Alfred W. McCoy (ed.), *Southeast Asia under Japanese Occupation*, 246–66. New Haven: Yale University Southeast Asia Studies.

Nérard, François-Xavier. 2004. *5% de vérité. La dénonciation dans l'URSS de Staline (1928–1941)*. Paris: Tallandier.

Nino, Carlos Santiago. 1996. *Radical Evil on Trial*. New Haven: Yale University Press.

Nordlinger, Eric A. 1972. Conflict Regulation in Divided Societies. *Occasional Papers in International Affairs* 29. Cambridge, Mass.: Harvard Center for International Affairs.

Nordstrom, Carolyn. 1997. *A Different Kind of War Story*. Philadelphia: University of Pennsylvania Press.

Nordstrom, Carolyn. 1992. The Backyard Front. In Carolyn Nordstrom and JoAnn Martin (eds.), *The Paths to Domination, Resistance, and Terror*, 260–74. Berkeley: University of California Press.

Nordstrom, Carolyn, and JoAnn Martin. 1992. The Culture of Conflict: Field Reality and Theory. In Carolyn Nordstrom and JoAnn Martin (eds.), *The Paths to Domination, Resistance, and Terror*, 3–17. Berkeley: University of California Press.

Nougayrede, Natalie. 2002. En Tchéthchénie, la jeune génération se radicalité dans la guérilla. *Le Monde*, 25 October, 7.

Novick, Peter. 1999. *The Holocaust in American Life*. New York: Houghton Mifflin.

Oberschall, Anthony. 2000. The Manipulation of Ethnicity: From Ethnic Cooperation to Violence and War in Yugoslavia. *Ethnic and Racial Studies* 23, 6:982–1001.

Okey, Robin. 1999. The Legacy of Massacre: The "Jacenovac Myth" and the Breakdown of Communist Yugoslavia. In Mark Levene and Penny Roberts (eds.), *The Massacre in History*, 263–82. New York: Berghahn Books.

O'Leary, Brendan, and John McGarry. 1993. *The Politics of Antagonism: Understanding Northern Ireland*. London: Athlone Press.

Olson, Mancur. 2000. *Power and Prosperity: Outgrowing Communist and Capitalist Dictatorships*. New York: Basic Books.

O'Neill, Bard E. 1990. *Insurgency and Terrorism: Inside Modern Revolutionary Warfare*. Washington: Brassey's.

O'Neill, Barry. 1999. *Honor, Symbols, and War*. Ann Arbor: University of Michigan Press.

O'Neill, Onora. 1991. Which Are the Offers *You* Can't Refuse? In R. G. Frey and Christopher W. Morris (eds.), *Violence, Terrorism, and Justice*, 170–95. Cambridge: Cambridge University Press.

Onishi, Norimitsu. 1999. Sierra Leone Measures Terror in Severed Limbs. *New York Times*, 22 August, 3.

Oppel, Richard A., Jr. 2005a. Magnet for Iraq Insurgents Is Test for U.S. Strategy. *New York Times*, 16 June, A1, A8.

Oppel, Richard A., Jr. 2005b. By Courting Sunnis, G.I.'s See Security Rise in a Sinister Town. *New York Times*, 17 July, 1, 4.

Ortiz Sarmiento, Carlos Miguel. 1990. *La violence en Colombie: Racines historiques et sociales*. Paris: L'Harmatan.

Orwell, George. 1937. *The Road to Wigan Pier*. London: V. Gollancz.

O'Sullivan, Patrick. 1983. A Geographical Analysis of Guerrilla Warfare. *Political Geography Quarterly* 2, 2:139–50.

Ourdan, Rémy. 2004. Cinq "hotlines" antiguérrilla pour inciter les Irakiens à la délation. *Le Monde*, 18 November, 2.

Overy, Richard. 1997. *Russia's War: A History of the Soviet War Effort, 1941–1945*. New York: Penguin.

Packer, George. 2003. War after the War. What Washington Doesn't See in Iraq. *New Yorker*, 24 November, 58–85.

Paczkowski, Andrzej. 1999. Nazisme et Communisme dans l'expérience et la mémoire Polonaise. In Henry Rousso (ed.), *Stalinisme et Nazisme: Histoire et mémoire comparées*, 307–30. Paris: Complexe.

Paget, Julian. 1967. *Counter-Insurgency Operations: Techniques of Guerrilla Warfare*. New York: Walker.

Paggi, Leonardo. 1996. *Storia e memoria di un massacro ordinario*. Rome: Manifestolibri.

Paige, Jeffery M. 1975. *Agrarian Revolutions: Social Movements and Export Agriculture in the Underdeveloped World*. New York: Free Press.

Paludan, Phillip Shaw. 1981. *Victims: A True Story of the Civil War*. Knoxville: University of Tennessee Press.

Parker, Geoffrey. 1994. Early Modern Europe. In Michael Howard, George J. Andreopoulos, and Mark R. Shulman (eds.), *The Laws of War: Constraints on Warfare in the Western World*, 40–58. New Haven: Yale University Press.

Paul, Benjamin D., and William J. Demarest. 1988. The Operation of a Death Squad in San Pedro la Laguna. In Robert M. Carmack (ed.), *Harvest of Violence: The Maya Indians and the Guatemalan Crisis*, 119–54. Norman: University of Oklahoma Press.

Pavone, Claudio. 1994. *Una guerra civile. Saggio storico sulla moralità nella Resistenza*. Turin: Bollati Boringhieri.

Paxson, Christina. 2002. Comment on Alan Krueger and Jitka Maleckova, "Education, Poverty, Political Violence, and Terrorism: Is There a Causal Connection?" Unpublished paper.

Payne, Stanley G. 1987. *The Franco Regime, 1936–1975*. Madison: University of Wisconsin Press.

Pécaut, Daniel. 1996. Réflexions sur la violence en Colombie. In Françoise Héritier (ed.), *De la violence*, 225–71. Paris: Odile Jacob.

Peluso, Nancy Lee, and Emily Harwell. 2001. Territory, Custom, and the Cultural Politics of Ethnic War in Western Kalimantan, Indonesia. In Nancy Lee Peluso and Michael Watts (eds.), *Violent Environments*, 83–116. Ithaca: Cornell University Press.

Peralta, Gabriel Aguilera, and John Beverly. 1980. Terror and Violence as Weapons of Counterinsurgency in Guatemala. *Latin American Perspectives* 7, 2–3:91–113.

Perez-Díaz, Victor M. 1993. *The Return of Civil Society: The Emergence of Democratic Spain*. Cambridge, Mass: Harvard University Press.

Perry, Elizabeth J. 1984. Collective Violence in China, 1880–1980. *Theory and Society* 13, 3:427–54.

Perry, Elizabeth J. 1980. *Rebels and Revolutionaries in North China, 1845–1945*. Stanford, Calif.: Stanford University Press.

Persaud, Raj. 2005. Winning Mental Ways. *Financial Times*, 10–11 September, W3.

Pervanic, Kemal. 1999. *The Killing Days*. London: Blake.

Peters, Krijn, and Paul Richards. 1998. "Why We Fight": Voices of Youth Combatants in Sierra Leone. *Africa* 68, 2:183–210.

Petersen, Roger D. 2002. *Understanding Ethnic Violence: Fear, Hatred, and Resentment in Twentieth-Century Eastern Europe*. Cambridge: Cambridge University Press.

Petersen, Roger D. 2001. *Resistance and Rebellion: Lessons from Eastern Europe*. Cambridge: Cambridge University Press.

Peterson, Scott. 2000. *Me against My Brother: At War in Somalia, Sudan, and Rwanda; A Journalistic Report from the Battlefields of Africa*. New York: Routledge.

Peterson, Scott. 1997a. Algeria's Real War: Ending the Cycle of Violence. *Christian Science Monitor*, 24 June.

Peterson, Scott. 1997b. Algeria's Village Vigilantes Unite against Terror. *Christian Science Monitor*, 5 November.

Petitfrère, Claude. 1981. *La Vendée et les Vendéens*. Paris: Gallimard/Julliard.

Pettigrew, Joyce. 2000. Parents and Their Children in Situations of Terror: Disappearances and Special Police Activity in Punjab. In Jeffrey A. Sluka (ed.), *Death Squad: The Anthropology of State Terror*, 204–25. Philadelphia: University of Pennsylvania Press.

Pezzino, Paolo. 1994. Risorgimento e guerra civile. Alcune considerazioni preliminari. In Gabriele Ranzato (ed.), *Guerre fratricide: Le guerre civili in età contemporanea*, 56–85. Turin: Bollati Boringhieri.

Pfaffenberger, Bryan. 1994. The Structure of Protracted Conflict: The Case of Sri Lanka. *Humboldt Journal of Social Relations* 20, 2:121–47.

Pigou, Piers. 2001. The Apartheid State and Violence: What Has the Truth and Reconciliation Commission Found? *Politikon* 28, 2:207–33.

Pike, Douglas. 1966. *Viet Cong: The Organization and Techniques of the National Liberation Front of South Vietnam*. Cambridge, Mass.: MIT Press.

Polgreen, Lydia. 2005. Civilians Bear Brunt of the Continuing Violence in Darfur. *New York Times*, 24 January, A3.

Poole, Michael A. 1995. The Spatial Distribution of Political Violence in Northern Ireland: An Update to 1993. In Alan O'Day (ed.), *Terrorism's Laboratory: The Case of Northern Ireland*, 27–45. Aldershot: Dartmouth.

Poole, Michael A. 1990. The Geographical Location of Political Violence in Northern Ireland. In John Darby, Nicholas Dodge, and A. C. Hepburn (eds.), *Political Violence: Ireland in a Comparative Perspective*, 64–82. Ottawa: University of Ottawa Press.

Popkin, Samuel L. 1979. *The Rational Peasant: The Political Economy of Rural Society in Vietnam*. Berkeley: University of California Press.

Portelli, Alessandro. 1997. *The Battle of Valle Giulia: Oral History and the Art of Dialogue*. Madison: University of Wisconsin Press.

Porter, Bruce. 1994. *War and the Rise of the State: The Military Foundations of Modern Politics*. New York: Free Press.

Posen, Barry. 1993. The Security Dilemma and Ethnic Conflict. *Survival* 35, 1:27–47.

Posner, Daniel. 2004. The Political Salience of Cultural Difference: Why Chewas and Tumbukas Are Allies in Zambia and Adversaries in Malawi. *American Political Science Review* 98, 4:529–45.

Pred, Allan. 1990. *Making Histories and Constructing Human Geographies: The Local Transformation of Practice, Power Relations, and Consciousness*. Boulder, Colo.: Westview Press.

Price, Jonathan J. 2001. *Thucydides and Internal War*. Cambridge: Cambridge University Press.

Prins, Gwyn. 1999. Civil and Uncivil Wars. *Civil Wars* 2, 1:117–29.

Prunier, Gérard. 2005. *Darfur: The Ambiguous Genocide*. Ithaca: Cornell University Press.

Prunier, Gérard. 1995. *The Rwandan Crisis: History of a Genocide*. New York: Columbia University Press.

Przeworski, Adam. 1991. *Democracy and the Market: Political and Economic Reforms in Eastern Europe and Latin America*. Cambridge: Cambridge University Press.

Przeworski, Adam, and Henry Teune. 1970. *The Logic of Comparative Social Inquiry*. New York: Wiley-Interscience.

Pye, Lucian W. 1964. The Roots of Insurgency and the Commencement of Rebellions. In Harry Eckstein (ed.), *Internal War: Problems and Approaches*, 157–79. New York: Free Press.

Pye, Lucian W. 1956. *Guerrilla Communism in Malaya: Its Social and Political Meaning*. Princeton, N.J.: Princeton University Press.

Pyszczynski, Tom, Jeff Greenberg, and Sheldon Solomon. 1997. Why Do We Need What We Need? A Terror Management Perspective on the Roots of Human Social Motivation. *Psychological Inquiry* 8, 1:1–20.

Race, Jeffrey. 1973. *War Comes to Long An: Revolutionary Conflict in a Vietnamese Province.* Berkeley: University of California Press.

Rajagopal, Balakrishnan. 2001. In Asia, Ethnic Cleansing in the Name of Progress. *International Herald Tribune,* 10 August.

Raleigh, Donald J. 2002. *Experiencing Russia's Civil War: Politics, Society, and Revolutionary Culture in Saratov, 1917–1922.* Princeton, N.J.: Princeton University Press.

Ramsey, Russell W. 1973. Critical Bibliography on La Violencia in Colombia. *Latin American Research Review* 8:3–44.

Randal, Jonathan C. 1983. *Going All the Way: Christian Warlords, Israeli Adventurers, and the War in Lebanon.* New York: Viking Press.

Ranzato, Gabriele. 1994. Un evento antico e un nuovo oggetto di riflessione. In Gabriele Ranzato (ed.), *Guerre fratricide: Le guerre civili in età contemporanea,* ix–lvi. Turin: Bollati Boringhieri.

Ranzato, Gabriele. 1988. Dies Irae. La persecuzione religiosa nella zona republicana durante la guerra civile spagnola (1936–1939). *Movimento Operaio e Socialista* 11: 195–220.

Rasenberger, Jim. 2005. Shadows on the Wall. *New York Times,* City Section, 23 January, 1.

Redfield, Robert. 1989. *The Little Community and Peasant Society and Culture.* Chicago: University of Chicago Press.

Reig Tapia, Alberto. 1996. Represión y esfuerzos humanitarios. In Edward Malefakis (ed.), *La guerra de España (1936–1939),* 571–602. Madrid: Taurus.

Reig Tapia, Alberto. 1990. *Violencia y Terror.* Los Berrocales del Jarama: Akal Universitaria.

Rejali, Darius. 2004a. Torture's Dark Allure. *Salon.com.* http://archive.salon.com_opinion/feature/2004/06/18/torture_1/index3.html.

Rejali, Darius. 2004b. Does Torture Work? *Salon.com.* http://archive.salon.com/opinion/feature/2004/06/21/torture_algiers/index2.html.

Reuters. 2005. 65 Kenyans Killed in Cattle-Rustling Violence. *New York Times,* 14 July, A5.

Rich, Paul B., and Richard Stubbs. 1997. Introduction: The Counter-Insurgent State. In Paul B. Rich and Richard Stubbs, *The Counter-Insurgent State: Guerrilla Warfare and State-Building in the Twentieth Century,* 1–25. New York: St. Martin's Press.

Richards, Paul. 1996. *Fighting for the Rain Forest: War, Youth, and Resources in Sierra Leone.* Oxford: James Currey.

Richardson, R. C. 1997. Introduction: Local Historians and the English Civil War. In R. C. Richardson (ed.), *The English Civil Wars: Local Aspects,* 1–13. Phoenix Mill: Sutton.

Riches, David. 1986. The Phenomenon of Violence. In David Riches (ed.), *The Anthropology of Violence,* 1–27. London: Blackwell.

Ricoeur, Paul. 1984. *Time and Narrative.* Chicago: University of Chicago Press.

Riste, Olav, and Berit Nökleby. 1973. *Norway, 1940–1945.* Oslo: Johan Grundt Tanum Forlag.

Robben, Antonius C. G. M. 1996. Ethnographic Seduction, Transference, and Resistance in Dialogues about Terror and Violence in Argentina. *Ethos* 24, 1:71–106.

Robben, Antonius C. G. M. 1995. Seduction and Persuasion. In Carolyn Nordstrom and Antonius C. G. M. Robben (eds.), *Fieldwork under Fire: Contemporary Studies of Violence and Survival,* 81–103. Berkeley: University of California Press.

Roberts, Adam. 1994. Land Warfare: From Hague to Nuremberg. In Michael Howard, George J. Andreopoulos, and Mark R. Shulman (eds.), *The Laws of War: Constraints on Warfare in the Western World*, 116–39. New Haven: Yale University Press.

Robinson, Geoffrey. 1995. *The Dark Side of Paradise: Political Violence in Bali.* Ithaca: Cornell University Press.

Rodriguez, Ernesto R., Jr. 1982. *The Bad Guerrillas of Northern Luzon: A Memoir of the Japanese Occupation in the Philippines.* Quezon City: J. Burgos Media Services.

Roesch, Otto. 1990. Renamo and the Peasantry: A View from Gaza. *Southern Africa Report* 6, 5:21–5.

Rohde, David. 2001. Warehouse of Death. *New York Times Magazine*, 11 March, 46.

Rohkrämer, Thomas. 1997. Daily Life at the Front and the Concept of Total War. In Stig Förster and Jörg Nagler (eds.), *On the Road to Total War: The American Civil War and the German Wars of Unification, 1861–1871*, 497–518. Cambridge: Cambridge University Press.

Roldán, Mary. 2002. *La violencia in Antioquia, Colombia, 1946–1953.* Durham: Duke University Press.

Romero, Mauricio. 2000. Changing Identities and Contested Settings: Regional Elites and the Paramilitaries in Colombia. *International Journal of Politics, Culture, and Society* 14, 1:51–69.

Ron, James. 2003. *Frontiers and Ghettos: State Violence in Serbia and Israel.* Berkeley: University of California Press.

Ron, James. 2000a. Boundaries and Violence: Repertoires of State Action along the Bosnia/Yugoslavia Divide. *Theory and Society* 29:609–40.

Ron, James. 2000b. Territoriality and Plausible Deniability: Serbian Paramilitaries in the Bosnian War. In Bruce B. Campbell and Arthur D. Brenner (eds.), *Death Squads in Global Perspective: Murder with Deniability*, 287–312. New York: St. Martin's Press.

Rose, David. 2004. Guantánamo Bay on Trial. *Vanity Fair*, January, 88–136.

Rosenau, William. 1994. Is the Shining Path the "New Khmer Rouge"? *Studies in Conflict and Terrorism* 17, 4:305–22.

Rosenberg, Tina. 1991. *Children of Cain: Violence and the Violent in Latin America.* New York: Penguin.

Rotella, Sebastian. 2002. U.N. Prosecutors Open Milosevic's War Crimes Trial. *Los Angeles Times*, 13 February, 1, 4.

Rothenberg, Gunther. 1994. The Age of Napoleon. Constraints on Warfare. In Michael Howard, George J. Andreopoulos, and Mark R. Shulman (eds.), *The Laws of War: Constraints on Warfare in the Western World*, 86–97. New Haven: Yale University Press.

Rothstein, Edward. 2005. Hate Crimes: What Is Gained When Forbidden Acts Become Forbidden Beliefs? *New York Times*, 19 September, E3.

Rousseau, Jean Jacques. 1964. *The First and Second Discourses.* Translated by Roger D. Masters and Judith R. Masters. New York: St. Martin's Press.

Rousseau, Jean Jacques. 1997[1762]. *The Social Contract and Other Later Political Writings.* Cambridge: Cambridge University Press.

Rousso, Henry. 1998. *La hantise du passé.* Paris: Textuel.

Roy, Beth. 1994. *Some Trouble with Cows: Making Sense of Social Conflict.* Berkeley: University of California Press.

Roy, Olivier. 1999. Etat et recompositions identitaires: L'exemple du Tadjikistan. In Jean Hannoyer (ed.), *Guerres civiles: Economies de la violence, dimensions de la civilité*, 221–34. Paris: Karthala.

Rubin, Elizabeth. 2001. Kabul Dispatch. Brothers in Arms. *New Republic Online*, 29 November. http://www.thenewrepublic.com/121001/reubin121001.html.

Rubio, Mauricio. 1999. *Crimen e impunidad: Precisones sobre la violencia*. Santafé de Bogotá: Tercer Mundo.

Rudebeck, Lars. 1975. Political Mobilisation in Guinea-Bissau. In Sam C. Sarkesian (ed.), *Revolutionary Guerrilla Warfare*, 431–51. Chicago: Precedent Publishing.

Rule, James B. 1988. *Theories of Civil Violence*. Berkeley: University of California Press.

Rummel, R. J. 1994. *Death by Government*. New Brunswick, N.J.: Transaction.

Rushdie, Salman. 1987. *The Jaguar Smile*. New York: Viking.

Sadowski, Yahya. 1998. *The Myth of Global Chaos*. Washington, D.C.: Brookings Institution Press.

Saint-Exupéry, Antoine. 1936. L'Espagne ensanglotée. *L'Intransigeant*, 12–19 August.

Salamanca Núñez, Camila. 2005. Massacres en Colombia 1995–2002: ¿Violencia Indiscriminada o Racional? Unpublished paper, Universidad de los Andes.

Salibi, Kamal S. 1988. *A House of Many Mansions: The History of Lebanon Reconsidered*. London: I. B. Tauris.

Salik, Siddiq. 1978. *Witness to Surrender*. Karachi: Oxford University Press.

Sambanis, Nicholas. 2004. What Is a Civil War? Conceptual and Empirical Complexities of an Operational Definition. *Journal of Conflict Resolution* 48, 6: 814–58.

Sambanis, Nicholas. 2000. Partition as a Solution to Ethnic War: An Empirical Critique of the Theoretical Literature. *World Politics* 52, 4:437–83.

Sambanis, Nicholas, and Ibrahim Elbadawi. 2002. How Many Wars Will We See? Explaining the Prevalence of Civil War. *Journal of Conflict Resolution* 46, 3:307–34.

Sánchez, Gonzalo. 2001. Introduction: Problems of Violence, Prospects for Peace. In Charles Bergquist, Ricardo Peñaranda, and Gonzalo Sánchez G. (eds.), *Violence in Colombia, 1990–2000: Waging War and Negotiating Peace*, 1–38. Wilmington, Del.: Scholarly Resources.

Sánchez, Gonzalo, and Donny Meertens. 2001. *Bandits, Peasants, and Politics: The Case of "La Violence" in Colombia*. Austin: University of Texas Press.

Sansom, Robert L. 1970. *The Economics of Insurgency in the Mekong Delta of Vietnam*. Cambridge, Mass.: MIT Press.

Sarkesian, Sam C. 1989. The American Response to Low-Intensity Conflict: The Formative Period. In David A. Charters and Maurice Tugwell (eds.), *Armies in Low-Intensity Conflicts: A Comparative Analysis*, 19–48. London: Brassey's Defense Publishers.

Sartori, Giovanni. 1970. Concept Misformation in Comparative Politics. *American Political Science Review* 64, 4:1033–53.

Sartori, Giovanni. 1969. From the Sociology of Politics to Political Sociology. In Seymour Martin Lipset (ed.), *Politics and the Social Sciences*, 65–100. New York: Oxford University Press.

Saul, John S., and Colin Leys. 1995. SWAPO: The Politics of Exile. In Colin Leys and John S. Saul, *Namibia's Liberation Struggle: The Two-Edged Sword*, 40–65. Athens: Ohio University Press.

Scheffler, Thomas. 1999. Religion, Violence and the Civilizing Process: The Case of Lebanon. In Jean Hannoyer (ed.), *Guerres civiles: Economies de la violence, dimensions de la civilité*, 163–85. Paris: Karthala.

Schell, Jonathan. 2000. An Account of the Destruction in Quang Ngai and Quang Tin. In *Reporting Vietnam: American Journalism 1959–1975*, 204–34. New York: Library of America.

Schell, Jonathan. 1967. *The Village of Ben Suc*. New York: Knopf.

Schelling, Thomas C. 1991. What Purpose Can "International Terrorism" Serve? In R. G. Frey and Christopher W. Morris (eds.), *Violence, Terrorism, and Justice*, 18–32. Cambridge: Cambridge University Press.

Scheper-Hughes, Nancy. 1992. *Death without Weeping: The Violence of Everyday Life in Brazil*. Berkeley: University of California Press.

Schlichte, Klaus. 1997. Magnitudes and Trends in Intrastate Violent Conflict. Paper presented at the International Conference on Violent Crime and Conflict, Courmayeur, Mont Blanc, Italy, 4–6 October.

Schmemann, Serge. 1999. *Echoes of a Native Land: Two Centuries of a Russian Village*. New York: Vintage.

Schmid, Alex P. 1983. *Political Terrorism: A Research Guide to Concepts, Theories, Data Bases, and Literature*. Amsterdam: SWIDOC.

Schmitt, Carl. 1992 [1963]. *Théorie du partisan*. Paris: Flammarion.

Schmitt, Carl. 1976. *The Concept of the Political*. New Brunswick, N.J.: Rutgers University Press.

Schmitt, Eric. 2003. Military in Iraq Is Warned of Attacks during Holidays. *New York Times*, 22 December, A20.

Schofield, Victoria. 1996. *Kashmir in the Crossfire*. London: I. B. Tauris.

Schofield, Victoria. 1984. *Every Rock, Every Hill: The Plain Tale of the North-West Frontier and Afghanistan*. London: Buchan & Enright.

Schoppa, R. Keith. 2001. Patterns and Dynamics of Elite Collaboration in Occupied Shaoxing County. In David P. Barrett and Larry N. Shyu (eds.), *Chinese Collaboration with Japan, 1932–1945: The Limits of Accommodation*, 156–79. Stanford, Calif.: Stanford University Press.

Schran, Peter. 1976. *Guerrilla Economy: The Development of the Shensi-Kansu-Ninghsia Border Region, 1937–1945*. Albany: State University of New York Press.

Schroeder, Michael J. 2000. "To Induce a Sense of Terror": Caudillio Politics and Political Violence in Northern Nicaragua, 1926–34 and 1981–95. In Bruce B. Campbell and Arthur D. Brenner (eds.), *Death Squads in Global Perspective: Murder with Deniability*, 27–56. New York: St. Martin's Press.

Schroeder, Michael J. 1996. Horse Thieves to Rebels to Dogs: Political Gang Violence and the State in the Western Segovias, Nicaragua, in the Time of Sandino, 1926–1934. *Journal of Latin American Studies* 28, 2:383–434.

Schulte, Theo J. 2000. Korück 582. In Hannes Heer and Klaus Naumann (eds.), *War of Extermination: The German Military in World War II, 1941–1944*, 315–28. New York: Berghahn Books.

Scott, A. O. 2004. Vengeance Is Ours, Says Hollywood. *New York Times*, 2 May, 24.

Scott, James C. 1990. *Domination and the Arts of Resistance: Hidden Transcripts*. New Haven: Yale University Press.

Scott, James C. 1985. *Weapons of the Weak: Everyday Forms of Peasant Resistance*. New Haven: Yale University Press.

Scott, James C. 1977a. Patron-Client Politics and Political Change in Southeast Asia. In Steffen W. Schmidt et al. (eds.), *Friends, Followers, and Factions: A Reader in Political Clientelism*, 123–46. Berkeley: University of California Press.

Scott, James C. 1977b. Protest and Profanation: Agrarian Revolt and the Little Tradition, Part I. *Theory and Society* 4, 1:1–38.

Scott, James C. 1977c. Protest and Profanation: Agrarian Revolt and the Little Tradition, Part II. *Theory and Society* 4, 2:211–46.

Seculić, Dušco. 2005. Structural Determinants of Nationalism in Croatia. Unpublished paper.

Seideman, Gay. 2001. Guerrillas in Their Midst: Armed Struggle in the South African Anti-Apartheid Movement. Paper presented at the 2001 Meeting of the Social Science History Association, Chicago, 15–18 November.

Seidman, Michael. 2002. *Republic of Egos: A Social History of the Spanish Civil War*. Madison: University of Wisconsin Press.

Selesky, Harold E. 1994. Colonial America. In Michael Howard, George J. Andreopoulos, and Mark R. Shulman (eds.), *The Laws of War: Constraints on Warfare in the Western World*, 59–85. New Haven: Yale University Press.

Semana. 2003. La Gran Redada. *Revista Semana*, 3 March. http://semana2.terra.com. co/opencms/opencms/Semana/articulo.html?id=73650#.

Sémelin, Jacques. 2000. Qu'est-ce qu'un crime de masse? Le cas de l'ex-Yougoslavie. *Critique Internationale* 6:143–58.

Sen, Amartya. 1986. Behaviour and the Concept of Preference. In Jon Elster (ed.), *Rational Choice*, 60–81. New York: New York University Press.

Senaratne, Jagath P. 1997. *Political Violence in Sri Lanka, 1977–1990: Riots, Insurrections, Counterinsurgencies, Foreign Intervention*. Amsterdam: VU University Press.

Sender Barayón, Ramón. 1989. *A Death in Zamora*. Albuquerque: University of New Mexico Press.

Senechal de la Roche, Roberta. 2001. Why Is Collective Violence Collective? *Sociological Theory* 19, 2:126–44.

Sengupta, Somini. 2005a. Vigilantes May Be Nepal's Secrete Weapon against Rebels. *New York Times*, 11 April, A3.

Sengupta, Somini. 2005b. For Afghans, Voting May Be a Life-and-Death Decision. *New York Times*, 16 September, A10.

Sengupta, Somini. 2005c. Where Maoists Still Matter. *New York Times Magazine*, 30 October, 64–69.

Sengupta, Somini. 2004. Sudan Government's Attacks Stoke Rebels' Fury. *New York Times*, 11 September, A1, A8.

Serrano, Secundino. 2002. *Maquis: Historia de la guerrilla antifranquista*. Madrid: Temas de Hoy.

Seybolt, Peter J. 2001. The War within a War: A Case Study of a County on the North China Plain. In David P. Barrett and Larry N. Shyu (eds.), *Chinese Collaboration with Japan, 1932–1945: The Limits of Accommodation*, 201–25. Stanford, Calif.: Stanford University Press.

Shalita, Nicholas. 1994. The Sudan Conflict. In Michael Cranna (ed.), *The True Cost of Conflict*, 135–54. New York: New Press.

Shanin, T. 1975. The Peasantry as a Political Factor. In Sam C. Sarkesian (ed.), *Revolutionary Guerrilla Warfare*, 267–89. Chicago: Precedent Publishing.

Shanker, Thom, and Steven Lee Myers. 2001. Increased US Activity to Aid Afghan Rebels. *New York Times*, 19 October, B2.

Shattuck, Kathryn. 2000. Beware the Cry of "NIYBY": Not in Your Backyard! *New York Times*, 11 May, F1.

Shave, David. 1994. The Peru Conflict. In Michael Cranna (ed.), *The True Cost of Conflict*, 113–33. New York: New Press.

Shaw, Brent. 2001. War and Violence. In G. W. Bowersock, Peter Brown, and Oleg Grabar (eds.), *Interpreting Late Antiquity: Essays on the Postclassical World*, 130–69. Cambridge, Mass.: Belknap Press.

Shaw, Bruno. 1975. Selections from Selected Works of Mao Tse-Tung. In Sam C. Sarkesian (ed.), *Revolutionary Guerrilla Warfare*, 205–35. Chicago: Precedent Publishing.

Sheehan, Neil. 1989. *A Bright Shining Lie: John Paul Vann and America in Vietnam*. New York: Vintage.

Shepherd, Ben. 2002. Hawks, Doves and *Tote Zonen*: A Wehrmacht Security Division in Central Russia, 1943. *Journal of Contemporary History* 37, 3:349–69.

Shils, Edward, and Morris Janowitz. 1948. Cohesion and Disintegration in the Wehrmacht in World War II. *Public Opinion Quarterly*, 2:280–315.

Shy, John. 1976. *A People Numerous and Armed: Reflections on the Military Struggle for American Independence*. New York: Oxford University Press.

Siegel, Daniel, and Joy Hackel. 1988. El Salvador: Counterinsurgency Revisited. In Michael T. Klare and Peter Kornbluh (eds.), *Low-Intensity Warfare: Counterinsurgency, Proinsurgency, and Antiterrorism in the Eighties*, 112–35. New York: Pantheon Books.

Silber, Laura, and Allan Little. 1997. *Yugoslavia: Death of A Nation*. New York: Penguin.

Silke, Andrew. 1998. In Defense of the Realm: Financing Loyalist Terrorism in Northern Ireland – Part One: Extortion and Blackmail. *Studies in Conflict and Terrorism* 21:331–61.

Simmel, Georg. 1955 [1908]. *Conflict*. Glencoe, Ill.: Free Press.

Simons, Anna. 1999. War: Back to the Future. *Annual Reviews of Anthropology* 28:73–108.

Siu, Helen F. 1989. *Agents and Victims in South China: Accomplices in Rural Revolution*. New Haven: Yale University Press.

Sivard, Ruth Leger. 1996. *World Military and Social Expenditures, 1996*. 16th ed. Washington, D.C.: World Priorities.

Sivard, Ruth Leger. 1987. *World Military and Social Expenditures, 1987–88*. 12th ed. Washington, D.C.: World Priorities.

Skinner, Jonathan. 1995. La guerre civile révolutionnaire: Oubli ou héritage? L'exemple de la presse vauclusienne de la IIe République. In Jean-Clément Martin (ed.), *La guerre civile entre histoire et mémoire*, 143–53. Nantes: Ouest Éditions.

Skocpol, Theda. 1979. *States and Social Revolutions: A Comparative Analysis of France, Russia, and China*. Cambridge: Cambridge University Press.

Sluka, Jeffrey A. 2000. Introduction: State Terror and Anthropology. In Jeffrey A. Sluka (ed.), *Death Squad: The Anthropology of State Terror*, 1–45. Philadelphia: University of Pennsylvania Press.

Sluka, Jeffrey A. 1989. *Hearts and Minds, Water and Fish: Support for the IRA and INLA in a Northern Irish Ghetto*. Greenwich, Conn.: JAI Press.

Smith, Adam. 1982 [1790]. *The Theory of Moral Sentiments*. Edited by D. D. Raphael and A. L. Macfie. Indianapolis: Liberty Fund.

Smith, Carol. 1988. Destruction of the Material Bases for Indian Culture: Economic Changes in Totonicapán. In Robert M. Carmack (ed.), *Harvest of Violence: The Maya Indians and the Guatemalan Crisis*, 206–31. Norman: University of Oklahoma Press.

Smith, Craig. 2005. U.S. and Iraq Step Up Effort to Block Insurgents' Routes. *New York Times*, 3 October, A6.

Smith, Craig. 2003. Paris Frees Airport Worker Who Was Framed as Terror Suspect. *New York Times*, 11 January, A5.

Smith, M. L. R. 1995. Holding Fire: Strategic Theory and the Missing Military Dimension in the Adademic Study of Northern Ireland. In Alan O'Day (ed.), *Terrorism's Laboratory: The Case of Northern Ireland*, 225–40. Aldershot: Dartmouth.

Smyth, Marie, and Marie-Therese Fay. 2000. *Personal Accounts from Northern Ireland's Troubles: Public Conflict, Private Loss*. London: Pluto Press.

Snow, Clyde Collins, and Maria Julia Bihurriet. 1992. An Epidemiology of Homicide: *Ningún Nombre* Burials in the Province of Buenos Aires from 1970 to 1984. In Thomas B. Jabine and Richard P. Claude (eds.), *Human Rights and Statistics: Getting the Record Straight*, 328–63. Philadelphia: University of Pennsylvania Press.

Snow, Donald M. 1997. *Distant Thunder: Patterns of Conflict in the Developing World.* Armonk, N.Y.: M. E. Sharpe.

Snyder, Timothy. 2003. The Causes of the Ukrainian-Polish Ethnic Cleansing, 1943. *Past and Present* 179:197–234.

Sofsky, Wolfgang. 1998. *Traité de la violence.* Paris: Gallimard.

Solomon, Robert C. 1994. Sympathy and Vengeance: The Role of the Emotions in Justice. In Stephanie H. M. Van Goozen, Nanne E. Van de Poll, and Joseph Sergeant (eds.), *Emotions: Essays on Emotion Theory,* 291–311. Hillsdale, N.J.: Lawrence Erlbaum Associates.

Sontag, Deborah. 2000. After Lebanon Convulsion, an Uncertain Landscape. *New York Times,* 25 May, A1.

Sorel, Georges. 1921. *Réflexions sur la violence.* Paris: Rivière.

Spencer, Jonathan. 2000. On Not Becoming a "Terrorist." Problems of Memory, Agency, and Community in the Sri Lankan Conflict. In Veena Das, Arthur Kleinman, Mamphela Ramphele, and Pamela Reynolds (eds.), *Violence and Subjectivity,* 120–40. Berkeley: University of California Press.

Spencer, Jonathan. 1992. Problems in the Analysis of Communal Violence. *Contributions to Indian Sociology* 26, 2:261–79.

Spencer, Jonathan. 1990. *A Sinhala Village in a Time of Trouble: Politics and Change in Rural Sri Lanka.* Delhi: Oxford University Press.

Spierenburg, Pieter. 1996. Long-Term Trends in Homicide: Theoretical Reflections and Dutch Evidence: Fifteenth to Twentieth Centuries. In Eric Johnson and Eric H. Monkkonen (eds.), *The Civilization of Crime: Violence in Town and Country since the Middle Ages,* 63–105. Urbana: University of Illinois Press.

Spinner, Jacquie. 2005. In a Calmer Fallujah, Marines Still Feel the Insurgents' Pulse. *Washington Post,* 16 February, A15.

Stacey, Robert C. 1994. The Age of Chivalry. In Michael Howard, George J. Andreopoulos, and Mark R. Shulman (eds.), *The Laws of War: Constraints on Warfare in the Western World,* 27–39. New Haven: Yale University Press.

Stanley, William. 1996. *The Protection Racket State: Elite Politics, Military Extortion, and Civil War in El Salvador.* Philadelphia: Temple University Press.

Stark, Rodney. 1997. *The Rise of Christianity: How the Obscure, Marginal Jesus Movement Became the Dominant Religious Force in the Western World in a Few Centuries.* New York: HarperCollins.

Starn, Orin. 1998. Villagers at Arms: War and Counterrevolution in the Central-South Andes. In Steve J. Stern (ed.), *Shining and Other Paths: War and Society in Peru, 1980–1995,* 224–57. Durham: Duke University Press.

Steinberg, Jacques. 2004. Source for USA Today Reporter Disputes Details of Kosovo Article. *New York Times,* 26 January, C1.

Stendhal. 1996. *L'abbesse de Castro.* Paris: Librio.

Stiles, T. J. 2002. *Jesse James: Last Rebel of the Civil War.* New York: Knopf.

St. John, Warren. 2002. Sorrow So Sweet: A Guilty Pleasure in Another's Woe. *New York Times,* 24 August, A17.

Stoll, David. 1999. *Rigoberta Menchú and the Story of All Poor Guatemalans.* Boulder, Colo.: Westview Press.

Stoll, David. 1993. *Between Two Armies: In the Ixil Towns of Guatemala.* New York: Columbia University Press.

Stone, Lawrence. 1972. *The Causes of the English Revolution: 1529–1642.* New York: Harper Torchbooks.

Stouffer, Samuel. 1949. *The American Soldier.* Princeton, N.J.: Princeton University Press.

Straus, Scott. 2004. The Order of Genocide: Race, Power, and War in Rwanda. Ph.D. dissertation, University of California, Berkeley.

Straus, Scott. 2000. Definitions and Sub-types: A Conceptual Analysis of Genocide. Unpublished paper, University of California, Berkeley.

Stubbs, Richard. 1989. *Hearts and Minds in Guerrilla Warfare: The Malayan Emergency, 1948–1960*. Singapore: Oxford University Press.

Suárez-Orozco, Marcelo. 1992. A Grammar of Terror: Psychocultural Reponses to State Terrorism in Dirty War and Post-Dirty War Argentina. In Carolyn Nordstrom and JoAnn Martin (eds.), *The Paths to Domination, Resistance, and Terror*, 219–59. Berkeley: University of California Press.

Suárez-Orozco, Marcelo. 1990. Speaking of the Unspeakable: Toward a Psychological Understanding of Responses to Terror. *Ethos* 18, 3:353–83.

Swain, Carol M. 1993. *Black Faces, Black Interests: The Representation of African Americans in Congress*. Cambridge, Mass.: Harvard University Press.

Swedenburg, Ted. 1995. *Memories of Revolt: The 1936–1939 Rebellion and the Palestinian National Past*. Minneapolis: University of Minnesota Press.

Sweets, John F. 1994. *Choices in Vichy France: The French under Nazi Occupation*. New York: Oxford University Press.

Tabbara, Lina Mikdadi. 1979. *Survival in Beirut: A Diary of Civil War*. London: Onyx Press.

Taber, Robert. 1965. *The War of the Flea: A Study of Guerrilla Warfare Theory and Practice*. New York: Lyle Stuart.

Tambiah, Stanley J. 1996. *Leveling Crowds: Ethnonationalist Conflict and Collective Violence in South Asia*. Berkeley: University of California Press.

Tarnopolsky, Noga. 1999. The Family That Disappeared. *New Yorker*, 15 November, 48–57.

Tarrow, Sidney G. 1994. *Power in Movement: Social Movements, Collective Action and Politics*. Cambridge: Cambridge University Press.

Taussig, Michael. 1987. *Colonialism, Shamanism, and the Wild Man: A Study in Terror and Healing*. Chicago: University of Chicago Press.

Tereshchuk, David. 2001. An Unreliable Witness. *New York Times Magazine*, 28 January, 66.

Terry, Nicholas. 2005. People's War or Civil War? The Struggle between Collaborators and Partisans in Central Russia and Belorussia, 1941–1944. Paper presented at the Conference on War Time Collaboration in Nazi Europe 1939–1945, EUI, Florence, 13–14 October.

Thaxton, Ralph. 1997. *Salt of the Earth: The Political Origins of Peasant Protest and Communist Revolution in China*. Berkeley: University of California Press.

Thayer, Thomas C. 1985. *War without Fronts: The American Experience in Vietnam*. Boulder, Colo.: Westview Press.

Thomas, Hugh. 1986. *The Spanish Civil War*. New York: Simon & Schuster.

Thompson, Ginger. 2003. El Quemado Journal; A Mexican Village Mourns Its Abducted Sons. *New York Times*, 28 July, A4.

Thompson, Ginger. 2001. Houses Divided; Why Peace Eludes Mexico's Indians. *New York Times*, 11 March, sec. 4:16.

Thompson, Robert. 1966. *Defeating Communist Insurgency*. New York: Praeger.

Thornton, Thomas P. 1964. Terror as a Weapon of Political Agitation. In Harry Eckstein (ed.), *Internal War: Problems and Approaches*, 71–99. New York: Free Press.

Thucydides. [1972]. *History of the Peloponnesian War*. Translated by Rex Warner. London: Penguin.

Thurston, Anne F. 1990. Urban Violence during the Cultural Revolution: Who Is to Blame? In Jonathan N. Lipman and Stevan Harrell (eds.), *Violence in China: Essays in Culture and Counterculture*, 149–74. Albany: State University of New York Press.

Tilly, Charles. 2003. *Politics of Collective Violence*. Cambridge: Cambridge University Press.

Tilly, Charles. 1992. *Coercion, Capital and European States*. London: Blackwell.

Tilly, Charles. 1985. War Making and State Making as Organized Crime. In Peter B. Evans, Dietrich Rueschemeyer, and Theda Skocpol (eds.), *Bringing the State Back*, 168–91. Cambridge: Cambridge University Press.

Tilly, Charles. 1978. *From Mobilization to Revolution*. New York: McGraw-Hill.

Tilly, Charles. 1975. Revolutions and Collective Violence. In Fred I. Greenstein and Nelson W. Polsby (eds.), *Handbook of Political Science: Macropolitical Theory*, 483–555. Reading, Mass.: Addison-Wesley.

Tilly, Charles. 1964. *The Vendée*. Cambridge, Mass.: Harvard University Press.

Timmons, Heather. 2005. Weakened British Unions Step Up Fight against Airlines and Their Suppliers. *New York Times*, 20 August, C3.

Tishkov, Valery. 2004. *Chechnya: Life in a War-Torn Society*. Berkeley: University of California Press.

Tishkov, Valery. 1999. Ethnic Conflicts in the Former USSR: The Use and Misuse of Typologies and Data. *Journal of Peace Research* 36, 5:571–91.

Tishkov, Valery. 1997. Political Anthropology of the Chechen War. *Security Dialogue* 28:425–37.

Tocqueville, Alexis de. 1988. *Democracy in America*. Edited by J. P. Mayer, translated by George Lawrence. New York: Harper & Row.

Tocqueville, Alexis de. 1933. *L'ancien regime*. Oxford: Blackwell.

Todorov, Tzvetan. 1996. *A French Tragedy: Scenes of Civil War, Summer 1944*. Hanover, N.H.: University Press of New England.

Toft, Monica Duffy. 2003. *The Geography of Ethnic Violence: Identity, Interests, and the Indivisibility of Territory*. Princeton, N.J.: Princeton University Press.

Tone, John Lawrence. 1994. *The Fatal Knot: The Guerrilla War in Navarre and the Defeat of Napoleon in Spain*. Chapel Hill: University of North Carolina Press.

Tong, James. 1991. *Disorder under Heaven: Collective Violence in the Ming Dynasty*. Stanford, Calif.: Stanford University Press.

Tong, James. 1988. Rational Outlaws: Rebels and Bandits in the Ming Dynasty. In Michael Taylor (ed.), *Rationality and Revolution*, 98–128. Cambridge: Cambridge University Press.

Toolis, Kevin. 1997. *Rebel Hearts: Journeys within the IRA's Soul*. New York: St. Martin's Griffin.

Trejo Osorio, Guillermo. 2004. Indigenous Insurgency: Protest, Rebellion, and the Politicization of Ethnicity in 20th Century Mexico. Ph.D. dissertation, University of Chicago.

Trinquier, Roger. 1964. *Modern Warfare: A French View of Counterinsurgency*. New York: Praeger.

Trotsky, Leon. 1965. *A History of the Russian Revolution*. 2 vols. London: Gollancz.

Trotsky, Leon. 1961. *Terrorism and Communism: A Reply to Karl Kautsky*. Ann Arbor, Mich.: Ann Arbor Paperbacks.

Trullinger, James W. 1994. *Village at War: An Account of Conflict in Vietnam*. Stanford, Calif.: Stanford University Press.

Tucker, Shelby. 2001. *Among the Insurgents: Walking through Burma*. London: Flamingo.

Tullock, Gordon. 1987. Autocracy. In Gerard Radnitzky and Peter Bernholz (eds.), *Economic Imperialism: The Economic Approach Applied Outside of the Field of Economics*, 365–81. New York: Paragon House.

Tyler, Patrick E. 2002. Ex-Soldier Fabricated Chechnya Story, Russian Officials Say. *New York Times*, 22 April, A2.

Tyler, Patrick E. 2001. Key Chechen Who Backed the Russians Dies in Battle. *New York Times*, 20 August, A8.

Tymowski, Andrej W. 2002. Apologies for Jedwabne and Modernity. *East European Politics and Societies* 16, 1:291–306.

Ucelay da Cal, Enric. 1995. La guerre civile espagnole et la propagande franco-belge de la Première Guerre mondiale. In Jean-Clément Martin (ed.), *La guerre civile entre histoire et mémoire*, 77–90. Nantes: Ouest Éditions.

Ung, Loung. 2000. *First They Killed My Father*. New York: Harper Collins.

University of Teachers for Human Rights. 1993. *Someone Else's War*. Colombo: Movement for Inter Racial Justice and Equality.

Upton, Anthony F. 1980. *The Finnish Revolution, 1917–1918*. Minneapolis : University of Minnesota Press.

Urbina, Ian. 2005. Revenge of the Perturbed IIL Readers Offer New Tactics. *New York Times*, 20 March, 35.

Urbina, Ian. 2004. As Energy Thieves Turn Crafty, Con Ed Turns Up Battle of Wits. *New York Times*, 5 May, A1, B9.

Uribe, Maria Victoria. 1990. *Matar, rematar y contramatar: Las masacres de la violencia en el Tolima, 1948–1964*. Bogotá: CINEP.

Valentino, Benjamin A. 2004. *Final Solutions: Mass Killing and Genocide in the 20th Century*. Ithaca: Cornell University Press.

Valentino, Benjamin A. 2000. Final Solutions: The Causes of Mass Killings and Genocides. *Security Studies* 9, 3:1–59.

Valentino, Benjamin A., Paul Huth, and Dylan Balch-Lindsay. 2004. "Draining the Sea": Mass Killing and Guerrilla Warfare. *International Organization* 58, 2: 375–407.

Van Creveld, Martin. 1991. *The Transformation of War*. New York: Free Press.

Van Evera, Stephen. 2001. Primordialism Lives! *APSA-CP* 12, 1:20–2.

Van Natta, Don. 2001. Hundreds of Arrests, but Promising Leads Unravel. *New York Times*, 21 October, B1.

Vargas Llosa, Mario. 1998. *Un barbare chez les civilisés*. Paris: Gallimard.

Vargas Llosa, Mario. 1994. *A Fish in the Water: A Memoir*. New York: Farrar, Strauss, Giroux.

Varshney, Ashutosh. 2003. Nationalism, Ethnic Conflict, and Rationality. *Perspectives on Politics* 1, 1:85–99.

Varshney, Ashutosh. 2002. *Ethnic Conflict and Civic Life: Hindus and Muslims in India*. New Haven: Yale University Press.

Varshney, Ashutosh. 2001. Ethnic Conflict and Civil Society: India and Beyond. *World Politics* 53, 3:362–98.

Verri, Pietro. 1961. *Osservazioni sulla tortura*. Edited by Gianluigi Barni. Milan: Rizzoli.

Verwimp, Philip. 2003. Testing the Double-Genocide Thesis for Central and Southern Rwanda. *Journal of Conflict Resolution* 47, 4:423–42.

Veyne, Paul. 1996. *Comment on écrit l'histoire*. Paris: Seuil.

Vick, Karl. 2002. In Kurdish Turkey, a New Enemy. Village Guards, Empowered during War, Turn Guns on Returnees. *Washington Post*, October 31, A18.

Vidal, Claudine. 1996. Le génocide des Rwandais tutsi: Cruauté délibérée et logiques de haine. In Françoise Héritier (ed.), *De la violence*, 327–66. Paris: Odile Jacob.

Vincent, Shaun. 1994. The Mozambique Conflict (1980–1992). In Michael Cranna (ed.), *The True Cost of Conflict*, 81–112. New York: New Press.

Viola, Lynne. 1993. The Second Coming: Class Enemies in the Soviet Countryside, 1927–1935. In J. Arch Getty and Roberta T. Manning (eds.), *Stalinist Terror: New Perspectives*, 65–98. Cambridge: Cambridge University Press.

Wageenar, Willem A. 1988. *Identifying Ivan: A Case Study in Legal Psychology*. Cambridge, Mass.: Harvard University Press.

Waghelstein, John D. 1985. *El Salvador: Observations and Experiences in Counterinsurgency*. Carlisle Barracks, Pa: US Army War College.

Wakin, Eric. 1992. *Anthropology Goes to War: Professional Ethics and Counterinsurgency in Thailand*. Madison: University of Wisconsin Center for Southeast Asian Studies.

Waldman, Amy. 2004. Afghan Strife Exposes Deep and Wide Ethnic Tensions. *New York Times*, 6 September, A3.

Waldman, Amy. 2003. Young Sri Lankans Are Lost to Forced Recruitment. *New York Times*, 6 January, A1.

Waldman, Amy. 2002a. Afghan Warlord's Rivals Link Him to U.S. Attacks. *New York Times*, 3 January, A15.

Waldman, Amy. 2002b. "Once Fertile Valley Left Arid by Taliban." *New York Times*, 7 January, A9.

Walter, Barbara F. 1997. The Critical Barrier to Civil War Settlement. *International Organization* 51, 3:331–60.

Walter, Eugene V. 1969. *Terror and Resistance*. New York: Oxford.

Walters, Richard H. 1966. Implications of Laboratory Studies of Aggression for the Control and Regulation of Violence. *Annals of the American Academy of Political and Social Science* 364:60–72.

Walzer, Michael. 1997. *Just and Unjust Wars: A Moral Argument with Historical Illustrations*. New York: Basic Books.

Wantchekon, Leonard. 2003. Clientelism and Voting Behavior: Evidence from a Field Experiment in Benin. *World Politics* 55, 3:399–422.

Warren, Kay B. 1998. *Indigenous Movements and Their Critics: Pan-Maya Activism in Guatemala*. Princeton, N.J.: Princeton University Press.

Watanabe, John M. 1992. *Maya Saints and Souls in a Changing World*. Austin: University of Texas Press.

Wax, Emily. 2002. Key to Conflict in Ivory Coast: Who Are Rebels? *Washington Post*, 24 October, A30.

Weber, Max. 1994. *Political Writings*. Edited by Peter Lassman and Ronal Speirs. Cambridge: Cambridge University Press.

Weiner, Tim. 2001. Gun Control Policy, Jalalabad Style: He Who Grabs All the Rifles Writes the Rules. *New York Times*, 23 November, B4.

Weinstein, Jeremy. 2003. Inside Rebellion: The Political Economy of Rebel Organization. Ph.D. dissertation, Harvard University.

Weinstein, N. D. 1980. Unrealistic Optimism about Future Life Events. *Journal of Personality and Social Psychology* 39:806–20.

Weir, Robert M. 1985. "The Violent Spirit," the Reestablishment of Order, and the Continuity of Leadership in Post-Revolutionary South Carolina. In Ronald Hoffman, Thad W. Tate, and Peter J. Albert (eds.), *An Uncivil War: The Southern Backcountry during the American Revolution*, 70–98. Charlottesville: University Press of Virginia.

Welch, Richard E. 1974. American Atrocities in the Philippines: The Challenge and the Response. *Pacific Historical Review*, 43:233–53.

Werth, Nicolas. 1998. Un état contre son peuple: Violences, répressions, terreurs en Union Soviétique. In Stéphane Courtois et al., *Le livre noir du communisme: Crimes, terreur, répression*, 39–312. Paris: Robert Laffont.

West, F. J., Jr. 1985. *The Village*. Madison: University of Wisconsin Press.

Westing, Arthur H. 1982. Research Communication: War as a Human Endeavor: The High-Fatality Wars of the Twentieth Century. *Journal of Peace Research* 19, 3:261–70.

White, Lynn T., III. 1989. *Policies of Chaos: The Organizational Causes of Violence in China's Cultural Revolution*. Princeton, N.J.: Princeton University Press.

White, Robert W. 1989. From Peaceful Protest to Guerrilla War: Micromobilization of the Provisional Irish Republican Army. *American Journal of Sociology* 94, 6: 1277–1302.

Wickham-Crowley, Timothy P. 1992. *Guerrillas and Revolution in Latin America: A Comparative Study of Insurgents and Regimes since 1956*. Princeton, N.J.: Princeton University Press.

Wickham-Crowley, Timothy P. 1991. *Exploring Revolution: Essays on Latin American Insurgency and Revolutionary Theory*. Armonk, N.Y.: M. E. Sharpe.

Wickham-Crowley, Timothy P. 1990. Terror and Guerrilla Warfare in Latin America, 1956–1970. *Comparative Studies in Society and History* 32, 2:201–37.

Wiesner, Louis A. 1988. *Victims and Survivors: Displaced Persons and Other War Victims in Viet-Nam, 1954–1975*. New York: Greenwood Press.

Wilensky, Harold L. 1967. *Organizational Intelligence: Knowledge and Policy in Government and Industry*. New York: Basic Books.

Wilkinson, Steven I. 2004. *Votes and Violence: Electoral Competition and Ethnic Riots in India*. Cambridge: Cambridge University Press.

Williams, Cratis D. 1975. The Southern Mountaineer in Fact and Fiction. Edited by Martha H. Pipes. *Appalachian Journal* 3:8–41.

Wills, Brian Steel. 2001. *The War Hits Home: The Civil War in Southeastern Virginia*. Charlottesville: University Press of Virginia.

Wilson, Gabrielle. 1970. *The Blood of Spain*. Philadelphia: Dorrance.

Wilson, Scott. 2004. Colombia Targeting Rebel Strongholds. *Washington Post*, 25 January, A14.

Wilson, Scott. 2003. "Peasant" Force Takes Shape in Colombia. *Washington Post*, 13 March, A11.

Wilson, Scott. 2002. Fewer Massacres in Colombia, but More Deaths. *Washington Post*, 24 June, A15.

Wines, Michael. 2003. Chechnya Weighs a Russian Offer of Self-Rule. *New York Times*, 23 March, A3.

Wines, Michael. 2001. Russians Recall the "Giant Mincer" That Was Afghanistan. *New York Times*, 29 September, B7.

Wintrobe, Ronald. 1998. *The Political Economy of Dictatorship*. Cambridge: Cambridge University Press.

Wolf, Eric R. 1969. *Peasant Wars of the Twentieth Century*. New York, Harper & Row.

Wood, Elisabeth Jean. 2003. *Insurgent Collective Action and Civil War in El Salvador*. Cambridge: Cambridge University Press.

Worchel, Stephen. 1974. Societal Restrictiveness and the Presence of Outlets for the Release of Aggression. *Journal of Cross-Cultural Psychology* 5:109–23.

Worden, Blair. 1985. Providence and Politics in Cromwellian England. *Past and Present* 109:55–99.

Wormald, Jenny. 1980. Bloodfeud, Kindred and Government in Early Modern Scotland. *Past and Present* 87:54–97.

Wou, Odoric Y. K. 1994. *Mobilizing the Masses: Building Revolution in Henan*. Stanford, Calif.: Stanford University Press.

Wyatt, Edward. 2005. Iraqi Refugee's Tale of Abuse Dissolves upon Later Scrutiny. *New York Times*, 21 January, A8.

Yang, Martin C. 1945. *A Chinese Village: Taitou, Shantung Province*. New York: Columbia University Press.

Yoo, Jieun. 2002. War Boundaries and Local Organization: Cases from the Korean War. Unpublished paper, University of Chicago.

Yoo, Jieun. 2001. The Chejudo Rebellions. Unpublished paper, University of Chicago.

Yoon, Taek-lim. 1992. Koreans' Stories about Themselves: An Ethnographic History of Hermit Pond Village in South Korea. Ph.D. dissertation, University of Minnesota.

Young, Marilyn B. 1991. *The Vietnam Wars, 1945–1990*. New York: Harper Perennial.

Young, Tom. 1997. A Victim of Modernity? Explaining the War in Mozambique. In Paul B. Rich and Richard Stubbs (eds.), *The Counter-Insurgent State: Guerrilla Warfare and State-Building in the Twentieth Century*, 120–51. New York: St. Martin's Press.

Zahar, Marie-Joëlle. 2001. Protégés, Clients, Cannon Fodder: Civil-Militia Relations in Internal Conflicts. In Simon Chesterman (ed.), *Civilians in War*, 43–65. Boulder, Colo.: Lynne Riener.

Zaretsky, Mark. 2003. City Soldier Gets a Break from War. *New Haven Register*, 8 December, A4.

Zemon Davis, Natalie. 1973. The Rites of Violence: Religious Riot in Sixteenth-Century France. *Past and Present* 59:51–91.

Zerrouky, Hassane. 1997. Le jeune capitaine et les paysans. *L'Humanité*, 17 October 1997.

Ziemke, Earl. 1964. Composition and Morale of the Partisan Movement. In John A. Armstrong (ed.), *Soviet Partisans in World War II*, 141–96. Madison: University of Wisconsin Press.

Zimmerman, Matilde. 2000. *Sandinista*. Durham, N.C.: Duke University Press.

Zimring, Franklin E., and Gordon J. Hawkins. 1973. *Deterrence: The Legal Threat in Crime Control*. Chicago: University of Chicago Press.

Zucchino, David. 2004. Sorting Friends from Foes. *Los Angeles Times*, 1 November, A1, A8–A9.

Zulaika, Joseba. 1988. *Basque Violence: Metaphor and Sacrament*. Reno: University of Nevada Press.

Zulaika, Joseba, and William Douglass. 1996. *Terror and Taboo: The Follies, Fables, and Faces of Terrorism*. New York: Routledge.

Zur, Judith N. 1998. *Violent Memories: Mayan War Widows in Guatemala*. Boulder, Colo.: Westview Press.

Zur, Judith N. 1994. The Psychological Impact of Impunity. *Anthropology Today* 10, 3:12–17.

Index

Other Books in the Series *(continued from page iii)*

Herbert Kitschelt, Zdenka Mansfeldova, Radek Markowski, and Gabor Toka, *Post-Communist Party Systems*

David Knoke, Franz Urban Pappi, Jeffrey Broadbent, and Yutaka Tsujinaka, eds., *Comparing Policy Networks*

Allan Kornberg and Harold D. Clarke, *Citizens and Community: Political Support in a Representative Democracy*

Amie Kreppel, *The European Parliament and the Supranational Party System*

David D. Laitin, *Language Repertories and State Construction in Africa*

Fabrice E. Lehoucq and Ivan Molina, *Stuffing the Ballot Box: Fraud, Electoral Reform, and Democratization in Costa Rica*

Mark Irving Lichbach and Alan S. Zuckerman, eds., *Comparative Politics: Rationality, Culture, and Structure*

Evan Lieberman, *Race and Regionalism in the Politics of Taxation in Brazil and South Africa*

Pauline Jones Luong, *Institutional Change and Political Continuity in Post-Soviet Central Asia*

Doug McAdam, John McCarthy, and Mayer Zald, eds., *Comparative Perspectives on Social Movements*

James Mahoney and Dietrich Rueschemeyer, eds., *Historical Analysis and the Social Sciences*

Scott Mainwaring and Matthew Soberg Shugart, eds., *Presidentialism and Democracy in Latin America*

Isabela Mares, *The Politics of Social Risk: Business and Welfare State Development*

Isabela Mares, *Taxation, Wage Bargaining, and Unemployment*

Anthony W. Marx, *Making Race, Making Nations: A Comparison of South Africa, the United States, and Brazil*

Joel S. Migdal, *State in Society: Studying How States and Societies Constitute One Another*

Joel S. Migdal, Atul Kohli, and Vivienne Shue, eds., *State Power and Social Forces: Domination and Transformation in the Third World*

Scott Morgenstern and Benito Nacif, eds., *Legislative Politics in Latin America*

Layna Mosley, *Global Capital and National Governments*

Wolfgang C. Müller and Kaare Strøm, *Policy, Office, or Votes?*

Maria Victoria Murillo, *Labor Unions, Partisan Coalitions, and Market Reforms in Latin America*

Ton Notermans, *Money, Markets, and the State: Social Democratic Economic Policies since 1918*

Roger D. Petersen, *Understanding Ethnic Violence: Fear, Hatred, and Resentment in Twentieth-Century Eastern Europe*

Simona Piattoni, ed., *Clientelism, Interests, and Democratic Representation*

Paul Pierson, *Dismantling the Welfare State? Reagan, Thatcher, and the Politics of Retrenchment*

Marino Regini, *Uncertain Boundaries: The Social and Political Construction of European Economies*